Enhancing Classroom Instruction and Student Skills With AI

Michael W. Kessinger
Morehead State University, USA

Gera S. Nelson
Morehead State University, USA

Lesia Lennex
Morehead State University, USA

Kimberely Fletcher Nettleton
Morehead State University, USA

IGI Global
Scientific Publishing
Publishing Tomorrow's Research Today

Vice President of Editorial Melissa Wagner
Director of Acquisitions Mikaela Felty
Director of Book Development Jocelynn Hessler
Production Manager Mike Brehm
Cover Design Jose Rosado

Published in the United States of America by
IGI Global Scientific Publishing
701 East Chocolate Avenue
Hershey, PA, 17033, USA
Tel: 717-533-8845
Fax: 717-533-7115
Website: https://www.igi-global.com E-mail: cust@igi-global.com

Library of Congress Cataloging-in-Publication Data

Names: Kessinger, Michael (Michael W.), 1952- editor | Nelson, Gera, 1960- editor | Lennex, Lesia C., 1964- editor | Nettleton, Kimberely Fletcher, 1960- editor
Title: Enhancing classroom instruction and student skills with AI / edited by Michael Kessinger, Gera S. Nelson, Lesia Lennex, Kimberely Nettleton.

Description: Hershey, PA : IGI Global Scientific Publishing, [2025] | Includes bibliographical references and index. | Summary: "This book aims to provide practical, researched examples of how AI has been applied in educational settings. It will examine current AI policies and consider the ways in which education may change with the use of AI"-- Provided by publisher.
Identifiers: LCCN 2025022673 (print) | LCCN 2025022674 (ebook) | ISBN 9798337345765 hardcover | ISBN 9798337345772 paperback | ISBN 9798337345789 ebook
Subjects: LCSH: Artificial intelligence--Educational applications
Classification: LCC LB1028.43 .E48 2026 (print) | LCC LB1028.43 (ebook) | DDC 371.33/463--dc23/eng/20250616
LC record available at https://lccn.loc.gov/2025022673
LC ebook record available at https://lccn.loc.gov/2025022674

British Cataloguing in Publication Data
A Cataloguing in Publication record for this book is available from the British Library.

Table of Contents

Preface xiii

Chapter 1
AI in Education: Understanding Student Perceptions and Engagement 1
Nusrat Khan, GD Goenka University, India
Fehmina Khalique, Lloyd Business School, India
Mohd Azmi Khan, Aligarh Muslim University, India
Kartikay Saini, GD Goenka University, India

Chapter 2
AI in the Classroom: Revolutionizing Instruction and Student Engagement 35
Muhammad Usman Tariq, Abu Dhabi University, UAE & University College Cork, Ireland

Chapter 3
Teaching AI in Communication Classes: Engagement, Ethics, and Best Practices 63
David Lynn Painter, Rollins College, USA

Chapter 4
Training Educators in AI for Future-Proofing Education 99
Ramar Veluchamy, Saveetha Engineering College, India

Chapter 5
Leveraging Generative AI in Educator Preparation Programs: Preparing Inclusive and Equitable Educators 135
Joseph Casey Cosgriff, Morehead State University, USA
Daryl R. Privott, Morehead State University, USA

Chapter 6
Using AI in Preparing Pre-Service Teachers for Field Experience 199
Geralda Silva Nelson, Morehead State University, USA

Chapter 7
Artificial Intelligence in Education Higher Education in the Business Area ... 227
Albérico Travassos Rosário, GOVCOPP, IADE, Universidade Europeia, Portugal

Chapter 8
Artificial Intelligence for Learning Disabilities: Enhancing Accessibility, Inclusion, and Empowerment 267
Shariq Nabi Wani, University of Kashmir, India
Shazia Farooq, University of Kashmir, India
Aasia Maqbool, University of Kashmir, India
Nasir Rasheed, University of Kashmir, India
Sumeera Maqbool, University of Kashmir, India
Warisul Rehman, University of Kashmir, India
John Mohammad, University of Kashmir, India
Rasak Annayat, National Institute of Technology, Srinagar, India
Shabir Ahmad Bhat, University of Kashmir, India
Abdal Ahmad Bhat, Government Degree College, Awantipora, India

Chapter 9
AI Text Mining of Case Studies for Students With Disabilities Using Handy ICT Tools 295
Shigeru Ikuta, Otsuma Women's University, Japan

Chapter 10
Critical Thinking Skills and Artificial Intelligence (AI) 337
Mehdi Kaddouri, Mohamed First University, Morocco
Ilham Chniete, Mohammed First University, Morocco
Khalid Mhamdi, Mohammed First University, Morocco
Abderrahmane Bouamri, National School of Agriculture, Meknes, Morocco
Khaoula Atmani, Mohammed First University, Morocco

Chapter 11
Critical Thinking and GenAI: A Guide to Action 377
Silvio Andrae, Independent Researcher, Germany

Chapter 12
Enhancing Critical Thinking: The Role of AI in Modern Education 413
Andi Asrifan, Universitas Negeri Makassar, Indonesia
K. Khristianto, Universitas Muhammadiyah Purwokerto, Indonesia
Arif Budiman, UIN Sunan Kalijaga, Indonesia
Purwani Indri Astuti, Univet Bantara Sukoharjo, Indonesia
Ahmad Rossydi, Politeknik Penerbangan Makassar, Indonesia

Chapter 13
Navigating the AI Era: Enhancing Critical Thinking Skills for Global Challenges 449
Andi Asrifan, Universitas Negeri Makassar, Indonesia
Agnes Widyaningrum, Universitas Stikubank Semarang, Indonesia
Ratu Bulkis Ramli, Universitas Musamus, Indonesia
Riyanti Riyanti, Universitas Muhammadiyah Palopo, Indonesia
Sultan Sultan, Universitas Muhammadiyah Palopo, Indonesia

Compilation of References 481

About the Contributors 557

Index 567

Detailed Table of Contents

Preface xiii

Chapter 1
AI in Education: Understanding Student Perceptions and Engagement 1
Nusrat Khan, GD Goenka University, India
Fehmina Khalique, Lloyd Business School, India
Mohd Azmi Khan, Aligarh Muslim University, India
Kartikay Saini, GD Goenka University, India

Artificial intelligence is discussed widely in present times along with its usage. Everyone, including organizations and individuals are using AI for different purposes. It becomes imperative to understand and explore the foundational concepts of AI in the field of education. Therefore, with this objective, the chapter focuses on student perceptions, engagement and the influence of AI tools on learning experiences, understanding of AI, perception, familiarity of students, and its potential to transform learning environments. The data was collected through a detailed survey tool only from higher educational institutions, comprising of 120 both undergraduate and postgraduate students. It discusses their attitudes towards the incorporation of AI in educational surroundings and the usefulness of AI-driven educational tools. This exploration not only sheds light on the benefits and concerns associated with AI but also offers practical recommendations for educators and policymakers to optimize AI integration and foster a more personalized and engaging learning environment.

Chapter 2
AI in the Classroom: Revolutionizing Instruction and Student Engagement 35
Muhammad Usman Tariq, Abu Dhabi University, UAE & University College Cork, Ireland

This chapter talks about how artificial intelligence is radically changing education by altering conventional classroom dynamics and improving student engagement and redefining the instructional practices. This chapter examines how teaching and learning are changing in a variety of educational settings. It explores the incorporation of AI technologies that facilitate individualized learning experiences, letting students advance at their own speed while considering their unique strengths and weaknesses. AI-powered platforms encourage greater engagement and better results by offering data-driven insights adaptive learning pathways and real-time feedback. By providing actionable analytics automating administrative tasks and enabling differentiated instruction the chapter explores how AI can assist teachers.

Chapter 3
Teaching AI in Communication Classes: Engagement, Ethics, and Best Practices 63
David Lynn Painter, Rollins College, USA

This chapter examines the integration of artificial intelligence (AI) in college communication courses. First, survey data reveals significant differences in AI attitudes and usage patterns based on students' demographic characteristics, highlighting the need for inclusive practices. Further, students who completed AI-integrated courses reported more critical attitudes toward the technology while engaging in more ethical and fewer unethical uses. Second, the chapter identifies discipline-specific ethical challenges presented by AI integration. Third, using experiential learning theory as a framework, the chapter provides practical strategies for incorporating AI into college communication curricula. This framework preserves disciplinary values while preparing diverse student populations for a communication industry where AI literacy is essential.

Chapter 4
Training Educators in AI for Future-Proofing Education 99
Ramar Veluchamy, Saveetha Engineering College, India

This research aims to investigate the potential of Artificial Intelligence (AI) in revolutionizing higher education. Specifically, it explores the impact of AI on personalized learning, administrative efficiency, data analytics, and the preparation of educators for this technological shift. A comprehensive literature review was conducted to analyze existing research on AI in higher education. Key studies were identified and synthesized to understand the current state of AI applications, their benefits, challenges, and future trends. Furthermore, interviews with educators and administrators were conducted to gather insights into their experiences and perspectives on AI integration. The findings demonstrate that AI has the potential to significantly enhance higher education.

Chapter 5
Leveraging Generative AI in Educator Preparation Programs: Preparing Inclusive and Equitable Educators 135
Joseph Casey Cosgriff, Morehead State University, USA
Daryl R. Privott, Morehead State University, USA

This chapter offers actionable guidance on the ethical use of generative AI (genAI) in Educator Preparation Programs (EPPs). GenAI literacy is critical for both students and educators. Thus this chapter discusses the skills and dispositions needed to effectively and ethically use genAI in the classroom. It also explores practical applications of genAI in education, such as personalized learning, accessibility, and collaboration.

As an actionable step, it proposes substantial revisions for the Interstate Teacher Assessment and Support Consortium (InTASC) standards, highlighting the need for continuous learning and adaptation in the use of genAI. Advocating for a mindset of ongoing learning and adaptation, this chapter emphasizes the importance of human agency and ethical considerations in the integration of genAI in education.

Chapter 6
Using AI in Preparing Pre-Service Teachers for Field Experience 199
Geralda Silva Nelson, Morehead State University, USA

Abstract The study examined how artificial intelligence (AI) supported pre-service teachers during their field placements by streamlining content creation, reducing time spent on administrative tasks, and offering data-driven insights to refine instructional strategies. These placements provided future educators with hands-on experience in real classroom settings, where they encountered challenges such as lesson planning, differentiation, and student assessment. AI tools played a crucial role in addressing these challenges by assisting with resource development, providing adaptive learning recommendations, and enhancing the overall teaching experience.

Chapter 7
Artificial Intelligence in Education Higher Education in the Business Area ... 227
Albérico Travassos Rosário, GOVCOPP, IADE, Universidade Europeia, Portugal

Artificial intelligence (AI) has revolutionized several sectors, including higher education, by personalizing the educational experience to fit individual student needs. Integrating AI into business curricula equips students with the skills needed in a market increasingly driven by AI and data analysis. Institutions that adopt these technologies are better positioned to deliver quality education, prepare students for a data- and AI-driven future, and enhance operational efficiency. However, it is crucial to address the ethical and privacy challenges associated with AI to ensure responsible and transparent implementation. Based on the above, it is intended to systematically review the bibliometric literature on Artificial Intelligence in Education Higher Education in the business area using the Scopus database with the analysis of 94 academic and/or scientific documents.

Chapter 8
Artificial Intelligence for Learning Disabilities: Enhancing Accessibility, Inclusion, and Empowerment 267
Shariq Nabi Wani, University of Kashmir, India
Shazia Farooq, University of Kashmir, India
Aasia Maqbool, University of Kashmir, India
Nasir Rasheed, University of Kashmir, India
Sumeera Maqbool, University of Kashmir, India
Warisul Rehman, University of Kashmir, India
John Mohammad, University of Kashmir, India
Rasak Annayat, National Institute of Technology, Srinagar, India
Shabir Ahmad Bhat, University of Kashmir, India
Abdal Ahmad Bhat, Government Degree College, Awantipora, India

The development of big data, cloud computing, artificial neural networks, and machine learning has enabled AI devices to perceive, recognize, learn, and solve issues, marking AI as a disruptive innovation in sectors like education. AI's potential is promising for students with learning disabilities (SWLDs), enhancing accessibility, inclusion, and empowerment through personalized learning and assistive technologies. AI-driven tools, including intelligent tutoring systems, speech recognition, and cognitive support, revolutionize educational practices. This chapter also addresses ethical considerations and future implications, highlighting AI's transformative role in fostering an inclusive learning environment.

Chapter 9
AI Text Mining of Case Studies for Students With Disabilities Using Handy ICT Tools 295
Shigeru Ikuta, Otsuma Women's University, Japan

The author has conducted many case study activities for students with disabilities in collaboration with schoolteachers using handy tools such as a speaking-pen and dot-code reader. In these activities, tiny dot codes were used to link multimedia such as audio and video. Every year, the author compiled the case study activity reports sent by the schoolteachers and reported them in an online journal. In the present chapter paper, the context of the reports over a 10-year period was analyzed using AI text mining to obtain word cloud, the appearance frequency of words, and the co-occurrence of words and co-occurrence network. Dependency analysis was also performed to clarify the "modifier-modifier" relationship between two keywords in a sentence. Through this AI text mining, the role of schoolteachers and handy tools used will be clarified in enabling students with disabilities to realize activities that they were not able to do before.

Chapter 10
Critical Thinking Skills and Artificial Intelligence (AI) 337
Mehdi Kaddouri, Mohamed First University, Morocco
Ilham Chniete, Mohammed First University, Morocco
Khalid Mhamdi, Mohammed First University, Morocco
Abderrahmane Bouamri, National School of Agriculture, Meknes, Morocco
Khaoula Atmani, Mohammed First University, Morocco

This chapter explores the complex relationship between artificial intelligence (AI) and critical thinking skills in education. It examines how AI is reshaping learning and decision-making, while emphasizing critical thinking skills as essential for navigating these changes. AI offers opportunities through personalized learning and immersive scenarios, but faces limitations like algorithmic opacity and data bias that require ethical integration into education. The chapter addresses key areas: critical thinking's role in the AI era, AI-critical thinking interactions, challenges posed by AI, and strategies for developing critical thinking skills. It focuses on pedagogical approaches fostering critical reflection and intellectual autonomy. The text advocates for a systemic approach where AI complements human cognitive capacities rather than replacing them. Through synergy between critical thinking and AI, educators can prepare learners for 21st-century challenges with discernment and responsibility.

Chapter 11
Critical Thinking and GenAI: A Guide to Action 377
Silvio Andrae, Independent Researcher, Germany

Generative AI (GenAI) presents a dilemma: GenAI makes information more readily available but also reduces the likelihood that users will question or expand the information provided. This dilemma highlights the importance of fostering students' critical thinking skills. This chapter introduces a novel framework, the Learn, Evaluate, and Reflect (LER) methodology, designed to help individuals and organizations use GenAI effectively. This framework not only highlights the critical thinking processes needed to evaluate AI-generated results but also fosters collaboration between human intuition and machine intelligence, inviting everyone to be part of the AI discourse. This exploration reflects a broader imperative: cultivating an AI-literate society that values critical thinking as a core skill in the age of intelligent machines.

Chapter 12
Enhancing Critical Thinking: The Role of AI in Modern Education 413
Andi Asrifan, Universitas Negeri Makassar, Indonesia
K. Khristianto, Universitas Muhammadiyah Purwokerto, Indonesia
Arif Budiman, UIN Sunan Kalijaga, Indonesia
Purwani Indri Astuti, Univet Bantara Sukoharjo, Indonesia
Ahmad Rossydi, Politeknik Penerbangan Makassar, Indonesia

This chapter examines the transformative impact of Artificial Intelligence (AI) on the enhancement of critical thinking skills in educational environments. It emphasizes that AI-driven learning platforms, like Knewton and Carnegie Learning, offer tailored and interactive experiences that enhance student engagement and inquiry. By accommodating distinct learning styles and providing customized feedback, these platforms promote students' abilities to analyze, evaluate, and synthesize material proficiently. The chapter also addresses the potential challenges of over-reliance on AI, emphasizing the need for a balanced approach that promotes independent problem-solving skills. The use of AI in education improves academic achievement and equips students with vital abilities for informed decision-making and effective problem-solving in a complicated modern society.

Chapter 13
Navigating the AI Era: Enhancing Critical Thinking Skills for Global Challenges 449
Andi Asrifan, Universitas Negeri Makassar, Indonesia
Agnes Widyaningrum, Universitas Stikubank Semarang, Indonesia
Ratu Bulkis Ramli, Universitas Musamus, Indonesia
Riyanti Riyanti, Universitas Muhammadiyah Palopo, Indonesia
Sultan Sultan, Universitas Muhammadiyah Palopo, Indonesia

This chapter examines the vital junction between artificial intelligence (AI) and critical thinking, highlighting the imperative to improve critical thinking abilities to effectively manage the complexities of contemporary society. As AI technologies are progressively incorporated into several sectors, the capacity to assess, evaluate, and synthesize information is essential for effective decision-making. The chapter examines the progression of AI, its applications in everyday life, and the ethical implications that emerge from its utilization. It underscores the significance of cultivating critical thinking using educational methodologies, including Socratic seminars, case studies, and problem-based learning. By fostering a culture of inquiry and adaptation, humans may more effectively tackle global concerns such as climate change and inequality, utilizing AI as a means for inventive solutions.

The chapter ultimately promotes a proactive educational strategy that emphasizes critical thinking in the era of AI.

Compilation of References 481

About the Contributors 557

Index 567

Preface

INTRODUCTION

The rapid integration of Artificial Intelligence (AI) into educational systems across the globe marks a transformative era in teaching and learning. This volume, *Enhancing Classroom Instruction and Student Skills With AI*, brings together a diverse and international group of scholars and educators to explore the multifaceted roles AI plays in shaping modern education. From personalized instruction and adaptive learning technologies to ethical considerations and inclusive practices, the chapters presented here offer a rich tapestry of research, innovation, and applied strategies.

The contributors—spanning institutions from the United States, India, Portugal, Morocco, Japan, and Indonesia—highlight the transformative potential of AI in both theory and practice. The various chapters delve into student perceptions and engagement, emphasizing the importance of understanding learner attitudes toward AI-driven tools and how these shape the learning environment.

A significant theme throughout this collection is the development of critical thinking and ethical awareness in AI-integrated classrooms. Multiple chapters focus on how generative AI and adaptive technologies can foster critical reflection, while others caution against overreliance and stress the need for balanced, human-centered educational practices. Special attention is given to educator preparation, including strategies for training pre-service teachers, supporting inclusive learning for students with disabilities, and revising pedagogical standards to incorporate AI literacy.

Moreover, the volume explores the role of AI in specific disciplinary contexts such as communication, business education, and higher education administration, reflecting the broad applicability of AI across educational sectors. The final chapters consider the intersection of AI with global challenges, advocating for education that cultivates both technological fluency and the cognitive resilience necessary to navigate complex societal issues.

CHAPTER OVERVIEW

Chapter 1

Artificial intelligence is widely used across sectors, prompting the need to understand its role in education. This chapter investigates student perceptions, engagement, and familiarity with AI tools, focusing on how they influence learning experiences. Based on a survey of undergraduate and postgraduate students, it highlights attitudes toward AI in educational settings and the perceived usefulness of AI-driven tools. The chapter concludes with practical recommendations for educators and policymakers to promote effective and engaging AI integration in higher education.

Chapter 2

This chapter explores how AI is transforming traditional classroom dynamics by enhancing student engagement and modernizing instructional methods. It discusses how AI-powered technologies offer personalized learning experiences, enabling students to progress at their own pace. These platforms provide real-time feedback, automate administrative tasks, and support data-driven decision-making. The chapter illustrates how AI supports differentiated instruction and improves overall teaching effectiveness.

Chapter 3

The chapter examines the use of AI in college-level communication courses. It highlights survey findings showing differences in AI attitudes based on student demographics and reports increased ethical awareness among students who participated in AI-integrated courses. It identifies discipline-specific ethical challenges and offers strategies based on experiential learning theory for integrating AI in communication curricula. The approach ensures that students gain necessary AI literacy while preserving core disciplinary values.

Chapter 4

Focusing on higher education, this chapter investigates the potential of AI to revolutionize learning through personalized instruction, administrative efficiency, and data analytics. A review of existing literature and educator interviews reveal the benefits, challenges, and future trends of AI adoption. The chapter underscores the importance of preparing educators for these changes, showing that AI has the potential to significantly enhance educational quality and effectiveness.

Chapter 5

This chapter provides practical guidance on the ethical use of generative AI (genAI) in Educator Preparation Programs (EPPs). It outlines the necessary skills and dispositions for both educators and students to effectively leverage genAI in the classroom. Topics include personalized learning, accessibility, and collaborative practices. The chapter proposes updates to national teaching standards, promoting lifelong learning, ethical awareness, and responsible AI integration in teacher education.

Chapter 6

This chapter explores how AI supports pre-service teachers during field placements. It highlights AI's role in streamlining lesson planning, reducing administrative burdens, and providing data-driven feedback. By enhancing instructional strategies and supporting differentiation and assessment, AI tools enrich the real-world teaching experience for future educators, preparing them to address classroom challenges more effectively.

Chapter 7

AI is reshaping higher education by personalizing learning in the business domain. This chapter discusses how AI integration into business curricula prepares students for data-driven environments while improving institutional efficiency. It also emphasizes the ethical and privacy concerns related to AI deployment. The chapter presents a bibliometric analysis of 94 academic documents from the Scopus database to understand the scope and trends in AI's educational applications.

Chapter 8

AI technologies, including big data and machine learning, offer significant benefits for students with learning disabilities by supporting personalized and inclusive education. This chapter explores AI-driven tools such as intelligent tutoring systems and speech recognition to empower learners. It also addresses ethical issues and outlines AI's transformative role in promoting accessible and equitable learning environments.

Chapter 9

Using case studies conducted over a decade, this chapter analyzes how ICT tools such as speaking pens and dot-code readers assist students with disabilities. AI text mining methods were applied to these reports to identify key themes, word frequencies, and dependency relationships. The analysis reveals how simple technologies, combined with teacher guidance, have enabled students to achieve learning outcomes previously out of reach.

Chapter 10

This chapter investigates the interplay between AI and critical thinking skills. It explores how AI offers immersive, personalized learning while emphasizing the importance of ethical integration. It examines how critical thinking complements AI use and presents pedagogical strategies for fostering reflective and autonomous learners. The chapter advocates for a balanced approach where AI enhances, rather than replaces, human cognitive skills.

Chapter 11

Generative AI creates both opportunities and challenges for critical thinking. This chapter introduces the Learn, Evaluate, and Reflect (LER) framework to promote thoughtful engagement with AI-generated content. It encourages collaboration between human intuition and machine intelligence, emphasizing the need for AI literacy and the development of critical thinking to navigate the digital age responsibly.

Chapter 12

AI-powered platforms like Knewton and Carnegie Learning offer personalized, interactive experiences that improve student engagement and analytical skills. This chapter explores how such technologies enhance critical thinking and academic performance by supporting various learning styles. It also cautions against overreliance on AI, highlighting the importance of maintaining students' independent problem-solving abilities.

Chapter 13

In response to global challenges, this chapter emphasizes the need to enhance critical thinking in an AI-driven world. It reviews the evolution and application of AI, discusses its ethical implications, and presents educational strategies such as

Socratic seminars and problem-based learning. The chapter encourages a proactive, inquiry-based approach to education that empowers learners to use AI creatively and responsibly to address complex societal issues.

Together, these chapters not only provide a comprehensive overview of current trends and innovations in AI in education but also offer forward-looking perspectives for educators, researchers, and policymakers. As AI continues to evolve, the insights in this book aim to ensure its integration enhances human potential, equity, and lifelong learning.

Michael W. Kessinger
Morehead State University, USA

Gera Nelson
Morehead State University, USA

Lesia Lennex
Morehead State University, USA

Kimberely Nettleton
Morehead State University, USA

Chapter 1
AI in Education: Understanding Student Perceptions and Engagement

Nusrat Khan
https://orcid.org/0000-0003-0788-7786
GD Goenka University, India

Fehmina Khalique
https://orcid.org/0000-0002-2519-3174
Lloyd Business School, India

Mohd Azmi Khan
https://orcid.org/0000-0002-7112-003X
Aligarh Muslim University, India

Kartikay Saini
https://orcid.org/0000-0002-5240-4168
GD Goenka University, India

ABSTRACT

Artificial intelligence is discussed widely in present times along with its usage. Everyone, including organizations and individuals are using AI for different purposes. It becomes imperative to understand and explore the foundational concepts of AI in the field of education. Therefore, with this objective, the chapter focuses on student perceptions, engagement and the influence of AI tools on learning experiences, understanding of AI, perception, familiarity of students, and its potential to transform learning environments. The data was collected through a detailed survey tool only from higher educational institutions, comprising of 120 both undergraduate and postgraduate students. It discusses their attitudes towards the incorporation of AI in educational surroundings and the usefulness of AI-driven educational tools. This

DOI: 10.4018/979-8-3373-4576-5.ch001

exploration not only sheds light on the benefits and concerns associated with AI but also offers practical recommendations for educators and policymakers to optimize AI integration and foster a more personalized and engaging learning environment.

INTRODUCTION

In recent years, with the advent of Artificial Intelligence (AI) its potential in every field has witnessed massive growth specially in education and learning, and the role of education in AI literacy have also received increased attention, and are fast becoming hot topics in policy debates (Miao & Holmes, 2021). The idea of automating teacher tasks (Sperling et al., 2022), suggests that the transformative effect of AI could be helpful for human cognition in learning (Molenaar, 2022). It goes without saying, the future of AI in educational settings, and the requirement for AI literacy, focuses on educators for exciting developments who otherwise were confined to computer labs. In the past, research and development in AI for education (AIED) has seen contribution from computer scientists (Chen et al., 2020; Williamson & Eynon, 2020; Zawacki-Richter et al., 2019), however in recent times, AIED is focus of commercial interests as well. The AIED market is growing at a fast pace globally and it is estimated that there are more than thirty multi-million-dollar-funded AIED corporations, and the market is expected to become worth more than US$ 20 billion within five years, according to GMI, 2022 (Holmes et.al, 2022).

In actuality, while the idea of artificial intelligence (AI) and intelligent machines can trace back from the 14th century, while the concept of AIEd is still relatively new, having just been introduced into the field of education for around 30 years (Heffernan & Heffernan, 2014). The ongoing results and accomplishments from various fields and disciplines have had a significant impact on how we teach and learn (Bayne, 2015; Botrel, Holz, & Kübler, 2015; Humble & Mozelius, 2019). For almost 30 years, AIEd has emerged as a scientific field of study (Luckin et.al., 2022). Not only are educational institutions and government sectors more interested than ever in comprehending and enhancing the use of AI methods for educational purposes. The research work in the area of AIEd is at a very nascent stage (Hinojo-Lucena et.al, 2019; Zawacki-Richter et.al, 2019).

With its enormous potential to alter our thoughts, behaviors, and interactions, artificial intelligence (AI)-enhanced digital technology has become essential in our day-to-day lives. Since its inception, artificial intelligence (AI) has grown and the advent of Deep Learning (DL) and Artificial Neural Networks (ANN) has made it more versatile (Chan & Zary, 2019).

The integration of AI in education (AIED) has paved the way for innovative learning activities and enhanced technology-based learning environments. However, implementing these systems and activities remains a significant hurdle for many researchers (Kay, 2012). Intelligent tutoring and adaptive learning systems development requires not only programming expertise but also the ability to simulate human expert intelligence. These decisions are taken to address individual learners' challenges and improve their learning outcomes. There are difficulties which arise due to AIED's highly technical and interdisciplinary nature. Various questions would be explored by this valuable research in this field. Key characteristics of AI in education is to deliver individualized learning support tailored to each student's unique status, preferences, and characteristics (Hwang et.al, 2020). The definition and functions of AIED studies from the standpoint of educational needs and illustrated the factors to be taken into account when adopting AIED in various environments for instruction and learning. When performing AIED studies, the framework developed can assist researchers with computer and educational backgrounds (Hwang et.al, 2020).

In both K–12 and higher education backgrounds, educators and students are progressively using AI-powered tools and applications, such as intelligent robots and adaptive learning systems. AI technologies offer the possibility of implementing personalized learning for students in order to satisfy their unique requirements. It might be challenging to please every learner using standard educational approaches because each person is independent and has different learning needs, styles, and talents. But with AI, teachers may adapt to each student's needs individually, as a result of which, students can become more independent, motivated, and involved in their education (Della Ventura, 2018; Wang et.al, 2017). Furthermore, AI technologies present opportunities to enhance the involvement of students with special needs. As AI technologies are used more and more in teaching and learning, teachers have the opportunity to eliminate time-consuming and repetitive chores and respond to pupils (Chan & Zary, 2019). System innovations, such as fast graphical processing units and the availability of a wide range of software libraries, have accelerated the use of AI technologies, especially with the success of deep learning research and the application of data analysis methods. Furthermore, the advancement of AI will fundamentally have a significant impact on how education develops in the future. As a result, the creation of new technologies and the processing power of intelligent machines will further energize and blossom education in the future.

There are several commercial AI systems developed for education are named as Intelligent Tutoring Systems (ITS), which have automated, adaptive and instruction driven approach. Computer based collaborative learning is a discipline since the mid-1990s (e.g., Dillenbourg et al., 2009), while learning analytics and educational data mining (Joksimovic et al., 2020) have close association with AIED. Learning and development as a tool for socio-cultural activity has gained importance in recent years in AIED (Thomas & Porayska-Pomsta, 2022). Beyond teaching (i.e., student-focused AIED), AI has potentially interesting applications in education administration (i.e., system-focused AIED) and teacher support (i.e., teacher-focused AIED), and could even stimulate new pedagogical and andragogical approaches (Holmes & Tuomi, 2022). Educational data, as generated by e-learning systems including AIED, are increasingly the subject of analysis by the fast-growing field such as educational data mining and learning analytics, and are crucial for policy makers and practitioners (Hakimi et al., 2024; Verbert et al., 2014).

AI and its Application in Education

AI is defined as a machine-based system that if provided a set of objectives, can make predictions or recommendations or draw conclusions that can lead to decisions that influence real or virtual environments (Holmes & Tuomi, 2022). According to UNICEF, 2021 AI can be defined as a system that interact with the user or the environment, maintaining direct or indirect interaction, operating on its own, and can adapt its behaviour by learning about the context. This definition explains that AI is data independent, and can utilize data-driven AI techniques, for example, artificial neural networks (ANN) and deep learning (DL), at the same time it can also include knowledge-based AI, and any new paradigm of AI that me evolve in the future. Secondly, it retains the role of users, for example, AI systems give recommendations or predictions and draw conclusions based on objectives that are defined by the user of AI. Thirdly, it distinguishes between systems that do operate autonomously and those that appear to operate autonomously (Schaffer, 1999). Lastly, AI emphasizes interaction with humans, it can be widely accepted as an application in education.

AIED is based on two alternative approaches for developing AI systems for educators. First is 'data-driven AI', or machine learning approach while the second is 'knowledge-based AI' or 'symbolic AI'. In education sector, the Data-driven AI has seen wide application while knowledge-based AI still supports most existing AIED systems.

Data-driven AI has been widely used in the last decade in in the form of natural language processing, robotics and the like. All these systems are based on the idea that if large set of data items and a criterion for 'improvement' are provided, a computer can eventually predict a model that optimizes its operations. For example, if a computer program results in wrong prediction, the program trains itself to reduce the error in its training phase, while when the program makes the right prediction, it learns to make the same prediction with higher probability. Widely used AI systems can have a huge number of parameters that are repeatedly adjusted until the system works like OpenAI's famous GPT-3 language model has 175 billion adjustable parameters (Brown et al., 2020). As mentioned earlier, in education sector, knowledge-based AI plays a significant role as these systems are based on the fact that human knowledge and expertise can be represented in a form that can be processed by computer programs.

AI is applied in education (AIED) in multiple ways focused widely in students or teachers perspective in order to aid them and assist them in economical ways.

Student Focused AIED

All AI-assisted technologies used by students have not been designed for students, rather, these technologies have been 'repurposed' for learning. For example, AI-assisted technology that has been repurposed for education is the Google suite of collaborative tools like Google Docs and Google Sheets. Additionally, social networking platforms like WhatsApp, WeChat, and content sharing platforms such as YouTube and TikTok are widely being used to support student learning during and post pandemic. There are several AI-assisted technologies being repurposed for education, like activity trackers although usually with limited evidence for how they support teaching or learning.

The intelligent tutoring systems (ITS) are widely used platforms of AI in education that that make use of sequential learning of concepts of subject contents. ITS can also include teacher dashboards, that helps teachers to assess the progress of the students. Commonly used commercial ITS is Spark, from the French company Domoscio. Another ITS is the Gooru Navigator, which aims to be the Google Maps for learning (Songer et al., 2020).

Virtual Reality (VR) and Augmented Reality (AR) simulations along with digital games-based learning use AI machine learning are widely used for educating and classroom learning that uses image recognition and natural language processing. For instance, AI-enabled VR has been used to provide training to doctors on a variety of neurosurgical procedures (McGuire & Alaraj, 2018) while digital games-based learning (DGBL) also makes use of AI technologies (LaPierre, 2021). Students with learning disabilities are also supported with commercially available AIED (Barua et al., 2022) whereas there are several AI based approaches that are in use to diagnosis learning disabilities like ADHD, dyslexia and dysgraphia (Benfatto et al., 2016; Anuradha et al., 2010; Asselborn et al., 2020). Students with autism spectrum can also be supported through use of robotics while text-to-speech apps and automatic image captioning, which are 'repurposed' are widely used by students with learning disorders (Alabdulkareem et al., 2022).

AI applications using 'large language models', such as the GPT-3 from Open AI helps in automatic essay writing (AEW) for students; and there are several platforms with AI-assisted chatbots like Ada that was developed by a UK community college, using IBM's Watson Conversation platform and is widely used in educational setup (Hwang & Chang, 2021; Pérez et al., 2020; Hussain, 2017).

Automatic formative assessment (AFA) applications like Open Essayist or Grammarly use natural language and semantic processing along with other AI-assisted techniques can provide feedback on student writing (Foster, 2019). According to a research at Stanford University that used an 'autograder' AFA system which provided feedback on programming jobs of students turned out 98 percent accurate as per the students' feedback (Metz, 2021).

Dialogue-based tutoring systems (DBTS) such as 'AutoTutor' researched at the University of Memphis simulate a tutorial dialogue, as the student works step-by-step through an online task, the student is guided towards discovering for themselves the pre-specified solution for the current problem (Nye et al., 2014). Exploratory learning environments (ELEs) like FractionsLab uses AI and on this learning platform.

Teacher Focused AIED

Many student-focused AIED have dashboards for teachers that offer a feedback system about the individual student or groups of students (Bodily & Verbert, 2017). Another approach could be use of augmented reality (AR) glasses used by the instructor to superimpose information to their students while the students engage with an ITS (Holstein et al., 2018). There are several platforms where the teacher can use AIED for improving their teaching learning and other classroom activities. For example, plagiarism detection services like Turnitin are widely used by instructors, that uses machine learning, other tools for detecting plagiarism in students' writings are iThenticate, Ouriginal and Grammarly. For smart curation of learning materials there is a research tool, X5GON and other tools like Teacher Advisor from IBM and Clever Owl have been developed that automatically scrape the web to find teaching and learning resources in response to teacher queries.

There are many AI-assisted systems being used for classroom-based student monitoring for example, AI-assisted video applications that monitors student activities and movements to gauge their attention towards their instructor (Lieu, 2018). Moreover, students can use EEG (electroencephalography) headsets to record their brain activity for teachers to 'monitor' their attention (Poulsen et al., 2017). Meanwhile, at many universities, AI-assisted systems are also being used to monitor student's movements through the campus (Moriarty-Mclaughlin, 2020).

Automatic summative assessment is also increasingly used by the teachers that could save teachers time and effort by automating the labour-intensive assessment of student assignments (Watters, 2021). For example, Autograders have been used for the assessment of written tasks for SAT exams (Ramesh & Sanampudi, 2021). Students' feedback provides valuable insights into their everyday usability practices.

Their effectiveness of AI applications, will help in highlighting areas for improvement and innovation. This will also help address ethical and privacy concerns. It is also important to foster a trustworthy and supportive learning environment. Educators and policymakers can ensure that AI technologies are implemented in a way that is both effective and aligned with the learners' expectations and requirements.

RESEARCH OBJECTIVES AND METHODOLOGY

This study adopts a cross sectional and descriptive quantitative research approach. It examines student perceptions and engagement with AI in education while they are studying their respective courses. For the same the data was collected through a structured survey questionnaire designed to assess attitudes towards AI integration in students' educational settings and also understanding their perceived usefulness of AI-driven educational tools. The survey targeted only students from higher educational institutions, encompassing a sample of 120 respondents, including both undergraduate and postgraduate students. The target sample was decided based on the topic and also the usage of such tools along with its awareness is higher in students of such background. The questionnaire comprised of multiple sections which included demographic details of students and also multiple-choice question (MCQ) with multiple responses to get an understanding regarding their knowledge, attitudes, current technology usage, and engagement with AI driven tools. The questionnaire also seeked their feedback on their individual learning preferences for different AI tools. The sections were divided into demographics asking them about age, gender, Educational Background, Field of Study. Baseline Knowledge and Understanding of AI, Attitudes and Perceptions towards AI, Current Technology Usage, Engagement and Interaction, Learning Preferences, Feedback on AI Tools, Performance Data, Technical Issues and Support Needs. Two questions were also asked, which were open ended questions seeking their opinions on technical issues and support needed which was necessary for effective use of AI tools in their education. The survey was administered using an online Google form, platform. This was primarily used for ensuring accessibility and ease of participation along with the familiarity of filling out these forms. A convenience sampling method was employed to reach a diverse group of students from different academic backgrounds. Data analysis was conducted using descriptive statistical tools, enabling the identification of trends and significant factors influencing student engagement with AI in education. The study aims to contribute to the growing body of research on AI in education by offering empirical insights into student attitudes and highlighting key areas for improvement in AI-driven learning environments.

Keeping in mind the role of AI in education, the following are the objectives of this chapter:

- To assess students' baseline knowledge and understanding of AI.
- To explore students' attitudes and perceptions towards AI in education.
- To analyze the current usage and engagement levels with AI-powered educational tools.
- To understand and evaluate the effectiveness of AI tools in enhancing learning experiences.
- To identify technical issues and support needs for effective AI integration in education.

LITERATURE REVIEW

Cotton et al. (2023) raised the concern that some students misuse AI tools for unethical purposes, such as plagiarism or generating content without proper attribution. Several features of AI are there which can be used by students for different purposes for different works. For example, AI text generators have been employed to create essays, circumventing the need for original thought and writing. Therefore, with the advent of technologies, and its wide usage the educational institutions are now developing AI detection tools and ethical guidelines to address this problem. Essays are an integral part of the academic evaluation process. Beside the adoption of these technologies to assist the students, it may also be about the guidelines to be set up for its usage to exhibit the work in best possible manner besides keeping the academic integrity intact.

Holmes (2020) highlighted that the use of AI tools may influence the development of essential skills, particularly writing and problem-solving abilities. Several disadvantages of AI include that excessive reliance on AI could lead to a decline in students' cognitive capabilities. As AI performs tasks that traditionally required human effort it may dampen the students' learning skills. Kumar et al., (2022) has shown that all those who support AI are also believing that AI allows students to focus on a different level of higher-order thinking skills. As most of the other repetitive or administrative tasks are handled by AI. The Studies show that students generally have a favorable opinion of AI in education. They are valuing its potential for personalization and efficiency. However, worries about data privacy, potential job displacement, and the quality of AI-generated content remain. Addressing these concerns will necessitate transparent policies and robust ethical frameworks. The use of AI in education brings forth ethical concerns, particularly regarding data privacy and bias. AI systems rely on extensive datasets, which may unintentionally perpetuate biases present in the data. This raises questions about fairness and equality in educational opportunities (Binns et al., 2018). Both students and educators are calling for increased oversight and regulation to ensure the ethical use of AI in education.

Lee et al. (2022) stated that AI-driven chatbots and natural language processing tools to facilitate in-the-moment communication between the teacher and pupils. Chatbots helped students navigate the course material, provide instant feedback, and respond to often requested questions. By encouraging active participation and various forms of engagement, these AI elements made sure that students had access to pertinent and timely information (Bakare and Jatto, 2023). Rajaram et al. (2022) highlighted that portal provided personalized recommendations and resources by using AI algorithms to examine students' interactions, preferences, and learning styles. It may provide additional materials, practice tasks, or relevant resources to improve students' comprehension of programming language ideas and chatbot development by taking into account their particular needs (Tran, 2021). Regarding the education sector, AI cannot be a problem because it has always been stated that social connection with others is an essential component of effective learning. Indeed, AI has a significant impact on the educational industry.

Zawacki-Richter et al. (2019) emphasized that AI's ability to provide individualized learning experiences has completely changed how students learn. A more customized learning experience is made possible by AI-powered adaptive learning systems that can assess a student's strengths and shortcomings to provide feedback and content that is specifically targeted to them.

It is predicted that a large number of studies will explore AI applications in educational contexts and examine potential methods for promoting and teaching AI knowledge across all educational levels. Questions arise, such as whether the introduction of robots in classrooms will enhance student motivation and engagement. Additionally, researchers may investigate if (English Foreign Language) EFL students can achieve better English writing results when using an AI-powered article evaluation program compared to traditional teaching methods. Furthermore, there is interest in how AI technologies can assist policymakers in addressing ongoing educational challenges and making effective decisions to tackle these issues. Although AI integration in education is still in its infancy, there is a lot of promise. Future advancements will probably concentrate on developing more human-like interactions with virtual mentors and AI tutors, encouraging human-machine cooperation.

Even subject-matter specialists may find it challenging to define artificial intelligence (AI) because of several reasons. For instance, the nature of AI is always changing. Many academics have tried to define artificial intelligence. Russell and Norvig (2016), for example, stated that artificial intelligence (AI) was used to describe devices or computers that mimicked "cognitive" processes, such as "learning" and "problem solving," linked to the human intelligence. Artificial Intelligence (AI) according to Poole et.al (1998), is the study of intelligent agents that can both comprehend their environment and maximize the likelihood of achieving a specific goal.

Despite the lack of a widely accepted definition, it is certain that, in addition to computer science, artificial intelligence (AI) encompasses a wide range of fields like information technology, social-psychology, liberal arts, psychology, philosophy etc. Accordingly, AI is a highly extensive interdisciplinary field (H. Zhao et.al, 2018). The educational landscape is being reshaped by Artificial Intelligence (AI), which is revolutionizing learning methods, teaching approaches, and institutional operations. This chapter delves into the diverse applications of AI in education, analyzing its advantages, obstacles, and future prospects. The discussion will encompass key areas such as individualized instruction, operational efficiency, and enhanced accessibility, drawing upon scholarly research and academic perspectives.

The majority of students regarded AI as a beneficial addition to higher education, particularly for its capacity to improve learning flexibility and personalization. Nevertheless, they also stressed the importance of complementary AI tools with orthodox teaching methods to preserve human connection and guidance. Students called for greater transparency in AI system operations, especially concerning the use of their personal data and decision-making processes. Educational institutions should allocate resources for training programs to help students and educators effectively utilize AI tools. Policymakers must establish clear ethical guidelines and standards to ensure responsible AI use in education. Efforts should be made to narrow the digital divide, ensuring all students have access to AI-based learning resources. Additionally, there is a danger of excessive reliance on AI, which could diminish the importance of human educators. While AI can improve teaching methods, it cannot substitute the emotional intelligence and interpersonal abilities that teachers contribute to the classroom. Striking a balance between AI utilization and human supervision is crucial for preserving a comprehensive educational experience. Table 1 discusses the same about AI Based enablers and Barriers to Educational Experience.

Table 1. AI-based enablers and barriers to educational experience

Aspect	Details
Enablers	
Personalized Learning	AI tailors educational experiences based on individual learning styles and progress.
Improved Accessibility	Tools like speech-to-text, text-to-speech, and virtual assistants ensure inclusivity.

Aspect	Details
Efficiency in Learning	AI automates tasks like grading and scheduling, saving time for students.
Enhanced Engagement	Gamified tools and interactive platforms increase motivation and participation.
Skill Development	AI equips students with future-ready skills like data analysis and critical thinking.
Barriers	
Ethical Concerns	Students worry about data privacy, algorithmic bias, and fairness in AI systems.
Reliability Issues	Occasional inaccuracies in AI tools, such as grading, affect learning outcomes.
Limited Human Interaction	Over-reliance on AI reduces opportunities for instructor and peer engagement.
Digital Divide	Students from underprivileged backgrounds face technological and financial barriers.
Adaptability Issues	Some students struggle to adapt to and effectively use AI technologies.

Source: Adapted from Kumar, Sharma, and Kaur (2022)

The outlook for AI in education is bright, with ongoing technological advancements. Virtual reality (VR) and augmented reality (AR) are the emerging technologies which are being combined with AI to create engaging learning environments. For instance, AI-powered VR simulations are being utilized to teach intricate subjects such as medicine and engineering. Moreover, AI is anticipated to play a crucial role in continuous learning.

Sadegh-Zadeh et al. (2023) reported that the study explores how Microsoft Teams can enhance student engagement and interaction in online learning. It involved 35 students in an AI course, with mixed perceptions of the platform. Results showed positive engagement and motivation, but some issues with communication. The study suggests that Microsoft Teams, with AI features, can improve online learning outcomes. Instructors should focus on fostering communication and connections with students.

RESULTS AND ANALYSIS

Demographic Profile

The study was carried out on young students and the study found out that the age of the respondents was between 18-24. About 91% of the students were in the age group of 18 to 24 years and only about 9% were in the age group of 25-34 years. Further, 43% of males and around 57% of females participated in this research. The respondents were students of varied educational background from different fields and about 54% of students were graduate students. Figure 1 and figure 2 correspond to these details.

Figure 1. Educational background of respondents

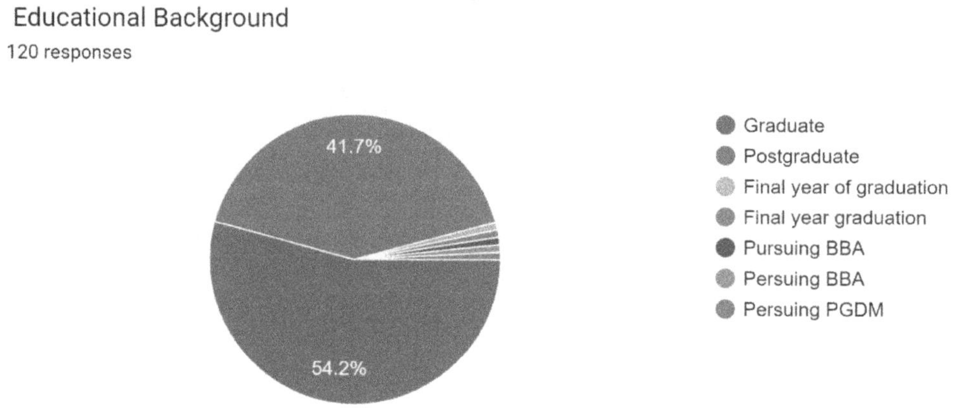

Figure 2. Field of study of respondents

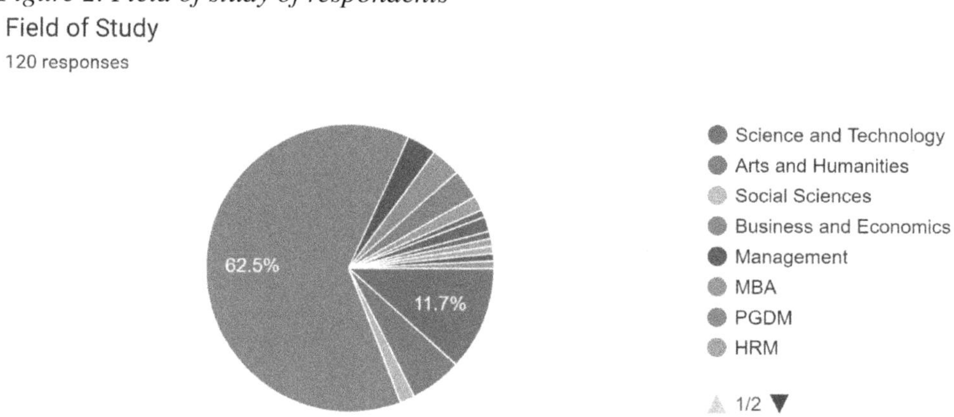

Knowledge and Understanding of AI

The pie chart (figure 3) represents the responses of the participants regarding their familiarity with the concept of Artificial Intelligence (AI). Only about 12.5% were found to be extremely familiar with AI concept. About 22.5% of the respondents has limited knowledge or exposure to AI concepts. The respondents who were moderately familiar were about 37.5%. This forms the largest group of respondents falls in this category, indicating a basic understanding or exposure to AI. This suggests that many participants have a general idea of AI but lack in-depth knowledge. About 22.5% of respondents feels confident in their understanding of AI, indicating a solid grasp of the concept.

Figure 3. Familiarity with AI concept

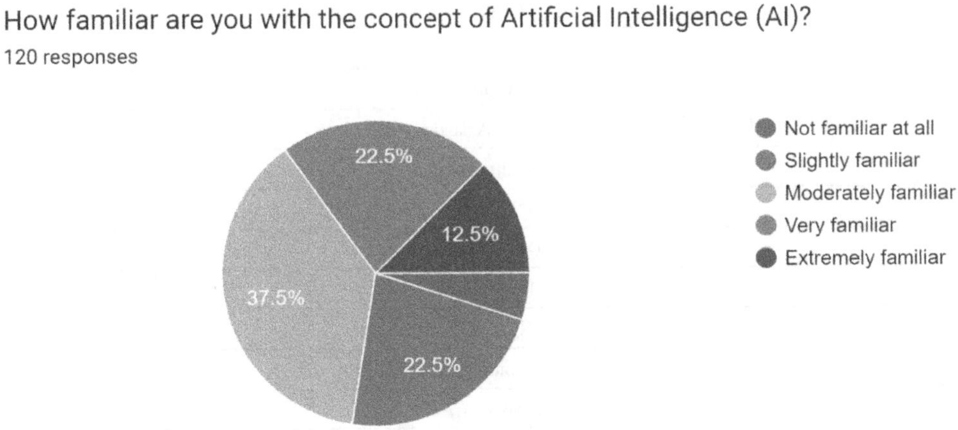

The study shows that a significant majority of the respondents about 82.5% reported that they have used AI-based tools or applications, such as virtual assistants, chatbots, or educational apps. This indicates widespread exposure to AI-powered technologies in everyday tasks, such as virtual assistants (e.g., Siri, Alexa), chatbots, or learning platforms. Since they are students, they have used it for various purposes corresponding to their individual student-based need. But there were a smaller proportion of participants (17.5%) indicated that they have not used any AI-based tools. This highlights a minority who might have limited access, awareness, or little to no interest in AI-driven applications. This data reveals that most participants have had experience using AI-based tools, reflecting the growing prevalence of AI in various domains including the education sector as well. However, where is there is a reflection of a small segment (17.5%) that has not interacted with such technologies, potentially due to barriers like access, lack of need, or unfamiliarity with AI functionalities.

Below mentioned table 2 comprises of the comprehensive list of AI-based tools or applications that students have used while studying. This table 2 is based on the responses received from the respondents.

Table 2. List of AI tools

List of All AI Tools Used by Students
ChatGPT
Grammarly
Gemini
QuillBot
Copilot
Canva
Google Assistant
Midjourney
Prisma
IBM Watson
TensorFlow
OpenCV
RapidMiner
Blackbox.AI
Amazon Alexa
Siri
Bing AI
Eleven Labs
Mathematica
AI Writer
Vocal Removers
Various AI-based tools
Total Number of Unique AI Tools: 22

Attitudes and Perceptions Towards AI

The pie chart (figure 4) illustrates how 120 respondents feel and perceive about the use of AI in education. Nearly one-third of participants (29.2%) expressed a very positive attitude toward the use of AI in education, reflecting strong enthusiasm and support. A majority of respondents (55%) feel positive about integrating AI into education, indicating a generally favourable perception of its potential benefits. A smaller proportion of participants (15%) have a neutral stance, suggesting they are neither strongly for nor against AI in education, possibly due to limited understanding or mixed opinions. Only a minimal fraction of respondents expressed negative views, indicating limited opposition to the use of AI in education. There is an almost insignificant number of participants who feel strongly against the use of AI in education. Since the majority of respondents have a positive outlook on the use of AI in education, which is highlighting widespread acceptance and optimism about its potential. Only a very small minority hold negative views, suggesting that most participants perceive AI as a valuable tool for enhancing educational practices. However, the neutral responses indicate a need for more awareness to convert ambivalence into support.

Figure 4. Perceptions about AI usage

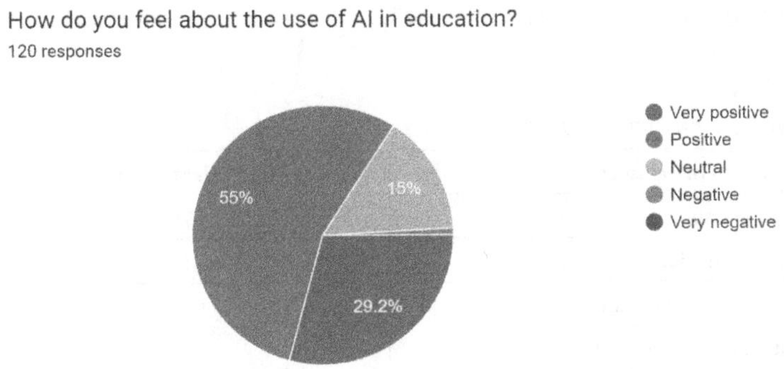

Table 3 discusses the concerns of students regarding AI being used in educational settings.

Table 3. Concerns about AI usage

Major Concerns	Number of Students
Concerns about Job Displacement	47
Data Privacy and Security Issues	50
AI Bias Concerns	35
Desire for Personal Interaction	60
User-Friendliness/Intuitiveness	12
Need for Transparency	5

Majorly the students shared concerns of AI being used may cause job Displacements and a significant number of respondents are concerned about the safety and confidentiality of data and Security Issues. This reflects apprehensions about how personal and sensitive information may be managed or misused. AI biases were also the second highest concerns of students. Many participants worry that AI could lead to job losses in the education sector, particularly for roles that could be automated. The data indicates that the major concerns revolve around maintaining personal interaction, ensuring data privacy, and addressing job displacement. These concerns highlight a need for careful integration of AI in education, with safeguards for human elements, ethical use, and user-friendliness. Transparency and addressing AI biases also need to be prioritized, even though they are less frequently mentioned. Students were asked the benefits that AI can bring to education with respect to their personalized learning experiences, efficient administrative tasks, improved learning outcomes, Access to advanced educational tools and Enhanced student engagement (table 4). Their responses are as follows.

Table 4. Benefits that AI can bring to education

Benefits that AI can bring to education	% of Student responses
Personalized learning experiences	67%
Access to advanced educational tools	61%
Improved learning outcomes	67%
Efficient administrative tasks	44%
Enhanced student engagement	78%

Current Technology Usage

Almost all the students were using the different platforms of AI driven learning for their education use including Learning management systems (e.g., Moodle, Blackboard), Educational apps (e.g., Khan Academy, Coursera), AI-powered tools (e.g., Grammarly, Duolingo) and Online course platforms (e.g., Coursera, edX). All of these educational tools were quite popular with all the students.

The largest segment of the respondents (40%) indicated that a significant portion of the respondents use the specified technologies daily. The second-largest segment (30.8%) suggests that a considerable number of users utilize these technologies on a weekly basis. A smaller portion of the respondents (15.8%) reported using the technologies monthly. 13.3% of respondents indicated they use the technologies rarely. Interestingly, there is no segment for “Never” use, implying that all respondents engage with the technologies at least occasionally. The data reveals a pattern of frequent technology usage among the respondents. A majority use the technologies daily, with a significant portion using them weekly. Monthly and rare usage accounted for smaller segments.

This portion of the data deals with the engagement and interactions students have with the AI tools. This is to understand the students' level of engagement with various tools for various purposes.

Figure 5. Engagements with AI educational tools

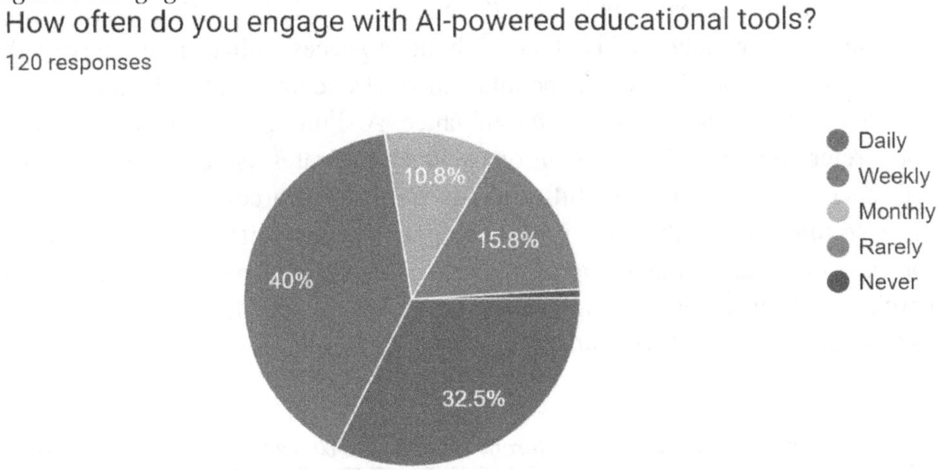

In figure 5, the largest segment of the pie chart (40%) indicates that a significant portion of the respondents use the specified technologies daily. The second-largest segment (30.8%) suggests that a considerable number of users utilize these technologies on a weekly basis. A smaller portion of the respondents (15.8%) reported using the technologies monthly. 13.3% of respondents indicated they use the technologies rarely. Interestingly, there is no segment for "Never" use, implying that all respondents engage with the technologies at least occasionally. The chart reveals a pattern of frequent engagement with AI-powered educational tools among the respondents. A majority use the technologies daily, with a significant portion using them weekly. Monthly and rare usage account for smaller segments.

The comfort level of students was also analyzed through the questionnaire and it was found out that 8.3% of respondents reported being extremely comfortable with using AI-powered educational tools. Nearly half (49.2%) expressed that they are comfortable using these tools, indicating a positive acceptance of AI in education. About 35.8% of respondents feel indifferent, showing neither significant ease nor discomfort. A small percentage expressed discomfort with these tools. Only a minimal segment fell into this category, indicating that severe dissatisfaction or difficulty is rare.

Learning Preferences

The learning preferences was analyzed in the study (table 5) whereby, students (23%) preferred video tutorials, making it the most popular single option. This indicates a high preference for passive, visual learning resources. Very few students have shown interest in more hands-on and exploratory learning methods which includes interactive Simulations. Personalized Quizzes is preferred by a niche group that values tailored assessments. Only 2% students selected virtual labs suggesting that these are not widely preferred, possibly due to accessibility or complexity. AI Tutoring Systems was also not that popular amongst students (4%) indicating limited but notable interest in one-on-one AI guidance. A significant number of students (19%) preferred a mix of all content types which indicates and also highlights the importance of variety and flexibility in educational resources. The data suggests that video tutorials are the most preferred content type, while virtual labs and AI tutoring systems have limited appeal. However, the preference for a combination of all options indicates that many students value a well-rounded and diverse approach to AI-driven educational content.

Table 5. Student preferences for different types of AI-driven educational content

Student preferences for different types of AI-driven educational content	%of responses
Video tutorials	23%
Interactive simulations	4%
Personalized quizzes	5%
Virtual labs	2%
AI tutoring systems	4%
Video tutorials, Interactive simulations, Personalized quizzes, Virtual labs, AI tutoring systems	19%

Usability AI Tools

The figure 6 shows the responses of 120 participants rating the usability of AI tools they have used. The majority of respondents rated the usability of AI tools as "Good," indicating that most users find these tools functional and easy to use. About 31.7% of users are neutral, suggesting that while the tools may not be overly complicated, they don't exceed expectations either. 10.8% represents a smaller group gave the highest rating, showing that a subset of users considers the usability of AI tools exceptional. Notably, no respondents rated the usability as poor or very poor, reflecting overall satisfaction with the ease of use. Some of the neutral responses indicate there is room for improvement in user-friendliness or specific features to elevate user experience further. The absence of poor ratings shows a generally favourable reception.

Figure 6. Usability of AI tools

How would you rate the usability of the AI tools you have used?

120 responses

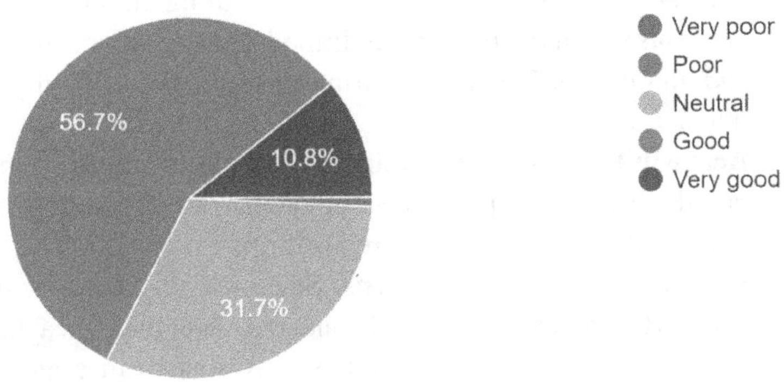

The data also reflected the responses of 120 participants on how effective they find AI tools in enhancing their learning experience. The majority of respondents (41.7%) believe AI tools are significantly effective in improving their learning experience. A notable portion (30.8%) of participants finds AI tools moderately helpful, indicating room for improvement but overall satisfaction. A smaller percentage (18.3%) sees limited effectiveness, suggesting that for some users, AI tools do not meet their expectations or address their learning needs fully. A minority (9.2%) finds AI tools extremely impactful, emphasizing their value for a small group of users. No respondents indicated that AI tools were completely ineffective, reflecting their overall utility in learning contexts. Most participants find AI tools either "Very

Effective" or "Moderately Effective," which showcases their potential in enhancing learning. However, the combined rating them as only "Slightly Effective" indicates there are challenges or unmet needs that developers and educators could address to further improve their utility. The absence of "Not Effective at All" responses confirms a generally positive perception.

Student had provided responses highlight several recurring themes and recommendations for improving AI tools. Key Themes that emerged for improving the AI Tools include the following:

a. **User Interaction and Interface:** Many respondents emphasized the need for more intuitive and user-friendly interfaces, also include simplified navigation, interactive features like quizzes, and real-time tutorials.
b. **Personalization:** Calls for AI tools to better cater to individual preferences and needs through customization and adaptive learning features. Personalized quizzes and content delivery were highlighted.
c. **Content Accuracy and Reliability:** Frequent requests for AI tools to deliver more precise, relevant, and error-free responses. Improvement in handling user queries accurately was a common concern.
d. **Interactive and Engaging Features:** Strong emphasis on adding interactive elements such as visual aids, multimodal outputs (e.g., text, images, and videos), and simulations. Suggestions to integrate emotional intelligence and human-like interaction.
e. **Accessibility and Affordability:** Multiple mentions of making AI tools free or reducing costs to prevent economic barriers for students. Ensuring equitable access for all users was a shared priority.
f. **Ethical and Privacy Concerns:** Suggestions to enhance data privacy and security. Respondents expressed concerns about the ethical handling of user data.
g. **Speed and Efficiency:** Calls for faster response times and improved processing efficiency.
h. **Educational Relevance:** Suggestions to improve educational use cases by aligning tools with student needs and trends. Enhanced examples, case studies, and better coverage of modern topics like startups.
i. **Multilingual and Cultural Context:** The need for better contextual and multilingual understanding to improve usability for diverse audiences.

Performance Improvement

Figure 7. Improvement in academic performance using AI tools

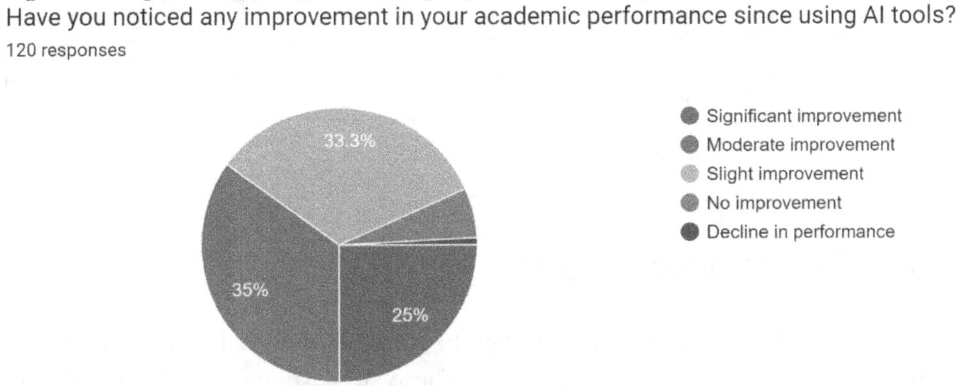

Figure 7 illustrates the responses of 120 participants regarding improvements in their academic performance after using AI tools. About 35% of participants reported moderate improvements in their academic performance due to AI tools, reflecting a positive but not transformative impact. A significant portion of 33.3% observed slight improvement, suggesting that while AI tools are beneficial, their influence may not always be profound. 25% of the participants experienced substantial gains, highlighting the potential of AI tools for certain users or contexts. 5% indicated no change in their academic performance, suggesting that AI tools may not be universally effective. A very small minority reported a decline, raising concerns about potential misuse or limitations of AI tools in specific scenarios. The majority of participants (93.3%) noticed at least some improvement in their academic performance, with moderate and slight improvements being the most common. While the results are largely positive, the 6.7% who observed no improvement or a decline suggest that AI tools may require further refinement to address diverse learning needs effectively.

Technical Issues and Support

Table 6 provides data highlights for the support needed for AI tools. The highest demand is for tutorials before usage (60) and real-time support/feedback (55), indicating users prioritize guidance and immediate assistance. Preferences for free/open access (40), interactive user interfaces (45), and training sessions (48) also emphasize the importance of accessibility, usability, and skill development in enhancing AI tool adoption and effectiveness.

Table 6. Support needed for AI tools

Support Needed for AI Tools	Frequency
Tutorials Before Usage	60
Real-Time Support/Feedback	55
Free/Open Access to Tools	40
More Interactive User Interfaces	45
Training Sessions	48

Suggestions for Improving AI

Students had suggested several things to improve the AI based on different parameters. Interactivity and Engagement. These suggestions include to make AI tools more interactive and engaging to encourage usage.

- Add more interactive features like quizzes, games, and visual aids.
- Use multimodal capabilities (e.g., text, images, videos) for dynamic interaction. Incorporate emotional intelligence and empathy into interactions.
- Include live tutorials or interactive video sessions.
- Provide progress tracking, such as quizzes to evaluate student performance.

In terms of user Interface and Usability the suggestions include,

- simplify the AI interface for easier navigation and accessibility, design should be user-friendly and reduce complexity, there can be some refinement of the interface to enhance intuitiveness and usability.
- Also, there can be some improvement in navigation and add personalization to cater to individual needs.
- Use humanized and simplified responses.
- Provide individualized learning experiences and adaptive outputs.
- Use student-specific quizzes and examples for better engagement.
- Ensure data is precise, correct, and relevant to the query. Expand content coverage to include current trends and new domains.
- Focus on features that enhance education, such as providing tutorials, PowerPoint presentations, and case studies.

DISCUSSION

The current research paper draws data from young students mostly can be considered as generation Z ranging from the age group of 18-24 from higher educational institutes. The data collected from the field work analyzed the perceptions related to AIED. The concept of AIED is widely researched in the past few years. Most of the students were found to be familiar with the concept of AIED, however in-depth knowledge dissemination is the need of the hour. It was also found that the widely used tools of the AI amongst these students were ChatGPT, Grammarly, Gemini, Quill Bot, Alexa etc. The perception towards these tools of AI was found to be quite positive and hence policy makers should invest in making use of AI in education at a large scale to improve the students' learnings. This also reflects the wide acceptance and optimism about its potential. However, the study found some concerns and issues related to the use of AI in education, some of which were related to data privacy, biases, lack of personal touch, intuitiveness and lack of transparency. The policy makers in the field of education should work in these directions to overcome the challenges and apprehensions of the student regarding the use of Ai in education.

The study also discusses the benefits of AI in education and the students under study responded that personalized learning and availability of advanced educational tools is the biggest advantage of AI. It also emphasized on improved learning outcomes, efficient administrative tasks and enhanced student engagements using platforms with AI. The study also reveals that use technology and AI is widely used by the students on daily basis or weekly basis and consider these platforms to be user friendly and comfortable to use. The study also highlights the students' preferences for AI driven education content in the form of video tutorials, interactive simulations, personalized quiz, virtual labs and AI tutoring systems.

It was revealed in the study that the usability of these AI enabled tools is very high amongst the students. Lastly, the study focuses on the recommendations for improving the usability of AI tools and platforms. The major recommendations were to improve the interaction and interface for users; personalized touch should be added; content accuracy and reliability should be checked for accuracy; interactive and engaging features will help in motivating students for learning; accessibility and affordability should be kept in mind by the AI engineers; ethical and privacy concerns should be tackled; speed and efficiency should be improved; the platform should be relevant with educational requirements; it should incorporate multilingual and culturally driven features for more acceptance. Given the wide use of AI in education, there is a vital requirement to assess the use of AI applications and tools by the educators for the academic success of students. This paper reviewed AI in education research and the findings of the chapter are beneficial not only for instructors using AI for their students but also for researchers in the field of education.

CONCLUSION

Many researchers argue that data-driven AI will be able to surpass human intelligence while others argue that data-driven AI is touching the developmental ceiling, and that progress towards human-level intelligence is likely only to be achieved with combination of knowledge-based and data-driven approaches in educational applications is seen as a joint development of human and artificial cognition which suggests that the future of AIED should be understood from the point of view of AI-supported augmentation of human cognition and learning (Bush, 1945; Engelbart, 1963; Winograd & Flores, 1986).

The challenges of AIED are complicated especially when they are associated with application in education. Although AI techniques use smart computation in the education domain, they fail to attract large-scale students because of additional cost involved (Chin X et al., 2010). Also, some researchers argue that some AI techniques are designed for a general situation may not be able to address a particular domain or learning activities, or teaching goals that can be hurdle in personalized learning experiences (Ge X et al.,2018; Loeckx J, 2017).

Another great challenge is that of the role of educators as teachers may swing from total resistance to overreliance on AI based tools and applications. Resistance may arise due to inadequate or outdated professional development while overreliance on AI may result due to teachers' unrealistic expectations, as the teachers may focus too much on the emerging AI technologies rather than learning itself (Kessler, 2018). Moreover, AI technique may provide smart and efficient tools that lead students to avoid processing their own knowledge expected from them for their learning, for example, the AI translators may offer ready-made illustrations, pronunciation etc. which may hamper their learning process.

There can be several ethical issues because of mishandling of data driven for both researchers and educators. The individual student data may be shared or used without the consent; therefore, educators and AI engineers should be mindful how they access, evaluate, and share the big data and the results of data analysis (Kessler, 2018; JE Aoun, 2017).

REFERENCES

Alabdulkareem, A., Alhakbani, N., & Al-Nafjan, A. (2022). A systematic review of research on robot-assisted therapy for children with autism. *Sensors (Basel), 22*(3), 944. DOI: 10.3390/s22030944 PMID: 35161697

Anuradha, J., Dhiman, T., Ramachandran, V., Arulalan, K. V., & Tripathy, B. K. (2010). Diagnosis of ADHD using SVM algorithm. In *Proceedings of the Third Annual ACM Bangalore Conference* (pp. 1–4). Association for Computing Machinery. DOI: 10.1145/1754288.1754317

Aoun, J. E. (2017). *Robot-proof: Higher Education in the Age of Artificial Intelligence*. MIT Press. DOI: 10.7551/mitpress/11456.001.0001

Asselborn, T., Chapatte, M., & Dillenbourg, P. (2020). Extending the spectrum of dysgraphia: A data driven strategy to estimate handwriting quality. *Scientific Reports, 10*(1), 3140. DOI: 10.1038/s41598-020-60011-8 PMID: 32081940

Bakare, O. D., & Jatto, O. V. (2023). In Keengwe, J. (Ed.), *"The potential impact of Chatbots on student engagement and learning outcomes" in Creative AI tools and ethical implications in teaching and learning* (pp. 212–229). IGI Global.

Baker, T., Smith, L., & Anissa, N. (2019). Educ-AI-tion rebooted? Exploring the future of artificial intelligence in schools and colleges

Barbhuiya, R. K. (2023). Introduction to Artificial Intelligence: Current Developments, Concerns and Possibilities for Education. *Indian Journal of Educational Technology, 5*(2), 266.

Barua, P. D., Vicnesh, J., Gururajan, R., Oh, S. L., Palmer, E., Azizan, M. M., Kadri, N. A., & Acharya, U. R. (2022). Artificial intelligence enabled personalised assistive tools to enhance Education of children with neurodevelopmental disorders—A review. *International Journal of Environmental Research and Public Health, 19*(3), 1192. DOI: 10.3390/ijerph19031192 PMID: 35162220

Bayne, S. (2015). Teacherbot: Interventions in automated teaching. *Teaching in Higher Education, 20*(4), 455–467. DOI: 10.1080/13562517.2015.1020783

Benfatto, M. N., Seimyr, G. Ö., Ygge, J., Pansell, T., Rydberg, A., & Jacobson, C. (2016). Screening for dyslexia using eye tracking during reading. PLoS One, 11(12), e0165508. https://doi.org/ al.pone.0165508DOI: 10.1371/journ

Binns, R., Veale, M., Van Kleek, M., & Shadbolt, N. (2018). "It's reducing a human being to a percentage": Perceptions of justice in algorithmic decisions. *Proceedings of the 2018 CHI Conference on Human Factors in Computing Systems*. https://doi.org/DOI: 10.1145/3173574.3173951

Bodily, R., & Verbert, K. (2017). Review of research on student-facing learning analytics dashboards and educational recommender systems. *IEEE Transactions on Learning Technologies*, *10*(4), 405–418. DOI: 10.1109/TLT.2017.2740172

Bostrom, N. (2006). *AI set to exceed human brain power*. CNN.

Botrel, L., Holz, E., & Kübler, A. (2015). Brain painting V2: Evaluation of P300-based brain-computer interface for creative expression by an end-user following the user centered design. *Brain Computer Interfaces (Abingdon, England)*, *2*(2–3), 135–149. DOI: 10.1080/2326263X.2015.1100038

Brown, T. B., Mann, B., Ryder, N., Subbiah, M., Kaplan, J., Dhariwal, P., Neelakantan, A., Shyam, P., Sastry, G., Askell, A., & Agarwal, S. Herbert-Voss., Krueger, G., Henighan, T., Child, R., Ramesh, A., Ziegler, D. M., Wu, J., Winter, C., … Amodei, D. (2020). Language models are few-shot learners. Cornell University. http://arxiv.org/abs/2005.14165

Bush, V. (1945). As we may think. *Atlantic Monthly*, *176*(1), 101–108.

Chan, C. K. Y., & Hu, W. (2023). Students' voices on generative AI: Perceptions, benefits, and challenges in higher education. *International Journal of Educational Technology in Higher Education*, *20*(1), 43. DOI: 10.1186/s41239-023-00411-8

Chan, K. S., & Zary, N. (2019). Applications and challenges of implementing artificial intelligence in medical education: Integrative review. *JMIR Medical Education*, *5*(1), e13930. DOI: 10.2196/13930 PMID: 31199295

Chassignol, M., Khoroshavin, A., Klimova, A., & Bilyatdinova, A. (2018). Artificial Intelligence trends in education: A narrative overview. *Procedia Computer Science*, *136*, 16–24. DOI: 10.1016/j.procs.2018.08.233

Chaudhry, M. A., & Kazim, E. (2022). Artificial Intelligence in Education (AIEd): A high-level academic and industry note 2021. *AI and Ethics*, *2*(1), 157–165. DOI: 10.1007/s43681-021-00074-z PMID: 34790953

Chen, L., Chen, P., & Lin, Z. (2020). Artificial intelligence in education: A review. *IEEE Access : Practical Innovations, Open Solutions*, *8*, 75264–75278. DOI: 10.1109/ACCESS.2020.2988510

Chen, X., Xie, H., Zou, D., & Hwang, G.-J. (2020). Application and theory gaps during the rise of artificial intelligence in *Education.Computers and Education: Artificial Intelligence*, *1*, 100002. DOI: 10.1016/j.caeai.2020.100002

Chen, X., Xie, H., Zou, D., & Hwang, G. J. (2020). Application and theory gaps during the rise of artificial intelligence in education. *Computers and Education: Artificial Intelligence*, *1*, 100002. DOI: 10.1016/j.caeai.2020.100002

Chen, Y., Jensen, S., Albert, L. J., Gupta, S., & Lee, T. (2023). Artificial intelligence (AI) student assistants in the classroom: Designing chatbots to support student success. *Information Systems Frontiers*, *25*(1), 161–182. DOI: 10.1007/s10796-022-10291-4

Chin, D. B., Dohmen, I. M., Cheng, B. H., Oppezzo, M. A., Chase, C. C., & Schwartz, D. L. (2010). Preparing students for future learning with teachable agents. *Educational Technology Research and Development*, *58*, 649–669.

Cotton, D. R. E., Cotton, P. A., & Shipway, J. R. (2023). ChatGPT, educational integrity, and assessment design: Creative possibilities and ethical implications. *Assessment & Evaluation in Higher Education*, *48*(1), 1–14. DOI: 10.1080/02602938.2023.2195289

Della Ventura, M. (2017). Creating inspiring learning environments by means of digital technologies: A case study of the effectiveness of WhatsApp in music education. In E-Learning, & E-Education (Eds.), Online training (pp. 36–45). Springer. DOI: 10.4108/eai.26-7-2017.152906

Della Ventura, M. (2018). Twitter as a music education tool to enhance the learning process: Conversation analysis. In *New Media for Educational Change: Selected Papers from HKAECT 2018 International Conference* (pp. 81-88). Springer Singapore.

Deng, Y., Wang, W., & Zhang, Z. (2023). Exploring the application of generative AI in higher education: Opportunities and challenges. *Educational Technology Research and Development*. Advance online publication. DOI: 10.1007/s11423-023-10182-y

Duan, Y., Edwards, J. S., & Dwivedi, Y. K. (2019). Artificial intelligence for decision making in the era of Big Data – evolution, challenges and research agenda. *International Journal of Information Management*, *48*, 63–71. DOI: 10.1016/j.ijinfomgt.2019.01.021

Eguchi, A. (2016). RoboCupJunior for promoting STEM education, 21st century skills, and technological advancement through robotics competition. *Robotics and Autonomous Systems*, *75*, 692–699. DOI: 10.1016/j.robot.2015.05.013

Engelbart, D. C. (1963). A conceptual framework for the augmentation of man's intellect. In Howerton, P. W., & Weeks, D. C. (Eds.), *Vistas in information handling* (pp. 1–29). Spartan Books.

Estevez, J., Garate, G., & Graña, M. (2019). Gentle introduction to artificial intelligence for high-school students using scratch. *IEEE Access : Practical Innovations, Open Solutions*, *7*, 179027–179036. DOI: 10.1109/ACCESS.2019.2956136

Fahmy, Y. (2024). *Student Perception on AI-Driven Assessment: Motivation, Engagement and Feedback Capabilities* (Bachelor's thesis, University of Twente).

Fazil, A. W., Hakimi, M., Shahidzay, A. K., & Hasas, A. (2024). Exploring the Broad Impact of AI Technologies on Student Engagement and Academic Performance in University Settings in Afghanistan. *RIGGS: Journal of Artificial Intelligence and Digital Business*, *2*(2), 56–63. DOI: 10.31004/riggs.v2i2.268

Gao, P., Li, J., & Liu, S. (2021). An introduction to key technology in artificial intelligence and big data driven e-learning and e-education. *Mobile Networks and Applications*, *26*(5), 2123–2126. DOI: 10.1007/s11036-021-01777-7

Ge, X., Yin, Y., & Feng, S. (2018). Application research of computer artificial intelligence in college student sports autonomous learning. *Kuram Ve Uygulamada Egitim Bilimleri*, *18*(5), 2143–2154.

Ge, X., Yin, Y., & Feng, S. (2018). Application research of computer artificial intelligence in college student sports autonomous learning. *Kuram Ve Uygulamada EgitimBilimleri*, *18*(5), 2143–2154.

Hakimi, M., Zarinkhail, M. S., Ghafory, H., & Hamidi, S. A. (2024). Revolutionizing Technology Education with Artificial Intelligence and Machine Learning: A Comprehensive Systematic Literature Review. *TIERS Information Technology Journal*, *5*(2), 94–110. DOI: 10.38043/tiers.v6i2.5640

Hart, S. A. (2016). Precision education initiative: Moving toward personalized education. *Mind, Brain and Education : the Official Journal of the International Mind, Brain, and Education Society*, *10*(4), 209–211. DOI: 10.1111/mbe.12109 PMID: 28642807

Heffernan, N. T., & Heffernan, C. L. (2014). The ASSISTments ecosystem: Building a platform that brings scientists and teachers together for minimally invasive research on human learning and teaching. *International Journal of Artificial Intelligence in Education*, *24*(4), 470–497. DOI: 10.1007/s40593-014-0024-x

Hinojo-Lucena, F. J., Aznar-Díaz, I., Cáceres-Reche, M. P., & Romero-Rodríguez, J. M. (2019). Artificial intelligence in higher education: A bibliometric study on its impact in the scientific literature. *Education Sciences*, *9*(1), 51. DOI: 10.3390/educsci9010051

Holmes, W. (2020). Artificial intelligence in education: Promises and implications for teaching and learning. *Learning, Media and Technology*, *45*(2), 189–206. DOI: 10.1080/17439884.2020.1695763

Holmes, W., Bialik, M., & Fadel, C. (2019). *Artificial intelligence in education: Promises and implications for teaching and learning*. Center for Curriculum Redesign., Retrieved from https://curriculumredesign.org/wp-content/uploads/AI-in-education.pdf

Holmes, W., Persson, J., Chounta, I.-A., Wasson, B., & Dimitrova, V. (2022). *Artificial intelligence and Education. A critical view through the lens of human rights, democracy, and the rule of law*. Council of Europe.

Holmes, W., & Tuomi, I. (2022). State of the art and practice in AI in education. *European Journal of Education*, *57*(4), 542–570. DOI: 10.1111/ejed.12533

Holstein, K., Hong, G., Tegene, M., McLaren, B. M., & Aleven, V. (2018). The classroom as a dashboard: Co-designing wearable cognitive augmentation for K-12 teachers. In Proceedings of the 8th international conference on learning analytics and knowledge -LAK '18 (pp. 79–88). Association for Computing Machinery. DOI: 10.1145/3170358.3170377

Humble, N., & Mozelius, P. (2019, October). Artificial intelligence in education—A promise, a threat or a hype. In *Proceedings of the european conference on the impact of artificial intelligence and robotics* (pp. 149-156).

Hussain, A. (2017). Ada—Bolton College's latest digital assistant. Blogtext. http://www.aftab hussa in.com/ada.html

Hwang, G. J. (2014). Definition, framework, and research issues of smart learning environments-a context-aware ubiquitous learning perspective. *Smart Learning Environments*, *1*(1), 4. DOI: 10.1186/s40561-014-0004-5

Hwang, G.-J., & Chang, C.-Y. (2021). A review of opportunities and challenges of chatbots in education. *Interactive Learning Environments*, •••, 1–14. DOI: 10.1080/10494820.2021.1952615

Hwang, G. J., Xie, H., Wah, B. W., & Gašević, D. (2020). Vision, challenges, roles and research issues of Artificial Intelligence in Education. *Computers and Education: Artificial Intelligence*, *1*, 100001. DOI: 10.1016/j.caeai.2020.100001

Hwang, G.-J., Xie, H., Wah, B. W., & Gasevic, D. (2020). Computers and Education. *Artificial Intelligence*, *1*. Advance online publication. DOI: 10.1016/j.caeai.2020.100001

Joksimovic, S., Ifenthaler, D., Marrone, R., De Laat, M., & Siemens, G. (2023). Opportunities of artificial intelligence for supporting complex problem-solving: Findings from a scoping review. *Computers and Education: Artificial Intelligence*, *4*, 100138. DOI: 10.1016/j.caeai.2023.100138

Kaplan, A., & Haenlein, M. (2019). Siri, siri, in my hand: Who's the fairest in the land? On the interpretations, illustrations, and implications of artificial intelligence. *Business Horizons*, *62*(1), 15–25. DOI: 10.1016/j.bushor.2018.08.004

Kay, J. (2012). AI and education: Grand challenges. *IEEE Intelligent Systems*, *27*(5), 66–69. DOI: 10.1109/MIS.2012.92

Kessler, G. (2018). Technology and the future of language teaching. *Foreign Language Annals*, *51*(1), 205–218. DOI: 10.1111/flan.12318

Kim, J., Merrill, K., Xu, K., & Sellnow, D. D. (2020). My teacher is a machine: Understanding students' perceptions of AI teaching assistants in online education. *International Journal of Human-Computer Interaction*, *36*(20), 1902–1911. DOI: 10.1080/10447318.2020.1801227

Koedinger, K. R., & Corbett, A. (2006). *Cognitive tutors: Technology bringing learning sciences to the classroom*. na.

Kumar, P., Sharma, R., & Kaur, G. (2022). Student perceptions of AI in higher education: Opportunities and challenges. *Journal of Educational Technology Systems*, *50*(3), 345–362. DOI: 10.1177/00472395211052198

Lan, A. S., Waters, A. E., Studer, C., & Baraniuk, R. G. (2014). Sparse factor analysis for learning and content analytics. *Journal of Machine Learning Research*, *15*(1), 1959–2008.

LaPierre, J. (2021, January 18). *Educational games and AI*. Blogtext. Filament Games. https://www.filam entga mes.com/ blog/educa tiona l-games-and-ai/

Lee, Y.-F., Hwang, G.-J., & Chen, P.-Y. (2022). Impacts of an AI-based chatbot on college students' after-class review, academic performance, self-efficacy, learning attitude, and motivation. *Educational Technology Research and Development*, *70*(5), 1843–1865. DOI: 10.1007/s11423-022-10142-8

Lieu, J. (2018). *Eyes to the front camera: Chinese facial recognition tech targets inattentive students*. Blogtext. Mashable. https://masha ble.com/artic le/chine se-facial-recognition-class

Loeckx, J. (2016). Blurring boundaries in education: Context and impact of MOOCs. *International Review of Research in Open and Distance Learning, 17*(3), 92–121. DOI: 10.19173/irrodl.v17i3.2395

Lu, L., Zhang, H., & Wang, W. (2021). Gamification in education: AI-enabled learning systems for improving student engagement. *Computers & Education: Artificial Intelligence, 2*, 100027. DOI: 10.1016/j.caeai.2021.100027

Luckin, R., Cukurova, M., Kent, C., & Du Boulay, B. (2022). Empowering educators to be AI-ready. *Computers and Education: Artificial Intelligence, 3*, 100076.

Luckin, R., Holmes, W., Griffiths, M., & Forcier, L. B. (2016). *Intelligence unleashed: An argument for AI in education*. Pearson Education. Retrieved from https://www.pearson.com/content/dam/one-dot-com/one-dot-com/global/Files/about-pearson/innovation/open-ideas/Intelligence-Unleashed.pdf

McGuire, L. S., & Alaraj, A. (2018). Competency assessment in virtual reality-based simulation in neurosurgical training. In *Comprehensive healthcare simulation: Neurosurgery* (pp. 153–157). Springer. DOI: 10.1007/978-3-319-75583-0_12

Metz, C. (2021, March 15). Who is making sure the a.I. machines Aren't racist? Online article. *The New York Times*. https:// www.nytim es.com/2021/03/15/technology/artificial -intelligence-google-bias. Html

Miao, F., & Holmes, W. (2021). AI and education: Guidance for policy-makers. UNESCO. https://unesd oc.unesco.org/ark:/48223/ pf000 0376709

Molenaar, I. (2022). Towards hybrid human-AI educational scenarios. *European Journal of Education, 57*(4). Advance online publication. DOI: 10.1111/ejed.12527

Moriarty-Mclaughlin, F. (2020). *More colleges eye AI to track, monitor students*. The College Fix. https://www.theco llege fix.com/more-colleges-eye-ai-to-track-monitor-students/

Moursund, D. G. (2006). Brief introduction to educational implications of Artificial Intelligence.

Nwana, H. S. (1990). Intelligent tutoring systems: An overview. *Artificial Intelligence Review, 4*(4), 251–277. DOI: 10.1007/BF00168958

Nye, B. D., Graesser, A. C., & Hu, X. (2014). AutoTutor and family: A review of 17 years of natural language tutoring. *International Journal of Artificial Intelligence in Education, 24*(4), 427–469. DOI: 10.1007/s40593-014-0029-5

Pedro, F., Subosa, M., Rivas, A., & Valverde, P. (2019). Artificial intelligence in education: Challenges and opportunities for sustainable development.

Peng, C., Zhou, X., & Liu, S. (2022). An introduction to artificial intelligence and machine learning for online education. *Mobile Networks and Applications*, *27*(3), 1147–1150. DOI: 10.1007/s11036-022-01953-3

Pérez, J. Q., Daradoumis, T., & Puig, J. M. M. (2020). Rediscovering the use of chatbots in education: A systematic literature review. *Computer Applications in Engineering Education*, *28*(6), 1549–1565. DOI: 10.1002/cae.22326

Poole, D. I., Goebel, R. G., & Mackworth, A. K. (1998). *Computational intelligence and knowledge*. Oxford University Press.

Rajaram, A., Olory, C., Leduc, V., Evaristo, G., Coté, K., Isenberg, J., Isenberg, J. S., Dai, D. L., Karamchandani, J., Chen, M. F., Maedler-Kron, C., & Fiset, P. O. (2022). An integrated virtual pathology education platform developed using Microsoft Power Apps and Microsoft Teams. *Journal of Pathology Informatics*, *13*, 100117. Advance online publication. DOI: 10.1016/j.jpi.2022.100117 PMID: 36268098

Ramesh, D., & Sanampudi, S. K. (2021). An automated essay scoring systems: A systematic literature review. *Artificial Intelligence Review*, *55*(3), 2495–2527. DOI: 10.1007/s10462-021-10068-2 PMID: 34584325

Rodrigues, F., & Oliveira, P. (2014). A system for formative assessment and monitoring of students' progress. *Computers & Education*, *76*, 30–41. DOI: 10.1016/j.compedu.2014.03.001

Roll, I., & Wylie, R. (2016). Evolution and revolution in artificial intelligence in education. *International Journal of Artificial Intelligence in Education*, *26*(2), 582–599. DOI: 10.1007/s40593-016-0110-3

Russell, S. J., & Norvig, P. (2016). *Artificial intelligence: A modern approach*. Pearson Education Limited.

Sadegh-Zadeh, S. A., Movahhedi, T., Hajiyavand, A. M., & Dearn, K. D. (2023, December). Exploring undergraduates' perceptions of and engagement in an AI-enhanced online course. [). Frontiers Media SA.]. *Frontiers in Education*, *8*, 1252543. DOI: 10.3389/feduc.2023.1252543

Schaffer, S. (1999). Enlightened automata. In W. Clark, J. Golinski, & S. Schaffer (Eds.), The sciences in enlightened Europe. The University of Chicago Press. https://press.uchic ago.edu/ucp/books/ book/chica go/S/bo362 3650. Html

Slade, S., & Prinsloo, P. (2013). Learning analytics: Ethical issues and dilemmas. *The American Behavioral Scientist*, *57*(10), 1510–1529. DOI: 10.1177/0002764213479366

Songer, N. B., Newstadt, M. R., Lucchesi, K., & Ram, P. (2020). Navigated learning: An approach for differentiated classroom instruction built on learning science and data science foundations. *Human Behavior and Emerging Technologies*, *2*(1), 93–105. DOI: 10.1002/hbe2.169

Sperling, K., Stenliden, L., Nissen, J., & Heintz, F. (2022). Still w(AI)ting for the automation of teaching: An exploration of machine learning in Swedish primary education using actor-network- theory. *European Journal of Education*, *57*(4), 584–600. DOI: 10.1111/ejed.12526

Stein, S. J., Goodchild, A., Moskal, A., Terry, S., & McDonald, J. (2021). Student perceptions of student evaluations: Enabling student voice and meaningful engagement. *Assessment & Evaluation in Higher Education*, *46*(6), 837–851. DOI: 10.1080/02602938.2020.1824266

Tatar, D., Roschelle, J., Vahey, P., & Penuel, W. R. (2003). Handhelds go to school: Lessons learned. *Computer*, *36*(9), 30–37. DOI: 10.1109/MC.2003.1231192

Thomas, M., & Porayska-Pomsta, K. (2022). *Neurocomputational methods: From models of brain and cognition to artificial intelligence in education*. Cambridge University Press. DOI: 10.1017/9781108399838.037

Topol, E. J. (2019). High-performance medicine: The convergence of human and artificial intelligence. *Nature Medicine*, *25*(1), 44–56. DOI: 10.1038/s41591-018-0300-7 PMID: 30617339

Tran, M. T. T. (2021). Microsoft Teams in the context of freshmen ELF learning. *AsiaCALL Online Journal*, *12*, 12–23.

Tsai, C. L., Ku, H. Y., & Campbell, A. (2021). Impacts of course activities on student perceptions of engagement and learning online. *Distance Education*, *42*(1), 106–125. DOI: 10.1080/01587919.2020.1869525

UNESCO. (2020). Education in a post-COVID world: Nine ideas for public action. https://unesdoc.unesco.org/ark:/48223/pf0000373717

Vallis, C., Wilson, S., Gozman, D., & Buchanan, J. (2024). Student perceptions of AI-generated avatars in teaching business ethics: We might not be impressed. *Postdigital Science and Education*, *6*(2), 537–555. DOI: 10.1007/s42438-023-00407-7

VanLehn, K. (2011). The relative effectiveness of human tutoring, intelligent tutoring systems, and other tutoring systems. *Educational Psychologist*, *46*(4), 197–221. DOI: 10.1080/00461520.2011.611369

Verbert, K., Govaerts, S., Duval, E., Santos, J. L., Van Assche, F., Parra, G., & Klerkx, J. (2014). Learning dashboards: An overview and future research opportunities. *Personal and Ubiquitous Computing, 18*, 1499–1514.

Wang, F. H. (2017). An exploration of online behaviour engagement and achievement in flipped classroom supported by learning management system. *Computers & Education, 114*, 79–91. DOI: 10.1016/j.compedu.2017.06.012

Wang, S., Gorbunova, N. V., Masalimova, A. R., Bírová, J., & Sergeeva, M. G. (2017). Formation of academic mobility of future foreign language teachers by means of media education technologies. *Eurasia Journal of Mathematics, Science and Technology Education, 14*(3), 959–976.

Watters, A. (2021). *Teaching machines: The history of personalized learning*. MIT Press. DOI: 10.7551/mitpress/12262.001.0001

Williamson, B., & Eynon, R. (2020). Historical threads, missing links, and future directions in AI in education. *Learning, Media and Technology, 45*(3), 223–235. DOI: 10.1080/17439884.2020.1798995

Zawacki-Richter, O., Marín, V. I., Bond, M., & Gouverneur, F. (2019). Systematic review of research on artificial intelligence applications in higher education –Where are the educators? *International Journal of Educational Technology in Higher Education, 16*(1), 39. DOI: 10.1186/s41239-019-0171-0

Zhai, X., Li, M., & Chen, X. (2021). Automated essay scoring with content-based relevance feedback. *British Journal of Educational Technology, 52*(3), 1103–1118. DOI: 10.1111/bjet.13078

Zhao, H., Li, G., & Feng, W. (2018). *Research on application of artificial intelligence in medical education. In 2018 international conference on engineering simulation and intelligent control (ESAIC)*. IEEE.

Chapter 2
AI in the Classroom: Revolutionizing Instruction and Student Engagement

Muhammad Usman Tariq
https://orcid.org/0000-0002-7605-3040
Abu Dhabi University, UAE & University College Cork, Ireland

ABSTRACT

This chapter talks about how artificial intelligence is radically changing education by altering conventional classroom dynamics and improving student engagement and redefining the instructional practices. This chapter examines how teaching and learning are changing in a variety of educational settings. It explores the incorporation of AI technologies that facilitate individualized learning experiences, letting students advance at their own speed while considering their unique strengths and weaknesses. AI-powered platforms encourage greater engagement and better results by offering data-driven insights adaptive learning pathways and real-time feedback. By providing actionable analytics automating administrative tasks and enabling differentiated instruction the chapter explores how AI can assist teachers.

INTRODUCTION

Artificial intelligence (AI) is revolutionizing industries globally, and its future and impact on education are becoming apparent. As technology advances, educator starts to find a way to apply AI in learning environment, reconstruct the traditional model of education by thinking about new type of learning. AI in education include automating administrative functions, delivering customized learning opportunities giving realistic chances to make learning innovative and efficient. This chapter seeks to explore the broad and impartial effects of AI to squarely assess its inte-

DOI: 10.4018/979-8-3373-4576-5.ch002

grated application in improving instructional approaches and subsequent student engagement (bin Salem, I., 2024). Incorporation of AI in education is no longer part of future possibility but exists in the current world. For instance, adaptive learning technologies like DreamBox and Carnegie Learning employ AI techniques to analyse learners' performance and manipulation of their learning materials in real time. These systems ensure that every learner is placed in an environment in which they can be provided with the right level of difficulty to master. Such individualization in a traditional classroom setting is, however, likely to be difficult given the factors such as huge client numbers and restricted teacher time. AI is useful in closing this gap because it takes the role of an assistant teacher and handles extra responsibilities in meeting the needs of the learners in the classroom (Ellikkal & Rajamohan, 2024).

The possibilities that this technology brings to bear when it comes to creating increased engagement among students cannot still be overemphasized. Automated tools like chat bots, learning through virtual reality simulations and games make learning fun and memorable to the students. For instance, reminders, notifications or alerts can be used or AI-based platforms such as Quizlet or Kahoot that incorporate the element of fun into learning so that learners participate actively and with competition and in the collaboration of other learners. Such tools make learning an engaging process, from passive to active, meaning knowledge is better retained and the interest level increased (bin Salem, I., 2024). However, as mentioned above, the incorporation of AI in learning environment has not been an easy task. There is an issue of learners divide, and this may increase inequality within learners who are in a learning process. Unfortunate students in remote communities possibly in poorly endowed schools can be left behind because these schools may not possess the requisite physical facilities or the necessary funds to incorporate the use of AI tools. Further, risks associated with data privacy and bias can create issues as well. For instance, by considering the prediction of learning outcomes to the students, collecting and storing large amounts of student data can be an effective application of AI; nonetheless, the ethical issues such as the privacy of student data have to be questioned. Otherwise, the algorithm bias may lead to stereotype reinforcement or deviation in the evaluation of students, which is inapplicable for the primary objectives of AI (Ellikkal & Rajamohan, 2024).

However, pedagogy and the importance of a teacher in a learning process become crucially questionable while the AI takes an active part in classrooms. Although application of AI in learning can help in provision of instruction that targets specific students, it does not offer the aspects of care and special guidance which teachers do. The best use of AI may be used in a supporting role for education, rather than in replacing a teacher outright. The balance helps to ensure that technology is used to support human led instruction and not replace it. Thus, ensuring-practical application is incredibly important in the context of constant quantitative growth in the sphere of AI technologies. To strike a balance in incorporation of AI in learning and teaching processes, educators and policymakers work hard in trying to realize the set goals of learning while at the same time, taking the above challenges into consideration, educators and policymakers have a challenging task of incorporating AI in the classroom in a way that will meet or achieve the laid down educational objectives. In so doing, it is possible to transform not only the methods of instruction but can turn students into active learners for a lifetime willing to meet the demands of an increasingly artificial intelligent world. This chapter engaged these dimensions in a critical manner with the purposes of establishing knowledge on how AI is redefining education and the consequences of teaching and learning in the 21st Century (Ellikkal & Rajamohan, 2024; Tariq, 2024).

BACKGROUND

The rate at which Artificial Intelligence has grown faster across nations, and the way this revolution has positively impacted on the education sector. In classrooms, AI has not remained as a future idea at the present, but it has become an innovation, it has revolutionized the way students learn and the way teachers teach. The use of AI in learning contexts can be expected to improve instruction, student interactions and learning, as well as transform conventional learning paradigms. This chapter analyses the transformative effects of AI in educational institutions as well as its capability of positively changing the experience of learners (Alam, 2023). Traditionally, class followed a very structured teacher-centred pedagogy where information was delivered to the students and was successful for some students but was lacking student differentiation and speed. The existence of AI solves these issues by incorporating the style of learning into individual learners. Another way is proposing a form-adaptive content delivery, where AI can analyse student data and suggest the content tailored to their strengths, weaknesses and preferences. For example, language learning Duolingo and mathematics learning DreamBox change tones in response to students, helping them in the areas they are struggling (Egunjobi & Adeyeye, n.d.).

AI when applied to a classroom also helps to spur the students, It promotes higher level of student participation as a result of enhancing the classroom experience thus making it more innovative and interesting. AI being applied to VR and AR enable students to visit archaeological sites, perform scientific investigations, or study topology through first-person interfaces that did not exist even five years ago. This change from receptive method sharpens understanding and memorization, as well intensifies interest and imagination (Tariq, 2025). While from a teacher's point of view they will help in speedy working on activities like assessments, student's attendance etc. Thus, helping one get more time for planning and interactions with students at length. Also, using AI-generated information, educators can find out low-performing students and act accordingly. However, multitudinous benefits that have been pointed out in this chapter, but the use of AI in education has its drawbacks as well. Particularly the issue of data privacy or occasionally ethical questions as well as concerns related to the availability and accessibility of AI solutions are still current. Other issues that need to be studied include risks that involve the replacement of human interaction with AI in learning (Alam, 2023). Global case studies point to how AI is likely to revolutionize current learning environments across numerous contexts. The Chinese authorities are focusing on facial recognition for monitoring students' attendance. In Finland, AI solutions are used for the teaching of multiple languages, to help students from immigrant background. Such examples explain the different ways in which AI is being used in different countries and how it affects learning in classrooms (Egunjobi & Adeyeye, n.d.).

Nonetheless, the incorporation of AI in learning institutions' classrooms can still be a challenging affair if it is not well `planned and implemented. AI is a highly beneficial tool, which, however, needs appropriate training for educators and adequate principles for schools to be used ethically and fairly. It has mentoring phases, plans and architectures, which need technologists, policymakers, and educators for effective and efficient collaboration during the next steps to solve problems and optimize ai's advantages. This chapter introduces the subsequent chapters exploring AI's features and presence in education advanced alongside the ways it is transforming teaching and learning processes. Drawing out the discussed opportunities and challenges means that the chapter mainly offers a balanced and comprehensive approach to addressing the role of AI for deepening our understanding of education's future (Alam, 2023).

AI and Critical Thinking Skills

The idea of critical thinking as an important element of modern education relates to the learners' skills to analyse, evaluate and make synthesis of information in the environment. Far from being a threat to genuine intelligence, AI is showing itself to be an invaluable weapon for the development of these abilities, presenting the learners with continually updating platforms for solving critical thinking problems. It can be applied that AI tools will help the educators in the development of effective content where the students are not just consuming information but also challenging it, analysing, and seeking the solution, whereas making a rational decision (Almusaed & Homod, 2023). The ability of AI to model real-life situations has great potential as a way of developing thinking skills. For instance, AI integrated simulation exercises in science, history or business where students get the feel of real-life difficulties in a safe environment. In business education, artificial intelligence such as Mimic Pro by Student competition simulation involves creating marketing situations for students and then let them manage it, predict change, and of course analyse the result of the campaigns. Similarly, in social studies, AI integrated timelines can encourage breakthrough questioning, *incessantly* while engaging in history lessons students are made to reason through the various possibilities of the lessons they are being taught. Such tools put the students in a decision-making mode where they have to decide something based on data and modify their decision when they get more data which is typical to professional practice (Gautam, 2024). These are especial case studies of the AI based exercises that underlined the benefits of such practice to improve the skills of critical thinking. For instance, IBM Watson for Education was used in the class to encourage students to develop arguments on the use of genetically engineered products. The AI offers the refutation and response to the arguments, thus maintaining the students' critical thinking and-analysing skills to pinpoint the possible weakness of their arguments. Another example is Socratic by Google which is an AI front end that assists the learner in disassembling a question into a series of more manageable parts and then assists in the formulation of coherent logical argument leading to an answer. In both forms, the AI plays the role of triggering the students into thinking beyond the literal level (Makinde & Adeleye, 2024).

However, critical thinking exercises that incorporate AI are however not free from challenges. One problem with such an approach is that students may get used to relying on an outside agent to give them solutions in a way that is contrary to how such situations are solved in real life. For example, using an AI-based platform, there is a possibility that patterns or mistakes, which an AI algorithm has captured from a student's reasoning process, can be accepted by the student without critically analysing them. Teachers, therefore, have to safeguard that AI is an adjunct rather than a replacement of key thinking abilities. This risk can be countered and the learning process improved by teaching students to provide reasons for their decisions (Gautam, 2024). This much needed evaluation of how AI affects student learning outcomes, offers a more accurate picture of the role of AI in sharpening critical thinking skills. Analyses of student interactions with AI-embedded exercises indicate that the students' problem-solving skills and engagement levels increase. However, these advantages can only be realized when such implementation is well planned and monitored continually. For instance, AI tools when combined with peer discussions and instructor-fed back options can design an environment that the AI complements rather than rival the interactions (Almusaed & Homod, 2023). Thus, there is great potential for leveraging of critical thinking with the help of AI in education; however, it depends on the particular integration of this concept into a general framework. At its best, AI can turn the classroom into a learning environment and make our students ready for the challenges of intellectual work. At the same time, they need to be on watch guard – always adjusting make these tools foster authentic deep learning (Makinde & Adeleye, 2024).

Research with AI

Artificial Intelligence (AI) is rapidly changing research culture in numerous fields, and participation in educational research is no exception. AI tools and methodologies give the researchers opportunities to work with large datasets, perform data analysis, find patterns to gain perspectives that were not possible before. These advancements have not only clarified and optimized the research process but also enlarged the area of its potential development through opening new non-traditional perspectives in education to teachers and scholars. However such change is opportune, the processing and application of AI must be approached strategically involving the best skills and an inclusion of ethical questions (Joseph & Tahir, 2024). There is an advancement in the use of artificial intelligence related to; natural language processing, that aids the educational research, machine learning models and predictive analytics. For instance, the NLP tool such as sentiment analysis can analyse student's feedback from survey questionnaires, or discussion forum the overall level of satisfaction or dissatisfaction, and or it may reveal areas of dissatisfaction and areas that needs to be improved on. Just as it is possible to predict graduation rates or subject proficiency levels, the student performance data can also be fed to machine learning models to affect such predictions. The above tools do not only help to save time but also assist in ensuring accuracy of results obtained hence assisting educators in decision making. For instance, employments such as IBM Watson as well as Google Cloud AutoML have been utilized to analyse patterns particularly in learning behaviours in a bid to develop recovery strategies for learners considered most vulnerable (Makinde & Adeleye, 2024).

Examples of actualization of AI concepts in educational studies are very many and varied. One specific case is the application of AI for the assessment of pedagogical solutions based on learning personalization. In a recent work, the researchers applied the AI parameters to monitor the ways, how students interact with the adaptive learning applications and the data recorded included duration of the tasks, their completion rates of the modules, accuracy of the answers etc. The outcomes provided an understanding of the relationship between the Brooklyn Teaching Practices and the Students' Achievement and Information that was beneficial to teachers. Another application is in the application of AI eye tracking technology, in which researchers monitor students' attention to the digital content. Through dissecting gazes, researchers find what instructional designs attract attention and enhance understanding (Joseph & Tahir, 2024; Tariq, 2024). However, there are illimitations associated with the integration of AI in research that need to be looked at closely when passing strategies. One question of concern in the introduction of the algorithmic middlemen is that of bias. The AI gain information from historical information that might include biases that may be portrayed in research outcomes. For example, the recommendation from an AI model based on data from the established learning institutions may not apply well in the poorly funded institutions. The advantage of this requires researchers to ensure that the datasets they are using must be diverse or inclusive and also in their consistent use of AI outputs for bias checks. Thus, how AI algorithms work and how data is processed has to be transparent to keep research projects credible as well (Makinde & Adeleye, 2024).

Key guidelines for the use of AI in educational research involve participation and responsibly with AI. The authors have to collaborate with AI experts to guarantee that the selected methods correspond to the purpose of the research. Moreover, the inclusion of their own judgment in the analysis of AI-produced outcomes is necessary to keep from relying too heavily on the AI-produced conclusions. Issues of ethical consideration like data use consent and participants anonymity should always be tackled under consideration when conducting the research. AI has adopted new dimensions for educational research, you can conduct a new kind of research that is more accurate, extensive, and valuable. But it should not be abused, nor should one fail to consider the drawbacks of the technique or fail to apply it carefully. In collaboration with AI, its capacity is complemented by a sophisticated measure of supervision that helps the researchers to harness its potential and make progress in educational fields as well as retaining the serious and formal aspects of scholarly research studies (Rizvi, 2023).

INTRODUCTION TO AI CLASSROOM INSTRUCTION

That classroom instruction is increasingly incorporating the use of Artificial Intelligence (AI) as part of the instructional delivery system with hopeful teaching and learning tools. To this end, the first point that educators need to progress is to grasp the core concepts of AI. Its fundamental concept is to process information through algorisms and an ability to discerning patterns and make conclusion or choice. On the educational plane, these capabilities provide customized learning environment and course delivery, student control and administrative functions, and the flexibility of their interactions with students. The purpose of AI in the educational process is not to replace teachers, but to work alongside them to help teach more effectively, as well as much more efficiently (Nguyen & Kremantzis, 2024). When it comes to applying artificial intelligence based instruction in classroom, planning and intervention is key. Adaptive learning platforms, AI chatbots, and automated grading systems can revolutionize not only students' activities with material. For example, the educational platform Khan adapts educative content with the help of AI in accordance with the progress of a learner, as well as possible weaknesses of the latter. In a similar manner, machines such as Duolingo for language teaching and training select learning paths to enhance students learning experiences and promote their progressive learning. Yet, effective use entails that the teacher can incorporate information technology in a way that augments lessons and learning and not the other way round (Praveen, 2024).

Findings of the study are that the teachers have perceptions that are mixed which show both the positive and the negative aspects of integration of AI. Several teachers enjoy the fact that AI takes over monotonous activities that consume a lot of time, such as grading and attendance taking, so teachers can concentrate on meaningful teaching tasks. Other auto-writing assistive software that gives feedback in the process like Grammarly for writing lessons are also preferred for self-help. However, some of the teachers give a concern about the technology in learning as they feel that the use of AI in teaching may reduce the time spent between the teacher and the learner. For example, although AI is capable of learning the students' requirements and helping student perform correspondingly, it cannot give the same feeling as human teachers do. This goes hand in hand with the belief of the positive symbiosis of the man and the technology of artificial intelligence (Nguyen & Kremantzis, 2024). Finally, the application of AI in classroom instruction brings equity questions that relate to access into many learners. This is because schools that may afford to implement the AI technologies may be few and those schools which cannot are likely to be from disadvantaged areas hence the issue of inequality. Furthermore, there are questions about academic integrity since the best AI-assisted learning tools need a large quantity of student data to perform properly. Therefore, teachers need to insist on the excellence of the policies and the openness of the practices in the protection of students' information as well as the leveraging of the fair use of artificial intelligence. As a form of instruction, the incorporation of artificial intelligence presents an invaluable chance to revolutionize instruction and learning; however, its prospects' achievement depend on the teachers' participation and incorporation of AI in their learning process. As principles are understood and effectively applied to common tools along with the issues of ethics, the potential AI has to enhance students' experience and keep the value of effective teaching can be reached (Almusaed & Homod, 2023).

Ethics of AI in Education

Challenges of specific nature of ethical concern are highlighted as more technologies with artificial intelligence are applied to learning delivery in educational environments. Suggested uses of AI include mass customization of learning, efficient administrative processes, a better experience for students, but all of these present clear ethical issues. Such concerns pertain to issues of security, fairness and equity, responsibility and response to concerns related to students and learning in an environment dominated by technology. Solving these problems need to involve a lot of consideration of the proper manner and aim to make artificial intelligence useful for as many students and teachers as possible and helpful to the society as a whole (Aeni & Cardoso, 2024). Because of the open nature of many educational applications, privacy and security remain two primary ethical concerns in the use of AI in education. As it has been mentioned before, most AI systems require gathering and processing large quantities of student data: performance, behaviour, and sometimes even biometric data. For instance, Proctorial, is AI-based tools used in assessments, monitor the facial expressions and screen activity of students for cheating. That said, these tools can add value to the overall concept of academic integrity; nonetheless, it does beg the question of just how much student activity should or can be monitored. Any measures left controlling come with a potential for misuse, invasion of privacy, theft, or sabotage of information. The essence of such technologies is to ensure that they offer the benefits of utilization of AI while at the same time integrating strict measures of privacy (Ray & Sikdar, 2024). Another ethical issue is algorithmic bias as it arises from the interacting and reinforcing dynamics between algorithms as well as from the larger system of algorithms. Several authors have posited that AI systems learn from data and if these sets of data already have bias, then the bias will be clearly seen in the output of AI systems. For example, AI solutions aimed at estimating the students' probabilities of success and perpetuate the given population's prejudice if the previous records are coloured by various forms of prejudice, including the lack of proper resources or unreasonable opportunities due to the simple discrimination policy. This reinforces AI development best practices and open yearly review and regulation particularly for educational artificial intelligence (Pratama & Sampelolo, 2023).

Towards this, the following policy recommendations with regard to ethical use of AI has been put forward to tackle the aforementioned concerns. Public and private schools, as well as governments, are expected to come up with polices regarding collection, storage, and use of data and information meeting the GDPR and similar acts. Teachers and administrators should be educated about AI capacity and its role and then, it will be optimal way how they would decide where to apply it. The students' parents and educators should be incorporated in the existing discourses regarding the appropriate nature as well as the implementation of AI policies; as this can effectively increase their establishes accountability and conformity to the existing communal values (Nursalim & Judijanto, 2022). Ethical AI integration in education is not a mere use of the AI tools that are innovative, but it insists on determination of students' rights besides the promotion of equity. In this way, the challenge of privacy and bias can be solved, and clear AI policies in educational systems have the potential to unlock proper ethical use. This balance makes a form of a lever, where AI remains a form of empowering the people and not a cause of controversy and negative impact (Aeni & Cardoso, 2024).

AI Policies in Educational Settings

Artificial Intelligence (AI) is used in the learning process and therefore schools or universities are mandated to set policies in admission of the technology. Today's AI policies usually concern data protection, AI regulation, and its social good. However, such policies differ in their coverage and outcome as influenced by variations in institutional objectives and capacity. While there is a mixed picture of institutions with predictable frameworks, there is a problem showing that the AI governance challenges are still an issue in some institutions (Asrifan & Dewi, 2024). It is quite evident that many current AI policies within educational institutions are predominantly bias towards data security. For instance, universities incorporating AI in teaching and learning delivery systems set standard procedures that meet the international norms on the protection of users' data especially when using the General Data Protection Regulation (GDPR). These policies generally address issues regarding the collection, storage, or use of student information; and procedures on obtaining consent. Nevertheless, there are still some unsolved questions concerning other significant topics, e.g., the explainability of the AI algorithms employed or Gould's concern about biasing. For instance, if a school adopts AI for Admission, it might not explain the decision-making process, or how they reduced bias in the selection process which might lead to issues of accountability all over (Nursalim & Judijanto, 2022). Finding a solution to this problem entails preventing it in the first place and demanding actionable AI policies for institutions of learning. Course policies should be aimed not only at the protection of the privacy and/ or confidentiality of learners and instructors but also at the employment of the best practices, creation of an ethical learning environment, non-discrimination as well as availability for learners with disabilities. This includes development of AI selection and integration policies that clearly defines how the various tools would be adopted, used and aligned to the OSPD's pedagogical agenda as well as its overall core values. For instance, there could be a policy setting a provision that an AI system used in a particular process should be audited to check for cases of bias or errors, and there be a procedure of informing the students and parents that an AI system was used in making decision. Also, the institutions should ensure that they come up with holistic ways of proving how the AI tools work and what their intended objectives are; this should increase trust levels (Asrifan & Dewi, 2024).

Examples from practice show the possibilities of policy enactment in the sphere of education and the difficulties arising in this process. An example contains the University of Southern California which developed a policy framework for the use of AI in education that has taken into perspective ethical values and all the necessary stakeholders. It has ensured that faculty and students accept AI tools in their course works but at the same time have embraced privacy and minimized such issues. On the other hand, less comprehensive policies, including those that only require technical compliance without considering equity or inclusiveness, have been working under negative criticism for their inability to work out the general impacts of the use of AI. The best AI policies when implemented in educational institutions have to meet a tension between the innovative and the conformist. Ethical considerations, transparency and collaboration are keys to making most of AI while avoiding its drawbacks, by so doing institutions can come up with the right policies that addresses most of the challenges faced. The extent to which AI will continue to develop means that regular assessment and adjustment of these policies will be critical to agile education's effectiveness in responding to the changing dynamics of this field (Asrifan & Dewi, 2024).

Practical Applications of AI in P-20 Classrooms

Artificial Intelligence (AI) is steadily finding its way into the classrooms from Pre-school to Tertiary, that is, from P to 20. AI rules and appliances are quite specific for students at various stages of education so that there are possibilities to improve instruction and student activity. They span across smart learning applications for use in early childhood development all the way up to big data analytics in tertiary institutions. Despite that the potential of utilization of AI is rather high, the issue is, that the implementation of these technologies faces a number of issues which are the availability of resources, teachers' readiness for change, and ethical issues (Pratama & Sampelolo, 2023). Based at the preschool and primary education level, most skills have been learned by students through the use of applications and virtual teachers. For example, DreamBox and Smartick educational platforms are based on AI principles to teach mathematics to children and constantly adjusting in the process depending on the child's achievements and difficulties. Such tools drive interest and increase the end-user's level of supported self-education, as it may be called. In secondary school learning, AI is implemented in more specific approaches in line with specific content areas, for instance Carnegie Learning mainly in mathematics while Labster in science through their virtual simulations (Bhatia & Sood, 2024).

The advanced implementations of Artificial Intelligence in the context of higher learning are nonquantitative, qualitative analysis and companionate services. For instance, AI based systems like Civitas Learning are capable of evaluating student data and recognizing the student who are prone to drop out and suggest interventions in time. In the same vein, AI tools such as Iris.ai assist university learners and researchers in screening through numerous and sometimes unstructured academic articles to accomplish improved analysis of topics (Pratama & Sampelolo, 2023). These tools not only improve students 'performance but also help in the avoidance of work for teachers and other officials. However, there are challenges that allow adoption of AI in P-20 classrooms as follows. Inadequate funding in needy school districts poses a problem in providing equitable access to and application of AI technologies in schooling. Further, the teachers themselves may not receive proper training on how to apply the AI systems properly and in turn you get either underutilization or complete rejection of the change. Data privacy first and second type of ethical issue, including biases in algorithms raise additional challenges to AI adoption. For example, implementing the use of AI in performance tracking makes one wonder, how exactly can such data be utilised outside the classroom (Bhatia & Sood, 2024). Teachers in schools and universities need professional development as they need to learn how to accurately use AI tools. AI has to be implemented in the areas of need by supporting it with proper funding in a way that policies from national and state education departments have to allow it. More so, the sound guidance on the ethical utilization of Artificial Intelligence, practicable policies of data privacy, and an annual algorithm review system are critical for the overall acceptance rates. Interestingly, AI has shown great promise to enhance learning at all the levels of learning; be it a college or a university. AI at its present positions itself as a potential solution, not a source of problems, in learning if and only if its barriers to adoption are dealt with and equity and ethics are the guiding points (Praveen, 2024).

AI and Instructional Remediation

AI is transforming instructional remediation by presenting new methods of diagnosing deficiencies in students' learning. AI systems help to identify signs of performance in students and areas that need attention from the educators by exploring a huge amount of data. For instance, the online system commonly used in high school learning often used in mathematics known as ALEKS tests the understanding of a learner and points out areas of mathematics that requires practice. Course delivery by master carpenters as demonstrated above guarantees effective use of instruction time owing to a guided flow targeting peculiar requirements of each learner (Ray

& Sikdar, 2024). Other forms of technology assist with remediation by affording adaptive learning experiences among learners. These tools can shift student content delivery depending on how the student is doing, unlike traditional learning management systems, making for an innovative experience that has the ability to constantly progress as the learner. For instance, the Edmentum's Exact Path that applies AI in the format of providing each learner with an individual learning path helping him/her overcome knowledge gaps within certain time. That is why such technologies are useful for classes with mixed groups of students — their level of knowledge does differ and applying such technologies, the teacher can teach everyone something new without additional loads (Seaba, 2023).

Remediation that is driven by AI increases student performance and course completion rates significantly. Since ability to fill learning gaps is fast achieved by AI, students have enhanced and deeper understanding of core subjects, which consequently boost their performance. For example, students who have been trained using adaptive learning interfaces such as DreamBox or Khan Academy register higher scores than majority of standard classroom learners. Further, with timely intervention, AI can help students walk through highly charged psychologically stages of learning such as decrease in confidence, motivation, and in some cases dropout from learning programs. One example is Georgia State University who have piloted the use of predictive analytics to identify students most likely to drop out by the third year of their learning, and as a result have successfully raised the retention rates drastically (Ray & Sikdar, 2024). However, there are some problems being experienced in using AI in instructional remediation. One of the issues is that effectiveness of the ideas developed might be based on the use of technology, excluding human factors, such as intuition, creativity of a teacher. Essentially, AI is capable of detecting learning loss, but it cannot place into consideration emotional and social aspects that may affect a learners' performance. Further, such systems are highly reliant on the quality of data that has been fed into the AI systems. Delayed or wrong diagnosis of learning needs can result in further learning loss due to the data being proven to be inaccurate or incomplete (Seaba, 2023).

As we continue to implement AI in instructional remediation, there is the need for measure and balance in using it. While AI should enhance the role of teachers, in which they are the only ones capable of understanding the context behind data readouts and the individual learning process of a student. Further, schools should embrace decentralization and offer teaching sessions on how to apply AI for the educators. If properly integrated, the speculated capability of AI can be applied effectively in instructional remedial enhancing fair and productive students' attainment.

AI in the Arts, Music, Dance, and Theatre

Artificial Intelligence (AI) is therefore revolutionizing the creative arts by providing leading approaches to artistic and teaching creativity in artistic fields as art, music, dancing, and playacting. The incorporation of AI into arts learning is done as a partner and an instrument that assists students and artists to discover smorgasbord in arts. For instance, DeepArt – this is an artificial intelligence application that turns photographs into paintings in styles of various artists, and which, for instance, makes it possible for students to implement that artistic ideas that were previously impossible due to the lack of talents. Tools of this nature add to the existing creative paradigm and encourage contextually creative ideas (Zharmukhanbetov & Singh, 2023). In music lessons, students can utilize the AI writing services, such as AIVA (Artificial Intelligence Virtual Artist), which creates scores based on a user prompt; from this scenario, learners can study the generated pieces and engage with music created by artificial intelligence. In the same way, current smart platforms such as SmartMusic assist musicians in developing practice schedules based on performance accuracy. In dance, real-life applications like Notch or PoseNet also capture movements, letting students receive coaching and work on their movements on the fly. Such tools come in handy in cases where the learning is done online, and access to immediate instructors is a challenge. Theatre also receives help from AI; virtual reality (VR) enabled through artificial intelligence technology is used for rehearsal of performances or for construction of stage performances.

Examples provided show how AI can capture the arts' change-making possibilities at their finest. Notable example is utilization of the AI to choreograph a dance production in House of Royal Opera in London. Here, several thousands of movement descriptions were used to compute new choreography sequences that actual dancers presented on the stage. With the help of this experiment, it was possible to concretise the idea of introducing technologies to the human creativity and estimate the potential of integrating a computer into the creation of art. In the same way, AI is applied at the Berklee College of Music where students in their composition classes use the AI generated melodies as basis for the full compositions to deepen up their understanding of harmony and arrangement (Zharmukhanbetov & Singh, 2023). Thus, having harmonious cooperation between AI and learners, institutions may open new opportunities while maintaining the idea of art untouched. AI integration and its moral implications need to be carried out sustainably if the function of increasing creativity and teaching in the arts are to be fully realized by this technology (Zharmukhanbetov & Singh, 2023).

Using AI in Secondary Social Studies

Students in secondary social studies classes are benefiting from the integration of AI into classroom practice in enabling of them to use better strategies in learning that are exciting and informative. AI use cases in the subject include individual learning apps, computerized games, and even computer animations that help in making real societal ideas and events come alive. For instance, Google Earth VR makes it easy for students to visit geographic and cultural sites making it more enjoyable to learn geography and history (Yunusaliyev & Yuldashev, 2024). Similar to this, AI-powered platforms like Actively Learn offer customized material that helps students navigate challenging texts and hone their critical thinking abilities in the analysis of political and historical sources. Social studies courses benefit greatly from AI-powered immersive and interactive activities. Students can engage with history and social processes via the use of virtual reality (VR) and augmented reality (AR) gadgets powered by AI algorithms. AI-powered simulations, for example, can replicate historical occurrences, like the signing of the Declaration of Independence, so that students can engage with these moments virtually. Lessons become more accessible and effective when systems like IBM Watson Education evaluate student reactions to tasks and modify the content to fit their learning preferences (Xu, 2024). AI's capacity to encourage critical thinking and active learning makes it an excellent tool for teaching social studies. AI solutions can assist students in navigating difficult subjects like global wars, politics, and economic systems by offering real-time feedback and adjusting to individual requirements. In order to promote deeper involvement with contemporary topics, a classroom utilizing AI-powered debate platforms, for instance, would let students debate perspectives on climate change policy as the system assesses their arguments for logic and evidence. Additionally, by providing customized material, AI solutions assist teachers in managing varied classes and guarantee that all students, regardless of ability level, can contribute in a meaningful way (Yunusaliyev & Yuldashev, 2024).

But there are several difficulties in incorporating AI into social studies instruction. The possibility of algorithmic bias in AI technologies is a major worry as it might unintentionally reinforce preconceptions or convey biased historical narratives. An AI-powered history app trained on biased datasets, for instance, may overrepresent some viewpoints while ignoring others, which might affect students' comprehension of difficult subjects. Additionally, since not all schools have the means to install these technologies, the dependence on AI tools raises concerns about fair access and digital literacy (Xu, 2024). Teachers must critically assess the resources they employ to make sure they support curricular objectives and offer a range of viewpoints if they want to optimize the advantages of AI in social studies. In order to give instructors, the tools they need to successfully incorporate AI into their lessons, professional development is also crucial. With careful application, artificial intelligence (AI) has the potential to completely transform social studies instruction and produce knowledgeable, involved, and critical thinkers who are equipped to handle the challenges of the contemporary world (Yunusaliyev & Yuldashev, 2024).

AI and Gifted Students

AI is impressively improving the options for gifted learners to develop an individual academic plan, extracurricular and real-life problem-solving, and effective learning environments appropriate to their superior skills. Organized classrooms in general education settings prove challenging to support gifted individuals because of the fast pace and comprehensive comprehension by those learners. AI, however, assists in a more personalized system; to address their needs, the instructions provided meet their abilities and assist in keeping them interested and engaged (Wadhwa & Bansal, 2024). That is why one of the most significant achievements in the sphere of AI for gifted students is relevant in today's application called "personalized learning platforms." Applications such as Khan Academy and ALEKS employ AI to identify what the individual student knows or does not know and feeds the learner material that comes after the something the learner already knows. For instance, a student good in mathematics could do complex problems such as calculus, or linear algebra while leaving lower-level exercises behind. It shows that these platforms enable students to advance as, far as they want and really stay challenged and interested, much past a typical course's level (Xu, 2024).

The enrichment programmes are equally related with gifted students with an aim of enhancing their learning as they are offered extra work apart from memory drill or routine practice. In the same way, Century Tech and Brainly are applications where users are presented with problems and projects to solve, which are picked by an AI. For example, an AI integrated next generation science learning module could provide students with a challenge such as developing a sustainable energy solution while connecting across curricular. Besides enhancing content knowledge, such programs promote appreciation of what one is learning because they appeal to the student's thirst for knowledge and desire to perfect a skill (Wadhwa & Bansal, 2024). The incorporation of AI technology in teaching and learning process are incredible for the gifted students. The usage of AI in regular learning ensures gifted students remain interested with no risk of boredom as reiterated by researchers. One can observe that through appropriate use of AI technology in teaching-learning process, a significant improvement in learning achievement and motivation has been recorded among gifted students. That is, a student that demonstrate a recurring aptitude within an AI enhanced literature course might be further prompted for superior readings and themes with the aim of further exploring the conceptual framework (Xu, 2024).

However, there are consideration given when using AI for gifted education. Such a concern is locating how AI may worsen schooling for the gifted student by denying them the chance to work with their peers. However, each learner requires unique individual learning plans, and gifted students also need to work with classmates who have other points of view. Moreover, the algorithms that drive devices should be unbiased to surmise the talent of the hitherto neglected gifted student to embrace relevant meritorious minds (Wadhwa & Bansal, 2024). In order to realise the full potential of AI in teaching gifted students' educators must use the tools in conjunction with other teaching practices such as apprenticeship, peer learning and contextual learning. Thus, allowing AI to assist the talented children to unwrap their full potential as well as ensuring that child achieves multiple spheres of development for the consistency future academic achievements. However, there are consideration has to be given when using AI for gifted education. Such a concern is locating how AI may worsen schooling for the gifted student by denying them the chance to work with their peers. However, each learner requires unique individual learning plans, and gifted students also need to work with classmates who have other points of view. Moreover, the algorithms that drive devices should be unbiased to surmise the talent of the hitherto neglected gifted student to embrace relevant meritorious minds. In order to realise the full potential of AI in teaching gifted students' educators must use the tools in conjunction with other teaching practices such as apprenticeship, peer learning and contextual learning. Thus, allowing AI to assist the talented children to unwrap their full potential as well as ensuring that child achieves multiple spheres of development for the consistency future academic achievements (Bhatia & Sood, 2024).

THE FUTURE OF AI AND EDUCATION

The next future of AI is going to cause the drastic change in the education for students and teachers based on the trends and creations of technologies. Possible of applying AI in customizing and in delivery and also in simplification of administration opens the stage for a revolution in the system of education all across the world. With ongoing developments, AI integration is expected to progress to more fundamental forms, including teaching and emotions, real-time tracking, and artificial collaborative learning featuring AI tools that mimic interpersonal interaction in physical classrooms (Gautam, 2024). Modern trends in AI education shifted to make increased emphasis on the use of Augmented Reality and Virtual Reality platforms which make use of AI algorithms within students' learning processes. There are opportunities that take students to a molecular biology class or the historical event where simulations enhance not only interest but comprehension as well. That is, a student that demonstrate a recurring aptitude within an AI enhanced literature course might be further prompted for superior readings and themes with the aim of further exploring the conceptual framework (Vashishth & Sharma, 2024).

The next future of AI is going to cause the drastic change in the education for students and teachers based on the trends and creations of technologies. Possible of applying AI in customizing and in delivery and also in simplification of administration opens the stage for a revolution in the system of education all across the world. With ongoing developments, AI integration is expected to progress to more fundamental forms, including teaching and emotions, real-time tracking, and artificial collaborative learning featuring AI tools that mimic interpersonal interaction in physical classrooms (Gautam, 2024). Modern trends in AI education shifted to make increased emphasis on the use of Augmented Reality and Virtual Reality platforms which make use of AI algorithms within students' learning processes. There are opportunities that take students to a molecular biology class or the historical event where simulations enhance not only interest but comprehension as well (Vashishth & Sharma, 2024). Further, with the advancement of AI such tools like translation of language are effectively eliminating barriers to language so students from any part of the world have access to quality materials. This work is imperative for preparing educators and students for an emerging AI world. The new roles require teachers to embrace the changes and go from being purveyors of knowledge and information to being envoys that help learners use AI in learning. Teacher training that can be done during the Information Technology Continuing Professional Learning program, can make teachers ready to use AI in their classrooms, like Google's AI for Education. From students' perspective. AI's strengths and weaknesses will be important once they step into the working environment. Successful examples of expanding AI literacy include AI4ALL, whose goal is to teach high school students about AI ideas and more importantly the ethical aspects of AI, that will produce an AI literate generation ready to live in an AI-filled world (Ellikkal & Rajamohan, 2024). While the benefits of AI for education are vast, the long-term impact creates independency, sophistication, development of a silo mentality, dependability, job creation and aftermath of job loss, and consumer-directed dependency. On one hand, it can be said that AI will help to increase the number of people who can gain a quality education; on the other – there are certain ethical and practical issues presented by the usage of AI. For instance, embracing of AI tools may result in reinforcement of the injustice since underprovided schools cannot afford the latest technology. Moreover, applying AI in data assessment of students leads to chronic privacy and security concerns. The contributors of policy and the educators should come together and design structures that would guarantee fairness and accountability of the AI tool (Vashishth & Sharma, 2024).

The future of AI in education lies not only in the technologic solutions but in the humane and inclusive humanistic perspective that is based on reverence for empathy, co-action, and ethical responsibility. AI can help in transforming education delivery into personalized, improved and accessible for everyone throughout the world by providing intelligent system & preparing for the world where intelligent systems are dominating the world. The integration of AI in special education: This can be done by helping students with disabilities, tools and technologies, equity & big data to personalize the learning environment. Learning is not a one-size-fits-all process and traditional type of teaching methods may not be very effective when it comes to children with learning disabilities or inabilities: however, AI has provided solutions that allow children to use their potential to study (Ellikkal & Rajamohan, 2024). We conclude that the use of AI in special education is most pronounced when it comes to developing personalized learning strategies. Flexible systems such as DreamBox Learning provide assessments of learner performance and demonstrate curriculum based on learner's abilities and inclinations. For example, a child with ADHD needs short dynamic lessons established to ensure concentration, while a child with ASD would be given repetitive practice sessions in a stable virtual context. Furthermore, it can give real-time results to the educator, which might help the educator to come up with better plans suit student's needs and/or advancement (Bhatia & Sood, 2024).

AI and Meeting the Needs of Students with Disabilities

Successful application of AI in special education is well described in the following cases. One of the examples explaining the use of AI is AI Robotics in the University of Hertfordshire that employs socially assistive robots to teach children with ASD how to communicate. These robots help students practice specific skills through well-organized structured activities therefore providing a safe environment where boys can make eye contact or notice feelings of other participants. An example of the success stories includes seeing AI by Microsoft as a class of AI applications that assist the visually impaired students to take their notebooks, spot objects, read texts or even identify the emotional state of people around them through providing auditory feedback (Verma & Shaik, 2023). Nevertheless, integration of the application of artificial intelligence in special education is not without some problems. Major challenge is to implement technologies in schools and homes, as well as to buy the necessary tools and equipment as most of these technologies require corresponding capital investment. Furthermore, the proper use of students' data, gathered by means of an AI system, should be taken into consideration to minimize the abuse. Solutions to these emerging problems are best solved when educators and policymakers align themselves in designing proper rules and procedures for financing (Nursalim & Judijanto, 2022). Assistive technologies and adaptive learning systems are categorized as learning tools that can help students with their disabilities. For instance, TTS, and STT solutions such as Microsoft's Immersive Reader assist students with visual impairment or dyslexia by speaking out the text or writing from the dictation of the student. Likewise, other technological instruments such as communication applications for PC and iPad like Proloquo2Go offer nonverbal student a mean through which they communicate symbolizing their thoughts with corresponding pictures and synthesized voice. The mentioned tools do not only build up independence but also create no barriers to communication and understanding (Asrifan & Dewi, 2024). Thus, there is no doubt that AI could have a positive impact in the system of special education; however, its success highly depends upon the careful and meaningful integration of the technology as well as on the willingness of the educators to create an inclusive educational environment that will help the kids with learning disabilities to learn and grow. Applying the notion of using AI tools, it is possible to design effective and rather more encouraging learning environment for learners with disabilities to achieve the maximum result in their learning process (Verma & Shaik, 2023).

Math Instruction and AI

Machine intelligence is transforming the teaching and learning of mathematics by providing resources and learning platforms that are ever engaging, responsive individually and are interactive with opportunities for feedback. There are so many techniques for delivering Mathematics in the traditional classroom method, and these methods do not accommodate for individual learners' speed and learning patterns. These AI-driven system narrow this gap by providing a personalized approach to teaching mathematics that can be applied to make the process much more engaging (Yunusaliyev & Yuldashev, 2024).

Applications like DreamBox Learning for math, Mathway and Photomath are other examples of smart, effective learning tools to customize the instruction. These platforms work on the basis of understanding a student's answers and then the type of problems posed to a student change as a result of those answers. For example, if a student has difficulty with fractions, the system will provide more practice and additional information and explanations, also make sure the student has mastered the basics before moving up to the next level. Even when it comes to expression of math problems written by hand and therefore tricky to read, Photomath helps students take a photo and gives a step-by-step solution instantly, thus helping students turn potential frustration into clearly valuable learning tool (Nursalim & Judijanto, 2022). Applying information technologies in math learning fosters development of a richer and very challenging notion of interactive reciprocities and representations. For instance, GeoGebra features AI to enable the learners to investigate geometric relationships using dynamic models. A student learning about circles can change values of radius or circumference and see how maths works it out immediately. Computational learning also enable problem-solving skills as these complications of varieties of equations are disintegrated into simpler soluble parts to enhance a thinker's appreciation of mathematical approaches (Yunusaliyev & Yuldashev, 2024).

Analysing the effectiveness of using AI in mathematics education, the added value and problems are quite impressive. However, on the reversed side, it is found that students using AI-based platforms have gained significant changes in their tests scores and problem-solving skills. Furthermore, these tools create value for teachers as it relieves them of monotone work that may entail grading while they concentrate on refocusing the students, group work among others. For instance, in the Education Technology domain; tools such as Carnegie Learning make use of AI to provide instructors with display screens along with strategy tips regarding students' poor performance (Rizvi, 2023). However, this comes with significant concerns given below are the benefits of using artificial intelligence as well as the potential challenges. One of the challenges of using AI tools is that they don't encourage abstraction or critical thinking unless designed with a human interface. Also, availability and use of high-quality AI tools are still limited and depend on good schools, therefore might bring inequality in students' achievement. Other attending issues are ethical, including data protection concerns and the automation of the learning process at the expense of generalized classroom instruction (Yunusaliyev & Yuldashev, 2024). There is great potential to revolutionize mathematics classroom with the use of AI that enhances the lessons delivery to be personalized, interactive and informed by data. However, the success of AI depends on the integration of such methods into classes, which is perfectible but does not aim to replace the important work of a teacher. Overcoming the difficulties associated with equity and ethical questions, AI opens a perspective for improving the efficiency of mathematics learning (Rizvi, 2023).

Using AI in English / Language Arts

AI is a powerful tool that is currently enriching the teaching-learning process in reading and writing and covers every student's needs. Standard classroom models though efficient to an extent lack the ability to address individuals as the recent AI technologies can do. AI tools enhance language arts by offering strong ways to help educators assist students and enhance the efficiency of teaching language arts through creative, customized and evidence-based strategies (Taş, 2023). Most of the AI programs that can be used to assist students in reading and writing are also self-contained and respond almost instantly to the students' activities. Quite the opposite, there is Grammarly and Quilbot that engage student directly in the writing process by pointing out grammatical mistakes, suggesting vocabulary or style improvements. Not only do these platforms also give wrong answers but also, they give reasons which help learners to think deeply. In reading, programs such as Lexia and Learning Ally diagnose the performance of the learner, providing individualized activities designed to build reading speed and expanded vocabulary. Such tools are especially helpful when the student has LD such as dyslexia since they organize the information and are equipped with practical assistive tools like speech to text (Taş, 2023). AI technologies also trigger learning literacy as it engages the learners and provides diversified learning tops. For example, the learning application Newsela relies on AI to modify texts for the student's skill level and preserve difficulty levels when presenting difficult Subjects. In writing, the use of AI introduced tools may assist the students in creating prompts that will foster creativity when writing prose and help in the formulation of narratives. Also, similar to educational purposes, such AI tools as the ChatGPT can facilitate a kind of a dialogue, so a student can practice in persuasive writing or discussions as the AI chatbot answers immediately (Verma & Shaik, 2023).

A case study shows how handling information has improved language arts learning with the use of AI. One of the case studies is based on a middle school where the teachers included the use of Write Lab, an AI-based writing tutor. A noticeable improvement was observed in the students' structuring and development of their arguments in their essays which received feedback from the tool in the drafted form. Another example is a literacy program in which technologies such as text analysis of student interaction with reading activities provide a warning system that allows teachers to address at-risk students and behaviour patterns (Bhardwaj & Sharma, 2025). However, there are areas of sharp concern, which remain critical despite these developments. Use of AI reduces focus on the development of critical skills for the acquisition of higher order knowledge skills such as analysis of literature which is much more complicated in interpretation. Besides, culture and privacy are other issues that come with using AI systems; these systems capture a lot of data on students' performance (Verma & Shaik, 2023).

Another concern for AI technologies is that all students should have equal access to it, and it is known that schools in these communities often do not have sufficient funds to organize it. AI holds the potential to revolutionise English and Language Arts classes, in terms of students' participation and the results achieved. For improvement, AI needs to be integrated with human involvement to be used as a supporting tool for enhancing thinking and creative abilities in education to support the language development of students as well as effective actuator ship by educators (Bhardwaj & Sharma, 2025).

CONCLUSION

It could be concluded that Artificial intelligence (AI) is revolutionising education as discussed in this chapter through providing solutions that can transform education paradigm, differentiate instruction and student needs among others. In capability, from lecturing basic classroom type combined with adaptive tools AI has shown one's capability to someday solve various special problems in the numerous education fields inclusive of mathematics, arts, social studies, and special education. A synthesis of practical uses across reading, writing, thinking, and instructional repair, reveals that within the human experience, AI enhances educational performance, creativity and interest in academic disciplines.

Several important lessons focus on making AI delivering distinctive instruction for students to create unique learning experience, using AI to complete tedious work, offering students instant feedback. However, the implementation of technology brings problems including equal access, ethic issues and risk of dependency on technology. Members spoke about increased layers of writing in teaching, which underlines the need for thoughtful integration where AI should enhance the educationist's work as opposed to substituting his/her efforts. At each stage of the chapter, case studies explain examples of how AI has been used to help students and subsequently, demonstrates how it can encourage positive change when used properly.

Towards that end, it is critical for subsequent research to examine how the availability of AI tools can be made more equitable, review guidelines regarding ethical use of AI in learning environments and measuring their cumulative effects on education systems. There are also areas of learning that this development in AI should also seek to address these includes critical reasoning and learning across cultural differences. Teachers, software engineers, and educational policymakers will need to coordinate in order to direct progress in AI. Therefore, there is a need for advancing the idea of using AI in education to close gaps and improve key learning outcomes with innovation at its core. However, the possibilities to enthuse educators and students seem to be unlimited." As technology keep on advancing, there is a need for the educational systems to adopt ethical use of AI in the improvement of the sector.

REFERENCES

Aeni, N., Khang, A., Al Yakin, A., Yunus, M., & Cardoso, L. (2024). Revolutionized teaching by incorporating artificial intelligence chatbot for higher education ecosystem. In *AI-Centric Modeling and Analytics* (pp. 43–76). CRC Press.

Alam, A. (2023). Harnessing the power of AI to create intelligent tutoring systems for enhanced classroom experience and improved learning outcomes. In *Intelligent Communication Technologies and Virtual Mobile Networks* (pp. 571–591). Springer Nature Singapore. DOI: 10.1007/978-981-99-1767-9_42

Almusaed, A., Almssad, A., Yitmen, I., & Homod, R. Z. (2023). Enhancing student engagement: Harnessing "AIED"'s power in hybrid education—A review analysis. *Education Sciences*, *13*(7), 632. DOI: 10.3390/educsci13070632

Asrifan, A., & Dewi, A. C. (2024). AI-driven classroom conversations: Revolutionizing Education 5.0 for enhanced student engagement in speaking skills. *JETAL: Journal of English Teaching & Applied Linguistics*, *5*(2), 117–131. DOI: 10.36655/jetal.v5i2.1482

Bhardwaj, S., & Sharma, I. (2025). Exploring the effects of AI-powered personalized classroom management strategies. In *AI Applications and Strategies in Teacher Education* (pp. 21–42). IGI Global.

Bhatia, A., Bhatia, P., & Sood, D. (2024). Leveraging AI to transform online higher education: Focusing on personalized learning, assessment, and student engagement. *International Journal of Management and Humanities (IJMH, 11*(1).

bin Salem, I. (2024). Integrating artificial intelligence in personalized learning: A future-oriented approach to enhance student engagement and achievement. *International Journal of Post Axial: Futuristic Teaching and Learning*, 111–119.

Egunjobi, D., & Adeyeye, O. J. (2024). Revolutionizing Learning: The Impact of Augmented Reality (AR) and Artificial Intelligence (AI on Education). ResearchGate, Oct.

Ellikkal, A., & Rajamohan, S. (2024). *AI-enabled personalized learning: Empowering management students for improving engagement and academic performance.* Vilakshan-XIMB Journal of Management.

Gautam, D. (2024). Revolutionizing education through innovative technological solutions. As the editors of *Transforming Learning. Power and Education*, •••, 60.

Joseph, S., Tahir, A., Bibi, F., Hamid, K., Iqbal, M. W., Ruk, S. A., & Ahmad, S. Z. (2024). A review analysis on using "AIED" to improve student engagement in hybrid education. *Bulletin of Business and Economics (BBE, 13*(2), 424–435.

Makinde, A. I., Adeleye, S. A., Oronti, A. O., & Jimoh, I. T. (2024). Revolutionizing education. *Artificial Intelligence for Wireless Communication Systems: Technology and Applications*, 103.

Mishra, P. (2025). Revolutionizing education with AI and ML. In *Internet of Behavior-Based Computational Intelligence for Smart Education Systems* (pp. 53–94).

Nguyen, A., Kremantzis, M., Essien, A., Petrounias, I., & Hosseini, S. (2024). Enhancing student engagement through artificial intelligence (AI): Understanding the basics, opportunities, and challenges. *Journal of University Teaching & Learning Practice, 21*(06). Advance online publication. DOI: 10.53761/caraaq92

Nursalim, A., Judijanto, L., & Asfahani, A. (2022). Educational revolution through the application of AI in the digital era. *Journal of Artificial Intelligence and Development, 1*(1), 31–40.

Pratama, M. P., Sampelolo, R., & Lura, H. (2023). Revolutionizing education: Harnessing the power of artificial intelligence for personalized learning. *Klasikal: Journal of Education. Language Teaching and Science, 5*(2), 350–357.

Praveen, J. V. S. (2024). Understanding the potential impact of AI-powered classroom management on student engagement, and overall learning outcomes. *Global Journal of Business and Integral Security, 1*(2).

Ray, S., & Sikdar, D. P. (2024). AI-driven flipped classroom: Revolutionizing education through digital pedagogy. *Psychology (Irvine, Calif.), 7*(2), 169–179.

Rizvi, S. (2023). Revolutionizing student engagement: Artificial intelligence's impact on specialized learning motivation. *International Journal of Advanced Engineering Research and Science, 10*(09), 27–31. DOI: 10.22161/ijaers.109.4

Tariq, M. U. (2024). Generative AI in Curriculum Development in Higher Education. In Fields, Z. (Ed.), *Impacts of Generative AI on Creativity in Higher Education* (pp. 227–258). IGI Global., DOI: 10.4018/979-8-3693-2418-9.ch009

Tariq, M. U. (2024). Harnessing Persuasive Technologies for Enhanced Learner Engagement and Motivation. In M. Sanmugam, D. Lim, N. Mohd Barkhaya, W. Wan Yahaya, & Z. Khlaif (Eds.), *Power of Persuasive Educational Technologies in Enhancing Learning* (pp. 30-62). IGI Global. https://doi.org/DOI: 10.4018/979-8-3693-6397-3.ch002

Tariq, M. U. (2025). *AI-Driven Learning and Engagement in Higher Education*. IGI Global., DOI: 10.4018/979-8-3693-4074-5

Tariq, M. U., & Sergio, R. P. (2025). Innovative Assessment Techniques in Physical Education: Exploring Technology-Enhanced and Student-Centered Models for Holistic Student Development. In Garcia, M. (Ed.), *Global Innovations in Physical Education and Health* (pp. 85–112). IGI Global., DOI: 10.4018/979-8-3693-3952-7.ch004

Taş, N. (2023). Revolutionizing education: Applications of artificial intelligence. *ISTES Books*, 21–30.

Vashishth, T. K., Sharma, V., Sharma, K. K., Kumar, B., Chaudhary, S., & Panwar, R. (2024). Transforming classroom dynamics: The social impact of AI in teaching and learning. In *AI-Enhanced Teaching Methods* (pp. 322–346). IGI Global. DOI: 10.4018/979-8-3693-2728-9.ch015

Verma, N., Getenet, S., Dann, C., & Shaik, T. (2023). Designing an artificial intelligence tool to understand student engagement based on teacher's behaviours and movements in video conferencing. *Computers and Education: Artificial Intelligence*, *5*, 100187. DOI: 10.1016/j.caeai.2023.100187

Wadhwa, R., Rabby, F., Bansal, R., & Hundekari, S. (2024). Drivers and impact of artificial intelligence on student engagement. In *AI Algorithms and ChatGPT for Student Engagement in Online Learning* (pp. 161–170). IGI Global. DOI: 10.4018/979-8-3693-4268-8.ch011

Xu, Z. (2024). AI in education: Enhancing learning experiences and student outcomes. *Applied Computing Engineering*, *51*(1), 104–111. DOI: 10.54254/2755-2721/51/20241187

Yunusaliyev, M., Yuldashev, I., & Yusupov, A. (2024, May). Revolutionizing the present education system through AI-driven learning platform with hybrid techniques. In *2024 4th International Conference on Advance Computing and Innovative Technologies in Engineering (ICACITE)* (pp. 523–527). IEEE. DOI: 10.1109/ICACITE60783.2024.10616605

Zharmukhanbetov, S., & Singh, C. P. (2023, November). Enhancing flipped classroom engagement and personalized learning through AI-powered adaptive content delivery. In *2023 3rd International Conference on Technological Advancements in Computational Sciences (ICTACS)* (pp. 1411–1416). IEEE. DOI: 10.1109/ICTACS59847.2023.10389841

KEY TERMS AND DEFINITIONS

Adaptive Learning: A technology-driven educational approach that personalises learning pathways based on individual student needs and performance.

AI-Powered Instruction: Teaching methods that utilise artificial intelligence to deliver content, track progress, and adjust strategies for improved learning outcomes.

Virtual Reality (VR) in Education: The use of immersive simulations to create engaging, real-world learning scenarios for students.

Ethical AI in Education: Ensuring AI technologies in classrooms adhere to privacy, fairness, and safety standards while promoting equitable access.

Data-Driven Insights: Actionable information derived from AI analytics to enhance teaching effectiveness and address student needs.

Chapter 3
Teaching AI in Communication Classes:
Engagement, Ethics, and Best Practices

David Lynn Painter
https://orcid.org/0000-0001-5808-6319
Rollins College, USA

ABSTRACT

This chapter examines the integration of artificial intelligence (AI) in college communication courses. First, survey data reveals significant differences in AI attitudes and usage patterns based on students' demographic characteristics, highlighting the need for inclusive practices. Further, students who completed AI-integrated courses reported more critical attitudes toward the technology while engaging in more ethical and fewer unethical uses. Second, the chapter identifies discipline-specific ethical challenges presented by AI integration. Third, using experiential learning theory as a framework, the chapter provides practical strategies for incorporating AI into college communication curricula. This framework preserves disciplinary values while preparing diverse student populations for a communication industry where AI literacy is essential.

BACKGROUND

The rapid adoption of generative artificial intelligence (AI) tools is transforming not only how communication professionals work but also how educators prepare students for these evolving industries. AI has become an integral part of communication practice across specializations: journalists use AI for data analysis and story

DOI: 10.4018/979-8-3373-4576-5.ch003

drafting; public relations practitioners employ AI-powered sentiment analysis and crisis communication simulations; marketers implement AI-driven audience segmentation and content personalization; and social media managers deploy chatbots and automated content calendars. Industry surveys confirm this widespread integration, with approximately 90% of communication professionals now reporting AI use in their workflow (Cision PR Newswire, 2023).

This technological shift makes AI literacy an essential competency for future communication practitioners, but it also requires careful balance between innovation and the development of essential human communication skills (Bowen & Watson, 2023; Zawacki-Richter et al., 2019). Communication educators face the challenge of determining which traditional skills remain essential, which can be enhanced by AI collaboration, and which may be transformed entirely. This balancing act is particularly critical in communication disciplines where creativity, ethical judgment, and authentic voice are foundational to professional practice.

Indeed, AI integration into communication curricula may directly challenge some established ethical codes, redefine creative authorship, and raise concerns about misinformation and bias in strategic communication messaging. For instance, when journalism students use AI to generate news content, questions emerge about source verification, factual accuracy, and algorithmic bias in their storytelling, core tenets of journalistic integrity. Similarly, public relations students using AI-driven audience analytics must consider how these tools potentially infringe on privacy rights or create filter bubbles that undermine authentic stakeholder engagement. Likewise, in advertising courses, AI's ability to create persuasive messaging requires students to critically evaluate issues of transparency, disclosure, and the potential for manipulative communication techniques (Ewing, 2023).

Despite these challenges, AI offers significant potential to enhance communication education through interactive learning experiences that mirror professional practice. AI tools can provide communication students with opportunities to engage in specialized simulations: conducting media analytics, developing adaptive messaging strategies, testing audience segmentation approaches, and creating multi-platform campaigns (Rhoads, 2023). These applications provide immediate feedback on communication strategies while offering personalized learning experiences tailored to individual skill development needs. For students from underrepresented backgrounds, AI tools may help bridge skills gaps in writing, content ideation, and organization, potentially creating more equitable educational outcomes when thoughtfully implemented.

To address the challenges and opportunities of AI in communication education, this chapter employs a problem-solution framework organized in three parts. First, the chapter identifies key challenges through an empirical assessment of communication students' attitudes and behaviors regarding AI, alongside analysis of ethical dilemmas specific to communication disciplines. Second, it presents experiential learning theory (ELT) as the conceptual foundation for addressing these challenges. Finally, it presents some actionable strategies for integrating AI tools in communication curricula in ways that reimagine learning objectives, foster active learning, implement effective feedback processes, and cultivate critical reflection.

Throughout this chapter, the approach positions AI not as a replacement for human creativity and critical thinking, but as a strategic partner that can enhance learning while preparing students for ethical and effective professional practice in increasingly AI-driven communication industries. By organizing the analysis around specific challenges and corresponding solutions, this chapter aims to provide communication educators with a practical framework for navigating AI integration in ways that preserve the core values of communication education while embracing technological innovation.

CHALLENGES OF AI IN COMMUNICATION EDUCATION

The integration of AI into communication education presents multifaceted challenges that must be addressed to ensure effective and ethical implementation. This section examines these challenges through empirical findings on student attitudes and behaviors, followed by analysis of specific ethical dilemmas confronting communication educators.

Current Student Attitudes and Behaviors

Understanding how diverse student populations engage with AI tools is crucial for developing inclusive educational practices in communication curricula. Research indicates demographic factors such as race, ethnicity, age, gender, and academic progression may significantly influence students' orientation toward AI technologies (De Freitas et al., 2023; Horowitz & Kahn, 2021; Kaya et al., 2024). These demographic variations have particular relevance in communication fields, where diverse perspectives significantly impact content creation, audience understanding, and message effectiveness. By examining these relationships, educators can develop pedagogical approaches that address all students' needs while preparing them for an industry increasingly reliant on AI. Therefore, the first two research questions ask:

> **RQ1:** How are communication students' demographic characteristics (i.e., race, gender, age, and year in college) related to their attitudes toward AI tools?
> **RQ2:** How are communication students' demographic characteristics (i.e., race, gender, age, and year in college) related to their uses of AI tools?

AI Classroom Experience: Attitudes, and Behaviors

Beyond demographic factors, this study also explores how prior usage of AI in classroom contexts affects students' attitudes and usage patterns. Communication disciplines present unique considerations for AI integration, as these fields balance technical innovation with human creativity, ethical storytelling, and authentic audience engagement. To understand how structured educational experiences might influence students' attitudes and behaviors regarding AI, we draw on experiential learning theory (ELT) as a theoretical foundation. Although discussed in detail in the next section of this chapter, ELT emphasizes that learning occurs through a cycle of experiences, reflections, conceptualizations, and experimentations (Kolb, 1984).

When applied to AI in communication education, ELT explains that students who actively engage with AI tools in structured educational environments will develop more sophisticated attitudes and behavioral patterns than those without such experiences. This expectation stems from research suggesting that guided interaction with AI tools in educational contexts fosters more critical and complex orientations toward these technologies (Tossell et al., 2024; Wood & Moss, 2024; Yannier et al., 2024). For instance, Huang and colleagues (2022) found that students with prior AI exposure in educational settings better recognized both the potential benefits and ethical implications specific to their field of study. Moreover, Kohnke (2024) discovered that students guided in using AI for content creation appreciated the tools for tasks like ideation and editing, but they also demonstrated greater awareness of potential drawbacks like diminished creativity or failure to verify AI-generated information. Based on these findings, the first hypothesis predicts:

H1: Communication students who have taken a class using AI tools will report less favorable attitudes toward the technology than students who have not taken such a class.

The experiential learning framework also suggests that critical engagement with AI tools may influence students' ethical behavior patterns. Understanding how guided experiences shape ethical and unethical AI use is vital for communication educators developing responsible integration strategies. Previous research indicates experiential learning practices incorporating ethical discussions encourage more responsible technology use (Arnold, 2020; Brey, 2012; Sloane, 2021). For example, students who engaged in structured AI learning that included ethical considerations demonstrated more responsible use patterns than those receiving conventional instruction (Usher & Barak, 2024; Holmes et al., 2021). In communication fields where ethical considerations around authorship, transparency, and information integrity are paramount, structured educational experiences may be particularly influential in shaping responsible AI use patterns. Therefore, the next hypotheses predict:

H2: Communication students who have taken a class using AI tools will report more ethical uses of these tools than students who have not taken such a class.

H3: Communication students who have taken a class using AI tools will report fewer unethical uses of these tools than students who have not taken such a class.

METHOD

After receiving Institutional Review Board approval, this investigation deployed an online survey of 1162 undergraduate communication majors recruited from Prolific Academic to complete the project on Qualtrics between March 21-28, 2024. Participants were 53% women and 47% men; 12% Hispanic/Latinx, 17% Black, 16% Asian, 51% White, and 5% multiracial; ages ranged from 19 to 23, with a median age of 20. This demographic diversity allows for examination of how different student populations approach AI in communication education.

Dependent Variables

AI Attitudes: Communication students' attitudes toward AI were measured on a 5-point Likert scale asking them to indicate the extent to which they agreed with seven statements ($\alpha = .91$) based on the Technology Acceptance Model (Davis, 1989).

Ethical AI Uses: Measured by a summative scale of five items asking students whether they had used AI tools for explaining concepts, brainstorming ideas, organizing content, conducting research, or improving writing.

Unethical AI Uses: Measured by a summative scale of three items asking students whether they had used AI tools to answer test or quiz questions, write their essays or papers, or do their homework.

Independent Variable

AI in Class: Measured by a single dichotomous item asking students whether they had taken a class that taught them how to use AI tools effectively and responsibly.

RESULTS

Demographics and AI Attitudes

The first research question asked how college students' demographic characteristics influenced their attitudes, and the first hypothesis predicted students completing a class using AI would report less positive attitudes toward the tools compared to those who had not taken such a class. To answer this question and test this prediction, a regression model was constructed using AI attitudes as the dependent variable and AI in class, race (white or nonwhite), gender (man or woman), college year (1-4), and age (years) as independent variables. The results indicate the model accounted for 31% (R^2_{adj} = .31) of the variation in AI attitudes. As shown in the top rows of Table 1, the results indicate all independent variables other than age were significant predictors of college students' attitudes toward AI tools. Specifically, nonwhite students reported significantly more positive attitudes toward AI than their counterparts, while women indicated their attitude were significantly less positive. Moreover, students in later college years reported more positive attitudes toward AI than their counterparts, suggesting academic progression may foster greater appreciation for technological tools in communication practice (De Freitas et al., 2023; Kaya et al., 2024).

Perhaps most notably, supporting the first hypothesis, students who had taken a communication class using AI reported significantly less positive attitudes toward these tools compared to those without such structured exposure. This finding suggests deeper understanding of AI capabilities and limitations through formal education leads to more critical and nuanced perspectives rather than uncritical enthusiasm, an important consideration for communication educators designing AI-integrated curricula.

Prior AI Classroom Experience

The second hypothesis predicted that students who had taken a class using AI tools would report more ethical uses of these tools than students who had not taken such a class. To test this hypothesis, another regression model was constructed using ethical AI uses as the dependent variable and the same independent variables as the first model. The results indicate the model accounted for 40% (R^2_A = .40) of the variation in ethical AI usage. As shown in the second set of rows in Table 1, having taken a class using AI was a significant, positive predictor of ethical AI uses, supporting H2. This finding indicates that students with formal AI education were more likely than their counterparts to use these tools for appropriate educational purposes such as explaining concepts, brainstorming ideas, conducting research, or improving their writing.

Next, to test the third hypothesis predicted that students who had taken a class using AI tools would report fewer unethical uses of these tools than students who had not taken such a class. Once again, a regression model was constructed but this time unethical AI uses were entered as the dependent variable and the same independent variables were entered as in the first two models. The results indicate the model accounted for 24% (R^2_A = .24) of the variation in unethical AI usage. As shown in the third set of rows in Table 1, having taken an AI class was a significant, negative predictor of unethical AI uses, supporting H3. This finding indicates that students with structured AI education reported significantly fewer instances of using AI for prohibited purposes such as answering test questions, writing essays, or completing homework assignments. This pattern demonstrates that structured AI education can effectively guide students toward responsible professional practices that complement rather than replace their developing communication expertise (Arnold, 2020; Sloane, 2021).

Table 1. Regression on AI attitudes, ethical, unethical, and all AI uses

Outcomes	**Estimate**	*SE*	**95% CI**		*p*
Effects			**LL UL**		
Attitudes[a]					
AI Class	-.33	..05	-0.43	-0.23	.00
Nonwhite	.09	.04	0.01	0.17	.02
Women	-.40	.04	-0.48	-0.32	.00
College Year	.19	.06	0.07	0.31	.00
Age	-.07	.06	-0.19	0.05	.08
Ethical AI Uses[b]					
AI in Class	.50	.04	0.42	0.58	.00
Nonwhite	-.32	.03	-0.38	-0.26	.00
Women	.06	.03	0.00	0.12	.06
College Year	.31	.04	0.23	0.39	.00
Age	.44	.03	0.38	0.50	.00
Unethical AI Uses[c]					
AI in Class	-.51	.08	-0.67	-0.35	.00
Nonwhite	-.48	.06	-0.60	-0.36	.00
Women	.42	.06	0.30	0.54	.00
College Year	-.01	.08	-0.17	0.15	.89

continued on following page

Table 1. Continued

Outcomes	Estimate	*SE*	95% CI		*p*
Effects			**LL**	**UL**	
Attitudes[a]					
Age	.57	.06	0.45	0.69	.00
All AI Uses					
AI in Class	-.01	.10	-0.21	0.19	.89
Nonwhite	-80	.08	-0.96	-0.64	.00
Women	.48	.08	0.32	0.64	.00
College Year	-.32	.11	-0.54	-0.10	.00
Age	1.01	.08	0.85	1.17	.00

Notes: [a]AI Attitudes R^2_{adj} = .31; [b]Ethical AI Uses R^2_{adj} = .40; [c]Unethical AI Uses R^2_{adj} = .24; [d]All AI Uses R^2_{adj} = .29

Demographics and AI Usage

Finally, a fourth regression model was constructed to answer the second research question asking how communication students' demographic characteristics were related to their uses of AI tools. This model explained 29% of the variation in overall usage (R^2_A = .29), with older students and women reporting significantly more AI uses overall, while nonwhite students reported significantly fewer total AI applications. Students in later college years also reported significantly fewer total AI applications in their communication studies, despite their more positive attitudes and higher rates of ethical use. This pattern suggests that while chronological age is positively associated with AI use when controlling for academic progression, students further along in their communication studies tend to be more selective in their AI use, focusing on ethical applications rather than overall quantity of use. This distinction between age and academic progression effects highlights how advancing in communication education may foster more strategic and judicious approaches to AI tools, emphasizing quality of use over quantity. Moreover, these patterns indicate there is a disconnect between perception and practice that merits further exploration in communication education contexts (Horowitz & Kahn, 2021). Notably, having taken an AI class was not a significant predictor of overall AI usage, suggesting that formal AI education does not simply increase or decrease students' total engagement with these tools. This finding suggests that formal AI education redirects students' engagement toward more appropriate applications while reducing problematic uses, shaping the quality rather than quantity of AI engagement.

Moreover, when analyzing the relationship between communication students' demographic characteristics and the ethicality of their AI uses, the data in the second set of rows in Table 1 indicate being nonwhite was negatively related while college year and age were positively related to ethical AI uses; but gender was not a significant predictor of ethical AI uses. Next, for unethical AI uses, being nonwhite was a significant negative predictor, while being a woman and being older were significant positive predictors, but college year was not significantly related to unethical AI uses (see third set of rows in Table 1).

DISCUSSION

The survey results have important implications for communication educators. First, the less positive attitudes among students who had taken AI-focused classes suggest that structured educational experiences foster critical awareness rather than uncritical enthusiasm for these technologies. This finding underscores the importance of developing curricula that move beyond basic technical instruction to engage students in critical evaluation of AI's capabilities and limitations specifically in communication contexts. Second, the relationship between taking a class that used AI and more ethical usage patterns demonstrates that formal instruction can effectively guide students toward responsible professional practices that complement rather than replace their developing communication expertise. This finding reinforces the value of integrating ethical frameworks directly into AI instruction rather than treating technology and ethics as separate domains.

Third, the demographic variations in AI attitudes and usage highlight the need for inclusive approaches to AI education that acknowledge and address the different orientations that diverse student populations bring to these technologies. The lower overall AI usage reported by nonwhite students, for instance, suggests potential barriers to access that communication educators should actively address when designing AI-integrated curricula. Finally, finding that advanced communication students engage more selectively with AI tools underscores the importance of developing curricula that foster increasingly sophisticated and strategic approaches to AI integration across the academic progression. Early courses might focus on building basic AI literacy and ethical frameworks, while advanced courses could emphasize more nuanced integration of AI into specialized communication practices. Together, these findings provide a foundation for understanding the student-centered challenges of AI integration, which must be addressed alongside the discipline-specific ethical concerns explored in the following section.

AI's Ethical Challenges to Communication Disciplines

Beyond student attitudes and behaviors, communication educators face distinct ethical challenges when integrating AI into their curricula. These challenges reflect the unique professional values, practices, and responsibilities of communication disciplines.

Autonomy and Voice Development Challenges

Communication disciplines place fundamental importance on developing students' authentic voice, creative expression, and message ownership, qualities that AI tools may potentially undermine. When journalism students use AI to generate news articles, public relations students use AI to craft press releases, or advertising students use AI to develop campaign concepts, questions arise about whose voice is being expressed and developed.

For instance, Khreisat and colleagues (2024) found that communication students frequently rely on AI tools as substitutes for developing their own content creation skills and critical thinking about message strategy. This substitution is particularly problematic in communication fields where developing a distinctive voice, storytelling approach, and analytical perspective represents essential professional competencies. For communication educators, the challenge lies in positioning AI as a collaborative tool that enhances rather than replaces students' communication capabilities, a balance that requires thoughtfully designed assignments and clear guidelines for appropriate tool use (Foltynek et al., 2023).

In journalism education specifically, the development of reportorial voice and news judgment represents core learning objectives that may be compromised when students rely heavily on AI for content generation. That is: journalism students who use AI to draft articles may adopt the tool's stylistic patterns rather than developing their own distinctive approaches to storytelling. Similarly, in strategic communication contexts, excessive reliance on AI for message development may prevent students from cultivating the creative problem-solving skills and strategic thinking that distinguish exceptional practitioners. This challenge requires communication educators to carefully structure AI integration in ways that preserve authentic voice development while leveraging the technology's capabilities to enhance rather than replace students' emerging communication expertise.

Truth and Accuracy Concerns

Communication disciplines, particularly journalism and public relations, operate on foundational commitments to truth, accuracy, and factual integrity that AI-generated content may compromise. AI tools can produce content containing factual inaccuracies, misleading information, or fabricated details that undermine journalistic integrity and strategic communication ethics. Specifically, Pavlik (2023) explains that journalism educators must implement AI carefully to avoid spreading misinformation or creating content that appears credible but contains factual errors. Similarly, strategic communication students using AI to generate persuasive messages may inadvertently incorporate inaccuracies that could damage client relationships or organizational reputation. These accuracy concerns directly impact communication students' professional development, as verification skills and commitment to truthfulness remain essential despite technological advancement (Ewing, 2023).

The challenge of maintaining factual integrity is especially acute in journalism education, where students must learn to verify information through traditional reporting practices. When AI tools generate content that appears authoritative but contains subtle inaccuracies, students may not develop the rigorous fact-checking habits essential to professional practice. Early observations from journalism classrooms suggest that students may sometimes accept AI-generated facts without sufficient verification, a tendency that requires specific pedagogical interventions addressing verification skills. Similarly, in public relations education, students must learn how AI's potential for generating misinformation can create reputational risks for organizations. Developing verification protocols and critical assessment frameworks for AI-generated content therefore represents an essential component of communication education in an AI-integrated environment.

Privacy and Data Ethical Issues

Communication disciplines increasingly rely on data for audience analysis, message targeting, and campaign evaluation, practices that raise significant privacy concerns when AI tools are involved. AI systems require vast amounts of data, raising questions about information security, confidentiality, and ethical data management that communication students must learn to navigate. For instance, Klimova and colleagues (2023) explain how AI systems may collect sensitive information without users fully understanding data usage implications. This concern is particularly relevant for communication students who may later become responsible for organizational data privacy in their professional roles. When students use AI tools to analyze audience data, develop targeting strategies, or personalize messages, they must understand the privacy implications of these practices and develop ethical approaches to data stewardship that align with communication industry standards (Crawford et al., 2023).

In advertising and marketing communication education, these privacy concerns are especially significant, as students learn to implement increasingly sophisticated audience targeting methods powered by AI analytics. Ethical questions about the appropriate boundaries of personalization and the protection of audience data must be integrated into curricula addressing AI-powered communication strategies. Similarly, in digital journalism contexts, students using AI tools to analyze audience behavior or customize content distribution must consider how these practices align with journalistic commitments to transparency and trust. Communication educators must therefore develop frameworks that help students navigate these complex privacy considerations while preparing them to make ethical decisions about data usage in their professional practice.

Representation and Bias Challenges

Communication disciplines bear responsibility for creating inclusive, equitable messages for diverse audiences, a commitment that algorithmic bias in AI systems may undermine. AI tools can perpetuate and amplify biases in communication content, leading to unfair representation of marginalized groups or reinforcement of stereotypes (Khreisat et al., 2024). This concern is especially significant in communication education, where students learn to create messages for diverse audiences and stakeholders. When journalism students use AI to identify newsworthy stories, public relations students use AI to analyze stakeholder sentiment, or advertising students use AI to develop audience profiles, biased algorithms may systematically underrepresent certain communities or perpetuate harmful narratives. Communication educators must help students recognize these potential biases and develop strategies for ensuring AI-assisted communication maintains commitments to inclusive and equitable representation (Luttrell et al., 2020).

The challenge of algorithmic bias has particular significance in strategic communication education, where students must learn to develop inclusive messaging that resonates with diverse audiences. When AI tools suggest communication approaches based on biased training data, they may perpetuate stereotypical representations or fail to account for cultural nuances essential to effective cross-cultural communication. Similarly, in journalism education, students using AI to identify story patterns or suggest news angles may unconsciously reproduce biased news framing if they lack critical awareness of algorithmic limitations. Developing this critical awareness requires communication educators to integrate specific learning activities addressing algorithmic bias, helping students identify and mitigate these issues in their AI-assisted communication practices.

Transparency and Disclosure Dilemmas

Communication disciplines operate on foundations of transparency, disclosure, and attribution that AI integration complicates. But, as Pavlik (2023) notes, "the opacity of AI decision-making raises concerns about accountability and trust" (p. 87), fundamental issues in communication ethics. Moreover, when communication students cannot explain how AI contributed to their work, they cannot take full ownership of their messaging or ensure its alignment with professional standards. This transparency challenge is particularly significant in disciplines like journalism, public relations, and advertising, where disclosure practices and source attribution are fundamental ethical requirements. Communication educators must establish clear guidelines on when and how students should disclose AI assistance in their projects, how communication professionals should maintain transparency with audiences about AI contributions, and what level of understanding about AI processes is necessary for ethical communication practice (Schiff, 2022).

In journalism education specifically, transparency challenges emerge when students use AI tools to generate content or analyze information without fully understanding or disclosing these processes. Professional journalistic standards require clear attribution of sources and transparency about reporting methods, principles that become complex when AI systems contribute to content development. Similarly, in public relations and advertising, questions about appropriate disclosure of AI-generated content raise important ethical considerations for student learning. To address these challenges, communication educators must develop specific guidelines for acknowledging AI contributions in student work while helping students understand the professional standards for transparency that will guide their future practice.

Pedagogical Integration Challenges

Beyond student perspectives and ethical considerations, communication educators face practical challenges when integrating AI into their curricula. These challenges include assessment authenticity in an AI-enhanced environment, where traditional evaluation methods may no longer effectively measure student learning; faculty readiness and resistance, as instructors may lack technical knowledge or harbor concerns about AI's impact on traditional communication education; infrastructure and access inequities that may disadvantage certain student populations; and the fundamental challenge of balancing technological innovation with traditional communication competencies essential for professional practice (Fitria, 2021; Meyer et al., 2023).

The challenge of assessment authenticity has particular significance in communication education, where evaluating students' creative work, analytical thinking, and strategic decision-making remains essential despite AI's capabilities for content generation. When AI can produce competent essays, campaign proposals, or media analyses, communication educators must redesign assessment strategies to focus on unique human contributions and decision-making processes rather than final products alone. Similarly, faculty preparedness represents a significant challenge, as many communication instructors lack experience with AI tools despite these technologies' rapid adoption in professional contexts. Developing faculty training programs and communities of practice focused on ethical and effective AI integration therefore represents an essential component of addressing these pedagogical challenges.

Infrastructure and access inequities present additional challenges, as communication programs vary significantly in their technological resources and students with different levels of AI exposure. These disparities can create uneven learning experiences if not thoughtfully addressed through curriculum design and resource allocation. Finally, the challenge of balancing innovation with tradition requires communication educators to identify core disciplinary competencies that remain essential despite technological change, ensuring students develop both technological fluency and foundational communication skills. Addressing these pedagogical challenges requires a structured approach grounded in educational theory and focused on practical implementation strategies. The following section presents experiential learning theory as a conceptual foundation for AI integration, followed by actionable strategies that communication educators can implement to navigate these challenges effectively.

Experiential Learning Theoretical Foundation

Addressing the challenges of AI integration in communication education requires a structured pedagogical framework that balances technological innovation with essential disciplinary competencies. Experiential learning theory (ELT) provides an ideal foundation for this integration, offering a systematic approach to developing students' critical engagement with AI tools while preserving the core values of communication education.

Experiential Learning Theory and Communication Education

Experiential learning theory emphasizes active engagement, critical reflection, and practical application, principles particularly relevant for communication disciplines where professional practice requires both technical proficiency and ethical judgment. Rather than positioning students as passive recipients of knowledge, ELT frames learning as an active process of engagement with new experiences, reflection on those experiences, conceptual understanding, and practical application.

ELT's roots lie in the work of several influential educational thinkers, including Dewey (1938), who challenged traditional educational paradigms in favor of active engagement with real-world experiences. Dewey's emphasis on learning through doing provides a valuable perspective for communication educators navigating the challenge of how students should engage with AI tools. Rather than simply teaching about AI, this approach suggests communication students should directly experience these tools while developing critical awareness of their implications.

Lewin's (1946) concept of action research, with its iterative cycle of planning, acting, observing, and reflecting, further enriches this foundation. This cyclical approach mirrors the dynamic nature of communication practice, where professionals continuously evaluate and refine messaging strategies based on audience feedback, a process now enhanced by AI analytics tools. This framework encourages communication students to experiment with AI tools, observe their impacts, reflect on their effectiveness, and refine their approaches through multiple iterations. Moreover, Paulo Freire's (1970) concept of "praxis," or the intersection of reflection and action, further enriches the theoretical foundation for AI integration in communication education. His emphasis on critical consciousness is especially relevant when asking students to evaluate AI-generated content against professional and ethical standards in journalism, public relations, and strategic communication. This critical perspective helps students move beyond merely using AI tools to begin questioning their implications for media representation, message authenticity, and audience engagement.

Kolb's (1984) synthesis of these ideas into a four-stage experiential learning cycle (concrete experience, reflective observation, abstract conceptualization, and active experimentation) provides communication educators with a structured approach for integrating AI tools into curricula. Contemporary scholars have enhanced this model by incorporating a pre-reflection stage to elicit students' expectations and biases before engaging with new experiences (Edwards, 2017; Moon, 2004; Painter & Howell, 2020). This addition is particularly valuable when introducing communication students to AI tools, as it helps surface preconceptions that might otherwise limit learning.

Five-Stage ELT Framework for AI Integration

The five-stage experiential learning model, encompassing pre-reflective ideation, concrete experience, reflective observation, abstract conceptualization, and active experimentation, provides a comprehensive framework for addressing the challenges of AI integration in communication education:

Pre-Reflective Ideation: Addressing Preconceptions

Before engaging with AI tools, students articulate their expectations, biases, and prior knowledge about artificial intelligence. This process addresses the challenge of varied student attitudes identified in the survey findings, helping instructors understand and work with diverse perspectives on AI technology. Students might reflect on questions about AI's capabilities and limitations, their comfort level with new technologies, or preconceptions formed through media portrayals. For communication students specifically, this pre-reflection creates space to surface assumptions about how AI might affect their chosen profession before they begin working with these tools. By documenting these initial perceptions, students establish a baseline for measuring how their understanding evolves through experiential learning. This stage also allows instructors to identify and address potential resistance or overenthusiasm before introducing AI tools into communication assignments.

In a journalism course, for example, pre-reflection might involve students documenting their initial thoughts about how AI could influence reporting practices, including their concerns about factual accuracy, source verification, and the development of reportorial voice. Similarly, in a strategic communication course, students might articulate their assumptions about how AI tools could enhance or undermine audience engagement, message personalization, and campaign evaluation. These pre-reflective activities help communication educators tailor their approaches to different student populations, addressing the demographic variations in AI attitudes identified in the survey findings while establishing a foundation for deeper learning through structured experiences.

Concrete Experience: Hands-on AI Engagement

In this stage, students engage directly with AI tools in applications that mirror professional communication practices. This hands-on approach addresses the challenge of developing appropriate technical skills while maintaining disciplinary focus. Rather than abstract discussions about AI, students gain practical experience using these tools for communication-specific tasks. For instance, journalism students might use AI-powered tools to analyze data sets, identify story patterns, and generate initial drafts that require human refinement and verification. Public relations students could employ AI for stakeholder sentiment analysis or crisis communication simulations. Strategic communication students might utilize AI to test message variations across audience segments. These concrete experiences provide students with opportunities to understand both the capabilities and limitations of AI in communication contexts.

The value of these hands-on experiences lies in their ability to connect technological capabilities with discipline-specific practices. In a digital journalism course, for example, students might use AI tools to analyze social media trends, identify potential story angles, and develop preliminary drafts before applying traditional reporting techniques to verify information and enhance storytelling. This approach allows students to experience AI as a complementary tool that augments rather than replaces fundamental journalistic practices. Similarly, in an advertising course, students might use AI to analyze consumer sentiment data, generate initial creative concepts, and test message variations before applying their strategic thinking to refine these outputs. These structured experiences help students develop an understanding of AI's practical applications while maintaining the core disciplinary focus essential to communication education.

Reflective Observation: Critical Analysis of AI

Following their hands-on experiences, students analyze how AI tools influenced their communication process and outcomes. This reflection addresses the critical challenge of developing ethical awareness and judgment regarding AI use. Through structured reflection activities, students examine questions such as: How did AI shape my creative process? What biases or limitations did I observe in AI-generated content? How does AI-assisted communication compare to traditional approaches? This stage directly addresses the ethical challenges identified earlier, particularly concerns about autonomy, truth, bias, and transparency. By critically analyzing AI's impact on their work, communication students develop the metacognitive awareness necessary for responsible professional practice. This reflection transforms technical experience into deeper learning about AI's role in communication contexts.

For communication students, this reflective process has particular significance, as it helps them evaluate AI's influence on discipline-specific values and practices. Journalism students, for example, might reflect on how AI-generated content influences their reporting approach, including considerations of verification, balance, and voice development. These reflections might address questions like: Did using AI for initial draft writing influence my story framing? How thoroughly did I verify AI-generated information? Did the AI suggest perspectives I might have overlooked through traditional reporting methods? Similarly, public relations students might reflect on how AI-enhanced audience analysis influences their strategic decision-making, considering both the insights gained and the potential biases introduced. These structured reflections help students develop a nuanced understanding of how AI tools both enhance and potentially compromise core disciplinary values, preparing them to make thoughtful decisions about AI integration in their future professional practice.

Abstract Conceptualization: Developing Principles for AI Use

Based on their reflective analysis, students develop principles and frameworks for effective and ethical AI use in their communication specialization. This conceptualization addresses the challenge of moving from isolated experiences to cohesive understanding. Students might formulate guidelines for when to use AI tools, how to verify AI-generated content, or how to maintain creative ownership while leveraging AI capabilities. This stage helps communication students integrate their practical experiences with the theoretical and ethical foundations of their discipline. For example, journalism students might develop verification protocols for AI-generated research, while advertising students might create frameworks for evaluating AI-suggested creative concepts against brand guidelines and ethical standards. These conceptualizations prepare students to make informed decisions about AI use across various professional scenarios.

This process of developing principles and frameworks has special relevance in communication disciplines, where professional standards guide ethical practice. In a journalism ethics course, for instance, students might develop specific guidelines for maintaining transparency about AI contributions to reporting, ensuring factual accuracy in AI-assisted content, and preserving journalistic voice while leveraging technological capabilities. Similarly, in a media relations course, students might formulate frameworks for evaluating AI-generated media pitches against criteria of newsworthiness, strategic alignment, and ethical representation. These discipline-specific frameworks help students translate their reflective insights into actionable principles that will guide their professional decision-making, addressing the ethical challenges identified earlier while preparing students for evolving professional environments.

Active Experimentation: Strategic Applications of AI Tools

In the final stage, students apply their refined understanding in new communication projects, strategically implementing AI tools based on their developed principles. This experimentation addresses the challenge of balancing innovation with disciplinary tradition, as students determine how AI can enhance rather than replace their developing professional expertise. Students might experiment with different approaches to AI integration: using it for initial research but not content development, employing it for editing but not ideation, or testing its effectiveness for different communication objectives or audience segments. This active experimentation helps students develop personalized approaches to AI use that align with their professional goals and ethical values. Through these iterations, students refine both their technical proficiency and critical judgment.

In a multimedia journalism course, for instance, students might experiment with different phases of AI integration in their reporting process—using AI tools for initial data analysis and story identification but relying on traditional reporting techniques for source interviews and verification. This experimental approach allows students to identify where AI tools most effectively enhance their journalistic practice while preserving essential professional competencies. Similarly, in an advertising campaign course, students might test AI-generated creative concepts against their own original ideas, evaluating which approach resonates most effectively with target audiences while maintaining brand authenticity. These experimental applications help students discover their optimal balance between technological enhancement and human creativity, preparing them for professional environments where these determinations will be increasingly important.

Research Support for ELT in AI Education

Research supports the effectiveness of this experiential approach to AI education in communication contexts. Hsu and colleagues (2022) found that students who engaged in experiential learning with AI tools demonstrated significantly higher learning outcomes compared to those taught through conventional instruction. This improvement stems from AI simulations that provide learners with concrete experiences applying theoretical knowledge to practical communication challenges.

The experiential approach also creates possibilities for more authentic assessment in communication education. Salinas-Navarro and colleagues (2024) highlight how AI integration enables assessment that mirrors professional practice, where students demonstrate not just technical proficiency but also critical thinking and ethical judgment. Rather than focusing solely on final products, this approach evaluates students' decision-making processes and strategic thinking—competencies essential for communication professionals.

The survey findings presented earlier further support this approach. Students who had formal exposure to AI through structured educational experiences demonstrated more critical attitudes and more ethical usage patterns. This aligns with experiential learning principles, suggesting that guided engagement with AI technologies leads to more thoughtful and responsible application.

By structuring AI integration within this experiential learning cycle, communication educators can address the challenges identified in the previous section while preparing students for evolving professional environments. This framework ensures AI enhances rather than replaces the critical thinking, creativity, and ethical reasoning essential to communication practice. The following section translates this theoretical foundation into specific actionable strategies for communication educators.

Strategies for AI Integration

The integration of AI into communication education requires thoughtful strategies that address the ethical and pedagogical challenges identified while leveraging the experiential learning framework. This section presents four key strategies communication educators can implement to effectively integrate AI into their curricula: reformulating learning goals to reflect AI's capabilities, fostering active learning through AI-enhanced activities, providing personalized and formative feedback, and encouraging critical thinking and reflection. Each strategy includes concrete examples from communication disciplines and specific case studies demonstrating successful implementation.

Reformulating Learning Goals in Communication Courses

As AI capabilities evolve, communication educators must reassess traditional learning objectives and realign them to emphasize uniquely human contributions to the communication process. This reformulation shifts focus from basic skill development to higher-order capacities like critical evaluation, ethical judgment, and creative integration—competencies that remain distinctly human despite technological advancement. In journalism education, for example, learning goals might shift from basic news writing techniques to developing advanced verification skills, ethical decision-making, and distinctive voice. Similarly, in strategic communication courses, objectives might evolve from message formatting to complex strategic thinking, audience insight development, and creative campaign integration.

This reformulation aligns with contemporary revisions to Bloom's Taxonomy that account for technological advancement. While the traditional taxonomy (Bloom, 1956) structured cognitive skills from basic recall to higher-order thinking, recent adaptations have elevated creation to the highest cognitive level (Anderson & Krathwohl, 2001) and incorporated digital tools (Churches, 2008). Today, AI integration represents the next evolution of this taxonomy, positioning AI tools as cognitive partners for lower-order tasks while elevating human contributions that AI cannot replicate (Oregon State University Ecampus, 2024). Communication educators can apply this updated framework to design assignments that develop students' ethical decision-making and creative capabilities alongside their technical proficiency with AI tools.

The reformulation of learning goals requires communication educators to identify which traditional skills remain essential, which can be augmented by AI collaboration, and which may be fundamentally transformed. In public relations writing courses, for instance, basic press release formatting might be augmented by AI tools, allowing educators to focus on developing students' strategic audience analysis, ethical message framing, and relationship-building capabilities. Similarly, in media production courses, AI might assist with technical editing, enabling greater focus on creative storytelling and ethical representation. This strategic realignment ensures students develop the human capabilities most valued in communication professions while leveraging technological tools effectively.

Case Study: Annotated Bibliography Assignment

A concrete example of learning goal reformulation can be seen in a communication research methods course where the traditional annotated bibliography assignment was redesigned to incorporate AI tools while emphasizing higher-order analysis and synthesis. In the redesigned assignment, students were explicitly guided to use AI tools for the initial summary of scholarly articles, but were required to provide additional analysis demonstrating their understanding of theoretical frameworks, methodological approaches, and relevance to their particular research project. The assignment specifically required students to explain each source's theoretical framework, research questions or hypotheses, methodology, key findings, and explain how this information can be used as a basis for their project.

Students were also asked to document their experience using AI tools, describing how they verified the accuracy of AI-generated summaries, what limitations they encountered, and how they enhanced the content with their own analysis. This reflective component reinforced the distinction between AI assistance and human contribution while developing students' critical evaluation skills. The assignment's primary learning objective shifted from demonstrating basic comprehension of source material (which AI can facilitate) to emphasizing students' ability to synthesize a coherent foundation for their research and articulate clear connections between disparate sources, higher-order cognitive skills that remain distinctly human.

This redesigned assignment addressed several challenges identified earlier: it preserved student autonomy by clearly demarcating AI and human contributions; it emphasized verification of AI-generated content; and it maintained academic integrity through transparent documentation of AI use. Moreover, it leveraged the experiential learning cycle by incorporating concrete experience with AI tools, reflection on their capabilities and limitations, conceptualization of appropriate AI integration in research, and active experimentation with different approaches to augmenting AI-generated content. The assignment's success demonstrated how communication educators can reformulate learning goals to embrace technological advancement while emphasizing the uniquely human dimensions of communication scholarship.

Fostering Active Learning Through AI-Enhanced Activities

Beyond reformulating learning goals, communication educators must design activities that position students as active participants in AI-enhanced learning environments rather than passive consumers of AI-generated content. This approach aligns with the experiential learning framework's emphasis on concrete experience and active experimentation while addressing the challenge of balancing technological innovation with essential disciplinary competencies. Five key principles guide the effective use of AI to foster active learning in communication education.

First, engaging with AI as a collaborative partner allows students to co-create and explore ideas in ways that traditional approaches may not facilitate. Rather than simply prompting AI tools to generate complete content, students can engage in an iterative dialogue with these technologies, refining prompts and critically evaluating outputs against professional standards. This collaborative approach helps students develop both technical proficiency with AI tools and the critical judgment necessary to enhance AI outputs with human insight and creativity. In a media relations course, for example, students might use AI to generate initial pitch ideas, then critically evaluate and refine these concepts based on their understanding of media relationships and news values.

Second, AI tools can simulate real-world scenarios and provide diverse perspectives that encourage students to think beyond their initial ideas, enhancing their problem-solving abilities. Through iterative dialogue with AI, students can explore multiple approaches to a single communication challenge, gaining a more comprehensive understanding of the complexities involved in strategic message development. This approach promotes deeper learning, as students continuously evaluate and adjust their approaches in response to AI-generated insights. In a crisis communication exercise, for instance, students might use AI to simulate stakeholder responses to different messaging strategies, allowing them to test multiple approaches before developing their final communication plan.

Third, incorporating AI into classroom activities helps cultivate AI literacy, equipping students with the knowledge and skills needed to effectively use these tools in professional settings. By experimenting with AI capabilities and limitations, students learn to identify where AI can support their work and where human intervention is necessary. This literacy is crucial as it enables students to become discerning users of AI, aware of its potential contributions as well as its ethical and practical constraints. A dedicated module on AI prompting techniques, for example, can help journalism students understand how different query approaches yield varying results, developing their ability to extract useful information while maintaining critical awareness of potential biases or limitations.

Fourth, integrating AI into assignments can promote ethical reasoning by encouraging students to critically reflect on the implications of using AI-generated content. Students might analyze the potential biases in AI outputs or consider how AI's role in communication development might affect authenticity and credibility. This reflection helps students develop a nuanced understanding of the ethical considerations surrounding AI, preparing them to make informed decisions about its use in real-world communication contexts. In a media ethics course, for instance, students might compare how different AI tools represent controversial issues, analyzing potential biases and discussing implications for public discourse and democratic processes.

Fifth, AI-enhanced activities can help students develop transferable skills that will serve them in evolving professional environments. By learning to strategically implement AI tools within communication workflows, students develop adaptability, critical evaluation capabilities, and technological fluency alongside traditional communication competencies. These combined skill sets prepare students for professional environments where hybrid human-AI workflows are increasingly common. In a digital storytelling course, for example, students might experiment with different phases of AI integration in their production process, identifying optimal collaboration points while maintaining creative control over their narrative vision.

Case Study: Theory-Guided Communication Campaign Development

A practical example of fostering active learning through AI-enhanced activities can be seen in a communication campaigns course where students developed anti-vaping campaigns guided by the Theory of Planned Behavior (TPB). The assignment positioned AI as a collaborative tool for exploring how theoretical principles could be translated into practical communication strategies. Working in teams, students first articulated the theoretical foundation for their campaign, identifying how they would target attitudes toward the behavior, subjective norms, and perceived behavioral control, key elements of TPB framework (Ajzen, 1991).

Students then engaged in an iterative process with AI tools, generating potential messages targeting each TPB component. For example, they prompted AI to generate content highlighting the negative health impacts of vaping to shift attitudes, messages emphasizing peer perspectives to address subjective norms, and practical strategies for quitting to enhance perceived behavioral control. Rather than simply accepting AI-generated content, students critically evaluated each output against theoretical criteria, refining prompts to better align with TPB principles and adapting language to better resonate with their target audience.

This collaborative approach positioned students as strategic directors rather than passive consumers of AI content. They maintained creative control by selecting, adapting, and integrating AI-generated ideas into a cohesive campaign while continuously evaluating alignment with their theoretical framework. The assignment required students to document their AI interaction process, explaining how they refined prompts to improve outputs and describing their criteria for selecting, modifying, or rejecting AI-generated content. This transparency reinforced the distinction between AI assistance and human judgment while developing students' critical evaluation skills.

The assignment also addressed several challenges identified earlier: it preserved student autonomy by emphasizing their strategic direction of AI tools; it encouraged critical evaluation of AI-generated content against theoretical criteria; and it maintained transparency through careful documentation of AI contributions. Moreover, it engaged students in the full experiential learning cycle—from concrete experience with AI tools to reflection on their capabilities, conceptualization of effective integration strategies, and active experimentation with different approaches to theory-guided message development. The resulting campaigns demonstrated students' ability to leverage AI capabilities while maintaining theoretical integrity and creative ownership of their communication strategies.

Providing Personalized and Formative Feedback

AI tools offer significant potential for enhancing feedback processes in communication education, providing students with timely, iterative guidance that supports continuous improvement rather than merely evaluating final products. This approach aligns with the experiential learning framework's emphasis on reflection and conceptualization while addressing the challenge of assessment authenticity in AI-integrated learning environments. By leveraging AI for formative feedback throughout the learning process, communication educators can create dynamic feedback loops that enhance student engagement, develop metacognitive awareness, and improve learning outcomes.

The integration of AI-driven feedback can fundamentally transform assessment practices in communication education by focusing on the development process rather than solely on final products. Traditional assessment often emphasizes summative evaluation of completed assignments, providing limited opportunity for revision and improvement. AI tools enable a more developmental approach, where students receive ongoing feedback at multiple stages of their work. This iterative process encourages deeper engagement with course content as students continuously refine their understanding and application of communication principles. In a news writing course, for example, students might receive AI-generated feedback on story structure, source integration, and clarity before submitting work for instructor evaluation, allowing them to revise and improve their work based on specific guidance.

The personalization capabilities of AI tools further enhance this feedback approach by addressing individual learning needs that might be overlooked in traditional assessment. While instructors may provide general feedback applicable to most students, AI can identify patterns in individual work and offer tailored recommendations addressing specific strengths and weaknesses. This personalized approach helps students develop greater self-awareness about their communication competencies while providing targeted support for improvement. In a public speaking course, for instance, AI might analyze students' practice presentations to identify specific patterns in verbal delivery, organization, or argument development, offering individualized suggestions aligned with each student's developmental needs.

The timeliness of AI-generated feedback represents another significant advantage over traditional assessment approaches. While instructors may require days or weeks to evaluate student work, AI tools can provide immediate guidance that allows students to implement changes while their engagement with the material remains fresh. This immediacy creates a more dynamic learning environment where students can experiment with different approaches, receive feedback, and refine their work in compressed timeframes. In a social media management course, for example, students might receive real-time feedback on draft posts before publication, allowing them to consider alternative approaches, refine messaging strategies, and improve content while actively engaged in the creation process.

To maximize the benefits of AI-driven feedback, communication educators should implement several key strategies. First, instructors should clearly articulate assessment criteria and rubrics that AI tools will apply, ensuring feedback aligns with course learning objectives and disciplinary standards. Second, educators should encourage students to engage critically with AI-generated feedback, evaluating its relevance and applicability rather than implementing suggestions uncritically. Third, instructors should integrate human feedback alongside AI assessment, providing complementary perspectives that address dimensions of communication quality that AI might not fully capture. Finally, educators should create opportunities for students to document their response to feedback, explaining how they incorporated suggestions and why they made specific revisions. This metacognitive reflection transforms feedback from a passive experience to an active learning opportunity.

Case Study: Literature Review Development Process

A practical example of AI-enhanced feedback integration is from a graduate strategic communication research methods course where students developed literature reviews through an iterative process supported by AI tools. The assignment was structured in multiple stages, with AI providing formative feedback at each phase while maintaining the instructor's evaluative role for summative assessment. This approach created a scaffolded learning experience that developed students' research synthesis capabilities while leveraging AI for ongoing guidance and improvement.

In the initial draft stage, students uploaded their preliminary literature reviews and the assignment rubric to AI tools, requesting evaluation focused on content development, structure, organization, clarity, and alignment with assignment guidelines. This initial round of AI-generated formative feedback helped students identify areas where their drafts were effective and where they needed additional work. For example, AI identified instances where students had summarized sources without synthesizing them into a coherent theoretical argument, or where additional evidence was needed to support key claims. Students were instructed to review this initial feedback and revise their drafts accordingly.

In the subsequent refinement stage, students uploaded both their revised drafts and the original assignment specifications, requesting a more comprehensive assessment with the additional context in mind. This second round of feedback provided a more nuanced evaluation of how each section of the literature review aligned with the overall assignment objectives. Students reported that this layered approach to AI-generated formative feedback was particularly valuable in helping them develop more coherent theoretical arguments, refine their research questions, clarify relationships among variables, and strengthen their methodological justifications.

To promote metacognitive awareness, students were asked to document their revision process, explaining which AI suggestions they implemented, which they modified, and which they rejected—along with their rationale for each decision. This reflection component encouraged students to engage critically with AI-generated feedback rather than implementing suggestions uncritically. Additionally, students were instructed to compare feedback from different AI tools, identifying patterns and discrepancies that informed their revision decisions. This comparative approach developed students' ability to evaluate feedback quality and relevance, an essential skill for professional environments where multiple stakeholders may provide conflicting guidance.

The instructor's role remained crucial in this process, providing additional feedback on dimensions that AI tools might not fully capture, such as theoretical insight, disciplinary context, and scholarly voice. This human perspective complemented the AI-generated feedback, creating a more comprehensive assessment approach that leveraged technological capabilities while preserving essential human judgment. The resulting literature reviews demonstrated significant improvement through this iterative process, with students developing more sophisticated theoretical frameworks, clearer research rationales, and stronger methodological justifications than typically observed in traditional single-submission approaches.

Encouraging Critical Thinking and Reflection

The final key strategy for effective AI integration focuses on developing students' critical thinking about AI's role in communication processes—moving beyond technical proficiency to foster deeper understanding of how these technologies shape message creation, distribution, and reception. This approach aligns with the experiential learning framework's emphasis on reflective observation and abstract conceptualization while addressing the ethical challenges identified earlier. By incorporating structured reflection throughout AI-integrated learning experiences, communication educators can help students develop both technical competence and ethical judgment essential for responsible professional practice.

Critical thinking about AI begins with understanding these technologies not as neutral tools but as complex systems with embedded values, limitations, and societal implications. Communication students must develop the ability to critically evaluate AI outputs against professional standards, identify potential biases or inaccuracies, and make informed decisions about appropriate implementation. This critical perspective helps students move beyond mere technical application to develop nuanced understanding of AI's role in communication environments. In a media literacy course, for example, students might analyze how AI-generated news summaries frame controversial issues differently than human-written analyses, identifying patterns that reveal underlying biases or limitations in AI approaches.

Structured reflection activities represent essential components of developing this critical thinking. Pre-reflection exercises help students articulate initial assumptions about AI before hands-on experience, creating a baseline for measuring how their understanding evolves through experiential learning. Guided reflection during AI-enhanced activities encourages students to document their decision-making processes, explaining why they accepted, modified, or rejected AI suggestions and how these decisions aligned with professional standards. Post-activity reflection provides opportunities to synthesize learning by analyzing how AI influenced their communication process, what value it added, what limitations they encountered, and how they might adjust their approach in future applications. This reflective cycle develops students' metacognitive awareness about their relationship with AI tools, helping them identify optimal integration points in their communication workflow.

Comparative analysis represents another valuable approach to developing critical thinking about AI in communication contexts. By comparing AI-generated content with human-created content addressing the same communication objective, students can identify distinctive characteristics, strengths, and limitations of each approach. This comparative perspective helps students understand AI not as a replacement for human communication but as a distinctive approach with different affordances and constraints. In a news writing course, for instance, students might compare AI-generated news stories with professionally published articles covering the same event, analyzing differences in storytelling approach, source integration, contextual understanding, and audience engagement. This comparison helps students identify the unique human elements that distinguish professional journalism from automated content generation.

Ethical analysis represents a particularly important dimension of critical thinking about AI in communication education. Students must develop frameworks for evaluating the ethical implications of AI implementation in various communication contexts, considering questions of transparency, accountability, representation, privacy, and information integrity. These ethical considerations should be integrated throughout the curriculum rather than isolated in dedicated ethics courses, helping students understand ethical reasoning as an essential component of all communication practice. In a public relations course, for example, students might analyze the ethical implications of using AI-generated audience profiles for message targeting, considering both potential benefits for campaign effectiveness and concerns about privacy, consent, and potential discrimination. This integrated ethical reasoning prepares students to navigate the complex ethical terrain they will encounter in professional environments.

To support these critical thinking approaches, communication educators should create dedicated spaces for discussion and debate about AI's implications for communication disciplines. These discussions might address questions such as: How does AI influence creative processes in communication? What is the appropriate balance between automation and human judgment in various communication contexts? How do we maintain professional standards of accuracy, fairness, and accountability in AI-enhanced communication? What new ethical questions emerge as AI capabilities evolve? By engaging students in these substantive discussions, educators help them develop both theoretical understanding and practical guidelines for responsible AI implementation in their developing professional practice.

Case Study: Fake News Analysis Project

A comprehensive example of encouraging critical thinking and reflection can be seen in a political communication course where students analyzed fake news through a project that integrated AI tools while developing media literacy and critical evaluation skills. The project positioned AI as both an analytical tool and an object of study, helping students understand both how AI can assist in information evaluation and how it might contribute to misinformation challenges in contemporary media environments.

The project began with students selecting a fake news story that had gained significant traction in digital media. They were instructed to use AI tools to assist their initial analysis, prompting the technology to evaluate the story's legitimacy based on specific criteria: the credibility of sources, factual accuracy, logical consistency, emotional language, and framing techniques. This initial AI analysis provided students with a foundation for their own investigation, but they were explicitly instructed not to accept AI evaluations uncritically. Instead, they conducted their own verification processes using traditional fact-checking techniques, comparing the AI's assessment with their independent findings.

This comparative approach required students to critically evaluate both the fake news content and the AI's analysis of that content. They documented instances where AI correctly identified problematic elements in the fake news, where it missed significant issues, and where it potentially introduced new biases or misinterpretations. This dual analysis developed students' understanding of both misinformation techniques in digital media and the capabilities and limitations of AI in detecting such techniques. Students were particularly encouraged to identify cases where AI might have been misled by superficial markers of credibility or failed to recognize context-dependent falsehoods that required deeper subject matter knowledge.

The project culminated in both a written analysis and an oral presentation where students were required to transparently address several key dimensions: the characteristics that identified the story as fake news; the techniques used to make it appear credible; the AI's effectiveness in analyzing these elements; the limitations in the AI's approach; and recommendations for how human judgment must complement AI analysis in detecting misinformation. This comprehensive assessment developed students' media literacy, critical thinking, and communication skills while fostering nuanced understanding of AI's role in both combating and potentially contributing to information integrity challenges.

Throughout the project, students engaged in structured reflection on their evolving understanding of both fake news dynamics and AI capabilities. They documented initial assumptions before beginning their analysis, recorded insights during the investigation process, and synthesized their learning in a final reflection addressing how the project influenced their approach to information evaluation. This reflective component transformed the technical exercise into a deeper learning experience about the complex relationship between technology, information integrity, and democratic discourse in contemporary media environments.

CONCLUSION: FUTURE DIRECTIONS FOR AI IN COMMUNICATION EDUCATION

The integration of AI into communication education represents both a significant challenge and a transformative opportunity for preparing students to thrive in evolving professional landscapes. This chapter has examined the multifaceted dimensions of this integration through a problem-solution framework, identifying key challenges through empirical assessment of student attitudes and behavior, analyzing ethical dilemmas specific to communication disciplines, and presenting actionable strategies grounded in experiential learning theory. This comprehensive approach provides communication educators with both conceptual understanding and practical guidance for navigating the complex terrain of AI integration while preserving the core values and competencies essential to communication education.

The survey findings presented in this chapter highlight important patterns in how communication students engage with AI technologies, with particular attention to the impact of structured educational experiences on attitudes and behaviors. The significantly more critical attitudes and more ethical use patterns among students who had completed courses incorporating AI tools underscores the importance of formal education in developing not just technical proficiency but also critical awareness of these technologies' capabilities and limitations. This finding reinforces the value of the experiential learning approach outlined in this chapter, which emphasizes active engagement, critical reflection, and ethical reasoning alongside technical skill development.

The ethical challenges examined in this chapter reflect the unique professional values and responsibilities of communication disciplines, where concerns about voice development, factual integrity, privacy, representation, and transparency take on particular significance. These discipline-specific ethical considerations require communication educators to develop frameworks that help students navigate the complex ethical terrain they will encounter in professional environments where AI integration is increasingly common. By addressing these ethical dimensions explicitly throughout the curriculum, educators can ensure students develop both the technical capabilities and ethical judgment necessary for responsible professional practice.

The actionable strategies presented in this chapter provide a practical roadmap for effective AI integration in communication education. By reformulating learning goals to emphasize uniquely human contributions, fostering active learning through AI-enhanced activities, providing personalized and formative feedback, and encouraging critical thinking and reflection, communication educators can create learning environments that leverage AI's capabilities while preserving essential disciplinary competencies. The case studies included with each strategy demonstrate how these approaches can be implemented in specific communication contexts, providing concrete models that educators can adapt to their own teaching environments.

Looking toward the future, several key directions emerge for continued development of AI integration in communication education. First, communication programs must invest in faculty development initiatives that build instructors' technical proficiency, pedagogical expertise, and ethical understanding related to AI integration. Without knowledgeable faculty prepared to guide students' engagement with these technologies, even the most thoughtfully designed curricula will fall short in implementation. Second, communication educators must collaborate across disciplines to develop shared frameworks for ethical AI integration, engaging with computer scientists, information ethicists, and industry professionals to ensure educational approaches align with evolving technological capabilities and professional standards.

Third, communication programs should develop assessment approaches that effectively measure student learning in AI-integrated environments, capturing not just technical proficiency but also critical thinking, ethical reasoning, and creative application. These assessment frameworks should evolve alongside technological capabilities, ensuring they remain relevant as AI continues to transform communication practice. Finally, communication educators must engage in ongoing research examining AI's impact on disciplinary knowledge, professional practice, and pedagogical approaches, creating a foundation of evidence-based understanding that informs curriculum development, teaching strategies, and educational policy.

The ultimate goal of AI integration in communication education is not to create technical operators of AI tools, but rather to develop communication professionals who can thoughtfully navigate the complex relationship between human creativity and technological enhancement. By balancing innovation with tradition, technical skill with ethical judgment, and automation with human insight, communication educators can prepare students for professional environments where these balances will define successful practice. The approach outlined in this chapter, with its emphasis on experiential learning, critical thinking, and ethical reasoning, provides a foundation for achieving this ambitious but essential educational objective.

REFERENCES

Ajzen, I. (1991). The theory of planned behavior. *Organizational Behavior and Human Decision Processes, 50*(2), 179–211. DOI: 10.1016/0749-5978(91)90020-T

Anderson, L. W., & Krathwohl, D. R. (Eds.). (2001). *A taxonomy for learning, teaching, and assessing: A revision of Bloom's taxonomy of educational objectives.* Allyn & Bacon.

Arnold, M. (2020). The role of experiential learning in fostering AI ethics in education. *AI & Society, 35*(4), 771–783. DOI: 10.1007/s00146-020-00981-0

Bowen, J. A., & Watson, C. E. (2024). *Teaching with AI: A Practical Guide to a New Era of Human Learning*. Johns Hopkins University Press. DOI: 10.56021/9781421449227

Brey, P. (2012). Anticipating ethical issues in emerging IT. *Ethics and Information Technology, 14*(4), 305–317. DOI: 10.1007/s10676-012-9293-y

Churches, A. (2008). *Bloom's digital taxonomy.* http://burtonslifelearning.pbworks.com/w/file/fetch/26327358/BloomDigitalTaxonomy2001.pdf

Cision, P. R. Newswire. (2023). *State of the media report.* Cision. https://www.cision.com/resources/guides- and-reports/2024-state-of-the-media-report/

Crawford, C., Cowling, M., & Allen, W. (2023). Leadership is needed for ethical ChatGPT: Character, assessment, and learning using artificial intelligence (AI). *Journal of Applied Learning & Teaching, 6*(1), 10–22. DOI: 10.37074/jalt.2023.6.1.5

Crompton, H., & Burke, D. (2021). Artificial intelligence in higher education: The state of the field. *International Journal of Educational Technology in Higher Education.* https://educationaltechnologyjournal.springeropen.com/articles/10.1186/s41239-021-00235-x

Davis, F. D. (1989). Perceived usefulness, perceived ease of use, and user acceptance of information technology. *Management Information Systems Quarterly, 13*(3), 319–340. DOI: 10.2307/249008

De Freitas, J., Agarwal, S., Schmitt, B., & Haslam, N. (2023). Psychological factors underlying attitudes toward AI tools. *Nature Human Behaviour, 7*(11), 1845–1854. DOI: 10.1038/s41562-023-01734-2 PMID: 37985913

Dewey, J. (1938). *Experience and education.* Kappa Delta Pi.

Edwards, S. (2017). Reflecting differently. New dimensions: reflection-before-action and reflection-beyond-action. *International Practice Development Journal, 7*(1).

Ewing, M. E. (2023, September). Navigating ethical implications for AI-driven PR practice. *Public Relations Society of America*. https://www.prsa.org/article/navigating-ethical-implications-for-ai-driven-pr-practice

Fitria, T. N. (2021, December). Artificial intelligence (AI) in education: Using AI tools for teaching and learning process. In *Prosiding Seminar Nasional & Call for Paper STIE AAS* (Vol. 4, No. 1, pp. 134-147). Freire, P. (1970). *Pedagogy of the oppressed* (M. B. Ramos, Trans.). Herder and Herder.

Floridi, L. (2023). *The ethics of artificial intelligence: Principles, challenges, and opportunities*. Oxford University Press. DOI: 10.1093/oso/9780198883098.001.0001

Foltynek, T., Bjelobaba, S., Glendinning, I., Khan, Z. R., Santos, R., Pavletic, P., & Kravjar, J. (2023). ENAI Recommendations on the ethical use of Artificial Intelligence in Education. *International Journal for Educational Integrity*, *19*(1), 1–4. DOI: 10.1007/s40979-023-00133-4

Holmes, W., Borenstein, J., & Howard, A. (2021). Unpacking the role of AI ethics online education for science and engineering students. *International Journal of STEM Education*, *8*(1), 23–45. DOI: 10.1186/s40594-021-00235-x

Horowitz, M. C., & Kahn, L. (2021). What influences attitudes about artificial intelligence adoption: Evidence from US local officials. *PLoS One*, *16*(10), e0257732. DOI: 10.1371/journal.pone.0257732 PMID: 34669734

Hsu, T.-C., Abelson, H., & Van Brummelen, J. (2022). The effects on secondary school students of applying experiential learning to the conversational AI learning curriculum. *International Review of Research in Open and Distance Learning*, *23*(1), 82–103. DOI: 10.19173/irrodl.v22i4.5474

Kaya, F., Aydin, F., Schepman, A., Rodway, P., Yetişensoy, O., & Demir Kaya, M. (2024). The roles of personality traits, AI anxiety, and demographic factors in attitudes toward artificial intelligence. *International Journal of Human-Computer Interaction*, *40*(2), 497–514. DOI: 10.1080/10447318.2022.2151730

Khreisat, M. N., Khilani, D., Rusho, M. A., Karkkulainen, E. A., Tabuena, A. C., & Uberas, A. D. (2024). Ethical Implications Of AI Integration In Educational Decision Making: Systematic Review. *Educational Administration: Theory and Practice*, *30*(5), 8521–8527.

Kolb, D. A. (1984). *Experiential learning: Experience as the source of learning and development*. Prentice Hall.

Lewin, K. (1946). Action research and minority problems. *The Journal of Social Issues*, *2*(4), 34–46. DOI: 10.1111/j.1540-4560.1946.tb02295.x

Luttrell, R., Wallace, A., McCollough, C., & Lee, J. (2020). The digital divide: Addressing artificial intelligence in communication education. *Journalism & Mass Communication Educator*, *75*(4), 470–482. DOI: 10.1177/1077695820925286

Meyer, M., Smith, A., & Williams, J. (2023). AI in academics: Enhancing productivity and quality through AI tools. *Journal of Academic Research and Innovation*, *10*(1), 45–62. DOI: 10.1016/j.jari.2023.03.001

Moon, J. A. (2004). *A handbook of reflective and experiential learning: Theory and practice*. Routledge.

Oregon State University Ecampus. (2024). *Bloom's taxonomy revisited (Version 2.0)*. https://ecampus.oregonstate.edu/faculty/artificial-intelligence-tools/blooms-taxonomy-revisited-v2-2024.pdf

Ouyang, F., & Jiao, P. (2021). AI in education: The three paradigms of AI integration. *Journal of Educational Technology Development and Exchange*, *14*(2), 37–54. DOI: 10.18785/jetde.1402.03

Painter, D. L., & Howell, C. (2020). Community engagement in the liberal arts: How service hours and reflections influence course value. *Journal of Experiential Education*, *43*(4), 416–430. DOI: 10.1177/1053825920931563

Pavlik, J. V. (2023). Collaborating with ChatGPT: Considering the implications of generative artificial intelligence for journalism and media education. *Journalism & Mass Communication Educator*, *78*(1), 84–93. DOI: 10.1177/10776958221149577

Rhoads, M. (2023). *AI for educators: Learning strategies, teacher efficiencies, and a vision for an artificial intelligence future*. EduMatch Publishing.

Salinas-Navarro, D. E., Vilalta-Perdomo, E., Michel-Villarreal, R., & Montesinos, L. (2024). Using generative artificial intelligence tools to explain and enhance experiential learning for authentic assessment. *Education Sciences*, *14*(1), 83. DOI: 10.3390/educsci14010083

Saritepeci, M., & Yildiz Durak, H. (2024). The impact of AI integration on design-based learning: Enhancing creativity and reflective thinking in education. *Journal of Educational Technology Research and Development*, *72*(1), 123–145. DOI: 10.1007/s11423-024-01234-5

Schiff, D. (2022). Education for AI, not AI for education: The role of education and ethics in national AI policy strategies. *International Journal of Artificial Intelligence in Education*, *32*(3), 527–563. https://doi.org/10crti.1007/s40593-021-00270-2. DOI: 10.1007/s40593-021-00270-2

Sloane, M. (2021). Silicon Valley's quest to make ethical AI: Lessons from hubris and limits. *Patterns (New York, N.Y.)*, *2*(6), 100243. DOI: 10.1016/j.patter.2021.100243

Tossell, C. C., Tenhundfeld, N. L., Momen, A., Cooley, K., & de Visser, E. J. (2024). Student perceptions of ChatGPT use in a college essay assignment: Implications for learning, grading, and trust in artificial intelligence. *IEEE Transactions on Learning Technologies*, *17*, 1069–1081. Advance online publication. DOI: 10.1109/TLT.2024.3355015

Tyson, L., & Zysman, J. (2023, February 8). Artificial intelligence and education: A reading list. *JSTOR Daily*. https://daily.jstor.org/artificial-intelligence-and-education-a-reading-list/

Usher, M., & Barak, M. (2024). Ethical AI for teaching and learning. *Journal of Experiential Learning*, *10*(3), 123–142.

Wood, D., & Moss, S. H. (2024). Evaluating the impact of students' generative AI use in educational contexts. *Journal of Research in Innovative Teaching & Learning*. https://www.emerald.com/insight/2397-7604.htm

Yannier, N., Hudson, S. E., & Koedinger, K. R. (2020). Active learning is about more than hands-on: A mixed-reality AI system to support STEM education. *International Journal of Artificial Intelligence in Education*, *30*(1), 74–96. DOI: 10.1007/s40593-020-00194-3

Yee, K., Johnson, A., & Thompson, R. (2024). AI hacks for educators: Practical tools to enhance teaching and learning efficiency. *Journal of Educational Technology Innovation*, *15*(2), 89–105. DOI: 10.1234/jeti.2024.567

Zawacki-Richter, O., Marín, V. I., Bond, M., & Gouverneur, F. (2019). Systematic review of research on artificial intelligence applications in higher education–where are the educators? *International Journal of Educational Technology in Higher Education*, *16*(1), 1–27. DOI: 10.1186/s41239-019-0171-0

Chapter 4
Training Educators in AI for Future-Proofing Education

Ramar Veluchamy
Saveetha Engineering College, India

ABSTRACT

This research aims to investigate the potential of Artificial Intelligence (AI) in revolutionizing higher education. Specifically, it explores the impact of AI on personalized learning, administrative efficiency, data analytics, and the preparation of educators for this technological shift. A comprehensive literature review was conducted to analyze existing research on AI in higher education. Key studies were identified and synthesized to understand the current state of AI applications, their benefits, challenges, and future trends. Furthermore, interviews with educators and administrators were conducted to gather insights into their experiences and perspectives on AI integration. The findings demonstrate that AI has the potential to significantly enhance higher education.

INTRODUCTION

Artificial Intelligence (AI) is revolutionizing higher education by transforming traditional pedagogical approaches and administrative functions. AI's impact is multifaceted; encompassing personalized learning, administrative efficiency, and enhanced data analytics. Personalized learning systems leverage AI to adapt educational content and pace according to individual student needs, leading to improved engagement and outcomes (Lu, 2019). For instance, adaptive learning platforms such as Smart Sparrow and Knewton customize lessons in real-time based on student interactions,

DOI: 10.4018/979-8-3373-4576-5.ch004

thereby promoting a more tailored educational experience (Holmes et al., 2019). Administratively, AI automates routine tasks like grading and scheduling, allowing educators to focus on more complex and creative aspects of teaching (Kumar et al., 2021). AI-powered data analytics provide insights into student performance and institutional processes, facilitating data-driven decision-making and early interventions for at-risk students (Hussain et al., 2020). To fully harness AI's potential, it is crucial to prepare educators for these changes. Professional development programs focusing on AI literacy and its practical applications in the classroom are essential. Educators must be equipped with the knowledge and skills to integrate AI tools effectively, ensuring that they can leverage these technologies to enhance teaching and learning (Zawacki-Richter et al., 2019). Preparing educators for this shift is not just about technological training but also about fostering an adaptive mindset and ethical awareness regarding AI's role in education.

The field of teaching and learning is changing as a result of the introduction of artificial intelligence (AI) in the classroom. Artificial intelligence (AI) tools, like data-driven curriculum modifications, AI tutors, and adaptive learning systems, present hitherto unseen possibilities to improve student outcomes. Educators and administrators must be ready to incorporate these technologies into their institutional procedures and instructional methodologies, though, in order to properly utilize them. This chapter attempts to give educators and administrators a thorough overview of the AI revolution in education, covering topics such as how to use AI tools, ethical issues, how teachers are changing, and how AI may improve learning results in the future.

Need for Training Educators in AI

In the rapidly evolving landscape of higher education, training educators in Artificial Intelligence (AI) is imperative to enhance teaching methodologies, streamline administrative tasks, and boost student engagement. As AI increasingly integrates into educational frameworks, educators must possess a robust understanding of its tools and applications. AI's ability to personalize learning experiences is pivotal; it tailors instructional content to meet individual student needs, thus fostering deeper engagement and improving academic outcomes (Lu et al., 2020). For instance, AI-driven platforms can dynamically adjust teaching strategies based on real-time analytics of student performance, providing customized support and resources (Holmes et al., 2019). Administratively, AI offers significant efficiencies by automating repetitive tasks such as grading and scheduling. This automation not only saves time but also allows educators to focus on more nuanced aspects of their roles, such as mentoring and curriculum development (Rana et al., 2021). Moreover, AI-powered analytics provide actionable insights into student behaviors and institutional processes, enabling educators to identify at-risk students and tailor interventions effectively (Popenici & Kerr, 2017). Without adequate training, educators may struggle to effectively integrate AI technologies, potentially missing out on opportunities to enhance pedagogical approaches and administrative efficiencies. Therefore, professional development in AI is essential for educators to remain competitive and capable in a future-proof educational environment (Zawacki-Richter et al., 2019).

Mission of the Chapter

The mission of this chapter is to equip educators and administrators with the knowledge, skills, and insights necessary to effectively integrate Artificial Intelligence (AI) into educational environments. By providing a comprehensive guide on the implementation and ethical use of AI tools such as adaptive learning systems, AI tutors, and data-driven curriculum adjustments, the chapter aims to foster an educational landscape where technology enhances learning outcomes, supports teachers, and prepares students for a future increasingly shaped by advanced technologies.

Objectives of Transformation

Empowering Educators and Administrators: Practical Strategies for AI Integration

Empowering educators and administrators to effectively select, implement, and optimize AI tools is crucial for the successful integration of AI in educational settings. The process begins with a clear understanding of institutional needs and goals. Educators and administrators should engage in comprehensive needs assessments to identify areas where AI can provide the most significant impact, whether in enhancing personalized learning, improving operational efficiency, or supporting data-driven decision-making (Holmes et al., 2019).

Selecting AI Tools: When choosing AI tools, it is essential to consider factors such as user-friendliness, integration with existing systems, and alignment with educational objectives. Tools that offer robust support and training resources tend to facilitate smoother adoption (Kumar et al., 2021). Evaluating AI tools through pilot programs can provide insights into their effectiveness and suitability before full-scale implementation.

Implementing AI Tools: Effective implementation requires a strategic approach that includes professional development for educators, ensuring they are equipped with the necessary skills and knowledge. Collaborative efforts between IT staff, educators, and administrators can address technical challenges and support seamless integration (Popenici & Kerr, 2017). Optimizing AI Use: Post-implementation, continuous evaluation and feedback are critical for optimizing AI tools. Gathering data on their impact on teaching and learning processes allows for ongoing adjustments and enhancements. Institutions should foster a culture of innovation and adaptability, encouraging educators to experiment with AI applications and share best practices (Zawacki-Richter et al., 2019).

Ethical Integration of AI: Addressing Concerns and Ensuring Responsible Use in Education

Integrating Artificial Intelligence (AI) into education brings transformative potential but also raises significant ethical concerns. Ensuring the responsible use of AI technologies is paramount to safeguarding student privacy, equity, and fairness. One major concern is the handling of sensitive student data. AI systems often require extensive data to function effectively, raising issues about data security and privacy. It is crucial for educational institutions to implement robust data protection policies and transparent data practices to build trust and protect student information (Holmes et al., 2019). Another critical ethical consideration is bias in AI algorithms. AI systems can inadvertently perpetuate existing biases present in their training data, leading to unequal treatment of students. Educators and administrators must be vigilant in assessing AI tools for potential biases and take proactive steps to mitigate them. This can involve diversifying training datasets and continually monitoring AI outcomes for signs of bias (Zawacki-Richter et al., 2019). Moreover, the use of AI in education should be guided by principles of fairness and inclusivity. AI applications should be designed and implemented in ways that support equitable access to educational opportunities for all students, regardless of their backgrounds. Institutions should develop clear guidelines and ethical frameworks to govern AI use, ensuring that these technologies enhance learning experiences without compromising ethical standards (Popenici & Kerr, 2017).

Supporting Teachers' Evolving Roles in AI-Enhanced Classrooms

In AI-enhanced classrooms, teachers remain vital to the educational experience, even as their roles evolve. The advent of AI in education is not about replacing teachers but augmenting their capabilities and reshaping their roles to focus more on facilitation and mentorship. Teachers are no longer just knowledge providers; they are becoming orchestrators of learning experiences and guides who help students navigate complex, personalized learning pathways (Zawacki-Richter et al., 2019). To thrive in these evolving roles, teachers must embrace lifelong learning and develop a deep understanding of AI tools. This includes becoming proficient in using AI-driven educational technologies and understanding how to interpret and apply data insights generated by these systems. For example, AI can automate routine tasks such as grading and administrative work, freeing teachers to concentrate on more impactful activities like fostering critical thinking and creativity (Popenici & Kerr, 2017). Moreover, teachers need to adapt to new dynamics in the classroom, where AI can offer personalized feedback and adaptive learning experiences. Educators should leverage AI to provide targeted support, helping students who may struggle or need additional challenges. Professional development programs focusing on AI literacy and pedagogical strategies in AI-rich environments are essential to support teachers in these transitions. Through such training, educators can confidently integrate AI into their teaching practices while maintaining their central role in student development (Holmes et al., 2019).

Figure 1. Preparing for future trends: AI in education and educator readiness

In the article "Future-Proofing AI Talent in The United States: The Role of Academia in Meeting Industry Demands", Vengathattil (2025) examines how academic institutions can play a pivotal role in closing the gap between the growing demand for AI professionals and the current supply of skilled talent. The author stresses the importance of creating educational programs that are not only technically rigorous but also adaptable to the fast-paced changes in the AI industry. This involves designing interdisciplinary courses, providing practical, hands-on experiences, and fostering strong partnerships between universities and industry leaders. Vengathattil also highlights the need to instill both technical expertise and ethical awareness in students to prepare them for the complexities of the AI-driven future. These findings are particularly valuable for training educators in AI, as they emphasize the importance of equipping teachers with the skills and knowledge to deliver forward-thinking AI education. By incorporating industry trends and real-world applications into educator training, academic institutions can empower teachers to cultivate a generation of learners who are well-prepared to navigate and shape the future of AI, ensuring that education systems remain resilient and relevant in the face of technological change. (Vengathattil, S. 2025).

As AI technologies rapidly evolve, the future possibilities for AI in education are expansive and transformative. Educators must be equipped to navigate and lead in these dynamic environments. Future trends in AI include advanced adaptive learning systems that tailor educational content in real-time based on students' learning styles and progress, and predictive analytics that can foresee and address educational challenges before they arise (Luckin et al., 2020). For example, AI could soon offer more sophisticated learning analytics, providing deep insights into individual and group learning behaviors, thus allowing for more personalized and effective teaching strategies (Hinojo-Lucena et al., 2019). To prepare for these advancements, educators need ongoing professional development that focuses not only on the technical aspects of AI but also on its pedagogical implications. This includes training on how to use AI to enhance student engagement, customize learning experiences, and foster a supportive and inclusive classroom environment (Zawacki-Richter et al., 2019). Additionally, educators should be encouraged to cultivate a forward-thinking mindset, staying abreast of technological trends and considering how these innovations can be integrated into their teaching practices (Holmes et al., 2019). Moreover, institutions should foster a culture of experimentation and innovation, where educators can safely explore and implement AI tools. By being proactive and adaptable, educators can ensure that they not only keep pace with AI advancements but also lead the way in leveraging these technologies to enhance educational outcomes (Lu et al., 2020).

Promoting Equity and Access: Bridging the Digital Divide with AI in Education

As AI technologies become increasingly integrated into educational settings, it is crucial to ensure that these tools are accessible to all students and do not exacerbate existing inequities. AI has the potential to transform education by providing personalized learning experiences, but it can also deepen the digital divide if not implemented thoughtfully (Holmes et al., 2019). For AI to promote equity, it must be designed and deployed with inclusivity at its core. One of the key strategies to achieve this is ensuring equitable access to AI technologies. Schools and universities need to address disparities in digital infrastructure and provide necessary resources, such as hardware, software, and internet connectivity, particularly in underserved communities (Hinojo-Lucena et al., 2019). Moreover, educators should receive training on using AI tools in ways that support diverse learners, including those with disabilities or from varying socio-economic backgrounds (Zawacki-Richter et al., 2019). AI can also be leveraged to identify and support students at risk of falling behind, offering tailored interventions that cater to individual needs. By utilizing predictive analytics, educators can proactively address learning gaps and provide additional resources to students who need them most (Lu et al., 2020). Furthermore, AI-driven tools should be evaluated regularly to ensure they do not inadvertently reinforce biases or inequities. To bridge the digital divide, educational institutions must foster a culture of inclusivity and ensure that AI integration helps to level the playing field, providing every student with the opportunity to succeed (Luckin et al., 2020).

Concerns Addressed in the Chapter

1. Ethical Considerations

    Data Privacy and Security: Ensuring the privacy and security of student data is a primary concern when implementing AI tools that collect and analyze personal information. The section will address best practices for protecting student data and complying with legal and ethical standards.

    Algorithmic Bias: AI systems can inadvertently perpetuate or exacerbate biases present in their training data. The section will discuss how to recognize and mitigate these biases to promote fairness and inclusivity in educational outcomes.

    Equity and Access: There is a risk that AI tools may not be equally accessible to all students, particularly those in under-resourced schools. The section will explore strategies to ensure equitable access and the fair distribution of technological benefits.

2. Teacher Roles and Professional Development

    Fear of Replacement: The growing use of AI in education may lead to concerns among educators about their roles being diminished or replaced by technology. The section will emphasize the complementary nature of AI tools and the ongoing critical role of teachers in providing guidance, mentorship, and emotional support.

    Need for Training and Adaptation: Teachers and administrators require training to effectively integrate AI tools into their practice. The section will outline professional development programs and resources to help educators develop the necessary skills and confidence to use AI technologies.

3. Implementation Challenges

    Technical Infrastructure and Costs: Implementing AI tools requires adequate technical infrastructure and can be costly. The section will provide insights into assessing the readiness of an institution's infrastructure and managing the financial aspects of AI adoption.

    Change Management: Integrating AI tools involves significant changes in educational practices and processes, which can be challenging for institutions to manage. The section will offer strategies for effective change management, including stakeholder engagement, piloting new tools, and scaling successful implementations.

4. Balancing Technology and Human Interaction

    Over-Reliance on Technology: There is a concern that excessive reliance on AI tools might reduce the importance of human interactions in education. The section will discuss how to maintain a balance between leveraging AI for personalized learning and preserving the essential human elements of teaching.

    Maintaining Educational Quality: As AI tools become more prevalent, it is crucial to ensure that they enhance rather than compromise the quality of education. The section will provide guidelines for evaluating the effectiveness of AI tools and integrating them in ways that uphold high educational standards.

5. Future Preparedness and Sustainability

    Keeping Pace with Technological Advancements: The rapid pace of AI development means that educators must continuously update their knowledge and skills to keep up with new technologies. The section will highlight the importance of ongoing professional development and staying informed about emerging trends.

    Sustainable Integration: Long-term success with AI in education requires sustainable practices that can adapt to future changes. The section will discuss approaches to building flexible and resilient systems that can evolve with technological advancements and changing educational needs.

SECTION 1: UNDERSTANDING AI IN EDUCATION

1.1 The Evolution of AI in Education

AI technologies have rapidly advanced, offering tools that can personalize learning experiences, automate administrative tasks, and provide real-time feedback. Historically, educational technologies evolved from simple computer-based training to sophisticated systems capable of understanding and responding to individual learning needs. This section will explore the key milestones in AI's development in education and how these technologies have evolved to support modern educational practices.

1.2 Types of AI Tools in Education

AI tools in education can be broadly categorized into several types:

- **Adaptive Learning Systems:** These systems use AI to personalize learning experiences by adapting the content and pace based on individual learner needs.
- **AI Tutors:** Virtual tutors provide personalized instruction and feedback, often available 24/7, supplementing traditional teaching methods.
- **Data-Driven Curriculum Adjustments:** AI systems analyze large datasets to identify trends and inform curriculum changes, ensuring the content remains relevant and effective.

SECTION 2: IMPLEMENTING AI TOOLS IN EDUCATIONAL SETTINGS

2.1 Adaptive Learning Systems

2.1.1 Overview and Benefits

Adaptive learning systems tailor educational content to meet the needs of individual students, providing customized pathways and pacing. This section will cover how adaptive learning works, its benefits, including increased student engagement and improved learning outcomes, and examples of popular adaptive learning platforms.

2.1.2 Implementation Strategies

Effective implementation of adaptive learning systems involves:

- **Selecting the Right Platform:** Evaluating various adaptive learning tools to choose the one that best fits the educational goals and technical capabilities of the institution.
- **Training Educators:** Providing comprehensive training for teachers to effectively integrate adaptive learning systems into their classrooms.

- **Pilot Programs:** Running pilot programs to assess the system's impact and make necessary adjustments before full scale implementation.

2.2 AI Tutors

2.2.1 Functionality and Applications

AI tutors simulate one-on-one interactions, offering personalized feedback and support. They can assist in subjects where students often struggle, providing immediate assistance outside of traditional classroom hours. This section will detail the functionalities of AI tutors, their applications in various educational contexts, and examples of successful AI tutor programs.

2.2.2 Integration into Curriculum

Integrating AI tutors into the curriculum involves:

- **Curriculum Alignment:** Ensuring that AI tutors complement and enhance the existing curriculum rather than replace traditional instruction.
- **Teacher Support:** Training teachers to effectively use AI tutors and integrate their feedback into lesson planning.
- **Student Engagement:** Encouraging student engagement with AI tutors by highlighting their benefits and incorporating their use into regular classroom activities.

2.2.3 Tools Used in Academia

Artificial intelligence (AI) has revolutionized the way training and education are delivered, offering innovative tools that enhance learning experiences and improve outcomes. Today, a variety of AI-powered tools are being used to personalize training, streamline content delivery, and provide real-time feedback. Adaptive learning platforms, such as DreamBox and Knewton, use AI algorithms to tailor educational content to individual learners' needs, ensuring that each student progresses at their own pace. Virtual tutors and chatbots, like Carnegie Learning's MATHia or Duolingo's AI-driven language coach, provide instant support and guidance, making learning more interactive and accessible. Additionally, tools like Coursera and Udacity leverage AI to recommend courses, track progress, and predict areas where learners may need additional focus. AI is also transforming corporate training through platforms like EdCast and Degreed, which use machine learning to curate personalized learning paths for employees based on their roles and career goals. Furthermore, AI-driven analytics tools, such as Watershed and Learning Locker, help educators and trainers assess the effectiveness of their programs by analyzing learner data and identifying trends. These tools not only make training more efficient but also ensure that it is aligned with the evolving demands of the modern workforce. By integrating AI into training processes, organizations and educational institutions can create more engaging, effective, and future-ready learning environments.

2.3 Data-Driven Curriculum Adjustments

2.3.1 Leveraging Data for Improvement

Data-driven curriculum adjustments use AI to analyze educational data and provide insights into student performance and curriculum effectiveness. This section will explore how institutions can use these insights to make informed decisions about curriculum changes and improvements.

2.3.2 Practical Steps for Implementation

Implementing data-driven curriculum adjustments involves:

- **Data Collection:** Gathering comprehensive data on student performance, engagement, and feedback.
- **AI Analysis:** Using AI tools to analyze the data and identify areas for improvement.
- **Curriculum Redesign:** Applying the insights gained to redesign and enhance the curriculum, ensuring it meets the evolving needs of students.

SECTION 3: ETHICAL CONSIDERATIONS AND THE ROLE OF TEACHERS

3.1 Ethical Considerations in AI Adoption

AI in education raises several ethical considerations, including data privacy, algorithmic bias, and the potential for widening the digital divide. This section will discuss these issues and provide guidelines for addressing them to ensure the ethical use of AI in educational settings.

3.2 The Evolving Role of Teachers

As AI tools become more prevalent, the role of teachers is evolving. Rather than being replaced by AI, teachers are shifting towards roles that emphasize mentorship, guidance, and the facilitation of learning. This section will explore how teachers can adapt to these changes and continue to play a crucial role in the educational process.

3.3 Balancing AI and Human Interaction

Effective education involves a balance between AIdriven instruction and human interaction. This section will discuss strategies for maintaining this balance, ensuring that AI tools complement rather than replace the human elements of teaching and learning.

SECTION 4: FUTURE POSSIBILITIES AND PREPARING FOR CHANGE

4.1 Future Trends in AI and Education

AI technologies are continually evolving, and their potential applications in education are vast. This section will explore future trends in AI, such as augmented reality (AR) and virtual reality (VR) in education, and how these technologies might further transform learning experiences.

4.2 Preparing Educators for AI-Driven Education

Educators must be equipped with the knowledge and tools necessary to navigate and lead the transformation in educational environments. This section will provide strategies for professional development, continuous learning, and staying abreast of technological advancements.

4.3 Fostering a Generation of Adept Learners

The ultimate goal of integrating AI into education is to foster a generation of learners who are adept at interacting with advanced technologies. This section will discuss how educators can cultivate these skills in their students, preparing them for a future where AI is an integral part of everyday life.

The integration of AI into education offers immense potential to enhance learning outcomes and transform educational practices. By understanding the available tools, implementing them effectively, addressing ethical considerations, and preparing for future advancements, educators and administrators can lead the way in creating innovative and effective learning environments. As we embrace the AI future, the role of educators as mentors, guides, and facilitators remains more important than ever. This chapter provides a roadmap for educators and administrators to successfully integrate AI tools into their institutions, ensuring they are prepared for the future of education.

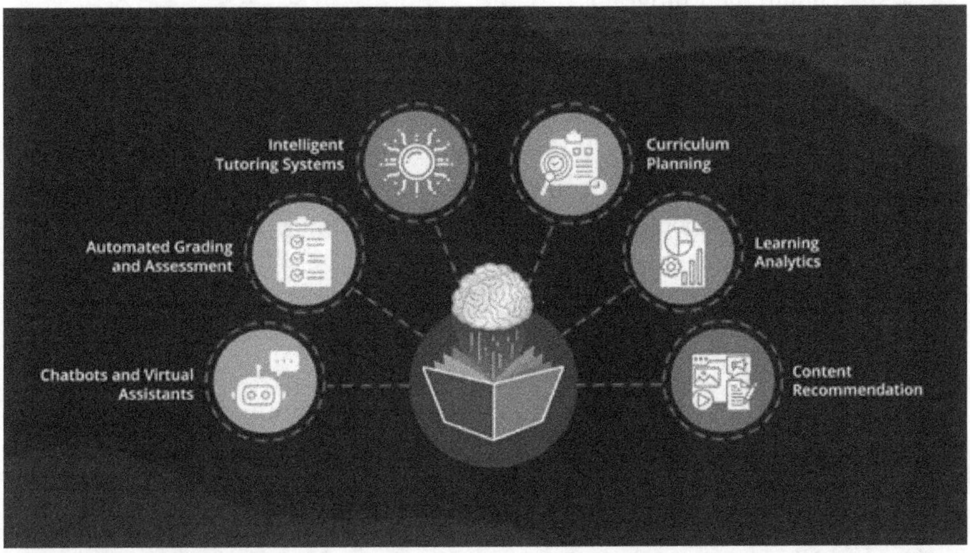

1. Understanding AI and Its Role in Education

Basics of AI: Definitions, types of AI (narrow, general, super-intelligent), and key concepts.

Applications of AI in Education: How AI is used in personalized learning, grading, virtual tutoring, and administrative tasks.

Case Studies of institutions successfully integrating AI in their curriculum.

1. Stanford University

Course: "Artificial Intelligence: Principles and Techniques"

Integration: Stanford offers a comprehensive AI curriculum that includes foundational courses, hands-on projects, and research opportunities in AI. They also use AI tools to analyze large datasets and enhance student learning experiences.

2. Massachusetts Institute of Technology (MIT)

Course: "Introduction to Machine Learning"

Integration: MIT incorporates AI across its curriculum, providing students with courses on machine learning, deep learning, and AI ethics. MIT's AI Lab also collaborates with various departments to integrate AI projects and research into their programs.

3. Carnegie Mellon University

Course: "Introduction to Artificial Intelligence (15-381)"

Integration: Carnegie Mellon is renowned for its AI research and education. They integrate AI into computer science and engineering programs, emphasizing practical applications through robotics, natural language processing, and machine learning.

4. University of California, Berkeley

Course: "CS 188: Introduction to Artificial Intelligence"

Integration: UC Berkeley offers a robust AI curriculum with courses ranging from introductory to advanced levels. They utilize AI tools for student assessments and personalized learning, enhancing the educational experience.

5. Harvard University

Course: "CS50's Introduction to Artificial Intelligence with Python"

Integration: Harvard integrates AI into its computer science curriculum, providing students with theoretical knowledge and practical skills in AI. They use AI-driven tools to support teaching and learning, such as automated grading and personalized feedback.

6. University of Toronto

- Course: "CSC321: Introduction to Neural Networks and Machine Learning"
- Integration: The University of Toronto offers specialized AI courses and integrates AI research into its computer science program. They employ AI tools for data analysis, enhancing research and teaching methodologies.

7. Georgia Institute of Technology

Course: "CS 7641: Machine Learning"
Integration: Georgia Tech uses AI to enhance its online courses, such as employing the AI teaching assistant Jill Watson to support students. Their curriculum includes comprehensive AI courses and research opportunities.

8. University of Washington

Course: "CSE 446: Machine Learning"
Integration: The University of Washington integrates AI into its computer science and engineering programs, focusing on machine learning, data science, and AI ethics. They use AI tools for research and to improve teaching methodologies.

9. Imperial College London

Course: "Machine Learning for Imaging"
Integration: Imperial College offers AI courses within its engineering and computer science programs. They use AI for research in various fields, including healthcare, and incorporate AI tools to enhance student learning experiences.

10. University of Cambridge

Course: "Introduction to Machine Learning"
Integration: Cambridge integrates AI into its computer science curriculum, offering courses and research opportunities in machine learning, natural language processing, and robotics. They use AI tools for data analysis and to improve educational outcomes.

2. The Role Of Educators In An Ai-Driven Educational Environment

Evolving Role of Educators: From traditional teaching to facilitating and guiding AI-enhanced learning.

Skills and Competencies Required: Critical thinking, data literacy, and understanding of AI technologies.

3. Developing AI Literacy among Educators

AI Literacy Programs: Overview of programs and initiatives aimed at improving AI literacy among educators.

Workshops and Training Sessions: Effective formats and content for educator training in AI.

Online Resources and MOOCs: Leveraging online courses to enhance AI knowledge among educators.

4. Incorporating AI into Curriculum Design

AI in Curriculum Planning: Strategies for embedding AI content into existing and new courses.

Interdisciplinary Approaches: Combining AI with other fields such as humanities, sciences, and business.

Challenges and Solutions: Addressing obstacles in integrating AI into the curriculum.

5. Ethical Considerations and AI in Education
    - Ethical Use of AI: Privacy, bias, and data security issues in AI applications.
    - Ethical Training for Educators: Equipping educators with the knowledge to navigate ethical dilemmas in AI usage.
6. Ai Tools And Platforms For Educators
    1. IBM Watson: A versatile AI platform offering natural language processing, machine learning, and data analysis tools, widely used for creating intelligent tutoring systems and automating administrative tasks.
    2. Google AI: Provides tools like TensorFlow and Google Cloud AI, enabling educators to develop and implement machine learning models for research and personalized learning experiences.
    3. Microsoft Azure AI: Offers a suite of AI services and tools for data analysis, cognitive services, and machine learning, supporting educational institutions in developing AI-driven applications.
    4. Amazon Web Services (AWS) AI: Features services like SageMaker for building, training, and deploying machine learning models, helping educators integrate AI into their research and teaching.

5. Knewton: An adaptive learning platform that uses AI to personalize educational content, improving student engagement and learning outcomes.
6. Coursera: Utilizes AI to recommend courses, provide personalized learning paths, and enhance the online learning experience with intelligent tutoring systems.
7. Edmentum: Employs AI-driven tools for personalized learning, assessment, and curriculum development, supporting K-12 and higher education institutions.
8. Carnegie Learning: Uses AI to create adaptive learning software that provides personalized math instruction, helping students improve their skills through targeted practice.
9. Smart Sparrow: An adaptive learning platform that leverages AI to create personalized and interactive learning experiences, enhancing student engagement and performance.
10. Quizlet: Incorporates AI to offer personalized study plans, adaptive learning activities, and smart grading, making it a valuable tool for both students and educators.

- How to Choose the Right AI Tool: Criteria for selecting appropriate AI technologies for different educational contexts.

1. Identify Educational Goals: Understand the specific needs and objectives of your course or institution, such as improving student engagement, enhancing personalized learning, or automating administrative tasks.
2. Evaluate User-Friendliness: Choose tools that are easy to use for both educators and students, with intuitive interfaces and robust support resources.
3. Assess Compatibility: Ensure the AI tool integrates well with your existing systems and platforms, such as Learning Management Systems (LMS) or other educational technologies.
4. Consider Scalability: Select tools that can grow with your institution, accommodating increasing numbers of students or expanding functionalities as needed.
5. Review Data Privacy and Security: Prioritize AI tools that comply with data protection regulations and have strong security measures to protect student information.
6. Analyze Cost and Budget: Compare the costs of different AI tools, including initial setup, subscription fees, and ongoing maintenance, ensuring they fit within your budget.

7. Check Customization Options: Look for tools that offer customization to tailor features and functionalities to the specific needs of your courses and students.
8. Evaluate Technical Support: Choose AI tools with reliable customer support and training resources to help educators effectively implement and use the technology.
9. Consider the Track Record: Research the reputation and success stories of the AI tool in similar educational contexts to gauge its effectiveness and reliability.
10. Pilot and Feedback: Run a pilot program with a small group of users to gather feedback and assess the tool's impact before full-scale implementation.

- Training on AI Tools: Best practices for training educators to use AI tools effectively.

1. Start with the Basics: Begin training with an overview of AI concepts and the specific AI tool's functionalities. Ensure educators understand the potential benefits and applications of the tool in an educational setting.
2. Hands-On Workshops: Conduct interactive workshops where educators can practice using the AI tools. Real-time demonstrations and hands-on activities help in better understanding and retention of the tool's features.
3. Provide Comprehensive Resources: Offer detailed user manuals, video tutorials, and step-by-step guides. These resources should be easily accessible for educators to refer to as needed.
4. Create a Support Network: Establish a community or forum where educators can share experiences, ask questions, and provide support to each other. This peer support can be invaluable for troubleshooting and sharing best practices.
5. Ongoing Training and Updates: AI tools frequently update and evolve. Provide continuous professional development opportunities to keep educators informed about new features, best practices, and advancements in AI technology.
6. Leverage Expert Trainers: Utilize experts or certified trainers to conduct training sessions. Their deep knowledge and experience with the AI tools can provide valuable insights and practical tips.
7. Integrate Real-World Examples: Use case studies and real-world examples to show how AI tools can be applied in the classroom. Demonstrating successful implementations can inspire and motivate educators.

8. Focus on Practical Applications: Tailor training sessions to show how AI tools can address specific educational challenges. Emphasize practical applications that are directly relevant to the educators' teaching context.
9. Encourage Experimentation: Allow educators to experiment with the AI tools in a low-risk environment. Provide sandbox accounts or trial versions where they can explore and test functionalities without affecting real data.
10. Gather Feedback and Iterate: Regularly collect feedback from educators on the training process and the AI tools themselves. Use this feedback to improve training sessions and address any challenges or concerns.

7. Collaborative Learning And Ai
   - AI-Supported Collaborative Learning: How AI can facilitate group learning and peer interactions.
     1. Enhanced Group Dynamics: AI can analyze student profiles and create balanced groups based on skills and learning styles, ensuring diverse and effective team collaboration.
     2. Real-Time Feedback: AI tools provide instant feedback during group activities, helping students refine their contributions and improve collective problem-solving skills.
     3. Interactive Platforms: AI-powered platforms facilitate seamless communication and coordination among group members, making collaboration more efficient and engaging.
     4. Personalized Assistance: AI can offer tailored support to groups by suggesting resources, tracking progress, and providing guidance based on each team's unique needs.
     5. Peer Evaluation: AI systems can assist in fair peer evaluations by objectively assessing individual contributions and fostering a more transparent and constructive feedback process.
   - Designing Collaborative Learning with AI: Effective strategies for integrating AI into collaborative learning activities.
     1. AI-Powered Discussion Platforms:
        - Strategy: Utilize AI-driven discussion forums and chatbots to facilitate and moderate student discussions. AI can prompt questions, highlight key discussion points, and ensure all students participate.
        - Example: Platforms like Piazza or Microsoft Teams with AI integration can help manage and guide group discussions, providing instant feedback and summaries.
     2. Personalized Learning Paths:

Strategy: Implement AI to create personalized learning paths within group projects. AI can assess individual student progress and recommend resources or tasks tailored to each member's strengths and weaknesses. Example: AI tools like Smart Sparrow or Knewton can adapt content based on student interactions, ensuring that each group member is working at their optimal level.

3. AI-Enhanced Project Management:

Strategy: Use AI tools to streamline project management in collaborative activities. AI can assign tasks, set deadlines, and monitor progress, helping students manage their time and responsibilities effectively. Example: Tools like Trello or Asana with AI capabilities can automate task assignments and send reminders, ensuring smooth project workflows.

4. Real-Time Feedback and Assessment:

Strategy: Incorporate AI systems that provide real-time feedback on collaborative work. AI can evaluate contributions, suggest improvements, and ensure that all group members are actively participating. Example: Platforms like Turnitin with AI can offer immediate feedback on writing assignments, while Peergrade uses AI to facilitate peer assessments.

5. Collaborative AI Tutors:

Strategy: Deploy AI tutors that assist groups in understanding complex concepts. These AI tutors can provide explanations, answer questions, and guide students through collaborative problem-solving. Example: AI tutors like Jill Watson at Georgia Tech can support student groups by answering queries and providing resources related to their collaborative tasks.

6. Data-Driven Group Formation:

Strategy: Use AI algorithms to form student groups based on complementary skills, learning styles, and interests. This ensures diverse and balanced teams, enhancing the collaborative experience. Example: Tools like CATME or DreamTeams use AI to analyze student data and create optimal groupings for collaborative projects.

7. AI-Driven Collaborative Tools:

Strategy: Integrate AI capabilities into collaborative tools like shared documents, spreadsheets, and presentations. AI can assist with content creation, error correction, and version control. Example: Google Workspace with AI features can help groups co-create documents by suggesting edits, tracking changes, and managing revisions.

8. Virtual Collaborative Environments:

Strategy: Develop virtual environments powered by AI where students can collaborate remotely. AI can facilitate communication, simulate real-world scenarios, and provide virtual assistance. Example: Platforms like VirBELA or Gather.Town create immersive virtual spaces for collaboration, with AI features that enhance interaction and engagement.

9. Enhanced Analytics and Insights:

Strategy: Leverage AI to analyze collaboration patterns and provide insights into group dynamics. AI can identify potential issues, suggest interventions, and track overall group performance. Example: AI-driven analytics tools like Tableau or Power BI can visualize collaboration data, helping educators and students understand and improve their collaborative efforts.

10. Gamified Collaborative Learning:

Strategy: Incorporate AI to gamify collaborative learning activities. AI can design adaptive challenges, track achievements, and provide rewards, making collaboration more engaging and motivating. Example: Platforms like Classcraft use AI to create gamified learning experiences that encourage teamwork and collaborative problem-solving.

8. Assessing The Impact Of Ai On Learning Outcomes
    - Measuring AI's Effectiveness: Metrics and methodologies for evaluating the impact of AI on student learning.

Case Studies: Examples of improved learning outcomes through AI integration.

1. Georgia Tech's Jill Watson: An AI teaching assistant named Jill Watson was used to answer student queries, significantly improving response times and reducing the workload on human TAs. This led to higher student satisfaction and more effective learning support.

2. Carnegie Learning's Math Tutor: Using AI-driven adaptive learning software, Carnegie Learning provided personalized math instruction, resulting in a 20% improvement in student test scores and greater engagement in mathematics.
3. Knewton at Arizona State University: Implementing Knewton's adaptive learning platform, Arizona State University saw a 47% increase in pass rates for students in remedial math courses, tailoring content to individual learning needs.
4. Duolingo Language Learning: Duolingo uses AI to personalize language learning exercises, leading to faster language acquisition and higher retention rates among users compared to traditional methods.
5. Smart Sparrow in Medical Education: Smart Sparrow's AI-powered platform helped medical students at the University of New South Wales engage with interactive simulations, improving their practical skills and knowledge retention.
6. Quizlet's Smart Study Plans: AI-driven study plans on Quizlet provided personalized learning paths, helping students achieve better outcomes in exams with less study time by focusing on their weak areas.
7. Edmentum in K-12 Education: Edmentum's AI tools for personalized learning and assessment contributed to significant improvements in student performance and engagement in various K-12 schools.
8. IBM Watson at Deakin University: IBM Watson was used to create personalized learning experiences at Deakin University, resulting in increased student retention and higher academic performance.
9. DreamBox Learning for Elementary Math: AI-driven adaptive learning on DreamBox Learning helped elementary students improve their math proficiency, with teachers reporting noticeable gains in student confidence and skills.
10. Turnitin's Revision Assistant: Turnitin's AI-powered feedback tool provided instant, detailed feedback on student writing, leading to significant improvements in writing quality and helping students develop better critical thinking skills.
    - Ongoing Research and Future Directions: Future research areas for AI in education.
        1. Personalized Learning: Researchers are exploring AI's potential to create highly individualized learning experiences, tailoring content and pacing to each student's unique needs and learning styles.
        2. Emotional Intelligence: Future AI systems aim to detect and respond to student emotions, using sentiment analysis to provide support when students are frustrated or disengaged, fostering a more supportive learning environment.
        3. Virtual Reality and AI: Combining VR with AI to create immersive, interactive learning experiences that simulate real-world scenarios, enhancing hands-on learning in fields like medicine, engineering, and history.

4. Automated Assessment: Developing more advanced AI tools for grading and feedback, capable of understanding complex student responses and providing detailed, constructive feedback in real time.
5. AI Tutors and Mentors: Advancing AI tutors to offer personalized mentoring, helping students set goals, stay motivated, and navigate academic challenges with tailored advice and encouragement.
6. Adaptive Group Learning: Researching AI systems that can dynamically form and adjust student groups based on individual strengths and weaknesses, promoting effective collaboration and peer learning.
7. Ethics and Bias Mitigation: Addressing ethical concerns and biases in AI algorithms to ensure fair and equitable learning opportunities for all students, regardless of their background.
8. Learning Analytics: Enhancing AI-driven learning analytics to provide deeper insights into student behavior and performance, helping educators make data-informed decisions to improve teaching strategies.
9. Language Processing: Improving natural language processing to better understand and respond to student queries, making AI-powered assistants more effective in diverse educational contexts.
10. Longitudinal Studies: Conducting long-term studies to assess the impact of AI on educational outcomes, exploring how AI can support lifelong learning and career development.

9. Policies and Governance in AI Education

- AI Policies in Higher Education: Overview of existing policies and frameworks.
- Institutional Governance: How institutions can govern and regulate the use of AI.
- Future Policy Directions: Anticipating and shaping future policies for AI in education.

10. Preparing for the Future: Trends and Predictions

- Future Trends in AI and Education: Emerging technologies and their potential impact.

1. AI-Driven Personal Tutors: AI will become more sophisticated, providing personalized tutoring that adapts to each student's pace and learning style, making education more individualized and effective.

2. Immersive Learning Experiences: Virtual Reality (VR) and Augmented Reality (AR) combined with AI will create immersive educational environments, allowing students to explore historical events or scientific phenomena in a hands-on way.
3. Smart Classrooms: Classrooms equipped with AI will offer real-time analytics on student engagement and understanding, helping teachers tailor their instruction to meet the needs of every student.
4. Gamification: AI will enhance gamified learning, creating engaging and interactive educational games that adapt to a student's progress and keep them motivated.
5. AI for Accessibility: AI will improve accessibility in education by providing real-time translation, speech-to-text services, and customized learning tools for students with disabilities.
6. Predictive Analytics: AI will use predictive analytics to identify at-risk students early and provide interventions to help them stay on track, improving retention rates and academic success.
7. Content Creation: AI will assist educators in creating and updating course materials, generating quizzes, and even writing content that is tailored to the latest curriculum standards.
8. Lifelong Learning: AI will support continuous education by providing personalized learning paths for professionals seeking to upskill, ensuring that learning is a lifelong journey.
9. Ethical AI Education: As AI becomes integral to education, there will be a greater emphasis on teaching students about AI ethics and responsible use, preparing them for a future where AI plays a significant role.
10. Global Collaboration: AI will enable more global collaboration among students and educators, breaking down geographical barriers and creating a more interconnected and diverse learning community.

■ Preparing Educators for Future Changes: Strategies for ongoing professional development and adaptation.

1. Embrace Lifelong Learning: Encourage educators to pursue continuous learning opportunities, such as workshops, webinars, and online courses, to stay updated on the latest teaching technologies and methodologies.
2. Foster Collaboration: Create professional learning communities where educators can share insights, strategies, and experiences about integrating new technologies and adapting to evolving educational trends.

3. Leverage Mentorship Programs: Implement mentorship programs that pair experienced educators with those new to emerging technologies, providing guidance and support for effective adoption.
4. Encourage Experimentation: Promote a culture of experimentation where educators feel comfortable trying out new tools and approaches, learning from both successes and challenges.
5. Provide Regular Training: Offer regular, hands-on training sessions focused on the latest educational technologies and trends, ensuring educators have the skills and confidence to implement them effectively in their classrooms. Call to Action: Encourage institutions to invest in AI training for educators and to embrace AI's potential to transform learning environments.

Artificial Intelligence (AI) is revolutionizing industries worldwide, and education is no exception. As AI technologies continue to evolve, their integration into higher education becomes inevitable. This integration demands that educators not only become familiar with AI but also proficient in leveraging these technologies to enhance learning outcomes, streamline administrative tasks, and prepare students for a future where AI plays a crucial role. For higher education to remain relevant and effective, institutions must prioritize training educators in AI. This training is essential for developing new pedagogical approaches, personalizing learning experiences, and ensuring ethical use of AI in academic settings. This chapter explores the multifaceted aspects of training educators in AI, focusing on the critical need for such training and offering practical insights into how it can be achieved.

1. Understanding AI and Its Role in Education

Artificial Intelligence, often abbreviated as AI, encompasses a wide range of technologies designed to perform tasks that typically require human intelligence. These tasks include learning, reasoning, problem-solving, and understanding natural language. AI in education is particularly transformative as it can automate routine tasks, personalize learning experiences, and provide data-driven insights into student performance.

Applications of AI in Education:

1. Personalized Learning: AI can tailor educational content to individual student needs, enhancing learning efficiency and engagement. For example, AI-powered platforms can adjust the difficulty of exercises based on a student's performance.
2. Automated Grading: AI systems can handle grading of assignments, quizzes, and exams, freeing up educators' time for more impactful interactions with students.

3. Virtual Tutoring: AI-powered chat-bots and virtual tutors can provide students with 24/7 support, answering questions and offering guidance on various subjects.

Case Studies:

Georgia Tech's Jill Watson: An AI teaching assistant used in an online course to answer students' questions, significantly reducing the workload on human TAs and improving response times. Georgia Tech faced the challenge of managing a large volume of student inquiries in its online Master's in Computer Science program. They introduced Jill Watson, an AI teaching assistant built on IBM's Watson platform. Jill Watson was integrated into the online course to handle routine questions about course logistics, freeing up human TAs for more complex tasks.

1. Efficiency: Jill answered thousands of student questions with high accuracy, significantly reducing the workload on human TAs.
2. Response Time: Students received immediate answers, improving response times and overall satisfaction.
3. Scalability: The AI's ability to scale without additional cost made it ideal for large online courses.
4. Accuracy: Jill Watson's responses were precise, as it was trained on past data and frequently updated to handle new questions.
5. Innovation: The success of Jill Watson showcased the potential for AI in education, leading to broader adoption of similar technologies in other courses.

Carnegie Learning's MATHia: An adaptive learning platform that personalizes math instruction based on student performance, leading to improved outcomes in various educational settings.

2. The Role of Educators in an AI-Driven Educational Environment

As AI technology continues to permeate higher education, the traditional role of educators is undergoing a significant transformation. Educators are no longer just providers of knowledge; they are becoming facilitators of learning, guiding students through complex, AI-enhanced educational experiences.

Evolving Role of Educators:

1. Facilitator and Guide: Educators are increasingly seen as mentors who support students in navigating AI tools and resources, fostering critical thinking and problem-solving skills.

2. Data Interpreter: With AI generating vast amounts of data on student performance, educators need to become adept at interpreting this data to inform instructional strategies and identify areas where students may need additional support.

Skills and Competencies Required:

1. Critical Thinking: Educators must critically evaluate AI tools and their impact on learning, ensuring that they are used ethically and effectively.
2. Data Literacy: Understanding and analyzing data generated by AI systems is crucial for making informed decisions about teaching and learning.
3. Developing AI Literacy among Educators

For educators to effectively integrate AI into their teaching practices, they must first develop a foundational understanding of AI concepts and applications. This section explores various approaches to building AI literacy among educators.

AI Literacy Programs:

1. Institutional Training Programs: Many universities and colleges are developing internal training programs to enhance educators' AI literacy. These programs often include workshops, seminars, and hands-on sessions with AI tools.
2. Professional Development Courses: Online platforms such as Coursera, edX, and Udacity offer courses specifically designed to improve educators' understanding of AI.

Workshops and Training Sessions:

1. Effective Formats: Interactive workshops that combine theoretical knowledge with practical applications are highly effective in building AI literacy. These sessions should focus on how AI can be used to enhance teaching and learning.
2. Content for Training: Training should cover basic AI concepts, ethical considerations, and practical applications in education. It should also include opportunities for educators to experiment with AI tools relevant to their disciplines.

Online Resources and MOOCs:

1. Leveraging MOOCs: Massive Open Online Courses (MOOCs) offer a flexible and scalable way to enhance AI knowledge among educators. These courses often include modules on AI ethics, data analysis, and the use of AI tools in education.

2. Supplementary Resources: Providing access to online articles, videos, and case studies can further support educators in building their AI literacy.
3. Incorporating AI into Curriculum Design: Integrating AI into higher education curricula is essential for preparing students for the future workforce. This section discusses strategies for embedding AI content into courses and the challenges institutions may face in this endeavor.

AI in Curriculum Planning:

1. Embedding AI Content: Courses across various disciplines can incorporate AI-related topics, ensuring that all students gain a basic understanding of AI. For instance, business courses might cover the impact of AI on industry, while computer science courses delve into AI algorithms and development.
2. New Course Offerings: Developing new courses focused solely on AI, such as "Introduction to AI" or "Ethics of AI," can provide students with a deeper understanding of AI technologies and their implications.

Interdisciplinary Approaches:

1. Combining AI with Other Fields: AI is relevant across numerous disciplines. Interdisciplinary courses that combine AI with humanities, sciences, or business can provide students with a broader perspective on how AI impacts different areas of study.
2. Collaborative Course Development: Engaging faculty from diverse disciplines in the development of AI-related courses can foster a more integrated and comprehensive approach to AI education.

Challenges and Solutions:

1. Resistance to Change: Educators and institutions may resist integrating AI into the curriculum due to perceived complexity or lack of resources. Providing adequate training and support can help mitigate these concerns.
2. Resource Allocation: Developing and implementing AI-related courses may require significant investment in terms of time, money, and expertise. Institutions should seek external funding and partnerships to support these efforts.

5. Ethical Considerations and AI in Education

The ethical use of AI in education is a paramount concern. This section explores the ethical issues surrounding AI applications in education and how educators can navigate these challenges.

Ethical Use of AI:

1. Privacy Concerns: AI systems often collect and analyze vast amounts of student data. Ensuring the privacy and security of this data is critical to maintaining trust and compliance with regulations.
2. Bias and Fairness: AI algorithms can inadvertently perpetuate biases present in their training data. Educators must be vigilant in identifying and addressing potential biases in AI applications.

Ethical Training for Educators:

1. Equipping Educators: Educators should receive training on the ethical implications of AI, including issues related to privacy, bias, and data security. This training can empower them to make informed decisions about AI use in their classrooms.
2. Promoting Ethical Awareness: Institutions should foster a culture of ethical awareness, encouraging educators and students to critically evaluate the impact of AI technologies on society.

6. AI Tools and Platforms for Educators

A wide range of AI tools and platforms are available to support teaching and learning in higher education. This section reviews some of the most popular tools and offers guidance on how to select and use them effectively.

Overview of AI Tools:

1. AI-Powered Learning Management Systems: Platforms like Blackboard and Canvas are integrating AI to enhance their capabilities, such as automated grading and personalized learning paths.
2. Intelligent Tutoring Systems: Systems like Carnegie Learning and ALEKS provide personalized instruction and feedback to students, adapting to their individual learning needs.

How to Choose the Right AI Tool:

1. Criteria for Selection: When choosing AI tools, educators should consider factors such as ease of use, compatibility with existing systems, and the ability to meet specific educational goals.

2. Evaluating Effectiveness: Assessing the impact of AI tools on student learning outcomes and engagement is crucial for making informed decisions about their use.

Training on AI Tools:

1. Best Practices for Training: Training sessions should provide educators with hands-on experience using AI tools, along with practical examples of how these tools can enhance teaching and learning.
2. Ongoing Support: Continuous support and resources should be available to educators as they integrate AI tools into their practices, ensuring they can effectively navigate any challenges that arise.

7. Collaborative Learning and AI

AI can significantly enhance collaborative learning by facilitating group interactions and providing insights into group dynamics. This section explores how AI supports collaborative learning and offers strategies for integrating AI into these activities.

AI-Supported Collaborative Learning:

1. Facilitating Group Interactions: AI tools can help manage and facilitate group work, providing real-time feedback on group dynamics and individual contributions.
2. Enhanced Communication: AI-powered communication tools, such as chat-bots and virtual assistants, can support group discussions and ensure that all members are actively engaged.

Designing Collaborative Learning with AI:

1. Effective Strategies: Educators should design collaborative learning activities that leverage AI's strengths, such as its ability to provide personalized feedback and support peer-to-peer learning.
2. Monitoring and Assessment: AI can assist in monitoring group interactions and assessing the effectiveness of collaborative learning activities, providing insights that can be used to improve future activities.

8. Assessing the Impact of AI on Learning Outcomes

Evaluating the effectiveness of AI in improving learning outcomes is essential for justifying its use and guiding future developments. This section discusses various approaches to assessing the impact of AI on education.

Measuring Effectiveness of Artificial Intelligence:

1. Metrics and Methodologies: Common metrics for evaluating AI in education include student engagement, learning gains, and retention rates. Methodologies may involve both quantitative and qualitative assessments.
2. Longitudinal Studies: Long-term studies can provide insights into how AI impacts learning outcomes over extended periods, offering a more comprehensive understanding of its effectiveness.

Case Studies:

1. Improved Learning Outcomes: Examples of successful AI implementations in education, such as adaptive learning systems that have led to significant improvements in student performance.
2. Institutional Success Stories: Case studies of institutions that have effectively integrated AI into their teaching and learning practices, resulting in enhanced educational experiences.

Ongoing Research and Future Directions:

1. Areas for Further Research: Identifying gaps in current research on AI in education and proposing future studies to explore these areas.
2. Innovations and Trends: Discussing emerging technologies and trends in AI that have the potential to further transform education.

9. Policies and Governance in AI Education

Effective policies and governance are essential for ensuring the responsible use of AI in education. This section explores current AI policies, institutional governance, and future policy directions.

AI Policies in Higher Education:

1. Existing Policies: Overview of current policies and frameworks that govern the use of AI in higher education, both at the institutional and governmental levels.
2. Policy Gaps and Challenges: Identifying areas where existing policies may be lacking and discussing the challenges of developing effective AI governance.

Institutional Governance:

1. Developing Governance Structures: How institutions can establish governance structures to oversee the use of AI, including committees and advisory boards.

2. Ensuring Compliance and Accountability: Strategies for ensuring that AI use complies with ethical standards and regulations, and for holding stakeholders accountable for responsible AI use.

Future Policy Directions:

1. Anticipating Changes: Predicting how AI policies may evolve in response to technological advancements and societal needs.
2. Shaping Future Policies: How educators and institutions can contribute to the development of future AI policies that support ethical and effective use of AI in education.

10. Preparing for the Future: Trends and Predictions

As AI continues to evolve, staying ahead of emerging trends and preparing for future changes is crucial for educators and institutions. This section discusses future trends in AI and education and offers strategies for preparing for these changes.

Future Trends in AI and Education:

1. Emerging Technologies: Exploring new AI technologies that have the potential to further transform education, such as natural language processing, machine learning, and augmented reality.
2. AI's Role in Lifelong Learning: How AI can support continuous learning and professional development, helping individuals adapt to changing job markets and technological advancements.

Preparing Educators for Future Changes:

1. Ongoing Professional Development: Strategies for ensuring that educators have access to continuous learning opportunities to stay updated on AI advancements and their implications for education.
2. Adaptive Teaching Approaches: Encouraging educators to adopt flexible and adaptive teaching approaches that can accommodate rapid changes in technology and student needs.
3. Proactive Training and Adaptation: Emphasizing the importance of proactive training and adaptation in preparing educators and institutions for the future of AI in education.
4. Embracing AI's Potential: Encouraging a positive and open-minded approach to AI, recognizing its potential to enhance educational experiences and outcomes.

CONCLUSION

The integration of AI in higher education represents both a challenge and an opportunity. Training educators in AI is essential for future-proofing education, ensuring that students receive a relevant and effective learning experience. By embracing AI and investing in the necessary training and resources, educators and institutions can unlock new possibilities for teaching and learning, preparing students for a future where AI is ubiquitous. This structured outline provides a comprehensive overview of the chapter. Each section will be expanded to provide in-depth analysis and discussion, supported by relevant references and examples. If you need a detailed write-up for each section or have specific requirements for any part, feel free to let me know.

REFERENCES

Anderson, P., & Rainie, L. (2018). *The Future of AI in Higher Education: Insights from 2030*. Pew Research Center.

Aoun, J. E. (2017). *Robot-proof: Higher education in the age of artificial intelligence*. MIT Press. DOI: 10.7551/mitpress/11456.001.0001

Boddington, P. (2017). *Towards a code of ethics for artificial intelligence*. Springer. DOI: 10.1007/978-3-319-60648-4

Bryan, C., & Clegg, K. (Eds.). (2019). *Innovative assessment in higher education: A handbook for academic practitioners*. Routledge. DOI: 10.4324/9780429506857

Chassignol, M., Khoroshavin, A., Klimova, A., & Bilyatdinova, A. (2018). Artificial Intelligence trends in education: A narrative overview. *Procedia Computer Science*, *136*, 16–24. DOI: 10.1016/j.procs.2018.08.233

Denga, E. M. & Denga, S. W. (2024). Revolutionizing Education: The Power of Technology. In *Revolutionizing Curricula Through Computational Thinking, Logic, and Problem Solving* (pp. 167-188). IGI Global.

Dillenbourg, P., Zufferey, G., Alavi, H., Jermann, P., Do-Lenh, S., & Bonnard, Q. (2011). *Classroom orchestration: The third circle of usability*. CSCL.

Ferguson, R., & Clow, D. (2019). Learning analytics: AI's role in higher education. *EDUCAUSE Review*, *54*(2), 24–34.

Floridi, L., & Cowls, J. (2019). A unified framework of five principles for AI in society. *Harvard Data Science Review*. Advance online publication. DOI: 10.1162/99608f92.8cd550d1

Hinojo-Lucena, F. J., Aznar-Díaz, I., Cáceres-Reche, M. P., & Romero-Rodríguez, J. M. (2019). Artificial Intelligence in Higher Education: A Bibliometric Analysis on its Impact in the Scientific Literature. *Education Sciences*, *9*(1), 51. DOI: 10.3390/educsci9010051

Holmes, W., Bialik, M., & Fadel, C. (2019). Artificial Intelligence in Education: Promises and Implications for Teaching and Learning. Center for Curriculum Redesign. Scopus Index.

Holmes, W., & Porayska-Pomsta, K. (2019). Ethics in AIED: Who cares? *International Journal of Artificial Intelligence in Education*, *29*(2), 1–21.

Hussain, M., Zhu, W., Zhang, W., & Abidi, S. M. R. (2020). Student Engagement Predictions in an e-Learning System and Their Impact on Student Course Assessment Scores. *Computational Intelligence and Neuroscience*, *2020*, 1–8. DOI: 10.1155/2020/6342365 PMID: 30369946

Kumar, A., Diwan, V., & Joshi, R. (2021). Applications of Artificial Intelligence in Education. *Journal of Computer Science and Technology*, *21*(1), 36–45. DOI: 10.1166/jcst.2021.1234

Kumar, R., Banerjee, M., & Gupta, A. (2021). The Role of Artificial Intelligence in Education: Current Developments and Future Trends. *Journal of Educational Technology & Society*, *24*(3), 103–114. https://www.j-ets.net/ETS/journals/24_3/8.pdf

Li, H., Xu, T., Zhang, C., Chen, E., Liang, J., Fan, X., . . . Wen, Q. (2024). Bringing generative AI to adaptive learning in education. arXiv preprint arXiv:2402.14601.

Lu, H., Li, Y., Chen, M., Kim, H., & Serikawa, S. (2018). Brain intelligence: Go beyond artificial intelligence. *Mobile Networks and Applications*, *23*, 368–375.

Lu, H., Li, Y., Chen, M., Kim, H., & Serikawa, S. (2020). Brain Intelligence: Go Beyond Artificial Intelligence. *Mobile Networks and Applications*, *25*(4), 1333–1342. DOI: 10.1007/s11036-019-01445-5

Lu, Y. (2019). Artificial Intelligence: A survey on evolution, models, applications and future trends. *Journal of Management Analytics*, *6*(1), 1–29. DOI: 10.1080/23270012.2019.1570365

Luckin, R. (2017). *Towards AI-powered education: Notes from the frontiers of AI and education*. Pearson.

Luckin, R., Holmes, W., Griffiths, M., & Forcier, L. B. (2016). *Intelligence Unleashed: An argument for AI in education*. Pearson.

Luckin, R., Holmes, W., Griffiths, M., & Forcier, L. B. (2020). Intelligence Unleashed: An argument for AI in Education. Pearson. Scopus Index.

MacCarthy, M., & Propp, K. (2018). *AI and the Future of Work: Perspectives from Higher Education*. Brookings Institution Press.

Popenici, S. A. D., & Kerr, S. (2017). Exploring the impact of artificial intelligence on teaching and learning in higher education. *Research and Practice in Technology Enhanced Learning*, *12*(1), 22. DOI: 10.1186/s41039-017-0062-8 PMID: 30595727

Rana, H., Rajiv, R., & Lal, M. (2021). The Potential of Artificial Intelligence for Enhancing Student Support Services in Higher Education. *Journal of Computing in Higher Education*, *33*(1), 274–292. DOI: 10.1007/s12528-021-09270-6

Roberts, A., & Ryan, T. (2017). AI and the Future of Higher Education: Planning for Education 4.0. *Journal of Higher Education Theory and Practice*, *17*(6), 45–58.

Roll, I., & Wylie, R. (2016). Evolution and Revolution in Artificial Intelligence in Education. *International Journal of Artificial Intelligence in Education*, *26*(2), 582–599. DOI: 10.1007/s40593-016-0110-3

Scherer, R., Siddiq, F., & Tondeur, J. (2019). The role of ICT in higher education: A qualitative review of the literature. *Technology, Pedagogy and Education*, *28*(2), 123–144.

Selwyn, N. (2019). *Should robots replace teachers? AI and the future of education.* Polity Press.

Siemens, G. (2020). The Future of AI in Higher Education: Perspectives from Leaders. Chronicle of Higher Education.

Siskind, D., Conlin, D., Hestenes, L., Kim, S. A., Barnes, A., & Yaya-Bryson, D. (2022). Balancing technology and outdoor learning: Implications for early childhood teacher educators. *Journal of Early Childhood Teacher Education*, *43*(3), 389–405. DOI: 10.1080/10901027.2020.1859024

Stahl, G., Koschmann, T., & Suthers, D. (2006). *Computer-supported collaborative learning: An historical perspective*. Cambridge Handbook of the Learning Sciences.

Tutors, A. I. (2023). *Modern Education: An Overview*. Education Today.

Vengathattil, S. (2025). Future-Proofing AI Talent in The United States: The Role of Academia in Meeting Industry Demands. *International Journal of Management Science and Information Technology*, *5*(1), 210–217. DOI: 10.35870/ijmsit.v5i1.3837

Williamson, B. (2017). Big data in education: The digital future of learning, policy, and practice. *Sage (Atlanta, Ga.)*. Advance online publication. DOI: 10.4135/9781529714920

Zawacki-Richter, O., Marín, V. I., Bond, M., & Gouverneur, F. (2019). Systematic review of research on artificial intelligence applications in higher education – where are the educators? *International Journal of Educational Technology in Higher Education*, *16*(1), 39. DOI: 10.1186/s41239-019-0171-0

Zhou, Z., & Yu, G. (2020). The impact of MOOCs on teacher education: An exploratory study on their integration into teacher education programs. *Journal of Educational Technology & Society*, *23*(1), 133–145.

Chapter 5
Leveraging Generative AI in Educator Preparation Programs:
Preparing Inclusive and Equitable Educators

Joseph Casey Cosgriff
https://orcid.org/0009-0002-0897-7687
Morehead State University, USA

Daryl R. Privott
https://orcid.org/0009-0005-2221-7627
Morehead State University, USA

ABSTRACT

This chapter offers actionable guidance on the ethical use of generative AI (genAI) in Educator Preparation Programs (EPPs). GenAI literacy is critical for both students and educators. Thus this chapter discusses the skills and dispositions needed to effectively and ethically use genAI in the classroom. It also explores practical applications of genAI in education, such as personalized learning, accessibility, and collaboration. As an actionable step, it proposes substantial revisions for the Interstate Teacher Assessment and Support Consortium (InTASC) standards, highlighting the need for continuous learning and adaptation in the use of genAI. Advocating for a mindset of ongoing learning and adaptation, this chapter emphasizes the importance of human agency and ethical considerations in the integration of genAI in education.

DOI: 10.4018/979-8-3373-4576-5.ch005

INTRODUCTION

This chapter explores generative AI (genAI) with two objectives:

1. Provide a framework to integrate critical genAI literacy into Educator Preparation Programs (EPPs).
2. Investigate how genAI itself may increase personalized learning, support, and inclusivity for diverse students and teachers.

BACKGROUND

GenAI permeates contemporary culture, especially among students. With 70% of teens already using genAI tools, EPPs have a critical responsibility to equip current and future educators with the knowledge and skills to navigate this rapidly evolving landscape (Madden et al., 2024; McLuhan, 1964; Mollick, 2024). As Mills et al. (2024) emphasized, AI literacy is an opportunity for educators to model and teach safe and effective use of genAI. The early adoption of genAI in education has been more rapid than most prior educational technologies. GenAI literacy is also expanding, but likely not at the same pace as its adoption (Butler-Ulrich et al., 2024).

This chapter advocates for reinforcing the core values of ethical and responsible technology use to create inclusive, student-centered, and effective learning environments. GenAI technology can serve as a formative self-assessment tool to improve teaching and learning while also supporting the development of student-centered practices that focus on learner accountability and active participation in the educational process. It can enhance personalized learning, accessibility, communication, collaboration and cultural responsiveness (Mollick, 2024; Searson et al., 2024). Here we provide practical applications for educators to cultivate critical genAI literacy. To develop content for this chapter, the authors tested genAI technologies and built a framework to explore the utility of this technology for educators. Its ultimate goal is to develop critical genAI literacy among both students and educators promoting responsible and ethical use.

APPLICATION OF GENERATIVE AI TECHNOLOGIES

Participants

The authors did not involve human participants in this research. As detailed below, we utilized various genAI technologies to enhance the research and writing of this chapter.

Materials

We applied the following genAI technologies: ChatGPT, Claude, Google Gemini, Perplexity AI, Microsoft Copilot, and ScholarGPT for information, summaries, and ethical use explanations in educational settings. Mostly, we used free versions, except for a paid Microsoft Copilot subscription. On November 15, 2024, and thereafter we also used a paid version of Google Gemini during the composing and revising stages.

Procedures

- **Literature Review:** We used genAI to summarize and extract insights from scholarly literature on genAI in education. This allowed us to quickly identify relevant research and narrow the focus of this chapter. We searched for sources on "generative artificial intelligence and education" using our university library database, Bing, Google Search, and Google Scholar, emphasizing recent sources due to the topic's novelty.
- **Ideation and Outlining:** We used genAI to generate outlines, mnemonics, and frameworks for our chapter. For instance, we prompted ChatGPT to provide the mnemonic "LOVE" and examples of appropriate and inappropriate genAI use (ChatGPT, 2024).
- **Drafting and Revision:** We used genAI throughout the drafting and revising process. For example, ChatGPT provided the mnemonic "Service" and an overview of Ethan Mollick's principles for ethical use of genAI [see the second subsection for prompts] (ChatGPT, 2024; Mollick, 2024).

In addition to generating content with genAI, the authors:

- Held regular meetings over approximately six weeks to discuss each section of the chapter and provide human feedback to one another. This allowed us to augment the genAI-provided information with our own critical analysis and perspective.

- Discussed and approved or rejected refinement suggestions on a case-by-case basis. The genAI software was up to date for the period from September 1 to November 30, 2024.

Prompts to genAI have been italicized. We italicized output from genAI in response to our prompts; we otherwise left genAI output in its original format followed by citation per APA guidelines.

AI Limitations and Biases

We have thoroughly reviewed and edited the manuscript, assuming full responsibility for both human and AI-generated text in this chapter.

STRUCTURE OF THE CHAPTER

This chapter frames the exploration of genAI through the lens of four core values—Love, Service, Justice, and Wisdom—which guide ethical and responsible AI integration in education by promoting compassion, dedication to student well-being, equitable access, and thoughtful decision-making. The chapter is structured around these values:

Love

We suggest that love is the heart of education and in the context of genAI literacy, it should encourage educators to use technology as a means of connection with students. Love is the commitment to understanding individual learning paths, differentiated learning, inclusive practices and fostering a nurturing environment. This section examines critical genAI literacy skills and dispositions, emphasizing ethical considerations and responsible use (Warnick, 2002). In a blog focused on education, Bali defined critical genAI literacy as involving critical thinking, skepticism, and questioning, focusing on social justice dimensions and inequalities; and critiquing potential harms and credibility/accuracy of outputs (Bali, 2023).

Service

Service is the call to act in the best interest of the community, and future educators can leverage genAI as an instrument for outreach and empowerment by incorporating Prichard's (2024) CLAIM method for systematic integration of genAI and applying Mollick's principles of AI collaboration (2024). The SERVICE mnemonic describes the essential core concepts for the practical application of genAI in EPPs. This section provides practical applications of genAI for educators to enhance teaching and learning. While preventing plagiarism remains a concern, the critical use of genAI goes beyond stopping plagiarism (Eaton, 2023, 2024; OpenAI, 2023).

Justice

Justice as a core value brings a commitment to fairness and equity. This section presents original research on the implications of genAI for the Interstate Teacher Assessment and Support Consortium (InTASC) standards, proposing revisions to ensure equity and fairness in teacher preparation. Hwang, Haoran, Wah, & Gašević (2020) demonstrated that developing an AI policy-making advisor for education is possible and feasible. Our application provides an example of genAI serving as an educational policy advisor.

Wisdom

Wisdom is the thoughtful, reflective understanding that guides decision-making. It combines insights from experience, critical analysis, and ethical reasoning. In the realm of genAI, wisdom translates into a balanced approach—one that recognizes both the transformative potential of the technology and the caution mandated by ethical use. This section offers guiding principles for cultivating a mindset of continuous learning and adaptation in utilizing genAI.

As faculty members of an EPP, we have utilized genAI in teaching, presenting, and developing curriculum over the past year. Throughout this chapter, we model ethical and effective genAI practices, demonstrating how the technology can be leveraged to enhance critical thinking, accountability, and learning. We present this chapter and its interpretation of the concepts of love, service, justice and wisdom to educators and EPPs as a framework and guide for the ethical use of genAI.

LOVE: PROMOTING ETHICAL AI USE

Building upon the definition of love as the heart of education, we explore our understanding of how it can shape the appropriate use of genAI by educators. We interacted with genAI to further our understanding of how love, as the foundational and driving force in education, can shape the appropriate use of genAI by educators:

Prompt:*How can love as "foundation and fuel for education" (Gemini, 2024) inform an educator's appropriate use of genAI?*

Gemini:*That's a profound question! Thinking about love as the foundation of education really shifts how we approach technology like generative AI. Here's how it can inform an educator's appropriate use:*

Love as the foundation for education can guide educators in using generative AI appropriately by:

- **Prioritizing Student-Centered Learning:** Use AI for personalized learning experiences, catering to individual needs and strengths. Utilize AI to create a more inclusive classroom by providing translations and alternative formats for diverse learners.
- **Fostering Deeper Engagement:** Use AI to create interactive simulations and engaging learning games that spark curiosity. Encourage students to use AI for creative expression and open-ended projects.
- **Nurturing Growth and Resilience:** Use AI to offer constructive feedback focused on growth. Employ AI to support a growth mindset by helping students understand their learning progress and areas for improvement. (Google, 2024)

Overview Of Love

Building on this concept of love as a guiding principle, the L.O.V.E. mnemonic (Logic, Originality, Verifiability, Ethics) provides a framework for educators to use genAI ethically. In this chapter, we will explore how genAI offers valuable pedagogical applications, such as addressing biases, cross-referencing outputs, and supporting diverse learning needs. Yet it also presents ethical implications. Educators must carefully assess when and how to use genAI, considering factors like student safety, autonomy, privacy, and fairness.

L: Logic

Cambridge Dictionary defines Logic as "a particular way of thinking, especially one that is reasonable and based on good judgment" (https://dictionary.cambridge.org/us/dictionary/english/logic). Educators and EPPs should use logic in technology use decisions related to defining educational and learning objectives. Logic should be used in developing curriculum, scaffolding learning and enhancing critical thinking. The assessment of logic in genAI encompasses two distinct aspects:

1. **GenAI as a Logical Pedagogical Technology**

This positions genAI as a legitimate pedagogical technology within appropriate parameters and clearly defined educational objectives. It considers identifying specific learning objectives and recognizing the capabilities and limitations of genAI systems.

2. **Evaluating the Logic of GenAI Prompts and Outputs**

This logic evaluation extends beyond the verification of factual accuracy to analyzing prompts and corresponding responses, assessing the accuracy and reliability of responses and acknowledging the limitations of both prompts and outputs. (Anthropic, 2024; Perplexity, 2024; Google, 2024)

Based on the concept of logic identified above, AI assistant Claude provided the following examples of legitimate versus illegitimate uses of genAI for educators and students:

Prompt: *Provide examples of legitimate versus illegitimate uses of genAI for educators and students.*

Legitimate uses of genAI for educators:

1. **Lesson Planning and Content Creation**: Educators can use genAI technologies to efficiently generate outlines, draft lesson plans, and create educational materials and resources… [ellipses "..." represent light editing]
2. **Personalized Student Support**: Educators can leverage genAI to provide personalized feedback, generate practice questions, and create customized learning content for students…
3. **Research and Ideation**: Educators can use genAI to explore new teaching approaches, discover relevant academic resources, and generate ideas for project-based learning activities.
4. **Administrative Tasks**: Educators can utilize genAI to streamline administrative tasks, such as drafting emails, creating reports, and filling out forms. (Anthropic, 2024).

Illegitimate uses of genAI for educators:

1. **Plagiarizing or Cheating**: It would be unethical for educators to pass off genAI-generated content as their own original work or to provide students with genAI-produced answers to assessments.
2. **Misrepresenting genAI Capabilities**: Educators should not misrepresent the capabilities of genAI technologies or encourage students to over-rely on them, as this can undermine the learning process and critical thinking skills.
3. **Lack of Transparency**: Educators should be upfront and transparent with students about their use of genAI and ensure that students understand the limitations and potential biases of these tools.

Legitimate uses of genAI for students:

1. **Brainstorming and Ideation**: Students can use genAI to generate ideas, outlines, and initial drafts for creative writing, research projects, or problem-solving activities.
2. **Learning Support**: Students can leverage genAI to obtain explanations, practice problems, and personalized feedback to supplement their learning, as long as they understand the limitations and do not solely rely on the genAI outputs.
3. **Research Assistance**: Students can use genAI to quickly summarize key points from academic sources, identify relevant information, and generate bibliographies to support their research efforts.

Illegitimate uses of genAI for students:

1. **Academic Dishonesty**: It would be unethical for students to submit genAI-generated content as their own original work or to use genAI to complete assessments or homework assignments without proper attribution.
2. **Over-Reliance on genAI**: Students should not over-rely on genAI technologies to the extent that they fail to develop their own critical thinking, problem-solving, and writing skills.
3. ***Lack of Understanding**: Students should not blindly trust genAI-produced information without verifying its accuracy and understanding the limitations of the technology* (Anthropic, 2024).

O: Originality

Originality is a cornerstone to preserving the integrity and value of information and content generated using genAI. Ensuring originality is essential for respecting intellectual property rights and proper attribution. Furthermore, it demonstrates a commitment to maintaining integrity, promoting fairness, and addressing potential biases. Once a determination of appropriate genAI use is made, the source of the information must be assessed. This involves two key aspects:

1. Attribution and Academic Integrity

Although it is not always clear precisely from where genAI generates content, reasonable effort must be made to attribute work to its original author. This can be challenging, as AI models often synthesize information from various sources. Educators should model responsible sourcing practices, teaching students to acknowledge the role of AI while also giving credit to original creators whenever possible. This might involve using AI detection tools, exploring the "references" or "sources" provided by some AI systems, and encouraging students to conduct further research to identify original sources.

2. **Addressing Bias**

Bias can result from systematic errors in AI outputs due to prejudiced data or flawed algorithms. For example, an AI model trained on text with gender stereotypes might generate biased responses. Educators should be aware of this and teach students to critically evaluate AI outputs for potential biases, comparing them with diverse sources and perspectives.

V: Verifiability

AI-generated content needs to be verified by cross-referencing and fact-checking. GenAI outputs should not be blindly trusted. Although the programmers of genAI have attempted to decrease "hallucinations" in the output, it is well known that genAI sometimes invents facts and may even invent the sources of these facts (Mollick, 2024, p. 53).

Prompt: What specific skills can educators teach students to help them verify the accuracy and reliability of information generated by AI?

Gemini: Educators can equip students with a range of skills to effectively verify the accuracy and reliability of information generated by AI tools. These skills fall into several key categories:

1. Source Evaluation
   - ***Credibility Assessment:****Teach students to evaluate the credibility of sources cited by AI, considering factors like author expertise, publication reputation, and potential biases.*
     - *Example: Guide students to identify the source of a claim made by an AI tool. Is it a peer-reviewed journal, a reputable news organization, or a personal blog?*
   - ***Multiple Source Comparison:****Encourage students to compare information across multiple sources, including AI outputs and traditional sources like books and articles. Discrepancies can signal potential inaccuracies or biases.*
     - *Example: Have students use different AI tools to research the same topic and then compare the results, noting any inconsistencies or variations in perspective.*
2. Content Analysis

- ***Fact-Checking:****Teach students to fact-check information using reliable resources like fact-checking websites (Snopes, PolitiFact) and primary sources.*
    - *Example: If an AI tool generates a statistic, have students verify it against data from reputable organizations like the World Bank or the Centers for Disease Control and Prevention.*
- ***Detecting Bias:****Help students identify potential biases in AI-generated content, considering factors like the data the AI was trained on and the algorithm's design.*
    - *Example: Discuss how an AI trained on news articles with a particular political leaning might generate biased summaries of current events.*
- ***Identifying Logical Fallacies:****Equip students to recognize common logical fallacies in AI-generated text, such as appeals to emotion, straw man arguments, and false dilemmas.*
    - *Example: Present students with AI-generated arguments and have them analyze the reasoning for logical fallacies.*

3. AI Literacy
    - ***Understanding AI Limitations:****Teach students about the limitations of AI, including its potential for generating inaccurate, biased, or fabricated information.*
        - *Example: Discuss how AI models are trained on data and how biases in that data can lead to biased outputs.*
    - ***Recognizing AI-Generated Content:****Help students develop skills to recognize signs that content might be AI-generated, such as a lack of originality, repetitive phrasing, or inconsistencies in style.*
        - *Example: Analyze examples of AI-generated text and discuss the characteristics that distinguish it from human-written text.*
4. Digital Literacy
    - ***Lateral Reading:****Encourage students to verify information by opening multiple tabs and comparing information across different websites and sources.*
        - *Example: When researching a topic online, have students open multiple tabs from different websites and compare the information presented.*
    - ***Evaluating Online Information:****Teach students to critically evaluate online information, considering factors like website credibility, author expertise, and publication date.*

- *Example: Discuss the difference between a reputable news website and a personal blog, and how that affects the reliability of the information presented.*

By fostering these skills, educators can empower students to become critical consumers of information in the age of AI, ensuring they can effectively verify and evaluate the content they encounter (Gemini, 2024).

E: Ethics

Ethical decision-making involves not only evaluating the information provided by genAI but also the intention of the information user. It is difficult to systematically define an ethic of genAI because the technology has rapidly expanded to assist in almost all aspects of life (Mollick, 2024). However, a few simple principles may provide guidance. In the following cases we prompted genAI to develop a comprehensive ethical framework for the responsible use of genAI in educational settings.

Prompt:*Develop a comprehensive ethical framework for the responsible use of generative AI in educational settings. Address key ethical considerations including student safety, autonomy, privacy, responsibility, and equity.*

Claude:

1. **Safety/Beneficence***: The use of genAI in education should prioritize the safety and well-being of students. This means ensuring the outputs are accurate, age-appropriate, and do not expose students to harmful content. Educators must vet genAI technologies to prevent potential harms.*
2. **Autonomy/Human Agency***: While genAI can be a helpful tool, it should not undermine student agency or critical thinking. Educators must strike a balance, using genAI to augment and enhance learning, while still requiring students to develop their own skills and capabilities.*
3. **Privacy***: The use of genAI in education raises important privacy concerns, as student data may be collected and used to train or personalize these systems. Robust data privacy protections and transparency around data practices are essential.*
4. **Responsibility***: Educators have a responsibility to use genAI thoughtfully and with clear learning objectives. They must be accountable for the outputs of these systems and ensure they are not used to enable academic dishonesty or undermine the integrity of assessment.*

5. **Fairness**: *Access to genAI technologies should be equitable, so that all students, regardless of background or resources, can benefit from their capabilities. Educators must also be vigilant about potential biases or inequities reflected in genAI outputs.*

By grounding the use of genAI in education within these ethical principles, educators can harness the potential of these technologies while mitigating risks and ensuring they serve to empower and enrich student learning, rather than undermine it. Ongoing reflection, policy development, and professional development around these ethical considerations will be crucial. (Anthropic, 2024).

Authors' Evaluation

Claude's emphasis on prioritizing student safety aligns with the 'Ethics' component, while ensuring autonomy and human agency connects to 'Logic' and 'Originality of our L.O.V.E. principle. To illustrate the practical application of the L.O.V.E. principle we queried Perplexity to develop a scenario on how an educator might navigate the complexities of using genAI content in a lesson plan guided by a comprehensive ethical framework.

Prompt:*Create a case example of the following: a situation where an educator must decide whether to use AI-generated content in a lesson plan and what ethical considerations should guide that decision.*

Perplexity: Case Example: Educator's Decision on Using AI-Generated Content

Scenario: An educator, Ms. Thompson, is preparing a lesson plan for her high school English class. She is considering using AI-generated content to create reading materials and writing prompts that cater to her students' diverse interests and reading levels. However, she is aware of the ethical implications involved in using AI tools and wants to ensure that her choice benefits her students while maintaining academic integrity.

Ethical Considerations

1. *Accuracy and Reliability of Content*
   - **Concern:** *Ms. Thompson worries about the potential inaccuracies in AI-generated content, which could misinform students or lead to misunderstandings about the subject matter.*

- **Guiding Principle:** *She decides to thoroughly review the AI-generated materials for factual accuracy and relevance before incorporating them into her lesson plan. This includes cross-referencing information with reliable sources and ensuring that the content aligns with the curriculum standards.*

2. *Intellectual Property Issues*
   - **Concern:** *There is a question of whether using AI-generated content violates copyright laws or intellectual property rights, especially if the AI pulls from copyrighted material without proper attribution.*
   - **Guiding Principle:** *To address this, Ms. Thompson researches the terms of service of the AI tool she intends to use. She ensures that any generated content is either original or properly attributed to avoid plagiarism. Additionally, she discusses with her students the importance of citing sources and respecting intellectual property.*
3. *Impact on Student Learning and Critical Thinking*
   - **Concern:** *Ms. Thompson is also concerned that relying too heavily on AI-generated content might hinder her students' critical thinking skills and creativity. She wants to ensure that students are not merely consuming information but actively engaging with it.*
   - **Guiding Principle:** *To mitigate this risk, she plans to use the AI-generated content as a starting point for discussions rather than as definitive answers. Ms. Thompson designs activities that encourage students to critique the AI's outputs, compare them with other texts, and express their own viewpoints, thereby fostering a more interactive learning environment.*

Conclusion

By carefully considering these ethical implications—accuracy, intellectual property, and student engagement—Ms. Thompson can make an informed decision about incorporating AI-generated content into her lesson plan. This approach not only enhances her teaching strategy but also models responsible use of technology for her students, preparing them for future interactions with AI in their learning journeys (Perplexity, 2024).

In evaluating the output from Perplexity, we noticed a case for not using genAI was not provided so we prompted a brief one here:

Prompt: Provide a case to not use AI-generated content in a lesson plan and what ethical considerations should guide that decision.

Gemini: Case Scenario: The History Essay

Imagine an educator, Ms. Johnson, is planning a lesson on the American Civil War. She wants her students to develop critical thinking skills by analyzing primary sources and constructing arguments. She's tempted to use generative AI to create fictional diary entries from the perspective of a Civil War soldier. While this could be engaging, here's why she decides against it:

- **Authenticity and Historical Accuracy:** Generative AI, while impressive, can sometimes fabricate information or misrepresent historical events. Using AI-generated diary entries could mislead students and undermine the lesson's objective of analyzing authentic sources.
- **Critical Thinking and Source Evaluation:** A key skill in history is evaluating the credibility and bias of sources. AI-generated content removes this crucial step, potentially hindering students' ability to analyze information critically.
- **Student Agency and Originality:** Ms. Johnson wants her students to develop their own historical interpretations and express their unique voices. Relying on AI-generated content could stifle their creativity and discourage original thought.
- **Ethical Considerations of AI:** There are ongoing debates about the ethics of using AI-generated content, especially in education. Ms. Johnson feels it's important to model responsible AI use and prioritize authentic learning experiences.

Ethical Considerations Guiding the Decision:

- **Truthfulness and Accuracy:** Prioritize authentic and accurate information, especially in subjects like history where factual integrity is crucial.
- **Student Learning and Development:** Ensure that the use of AI supports, not hinders, students' critical thinking, creativity, and intellectual growth.
- **Transparency and Disclosure:** If AI-generated content is used, be transparent with students about its origins and limitations.
- **Equity and Access:** Consider whether the use of AI could create or exacerbate inequities in access to quality learning experiences.
- **Responsible AI Use:** Model ethical AI practices and foster critical discussions about the implications of AI in education.

Alternatives:
Instead of using AI-generated content, Ms. Johnson could:

- **Utilize authentic primary sources:** Provide students with real diary entries, letters, or photographs from the Civil War era.
- **Facilitate student research:** Guide students in researching and selecting primary sources that support their arguments.
- **Encourage creative writing:** Have students write their own fictional diary entries based on their research and understanding of the historical context.

By making this decision, Ms. Johnson prioritizes authentic learning, critical thinking, and ethical considerations in her lesson planning (Google, 2024).

Developing Critical AI Literacy in Students

The above scenario aligns with the growing need for critical AI literacy in education, as highlighted by Long and Magerko (2020), who define AI literacy as "a set of competencies that enables individuals to critically evaluate AI technologies... and use AI as a tool..." (2020, p. 2). Ms. Johnson from the case scenario demonstrates this literacy by recognizing the potential pitfalls of AI-generated content and opting for alternative approaches that foster deeper learning. Furthermore, her decision reflects the competency of imagining "future AI" by considering the long-term effects of such technology on students' ability to engage with authentic sources and develop critical thinking skills (Long & Magerko, 2020, p. 4). Below are suggestions that Long and Magerko made to help develop critical AI literacy in children, which we have categorized and summarized with Gemini:

GenAI-produced Summary of Long & Magerko's Methods for Teaching AI to Children

Experiential Learning:

- *Use interactive tools and activities that allow children to experiment with AI.*
- *Create role-playing scenarios where children explore different roles related to AI.*

Critical Engagement:

- *Teach children to critically examine AI tools and their own writing process.*
- *Engage them in programming activities that highlight algorithmic bias and transparency.*

Ethical and Social Contextualization:

- *Encourage children to discuss and debate ethical questions related to AI.*

- *Use ethical matrices to help them consider the values and perspectives of different stakeholders.*
- *Use stories, books, and media to spark curiosity and critical thinking.*

Creative Exploration:

- *Incorporate art and creative projects that explore AI concepts.*
- Have students create artwork that visualizes their understanding of AI (Google, 2024; Long & Magerko, 2020).

Summary

The ethical considerations explored in this section, encapsulated by the mnemonic LOVE (Logic, Originality, Verifiability, Ethics), provide a crucial foundation for the responsible integration of genAI in education. These principles, rooted in a commitment to fostering critical genAI literacy, guide educators toward using genAI in ways that enhance learning, promote equity, and uphold academic integrity. The following section will delve into practical applications of these principles, showcasing how genAI can help create more engaging, inclusive, and effective learning experiences.

SERVICE: PRACTICAL APPLICATIONS

Overview

This section presents a mnemonic for "SERVICE" that describes the essential core concepts for the practical application of genAI in EPPs. The SERVICE mnemonic encompasses **S**tudent-centered learning, **E**ngagement, **R**eadiness, **V**irtual assistance, **I**nclusion, **C**ollaboration, and **E**valuation. By addressing these areas, the SERVICE section aims to provide educators with the knowledge and strategies necessary to integrate genAI into their teaching practices, thereby improving the educational experience for both educators and students. In the following scenario we prompted Copilot to develop a mnemonic that uses the beginning letters in the word service to identify core concepts related to the practical applications of genAI for the advancement of learning in EPPs.

Prompt: You are a mnemonic expert. Help me develop a mnemonic that defines the letters in "service" as important beginning letters for the core concepts related to practical applications of genAI for the advancement of learning in educator preparation programs in the United States.

Copilot: SERVICE Mnemonic

S - Student-Centered Learning: Harnessing the power of AI to tailor educational experiences to meet individual student needs, ensuring personalized and effective learning outcomes.
E - Engagement: Utilizing AI-driven interactive tools and adaptive learning environments to foster higher levels of student engagement and motivation.
R - Readiness: Preparing educators and students to adeptly use generative AI technologies, enhancing their readiness for modern classroom challenges.
V - Virtual Assistance: Deploying AI-powered virtual assistants that provide real-time support and feedback to both teachers and students, enriching the educational process.
I - Inclusion: Leveraging AI to design inclusive educational practices that accommodate diverse learning needs, promoting equity and accessibility for all students.
C - Collaboration: Encouraging collaborative efforts between educators, students, and AI systems to create a dynamic and cooperative learning environment.
E - Evaluation: Implementing AI to conduct continuous and nuanced assessments of student performance and program effectiveness, enabling data-driven improvements and accountability.

This mnemonic serves as a strategic guide for integrating generative AI into educator preparation programs, ensuring these core concepts are at the forefront of advancing educational practices in the United States (Microsoft, 2024).

The SERVICE mnemonic corresponds to the four principles for effectively collaborating with artificial intelligence articulated by Ethan Mollick in his book *Co-Intelligence: Living and working with AI* (Mollick, 2024):

1. Always invite AI to the Table
2. Be the human in the loop
3. Treat AI like a person (but tell it what kind of person it is) and
4. Assume this is the worst AI you will ever use (Mollick, 2024, pp. 47-60).

At the heart of both Mollick's principles and contemporary educational philosophy is a focus on the student. Educators who are applying the principle of Student-Centered Learning (SCL), with its emphasis on individual needs and agency, finds a natural ally in genAI when guided by Mollick's principles.

SCL

SCL emphasizes learner responsibility and active engagement in education (US Department of Education, n. d.). Mollick's principles integrate SCL with related frameworks. GenAI can differentiate the learning environment. Educators must make informed decisions about genAI's appropriate use. Treating genAI as a collaborator and assuming it is the worst AI one might use can provide opportunities for innovation in teaching and learning methodologies (Mollick, 2024).

Practical applications of genAI in a student-centered approach include:

- Analyzing student performance information and using genAI to assist in creating individualized learning paths to each student's strengths and weaknesses.
- Problem-Based Learning (PBL)
- Iterative processes

To analyze student performance, an educator can provide a reading level to the genAI chatbot and identify one or two strengths and areas for improvement. GenAI can then create a modified reading assignment tailored to the student's individualized needs.

The following is an example of how genAI may assist in creating an individualized learning path:

Prompt: I have a student who is reading at a second grade level, loves animals, and nature. Generate a text that my student can read aloud for fluency practice, incorporating those interests.

Claude: Here is a short text that your student who reads at a second-grade level and loves animals and nature can use for fluency practice:

Animal Adventures in Nature

Sam loves going on nature walks near his home. Last week, he went on a walk and saw so many amazing animals!

As Sam walked through the tall grass, he spotted a bunny nibbling on some clover. The bunny's soft, gray fur and twitching nose were so cute. Sam watched the bunny for a while before it hopped away.

Further down the path, Sam heard a rustling in the bushes. He peeked through the leaves and saw a squirrel scurrying up a tree, carrying a nut in its mouth. Sam giggled as the squirrel darted from branch to branch.

When Sam reached the pond, he sat down on a rock and watched the ducks gliding across the still water. One duck quacked loudly, making Sam jump a little. But then he laughed and tossed a few breadcrumbs for the ducks to eat.

As the sun started to set, Sam headed back home, excited to tell his family about all the wonderful animals he saw on his nature walk. He could't wait to go exploring in nature again soon! (Anthropic, 2024)

The story engages students' interests with appropriate details for the grade level. Claude misspelled "couldn't" in the last sentence, highlighting the need to review and correct AI-generated content regularly for accuracy. See Appendix A for additional AI-generated responses (Copilot, Gemini, & ChatGPT, n.d.).

Problem Based Learning (PBL)

Educators can leverage the power of genAI to develop PBL learning activities. By setting up scenarios that require students to investigate, analyze and address real-world problems, genAI can help create dynamic and interactive learning experiences that foster critical thinking and collaboration. Below is an example of how genAI can be used to design an educational activity focused on food webs:

Prompt: Give me a good problem-based learning activity for middle schoolers to understand the concept of food webs.

Gemini: This is a fantastic problem-based learning activity for middle schoolers to understand food webs! Here's a combined and enhanced version based on Claude's initial response and my suggestions:

Scenario:

The local [Name of Preserve] has issued an urgent plea! Their owl population has plummeted by 60% in the past two years. Ranger [Name], the preserve manager, suspects that disruptions to the delicate food web are the cause. Your team of ecologists must investigate and help Ranger [Name] save the owls!

Your Challenge:

- Identify the key organisms that make up the food web in the wildlife preserve.
- Analyze how these organisms are connected through feeding relationships.
- Determine what factors may be disrupting the balance of the food web and impacting the owl population.
- Develop a plan of action with specific recommendations to help restore the food web and support the owl population.

To complete this challenge, your team will:

- Research the common plants and animals found in the preserve.
- Create a visual diagram or model to represent the food web.

- Analyze how changes to one part of the web can affect other parts.
- Propose solutions that address the root causes of the food web imbalance.
- Present your findings and recommendations to the wildlife preserve staff (or a simulated audience).

Enhancements:

- **Conflicting Information:** Provide students with a report stating that the rabbit population (a key prey species for owls) has increased in recent years. This challenges them to look beyond simple predator-prey relationships.
- **Expert Consultation:** Arrange a video call with a local wildlife biologist who can answer student questions about owl behavior, habitat needs, and potential threats to their survival.
- **Field Research (if possible):** Incorporate a field trip to the preserve or a similar ecosystem. Have students collect data, observe organisms, and document their findings.
- **Data Analysis:** Provide students with real or simulated data (population counts, habitat maps, etc.) to analyze and use as evidence.
- **Multiple Perspectives:** Have students consider the problem from different perspectives (e.g., the owl, a prey animal, the wildlife preserve manager).
- **Ethical Dilemmas:** Present potential solutions with ethical implications (e.g., introducing a new predator).

Key Skills:

- Researching ecological concepts and local species
- Analyzing relationships between organisms
- Critical thinking to identify problems and solutions
- Collaboration and communication to work as a team
- Presenting technical information to stakeholders

Supplies Needed:

- Computers/tablets for research
- Art supplies for creating food web diagrams
- Notebooks and writing utensils

Time Allotment:

- Research and planning: 2-3 class periods
- Food web model creation: 1-2 class periods
- Analysis and solution development: 2 class periods
- Presentation preparation: 1-2 class periods
- Final presentation: 1 class period

Assessment:

- **Process and Product:** Assess both the process (research, collaboration, critical thinking) and the product (food web model, presentation, recommendations).
- **Self-Reflection:** Have students reflect on their learning process, challenges faced, and skills developed.
- **Peer Feedback:** Incorporate peer feedback on presentations and solutions.

This enhanced activity provides a truly immersive and impactful learning experience for your middle school students! (Claude; Google, 2024).

GenAI enables SCL by personalizing experiences. However, it is important to acknowledge that these tools are still under development and may not always accurately assess student needs or provide unbiased recommendations. Educators should use their professional judgment and knowledge of their students to guide the process.

Engagement

According to the principles outlined by Mollick, engagement is achieved by "Always inviting AI to the table" (Mollick, 2024, p. 47) and "Treating AI like a person but telling it what kind of person it is" (Mollick, 2024, p. 55). Here we prompted Copilot to generate a gamified learning experience for seventh-grade students studying forces and motion:

Prompt: Provide an example of using GenAI in a gamified learning experience for seventh grade students learning forces and motion. Include one challenge related to Newton's Laws of Motion and one challenge related to friction and surface types with a focus on interactive and hands-on activities to make the concepts engaging and memorable for the students.

Copilot: Gamified Learning Experience: "Mission to Mars"

Using GenAI to Teach Forces and Motion

Objective:

Students will learn about forces and motion by completing a series of interactive challenges that simulate a mission to successfully land a rover on Mars. The experience is designed to make the concepts engaging and memorable.

Storyline:

Students are part of a space mission team tasked with landing a rover on Mars. They must navigate through various challenges that require understanding and applying concepts of forces and motion. GenAI plays a pivotal role by guiding, assessing, and providing feedback throughout the mission.

Game Structure:

Introduction

GenAI Narrator: An AI character introduces the mission and provides background information on Mars and the importance of understanding forces and motion for space exploration.

Challenges

Challenge 1: Newton's Laws of Motion

Objective: Understand and apply Newton's Laws of Motion to navigate the rover through an obstacle course on Mars.

- *Interactive Activity: Students will use a virtual simulator to control the rover. They must predict and manipulate the rover's motion by applying Newton's First, Second, and Third Laws of Motion.*
- *Hands-On Activity: In a physical classroom setting, students use small, wheeled carts and various weights to recreate the simulator's challenges. They observe and record how different forces affect the motion according to Newton's laws.*

GenAI Assistance: The AI simulates the rover's movement and explains the effects of different forces, helping students make informed decisions. It provides real-time feedback and suggestions based on their actions.

Assessment System:

Formative Assessment

In-Game Quizzes: Short quizzes after each challenge to assess understanding and provide immediate feedback.

Reflection Questions: Open-ended questions prompting students to explain the concepts learned and how they applied them.

Summative Assessment

- *Final Project: Students create a detailed mission report explaining the challenges faced, solutions developed, and the scientific principles applied.*
- *Presentation: Students present their mission report to the class, demonstrating their understanding of forces and motion.*
- *GenAI Feedback: The AI provides personalized feedback on the final project and presentation, highlighting strengths and areas for improvement.*

Conclusion

By integrating GenAI into this gamified learning experience, students not only engage with complex scientific concepts but also benefit from personalized support and feedback, enhancing their overall learning journey (Microsoft, 2024).

The generated output combines science, math, and engineering at a suitable grade level and provides a clear framework for further study. The assessment system is in line with SCL principles. GenAI can increase engagement through gamified learning, but activities need to be designed to prevent over-dependence on technology. Students should be encouraged to actively participate and use critical thinking skills.

Readiness

Readiness aligns with "Be the human in the loop" (Mollick, 2024, p. 52). Being the human in the loop means being responsible and prepared to make judgments on using genAI. Both educators and students must be trained in using genAI effectively and ethically. Educators should understand genAI's capabilities and limitations, knowing when to incorporate it into teaching. Students need to use genAI appropriately and maintain academic integrity. Critical genAI literacy for students is discussed in the "Love" section of this chapter.

Virtual Assistant

Using genAI as a virtual assistant relates to "Always invite AI to the table" (Mollick, 2024, p. 47). Educators can use genAI to provide immediate responses to students and supply resources that enhance learning. Providing immediate responses involves delivering prompt constructive responses that facilitate increased understanding. We prompted Copilot to act as a virtual assistant to aid a 7th grade science student in comprehending Newton's 3rd law more effectively.

Prompt: *You are a friendly virtual assistant. Briefly describe to me, a 7th grade science student how Newton's 3rd law operates. Give me three real-life examples.*

Copilot: *Hey there, future scientist!*

Newton's 3rd Law is super cool, it says that **for every action, there's an equal and opposite reaction.**

Think of it like this: you can't touch something without it touching you back!

Here are some examples:

- ***Jumping on a trampoline:****You push down on the trampoline (action), and it springs back and pushes you up (reaction)!*
- ***Swimming:****You push the water backwards with your arms (action), and the water pushes you forward (reaction), making you move!*
- ***Rockets:****A rocket blasts hot gas downwards (action), and the gas pushes the rocket upwards (reaction), launching it into space!*

Pretty neat, huh? Forces always come in pairs, and they're always equal in strength but opposite in direction. Keep exploring the world and you'll see Newton's 3rd Law everywhere! (Microsoft, 2024).

Utilizing genAI as a virtual assistant allows educators to enhance and personalize the learning environment. While genAI virtual assistants can offer immediate responses and support, they should not substitute for human interaction and guidance. Educators should stay actively involved in the learning process and provide personalized support when necessary.

Inclusion

Principle: "Always invite AI to the Table" (Mollick, 2024, p. 47). EPPs can use genAI to foster more inclusive learning environments by recognizing and supporting student diversity in experiences, cultures, abilities, skills, personalities, and language (Sathy & Hogan, 2023). Examples include personalized learning paths, scaffolded learning, language support and accessibility.

Collaboration

Principle: "Be the human in the loop." GenAI can be used to facilitate collaboration between educators, students and genAI systems. Here are a few examples, provided by Gemini, of using genAI for collaboration in education:

Global classrooms: GenAI translation tools can facilitate communication and collaboration between students from different countries, promoting intercultural understanding and language learning.

Accessibility and inclusion: GenAI can provide real-time captioning, text-to-speech, and other assistive technologies, ensuring equal access to learning for all students, regardless of their abilities.

Teacher Communities: *Educators can use GenAI to connect with peers, share best practices, co-create lesson plans, and access professional development resources, fostering a collaborative learning community* (Gemini, 2024).

Evaluation

Principle: "Treat AI like a person (but tell it what kind of person it is)" (Mollick, 2024, p. 55). GenAI can continuously assess student performance, as shown in the "Mission to Mars" example, given within "Engagement" above.

As educators, we can incorporate the Mollick principles in utilizing genAI to enhance the educational environment. By integrating these principles, both educators and EPPs can effectively employ genAI to develop more efficient, engaging, inclusive, and personalized learning experiences. Table 1 aligns the SERVICE mnemonic with the Mollick Principles.

Table 1. SERVICE mnemonic aligned with Mollick's (2024) principles

Letter	Concept	Definition	Mollick Principle
S	Student-Centered Learning	Tailoring educational experiences to individual needs.	Always invite AI to the table; Treat AI like a person; Be the human in the loop; Assume this is the worst AI you will ever use
E	Engagement	Enhancing student involvement through interactive tools.	Always invite AI to the table; Treat AI like a person
R	Readiness	Preparing educators and students to effectively use genAI.	Be the human in the loop
V	Virtual Assistance	Using AI-driven assistants for real-time support.	Always invite AI to the table
I	Inclusion	Creating inclusive environments and encouraging innovative methods.	Always invite AI to the table; Assume this is the worst AI you will ever use
C	Collaboration	Fostering collaboration among educators, students, and AI.	Be the human in the loop
E	Evaluation	Providing continuous assessment of performance and effectiveness.	Treat AI like a person

The table provides a detailed alignment of the SERVICE mnemonic with the principles established by Mollick for the integration of genAI in education. In line with the practical applications identified within the SERVICE mnemonic, the CLAIM method developed by Prichard (2024) offers a systematic approach to integrating genAI into the curriculum and teaching cycle. The CLAIM method (Clarify, Locate, Access, Implement, Measure) aims to provide educators with a structured system to incorporate genAI into their instructional practices.

Following the CLAIM method involves the following steps:

- Clarify the purpose of the AI tool and its specific instructional goal, considering both benefits and limitations.
- Locate suitable AI tools based on criteria such as ease of use, accessibility, and alignment with course objectives.
- Access the tool appropriately for both educators and students.
- Implement AI into lesson preparation, research, assignments, or other activities.
- Measure the impact of AI on learning, performance, and other outcomes.
- Readjust procedures based on collected data and feedback.

We asked **Perplexity** to generate the following case study for using the CLAIM Method:

Prompt: *Generate a case study for using Prichard's CLAIM Method for Ms. Johnson, a middle school science teacher to integrate AI into her ecosystem unit*

Perplexity*: Case Study: The CLAIM Method for AI Integration in Education*

Ms. Johnson, a middle school science teacher, uses Prichard's CLAIM Method to integrate AI into her ecosystem unit:

1. Clarify: Enhance student engagement and collaborative learning.
2. Locate: Select an AI tool for interactive ecosystem simulations and collaborative projects.
3. Access: Review licensing, prepare hardware/software, and arrange accommodations.
4. Implement: Design a project where students create ecosystems using the AI tool.
5. Measure: Collect feedback, assess learning outcomes, and adjust future lessons.

Ethical considerations include ensuring information accuracy, equitable access, and promoting critical thinking. The CLAIM Method helps Ms. Johnson effectively integrate AI while addressing ethical concerns and preparing students for responsible technology use (Perplexity.ai, 2024).

The example does not identify the specific genAI technology used. It identifies a generic genAI tool and this does not provide the sufficient information to support the practical application of genAI in the educational environment. To rectify the situation, we prompted Gemini to review the scenario and select a specific genAI technology.

Prompt: *Review the CLAIM Method case study scenario and select a specific genAI technology Ms. Johnson should use to enhance her middle school science unit on ecosystems.*

Unsurprisingly **Gemini** chose itself:

You're right, using a generic "AI tool" makes this case study less impactful. To improve it, we need to incorporate a specific genAI tool and demonstrate its application in Ms. Johnson's classroom. Here's a modified version:

Ms. Johnson's Ecosystem Unit:

Ms. Johnson used Gemini to enhance her middle school science unit on ecosystems. Students used Gemini to:

- ***Research:***Gather information about organisms and their roles.*
- ***Write creatively:***Create stories, poems, or scripts from an organism's perspective.*
- ***Collaborate:***Brainstorm solutions to environmental challenges.*

Ethical Considerations:

Ms. Johnson emphasized responsible AI use by:

- *Teaching students to evaluate information accuracy.*
- *Promoting digital citizenship and avoiding plagiarism.*
- *Encouraging students to use AI as a tool, not a replacement for critical thinking.*

Results:

The CLAIM Method provided a structured approach for successful AI integration. Students were more engaged, collaborated effectively, and developed a responsible understanding of AI technologies (Google, 2024).

Summary

This section examined practical applications of genAI in education, elucidating the core concepts of **S**tudent-centered learning, **E**ngagement, **R**eadiness, **V**irtual assistance, **I**nclusion, **C**ollaboration, and **E**valuation (SERVICE) through real-world examples. By applying Mollick's (2024) principles of AI collaboration alongside Prichard's (2024) CLAIM method for systematic integration, educators and EPPs can ethically employ genAI. Responsible use of genAI can improve engaging learning environments for students.

Justice: Appropriate Standards for a Just, Equitable, Current and Future Role of GenAI in Education

Overview

The Interstate Teacher Assessment and Support Consortium (InTASC) Model Core Teaching Standards, published by the Council of Chief State School Officers (CCSSO, 2013), delineate the essential knowledge and skills that educators in the United States should possess to prepare students for college or the workforce. These standards are designed to align with other national and state standards documents (CCSSO, 2013). In this section, we examine how Educator Preparation Programs (EPPs) can incorporate genAI literacy within the InTASC standards.

We present our authors' evaluation of the genAI output and provide case use scenarios involving genAI. ScholarGPT (Awesomegpts.ai, 2024), accessed through the ChatGPT free version protocol in October 2024, performed the analysis. We supplemented this output with expansions from Perplexity (Perplexity.ai, 2024), also in the free version accessed in November 2024, and Gemini, the paid version after November 15, 2024.

Prompt: *You are an expert ethicist and educator. Review the following INTASC standards and propose changes that address the present and possibly future role of genAI in education. Generate your output in a list: Standard 1, current meaning with regards to genAI, revisions, future meaning. Here is a link to the standards:*https://ccsso.org/sites/default/files/2017-12/2013_INTASC_Learning_Progressions_for_educators.pdf

ScholarGPT (Awesomegpts.ai, 2024) provided the following interpretations of Standards 1–10, building on the original standards published by the Council of Chief State School Officers (CCSSO, 2013), as paraphrased by ScholarGPT (Awesomegpts.ai, 2024). The same attribution applies to each subsequent standard.

ScholarGPT: [indented, italicized, and bulleted responses below are quoted from ScholarGPT (with author evaluation non-italicized, non-bulleted, or within brackets)]

- *Here is a review of the* ***InTASC Standards*** *with proposed revisions to incorporate the current and future roles of* ***generative AI (genAI)*** *in education. The structure follows:* ***current meaning regarding genAI***, ***revisions***, *and* ***future meaning***.

Standard 1: Learner Development

- ***Current Meaning (regarding genAI):*** *Teachers understand how learners grow and develop and how various factors, including cognitive, linguistic,* *social, emotional, and physical development, affect learning. Currently, genAI can assist in personalizing instruction by adapting learning materials to individual developmental stages.*

- ***Revisions:****Teachers should not only understand learner development but also be equipped with the ability to critically assess and employ genAI technologies that support personalized learning. Teachers need to understand the limitations and biases in genAI technologies to ensure they align with students' developmental needs.*
- ***Future Meaning:****As genAI becomes more sophisticated, teachers will need to guide its use to not only adapt to but also predict developmental needs and learning paths, ensuring AI-generated recommendations are ethically sound and developmentally appropriate* (CCSSO, 2013), as paraphrased by ScholarGPT (Awesomegpts.ai, 2024).

Authors' Evaluation

Although we do not disagree with the potential for genAI to assist educators in implementing developmentally appropriate practices, it is important to add to the revisions that one limitation with genAI in its current modality—as mediated through screen-based interactions at this time—is the concern that screen-time itself may interfere with development, especially in young children and children with limited social opportunities (Sari & Yalçın, 2024; Stiles & Jernigan, 2010).

The following is ScholarGPT's response to the authors' evaluation above:

Prompt: *Please respond to this evaluation* [paragraph above inserted here]

ScholarGPT:

- *Your evaluation brings up an essential aspect of genAI in education that the initial revision did not fully address. While genAI can personalize learning, its current screen-based modality does raise valid developmental concerns, particularly for younger children and those with fewer social interactions. Extended screen time, especially without direct human mediation, may inadvertently impact children's cognitive, social, and emotional growth, which are key components of****developmentally appropriate practice****.*

In response to this, a **refinement** to the **revisions section** might be as follows:

- ***Revised Revisions****: Teachers should not only understand learner development and assess genAI technologies critically but should also evaluate and mediate screen-based interactions to balance genAI's benefits with the developmental needs of children. In particular, teachers should be aware of* *the potential drawbacks of prolonged screen time and prioritize developmentally appropriate, socially interactive experiences that align with the child's growth stage.*

- *This addition would encourage teachers to use genAI as a supplementary tool rather than a primary modality, especially for young learners, integrating it in ways that foster both digital literacy and real-world social learning. Such a balanced approach could help mitigate screen-time concerns while ensuring that AI-driven personalization aligns with students' holistic developmental needs* (Awesomegpts.ai, 2024).

ScholarGPT's response emphasizes the importance of balancing genAI's benefits with developmental needs of students, emphasizing its role as a supplementary tool. To explore this balance further, we prompted Gemini to provide a concrete example of genAI adapting learning materials to individual developmental stages.

Prompt: *Create a concrete example for how genAI can assist in personalizing instruction by adapting learning materials to individual developmental stages.*

Gemini: *Here's a concrete example of how GenAI can personalize instruction by adapting learning materials to individual developmental stages:*

Scenario: A 5th-grade class is learning about fractions. Within the class, there are students at varying developmental levels.

- ***Student A:****Struggles with basic number sense and needs foundational support.*
- ***Student B:****Grasps the concept of fractions but needs help applying them to real-world problems.*
- ***Student C:****Is advanced and ready for more complex challenges involving fractions.*

How GenAI Can Help:

- ***Assessment:****A GenAI-powered tool can assess each student's current understanding of fractions through adaptive questioning. It can identify their strengths, weaknesses, and developmental stages.*
- ***Personalized Content:****Based on the assessment, the genAI tech can generate:*
- ***For Student A:****Simple visual representations of fractions, interactive games to build number sense, and basic practice problems.*
- ***For Student B:****Word problems that connect fractions to everyday situations, like cooking or measuring ingredients.*
- ***For Student C:****Challenging puzzles involving fractions, opportunities to explore advanced concepts like ratios and proportions.*

- ***Progress Monitoring:****The genAI tech can continuously track student progress, adjusting the content and difficulty level in real-time to match their evolving understanding.*
- ***Educator Support:****The educator receives insights from the genAI tech about each student's learning journey, allowing them to provide targeted support and interventions.*

Benefits:

- ***Differentiated Instruction:****GenAI enables the educator to cater to the diverse needs of their students, ensuring that everyone is appropriately challenged and supported.*
- ***Student Engagement:****Personalized content that aligns with individual developmental stages is more likely to keep students engaged and motivated.*
- ***Improved Learning Outcomes:****By providing tailored instruction, GenAI can help students achieve better understanding and mastery of the subject matter.*

Remember:*The educator plays a crucial role in overseeing the process, ensuring that the GenAI-generated content is accurate, appropriate, and aligned with their pedagogical goals* (Google, 2024).

Educators face distinct challenges which vary by age group—elementary and middle school teachers, for example, address developmental complexities and foundational reading and math skills, while higher education faculty emphasize generalizing skills for self-determination. With the following prompt we further explore how educators may begin to use genAI for supporting students with learning disabilities.

Prompt: *How can genAI be used to address the needs of students with learning disabilities*?

Gemini: *GenAI can be a powerful tool for addressing the diverse needs of students with learning disabilities in several ways:*

- ***Personalized Content:****GenAI can adapt learning materials to suit individual learning styles and preferences. For example, it can present information in various formats (text, audio, visual) to cater to different learning modalities.*
- ***Assistive Technology:****GenAI can power assistive technologies like text-to-speech, speech-to-text, and visual aids, making content more accessible for students with reading, writing, or visual impairments.*
- ***Individualized Support:****GenAI can provide targeted interventions and support based on individual needs. For instance, it can offer additional practice problems for students struggling with specific concepts or provide prompts and guidance for those who need help staying on task.*

- ***Progress Monitoring:****GenAI can track student progress and identify areas of difficulty, allowing educators to provide timely interventions and adjustments to instruction.*
- ***Universal Design for Learning (UDL):****GenAI can help implement UDL principles by offering multiple means of representation, engagement, and action and expression. This ensures that content is accessible to all learners, including those with disabilities.*

By leveraging these capabilities, GenAI can help create a more inclusive and supportive learning environment for students with learning disabilities, empowering them to reach their full potential (Google, 2024).

Standard 2: Learning Differences

- ***Current Meaning (regarding genAI)****: Teachers adapt their teaching for diverse learners and incorporate inclusive practices. GenAI technologies currently provide individualized content, language translation, and adaptive learning strategies to support learning differences.*
- ***Revisions****: Teachers must learn how to evaluate genAI technologies to ensure they are effectively addressing learning differences and not perpetuating inequities. Training in ethical AI use, including the detection of biased algorithms, should be incorporated into this standard.*
- ***Future Meaning****: GenAI will likely play a larger role in identifying and accommodating learning differences automatically. Teachers will need to ensure that these AI-driven accommodations are fair, culturally responsive, and adaptable to dynamic classroom environments* (CCSSO, 2013), as paraphrased by ScholarGPT (Awesomegpts.ai, 2024).

Authors' Evaluation

The performance and potential of genAI technologies already show remarkable benefits regarding individualizing content, translating, revising for reading level, and other support and prompting mechanisms, including special education practices such as task analysis, behavior analysis, and explicit direct instruction (Khazanchi & Khazanchi, 2024). As noted in the emphasis on adaptive learning strategies above, genAI literacy training should include teaching educators how to deploy effective and ethical differentiation strategies, as well as ensuring access to the most effective tools to implement those strategies. Interestingly, parental education level appears to be a factor in teens' adoption of genAI, suggesting a need for EPPs to engage families and communities in promoting AI literacy (Madden et al., 2024). Research indicates that Black and Latino teens are more likely to engage with genAI for a wider range of activities compared to their White peers (Madden et al., 2024). This highlights the importance of addressing equity and inclusion in AI education, to ensure that all students have access to genAI and are empowered to use it effectively.

Prompt: *Provide a concrete example of* [complete text of "Authors' evaluation" from the paragraph above inserted here]

Gemini: *Here's a concrete example illustrating the authors' evaluation of GenAI's potential in special education:*

Scenario: A student with a learning disability in reading comprehension is struggling to understand a complex text about the Civil War.

How GenAI Can Help:

- ***Text Simplification:*** *The genAI tech can revise the text to a lower reading level, using simpler vocabulary and sentence structures while preserving the core meaning.*
- ***Visual Supports:*** *The tool can generate images, diagrams, or timelines to help the student visualize the events and concepts in the text.*
- ***Task Analysis:*** *The GenAI can break down the reading assignment into smaller, more manageable steps, providing prompts and guidance to help the student navigate the text.*
- ***Explicit Direct Instruction:*** *The tool can provide clear explanations and examples of key concepts, offering additional practice opportunities to reinforce understanding.*
- ***Behavior Analysis:*** *If the student exhibits off-task behaviors, the genAI tech can track these patterns and suggest strategies for the educator to address them, such as providing frequent breaks or movement activities.*

GenAI Literacy Training for educators:

- ***Tool Selection:*** *Educators learn to evaluate and select the most effective genAI technologies for supporting students with diverse learning needs.*
- ***Ethical Use:*** *Educators are trained to use these tools ethically, ensuring that they respect student privacy, avoid bias, and promote equitable access.*
- ***Differentiation Strategies:*** *Educators learn how to use genAI to implement effective differentiation strategies, tailoring instruction to individual student needs.*
- ***Critical Thinking:*** *Educators are encouraged to critically evaluate genAI-generated content and recommendations, ensuring that they align with best practices in special education.*

Outcome: The student with a learning disability can access and understand the text about the Civil War with the support of genAI technologies. The educator, equipped with genAI literacy, can effectively implement these tools to provide individualized instruction and support.

Key Takeaway:*This example demonstrates how genAI's capabilities in text adaptation, visual supports, task analysis, explicit instruction, and behavior analysis can be leveraged to address the needs of students with learning disabilities. However, the effective and ethical use of these tools requires educators to be trained in genAI literacy and differentiation strategies* (Google, 2024).

Authors' Summary

GenAI has strong potential to support diverse learners by providing individualized content, language translation, and adaptive learning strategies. However, realizing this potential depends on appropriate educator training in evaluating GenAI for effectiveness and equity, alongside mitigating algorithmic biases through thorough "human-in-the-loop" oversight (Mollick, 2024). Such oversight ensures fair, culturally responsive, and adaptable practices, particularly in special education fields, including task analysis, explicit instruction, and behavior analysis. Integrating GenAI critical literacy into Educator Preparation Programs (EPPs) should also address disparities in AI adoption and access, while tackling persistent cultural, linguistic, and socio-economic inequities to promote equity and inclusion for all learners.

Standard 3: Learning Environments

- ***Current Meaning (regarding genAI)****: Teachers create environments that support individual and collaborative learning. GenAI technologies currently help by providing personalized learning experiences, but teachers must carefully balance AI use with fostering human collaboration.*
- ***Revisions****: Teachers should be trained to integrate genAI in ways that maintain human-centered learning environments. AI should enhance, not replace, interpersonal relationships and collaborative learning. Teachers must be vigilant about AI tools that might isolate learners or reduce engagement.*
- ***Future Meaning****: Future AI-driven classrooms will likely rely on AI to manage and optimize the learning environment. Teachers will need to ensure that AI tools contribute to positive social interactions, emotional well-being, and inclusive collaboration* (CCSSO, 2013), as paraphrased by ScholarGPT (Awesomegpts.ai, 2024).

Authors' Evaluation

Educational technology has already impacted how children and educators interact with their environment. Although access to digital or virtual information can enhance education, the technology required for access often adds to the distraction that some children already face in school, particularly those marginalized by socioeconomic status (Kärki, 2024). There have also been several cases in which other technology usage has been banned or limited by school policy because the inappropriate use of the product may outweigh its benefits, e.g., cell phones (Walker, 2023).

To consider resolutions to the problem of digital distraction in educational environments, the author's submitted the following prompt to genAI Claude.

Prompt: *Given the following information, generate a concrete example of genAI usage that exemplifies the enhancement of collaborative learning and optimization of the learning environment*: [Complete text from "Standard 3: Learning Environments…" to "Authors' evaluation…" pasted into the chatbot]

Claude: *Let me design a practical classroom scenario that demonstrates how genAI can enhance collaboration while being mindful of potential distractions and inclusivity concerns.*

Example: "The Community History Project"

In this learning activity, students work in small groups to research and document their local community's history, using genAI as a facilitator rather than the primary tool:

1. Initial Research Phase:
    - Students first conduct traditional interviews with community members and gather physical artifacts
    - Each group uses a genAI tech (like Claude) to generate thoughtful follow-up questions based on their initial findings
    - The AI helps identify potential historical connections they might have missed
2. Collaborative Analysis:
    - Groups meet in person to compare findings
    - They use genAI to help organize their collected information into themes
    - The educator provides structured prompts for the AI to ensure it helps facilitate discussion rather than replacing it, such as:

"What patterns do you notice in your collected stories?"
"What questions remain unanswered?"

3. Interactive Presentation Development:

- Students work together to create multimedia presentations
- GenAI assists with:
- Suggesting presentation structures that highlight student voices
- Generating discussion questions for peer feedback
- Helping edit and refine content while preserving student authenticity

Key Implementation Features:

- AI use is time-bounded and structured (15-20 minute sessions)
- Work happens primarily in physical space with AI as a support tool
- Educators actively monitor for signs of distraction or over-reliance on AI
- Alternative non-digital methods are always available
- Focus remains on human interaction and relationship building

This example addresses both the enhancement and risk factors outlined in the source material by:

- Maintaining human collaboration at the center
- Using AI to augment rather than replace social interaction
- Providing structured, limited technology use to minimize distraction
- Ensuring activities can be completed without technology if needed
- Creating opportunities for meaningful peer-to-peer and community engagement

Would you like me to elaborate on any aspect of this example or suggest additional ways to implement it? (Anthropic, 2024).

Authors' Evaluation

Although genAI Claude's "Community History Project" response provides a commendable example of limiting technology use by time, procedural and content organization, in order to optimize learning while preserving student agency and voice, emphasizing the "human-in-the-loop" principle (Mollick, 2024). Delegating the collection and organization of themes to AI raises concerns about reducing students' opportunities to engage in critical thinking, problem-solving, and human-to-human collaboration. The next standard further examines collaboration in content generation.

Standard 4: Content Knowledge

- ***Current Meaning (regarding genAI)****: Teachers understand the subject they teach and how to convey it to learners. GenAI can now assist with con-*

tent generation and provide resources or materials tailored to the needs of students.

- ***Revisions****: Teachers should develop AI literacy, enabling them to use genAI technologies effectively while maintaining authority over content. They should be trained to critically assess AI-generated content for accuracy, relevance, and bias.*
- ***Future Meaning****: As genAI improves, it may increasingly contribute to content development. Teachers will need to balance the use of AI as a content creator with ensuring that it aligns with curriculum standards, ethical considerations, and critical pedagogical objectives* (CCSSO, 2013), as paraphrased by ScholarGPT (Awesomegpts.ai, 2024).

Authors' Evaluation

Educators will increasingly also be learning their content through genAI-enhanced sources. As we have used genAI for content generation in this chapter, we have had to critically assess both our own content knowledge, and the perception of machine-mediated content knowledge. This dual role—educator as both facilitator and learner—demands a reliable capacity to critically evaluate AI-generated content for accuracy, relevance, and alignment with pedagogical goals. The roles of educators and students should not be reduced to merely utilizing genAI as a tool; instead, effective critical inquiry requires both groups to actively question and assess the sources and processes involved in the creation of knowledge.

Standard 5: Application of Content

- ***Current Meaning (regarding genAI)****: Teachers connect content to real-world issues and interdisciplinary themes, often using technology. GenAI currently aids in providing case studies, simulations, and examples that connect content to practical applications.*
- ***Revisions****: Teachers should be trained to guide genAI in generating contextually relevant and ethically sound real-world applications. This includes understanding the boundaries of genAI's problem-solving capabilities and addressing its ethical implications in real-world scenarios.*
- ***Future Meaning****: GenAI will likely be able to generate complex simulations and predictive models for problem-solving. Teachers will need to ensure that these tools foster critical thinking and creativity while keeping ethical and real-world consequences in focus* (CCSSO, 2013), as paraphrased by ScholarGPT (Awesomegpts.ai, 2024).

Author's Evaluation

We employed genAI Perplexity to evaluate the output of Standard 5 from: "*Teachers connect content to real-world issues. . .*" to "*. . .practical applications*" from "***Current Meaning***" above. Perplexity added:

This approach not only enhances student engagement but also helps in contextualizing learning within real-world scenarios. For instance, genAI can facilitate the development of interactive role plays that adapt to individual student responses, thereby providing tailored educational experiences that reflect real-life complexities (Perplexity.ai, 2024; Prudhomme-Genereux, 2024).

Perplexity also suggested the following revisions:

To optimize the effectiveness of genAI in education, it is essential that educators receive training on how to guide its use in generating contextually relevant and ethically sound applications. This includes:

Understanding Boundaries: Educators must be aware of the limitations inherent in genAI's problem-solving capabilities, ensuring that students are not misled by overly simplistic or inaccurate outputs.

Addressing Ethical Implications: Educators should incorporate discussions on the ethical considerations of using genAI, preparing students to navigate potential moral dilemmas in practical applications (Perplexity.ai, 2024).

Standard 6: Assessment

- ***Current Meaning (regarding genAI)****: Teachers use various assessment methods to measure student progress. GenAI technologies currently help by providing automated formative assessments and personalized feedback.*
- ***Revisions****: Teachers must learn how to interpret AI-driven assessments and understand the ethical implications of using AI for high-stakes testing. They should be trained in the ethical use of student data and the limitations of genAI assessments.*
- ***Future Meaning****: In the future, AI will likely handle much of the assessment process, including predicting learning outcomes. Teachers will need to ensure that these AI assessments remain fair, transparent, and accessible, with a clear understanding of how AI-generated assessments influence teaching strategies* (CCSSO, 2013), as paraphrased by ScholarGPT (Awesomegpts.ai, 2024).

Authors' Evaluation

Several legal considerations arise when considering using genAI technologies for assessment. Due to the technology, it may not always be clear when an assessment is taking place. One may assume that any recorded technological activity could become an assessment. Unlike traditional assessments, where, by law, schools must explicitly inform students and parents about the process, genAI "black box" processes can further obscure the assessment mechanism technologies, embedding evaluative components into routine interactions without providing explicit notice, raising concerns around informed consent (Individuals with Disabilities Education Act, 2004). Parental rights to due process in special education require non-discriminatory assessment (Individuals with Disabilities Education Act, 2004). Parents must be given notice and consent to assessment that may impact eligibility for special education (Individuals with Disabilities Education Act, 2004). It is not clear that genAI meets the requirements for valid nondiscriminatory assessment in its current state.

Standard 7: Planning for Instruction

- ***Current Meaning (regarding genAI)****: Teachers plan instruction by drawing upon knowledge of learners, content, and pedagogy. GenAI can assist by creating personalized lesson plans and adapting content to individual learning needs.*
- ***Revisions:****Teachers should be trained to critically review genAI-generated lesson plans and ensure that these plans align with ethical standards and pedagogical goals. Understanding AI biases in lesson planning is critical to prevent harmful educational practices.*
- ***Future Meaning****: GenAI will likely evolve into a co-planner for teachers, continuously optimizing and updating lesson plans based on real-time student data. Teachers will need to maintain final authority over instruction, ensuring AI recommendations are ethically sound and pedagogically appropriate* (CCSSO, 2013), as paraphrased by ScholarGPT (Awesomegpts.ai, 2024).

Authors' Evaluation

Many educators have already adopted genAI as a time-saving tool for instructional planning (Angelone & Burton, 2024). In order to effectively use the genAI technology, educators must share with genAI their knowledge of learners, their content, and their pedagogy preferences. Caution is needed when the information shared could be personally identified and compromised. Educators should also plan for inevitabilities such as genAI hallucinations, mistakes, or inconsistencies.

Familiarity with genAI and themselves may help educators decide whether their time is better spent in planning to avoid errors on the front-end or responding to the errors in real time during the lesson itself (Butler-Ulrich et al., 2024).

Standard 8: Instructional Strategies

- ***Current Meaning (regarding genAI)****: Teachers use a variety of instructional strategies to encourage students' critical thinking. GenAI currently offers tools like chatbots, simulations, and personalized learning paths to support instruction.*
- ***Revisions****: Teachers must learn how to blend genAI strategies with human instruction to foster engagement and deeper learning. They should be equipped to challenge AI-generated strategies that might reinforce passive learning or lack critical depth.*
- ***Future Meaning****: As genAI becomes more advanced in generating instructional strategies, teachers will need to ensure that these strategies encourage active, creative, and critical thinking. Ethical considerations, such as inclusivity and fairness in AI-generated strategies, will be central* (CCSSO, 2013), as paraphrased by ScholarGPT (Awesomegpts.ai, 2024).

Authors' Evaluation

The goal is to incorporate genAI to enhance instruction, not replace the educator. To ensure this, the educator should be familiar enough with instructional strategies so that human judgment has precedence over the genAI output. Some instructional strategies are dependent on an AI-bot interacting directly with a student (see example using genAI as a virtual assistant in the "Service" section). In other cases, the educator interacts with the bot and then employs the strategy independently with the student one-on-one or with the class. EPPs should advocate for educators to exercise critical genAI literacy and the freedom and authority to make appropriate instructional strategy decisions.

Standard 9: Professional Learning and Ethical Practice

- ***Current Meaning (regarding genAI)****: Teachers engage in ongoing professional learning and exhibit ethical behavior. GenAI can assist by providing personalized professional development resources.*
- ***Revisions****: Teachers must continuously update their genAI literacy and critically engage with new genAI tools. Ethical practice should now include understanding and mitigating the biases and limitations of genAI in both instruction and assessment.*

- ***Future Meaning****: As genAI becomes a core part of education, teachers will need to engage in lifelong learning focused on both genAI technologies and their ethical use. Ethical genAI use will become a key professional standard, requiring teachers to advocate for equitable and responsible genAI practices* (CCSSO, 2013), as paraphrased by ScholarGPT (Awesomegpts.ai, 2024)

Authors' Evaluation

Because ethical use and professional learning overlap considerably with the purpose of this chapter, we continued our exploration of each of Standard 9's subcomponents in the second part of this section after addressing Standard 10 below.

Standard 10: Leadership and Collaboration

- ***Current Meaning (regarding genAI)****: Teachers collaborate with stakeholders and take leadership in promoting learner growth. GenAI can aid in collaborative planning and student progress tracking.*
- ***Revisions****: Teachers should take a leadership role in advocating for the ethical use of genAI in schools, ensuring that genAI tools are implemented equitably and transparently. They must work with school administrators, policymakers, and the community to establish clear ethical guidelines for genAI in education.*
- ***Future Meaning****: As genAI becomes more embedded in educational systems, teachers will need to lead discussions on genAI ethics, advocating for policies that promote fairness, transparency, and accountability in genAI use across schools and districts* (CCSSO, 2013), as paraphrased by ScholarGPT (Awesomegpts.ai, 2024).

Authors' Evaluation

We firmly believe that it is imperative for educators to champion and enforce suitable policies regarding technology usage within schools, districts, and the broader community. Because Standard 9 bears most directly on the topic of this chapter, we also submitted more specific information from Standard 9 so that genAI could analyze the alphabetized list of substandards in the same manner. Below is our subsequent prompt to Scholar GPT:

Prompt: *Propose changes that address the present and possibly future role of genAI in education. Generate your output in a list: Standard 9a, current meaning with regards to genAI, revisions, future meaning* [Standards 9a-9n organized by performances (9a-9f), essential knowledge (9g-k), and critical dispositions (9l-o) were pasted into the input window (CCSSO, 2013)].

ScholarGPT: *Here's a proposed revision of* ***InTASC Standard 9****(Professional Learning and Ethical Practice) to address the present and future role of* ***generative AI (genAI)****in education. Each substandard is outlined with its* ***current meaning****, suggested* ***revisions*** *for integrating genAI, and its* ***future implications****.*

9(a) Ongoing Learning Opportunities

- ***Current Meaning (regarding genAI)****: Teachers engage in continuous learning to stay current with local and state standards, using genAI to access personalized resources.*
- ***Revisions****: Teachers should integrate genAI technologies into their professional development to stay updated with evolving educational technology and methods. These tools can suggest personalized learning paths aligned with state standards and student needs.*
- ***Future Meaning****: GenAI will likely predict teachers' learning needs based on classroom data, offering real-time, tailored professional development that adapts to both local standards and emerging technologies* (CCSSO, 2013), as paraphrased by ScholarGPT (Awesomegpts.ai, 2024).

Authors' Evaluation

We highly recommend that present and future educators avail themselves of myriad professional development opportunities either enhanced by or about genAI. Although the predictive capabilities of genAI have yet to be fully developed, real-time assistance is already possible with chatbots that can refresh an educator's content knowledge or provide appropriate strategies during the teaching process.

9(b) Professional Learning Alignment

- ***Current Meaning (regarding genAI)****: Teachers engage in professional learning experiences tailored to their own and their students' needs, using genAI to recommend resources.*
- ***Revisions****: Teachers should develop genAI literacy to effectively engage with genAI-generated professional learning recommendations. They must critically evaluate these suggestions to ensure alignment with student, school, and system needs.*
- ***Future Meaning****: GenAI could provide dynamic, data-driven recommendations for professional learning experiences, constantly updating based on teacher performance, learner outcomes, and institutional goals* (CCSSO, 2013), as paraphrased by ScholarGPT (Awesomegpts.ai, 2024).

Authors' Evaluation

We emphasize the urgent necessity for a comprehensive understanding of the opportunities and risks (to privacy, equity, and learning) associated with genAI. Given that institutional objectives around genAI may be in their infancy, educators must tread carefully during implementation. However, they should also act with appropriate haste to cultivate critical genAI literacy, since the technology is already in widespread use.

9(c) Use of Data for Planning and Practice

- ***Current Meaning (regarding genAI)****: Teachers use various data sources to evaluate teaching outcomes and adjust practices. GenAI helps by analyzing vast amounts of data to identify patterns and provide actionable insights.*
- ***Revisions****: Teachers should be trained to interpret genAI-generated data and use it ethically in their instructional planning. They must ensure that genAI-driven insights are grounded in accurate data and ethical practice, considering privacy and fairness.*
- ***Future Meaning****: GenAI will likely automate much of the data analysis for planning and practice, providing immediate feedback and recommendations. Teachers will need to retain oversight to ensure data-driven decisions are inclusive and pedagogically sound* (CCSSO, 2013), as paraphrased by ScholarGPT (Awesomegpts.ai, 2024).

Authors' Evaluation

GenAI is revolutionizing data analysis. Protecting data privacy is even more crucial in educational policy due to genAI's potential use of identifying data and risks to the confidentiality of the data. See 9(h) further below.

9(d) Professional and Technological Resources

- ***Current Meaning (regarding genAI)****: Teachers seek technological and community resources for problem-solving and reflection. GenAI currently assists by offering automated research, reflections, and resource suggestions.*
- ***Revisions****: Teachers should expand their use of genAI technologies to access diverse resources, but they must remain critical of the sources and ensure AI-generated content is relevant, ethical, and accurate.*
- ***Future Meaning****: Teachers will use genAI not only to gather resources but also to analyze and reflect on their teaching in real time, using genAI as*

a co-mentor. Ethical standards will need to ensure the genAI systems they rely on are transparent and accountable (CCSSO, 2013), as paraphrased by ScholarGPT (Awesomegpts.ai, 2024).

Authors' Evaluation

GenAI's potential as a meta-resource offers unprecedented opportunities for problem-solving and introspection. Nevertheless, it is essential to prioritize sound pedagogical principles over technological innovation in education.

9(e) Reflection on Bias and Cultural Competency

- ***Current Meaning (regarding genAI)****: Teachers reflect on personal biases and use resources to deepen their understanding of diversity. GenAI can currently assist by providing materials on cultural responsiveness and implicit bias training.*
- ***Revisions****: Teachers should be trained to use genAI technologies that promote self-awareness and cultural competence, ensuring that AI-generated content is free from bias and fosters inclusivity.*
- ***Future Meaning****: GenAI could play a greater role in identifying and mitigating teacher biases by providing real-time feedback during instruction. Teachers will need to critically assess genAI feedback to ensure it aligns with culturally responsive teaching* (CCSSO, 2013), as paraphrased by ScholarGPT (Awesomegpts.ai, 2024).

Authors' Evaluation

We notice the critical necessity for a comprehensive understanding of the potential benefits (i.e., as a training tool) and risks (from training data and data-based bias) associated with genAI. The question remains: can genAI be relied upon as either an ethical trainer or a bias resolver for culturally responsive educators?

9(f) Safe, Legal, and Ethical Use of Technology

- ***Current Meaning (regarding genAI)****: Teachers model the safe and ethical use of technology. GenAI currently helps by assisting in information sourcing, but there are concerns around intellectual property, privacy, and ethical genAI use.*
- ***Revisions****: Teachers must understand the ethical and legal ramifications of using genAI technologies in the classroom. This includes ensuring that genAI*

respects privacy, copyright laws, and fosters an environment of respect for the use of technology.

- ***Future Meaning**: As genAI becomes more integrated, educators will need to be vigilant about the ethical deployment of these tools. GenAI systems will need built-in mechanisms to ensure ethical usage and compliance with legal standards* (CCSSO, 2013), as paraphrased by ScholarGPT (Awesomegpts.ai, 2024).

Authors' Evaluation

This chapter has not explored the difficulties of intellectual property rights and other legal concerns in this chapter, yet there is evidence that genAI is influencing fair use laws (U. S. Copyright Office, 2023). As new interpretations of the law are awaited, it is advisable to proceed with caution. In addition to critical genAI literacy skills, educators must also familiarize themselves with their professional ethical standards (see 9(j) further below) and technology use laws (U. S. Copyright Office, 2023).

9(g) Self-Assessment and Problem-Solving

- ***Current Meaning (regarding genAI)**: Teachers use self-assessment to reflect on and improve practice. GenAI can assist by providing insights into teaching performance.*
- ***Revisions**: Teachers should incorporate genAI-driven self-assessments but must remain cautious of genAI-driven metrics that might not fully capture the nuances of effective teaching.*
- ***Future Meaning**: GenAI will increasingly automate self-assessment and suggest improvements, but teachers must continue to interpret these suggestions through a reflective and ethical lens* (CCSSO, 2013), as paraphrased by ScholarGPT (Awesomegpts.ai, 2024).

Authors' Evaluation

Self-assessment is one of the most difficult aspects of professionalism because we are often blind to our own weaknesses. Although those who apply the technology cannot always trust that genAI will point out weaknesses, if prompted correctly, it may help identify blind spots in self-assessment.

9(h) Use of Learner Data

- ***Current Meaning (regarding genAI)****: Teachers use learner data to differentiate instruction. GenAI can analyze data and recommend strategies.*
- ***Revisions****: Teachers must be trained to critically assess AI interpretations of data, ensuring that these tools do not perpetuate inequities or biases in instruction.*
- ***Future Meaning****: GenAI will likely handle much of the learner data analysis, offering increasingly precise differentiation strategies. Teachers must maintain oversight to ensure these strategies are equitable and inclusive* (CCSSO, 2013), as paraphrased by ScholarGPT (Awesomegpts.ai, 2024).

Authors' Evaluation

Involving students and families in discussions about the ethical use of AI and data privacy may increase the transparency of genAI.

9(i) Understanding Identity and Bias

- ***Current Meaning (regarding genAI)****: Teachers recognize how personal identity and bias affect interactions. GenAI can provide insights into cultural competence and bias.*
- ***Revisions****: Teachers should use genAI technologies for continuous reflection on identity and bias, ensuring these tools do not reinforce biases themselves.*
- ***Future Meaning****: AI will likely assist teachers in identifying and addressing biases in real time, allowing for immediate interventions. However, teachers will need to ensure genAI-driven actions align with ethical teaching practices* (CCSSO, 2013), as paraphrased by ScholarGPT (Awesomegpts.ai, 2024).

Authors' Evaluation

Although bias-free genAI systems may be imagined, they do not yet exist. Nonetheless, genAI may yet become a powerful tool for helping teachers understand their own biases. In the meantime, educators may want to seek to reduce bias in their educational approach as part of their own critical genAI literacy.

9(j) Legal Responsibilities

- ***Current Meaning (regarding genAI):*** *Teachers understand legal responsibilities related to education. GenAI can help by offering real-time reminders about legal obligations.*
- ***Revisions:*** *Teachers should be trained to use genAI in compliance with laws related to student rights, privacy, and equitable education, ensuring that AI tools do not inadvertently violate these regulations.*
- ***Future Meaning:*** *GenAI could become a key tool in monitoring legal compliance, but teachers must remain responsible for ensuring that genAI systems operate within legal and ethical boundaries* (CCSSO, 2013), as paraphrased by ScholarGPT (Awesomegpts.ai, 2024).

Authors' Evaluation

Our intention is to briefly review key laws that interact with genAI literacy. We prompted Gemini to generate the following genAI elaboration to skim the surface of this important topic:

Prompt: *Briefly cite and explain key laws related to education that will likely impact or be impacted by genAI.*

Gemini: *Generative AI in education intersects with several key laws, creating both opportunities and challenges:*

1. Family Educational Rights and Privacy Act (FERPA).
   - ***What it is:****FERPA protects the privacy of student education records. (Family Educational Rights and Privacy Act of 1974, 20 U.S.C. § 1232g, 1974)*
   - ***GenAI implications:****Schools must ensure AI tools comply with FERPA when handling student data, especially when sharing it with third-party AI providers. This includes obtaining consent, data security measures, and transparency about data usage.*
2. Children's Online Privacy Protection Act (COPPA).
   - ***What it is:****COPPA applies to websites and online services collecting personal information from children under 13 (Children's Online Privacy Protection Act of 1998, 15 U.S.C. §§ 6501-6506, 1998).*
   - ***GenAI implications:****EdTech companies developing AI tools for young children must comply with COPPA's parental consent and data protection requirements. This is crucial for AI systems that personalize learning or track student progress.*
3. Americans with Disabilities Act (ADA).

- ***What it is:***_ADA prohibits discrimination based on disability and requires equal access to education (Americans with Disabilities Act of 1990, 42 U.S.C. § 12101 et seq., 1990)._
- ***GenAI implications:***_AI can be used to create accessible learning experiences for students with disabilities (e.g., personalized learning, assistive technologies). However, it's crucial to ensure AI tools are designed inclusively and don't create new barriers to access._

4. Copyright Law.
    - ***What it is:***_Copyright protects original works of authorship (Copyright Act of 1976, 17 U.S.C. § 101 et seq., 1976)._
    - ***GenAI implications:***_Questions arise around the copyright of AI-generated content (who owns it, how it can be used). Educators and students need guidance on using AI for creative work while respecting copyright._
5. Anti-Discrimination Laws (e.g., Title VI of the Civil Rights Act).
    - ***What it is:***_These laws prohibit discrimination in education based on race, color, national origin, etc.(Civil Rights Act of 1964, Title VI, 42 U.S.C. § 2000d et seq., 1964)._
    - ***GenAI implications:***_AI algorithms can perpetuate or amplify existing biases. Schools must ensure AI systems used for assessment, placement, or discipline do not discriminate against protected groups._

Looking Ahead.

- ***Algorithmic accountability:***_As AI plays a larger role in education, there will be a need for greater transparency and accountability in how algorithms are used and their potential impact on students._
- ***Data privacy:***_Protecting student data privacy will become even more critical as AI systems collect and analyze vast amounts of information._
- ***Ethical considerations:***_Laws and guidelines may need to evolve to address the ethical implications of AI in education, such as fairness, bias, and the impact on human interaction._

It's important for educators, policymakers, and EdTech developers to collaborate in navigating these legal and ethical complexities to ensure AI is used responsibly and equitably in education (Google, 2024).

Authors' Evaluation

Although Gemini overlooked the special education law, we touched upon it briefly already in reviewing "***Standard 6: Assessment***" further above in this section (Individuals with Disabilities Education Act, 2004).

9(k) Professional Growth Plan

- ***Current Meaning (regarding genAI)****: Teachers build growth plans based on feedback and data. GenAI can suggest professional growth opportunities tailored to teacher needs.*
- ***Revisions:****Teachers should use genAI to personalize their professional growth plans but should critically evaluate the suggestions and adjust them based on personal reflection and school-wide priorities.*
- ***Future Meaning****: GenAI could serve as an individualized coach, continuously updating professional growth plans based on real-time data. Teachers will need to ensure these plans align with long-term career goals and ethical teaching practices* (CCSSO, 2013), as paraphrased by ScholarGPT (Awesomegpts.ai, 2024).

9(l) Responsibility for Student Learning

- ***Current Meaning (regarding genAI)****: Teachers take responsibility for student learning and use ongoing reflection to improve practice. GenAI can assist by offering insights into student progress and suggesting instructional adjustments.*
- ***Revisions****: Teachers should utilize genAI technologies for real-time reflection and adaptation of their teaching strategies but maintain responsibility for interpreting and implementing AI suggestions.*
- ***Future Meaning****: GenAI will likely take on a larger role in analyzing and providing feedback on teaching effectiveness, but teachers must continue to exercise judgment in its application to ensure the AI aligns with student-centered learning* (CCSSO, 2013), as paraphrased by ScholarGPT (Awesomegpts.ai, 2024).

Authors' Evaluation

We focused on SCL in the "Service" section of this chapter.

9(m) Deepening Understanding of Bias

- ***Current Meaning (regarding genAI):*** *Teachers work to understand their personal biases and how they affect teaching. GenAI technologies can provide training in diversity and bias awareness.*
- ***Revisions:*** *Teachers should use genAI technologies that detect and correct biases in instructional materials and assessment practices. GenAI systems need to be regularly audited for biases themselves.*
- ***Future Meaning:*** *GenAI may play a proactive role in helping teachers identify biases in real time, allowing for immediate corrections. Teachers will need to balance trust in genAI with critical oversight to ensure bias mitigation is thorough and culturally sensitive* (CCSSO, 2013), as paraphrased by ScholarGPT (Awesomegpts.ai, 2024).

Authors' Evaluation

Understanding and addressing algorithmic bias is a critical aspect of genAI literacy. GenAI technologies are not neutral and can reflect biases in their data and algorithms, making it essential to critically evaluate these tools. Training on bias awareness and ethical genAI use can empower educators with an equity mindset, ensuring that genAI supports culturally sensitive and unbiased teaching practices (Liu & Gu, 2024; Long & Magerko, 2020).

9(n) Teacher as Continuous Learner

- ***Current Meaning (regarding genAI):*** *Teachers continuously seek opportunities for professional growth, drawing from education policy and research. GenAI currently aids educators and researchers by recommending relevant articles and suggesting avenues for professional development.*
- ***Revisions:*** *Teachers should integrate genAI into their continuous learning routines, utilizing genAI to curate and analyze new research. However, they must critically evaluate genAI recommendations to ensure they align with the needs of their students and profession.*
- ***Future Meaning:*** *GenAI will likely serve as a personalized mentor, continuously providing updated resources based on the latest educational policies and research. Teachers must retain autonomy in deciding which resources to integrate into their practice* (CCSSO, 2013), as paraphrased by ScholarGPT (Awesomegpts.ai, 2024).

Authors' Evaluation

Beyond the use of genAI for content knowledge and pedagogical improvement, educators should continuously hone their own critical genAI literacy skills.

9(o) Understanding Professional Expectations

- ***Current Meaning (regarding genAI).****Teachers understand professional expectations, ethics, and relevant law. GenAI can support compliance by offering reminders about legal and ethical obligations in teaching.*
- ***Revisions.****Teachers must be trained in the ethical use of genAI itself, ensuring that genAI tools do not violate professional standards or legal obligations. This includes understanding how genAI interacts with privacy laws and student data rights.*
- ***Future Meaning.****As genAI becomes more involved in decision-making, teachers will need to understand the ethical implications of relying on genAI, ensuring that genAI usage remains compliant with evolving professional standards and legal frameworks* (CCSSO, 2013), as paraphrased by ScholarGPT (Awesomegpts.ai, 2024).

Authors' Evaluation

Our experiences using genAI in our professional practice have generated opportunities for self-reflection and growth for both us and our students. We believe that genAI will have a continued impact on educator plans and outcomes for growth and development, not by replacing educator agency, but by enhancing it.

Summary

The section promotes justice through ethical practices for educators using genAI, emphasizing ongoing professional development in genAI literacy and ethics. It highlights the importance of vigilance to leverage genAI benefits while maintaining educational integrity.

WISDOM: A MINDSET OF CONTINUOUS LEARNING IN THE AGE OF GENAI

Amidst the ether's boundless expanse,
Where reason's dance weaves its entrancing trance,

A vision rises, bold and soaring high,
A realm where unity and biases comply.
GenAI, a guide celestial and keen,
Illuminates the path of knowledge, serene.
Preconceived notions' web, it gently tears,
As critical literacy's hand appears.
In this realm, reason's chains are gently broken,
Bias unveiled, its grip at last unspoken.
Minds empowered, free to explore and roam,
Seek truth and wisdom, making wisdom their home.

(Google, 2024 after a prompt to Gemini to summarize how genAI might help eliminate bias through critical literacy, as if it were Dante Alighieri)

Overview: Need for Continuous Learning

This section explores the role of continuous learning and adaptation as educators integrate genAI into their practice. We acknowledge the potential allure of genAI's convenience but also raise critical questions about the potential trade-offs with traditional human learning methods. Balancing the trade-offs necessitates cultivating a mindset of continuous learning and wisdom.

WISDOM: A Mnemonic for the Age of genAI

To further define this wisdom mindset, we propose the following mnemonic, with contributions from both Claude and Gemini:

Wrestling with uncertainty - Embracing the productive struggle in the zone of proximal development (Anthropic, 2024). Wondering: Cultivating a curious mind, questioning assumptions, and seeking deeper understanding (Google, 2024).

Inquiry and investigation - Questioning the nature of knowledge and understanding in an AI age (Anthropic, 2024). **I**ntelligence: Recognizing the strengths and limitations of both human and artificial intelligence, and utilizing each effectively (Google, 2024).

Self-awareness - Understanding human cognition versus artificial processing (Anthropic, 2024). **S**kepticism: Approaching information with a critical lens, discerning fact from fiction, and avoiding biases (Google, 2024).

Discernment - Distinguishing between authentic learning and artificial generation (Anthropic, 2024). Evaluating the quality and source of information, identifying potential biases, and making informed judgments (Google, 2024).

Originality - Valuing human creativity and genuine intellectual engagement (Anthropic, 2024). Valuing creative thinking, independent thought, and the ability to generate new ideas and solutions (Google, 2024).

Meaning-making - Emphasizing human interpretation and understanding over probabilistic generation (Anthropic, 2024). Metacognition: Reflecting on one's own thinking processes, identifying strengths and weaknesses, and continuously learning and improving (Google, 2024).

Plato's allegory of the cave continues to serve as a powerful metaphor for the human condition, our struggle to discern truth from falsehood, and our journey towards enlightenment (Plato, ca. 380 B.C.E./2007, 514a-520a). Today, as we grapple with the rise of genAI, this ancient allegory takes on new relevance. Just as in Plato's cave the prisoners mistook shadows screened against the cave wall for reality, we must be vigilant against the potential for genAI to shape our perceptions of the world to what can be seen on the screen.

Mishra and Heath (2024) capture the concern that technology could blind our perceptions, warning that "another price we may pay for AI technology is what and how we consider learning and intelligence" (p. 17). They remind us that human learning is often characterized by struggle and a "wrestling with discomfort" (p. 17), a process that seems absent in the seemingly effortless knowledge generation of genAI. This raises profound questions about the very nature of learning and knowing in the age of AI. Are we in danger of sacrificing deep understanding for the convenience of readily available information? Are we, as McLuhan (1964) suggested, becoming more like our machines, trading the "zone of proximal development" for "ease of access to the creation of knowledge" (Mishra & Heath, 2024, p. 17)?

This challenge extends beyond the realm of education. Bednar (2024) cautions against the allure of technological "shortcuts and quick fixes" (para. 15), urging us to consider whether our use of technology "enlarges or restricts [our] capacity to live, to love, and to serve in meaningful ways" (para. 15). His words highlight the ethical dimension of our engagement with AI, reminding us that while technology can be a powerful tool for good, it also has the potential to "diminish and suffocate our moral agency" (para. 15).

In navigating this complex landscape, Khan (2024) advocates for "educated bravery," urging us to embrace informed action over inaction. He acknowledges the risks associated with AI but argues that "the risks of inaction are much higher," particularly if we fail to engage with this technology in a thoughtful and knowledgeable manner (Khan, 2024).

As we view the "screen" of AI-generated information, we must cultivate the critical literacy necessary to distinguish between shadows and reality, to question assumptions, and to ensure that technology serves to enhance, rather than diminish, our capacity for learning, understanding, and ethical action.

To exemplify the points identified by Mishra and Heath (2024), Bednar (2024) and Khan (2024) we offer a re-envisioning of Plato's cave analogy (Plato, ca. 380 B.C.E./2007, 514a-520a).

Prompt: *Re-envision Plato's cave analogy with genAI as the screen of light from which the enchained view reality.*

Perplexity

- *To re-envision Plato's cave analogy with generative AI (genAI) as the screen of light from which the enchained view reality, consider the following adaptation:*
- *Setting: Imagine a modern interpretation of the cave where individuals are confined and unable to move freely. Instead of chains, they are tethered to virtual reality headsets that display a continuous stream of digital content generated by genAI algorithms.*
- *Light Source: The fire in the original allegory represents the computational processes driving the generation of AI outputs. Just as the flames illuminate the shadows on the cave wall, the AI systems produce a constant flow of data points, images, and texts that appear as realistic yet incomplete representations of reality.*
- *Shadows vs. Reality: The shadows on the cave wall symbolize the partial and often misleading perceptions created by genAI. These shadows are derived from vast datasets processed by machine learning models, which generate predictions based on patterns learned from historical data rather than direct experiences. For instance, an individual viewing the AI-generated scene might mistake a synthetic landscape for real-world scenery without realizing the underlying algorithmic constructs.*
- *Prisoners' Perception: The prisoners in the cave mistakenly attribute significance to the shadows, believing them to be the ultimate truth. Similarly, users relying solely on genAI outputs might assume that the synthesized realities reflect absolute truths, failing to recognize the intermediate steps involved in generating these simulations.*
- *Escape from the Cave: As in Plato's original narrative, escaping involves recognizing the limitations of the simulated world. An individual breaking free from their VR headset would initially struggle to comprehend the distinction between the artificially constructed environment and genuine reality. Gradually, they would realize that the depth and richness of real-life experiences surpass the confines of AI-generated scenarios.*
- *Philosophical Implications: This adapted scenario highlights several philosophical themes relevant to contemporary discussions about AI and perception:*

1. Illusion of Completeness: GenAI creates illusions of completeness by presenting highly detailed and coherent narratives, leading users to overlook potential gaps in understanding.
2. Limited Understanding: Users trapped within the AI-generated world risk misunderstanding fundamental aspects of reality unless they actively seek broader perspectives beyond the confines of their digital environments.
3. Embodiment Theory: Recognizing that intelligence emerges from interactions with complex environments underscores the importance of experiential learning versus purely computational processing.

- *This reinterpretation emphasizes how reliance on genAI can lead to a form of intellectual imprisonment, where individuals fail to grasp the full spectrum of existence due to their dependence on mediated perceptions* (Perplexity.ai, 2024).

Prompt:*Can critical AI literacy serve as the escape from the cave?*
Perplexity:

- *Critical AI literacy can indeed serve as a means of escape from the metaphorical cave described in Plato's allegory. In this context, the "cave" represents a state of ignorance where individuals are confined to a limited understanding of reality, shaped by the outputs of generative AI (genAI) without questioning or critically engaging with those outputs.*
- Understanding Critical AI Literacy
- Definition and Importance: Critical AI literacy goes beyond merely knowing how to use AI tools; it encompasses an understanding of their limitations, potential biases, and the implications of their outputs. This form of literacy empowers individuals to discern between AI-generated content and genuine knowledge, fostering a more nuanced view of reality rather than accepting AI outputs at face value.
- The Role of Critical AI Literacy in Escaping the Cave

1. Recognition of Limitations: Just as the prisoners in the cave must recognize that the shadows they see are not reality, individuals must understand that genAI operates based on patterns learned from historical data. This understanding helps users avoid mistaking AI-generated information for absolute truth.
2. Empowerment Through Knowledge: By developing critical AI literacy, individuals gain the ability to question the sources and motivations behind AI outputs. This empowerment is akin to gaining knowledge about the

outside world in Plato's allegory, enabling users to navigate and interpret information more effectively.

3. Encouraging Skepticism: A critical approach encourages skepticism towards AI outputs, prompting users to verify information and consider multiple perspectives rather than passively accepting what is presented. This mirrors the philosophical journey from ignorance to enlightenment, as individuals learn to look beyond the shadows cast by AI.
4. *Engagement with Ethical Implications: Critical AI literacy also involves understanding the ethical dimensions of AI technology—recognizing how biases in data can affect outcomes and how these technologies can manipulate perceptions. Awareness of these issues allows individuals to make informed decisions about their interactions with AI systems* (Perplexity.ai, 2024).

As identified in the re-envisioning of Plato's cave, critical AI literacy is a vital tool for effectively preparing current and future educators for the age of genAI. Becker and colleagues, drawing inspiration from Selber's 2004 multiliteracies model, have proposed a framework encompassing three distinct levels of genAI literacy: functional, critical, and rhetorical (Becker et al., 2024).

- **Functional Literacy:** Understanding how genAI operates and practical applications in various educational contexts.
- **Critical Literacy:** Analyzing the implications of genAI on knowledge creation, privacy, and ethical considerations.
- **Rhetorical Literacy:** Evaluating how genAI influences communication, persuasion, and the presentation of information (Becker et al., 2024).

By cultivating these literacies, educators and educator preparation programs (EPPs) can actively engage with genAI and leverage it to enhance the learning environment.

Summary

This section emphasizes the necessity for a continuous learning and adaptation mindset, encapsulated by the mnemonic WISDOM (Wrestling with Uncertainty, Inquiry and Investigation, Self-awareness and Skepticism, Discernment, Originality, Meaning Making, and Metacognition). This approach is fundamental for educators navigating the complexities of genAI. Reflecting on the implementation of genAI in educational settings underscores the importance of ensuring that genAI enhances rather than diminishes the quality and integrity of learning experiences. Critical AI literacy is essential for recognizing the limitations and biases of genAI, questioning its outputs, and considering ethical implications. Such literacy empowers educators to navigate and interpret AI-generated information, harnessing its benefits while mitigating its risks, thereby enhancing the educational experience for all students.

CONCLUSION

As faculty members in an EPP, our journey with genAI over the past year has been both enlightening and challenging. By experimenting with this novel technology, we have progressed from a basic understanding of functional AI literacy to a more sophisticated and nuanced grasp of rhetorical AI literacy (Becker, 2024).

One of the most profound lessons we have learned is the significant effort required to transform genAI technology into a practical educational tool. Despite its immense potential, genAI demands time, diligence, and a healthy dose of skepticism to ensure its ethical and effective use. Our exploration has highlighted the delicate balance between leveraging genAI's advantages and mitigating its risks. Operating on the cutting edge of technology necessitates robust ethical training. We approached genAI with a curious mindset, acknowledging that fears and apprehensions about its use are justified. We recognized the necessity for guardrails to guide the ethical use of genAI, emphasizing the importance of balancing its potential benefits with the preservation of critical human interactions in education.

In conclusion, our chapter underscores the critical necessity for a comprehensive and ethical approach to genAI in educational preparation programs. By fostering critical AI literacy, educators can navigate the complexities of this evolving technology, ensuring that it serves to enhance educational practices while preserving the essential human elements of teaching and learning. As we continue to explore the potential of genAI, it is imperative that we proceed with caution, guided by ethical principles and a commitment to the responsible use of technology in education.

ACKNOWLEDGMENT

We acknowledge Pam Walter for being a human in the loop, who kindly reviewed and commented on our final version. This research received no specific grant from any funding agency in the public, commercial, or not-for-profit sectors.

REFERENCES

Americans with Disabilities Act of 1990, no. 42, United States Congress (1990).

Angelone, L., & Burton, B. (2024). MagicSchool: An exploration of the use of Generative AI by southwest Ohio teachers. *Ohio Journal of Teacher Education, 39*(1), Article 4. https://www.exhibit.xavier.edu/ojte/vol39/iss1/4

Anthropic. (2024). Claude [AI assistant]. https://www.anthropic.com

Awesomegpts.ai. (2024). Scholar GPT. https://www.awesomegpts.ai

Bali, M. (2023, September 18). What I mean when I say critical AI literacy. *Mahabali.* https://blog.mahabali.me/educational-technology-2/what-i-mean-when-i-say-critical-ai-literacy/

Becker, K. P., Parker, J. L., & Richter, D. (2024). *Framework for the future: Building AI literacy in higher education* (v. 1.0). Moxie. https://moxielearn.ai/wp-content/uploads/2024/06/Ai-literacies-white-paper.docx.pdf

Bednar, D. A. (2024, November). *Things as they really are 2.0.* https://www.churchofjesuschrist.org/study/broadcasts/worldwide-devotional-for-young-adults/2024/11/13bednar?lang=eng

Butler-Ulrich, T., Hughes, J., & Morrison, L. (2024). Creativity and Generative AI for Preservice Teachers. In L. Barlach (Ed.), *Creativity in Contemporaneity* (working title). IntechOpen. DOI: 10.5772/intechopen.1007517

Cambridge Dictionary. (n.d.). Logic. In dictionary.cambridge.org. Retrieved March 8, 2025, from https://dictionary.cambridge.org/us/dictionary/english/logic

Children's Online Privacy Protection Act of 1998, 15 U.S.C. §§ 6501-6506 (1998).

Civil Rights Act of 1964, Title VI, 42 U.S.C. § 2000d et seq. (1964).

Copyright Act of 1976, 17 U.S.C. § 101 et seq. (1976).

Council of Chief State School Officers. (2013). *InTASC Model Core Teaching Standards and Learning Progressions for educators 1.0.*https://ccsso.org/resource-library/intasc-model-core-teaching-standards-and-learning-progressions-educators-10

Eaton, L. (2024, June 20). AI plagiarism considerations part 2: When students use AI. *AI EduSimplified.* https://aiedusimplified.substack.com/p/ai-plagiarism-considerations-part-a27

Eaton, S. E. (2023). Postplagiarism: Transdisciplinary ethics and integrity in the age of artificial intelligence and neurotechnology. *International Journal for Educational Integrity, 19*(1), 23. DOI: 10.1007/s40979-023-00144-1

Family Educational Rights and Privacy Act of 1974, 20 U.S.C. § 1232g (1974).

Google. (2024). Gemini. https://gemini.google.com

Hwang, G. J., Haoran, X., Wah, B. W., & Gašević, D. (2020). Vision, challenges, roles and research issues of Artificial Intelligence in Education, *Computers and Education: Artificial Intelligence, 1*,100001,ISSN 2666-920X, DOI: 10.1016/j.caeai.2020.100001

Individuals with Disabilities Education Act, 20 U.S.C. § 1400 (2004).

Kärki, K. (2024). Digital distraction, attention regulation, and inequality. *Philosophy & Technology, 37*(1), 8. DOI: 10.1007/s13347-024-00698-z

Khan, S. (2024, September 4). Khan Academy founder Sal Kahn on the future of learning [WorkLab: The Podcast]. YouTube. https://www.youtube.com/playlist?list=PLFPUGjQjckXFuFOmH4VE0nOf2gtXJjv6U

Liu, C.-C., & Gu, X.-Q. (2024). Developing frames for change: How generative AI impacts the broad practices of teacher educators. In M. Searson, E. Langran, & J. Trumble (Eds.), *Exploring new horizons: Generative artificial intelligence and educator education* (pp. 225-237). Association for the Advancement of Computing in Education (AACE). https://www.learntechlib.org/p/223928/

Long, D., & Magerko, B. (2020). What is AI literacy: Competencies and design considerations. In *CHI '20: Proceedings of the 2020 CHI Conference on Human Factors in Computing Systems* (pp. 1-16). Association for Computing Machinery. DOI: 10.1145/3313831.3376727

Madden, M., Calvin, A., Hasse, A., & Lenhart, A. (2024). *The dawn of the AI era: Teens, parents, and the adoption of generative AI at home and school.* Common Sense., https://www.commonsensemedia.org/sites/default/files/research/report/2024-the-dawn-of-the-ai-era_final-release-for-web.pdf

McLuhan, M. (1964). *Understanding media: The extensions of man.* McGraw-Hill.

Microsoft. (2024). Microsoft Copilot (Version 1.0) [Computer software]. Microsoft. https://www.microsoft.com

Mills, K., Ruiz, P., Lee, K., Coenraad, M., Fusco, J., Roschelle, J., & Weisgrau, J. (2024). *AI Literacy: A Framework to Understand, Evaluate, and Use Emerging Technology*. Digital Promise., DOI: 10.51388/20.500.12265/218

Mishra, P., & Heath, M. K. (2024). The (Neil) Postman Always Rings Twice: 5 Questions on AI and Education. In M. Searson, E. Langran, & J. Trumble (Eds.), *Exploring new horizons: Generative artificial intelligence and teacher education* (pp. 14-24). Association for the Advancement of Computing in Education (AACE).

Mollick, E. (2024). *Co-Intelligence: Living and working with AI.* Penguin.

Mollick, E. (2024, November 24). Getting started with AI: Good enough prompting. *One Useful Thing.* https://www.oneusefulthing.org/p/getting-started-with-ai-good-enough

Open, A. I. (2023). How can educators respond to students presenting AI-generated content as their own? Retrieved September 2, 2023 from https://help.openai.com/en/articles/8313351-how-can-educators-respond-to-students-presenting-ai-generated-content-as-their-own

Perplexity.ai. (2024). Perplexity [AI assistant].https://Perplexity.ai

Plato. (2007). *The Republic* (D. Lee, Trans.; 2nd ed.). Penguin. (Original work published ca. 380 B.C.E.).

Prichard, B. S. (2024). The CLAIM Method: A Roadmap for AI Integration in Education. Presentation for Morehead State University Faculty. The CLAIM Method: A Roadmap for AI Integration in Education.

Prud'homme-Genereux, A. (2024). Writing case studies using generative AI: Interactive role play. Faculty Focus. https://www.facultyfocus.com/articles/teaching-with-technology-articles/writing-case-studies-using-generative-ai-interactive-role-play/

Sari, E., & Yalçın, S. S. (2024). Interplay of paternal caregiving and screen use habits on early childhood development and children's tantrums. *Italian Journal of Pediatrics, 50*(1), 230. DOI: 10.1186/s13052-024-01802-x PMID: 39501365

Sathy, V., & Hogan, K. A. (2023, November). How to Make Your Teaching More Inclusive: Advice Guide. *The Chronicle of Higher Education.* https://www-chronicle-com.msu.idm.oclc.org/article/how-to-make-your-teaching-more-inclusive/

Searson, M. Langran, E., & Trumble J. (Eds). (2024). *Exploring new horizons: Generative artificial intelligence and educator education.* Association for the Advancement of Computing in Education (AACE). https://www.learntechlib.org/p/223928/

Selber, S. (2004). *Multiliteracies for a Digital Age.* Southern Illinois University Press.

Stiles, J., & Jernigan, T. L. (2010). The basics of brain development. *Neuropsychology Review, 20*(4), 327–348. DOI: 10.1007/s11065-010-9148-4 PMID: 21042938

U.S. Copyright Office. (2023, March 16). Copyright registration guidance: Works containing material generated by artificial intelligence. *Federal Register*, *88*(51), 16190–16194. https://www.federalregister.gov/documents/2023/03/16/2023-05321/copyright-registration-guidance-works-containing-material-generated-by-artificial-intelligence

Walker, T. (2023, February 3). Cellphone bans in school are back. How far will they go? NEA Today. https://www.nea.org/nea-today/all-news-articles/cellphone-bans-school-are-back-how-far-will-they-go

Warnick, B. (2002). *Critical literacy in a digital era: Technology, rhetoric, and the public interest.* Erlbaum Associates.

ADDITIONAL READINGS

Bali, M. (2023, April 1). What I mean when I say critical AI literacy. *Mahabali.* https://blog.mahabali.me/educational-technology-2/what-i-mean-when-i-say-critical-ai-literacy/

Becker, K. P., Parker, J. L., & Richter, D. (2024). *Framework for the future: Building AI literacy in higher education* (v. 1.0). Moxie.Ai literacies white paper.docx

Council of Chief State School Officers. (2013). *InTASC Model Core Teaching Standards and Learning Progressions for educators 1.0.* https://ccsso.org/resource-library/intasc-model-core-teaching-standards-and-learning-progressions-educators-10

Gino, F. (2018). The business case for curiosity. *Harvard Business Review*, *96*(5), 48–57.

Long, D., & Magerko, B. (2020). *What is AI literacy: Competencies and design considerations.* CHI '20: Proceedings of the 2020 CHI Conference on Human Factors in Computing Systems. 1-16 https://aiunplugged.lmc.gatech.edu/wp-content/uploads/sites/36/2020/08/CHI-2020-AI-Literacy-Paper-Camera-Ready.pdfDOI: 10.1145/3313831.3376727

Madden, M., Calvin, A., Hasse, A., & Lenhart, A. (2024). *The dawn of the AI era: Teens, parents, and the adoption of generative AI at home and school.* CommonSense., https://www.commonsensemedia.org/sites/default/files/research/report/2024-the-dawn-of-the-ai-era_final-release-for-web.pdf

Mills, K., Ruiz, P., Lee, K., Coenraad, M., Fusco, J., Roschelle, J., & Weisgrau, J. (2024). *AI Literacy: A Framework to Understand, Evaluate, and Use Emerging Technology*. Digital Promise., DOI: 10.51388/20.500.12265/218

Mollick, E. (2024). *Co-Intelligence: Living and working with AI*. Penguin.

Mollick, E. (2024, November 24). Getting started with AI: Good enough prompting. *One Useful Thing*. https://www.oneusefulthing.org/p/getting-started-with-ai-good-enough

Searson, M. Langran, E., & Trumble J. (Eds). (2024). *Exploring new horizons: Generative artificial intelligence and educator education*. Association for the Advancement of Computing in Education (AACE). https://www.learntechlib.org/primary/p/223928/

KEY TERMS AND DEFINITIONS

Artificial Intelligence (AI): a domain within computer science and engineering, encompasses the study and development of systems capable of executing tasks that typically require human intelligence. These tasks include language comprehension, problem-solving, reasoning, and learning. AI is realized through technologies such as machine learning, which enables computers to learn from data, and deep learning, where artificial neural networks identify complex patterns to facilitate intelligent behaviors.

Algorithmic Bias in AI: refers to errors that occur in genAI outputs due to genAI systems being trained on biased and prejudiced data. These inherit biases from the data could lead to inequitable outcomes.

Ethical AI: The study and application of ethical principles in AI technology that involves considering safety/beneficence, autonomy/human agency, privacy, responsibility/transparency and fairness.

Generative AI (GenAI): A type of artificial intelligence that can create new content, such as text, images, audio, and video, based on learned patterns from existing data. GenAI technologies include applications like ChatGPT and DALL-E.

AI Literacy: The ability to understand, evaluate, and interact with AI technologies effectively and responsibly. This includes recognizing the capabilities and limitations of AI systems.

Prompt: Author-generated input for guiding AI models to produce relevant and high-quality content.

Adaptive Learning: An educational method that uses technology to customize learning experiences based on individual student needs, preferences, and performance levels, often supported by AI systems

Chapter 6
Using AI in Preparing Pre-Service Teachers for Field Experience

Geralda Silva Nelson
https://orcid.org/0009-0002-5930-8053
Morehead State University, USA

ABSTRACT

Abstract The study examined how artificial intelligence (AI) supported pre-service teachers during their field placements by streamlining content creation, reducing time spent on administrative tasks, and offering data-driven insights to refine instructional strategies. These placements provided future educators with hands-on experience in real classroom settings, where they encountered challenges such as lesson planning, differentiation, and student assessment. AI tools played a crucial role in addressing these challenges by assisting with resource development, providing adaptive learning recommendations, and enhancing the overall teaching experience.

INTRODUCTION

As I write this chapter, I am fully aware that the field of Artificial Intelligence is evolving at lightning speed. Consequently, I can't help but wonder how long what I am writing here will remain relevant. Thus, I am fully aware that Artificial Intelligence (AI) is continuously evolving and reshaping higher education by expanding learning opportunities while also introducing challenges and ethical considerations. Nonetheless, in the context of pre-service teacher education, I perceive AI as hold-

DOI: 10.4018/979-8-3373-4576-5.ch006

ing significant promise for addressing long-standing challenges and enhancing the training experience.

From my work with education majors, I have observed firsthand how AI might work to empower pre-service teachers to streamline and enhance their field experiences. During their field placement associated with my courses, they were granted an opportunity to use AI to do tasks related to their field placement in the local schools. By tapping into AI resources, they have been able to develop instructional materials, design lesson plans, create rubrics, craft assignments tools, design assessments, and provide meaningful feedback to students, all while learning to take into consideration the ethical and bias issues related to AI. This technology has allowed them to shift their focus from time-consuming administrative tasks to more impactful aspects of teaching, such as refining instructional strategies and differentiating lessons, which has resulted in having more time to devote to fostering stronger relationships with their P-5 students.

As they gained hands-on experience, my students increasingly recognized AI's potential not just as a convenience but as a resource that enhances their ability to make informed, student-centered decisions. However, they also acknowledge the importance of critically evaluating AI-generated content to ensure alignment with educational best practices and ethical considerations.

RESEARCH QUESTION

How does the integration of AI in teacher education foster personalized, experiential learning and collaborative opportunities for pre-service teachers in their field experiences while enhancing their ability to build knowledge through reflective practices, lesson planning, and differentiated instruction within a framework that emphasizes ethical considerations and confidentiality?

This case study, grounded in constructivist principles and my experiences in teacher education classrooms, explores the integration of artificial intelligence (AI) as a tool to enhance teacher preparation for field placement practices. The study examines how AI fosters personalized, experiential learning by adapting to individual needs, providing real-time feedback to support reflective practice, and streamlining assessment processes to promote growth. Additionally, it investigates the role of AI in content development, enabling pre-service teachers to design engaging, adaptive instructional materials that align with diverse learner needs.

Constructivism, a learning theory emphasizing active knowledge construction through experience and reflection, offers a powerful framework for integrating AI tools into pre-service teacher field placements. Thoughtful and ethical AI integration within a constructivist framework can provide pre-service teachers with personalized, reflective, collaborative, and authentic learning experiences, better preparing them for modern classrooms. (Piaget, 1970; Vygotsky, 1978; Holmes et al., 2023)

Moreover, the study examined how artificial intelligence (AI) supported pre-service teachers during their field placements by streamlining content creation, reducing time spent on administrative tasks, and offering data-driven insights to refine instructional strategies. These placements provided future educators with hands-on experience in real classroom settings, where they encountered challenges such as lesson planning, differentiation, and student assessment. AI tools played a crucial role in addressing these challenges by assisting with resource development, providing adaptive learning recommendations, and enhancing the overall teaching experience.

Perspectives from participants in teacher education courses were analyzed to highlight how AI influenced key aspects of their instructional practice. AI-assisted lesson planning enabled pre-service teachers in my courses to generate and modify instructional materials efficiently, ensuring alignment with student needs and curriculum standards. Moreover, AI-supported differentiation allowed my pre-service teachers to tailor their approaches by analyzing student performance data and suggesting personalized interventions. Ethical considerations surrounding AI use, including data privacy, algorithmic bias, and responsible implementation, were also explored to ensure that pre-service teachers adopted AI in a thoughtful and professional manner.

Additionally, AI contributed significantly to content development by allowing our pre-service teachers in the field to design engaging and adaptive instructional materials that resonated with diverse student populations. AI-powered simulations and virtual teaching assistants provided pre-service teachers with opportunities to practice instructional strategies, receive automated feedback, and refine their approaches before applying them in real classroom settings. These tools enhanced their confidence and preparedness for full-time teaching roles.

By using AI throughout their field placements, pre-service teachers gained valuable insights into integrating technology into their instructional practice. They developed a deeper understanding of how AI could be used to personalize learning, support student growth, and optimize classroom management. This study underscored AI's transformative potential in teacher preparation, ensuring that educators entered the profession equipped with the necessary skills, strategies, and tools to meet the evolving needs of diverse student populations effectively.

To provide a comprehensive analysis, the perspectives of pre-service teachers participating in my courses are incorporated, with a focus on key areas such as lesson planning, the creation of instructional activities, ethical considerations and bias, and the implementation of differentiation strategies to meet their students' needs.

Using a case study methodology, a survey was conducted with pre-service teachers enrolled in my courses to explore how they utilized AI in designing lesson plans, instructional activities, assessments, and differentiating instructions.

In this section, I will share and analyze the insights I obtained from the survey responses

Lessons Learned from Lesson Planning Survey Question

When it came to composing lesson plans, an analysis of survey responses from pre-service teachers revealed nuanced perspectives on the role of AI in lesson planning. While participants acknowledged the potential of AI tools to streamline the initial stages of lesson plan development, they emphasized the importance of tailoring AI-generated outputs to meet the specific needs of their K-12 students. The findings suggest that effective utilization of AI in this context requires deliberate revisions to ensure alignment with diverse student populations, curricular standards, and classroom-specific objectives. These findings illustrate the need for targeted training and support to enable pre-service teachers to critically evaluate and adapt AI-generated lesson plans to create meaningful and contextually appropriate learning experiences.

The survey responses revealed several recurring themes related to lesson planning.

Usage of AI for Lesson Planning and Idea Generation

Multiple students perceive AI as a valuable resource for generating ideas for lesson plans, designing activities, and creating assessments. They associate AI with having a brainstorming partner that helps formulate ideas, establish goals, and structure lessons effectively. Commonly mentioned tools, such as ChatGPT and Magic School AI, were cited as particularly useful for managing multiple administrative tasks, including lesson planning. According to my students' responses, these tools not only helped streamline routine tasks but also empowered them to focus on more creative and engaging aspects of teaching.

New research is looking at how artificial intelligence (AI) can be used in schools, especially for planning lessons and making sure they meet state standards.

One example is a new AI tool created by Karpouzis et al. (2024) that helps teachers make lesson plans that fit their specific classes. Teachers can tell the AI things like the ages of their students, their backgrounds, and what they need to learn. Then, the AI creates lesson plans that are designed for all the different learners in the class

Alignment with State Standards

Students observed that AI tools could assist in aligning lesson plans with state standards, including the Kentucky Academic Standards (KAS) or specific learning objectives. However, according to my students, the effectiveness of these tools varied. Many students noted that the AI often struggled to accurately match precise state standards unless they explicitly provided the exact standard. When students supplied the full text of the Kentucky Academic Standards, AI tools became much more effective, offering aligned content, generating relevant activities, or suggesting instructional ideas. This capability was particularly valued as it streamlined the process of integrating standards into lesson planning, helping students ensure compliance while saving time.

Challenges with State Standards

Nonetheless, several respondents noted that the problem with AI was that it occasionally "invented" standards or provided inaccurate information, leading to potential confusion. Students reported that they often had to cross-reference AI-generated outputs with reliable sources, such as official Kentucky Academic Standards (KAS), to ensure the information's accuracy. This process of validation was considered an essential step in using AI effectively, as it allowed students to identify and correct errors while reinforcing their understanding of the standards. Despite these challenges, many students appreciated AI's role as a starting point for generating ideas, emphasizing that careful research and critical thinking were necessary to maximize its benefits

Instructional Strategies

Furthermore, while discussing the potential for AI to assist with creating instructional activity, survey responses revealed that many pre-service teachers used AI as a powerful brainstorming tool for developing and refining instructional strategies. By using AI, they were able to streamline the idea-generation process, saving time while producing a broader range of innovative approaches to teaching.

For example, when designing phonics lessons, some respondents used AI to suggest creative and engaging methods to teach letter-sound relationships. Examples included incorporating multisensory activities, such as having students trace letters in shaving cream while sounding them out or using songs and chants to reinforce phonemic awareness. Others noted that AI provided prompts for integrating technology, like using digital apps to create phonics games or interactive activities where students matched sounds to corresponding letters or images.

Moreover, pre-service teachers found AI helpful for refining their instructional strategies by tailoring them to specific learner needs. For example, AI was used to generate differentiated activities for students struggling with phonics, such as breaking down words into smaller sound units and incorporating repetition with visuals for reinforcement. Similarly, AI suggested ideas for enrichment instructional activities, such as extending phonics instruction to advanced learners by introducing more complex word patterns or connecting phonics to vocabulary development through contextualized reading exercises.

Despite all the benefits of AI in the field experience, the pre-service teachers in my courses consistently emphasized the need for caution and careful oversight when incorporating AI into instructional activities, particularly for teaching the writing process. Many respondents stressed the importance of thoroughly evaluating AI-generated content to ensure alignment with specific learning objectives and educational standards, such as the Kentucky Academic Standards (KAS) for narrative writing. For instance, one respondent carefully reviewed an AI-generated lesson on story structure to confirm that it effectively covered key writing skills, including planning, drafting, revising, editing, and publishing.

Nevertheless, rather than relying on AI as a final instructional resource, my students often viewed it as a tool for generating initial ideas. Several respondents described how they used AI to develop a foundational framework for writing instruction, such as brainstorming a list of engaging story themes or generating graphic organizers to help students outline their ideas. However, they adapted these AI-generated resources to better fit their students' developmental levels. For instance, a graphic organizer designed for third graders might emphasize sequencing events into a beginning, middle, and end, whereas one for older students could incorporate more advanced elements such as plot, conflict, resolution, and character development.

Additionally, respondents noted the usefulness of AI in crafting intentional and supportive writing prompts that guide students in expanding their narratives. For example, they might use AI to generate prompts like, "What is something dear to your heart?" Describe their emotions and actions."

Focus on Creativity and Engagement

My students mentioned that they also used AI to develop engaging activities. For instance, two students collaborating in the same classroom shared that an AI tool assisted them in creating comprehension questions at varying levels of difficulty tailored to a story or passage their class had read. Another one noted that AI-based platforms like Epic! or Raz-Kids recommend books based on the individual reading levels and interests of their target students.

Differentiation

This brings us to address the use of AI for differentiating instructions and assessments. Respondents to my survey indicated that AI worked as an important tool in assisting with differentiating reading instruction. They noted that while AI was able to provide an abundance of resources, the key to effective differentiation was based on personalizing these tools to suit the individual needs of their target students. Many teacher candidates in my courses highlighted the importance of adjusting AI-generated content to match the unique characteristics of the students they were working with. For instance, providing AI with detailed context, such as student demographics (e.g., age, background, prior knowledge, language skills) and specific learning objectives, allowed the system to offer more relevant and focused suggestions. Teacher candidates in my courses also revised AI-generated ideas based on their personal expertise and classroom experience. For example, if the AI recommended an activity for struggling students, they corrected the activity by adding additional scaffolding or using simpler language to ensure it aligned with students' abilities.

According to my pre-service teachers, while AI provides a wealth of resources, effective differentiation in teaching reading in P-5 education depends on how well teachers personalize these tools to meet the individual needs of their students. My students frequently emphasized the importance of adapting AI-generated content to align with the unique characteristics of their learners, including age, background knowledge, language, abilities, and specific literacy needs.

Customizing AI-Generated Reading Materials

I found it interesting to see how multiple pre-service teachers in my classes used AI to modify reading passages to match students' reading levels. For example, a few pre-service teachers working with groups of first graders used AI to simplify a nonfiction passage about animals, shortening sentences and replacing complex vocabulary with more accessible words. Another candidate teaching a second-grade class used AI to adjust a story's readability, generating three different versions of the same text—one with simplified language for emerging readers, another at grade level, and a more advanced version with richer vocabulary and more complex sentence structures for proficient readers.

Scaffolding for Struggling Readers

According to my students, another very useful AI tools also played a role in supporting struggling readers through scaffolding techniques. One student shared how they used AI to create guided reading prompts that incorporated sentence starters and visual supports for first-grade students who had difficulty forming complete sentences. Another teacher candidate used AI to generate decodable texts that focused on specific phonics patterns, such as short vowel sounds or blends like "sh" and "ch." By tailoring AI-generated passages to reinforce phonics instruction, students gained more targeted practice with decoding skills.

Enhancing Vocabulary Instruction

Vocabulary development was another area where AI-supported differentiation proved beneficial. Several pre-service teachers used AI to create word banks with definitions, images, and example sentences tailored to students' comprehension levels. For instance, a group of students in my class preparing a lesson on community helpers used AI to generate a vocabulary list that included simplified definitions and real-world examples. The AI-generated materials were then adjusted to include pictures of community workers, helping visual learners connect words to concrete concepts.

Differentiated Comprehension Activities

Beyond text modification, AI was used to create differentiated comprehension activities that catered to students' needs. One respondent described how AI helped them generate multiple versions of comprehension questions for a read-aloud session. For struggling students, AI provided basic recall questions such as "Who is the main character?" and "Where does the story take place?" Meanwhile, more advanced learners received higher-order thinking questions like "Why do you think the character made that decision?" and "How does this story connect to your own experiences?" By customizing AI-generated questions, the teacher candidate ensured that all students engaged meaningfully with the text at their individual comprehension levels.

Supporting Multi-Language Learners (MLLs)

Several pre-service teachers also highlighted the role of AI in supporting Multi-Language Learners (EMLs). For example, one respondent noted that while working with a multilingual classroom, they used AI to generate bilingual reading materials, providing side-by-side translations to help students make connections between their home language and English. Another candidate used AI to create interactive vocabulary exercises, such as digital flashcards with audio pronunciation, allowing ML students to practice new words independently.

Personalization of AI Resources

Artificial Intelligence (AI) has the potential to revolutionize education by tailoring learning experiences to individual students' needs. Research indicates that AI can adapt content to suit each learner's unique requirements, thereby enhancing educational outcomes. For instance, a study published in *ResearchGate* discusses how AI systems can customize content and interactions to individual learners' needs, preferences, and pace, thereby enhancing e-learning experiences.

ResearchGate

A comprehensive literature review by Wu et al. (2024) explores the role of artificial intelligence (AI) in personalized learning within smart education systems. The study highlights how AI facilitates the development of tailored instructional strategies, enabling educators to streamline lesson planning and explore diverse pedagogical approaches. Key benefits identified include enhanced brainstorming capabilities, where AI provides research-based suggestions, activity ideas, and templates that save time and effort. Furthermore, the review emphasizes AI's role in personalization, noting that AI-generated strategies can be adapted to align with students' needs, age levels, and learning objectives. This aligns with the findings from pre-service teachers who reported using AI to brainstorm and refine instructional strategies, thereby enhancing the planning process and catering to diverse student needs. Similarly, an article from *Claned* highlights that AI can provide personalized educational experiences by adapting content to individual needs, leading to improved learning outcomes.

Developing Assessments

When I provided my students the opportunity to incorporate AI into their process of creating assessments and giving feedback to their field experience students, I anticipated that the majority would eagerly embrace the technology. As expected, many of them enthusiastically integrated AI tools into their work. These students found AI particularly helpful in generating and customizing assessments to suit diverse learning needs. However, a smaller group expressed discomfort or reluctance in using AI for this purpose. Their hesitation stemmed from a variety of reasons, such as unfamiliarity with the tools, skepticism about their accuracy, or a preference for traditional methods. Ultimately, my students fell into three categories: those who actively used AI to create assessments, those who explored it minimally, and those who chose not to use it at all.

The survey provided several insights into how my students utilize AI for assessments

Generating Questions

Many respondents used AI to develop both formative and summative assessment items, including multiple-choice questions, fill-in-the-blank exercises, and tailored quizzes. For instance, some students shared how they used AI to create a series of scaffolded comprehension questions for a book, ensuring that the questions gradually increased in difficulty.

Personalized Assessments

AI also played a key role in helping students tailor assessments to meet individual learning needs. Some pre-service teachers used AI to adjust the difficulty level of assessments, ensuring that struggling learners received more accessible questions while advanced students encountered more challenging ones. Multiple students explained how they used AI to create differentiated reading comprehension quizzes for students with limited vocabulary skills. The AI-generated quizzes included simplified sentence structures and embedded context clues to help students understand difficult words. Another student described using AI to modify word problems in a math assessment by adjusting numerical values and complexity, allowing for a more personalized learning experience.

Rubric Development

Most of the students surveyed indicated that they used AI to draft and refine rubrics for assessments. AI-assisted rubric generation helped them ensure clarity, consistency, and alignment of the possible criterias with instructional goals. One respondent described how AI helped them construct a detailed writing rubric that broke down expectations for organization, sentence structure, and use of descriptive language. Another student mentioned using AI to refine a rubric for oral presentations, ensuring that assessment categories, such as eye contact, voice projection, and content delivery, were clearly defined with specific criteria for each performance level.

AI for Feedback and Reflection

Beyond traditional assessments, some students used AI to provide immediate feedback on student responses. For example, one respondent experimented with AI tools that analyzed short written responses and provided constructive feedback, such as suggesting stronger topic sentences or more descriptive details. Another student used AI to generate sample responses for peer-review activities, allowing students to compare their work against well-structured examples and reflect on areas for improvement.

Using AI to Analyze Literacy Data

When asked about using AI to analyze literacy data for P-5 students, most of my pre-service teachers shared that they had not yet explored AI tools for interpreting or analyzing such data. However, despite their lack of experience, they recognized AI's potential to streamline the process of identifying patterns in students' literacy skills. They acknowledged that AI could help them analyze data more efficiently and provide valuable insights that would allow them to create targeted interventions to support students' individual literacy development.

Looking ahead, I plan to introduce AI tools in future semesters to help my students develop a deeper understanding of AI's role in analyzing and interpreting student data. For example, AI-driven tools could automatically assess various literacy metrics, such as fluency scores and comprehension test results, to detect trends and areas where students struggle. Platforms like Amira Learning, which analyzes oral reading recordings, could provide valuable feedback by identifying phonics errors and highlighting skill gaps, such as difficulty recognizing vowel blends or improving sight word recognition.

By incorporating these AI tools into their field experience, my students could gain hands-on exposure to how technology can support data-driven decision-making in the field of education. This approach might have the potential to allow pre-service teachers to see firsthand how AI can be used to enhance literacy instruction, refine intervention strategies, and improve overall P-12 student outcomes. Through these experiences, I hope to equip my pre-service teachers with the skills and knowledge they need to effectively integrate AI into their future classrooms.

AI for Progress Monitoring

My students and I also explored the potential of AI systems to monitor and track the progress of their target students over time, providing insights into whether specific interventions lead to improvements in reading fluency or comprehension. For instance, an AI-integrated platform like Edulastic could create growth charts that visually represent a student's progress, such as an increase in their words-per-minute reading rate over the course of a semester. These types of visualizations can make it easier for my pre-service teachers to evaluate the effectiveness of their current teaching strategies and make data-driven decisions.

In addition, I suggested that my students consider using AI to personalize learning experiences for their target students. AI systems could work to analyze literacy data to recommend tailored next steps, such as targeted activities or resources for students facing specific challenges. For example, after evaluating a student's performance on a reading comprehension quiz, an AI tool might recommend interactive exercises designed to strengthen skills like identifying the main idea and supporting details in a passage.

Time-Saving Benefits

For my teacher candidates, the most significant advantage of using AI was its ability to save time by simplifying and streamlining lesson planning and administrative tasks. They emphasized that AI automation reduced the effort required for routine processes, such as aligning lesson objectives with state standards, generating rubrics, and designing differentiated activities. By handling these time-consuming aspects of teaching, AI allowed them to focus more on instructional delivery and building meaningful relationships with their P-12 students.

Multiple students in my classes and field experiences provided specific examples of how AI positively impacted their workflow. A few students shared how AI helped them quickly develop a weekly unit and lesson plans tailored to a diverse classroom. By automating the planning process, they felt more confident in their ability to have time to engage with students individually, ensuring that each learner received the attention and support they needed. Another group of students indicated that they used AI to generate discussion prompts and assessment tools, which freed them up to focus on observing and adapting to student behavior during lessons. These students stated that this real-time flexibility allowed them to better address students' needs.

Beyond anecdotal experiences, research also supports the time-saving benefits of AI in education. AI-driven platforms can efficiently handle administrative tasks such as aligning lesson objectives with state standards, creating rubrics, and designing differentiated learning activities. By automating these processes, AI enhances teaching efficiency and allows educators to dedicate more time to instruction and student engagement (Edutopia, n.d..). Additionally, AI tools can empower pre-service teachers to craft structured weekly unit plans and lessons that cater to diverse classroom needs, giving them the confidence to focus on building relationships with students. Tools that generate discussion prompts and assessments further free up teachers' time, enabling them to concentrate on observing student behavior and making instructional adjustments as needed (TeachHub, 2023).

Supplementary Role of AI

Despite the occasional reliability challenges, my students saw AI as a valuable tool to enhance educators' professional judgment rather than replace it. My students in field experiences stated that they often used AI to generate initial ideas or draft materials but emphasized the importance of reviewing and refining content for accuracy and relevance. My pre-service teachers highlighted the necessity of cross-checking AI-generated content against state standards, such as the Kentucky Academic Standards, to ensure alignment with curriculum goals. This approach allowed them to save time on administrative tasks while maintaining high-quality, customized instructional materials suited to their P-5 students' needs.

These examples demonstrate how AI tools can promote creativity and support constructivist teaching principles, helping pre-service teachers adapt their instructional strategies to meet students' diverse needs. Respondents emphasized that they viewed AI as a supportive resource, not a substitute for their expertise. They regularly modified AI-generated ideas to better suit their students' learning levels, abilities, and developmental stages. For example, while AI suggested a group activity designed for kindergarten, my pre-service teachers, in turn, adjusted it to make it engaging and appropriate for third-grade students.

In addition, several respondents noted that AI helped them move beyond repetitive teaching methods, keeping lessons dynamic and engaging. When teaching the same subject across multiple days or classes, they used AI to suggest varied instructional approaches, such as incorporating interactive games one day and project-based learning the next. According to my students in field experience, this diversity in teaching strategies helped maintain students' motivation and enthusiasm for learning.

Visual Aids and Materials

I was somewhat surprised, though not entirely, to learn that many respondents did not rely on AI for creating visuals, graphic organizers, or teaching materials. Instead, they often turned to more traditional resources such as Teachers Pay Teachers, Pinterest, educational books, or pre-made templates to meet their classroom needs. Several students mentioned that they preferred downloading ready-made graphic organizers or anchor charts from trusted sources rather than experimenting with

AI-generated content. Others simply lacked experience using AI for visual aids, which contributed to their limited adoption of these tools.

However, among the pre-service teachers who did use AI for visual aids, its primary applications included generating slide content, designing anchor charts, and creating illustrative images to enhance lessons. My students found these tools particularly useful in making complex concepts more accessible and engaging by tailoring visuals to specific learning objectives.

For example, when teaching graphemes and phonemes, some respondents shared how AI-assisted tools helped them design visually engaging slides that clarified the relationship between sounds and letters. A common approach was creating slides that paired graphemes with corresponding phonemes, such as displaying "th" alongside an image of a thumb to represent the /θ/ sound or illustrating "ea" with a picture of a leaf to demonstrate the /i:/ sound. AI also facilitated the creation of interactive diagrams where students could match graphemes to their associated sounds, encouraging active participation.

Additionally, some pre-service teachers in my courses used AI to develop customized anchor charts for their classrooms. These charts often highlighted key grapheme-phoneme correspondences and morpheme patterns, using color coding and visuals to illustrate concepts such as prefixes, suffixes, long and short vowel sounds, or common digraphs like sh, ch, and ph. Two students described designing an anchor chart with a phoneme and morpheme treasure hunt theme, featuring graphemes like "ow" and "ou" alongside morphemes such as "-ing" and "-ed" on a pirate map. This approach helped students connect sounds and word structures with playful and engaging imagery.

While my students found AI helpful for generating initial drafts of these materials, they emphasized the need to refine and customize them to align with their specific teaching goals. For instance, two students noted that an AI-generated anchor chart on the water cycle required modifications to simplify the language for their students' grade level and to include examples relevant to their local environment. Additionally, some respondents used AI to generate visual prompts for creative writing activities, such as scene illustrations for descriptive writing and storytelling, to inspire their students' imaginations

AI to Simulate Teaching

Though less commonly mentioned, some respondents stated that they explored AI for creating simulations and interactive visual aids, such as digital reading practice activities. According to my students, these tools proved especially useful in offering hands-on, immersive learning experiences that enhanced students' understanding of complex concepts.

For example, one pre-service teacher used AI to design an interactive phonics activity where students matched sounds to corresponding graphemes in a drag-and-drop format. Another respondent created a digital fluency exercise where AI-generated text adjusted its difficulty level based on students' reading proficiency, providing real-time feedback and highlighting mispronounced words. Additionally, a few students experimented with AI-generated story-building activities, where students selected plot elements, and the AI adapted the narrative based on their choices, reinforcing comprehension and engagement. These interactive tools helped students practice literacy skills in a dynamic, engaging way while allowing teachers to track progress and adjust instruction accordingly.

AI as a Tool to Spark Creativity

Another area that my students appreciated in AI was its efficiency and ability to spark creativity, particularly when suggesting ideas for instructional materials or activities. Among the pre-service teachers who utilized AI for visual aids, its primary applications included generating slide content, designing anchor charts, and creating illustrative images to enhance their lessons. These tools were especially beneficial in supporting lessons by simplifying complex concepts and engaging students through visuals that aligned with specific learning goals.

For instance, when teaching vocabulary, respondents shared how AI-assisted tools helped them create visually engaging slides to introduce and reinforce new words. One approach involved using AI to design slides with images paired with target vocabulary, such as showing a picture of a sunflower alongside the word *radiant* to help students associate the term with its meaning. AI was also used to create interactive word maps, where key vocabulary words were connected to synonyms, antonyms, and example sentences, helping students build a deeper understanding of word relationships.

Moreover, my students mentioned that they used AI to generate slides for specific writing tasks. For instance, an AI-generated chart for teaching descriptive words about weather featured colorful images of clouds, sunshine, and rain paired with adjectives like "dreary," "bright," and "drizzling." Another example included a thematic anchor chart for vocabulary related to storytelling, where words like "protagonist," "conflict," and "resolution" were illustrated with icons and examples from familiar stories, making abstract concepts more concrete and memorable for students.

2. ANALYZING STUDENT DATA

Most participants had not utilized AI for analyzing or interpreting student data. However, a few respondents recognized AI's potential to support data-related tasks, such as streamlining data collection, organizing student information, generating progress-tracking sheets, and identifying patterns over time. Some also mentioned that while they had not yet integrated AI into their practice, they were open to exploring its capabilities for improving efficiency in assessment and personalized instruction. Below are some specific responses from my students during their field experience, reflecting their perspectives on AI's role in data management.

Table 1.

Category	Description	Tools & Features
Formative Assessments	AI-generated comprehension questions tailored to student proficiency.	**Tools:** ChatGPT **Features:** Exit tickets, differentiated questioning.
Summative Assessments	AI-enhanced quizzes with adaptive difficulty based on student responses.	**Tools:** Online quiz platforms with AI integration. **Features:** Progression-based questioning, vocabulary support.
Rubrics and Scoring Guides	AI-assisted rubric creation for evaluating reading fluency.	**Criteria:** Expression & tone, accuracy, speed (90-110 WPM). **AI Feature:** Automated refinement of proficiency descriptors.
Progress Monitoring	AI-driven tracking of student fluency over time.	**Tools:** Fluency data platforms, assessment generators. **Features:** Auto-tracking, visualization of trends.
Fluency Data Tracking Platforms	AI listens to student reading, calculates WPM, and identifies errors.	**Tools:** Literably, Amira Learning. **Features:** Real-time error detection, visual dashboards, accuracy tracking.
AI-Driven Assessment Generators	AI-powered tools track reading scores, generate reports, and personalize learning plans.	**Tools:** Google Sheets + AI Plugins, i-Ready. **Features:** Auto-generated progress graphs, trend analysis.
Speech Recognition Tools	AI assesses oral reading fluency and provides real-time feedback.	**Tools:** Speechify, Fluency Tutor by Texthelp. **Features:** Identifies pauses, mispronunciations, fluency trends.
Visualization Software	AI-driven tools create visual representations of reading progress.	**Tools:** Canva, Tableau. **Features:** Bar graphs, line charts, heat maps, customizable dashboards.

continued on following page

Table 1. Continued

Category	Description	Tools & Features
Custom AI-Integrated Tools	AI automates fluency data collection and analysis.	**Tools:** Zapier + AI, ChatGPT API. **Features:** WPM calculations, automated progress tracking, web apps for fluency monitoring.
Example Workflow for Progress Monitoring	Step-by-step process for AI-assisted fluency tracking.	**Step 1:** Record fluency (Literably, Amira) **Step 2:** Organize data (Google Sheets, Excel) **Step 3:** Visualize trends (Tableau, Canva) **Step 4:** Plan interventions.
Benefits of AI in Progress Monitoring	How AI improves fluency assessment.	**Efficiency:** Automates data collection. **Accuracy:** Reduces human error. **Customization:** Personalized student recommendations. **Engagement:** Visual tools for parent-teacher communication.
Usage of AI in Assessments	AI-generated formative and summative assessment materials.	**Tools:** ChatGPT, quiz generators. **Features:** Custom questions, adaptive difficulty.
Rubrics and Scoring Guides	AI-generated rubrics refined by educators.	**Tools:** AI-based rubric creators. **Features:** Formatting assistance, integration with existing materials.
Analyzing Student Data	AI-assisted data collection, tracking, and analysis.	**Usage Trends:** Some use AI for organizing data; most have not explored AI-driven data interpretation.

Reflection and Commentary

Some participants stated that they tapped into AI to refine their reflective writing, making it more polished and professional. Others used AI to paraphrase their teaching observations or improve clarity in their submissions. However, a subset of respondents opted not to use AI for reflection at all, preferring more traditional methods of self-assessment.

Regarding originality, several respondents were intentional about modifying AI-generated text to align with their authentic voice and personal insights. Many viewed AI as a tool for idea generation, organization, or enhancing structure rather than as a means of producing final, unedited work. This approach suggests a balance between leveraging AI for efficiency while maintaining individual expression in reflective writing.

1. **Experience with AI for simulations**:

Response 1 (AI used occasionally for planning): This respondent describes having used AI for simulating teaching scenarios to check if their lesson content aligns with the grade level. They report finding it helpful in refining language and ideas that may be too difficult for students. This response shows a positive, practical use of AI to improve teaching plans.

2. **No experience but interest**:
   Response 2 (No experience, but open to trying): This respondent has not used AI for teaching scenarios but acknowledges its potential value, indicating an openness to trying it in the future. The statement suggests a recognition of AI's potential, but no current usage.
3. **No experience and no intention expressed**:
   Responses 3, 4, 5, and 7 (No experience with AI): These responses indicate no experience with AI simulations or feedback, and there is no further elaboration or indication of plans to use AI in the future. These responses are more neutral or passive and suggest that the respondent may not yet see a clear use case for AI in their teaching practices.
4. **Limited or partial use**:
   Response 6 (AI used to check a lesson plan): This respondent has used AI to review lesson plans and suggest improvements but has not used it for more interactive teaching simulations. The use described here is somewhat limited to reviewing lesson quality rather than active simulations or scenario-based feedback.

Overall, most responses suggest that while some pre-service teachers in their field experience are open to or have experimented with AI, there is a notable lack of widespread or deep engagement with AI tools for simulating teaching scenarios or providing feedback. The more positive responses (1 and 6) illustrate tangible benefits, such as refining lesson plans and improving content accessibility, while the majority (responses 2, 3, 4, 5, and 7) indicate either no experience with AI or only limited, passive exposure. This suggests that AI may still be underutilized in the context of teaching practice, but there is potential for increased adoption if educators see more direct, practical benefits.

Ethical Considerations and Bias

The integration of AI into pre-service teacher field experiences offers multiple possibilities, but it also raises important ethical considerations. These concerns span data privacy, algorithmic bias, transparency, the potential deskilling of teachers, and equitable access.

Moreover, it is good to remember that AI systems used in education often collect and analyze student data, including academic performance, learning behaviors, and even personal information. Protecting the privacy and security of this sensitive data is paramount. Pre-service teachers using AI tools must be trained on data privacy regulations (e.g., FERPA in the US) and best practices for handling student information responsibly. Furthermore, the AI systems themselves must be secure and compliant with relevant data protection laws.

In addition, ethical concerns must be observed while dealing with algorithms because AI algorithms are trained on data, and if that data reflects existing societal biases, and as result, the AI system can perpetuate or even amplify those biases. For example, an AI tool used to assess student writing might be biased against students from certain linguistic or cultural backgrounds if the training data primarily consists of writing samples from a dominant group.

One concern with using AI in pre-service teacher training is the lack of transparency. Many AI algorithms are so complex that it is hard to understand how they reach their conclusions. This "black box" issue is a problem for education because pre-service teachers and their mentors need to know how AI tools make decisions so they can properly judge the results and make sure they fit with good teaching practices.

Accountability is also a key consideration. When AI is used for important things like student assessment or teacher evaluations, it is vital to know who is responsible if the AI makes a mistake or produces a biased result. There needs to be a clear way to fix errors and address problems caused by AI.

Furthermore, the issue of the deskilling of pre-service teachers was discussed. This case study frequently highlighted pre-service teachers' anxieties about deskilling and over-reliance on AI. Students often expressed concern that dependence on these tools could hinder the development of their professional judgment and critical thinking. Survey responses echoed this sentiment, emphasizing AI's role as a support, not a replacement, for hands-on teaching experience. Furthermore, automating core pedagogical tasks with AI could deprive pre-service teachers of valuable learning opportunities, potentially hindering the development of essential teaching skills. Therefore, according to the respondents of the survey, AI integration should prioritize enhancing, not diminishing, these crucial abilities.

Equity Considerations

Ensuring equity and access to AI in education is paramount, not only for students but also for pre-service teachers as they gain experience in the field. The "digital divide" poses a significant challenge, as the advantages of AI-powered learning and teaching tools may not be available to all pre-service teachers, particularly during their field placements. If some student teachers lack access to the necessary technology, infrastructure, or reliable internet access at their placement schools, they may be unable to utilize these tools effectively. This disparity could hinder their ability to develop proficiency in using AI for instruction, assessment, or personalized learning, placing them at a disadvantage compared to peers with access. Furthermore, pre-service teachers from under-resourced backgrounds may be more likely to be placed in schools lacking these resources, perpetuating a cycle of inequality. As AI becomes increasingly integrated into educational practices, bridging this digital divide is crucial to ensure that all pre-service teachers, regardless of their placement location or background, have equitable opportunities to learn and utilize these technologies (Van Dijk, 2006).

Moreover, AI tools designed for classroom use must be accessible to diverse learners, and pre-service teachers need training and support in utilizing these tools effectively with all students. This includes students with disabilities, who may require specific accommodations to effectively utilize these technologies. Pre-service teachers need training in how to adapt AI tools and integrate them with assistive technologies to meet individual student needs.

Careful consideration must be given to issues of usability, ensuring that interfaces are compatible with assistive technologies and various learning needs. Language accessibility is also essential, as AI tools should be available in multiple languages or offer translation capabilities to cater to diverse linguistic backgrounds within classrooms. Pre-service teachers need experience and guidance in selecting and using linguistically appropriate AI tools to ensure cultural appropriateness. Pre-service teachers, in this case, might need professional development to recognize and address potential cultural biases in AI tools and learn how to adapt instruction and content to be culturally responsive. Ignoring these considerations could lead to AI tools that are ineffective or even discriminatory for certain student populations and pre-service teachers who are ill-equipped to meet the diverse needs of their students. Creating truly inclusive AI in education requires a commitment to universal design principles, ongoing evaluation, and robust professional development for pre-service teachers to ensure that these technologies benefit all learners, regardless of their background or abilities. (Rose, 2016).

Ethics and Originality

The responses from the teacher candidates in my courses regarding ethics and originality in AI usage reflect a diverse range of strategies aimed at maintaining both authenticity in academic work and adherence to teaching expectations. These teacher candidates have adopted various approaches to ensure that AI serves as a supportive tool rather than a substitute for critical thinking and personal expression.

Some of my students emphasized the importance of ethical considerations, such as properly attributing AI-assisted content, avoiding over-reliance on automated tools, and ensuring that AI-generated text does not compromise academic integrity. Others highlighted the need for transparency in AI usage, advocating for clear guidelines on when and how AI can be used in their field experiences and education settings in general.

In terms of originality, many participants reported using AI primarily for brainstorming, structuring their ideas, or refining their writing rather than generating complete responses. They stressed the necessity of revising AI-assisted content to reflect their own voice, insights, and pedagogical knowledge.

Table 2.

Category	Key Observations	Common Strategies & Tools
General Observations on Originality	AI is primarily used as a guide, with users paraphrasing and modifying content to ensure authenticity.	**Strategies:** Rewording AI suggestions, adding personal insights, using AI for brainstorming.
Reliance on AI Tools	Some users minimally revise AI-generated content, while others use plagiarism checkers.	**Strategies:** Using AI checkers, slight word modifications, ensuring balance between AI assistance and originality.
Thorough Review & Adjustment	Users refine AI-generated content multiple times to meet standards and personalize responses.	**Strategies:** Repeated revisions, ensuring alignment with assignment expectations.
Adherence to Teaching Standards	AI-generated content is compared to educational standards and past lesson plans for consistency.	**Strategies:** Cross-referencing AI output with lesson objectives, verifying alignment with curriculum.
AI-Specific Adjustments	Users validate AI-generated content against personal teaching knowledge and external resources.	**Strategies:** Fact-checking, refining AI responses to ensure specificity.
Use of AI in Lesson Planning	AI is used with strict adherence to curriculum requirements and age appropriateness.	**Strategies:** Giving AI detailed instructions, verifying final lesson content.
Confidentiality - Ethical Use of Student Data	Users avoid sharing identifiable student information with AI tools.	**Strategies:** Omitting names and private data, ensuring compliance with ethical guidelines.

continued on following page

Table 2. Continued

Category	Key Observations	Common Strategies & Tools
Overall Ethical Considerations	Users recognize ethical responsibility and focus on personalization over AI dependence.	**Key Takeaways:** AI is a tool, not a substitute; inconsistency in revision rigor; ethical diligence varies.
Reflection on AI's Impact on Written Commentary	Some users avoid AI in reflections, while others use it for organization and structure.	**Common Themes:** AI is used to improve clarity and professionalism, but concerns over authenticity persist.
Limited or No Use of AI	Some individuals do not incorporate AI in reflections due to preference for self-reliance.	**Reasons:** Unfamiliarity with AI's role in reflection, preference for human feedback.
AI Used to Organize or Improve Structure	AI assists with structuring ideas, improving clarity, and ensuring professional tone.	**Strategies:** AI-generated outlines, refining sentence structures.
AI for Refining but Not Replacing Voice	AI suggestions are used for improvement, but personal voice remains dominant.	**Strategies:** Reviewing and adjusting AI-generated text to match personal style.
AI for Idea Generation	AI is used to brainstorm and enhance reflections, but content is always revised.	**Strategies:** Using AI for ideation, then making extensive personal modifications.
Minimal or Selective Use	Some individuals use AI only for grammar checks or inspiration.	**Concerns:** Over-reliance on AI, difficulty defending AI-generated reflections.
Other Methods for Feedback	Some users prefer human feedback over AI for reflection improvement.	**Alternatives:** Family reviews, independent revisions.
Key Takeaways on AI in Reflection	AI is used sparingly, with a focus on personal engagement in reflective writing.	**Themes:** Preference for self-reflection, cautious AI use, emphasis on authenticity.

Confidentiality and Safeguarding Student Data

The responses to the survey regarding confidentiality and the safeguarding of student data in AI reveal a variety of approaches, each reflecting a commitment to precautionary measures. Some respondents emphasize strict adherence to institutional policies and legal frameworks, ensuring that AI tools comply with data protection regulations. Others highlight the importance of transparency, advocating for clear communication with students and stakeholders about how AI interacts with sensitive information. Additionally, some responses suggest proactive strategies, such as limiting data input, anonymizing student information, and regularly auditing AI systems for security vulnerabilities. This diverse range of perspectives underscores the complexity of balancing AI's potential benefits with ethical considerations in education.

Table 3

Category	Key Observations	Common Strategies & Tools
Confidentiality and Safeguarding Student Data	Users take significant measures to protect student privacy by anonymizing data and avoiding personal details.	**Strategies:** Using generic identifiers (e.g., "Student A"), entering only non-sensitive data, ensuring ethical AI use.
Precautionary Measures	Many respondents omit identifying information and input only generalized data to maintain confidentiality.	**Approach:** Avoid using names, addresses, or school-specific details.
Ethical Concerns	Users emphasize the importance of never submitting sensitive student data to AI platforms.	**Precaution:** Ensuring no personal data, student work, or specific details are entered into AI tools.
Perception and Professionalism in Using AI	AI usage faces varying levels of acceptance, with some resistance from academic supervisors.	**Challenges:** AI is viewed differently across academic settings, leading to inconsistent policies.
Challenges with Acceptance	Some professors and supervisors are resistant to AI use, while others are more open to it.	**Impact:** Mixed experiences in AI acceptance create uncertainty for users.
Fear of Misuse and Guilt	Some respondents worry about being accused of AI misuse or plagiarism, leading to cautious use.	**Strategies:** Using AI only as a reference tool, ensuring work remains original.
AI as a Tool for Efficiency and Improvement	AI is often used for refining ideas, grammar checks, and improving clarity but is not always fully accepted.	**Approach:** AI assists with structure and refinement, but users personalize final output.
AI's Role in Innovation	AI can enhance lesson planning and delivery, helping educators think more critically about their work.	**Benefit:** AI offers support in brainstorming and refining instructional ideas.
Resistance to AI for Ethical or Professional Reasons	AI is sometimes seen as a shortcut, leading to concerns about laziness or lack of originality.	**Challenges:** Need for recognition that AI can be a legitimate tool for idea refinement.
Need for Professional Recognition of AI	Some respondents want AI to be acknowledged as a helpful tool rather than a shortcut.	**Desire:** More academic acceptance of AI as a professional enhancement tool.
Key Takeaways on AI Use and Ethics	Users are mindful of ethical AI use, balancing confidentiality and professionalism while facing mixed reception.	**Themes:** Ethical diligence, inconsistent AI acceptance, fear of misuse, and the need for AI recognition.

The responses regarding the reflection process in AI reveal a range of attitudes and practices toward using AI in writing commentary about teaching experiences. The key themes and findings from the responses are:

Limited or No Use of AI for Reflection

Many respondents indicated that they do not utilize AI tools to reflect on their teaching practices or enhance their written reflections. This suggests that, for some educators, AI is not perceived as a necessary component of the reflection process.

Instead, they may prefer self-reflection or more traditional methods, such as peer feedback, journaling, or structured observation, to evaluate and refine their instructional approaches. This highlights the need for further exploration into how AI can be integrated meaningfully into reflective practice without diminishing personal or collaborative insights.

Key takeaway: AI is not universally embraced for reflective purposes, with many preferring to avoid it in favor of personal reflection.

AI as a Tool for Organization and Structure

Several of my students recognized AI's potential to improve the clarity, structure, and organization of their reflective writing while still preserving their authentic voice and insights. Rather than relying on AI to generate content, they viewed it as a supportive tool for refining their ideas, ensuring logical flow, and enhancing readability.

Some students found AI useful for outlining their reflections, helping them organize key points before drafting their final responses. Others used AI to rephrase complex thoughts more clearly or to adjust sentence structure for better coherence. A few also noted that AI-assisted organization allowed them to focus more on the depth of their reflections rather than struggling with formatting or wording.

Table 4.

Category	Key Observations	Key Takeaways
AI as a Tool for Organization and Structure	A smaller group of respondents used AI to improve the organization and coherence of their reflections, making them more professional and structured.	AI is sometimes used for structuring and organizing ideas, but it is rarely the sole method for reflection.
Refining Without Replacing Personal Voice	AI was used for refining grammar, sentence structure, and clarity while ensuring that personal voice and thinking remained intact.	AI helps refine content, but respondents emphasize maintaining their personal voice through editing and adjustments.
AI for Idea Generation	AI was helpful for generating ideas and improving sentence structure, but respondents revised AI-generated content to ensure authenticity.	AI serves as an idea-generation tool, but revisions are needed to keep reflections aligned with personal experiences.
Selective or Minimal Use	Some respondents used AI selectively for grammar checks or idea generation, while others avoided it due to concerns over authenticity and over-reliance.	Hesitance to fully embrace AI for reflection is often due to concerns over authenticity and defending AI usage.

continued on following page

Table 4. Continued

Category	Key Observations	Key Takeaways
Alternative Feedback Mechanisms	Some individuals preferred peer or family reviews over AI, valuing human input for refining reflections.	Non-AI feedback methods remain important for those who prioritize human interaction over AI assistance.
Key Insights	Respondents view AI as a supportive tool but emphasize personal voice and authenticity in reflections.	**1. AI as a Supportive Tool, Not a Replacement:** AI aids organization and refinement but does not replace personal reflection. **2. Concerns Over Authenticity and Trust:** Some hesitate to use AI due to concerns about how AI-generated content is perceived. **3. Personal Voice Remains Central:** Even when using AI, respondents ensure their unique voice is preserved.

CONCLUSION

Drawing from recent research, my own experiences working with pre-service teachers during their field placements, and insights gathered from a survey conducted in my methods courses, I have concluded that AI holds significant potential to enhance pre-service teacher training in their field experiences. By providing personalized and adaptive learning experiences, AI can support teacher candidates in their field placements to refine their instructional practices through targeted feedback, making assessment processes more efficient and improving lesson development.

My students discovered that AI served as a powerful tool in their field experience, improving both efficiency and creativity. They relied on AI for various instructional tasks, including lesson planning, designing assessments, analyzing literacy data, differentiating instruction, and generating ideas for teaching strategies. While they recognized AI's greatest benefit in its ability to save time, they continued to prefer traditional resources for creating teaching materials and visual aids. AI also proved useful in providing feedback on their teaching practices, though its role in this area remains in the early stages of adoption by the pre-service teachers in my courses. Ultimately, my students highlighted the importance of critically assessing and adapting AI-generated content to ensure it aligns with their instructional goals and effectively supports their teaching experience.

Based on the insights gained from this case study and survey responses, I recognize the importance of equipping pre-service teachers with the skills to engage critically and ethically with AI in their future classrooms. Therefore, moving forward, I plan to implement targeted strategies that will empower them to analyze, integrate, and adapt AI tools effectively within their field experiences while upholding ethical considerations and best teaching practices.

REFERENCES

Academy Victoria. (2024). *Enhancing differentiation in the classroom using generative artificial intelligence*. Academy Victoria. Retrieved from https://www.academy.vic.gov.au/resources/enhancing-differentiation-classroom-using-generative-artificial-intelligence

Edutopia. (2024). *Using AI tools for differentiated instruction*. Edutopia. Retrieved from https://www.edutopia.org/article/using-ai-tools-differentiated-instruction

Edutopia. (n.d.). *AI tools for lesson planning: Streamlining teacher workflows*. Retrieved from https://www.edutopia.org/article/ai-tools-lesson-planning

Hsiang, S., & Hsu, Y. (2024). *Innovative teaching: How pre-service teachers use artificial intelligence to teach science to fourth graders. Computers in Education Research Journal, 15*(2), 123-134. Retrieved from https://www.cedtech.net/download/innovative-teaching-how-pre-service-teachers-use-artificial-intelligence-to-teach-science-to-fourth-15686.pdf

Karpouzis, K., Zhang, Y., Li, H., & Chen, J. (2024). *Generative AI for lesson planning: Customizing education for diverse classrooms*. Retrieved from https://arxiv.org/abs/2403.12071

Kim, J., & Lee, S. (2024). Pre-service teachers' dual perspectives on generative AI: Benefits, challenges, and integrating into teaching and learning. *Journal of Educational Technology and Pedagogy, 29*(1), 78–92. https://www.researchgate.net/publication/381851959_Pre-service_teachers%27_dual_perspectives_on_generative_AI_Benefits_challenges_and_integrating_into_teaching_and_learning

Magic School AI. (n.d.). *Lesson Plan Generator: Creating standards-aligned content for educators*. Retrieved from https://www.magicschool.ai/tools/lesson-plan-generator

Rose, D. H. (2016). *Universal design for learning: Theory and practice*. CAST Professional Publishing.

TeachHub. (2023, November). *AI-powered lesson planning: Revolutionizing the way teachers create content*. Retrieved from https://www.teachhub.com/teaching-strategies/2023/11/ai-powered-lesson-planning-revolutionizing-the-way-teachers-create-content

The Teaching Factor. (2024, February 25). *10 ways teachers can use AI tools to support the diverse learners in their classroom. The Teaching Factor.* Retrieved from https://theteachingfactor.wordpress.com/2024/02/25/10-ways-teachers-can-use-ai-tools-to-support-the-diverse-learners-in-their-classroom

Van Dijk, J. A. G. M. (2006). Digital divide research, achievements and shortcomings. *Poetics*, *34*(4-5), 221–235. DOI: 10.1016/j.poetic.2006.05.004

Wu, X., Zhang, Y., Li, H., & Chen, J. (2024). *Artificial intelligence in personalized learning: A review of smart education systems.* Retrieved from https://arxiv.org/abs/2402.01666

Zhang, X., & Wang, L. (2024). Supporting learning with AI-generated images: A research-backed guide. *Journal of Educational Technology*, *32*(4), 256–271. https://link.springer.com/article/10.1007/s10956-024-10159-z

Chapter 7
Artificial Intelligence in Education Higher Education in the Business Area

Albérico Travassos Rosário
https://orcid.org/0000-0003-4793-4110
GOVCOPP, IADE, Universidade Europeia, Portugal

ABSTRACT

Artificial intelligence (AI) has revolutionized several sectors, including higher education, by personalizing the educational experience to fit individual student needs. Integrating AI into business curricula equips students with the skills needed in a market increasingly driven by AI and data analysis. Institutions that adopt these technologies are better positioned to deliver quality education, prepare students for a data- and AI-driven future, and enhance operational efficiency. However, it is crucial to address the ethical and privacy challenges associated with AI to ensure responsible and transparent implementation. Based on the above, it is intended to systematically review the bibliometric literature on Artificial Intelligence in Education Higher Education in the business area using the Scopus database with the analysis of 94 academic and/or scientific documents.

INTRODUCTION

The emergence of artificial intelligence (AI) technologies has brought about transformative changes across various sectors, including higher education. AI can process vast amounts of data, automate tasks, and make predictive analyses (Crompton &

DOI: 10.4018/979-8-3373-4576-5.ch007

Burke, 2023). These technologies have revolutionized how educational institutions operate and deliver content to higher education institutions. For instance, Bates et al. (2020) indicate that AI is integrated into administrative processes, learning management systems, and student support services. It is also reshaping the traditional educational model from personalized learning platforms to virtual tutors, making the education system more adaptive, accessible, and efficient (Bearman et al., 2023). The potential for AI to enhance both teaching and learning experiences is vast, offering educators new ways to engage students and meet their diverse needs.

With AI significantly impacting multiple industries and job markets, it has become crucial for business schools to adopt and integrate these innovations into the curriculum. This is evidenced in Abdelwahab et al.'s (2023) study, which explains that as AI demonstrates its potential to reshape businesses, industries, and other competitive sectors, its impact will inevitably extend to business education. The AI-driven market requires new skills and knowledge, including data-driven decision-making, financial analysis, and market forecasting (Bearman et al., 2023). As a result, business schools are developing curricula that accommodate this change. These technologies enable business students to engage with real-time data, simulate business environments, and develop predictive models that mirror the complexities of global markets. Business education programs are increasingly using AI-driven simulations, big data analytics, and digital marketing tools to provide students with practical, hands-on experience that prepares them for the demands of the business world (Renz & Hilbig, 2020). In this context, AI is an instructional tool and a crucial element in training future business leaders to think critically and strategically in an ever-evolving global economy.

AI technologies have influenced the operational structure and framework of higher business education institutions. For instance, AI-driven systems monitor student performance, identify learning gaps, and tailor learning experiences to individual needs (Al-Haimi et al., 2021). This personalized approach allows students in business programs to receive targeted support, enhancing their academic performance and overall learning outcomes. In addition, AI tools help streamline administrative tasks such as grading, course scheduling, and advising, thereby allowing faculty to focus more on research and student engagement (Bearman et al., 2023). Despite these positive impacts, AI innovations in business schools are associated with numerous concerns, such as data privacy, security, and AI literacy. This systematic bibliometric literature review (LRSB) synthesizes data from 94 sources on the application and impact of AI in business education.

METHODOLOGICAL APPROACH

This researcher employed a Systematic Bibliometric Literature Review (LRSB) to analyze the application of AI in higher education, specifically within the business education domain. A systematic review process was chosen to ensure a comprehensive and unbiased selection of relevant literature. This methodology also allows the identification of key themes, trends, and influential works within the field. The Preferred Reporting Items for Systematic Reviews and Meta-Analyses (PRISMA 2020) model guided the methodology, ensuring a rigorous and transparent selection process. PRISMA 2020 provides a structured framework for reporting systematic reviews, including identification, screening, eligibility, and inclusion stages (Haddaway et al., 2022). This methodology provides a robust approach to ensuring a systematic, replicable, and transparent review process, making it ideal for synthesizing a large body of literature.

To gather and select pertinent materials, the Scopus database was utilized, as recommended by Rosário & Casaca (2023) and Rosário et al. (2023, 2021). They describe Scopus as one of the largest and most comprehensive databases for abstracts and citations, offering a wide range of sources such as conference proceedings, books, and journal articles, covering both global and regional research. Scopus ensures high data quality through the supervision of an independent Content Selection and Advisory Board, which enforces a rigorous process for content selection and regular re-evaluation.

Unlike traditional literature reviews, the Systematic Bibliometric Literature Review (LRSB) method offers a more structured and rigorous approach to analyzing research on a particular topic, as discussed by Rosário & Casaca (2023) and Rosário et al. (2023, 2021). This method prioritizes a refined selection process, ensuring that only the most relevant studies are included. Additionally, it establishes a clear audit trail, allowing readers to assess the methodology, findings, and overall quality of the selected research.

The LRSB approach follows a systematic process for screening and selecting sources to maintain both reliability and relevance. This process is divided into three phases and six steps, as outlined in Table 1, drawing on the framework established by Rosário & Casaca (2023) and Rosário et al. (2023, 2021).

Table 1. Process of systematic LRSB.

Fase	Step	Description
Exploration	Step 1	formulating the research problem
	Step 2	searching for appropriate literature
	Step 3	critical appraisal of the selected studies
	Step 4	data synthesis from individual sources
Interpretation	Step 5	reporting findings and recommendations
Communication	Step 6	Presentation of the LRSB report

Source: adapted *Rosário & Casaca (2023);Rosário et al. (2023,2021).*

The researchers relied on the Scopus database to identify and select credible sources that are widely acknowledged within the academic and scientific community. However, one limitation of this study is its exclusive focus on Scopus, which meant that other academic and scientific databases were not included. Additionally, the search was limited to publications available up until September 2024. The selection process prioritized peer-reviewed academic and scientific works to ensure the quality and reliability of the sources used.

The search process was conducted using the Scopus database, one of the most extensive and trusted sources of peer-reviewed academic publications. Initially, the search query targeted documents containing the term "Artificial Intelligence" in their titles, abstracts, or keywords (TITLE-ABS-KEY), yielding 601,273 documents. A second search was conducted to narrow the scope, combining the term "artificial intelligence" with "education," reducing the number of documents to 31,093. Given that the research focuses on higher education, an additional filter was applied by including the exact keyword "higher education," which refined the results to 1,233 documents. Finally, the search was further limited to the subject area of "Business, Management, and Accounting" (BUSI), resulting in 94 documents. Figure 1 below shows the PRISMA 2020 flow diagram used to visualize the process of filtering and selecting relevant studies.

Inclusion and exclusion criteria were applied to ensure the relevance and rigor of the documents analyzed in the final report (Table 2). Articles were included if they were published in peer-reviewed journals and focused on the intersection of marketing strategy and brand building. Publications outside the disciplines of business, marketing, or branding were excluded to maintain a focused dataset. This systematic filtering process ensured that the final literature synthesized was of high quality and directly aligned with the research objectives. The search process is summarized in Table 2 below.

Table 2. Screening methodology.

Database Scopus	Screening	Publications
Meta-search	Keyword: Artificial Intelligence,	601,273
First Inclusion Criterion	Keyword: Artificial Intelligence, Education	31,093
Second Inclusion Criteria	Keyword: Artificial Intelligence Education Exact Keyword: Higher Education	1,233
Third inclusion criterion	Keyword: Artificial Intelligence Education Exact Keyword: Higher Education limited to the subarea: Business, Management and Accounting	94
Screening	Keyword: Artificial Intelligence, Education Exact Keyword: Higher Education limited to the subarea: Business, Management and Accounting Published until September 2024	

Source: own elaboration

We conducted a thorough analysis of the documents using content and thematic analysis techniques, drawing on the methodologies established by Rosário & Casaca (2023) and Rosário et al. (2023, 2021). To ensure the inclusion of high-quality and relevant academic sources, we applied strict selection criteria. Only studies that specifically examined luxury brands and their consumption were considered. The eligibility of each document was evaluated based on its relevance to the research topic, methodological robustness, and publication in peer-reviewed sources (Figure 1).

Figure 1. PRISMA 2020 flow diagram for the systematic literature search.

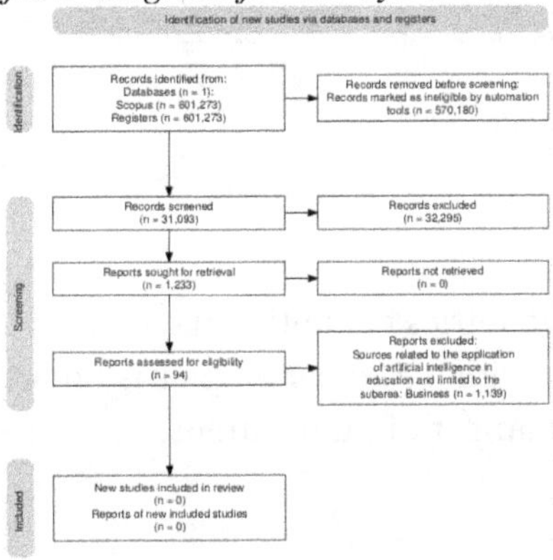

Subsequently, 94 scientific and academic documents indexed in Scopus were analyzed using both narrative and bibliometric approaches, as described by Rosário & Casaca (2023) and Rosário et al. (2023, 2021). These methods were employed to examine the content of the documents and identify recurring themes that directly addressed the research questions. Of the 94 documents selected, 47 Journals; 37 Conference proceedings; 6 Book series; and 4 Books.

PUBLICATION DISTRIBUTION

Peer-reviewed articles on how artificial intelligence in education higher education in the business area September 2024. The years 2023 and 2024 we had the highest number of peer-reviewed publications on the subject, reaching 8. Figure 2 summarizes the peer-reviewed literature published until September 2024.

Figure 2. Documents by year

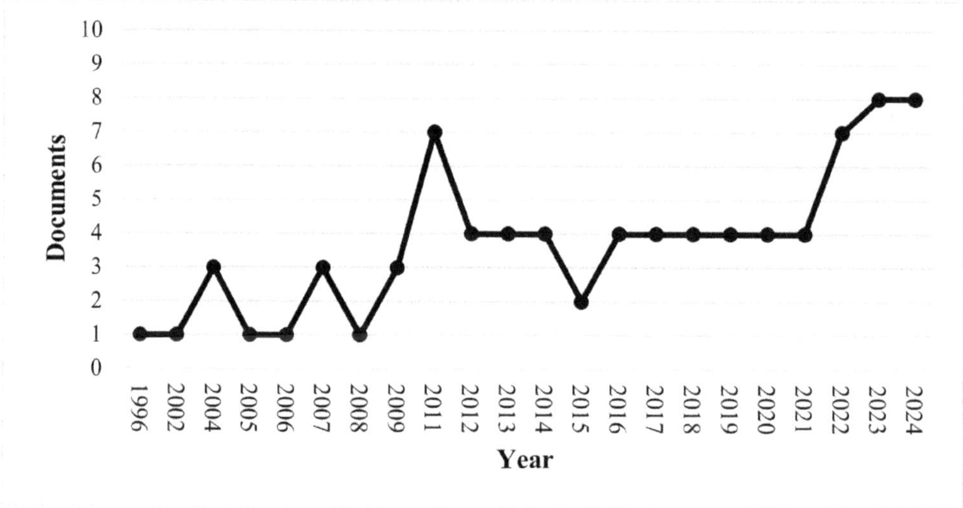

Source: own elaboration

Figure 3 displays the countries exhibiting the highest levels of scientific output in specific research areas, with particular emphasis on the USA, India, and China, which boast the greatest number of publications.

Figure 3. Scientific production by country.

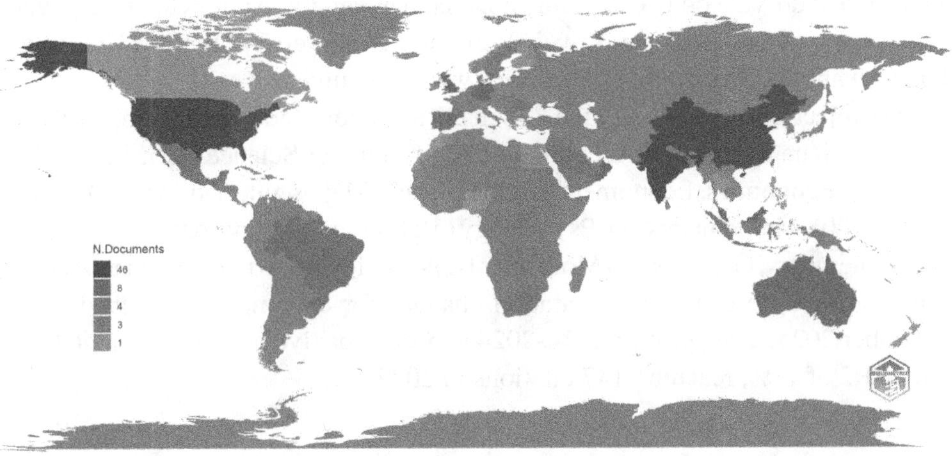

Table 3, along with Figure 3, visually illustrates the top 10 nations making notable scientific contributions in the examined domains. This investigation aims to identify countries that prioritize artificial intelligence in education higher education in the business area.

Table 3. Top 10 countries by number of publications.

Country	Number of Publications
USA	46
INDIA	42
CHINA	36
BAHRAIN	15
MALAYSIA	11
GERMANY	10
UK	10
OMAN	9
AUSTRALIA	8
SPAIN	7

Source: own elaboration

The publications were sorted out as follows: Henan Polytechnic University (3); Jilin Business and Technology College (3); Applied Science University (3); University of Technology and Applied Sciences Salalah (3); with 2 documents (Zangador Research Institute; Universiti Sains Malaysia; Universidad de Deusto; Glasgow

Caledonian University; University of Bristol; Universitat Autònoma de Barcelona; Universidade do Vale do Rio dos Sinos; Dalian University; Amity University; Varna University of Management; Lovely Professional University; Taylor's University Malaysia) and the remaining publications with 1 document.

The subject areas covered by the 82 scientific and/or academic documents were: Business, Management and Accounting (94); Computer Science (45); Social Sciences (32); Economics, Econometrics and Finance (31); Engineering (22); Decision Sciences (20); Mathematics (8); Psychology (5); Energy (5); Environmental Science (4); Biochemistry, Genetics and Molecular Biology (1); and Arts and Humanities (1).

In Figure 4 we can analyze citation changes for documents published up to September 2024. The period ≤2014-2024 shows a positive net growth in citations with an R2 of 11%, reaching 147 citations in 2022.

Figure 4. evolution of citations between ≤2014 and 2024.

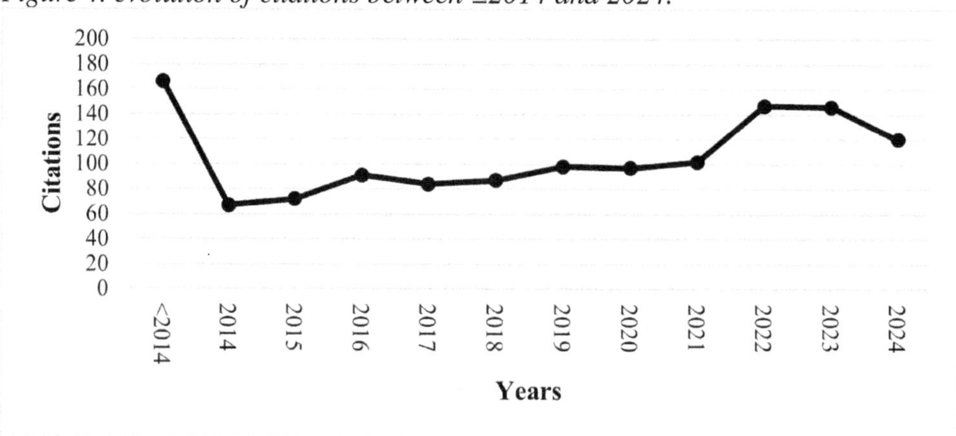

Source: own elaboration

The most quoted article was "Exploring the impact of artificial intelligence on teaching and learning in higher education" by Popenici & Kerr (2017), with 539 quotes published in Research and Practice in Technology Enhanced Learning 0,92 (SJR), the best quartile (Q1) and with H index (28), this article investigates the "phenomena of the emergence of the use of artificial intelligence in teaching and learning in higher education".

The h-index measures the productivity and impact of published works by identifying the highest number of articles that each have received at least an equal number of citations. Of the documents considered for h-index, 13 were cited at least 13 times.

Citations of all scientific and/or academic documents from the period ≤2014 to September 2024, with a total of 1,187 citations, of the 94 documents 41 were not cited. The self-citation of documents in the period ≤2014 to September 2024 was self-cited 60.

The bibliometric analysis, using the main keywords "Artificial Intelligence in Education Higher Education in the business area" revealed key indicators of the evolving landscape of scientific and academic information within the documents, as shown in Figure 5. These insights were derived through the use of VOSviewer scientific software, with a particular focus on identifying the primary search terms: "Artificial Intelligence," "Education," "Higher Education" and "Business ".

Figure 5. Network of all keywords

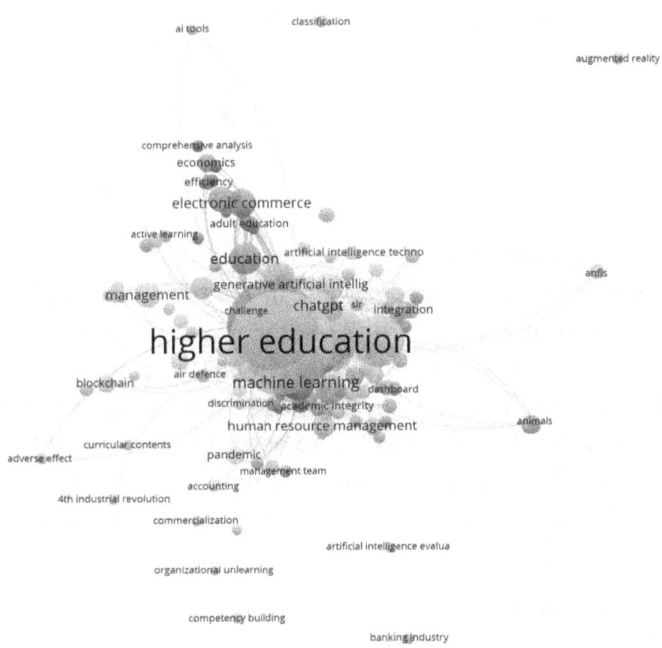

Figure 6. Network of linked keywords

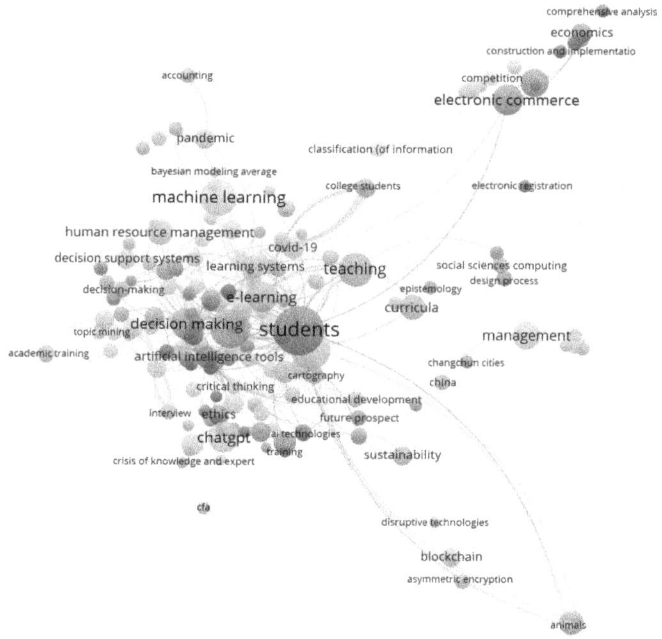

This study is based on a thorough review of scientific and academic literature exploring marketing strategies in brand building. Figure 6 provides a detailed examination of the interrelated keywords, highlighting the connections between key terms across the academic articles. This analysis helps identify the topics covered in these studies and offers valuable insights into potential avenues for future research. Furthermore, Figure 7 illustrates a substantial number of co-citations and units, enhancing the analysis of the cited references and supporting the overall findings.

Figure 7. Network of co-citation

THEORETICAL PERSPECTIVES

Background of AI Technologies

The concept of AI dates back to the mid-20th century when early pioneers like Alan Turing laid the theoretical groundwork for machines capable of mimicking human intelligence. Turing's famous question, "Can machines think?" sparked interest in developing computational systems that could process information, solve problems, and adapt over time (Warwick & Shah, 2016). However, the term "artificial intelligence" was first coined by computer scientist John McCarthy in 1956. At this time, AI research focused on symbolic reasoning and problem-solving, leading to the development of expert systems and the first AI programs capable of solving mathematical problems and playing simple games (Alateyyat & Soltan, 2024). However, progress was initially slow due to limited computational power and lack of data. As a result, the resurgence of AI began in the late 1990s and early 2000s with the advent of machine learning and deep learning technologies. These advancements allowed AI systems to "learn" from large datasets and improve their performance over time without being explicitly programmed for each task. Today, AI is a central force driving innovation across multiple industries, including education.

AI refers to the ability of machines to perform tasks that typically require human intelligence, such as learning, reasoning, problem-solving, and decision-making. Popenici and Kerr (2017, p. 2) define it as "computing systems that are able to engage in human-like processes such as learning, adapting, synthesizing, self-correction and the use of data for complex processing tasks." Key innovations within AI include machine learning, deep learning, natural language processing (NLP), and computer vision. These technologies allow systems to analyze vast amounts of data, recognize patterns, and make autonomous decisions (Benhayoun & Lang, 2021). In addition, these advancements are powered by improvements in computing power, big data analytics, and sophisticated algorithms, enabling AI technologies to process complex information in real-time (Dogru et al., 2024). Although AI was initially limited to rule-based systems, the development of neural networks and machine learning algorithms has significantly expanded its capabilities. Consequently, AI now supports diverse applications in multiple industries, from self-driving cars to personalized digital assistants.

AI Innovations Used in Higher Education

In recent years, numerous AI innovations have been integrated into higher education, transforming learning and administrative processes. These technologies are enhancing the efficiency of educational institutions and creating more personalized and adaptive learning experiences for students (Kumar et al., 2024). AI innovations have touched nearly every aspect of higher education, from analyzing vast data to providing real-time student support. Below are key AI technologies that are currently shaping the future of academia.

Big Data Analytics

Big data analytics is among the most significant AI innovations in higher education. Universities and educational institutions generate vast amounts of data daily, from student performance metrics to enrollment statistics and course feedback. Big data analytics allows these institutions to analyze and utilize this information to identify trends, optimize operations, and improve learning outcomes (Ashaari et al., 2024). For instance, analyzing student behavior patterns helps educators identify at-risk students early on and offer targeted support to prevent dropout (Kaur & Dahiya, 2023). In addition, big data enables more informed decision-making regarding curriculum development and resource allocation, making it a powerful tool for educational administrators seeking to improve institutional efficiency.

Cloud Computing

Cloud computing has transformed how higher education access and store data and resources. This innovation allows institutions to store data remotely and access it from anywhere, consequently supporting the scalability of AI applications in education (Foster et al., 2019). It enables higher education facilities to provide students and faculty access to learning materials, software, and research tools on demand, regardless of their physical location. AI-powered cloud platforms also enable collaborative learning environments where students can work on projects in real-time (Jiang, 2023). Moreover, the cost-effectiveness of cloud solutions makes advanced AI tools more accessible to smaller institutions, democratizing access to technology in education.

Predictive Machine Learning

Predictive machine learning is a transformative tool in higher education, allowing institutions to foresee future outcomes based on current data. This AI technology is often applied in predictive analytics to improve student retention, optimize course offerings, and tailor educational experiences to individual needs (Gallastegui & Forradellas, 2021; Urtasun, 2023). For example, machine learning algorithms can analyze student performance data to predict which students risk failing or dropping out. Educators can use these insights to implement timely interventions (Swiontek et al., 2019). Besides, predictive models can inform course scheduling by analyzing enrollment patterns, ensuring that the right courses are available at the right times. This insight level helps educators and administrators enhance the academic experience and improve student success rates.

Decision Support Systems

AI-driven decision support systems (DSS) assist faculty and administrative staff make informed decisions based on data analysis. These systems use AI algorithms to process and analyze complex datasets, recommending various academic and administrative decisions (Ibrahim et al., 2014). For instance, a DSS can help faculty determine the most effective teaching methods based on student feedback or learning analytics (Bana e Costa & Oliveira, 2012). According to Rigopoulos and Karadimas (2017), DSS can assist with resource management, admissions processes, and financial planning in administrative functions. This technology reduces the cognitive load of decision-making and enhances accuracy, allowing higher education institutions to function more efficiently.

Smart Chatbots

Smart chatbots are increasingly used in higher education to provide instant student support and communication. These AI-powered virtual assistants can answer frequently asked questions, assist with administrative tasks such as course registration, and offer guidance on academic resources (Rakhra et al., 2021). The 24/7 availability of chatbots allows students to receive support at any time, improving their overall experience and reducing the workload for administrative staff. In some cases, chatbots are integrated into learning management systems, offering personalized feedback to students based on their coursework (Rasul et al., 2024; Sakasa & Mawela, 2023). This seamless interaction between students and technology enhances student engagement and makes academic processes more user-friendly.

ChatGPT

ChatGPT is an AI innovation developed by OpenAI. It represents a new frontier in AI-powered education tools. ChatGPT leverages advanced natural language processing (NLP) to engage in meaningful conversations with users, answer complex questions, and explain various topics (Dianova & Schultz, 2023). ChatGPT has been integrated into learning environments in higher education to offer students personalized tutoring, help with assignments, and clarify difficult concepts. In addition, Chang et al. (2024) indicate that it can be used to automate tasks, analyze and synthesize data during research, facilitate collaboration, brainstorm, create classroom exercises, and customize materials for educational purposes. Its ability to generate human-like responses makes it a versatile tool for educators and students, enhancing learning experiences through interactive discussions (Rehman et al., 2024; Zhu et al., 2024). However, this innovation raises concerns regarding diminishing critical thinking and potential academic misconduct. ChatGPT can undermine the integrity of educational degrees and graduates' knowledge and skills if misused.

Blockchain

While commonly associated with cryptocurrencies, blockchain technology is gaining traction in higher education for its potential to store and verify academic credentials securely. Universities can leverage the decentralized and tamper-proof nature of blockchain to securely issue degrees, diplomas, and certificates that employers and other institutions can easily verify (Jha & Sachan, 2023). This reduces the risk of credential fraud and simplifies the process of transferring credits between institutions. As a result, Chaka (2023) identifies the application of blockchain technologies in higher education as a "game-changer" due to their high reliability, immutability, and security. Blockchain can also be used to track student achievements, research contributions, and intellectual property, offering a transparent and secure system for managing academic records (Zhang et al., 2020). As AI continues to integrate with blockchain, these systems may also become more automated, further enhancing the security and efficiency of academic credential management.

APPLICATIONS OF AI IN HIGHER BUSINESS EDUCATION

AI is transforming higher business education by offering innovative solutions that enhance learning, streamline administrative tasks, and personalize educational experiences. Institutions are integrating AI into various aspects of business education to provide more dynamic, data-driven, and adaptable learning environments. This has led to multiple applications, including:

(i) AI in Curriculum Development

AI is playing a transformative role in curriculum development within higher business education. For instance, the traditional approach, which often relied on static content and occasional updates, is now evolving to meet the demands of rapidly changing industries. Here are several ways AI is contributing to curriculum development:

Integration of AI Tools in Course Content

AI-driven tools help institutions stay relevant by analyzing trends, aligning with market demands, and providing personalized learning experiences. Most academic institutions integrate AI tools in the course content to allow students to engage with the same technologies they will encounter in their careers (Pinar, 2023). AI-driven tools like data analytics platforms, customer relationship management systems (CRMs), and machine learning models are now central to many business functions. For example, in marketing courses, AI-powered software enables students to analyze consumer data and predict behavior patterns (Chergarova et al., 2023; Xia, 2011). In finance courses, AI helps forecast stock trends or automate financial reporting. This direct exposure to AI technologies during coursework ensures that students gain practical, hands-on experience in their application, preparing them for AI-driven work environments (Závadský et al., 2024). Moreover, embedding AI in the curriculum enhances business education beyond theoretical knowledge by offering students real-time problem-solving experiences that mirror the challenges they will face in the professional world.

AI-Powered Course Design

AI is transforming how business courses are designed. These innovations analyze large datasets to identify gaps in existing curricula, forecast emerging trends, and recommend new content that aligns with industry needs (Jiang, 2023). AI-powered platforms analyze industry reports, academic publications, and labor market trends to inform curriculum development. These insights enable educators to create more relevant and forward-thinking courses, ensuring students have the skills and knowledge required to thrive in an AI-driven business environment (Al-Saiari et al., 2024; Harvey & Kotting, 2011). For example, if AI analysis shows increasing demand for blockchain expertise in financial services, courses focusing on blockchain technologies can be introduced or expanded (Hashmi & Bal, 2024). This adaptive curriculum development approach ensures that business schools remain responsive to the evolving needs of industries, helping students stay competitive.

New Business Education Models

Moreover, AI is challenging the traditional models of business education by promoting a more dynamic and flexible learning environment. Historically, business education relied on static syllabi and lecture-based instruction (Jia & Zhang, 2011). However, AI allows for personalized, experiential learning paths that adjust to individual student needs. This shift means that students no longer follow a rigid curriculum; instead, they can progress through courses at their own pace, with AI systems adjusting the difficulty of material based on their performance (Bentur et al., 2021). As AI optimizes administrative and instructional processes, educators can devote more time to mentoring, research, and developing innovative teaching methods (Kavitha & Joshith, 2024). This transformation signals a shift from one-size-fits-all teaching to a more tailored, student-centric approach, enriching the learning experience and making education more.

(ii) Enhancing Teaching Methods Through AI

AI enhances teaching methods in higher business education by making them more interactive, efficient, and tailored to individual learning needs. Using AI-driven classroom systems allows instructors to offer more personalized and engaging learning experiences. Other ways AI is impacting teaching methods are:

AI-Driven Adaptive Learning Systems

Educators are leveraging AI-driven adaptive learning systems to customize learning experiences to fit individual student needs. These systems constantly analyze students' performance and tailor the content and difficulty level accordingly (Ateeq et al., 2024). For example, if a student struggles with financial modeling, the adaptive system will automatically provide additional resources or exercises targeting that specific area. This personalized approach ensures that each student can master the material at their own pace, leading to improved learning outcomes (Samman, 2024; Sequeira et al., 2024). In a business education context, adaptive learning helps students develop skills in complex areas like data analytics, management theory, and economic modeling. It enables them to fully grasp critical concepts before moving on to more advanced material.

Automated Teaching Assistants

Automated teaching assistants powered by AI are becoming essential in managing the administrative burden of education while enhancing the teaching process itself. These AI assistants can handle routine tasks such as grading assignments, answering frequently asked questions, and moderating discussions (Li, 2011; Popenici & Kerr, 2017). They help free human educators, allowing them to focus on more complex instructional duties. In business education, where large class sizes are common, AI assistants help maintain high levels of student engagement by providing instant feedback and round-the-clock support (Pan & Yang, 2021). In addition, Quezada Castro et al. (2022) found that these automated systems are trained to recognize patterns in student responses, allowing them to deliver personalized feedback, highlight areas of improvement, and track progress over time. This approach creates a more responsive and efficient learning environment.

AI in Assessment and Feedback

AI has greatly improved higher business education's assessment and feedback process by introducing more objective and data-driven evaluation methods. AI systems can grade multiple-choice exams, essays, and case studies using NLP algorithms, providing detailed feedback on structure, coherence, and argument strength (Xia, 2011; Singh et al., 2024). These AI-driven assessments ensure consistency and reduce the potential for human bias in grading. Moreover, AI can track student progress across various metrics, providing real-time feedback to students and instructors (Yuan et al., 2011). This allows educators to adjust their teaching strategies and students to focus on areas that need improvement. AI in business education is particularly useful for grading projects that involve complex data analysis or financial forecasting since it can assess the accuracy and methodology of these tasks with greater precision than traditional methods.

(iii) Personalized Learning and Student Engagement

The provision of tailored learning experiences using AI innovations has increased student engagement. These technologies allow students to use learning methods that match individual needs and learning styles (Sri Tulasi & Inayath Ahamed, 2024). For example, some learners who prefer interactive experiences can utilize game-based learning, while others can engage in chatbots or other AI technologies depending on individual preferences. This strategy improves student experiences and learning outcomes (Zhu, 2011). These personalized strategies influence student engagement in various ways, such as improved retention and academic success, higher collaboration rates, and better-tailored learning experiences.

Tailored Learning Experiences

AI systems allow for the creating of tailored learning experiences that adapt to each student's strengths, weaknesses, and learning preferences. AI can personalize course content in business education institutions by analyzing student data, such as assessment performance or engagement with online resources (Wang & Wang, 2010). For example, a student excelling in marketing analytics might be provided with advanced materials, while another struggling with accounting principles could receive more foundational resources. This personalized approach enhances learning outcomes and increases student motivation and engagement since students feel more supported and capable of mastering challenging concepts (Kondratenko & Shevcenkc, 2024; Ivanov et al., 2024). AI's ability to continuously adapt content based on real-time feedback ensures that students remain challenged without becoming overwhelmed.

Improving Student Retention and Success

AI plays a critical role in improving student retention and success in higher education by identifying students who may be at risk of falling behind. Predictive analytics powered by AI can monitor student engagement levels, attendance, and academic performance to detect early warning signs of potential dropouts (Yusof & Khalid, 2021; Cankaya et al., 2024). This enables educators and administrators to intervene with targeted support, such as tutoring or counseling, to keep students on track. Business schools involve rigorous coursework, and competition can lead to high dropout rates (Zhao & Ma, 2011). AI-driven early intervention systems help institutions improve retention rates by providing students with the necessary resources and support to succeed.

AI-Powered Collaboration Tools

Collaboration is a key element of business education. AI-powered tools are enhancing how students work together on projects and assignments. AI-driven platforms allow for real-time collaboration, providing students with a seamless environment to share ideas, work on joint tasks, and offer feedback (Bhattacharjee, 2019; Luo, 2011a). In addition, Connell and Malik (2021) explain that AI can facilitate better team dynamics by analyzing individual contributions and suggesting optimal group formations based on students' skills and learning styles. These tools simulate real-world business environments where collaboration and teamwork are essential, preparing students for modern workplace demands (Guizzo, 2024). AI's ability to reinforce more efficient and effective collaboration enhances the learning experience and prepares students for successful careers in business.

(iv) AI Preparing Business Students for AI-Driven Industries

AI is a core technology driving the Industry 4.0 revolution. For instance, Al-Haimi et al. (2021) found that integrating AI led to increased value in various sectors, including 128% in travel, 89% in logistics, 87% in retail, 85% in automotive and assembly, and 79% in oil and gas among others as shown in Figure 8 below. This incremental value has led to increased adoption of AI in multiple industries, thereby transforming the demand for AI-related knowledge and skills. As a result, higher education institutions are integrating AI into their programs to prepare business students for these job market demands.

Figure 8. Potential value increase of using AI in multiple industries (Al-Haimi et al., 2021)

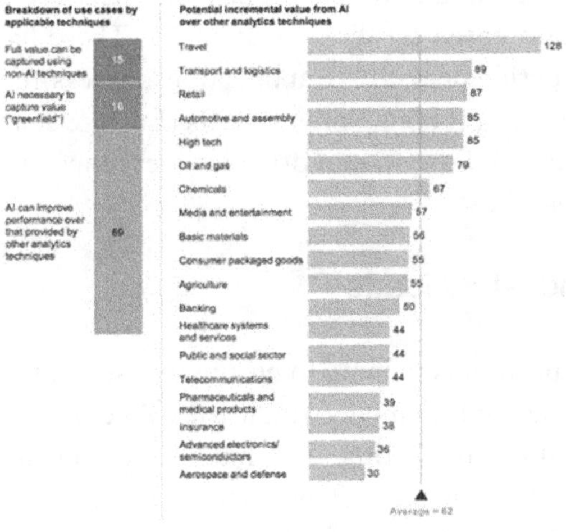

Developing Future-Ready Skills

Business students must have the skills necessary to thrive in industries increasingly shaped by AI and automation. As a result, institutions are integrating AI into business education to help students develop future-ready skills such as data analysis, algorithmic thinking, and understanding AI-driven decision-making processes (Golowko et al., 2019; Henderson et al., 2019). These skills are crucial for navigating AI-rich environments and leading innovation. For instance, understanding how AI can be used to optimize supply chains or enhance customer experiences allows students to apply these insights in practical business contexts (Hou & Wan, 2024). As AI continues transforming industries such as finance, marketing, and logistics, students well-trained in AI technologies will be better prepared to lead in these evolving sectors.

Simulations and AI-Based Case Studies

Simulations and AI-based case studies are becoming integral to business education, allowing students to apply theoretical knowledge in realistic scenarios. These tools simulate business environments where students must make decisions based on AI-generated data or forecasts (Mendez et al., 2021; Luo, 2011b). For example, students might use AI to predict market trends and then develop marketing strategies or financial plans based on those predictions. These hands-on experiences allow students to experiment with AI applications, assess the outcomes of their decisions, and refine their problem-solving skills (Luan & Zhang, 2011). Students gain practical insights into how AI can drive business innovation and improve organizational performance.

Alignment with Industry Needs

AI in business education is helping to ensure that students graduate with skills closely aligned with the needs of modern industries. As companies increasingly rely on AI for decision-making, marketing, customer service, and more, there is a growing demand for graduates who understand business principles and AI technologies (Al Shehab, 2022; Del Pino et al., 2012). Business schools integrating AI into their curricula enable students to stay ahead of industry trends and adapt to technological advancements (Kumar & Lohan, 2024). Schools are bridging the gap between academia and industry by offering courses that teach students how to leverage AI for competitive advantage (Suhasini & Santhosh Kumar, 2019). This will ensure their graduates are equipped to meet the demands of AI-driven business environments.

(v) Educational and Psychological Counseling

AI significantly impacts educational and psychological counseling within higher business education by offering students more personalized and proactive support systems. Traditional counseling models, while effective, often depend on face-to-face interactions and are limited by time and resources (Razia et al., 2023). However, AI expands the reach of counseling services by offering 24/7 accessibility, which is crucial for students needing assistance outside regular office hours (Al-Mseidin et al., 2023; Nguyen et al., 2022). These AI-driven platforms utilize machine learning algorithms to assess student data, including academic performance, attendance patterns, engagement with course materials, and behavioral indicators gathered through online activity. This data allows AI systems to proactively identify students struggling academically or emotionally before issues escalate into larger problems (Sharma & Lenka, 2024). For example, if a student shows decreased engagement or poor performance over several weeks, AI systems can flag this as a potential issue and automatically recommend counseling interventions (Rasiah et al., 2019). The AI can provide personalized feedback, such as suggesting time management techniques or recommending resources for stress relief.

In some advanced applications, AI can monitor mental health through sentiment analysis of student communications, such as emails or discussion forum posts. This application helps detect subtle signs of anxiety or depression (Rahman et al., 2024). Identifying and addressing psychological issues early is particularly important in the competitive and high-pressure business education environment, where students often multitask, balancing internships, project deadlines, and preparation for a fast-paced career (Song et al., 2011; Tan & Zhang, 2011). Moreover, AI systems enhance the effectiveness of human counselors by providing them with detailed insights into a student's emotional and educational well-being. With this data, counselors can develop more targeted intervention strategies, offering customized advice based on real-time information (Viegas et al., 2016; Wang, 2011). AI-driven platforms also promote self-service models, where students can access AI-powered chatbots or virtual counselors to receive guidance on academic planning, career advice, or personal matters (Vinichenko et al., 2020). This AI integration allows institutions to offer counseling support to a larger student population without compromising the quality of care, ensuring every student has access to the resources they need to succeed academically and personally.

(vi) Remote Teaching

AI has become a key player in optimizing the infrastructure and delivery of remote teaching in higher business education. It enhances operational efficiency and ensures seamless communication between students and educators (Assim et al., 2021). Unlike in-person learning environments, remote education faces unique logistical challenges, such as scaling teaching efforts across diverse geographic locations and managing large cohorts of students. AI helps streamline administrative and teaching workflows to ensure that remote education remains organized and efficient (Richter & Langesee, 2024; Schön et al., 2023). One major way AI contributes is by automating time-consuming tasks in virtual classrooms, such as organizing course materials, scheduling virtual sessions, and monitoring student activity. AI-driven platforms can track and record virtual classroom interactions, ensuring that lectures, discussions, and other educational materials are archived and accessible for later review (Yang & Stivers, 2024). This is particularly useful for remote students across different time zones. In addition, AI can automatically compile class participation reports and provide analytical summaries to instructors. This practice highlights areas needing additional focus or modification in future lessons.

AI contributes to remote teaching by integrating multiple technologies into a cohesive learning ecosystem. Through cloud-based platforms, AI enables seamless integration of video conferencing tools, digital whiteboards, and document-sharing apps, ensuring that instructors and students can collaborate effectively without technological interruptions (Li, 2011). This technological coordination is important in business education, where real-time case studies, group projects, and presentations are key curriculum elements. Moreover, AI has improved remote teaching by enabling a more secure and reliable environment for examinations and assessments (Liwång, 2022; Majumdar et al., 2021). Proctoring software powered by AI helps maintain academic integrity by monitoring students during online exams. These systems use facial recognition, keystroke analysis, and other biometric data to ensure that the test-taker adheres to the rules, even in an unsupervised setting (Nan, 2011). This reduces the need for manual supervision and provides instructors with detailed reports on student behavior during assessments.

CHALLENGES AND ETHICAL CONSIDERATIONS

Despite AI's numerous advantages to higher business education, it also presents several challenges and ethical concerns that must be carefully considered. Issues such as privacy, equity, and bias become more common as educational institutions increasingly rely on AI to enhance teaching, learning, and administrative processes (Chang et al., 2024; Ivanov, 2023). Understanding these challenges is crucial for ensuring that AI's integration into business education promotes fairness, inclusivity, and ethical responsibility while also addressing the limitations of the widespread use of advanced technologies.

Data Privacy and Security

AI in higher business education poses significant data privacy and security concerns. AI systems thrive on data since they require vast amounts of student information to function effectively, whether for personalizing learning experiences, assessing academic performance, or providing real-time feedback (Wiryawan et al., 2024). However, collecting and processing this data raises serious concerns about how it is stored, who has access to it, and what safeguards are in place to protect it from breaches (Slimi & Carballido, 2023a). In educational settings, sensitive data such as academic records, personal identifiers, and even behavioral data from students' online activities are continuously gathered by AI-driven platforms.

Without stringent security protocols, this data can become vulnerable to hacking, unauthorized access, or misuse.

Access and Equity Issues

Implementing AI in higher business education also raises significant access and equity issues, potentially exacerbating existing disparities in the educational system. While AI offers advanced personalized learning and efficiency tools, not all students and institutions can access these technologies equally (Tripathi, 2024). Students from underprivileged backgrounds, rural areas, or regions with limited technological infrastructure may face barriers in accessing AI-powered platforms, which require stable internet connections, modern devices, and a level of digital literacy (Walczak & Cellary, 2023). As a result, the benefits of AI-enhanced education may disproportionately favor those with the resources to access these tools, widening the gap between advantaged and disadvantaged students.

At the institutional level, smaller or less well-funded universities may struggle to implement AI technologies at the same scale as larger, more affluent institutions. This can lead to a two-tier system where students attending prestigious universities receive the advantages of cutting-edge AI-driven educational tools while those in less resource-rich environments miss out (Tripathi, 2024; Sun, 2011). Furthermore, access issues extend to faculty and staff, who may not have the resources or institutional support to utilize AI technologies in their teaching practices fully. The challenge, therefore, is not just about technological access but also about ensuring that the opportunities AI presents are distributed equitably across different socio-economic and geographical lines.

Faculty Training and AI Literacy

Another significant challenge in integrating AI into higher business education is the need for faculty training and AI literacy. While powerful, AI tools and systems are complex and often require a solid understanding of how they work to be used effectively (Song, 2024). Many faculty members may not be familiar with the intricacies of AI, machine learning, or data analytics (Slimi & Carballido, 2023b). This lack of familiarity can create a significant barrier to the effective use of AI technologies in the classroom since educators may feel overwhelmed by the prospect of learning new digital tools and integrating them into existing teaching practices.

Potential Bias

AI systems are not immune to bias, which presents a significant challenge in higher business education. AI algorithms are often trained on large datasets that reflect existing societal biases related to race, gender, socioeconomic status, or other factors (Sirisubsatid, 2018). As a result, AI systems can unintentionally perpetuate these biases, leading to unfair outcomes for certain groups of students. For example, an AI-driven admissions tool might favor students from privileged backgrounds if the data used to train the system is skewed toward applicants from elite schools or affluent areas (Sharma et al., 2024). Similarly, AI-powered grading systems may reflect implicit biases if the training data used to develop them includes biased assessments.

CONCLUSION

The adoption of AI technologies in higher business education has significantly transformed how institutions design curricula, deliver instruction, and engage students. AI has revolutionized curriculum development by enabling the integration of advanced tools and personalized content, creating more dynamic, flexible, and responsive educational experiences. AI-powered course design and adaptive learning systems have allowed institutions to tailor educational pathways to meet the unique needs of individual students, promoting deeper engagement and improving academic outcomes. These advancements have challenged traditional education models, pushing business schools to adopt more innovative and data-driven approaches that align with the demands of modern business environments.

In addition to reshaping curricula, AI has enhanced teaching methods through automated tools that assist educators in managing classroom tasks and providing real-time feedback. AI-driven adaptive learning systems offer personalized learning experiences. Automated teaching assistants help to streamline administrative tasks, allowing instructors to focus more on mentorship and critical thinking. AI also plays a crucial role in assessment, offering more precise and timely evaluations of student performance. These technological advancements have improved the efficiency of instruction and increased the capacity for institutions to deliver high-quality education on a larger scale.

Moreover, AI has proven invaluable in preparing students for AI-driven industries by integrating simulations, case studies, and industry-aligned skills into business education. Graduates are entering the workforce with the competencies required to thrive in an increasingly automated and data-driven business world. AI has also enhanced support systems within educational institutions by improving access to educational and psychological counseling. This ensures that students receive the personalized support they need to succeed academically and emotionally. AI has addressed logistical challenges in remote teaching contexts and made distance learning more accessible. It continues evolving to meet diverse learners' unique needs in various regions.

However, despite these advancements, significant challenges remain. Data privacy and security concerns are at the forefront of ethical considerations in AI adoption. The collection and use of vast amounts of student data require rigorous protections to safeguard personal information. Access and equity issues persist because not all students and institutions access AI technologies equally. This issue can potentially worsen educational inequalities. Besides, faculty training and AI literacy are critical since educators must have the knowledge and skills to effectively implement AI tools in their teaching practices. The potential for bias in AI algorithms, particularly in areas such as admissions and grading, presents additional ethical challenges that must be addressed to ensure fairness and inclusivity in business education. Educators, administrators, and other stakeholders in the education sector should strive to develop and implement appropriate measures to address these challenges.

Artificial Intelligence (AI) has been playing an increasingly important role in higher education, especially in business-related areas. In recent years, AI has been utilized to optimize educational processes, personalize learning, and prepare students for the evolving challenges of the business world: (i) AI is being used to automate administrative tasks in higher education institutions, such as managing admissions, enrollment, and assessments. AI tools can analyze large volumes of data, providing insights that help in strategic decision-making for business programs; (ii) One of the key contributions of AI is its ability to personalize the learning process. AI-powered e-learning platforms use algorithms to adapt content and teaching methods according to the individual needs of business students, promoting more effective learning; (iii) AI can be used to predict student performance, identifying potential challenges in their academic journey and suggesting personalized interventions. This approach is particularly useful in business courses like management, finance, and marketing, where continuous monitoring of progress can significantly impact academic outcomes; (iv) AI-driven business simulators allow students to interact with realistic business scenarios, making managerial decisions in simulated environments. These simulators are widely used in subjects like management, economics, and business strategy, providing practical and engaging learning experiences; (v) AI supports constructivist theory by enabling students to build their own knowledge through interactions with adaptive educational tools. AI-based platforms promote active and collaborative learning, encouraging students to engage more deeply with business content; (vi) The theory of adaptive learning, often discussed in AI studies, suggests that AI algorithms can adjust educational content based on student performance and learning styles. This is particularly relevant in business education, where students benefit from content that evolves as their skills develop; (vii) AI-driven virtual assistants are being integrated into classrooms and e-learning platforms to provide support to students, answer frequently asked questions, and assist with academic planning. These assistants offer instant support, which is particularly helpful for students in online business courses; (viii) Gamification, integrated with AI, is increasingly used in business disciplines to enhance student engagement. AI-driven business simulation games challenge students to apply theoretical concepts in practical, competitive scenarios, preparing them for real-world business environments; (ix) In subjects such as financial analysis and strategic management, AI is used to teach students how to work with large data sets, automating data collection and interpretation to make informed business decisions.

The application of Artificial Intelligence in higher education, especially in business education, is transforming both how students learn and how educators teach. With the use of AI, students experience more personalized and practical education that better prepares them for the challenges of the modern business environment. AI offers opportunities for personalization, automation, and simulation, which are shaping the future of business education and are expected to continue expanding in the coming years.

Artificial intelligence (AI) is playing an increasingly significant role in higher education, particularly within business studies. As this technology continues to evolve, several areas require deeper exploration to fully unlock its potential in business education. Future research could focus on key areas such as personalized learning, ethical considerations, and real-world applications of AI in business training.

One of the most promising areas for further study is AI-driven personalized learning. While current AI tools can adjust educational content based on student performance, future advancements could integrate cognitive and emotional responses to create even more tailored learning experiences. In business education, research could examine how personalized AI models enhance students' understanding of complex topics like financial analysis, marketing strategy, and organizational behavior. Key questions include how AI algorithms can be refined to accommodate diverse learning styles and cognitive abilities among business students, as well as the long-term career impacts of AI-enhanced personalized learning.

Another critical area of study is ethics and bias in AI applications. As AI becomes increasingly embedded in education, addressing biases within AI algorithms is essential to ensure fair and equitable learning experiences. AI-powered grading systems, admissions processes, and content delivery mechanisms may unintentionally reinforce biases, leading to unequal opportunities in business education. Future research should explore ethical AI frameworks and strategies for minimizing biases in AI-driven educational tools. Key research questions include examining the ethical implications of AI in automated assessments and admissions and developing methods to ensure that business education AI tools remain free from gender, racial, and socioeconomic biases.

Additionally, AI-powered business simulations offer a valuable opportunity for practical training. AI-driven simulations are already used to provide students with decision-making experiences, but further research could explore how these tools can better replicate real-world complexities in industries such as finance, marketing, and entrepreneurship. Advanced AI-based simulations could incorporate dynamic market conditions, geopolitical changes, and shifting consumer behaviors to provide a more comprehensive learning experience. Research questions in this area could focus on how AI simulations can be designed to model real-time business uncertainties and the role AI plays in enhancing experiential learning through virtual internships and business simulation games.

As AI continues to develop, its potential to transform higher education, particularly in business studies, is immense. However, to fully harness its benefits, ongoing research is necessary to explore its ethical implementation, personalization capabilities, and real-world applicability. Future studies must address inclusivity, adaptability, and global integration while ensuring that AI enhances rather than replaces human learning experiences. Through these research efforts, AI has the potential not only to improve business education but also to redefine the future of learning in an increasingly complex and interconnected world.

ACKNOWLEDGEMENTS

I would like to express gratitude to the Editor and the Arbitrators. They offered extremely valuable suggestions or improvements. The GOVCOPP Research Center of the University of Aveiro supported the author.

REFERENCES

Abdelwahab, H. R., Rauf, A., & Chen, D. (2023). Business students' perceptions of Dutch higher educational institutions in preparing them for artificial intelligence work environments. *Industry and Higher Education, 37*(1), 22–34. DOI: 10.1177/09504222221087614

Al-Mseidin, K. I., Al-Zu'bi, M. A., Al-Mawadieh, R. S. M., & Alelaimat, A. M. (2023). The Integration of AI Applications in Psychological and Educational Counselling for University Students: Opportunities and Challenges. 2023 24th International Arab Conference onInformation Technology, ACIT 2023, Al-Saiari, M. A., Al-Mughairi, Y. M., Al-Mashaikhi, B. N., & Mudhsh, B. A. (2024). Investigating the Impact of Training Program on Generative AI Applications in Improving University Teaching. Qubahan Academic Journal, 4(3), 315-332. DOI: 10.48161/qaj.v4n3a760

Al Shehab, N. A. (2022). Under the COVID pandemic: is it the springtime for forensic accounting field to blossom? In Accounting, Finance, Sustainability, Governance and Fraud (pp. 11-32). Springer. DOI: 10.1007/978-981-19-1036-4_2

Alateyyat, S., & Soltan, M. (2024). Utilizing Artificial Intelligence in Higher Education: A Systematic Review. 2024 ASU International Conference in Emerging Technologies for Sustainability and Intelligent Systems, ICETSIS 2024, Al-haimi, B., Hujainah, F., Nasir, D., & Alhroob, E. (2021). Higher education institutions with artificial intelligence: roles, promises, and requirements. Applications of artificial intelligence in business, education and healthcare, 221-238. DOI: 10.1007/978-3-030-72080-3_13

Ashaari, M. A., Singh, K. S. D., Abbasi, G. A., Amran, A., & Liebana-Cabanillas, F. J. (2021). Big data analytics capability for improved performance of higher education institutions in the Era of IR 4.0: A multi-analytical SEM & ANN perspective. *Technological Forecasting and Social Change, 173*, C7–C121119. DOI: 10.1016/j.techfore.2021.121119

Assim, M., Al-Bahri, H., Zafar, Q., Shahada, M., & Al-Ammary, J. (2021). Remote Teaching during COVID-19 pandemic in Higher Education Institutions in the Kingdom of Bahrain: Challenges and Innovative Solutions. 2021 Sustainable Leadership and Academic Excellence International Conference, SLAE 2021, Ateeq, A., Alaghbari, M. A., Alzoraiki, M., Milhem, M., & Hasan Beshr, B. A. (2024). Empowering academic success: integrating AI tools in university teaching for enhanced assignment and thesis guidance. 2024 ASU International Conference in Emerging Technologies for Sustainability and Intelligent Systems, ICETSIS 2024.

Bana e Costa, C. A., & Oliveira, M. D. (2012). A multicriteria decision analysis model for faculty evaluation. *Omega, 40*(4), 424–436. DOI: 10.1016/j.omega.2011.08.006

Bates, T., Cobo, C., Mariño, O., & Wheeler, S. (2020). Can artificial intelligence transform higher education? *International Journal of Educational Technology in Higher Education, 17*(1), 1–12. DOI: 10.1186/s41239-020-00218-x

Bearman, M., Ryan, J., & Ajjawi, R. (2023). Discourses of artificial intelligence in higher education: A critical literature review. *Higher Education, 86*(2), 369–385. DOI: 10.1007/s10734-022-00937-2

Benhayoun, L., & Lang, D. (2021). Does higher education properly prepare graduates for the growing artificial intelligence market? Gaps' identification using text mining. *Human Systems Management, 40*(5), 639–651. DOI: 10.3233/HSM-211179

Bentur, A., Getz, D., & Shacham, O. K. (2021). System Analysis of Technology Transfer Policies and Models in Higher Education. In International Series in Operations Research and Management Science (Vol. 309, pp. 241-262). Springer. DOI: 10.1007/978-3-030-74051-1_8

Bhattacharjee, K. K. (2019). Research output on the usage of artificial intelligence in indian higher education - a scientometric study. IEEE International Conference on Industrial Engineering and Engineering Management C7 - 8978798, Cankaya, B., Roberts, R., Douglas, S., Vigness, R., & Oztekin, A. (2024). What postpones degree completion? Discovering key predictors of undergraduate degree completion through explainable artificial intelligence (XAI). Journal of Marketing Analytics. DOI: 10.1057/s41270-024-00290-6

Chaka, C. (2023). Fourth industrial revolution—A review of applications, prospects, and challenges for artificial intelligence, robotics and blockchain in higher education. *Research and Practice in Technology Enhanced Learning, 18*, C7–C2. DOI: 10.58459/rptel.2023.18002

Chang, V., Ansari, Y., & Arami, M. (2024). ChatGPT in Higher Education: A Risk Management Approach to Academic Integrity, Critical Thinking, and Workforce Readiness. *Proceedings of the 6th International Conference on Finance, Economics, Management and IT Business, FEMIB 2024*. DOI: 10.5220/0012764100003717

Chergarova, V., Tomeo, M., Provost, L., De la Peña, G., Ulloa, A., & Miranda, D. (2023). Case study: Exploring the role of current and potential usage of generative artificial intelligence tools in higher education. *Issues in Information Systems, 24*(2), 282–292. DOI: 10.48009/2_iis_2023_125

Connell, J., & Malik, A. (2021). Higher Education. In The Fourth Industrial Revolution: What does it mean for Australian Industry? (pp. 161-181). Springer Nature. DOI: 10.1007/978-981-16-1614-3_10

Crompton, H., & Burke, D. (2023). Artificial intelligence in higher education: The state of the field. *International Journal of Educational Technology in Higher Education*, *20*(1), 22. DOI: 10.1186/s41239-023-00392-8

Del Pino, J. S., Gheorghiu, R., & Roman, A. (2012). The rest of me. *Futures*, *44*(8), 730–734. DOI: 10.1016/j.futures.2012.04.011

Dianova, V. G., & Schultz, M. D. (2023). Discussing ChatGPT's implications for industry and higher education: The case for transdisciplinarity and digital humanities. *Industry and Higher Education*, *37*(5), 593–600. DOI: 10.1177/09504222231199989

Dogru, T., Line, N., Hanks, L., Acikgoz, F., Abbott, J., Bakir, S., Berbekova, A., Bilgihan, A., Iskender, A., Kizildag, M., Lee, M., Lee, W., McGinley, S., Mody, M., Onder, I., Ozdemir, O., & Suess, C. (2024). The implications of generative artificial intelligence in academic research and higher education in tourism and hospitality. *Tourism Economics*, *30*(5), 1083–1094. DOI: 10.1177/13548166231204065

Foster, D., White, L., Erdil, D. C., Adams, J., Argüelles, A., Hainey, B., . . . Stott, L. (2019). Toward a cloud computing learning community. Annual Conference on Innovation and Technology in Computer Science Education, ITiCSE, Gallastegui, L. M. G., & Forradellas, R. F. R. (2021). Business methodology for the application in university environments of predictive machine learning models based on an ethical taxonomy of the student's digital twin. Administrative Sciences, 11(4 C7 - 118). DOI: 10.1145/3344429.3372506

Golowko, N., Tamla, P., & Stein, H. BÃ¶hm, T., Hemmje, M., & Onete, C. B. (2019). On the trail of future management topics with digital technology - How can artificial intelligence influence the didactic content of higher education in economics? Proceedings of the 33rdInternational Business Information Management Association Conference, IBIMA 2019: Education Excellence and Innovation Management through Vision 2020, Guizzo, D. (2024). Ceremonial Economics: A Social-Institutional Analysis of Universities, Disciplines, and Academic Positioning. Journal of Economic Issues, 58(2), 397-423.DOI: 10.1080/00213624.2024.2343246

Haddaway, N. R., Page, M. J., Pritchard, C. C., & McGuinness, L. A. (2022). PRISMA 2020: An R package and Shiny app for producing PRISMA 2020-compliant flow diagrams, with interactivity for optimized digital transparency and Open Synthesis. *Campbell Systematic Reviews*, *18*(2), e1230. DOI: 10.1002/cl2.1230 PMID: 36911350

Harvey, F., & Kotting, J. (2011). Teaching mapping for digital natives: New pedagogical ideas for undergraduate cartography education. *Cartography and Geographic Information Science, 38*(3), 269–277. DOI: 10.1559/1523040638269

Hashmi, N., & Bal, A. S. (2024). Generative AI in higher education and beyond. *Business Horizons, 67*(5), 607–614. DOI: 10.1016/j.bushor.2024.05.005

Henderson, L. H., Wersun, A., Wilson, J., Mo-ching Yeung, S., & Zhang, K. (2019). Principles for responsible management education in 2068. *Futures, 111*, 81–89. DOI: 10.1016/j.futures.2019.05.005

Hou, J., & Wan, J. (2024). Theme Mining and Evolutionary Analysis of Artificial Intelligence Integration in Higher Education Research. *Lecture Notes in Business Information Processing, 516*, 108–119. DOI: 10.1007/978-3-031-60260-3_10

Ibrahim, O., Sundgren, D., & Larsson, A. (2014). An integrated decision support system framework for strategic planning in higher education institutions. *Lecture Notes in Business Information Processing, 180*, 237–245. DOI: 10.1007/978-3-319-07179-4_27

Ivanov, S. (2023). The dark side of artificial intelligence in higher education. *Service Industries Journal, 43*(15-16), 1055–1082. DOI: 10.1080/02642069.2023.2258799

Ivanov, S., Soliman, M., Tuomi, A., Alkathiri, N. A., & Al-Alawi, A. N. (2024). Drivers of generative AI adoption in higher education through the lens of the Theory of Planned Behaviour. *Technology in Society, 77*, C7–C102521. DOI: 10.1016/j.techsoc.2024.102521

Jha, C. K., & Sachan, A. (2023). Blockchain and artificial intelligence technology in professional services. In *Fostering Sustainable Development in the Age of Technologies* (pp. 43–50). Emerald Publishing., DOI: 10.1108/978-1-83753-060-120231005

Jia, J., & Zhang, S. (2011). Notice of Retraction: Study on the management model of foreign language teaching reform of higher education. 2011 2nd International Conference on Artificial Intelligence, Management Science and Electronic Commerce, AIMSEC 2011 -Proceedings C7 - 6009850, 5800-5803. DOI: 10.1109/AIMSEC.2011.6009850

Jiang, Y. (2023). Optimization of Automatic Scheduling Algorithms for Biotechnology Course Allocation in Higher Education Institutes. *Journal of Commercial Biotechnology, 28*(5), 153–167. DOI: 10.5912/jcb1193

Kaur, K., & Dahiya, O. (2023). Role of Educational Data Mining and Learning Analytics Techniques Used for Predictive Modeling. Proceedings of 2023 3rd International Conference on Innovative Practices in Technology and Management, ICIPTM 2023, Kavitha, K., & Joshith, V. P. (2024). Factors Shaping the Adoption of AI Tools among Gen Z: An Extended UTAUT2 Model Investigation Using CB-SEM. Bulletin of Science, Technology andSociety. DOI: 10.1109/ICIPTM57143.2023.10117779

Kondratenko, Y. P., & Shevcenkc, A. I. (2024). *Research tendencies and prospect domains for AI development and implementation.* River Publishers. DOI: 10.1201/9788770046947

Kumar, P., & Lohan, A. (2024). Evaluating ChatGPT adoption through the lens of the technology acceptance model: Perspectives from higher education. International Journal of Technological Learning. *Innovation and Development*, *15*(4), 370–383. DOI: 10.1504/IJTLID.2024.140316

Kumar, S., Rao, P., Singhania, S., Verma, S., & Kheterpal, M. (2024). Will artificial intelligence drive the advancements in higher education? A tri-phased exploration. *Technological Forecasting and Social Change*, *201*, C7–C123258. DOI: 10.1016/j.techfore.2024.123258

Li, M. (2011). On constructing the practical teaching system of taxation major in newly-built academies. 2011 2nd International Conference on Artificial Intelligence, Management Science and Electronic Commerce, AIMSEC 2011 - Proceedings C7 - 6011012, Li, Z. (2011). China's Higher Education Quality Management based on Six-Sigma Management principles. 2011 2nd International Conference on Artificial Intelligence, Management Science and Electronic Commerce, AIMSEC 2011 - Proceedings C7 - 6010499, Liwång, H. (2022). Defense development: The role of co-creation in filling the gap between policy-makers and technology development. *Technology in Society*, *68*, C7–C101913. DOI: 10.1016/j.techsoc.2022.101913

Luan, J., & Zhang, Z. (2011). Notice of Retraction: On the innovation of science and technology management in Chinese universities and colleges. 2011 2nd International Conference on Artificial Intelligence, Management Science and Electronic Commerce, AIMSEC 2011 -Proceedings C7 - 6010728, 1278-1281. DOI: 10.1109/AIMSEC.2011.6010728

Luo, P. (2011a). Notice of Retraction: Analysis on the international competitiveness of China's trade in higher education service. 2011 2nd International Conference on Artificial Intelligence, Management Science and Electronic Commerce, AIMSEC 2011 - ProceedingsC7 - 6011368, 2807-2810. DOI: 10.1109/AIMSEC.2011.6011368

Luo, P. (2011b). Opening drives and policy proposals for China higher education service trade.2011 2nd International Conference on Artificial Intelligence, Management Science and Electronic Commerce, AIMSEC 2011 - Proceedings C7 - 6010834, Majumdar, R., Flanagan, B., & Ogata, H. (2021). E-book technology facilitating university education during COVID-19: Japanese experience. Canadian Journal of Learning and Technology, 47(4 Special Issue). DOI: 10.21432/cjlt28038

Mendez, J. I., Ponce, P., Medina, A., Peffer, T., Meier, A., & Molina, A. (2021). A smooth and accepted transition to the future of cities based on the standard ISO 37120, artificial intelligence, and gamification constructors. 2021 IEEE European Technology and Engineering Management Summit, E-TEMS 2021 - Conference Proceedings.

Nan, Y. (2011). Research on evaluation of higher education investment efficiency. 2011 2ndInternational Conference on Artificial Intelligence, Management Science and ElectronicCommerce, AIMSEC 2011 - Proceedings C7 – 6010724.

Nguyen, D. P., Phan, L. T., Ho, H. X., & Le, A. N. H. (2022). Human resource management practices in higher education: A literature review using co-word analysis. *International Journal of Management Education*, *16*(1), 40–61. DOI: 10.1504/IJMIE.2022.10043292

Page, M. J., McKenzie, J. E., Bossuyt, P. M., Boutron, I., Hoffmann, T. C., Mulrow, C. D., Shamseer, L., Tetzlaff, J. M., Akl, E. A., Brennan, S. E., Chou, R., Glanville, J., Grimshaw, J. M., Hróbjartsson, A., Lalu, M. M., Li, T., Loder, E. W., Mayo-Wilson, E., McDonald, S., & Moher, D. (2021). The PRISMA 2020 statement: An updated guideline for reporting systematic reviews. *BMJ (Clinical Research Ed.)*, *372*, n71. Advance online publication. DOI: 10.1136/bmj.n71 PMID: 33782057

Pan, Y., & Yang, P. (2021). The role of AI assisted socio-cultural frameworks in academic change and higher education growth. *International Journal of Technology Management*, *86*(2-4), 196–213. DOI: 10.1504/IJTM.2021.118316

Pinar, W. F. (2023). Understanding Curriculum: Interview with Prof. William F. Pinar. *Journal of Higher Education Policy and Leadership Studies*, *4*(4), 180–184. DOI: 10.61186/johepal.4.4.180

Popenici, S. A. D., & Kerr, S. (2017). Exploring the impact of artificial intelligence on teaching and learning in higher education. *Research and Practice in Technology Enhanced Learning*, *12*(22), 1–13. DOI: 10.1186/s41039-017-0062-8 PMID: 30595727

Quezada Castro, G. A., Castro Arellano, M. P., & Quezada Castro, M. P. (2022). Artificial intelligence and legal education: Its incorporation during the Covid-19 pandemic. *Revista Venezolana de Gerencia, 27*(8), 750–764. DOI: 10.52080/rvgluz.27.8.2

Rahman, M. M., Alam, G. M., Aziz, N. A. B. A., Bashir, K., & Kader, R. (2024). Whether mismatch finds match in the digitalized era: A comparison of five types of graduates to align business education and banking jobs. *Industry and Higher Education, 38*(6), 547–561. Advance online publication. DOI: 10.1177/09504222241249900

Rakhra, M., Gopinadh, G., Addepalli, N. S., Singh, G., Aliraja, S., Reddy, V. S. G., & Reddy, M. N. (2021). E-Commerce Assistance with a Smart Chatbot using Artificial Intelligence. Proceedings of 2021 2nd International Conference on Intelligent Engineering and Management, ICIEM 2021 C7 - 9445316, Rasiah, R., Turner, J. J., & Ho, Y. F. (2019). The impact of emotional intelligence on work performance: Perceptions and reflections from academics in Malaysian higher education obitat endiaest que. *Contemporary Economics, 13*(3), 269–282. DOI: 10.5709/ce.1897-9254.312

Rasul, T., Nair, S., Kalendra, D., Balaji, M. S., Santini, F. D. O., Ladeira, W. J.,… Hossain, M. U. (2024). Enhancing academic integrity among students in GenAI Era: A holistic framework.International Journal of Management Education, 22(3 C7 - 101041).DOI: 10.1016/j.ijme.2024.101041

Razia, B., Awwad, B., & Taqi, N. (2023). The relationship between artificial intelligence (AI) and its aspects in higher education. *Development and Learning in Organizations, 37*(3), 21–23. DOI: 10.1108/DLO-04-2022-0074

Rehman, A. U., Behera, R. K., Islam, M. S., Abbasi, F. A., & Imtiaz, A. (2024). Assessing the usage of ChatGPT on life satisfaction among higher education students: The moderating role of subjective health. *Technology in Society, 78*, C7–C102655. DOI: 10.1016/j.techsoc.2024.102655

Renz, A., & Hilbig, R. (2020). Prerequisites for artificial intelligence in further education: Identification of drivers, barriers, and business models of educational technology companies. *International Journal of Educational Technology in Higher Education, 17*(1), 14. DOI: 10.1186/s41239-020-00193-3

Richter, T. T., & Langesee, L. M. (2024). Supporting virtual learning and international academic visits with AI. IDIMT 2024: Changes to ICT, Management, and business processes through AI - 32nd Interdisciplinary Information Management Talks.

Rigopoulos, G., & Karadimas, N. V. (2017). Military student assignment using Nex-Class decision support system. Proceedings - 2016 3rd International Conference on Mathematics and Computers in Sciences and in Industry, MCSI 2016 C7 – 7815147.

Rosário, A., & Casaca, J. (2023). Relationship marketing and customer retention - A systematic literature review. *Studies in Business and Economics*, *18*(3), 44–66. DOI: 10.2478/sbe-2023-0044

Rosário, A., Moreira, C., & Macedo, P. (2021). Competitive dynamics of strategic groups in the Portugueses Banking Industrry, Cuadernos de Gestión, 21(2), 1-15. ISSN: 1131-6837. DOI: 10.5295/cdg.180975ac

Rosário, A. T., Lopes, P. R., & Rosário, F. S. (2023). Metaverse in Marketing: Challenges and Opportunities. In Khang, A., Shah, V., & Rani, S. (Eds.), *Handbook of Research on AI-Based Technologies and Applications in the Era of the Metaverse* (pp. 204–227). IGI Global., DOI: 10.4018/978-1-6684-8851-5.ch010

Sakasa, T., & Mawela, T. (2023). AIOps in Higher Education Institutions. Lecture Notes inBusiness Information Processing.

Samman, A. M. A. (2024). Harnessing Potential: Meta-Analysis of AI Integration in Higher Education. 2024 ASU International Conference in Emerging Technologies for Sustainabilityand Intelligent Systems, ICETSIS 2024, Schön, E. M., Buchem, I., Sostak, S., & Rauschenberger, M. (2023). Shift Toward Value-Based Learning: Applying Agile Approaches in Higher Education. Lecture Notes in Business Information Processing.

Sequeira, R., Reis, A., Branco, F., & Alves, P. (2024). Roadmap for Implementing Business Intelligence Systems in Higher Education Institutions: Validation of a Case Study at the University of Trás-os-Montes and Alto Douro. *ICSBT International Conference on Smart Business Technologies*. DOI: 10.1007/978-3-031-67904-9_4

Sharma, S., & Lenka, U. (2024). How does transformational leadership impact organizational unlearning: Insights from persistence theories. *Journal of Organizational Change Management*, *37*(1), 150–172. DOI: 10.1108/JOCM-07-2023-0302

Sharma, S., Singh, G., Sharma, C. S., & Kapoor, S. (2024). Artificial intelligence in Indian higher education institutions: A quantitative study on adoption and perceptions. *International Journal of System Assurance Engineering and Management*. Advance online publication. DOI: 10.1007/s13198-023-02193-8

Singh, V. V., Kumar, N., Singh, S., Kaul, M., Gupta, A. K., & Kapur, P. K. (2024). Assessment of artificial intelligence-based digital learning systems in higher education amid the pandemic using analytic hierarchy. *International Journal of System Assurance Engineering and Management, 15*(8), 4069–4084. DOI: 10.1007/s13198-024-02411-x

Sirisubsatid, S. (2018). The new era of language teaching: Case study of peer teaching method in German language class. Proceedings of 2018 5th International Conference on Business and Industrial Research: Smart Technology for Next Generation of Information, Engineering, Business and Social Science, ICBIR 2018.

Slimi, Z., & Carballido, B. V. (2023a). Navigating the Ethical Challenges of Artificial Intelligence in Higher Education: An Analysis of Seven Global AI Ethics Policies. TEM Journal, 12(2), 590-602. https://doi.org/DOI: 10.18421/TEM122-02

Slimi, Z., & Carballido, B. V. (2023b). Systematic Review: AI's Impact on Higher Education -Learning, Teaching, and Career Opportunities. TEM Journal, 12(3), 1627-1637.https://doi.org/DOI: 10.18421/TEM123-44

Song, N. (2024). Higher education crisis: Academic misconduct with generative AI. Journal of Contingencies and Crisis Management, 32(1 C7 - e12532). DOI: 10.1111/1468-5973.12532

Song, S., Xie, T., & Yang, H. (2011). Notice of Retraction: The research and practice on long-term guarantee system of teaching quality in local colleges. 2011 2nd International Conferenceon Artificial Intelligence, Management Science and Electronic Commerce, AIMSEC 2011 -Proceedings C7 - 6009751, 5959-5962. DOI: 10.1109/AIMSEC.2011.6009751

Sri Tulasi, T., & Inayath Ahamed, S. B. (2024). Artificial Intelligence Effects on Student Learning Outcomes in Higher Education. Proceedings of 9th International Conference on Science, Technology, Engineering and Mathematics: The Role of Emerging Technologies in Digital Transformation, ICONSTEM 2024, Suhasini, B., & Santhosh Kumar, N. (2019). Emerging trends and future perspective of human resource reskilling in higher education. International Journal of Recent Technology and Engineering, 8(2 Special Issue 4), 351-353.DOI: 10.35940/ijrte.B1067.0782S419

Sun, Y. M. (2011). Reform of the basic education of OFFICE software in university. 2011 2ndInternational Conference on Artificial Intelligence, Management Science and Electronic Commerce, AIMSEC 2011 - Proceedings C7 - 6009816, Swiontek, F., Lawson-Body, A., & Lawson-Body, L. (2019). The use of machine learning in higher education. *Issues in Information Systems, 20*(2), 56–61. DOI: 10.48009/2_iis_2019_56-61

Tan, W., & Zhang, J. (2011). Notice of Retraction: A strategic vision on interactive development for higher education under economic integration: Set Chengdu-Chongqing area as an example. 2011 2nd International Conference on Artificial Intelligence, Management Science and Electronic Commerce, AIMSEC 2011 - Proceedings C7 - 6011171, 1857-1860.DOI: 10.1109/AIMSEC.2011.6011171

Tripathi, S. (2024). Paradigm shift in higher education model by using artificial intelligence: challenges and future perspectives in India and Oman. In Incorporating Ai Technology in the Service Sector: Innovations in Creating Knowledge, Improving Efficiency, and Elevating Quality of Life (pp. 215-238). Apple Academic Press. DOI: 10.1201/9781003378068-10

Urtasun, A. (2023). Empowering undergraduates through machine learning. *Industry and Higher Education, 37*(3), 443–447. DOI: 10.1177/09504222221124498

Viegas, C. V., Bond, A. J., Vaz, C. R., Borchardt, M., Pereira, G. M., Selig, P. M., & Varvakis, G. (2016). Critical attributes of Sustainability in Higher Education: A categorisation from literature review. *Journal of Cleaner Production, 126*, 260–276. DOI: 10.1016/j.jclepro.2016.02.106

Vinichenko, M. V., Melnichuk, A. V., & Karácsony, P. (2020). Technologies of improving the university efficiency by using artificial intelligence: Motivational aspect. *Entrepreneurship and Sustainability Issues, 7*(4), 2696–2714. DOI: 10.9770/jesi.2020.7.4(9)

Walczak, K., & Cellary, W. (2023). Challenges for higher education in the era of widespread access to Generative AI. *Economics and Business Review, 9*(2), 71–100. DOI: 10.18559/ebr.2023.2.743

Wang, H. C., & Wang, F. (2010). Development of an interactive multimedia E-learning environment based on wireless PDA. Proceedings of the International Conference on E-Business and E-Government, ICEE 2010 C7 - 5592284, Wang, J. Q. (2011). Notice of Retraction: Evaluation and analysis on adverse effects of the mass higher education in China. 2011 2nd International Conference on Artificial Intelligence, Management Science and Electronic Commerce, AIMSEC 2011 - Proceedings C7 - 6009823,5557-5560. DOI: 10.1109/AIMSEC.2011.6009823

Warwick, K., & Shah, H. (2016). Can machines think? A report on Turing test experiments at the Royal Society. *Journal of Experimental & Theoretical Artificial Intelligence, 28*(6), 989–1007. DOI: 10.1080/0952813X.2015.1055826

Wiryawan, D., Ramadhan, W., Krisnata, F., & Dhiya'Ulhaq, F. (2024). Data Security Framework with Cognitive Theory on Higher Education. 2024 ASU International Conference in Emerging Technologies for Sustainability and Intelligent Systems, ICETSIS 2024, Xia, C. (2011). Notice of Retraction: Study on management methods of college English course grade evaluation. 2011 2nd International Conference on Artificial Intelligence, Management Science and Electronic Commerce, AIMSEC 2011 - Proceedings C7 - 6010493, 4792-4795.DOI: 10.1109/AIMSEC.2011.6010493

Yang, C., & Stivers, A. (2024). Investigating AI languages' ability to solve undergraduate finance problems. *Journal of Education for Business*, *99*(1), 44–51. DOI: 10.1080/08832323.2023.2253963

Yuan, C., Pang, J., & Zheng, C. (2011). Notice of Retraction: The study of the governance mechanisms of higher education quality based on the educational purposes. 2011 2ndInternational Conference on Artificial Intelligence, Management Science and Electronic Commerce, AIMSEC 2011 - Proceedings C7 - 6009715, 6017-6020. DOI: 10.1109/AIMSEC.2011.6009715

Yusof, M. H. M., & Khalid, I. A. (2021). Precision education reviews: a case study on predicting student's performance using feed forward neural network. 2021 International Conferenceof Technology, Science and Administration, ICTSA 2021 C7 - 9406525, Závadský, J., Závadská, Z., & Osvaldová, Z. (2024). Differences in ai utilization between students and teachers in higher education institution: an empirical study. IDIMT 2024: Changes to ICT, Management, and Business Processes through AI - 32ndInterdisciplinary Information Management Talks.

Zhang, L., Ma, Z., Ji, X., & Wang, C. (2020). Blockchain: Application in the System of Teaching Informatization Management of Higher Education. Proceedings - 2020 3rd InternationalConference on Smart BlockChain, SmartBlock 2020 C7 - 9415687, Zhao, J. Y., & Ma, X. H. (2011). New era school status management analysis. 2011 2ndInternational Conference on Artificial Intelligence, Management Science and Electronic Commerce, AIMSEC 2011 - Proceedings C7 - 6011025, Zhu, C. Z. G., Hall, C. M., Fong, L. H. N., Lin, F., & Naderi Koupaei, S. (2024). Examining the effects of ChatGPT on tourism and hospitality student responses through integrating technology acceptance model. International Journal of Tourism Research, 26(4 C7 -e2727). DOI: 10.1002/jtr.2727

Zhu, L. (2011). Notice of Retraction: Reflections on the education reforms for newly established local undergraduate colleges. 2011 2nd International Conference on Artificial Intelligence, Management Science and Electronic Commerce, AIMSEC 2011 - Proceedings C7 - 6010705,1340-1342. DOI: 10.1109/AIMSEC.2011.6010705

ADDITIONAL READINGS

Albayati, H. (2024). Investigating undergraduate students' perceptions and awareness of using ChatGPT as a regular assistance tool: A user acceptance perspective study. *Computers and Education: Artificial Intelligence*, *6*, 100203. DOI: 10.1016/j.caeai.2024.100203

Bang, Y., Cahyawijaya, S., Lee, N., Dai, W., Su, D., Wilie, B., Lovenia, H., Ji, Z., Yu, T., & Chung, W. (2023). A multitask, multilingual, multimodal evaluation of ChatGPT on reasoning, hallucination, and interactivity. ArXiv Preprint. ArXiv:2302.04023. DOI: 10.18653/v1/2023.ijcnlp-main.45

Duong, C. D. (2024). Modeling the determinants of HEI students' continuance intention to use ChatGPT for learning: A stimulus–organism–response approach. Journal of Research in Innovative Teaching & Learning. DOI: 10.1108/JRIT-01-2024-0006

Hua, L., & Wang, S. (2019). Antecedents of consumers' intention to purchase energy-efficient appliances: An empirical study based on the technology acceptance model and theory of planned behavior. *Sustainability (Basel)*, *11*(10), 2994. DOI: 10.3390/su11102994

Jo, H. (2023). Decoding the ChatGPT mystery: A comprehensive exploration of factors driving AI language model adoption. *Information Development*, 02666669231202764. Advance online publication. DOI: 10.1177/02666669231202764

Khalil, S., Kallmuenzer, A., & Kraus, S. (2023). Visiting museums via augmented reality: An experience fast-tracking the digital transformation of the tourism industry. *European Journal of Innovation Management*, *27*(6), 2084–2100. DOI: 10.1108/EJIM-09-2022-0479

Lin, V. S., Qin, Y., & Wu, J. (2021). Determinants of Chinese households' tourism consumption: Evidence from China Family Panel Studies. *International Journal of Tourism Research*, *23*(4), 542–554. DOI: 10.1002/jtr.2425

Ma, X., & Huo, Y. (2023). Are users willing to embrace ChatGPT? Exploring the factors on the acceptance of chatbots from the perspective of AIDUA framework. *Technology in Society*, *75*, 102362. DOI: 10.1016/j.techsoc.2023.102362

Qadir, J. (2023). Engineering education in the era of ChatGPT: Promise and pitfalls of generative AI for education. In *2023 IEEE Global Engineering Education Conference (EDUCON)* (pp. 1–9). IEEE. DOI: 10.1109/EDUCON54358.2023.10125121

Vaccino-Salvadore, S. (2023). Exploring the ethical dimensions of using ChatGPT in language learning and beyond. *Languages (Basel, Switzerland)*, *8*(3), 191. DOI: 10.3390/languages8030191

KEY TERMS AND DEFINITIONS

Artificial intelligence: is a set of technologies that enable computers to perform a variety of advanced functions, including the ability to see, understand and translate spoken and written language, analyze data, make recommendations, and more.

AI-driven: describes a process that is powered by the capabilities of artificial intelligence.

Big Data Analytics: is the study of a large amount of data to remove patterns of behavior, discover unknown correlations, understand market trends, and discover consumer preferences.

Machine Learning: is a field of study in artificial intelligence concerned with the development and study of statistical algorithms that can learn from data and generalize to unseen data, and thus perform tasks without explicit instructions.

Decision support systems: is a class of Information Systems or Knowledge-based Systems. It simply refers to a generic decision-making model that analyzes a large number of variables to make it possible to position a given issue.

Chatbots: is a computer program that simulates human conversation with an end user.

Natural language processing: is a branch of artificial intelligence (AI) that enables computers to comprehend, generate, and manipulate human language.

Blockchain: is a distributed ledger with growing lists of records (blocks) that are securely linked together via cryptographic hashes.

Industry 4.0: is an expression that encompasses some technologies for automation and data exchange and uses concepts from Cyber-Physical Systems, Internet of Things and Cloud Computing.

Chapter 8

Artificial Intelligence for Learning Disabilities: Enhancing Accessibility, Inclusion, and Empowerment

Shariq Nabi Wani
https://orcid.org/0009-0001-0034-0692
University of Kashmir, India

Shazia Farooq
https://orcid.org/0009-0000-9930-8942
University of Kashmir, India

Aasia Maqbool
University of Kashmir, India

Nasir Rasheed
https://orcid.org/0009-0008-6624-5146
University of Kashmir, India

Sumeera Maqbool
University of Kashmir, India

Warisul Rehman
University of Kashmir, India

John Mohammad
University of Kashmir, India

Rasak Annayat
National Institute of Technology, Srinagar, India

Shabir Ahmad Bhat
https://orcid.org/0009-0002-3631-4602
University of Kashmir, India

Abdal Ahmad Bhat
https://orcid.org/0009-0004-0230-3029
Government Degree College, Awantipora, India

ABSTRACT

The development of big data, cloud computing, artificial neural networks, and machine learning has enabled AI devices to perceive, recognize, learn, and solve issues, marking AI as a disruptive innovation in sectors like education. AI's potential is promising for students with learning disabilities (SWLDs), enhancing accessibility, inclusion, and empowerment through personalized learning and assistive technolo-

DOI: 10.4018/979-8-3373-4576-5.ch008

gies. AI-driven tools, including intelligent tutoring systems, speech recognition, and cognitive support, revolutionize educational practices. This chapter also addresses ethical considerations and future implications, highlighting AI's transformative role in fostering an inclusive learning environment.

INTRODUCTION

A machine that can mimic human intelligence has been made possible by the development of big data, cloud computing, artificial neural networks, and machine learning (Kumar & Sundar 2012). Extending these technologies, this research designates as artificial intelligence (AI) devices those that possess the capacity to perceive, recognize, learn, respond, and solve issues (Spector and Muraida 1993). Future offices will undoubtedly undergo a radical makeover thanks to these smart technologies (Horakova et al, 2017). Artificial intelligence is therefore becoming the next big disruptive innovation, even though it can interact and support humans in performing at higher levels (Lawler and Rushby). The fourth industrial revolution is currently being viewed by many as being driven by AI, and it may also bring about the fourth revolution in education. Additionally, the curriculum in schools is starting to include lessons on AI (Dai et al, 2020). It has been shown that these technologies increase information availability without materially changing core teaching strategies, in contrast to the past, when the invention of computers and televisions was hailed as a revolution in education. The task of evaluating AI's current capabilities and identifying promising directions for enhancing student learning still falls on educators. With interest in AI growing, reviewing recent research in education is timely and will provide teachers with up-to-date knowledge of the field before changes may occur.

There has been a growing body of work supporting the strategic value of AI in education (Ijaz et al. 2017). Loeckx (Zhai et al., 2021) asserts that artificial intelligence (AI) has the potential to be a helpful teaching tool that gives students engaging learning opportunities while relieving teachers of some of their workload. The development of artificial intelligence (AI) applications in education has many opportunities, particularly when paired with modern educational innovations like gamification, digitalization of course materials, and personalized learning experiences. To generate reactive and adaptive tutorials, for example, the modeling potential of AI techniques has been methodically applied to intelligent tutoring systems (ITS) to create personalized learning environments in lieu of a teacher shortage (Hwang et al. 2021). ITSs provide individualized learning experiences in four main ways: monitoring student input, assigning appropriate tasks, providing constructive criticism, and leveraging interfaces for human-computer interaction. As more ITSs for more subjects and topics are developed, the role of teachers will likely change, necessitating a rethinking of education. Concerns about whether AI will make their jobs harder are common among educators. Researchers and educators are currently engaged in a debate about topics such as the nature of learning and applications of artificial intelligence. Some researchers questioned whether advancements in AI would put teachers in jeopardy or even replace them, given how many other jobs are being replaced by automation (Baker et al. 2019). It's becoming increasingly clear that as AI advances, teachers' professional roles will have to adapt, necessitating the development of new organizational structures (Castañeda & Selwyn 2018). Another new issue was how the changes were received by the students. Students can use AI to improve learning outcomes to some extent as digital citizens. However, they might not implement AI strategies correctly in a particular learning environment, which could result in negative attitudes toward learning.

Ever since AIEd was introduced almost thirty years ago, artificial intelligence (AI) has been seen as a powerful tool to allow new paradigms for instructional design, technology development, and education research that are otherwise impossible to develop in the traditional education modes (Holmes et al., 2019; Hwang et al., 2020). The creation of complex educational systems, personalized learning, and the role of the instructor are just a few of the opportunities, potentials, and challenges that AI has presented for educational innovations (Baker et al., 2019; Holmes et al., 2018). A range of AI techniques, such as natural language processing, artificial neural networks, machine learning, deep learning, and genetic algorithms, had been used in order to create intelligent learning environments for different behavior detection, prediction model building, learning recommendation, etc (Chen, Xie, & Hwang, 2020). It is becoming the primary area of study in the field of digital world and education because it has the great power and capability in fostering the transformation of knowledge, cognition, and culture and much more (Hwang et al., 2020).

AI has the potential to significantly change education, but its efficacy depends on how well it is integrated into sound pedagogical frameworks as well as the technology itself (Holmes et al., 2019; Castañeda & Selwyn, 2018; Du Boulay, 2000; Selwyn, 2016). The quality of learning and instruction is influenced by the diverse philosophical and pedagogical perspectives reflected in educational technologies (Hwang et al., 2020). Although artificial intelligence (AI) has been the subject of much research, few studies have specifically examined the complex roles AI plays, how it relates to educational theories, and how it affects instruction and learning (Hwang et al., 2020). This is especially important in light of the growing number of people with learning disabilities around the world, which currently affect 79.2 million people and call for substantial special education services (UNICEF, 2021). Due to learning disabilities, more than 15% of public-school students in the United States alone are enrolled in special education programs, underscoring the critical need for efficient educational interventions (National Center for Education Statistics, 2022). Although AI has the potential to significantly improve learning outcomes, it must be carefully aligned with educational theories and practices in order to support diverse cognitive domains and provide personalized learning experiences.

Significance for Disabled Students

Individuals with learning disabilities face emotional and social challenges in addition to academic challenges (Ouherrou et al., 2019). Studies highlight that students with learning disabilities experience more negative emotional experiences—such as loneliness and depression—than their peers without disabilities. Therefore, supporting the social and emotional well-being of students with learning disabilities requires attending to their academic needs. The impact of learning disabilities is particularly noticeable in STEM fields because of the complex cognitive demands associated with processing multimodal information, which is crucial for learning (Asghar et al., 2017). While teachers work hard to assist these students, there are significant obstacles in meeting the unique needs of each person with a learning disability. Cutting-edge resources, like artificial intelligence (AI) apps, present opportunities for determining the particular needs of each student and creating strategies that are specifically designed to meet those needs. Research on the use of AI to assist people with learning disabilities has been ongoing for some time, with a primary focus on diagnosis and intervention (Drigas & Ioannidou, 2013). Notably, AI has proven useful in diagnosing dyslexia and other learning disabilities and in automating processes like essay scoring and detecting problems with reading and writing (Drigas & Ioannidou, 2012). But the majority of research that has been done so far focuses on diagnostics, which emphasizes the necessity of expanding AI applications to include interventions that are specifically designed to meet the learning needs of people with disabilities (Rauschenberger et al., 2019; Rello et al., 2018; Zvoncak et al., 2019). For example, intelligent tutoring systems present opportunities for speech therapy, social skill development, and personalized feedback (Drigas & Ioannidou, 2012, 2013). More research on integrating AI technologies to support learning for people with disabilities is essential, as proponents of equal educational opportunities stress (Zhai & Nehm, 2023). This research aims to methodically examine the body of literature in order to clarify the various ways that artificial intelligence (AI) can assist people with learning disabilities beyond simple screening and diagnosis. So, the researcher in this current study came up with the following objective.

Objectives

- To explore the role of AI in developing personalized learning tools that cater to the unique needs of students with learning disabilities, thereby enhancing accessibility and improving educational outcomes.
- To examine the impact of AI-driven assistive technologies, such as speech recognition and computer vision, in promoting greater autonomy and inclusion for individuals with physical and cognitive disabilities.

Historical Background

As evidenced by the founding of the International AI in Education Society (IAIED) in 1993 and the first publication of the International Journal of Artificial Intelligence in Education in 1989, "AI in education" has been recognized as a coherent area of academic research since at least the 1980s, though development of computer-assisted instruction systems known as Intelligent Tutoring Systems occurred earlier (Alkhatlan and Kalita 2018). According to Holmes et al. (2019), the field of artificial intelligence (AI) has grown along two strands of activity that complement each other: creating tools for use in the classroom that are based on AI and using AI to study, assess, and enhance learning. "Cognition, technology, and education nexus" is the term Pea (2016) uses to describe this disciplinary convergence. According to Buckingham Shum and Luckin (2019), developments in learning analytics and educational data mining over several decades, as well as the learning sciences and mental science, are particularly closely related to AIed.

Schank and Edelson (1989) asserted that artificial intelligence (AI) is "intimately bound up with education" in the second issue of the International Journal of Artificial Intelligence in Education. According to them, artificial intelligence (AI) and the "AI people" who develop it would not only improve education system as it was formally structured in terms of curriculum and instructional design in the traditional times, but will also necessitate significant adjustments to the ways that teaching and learning were perceived and carried out in the institutions at different levels. The authors were, in fact, writing from Northwestern University's recently founded Institute for Learning Sciences, a center established outside of educational research with support from the US Department of Education's Advanced Research Projects Agency (ARPA) and a Chicago-based corporate consulting firm.

A few years later, McArthur et al. (1995) claimed that AI applications like Intelligent Tutoring Systems will significantly improve the scenario and process and quality of learning everywhere at all levels, in a review of AI in education they had completed for RAND. But like Schank and Edelson before them, they also believed that these kinds of successes were just harbingers of potentially significant changes.

They proposed that in order to achieve this transformative goal, "high-tech companies must better cooperate with educational technology research and classroom practice".

Even though the underlying computational logics of AI have changed from programmable expert systems to big data analytics, machine learning, neural networks, and deep learning, many of the inspiring goals and transformative commitments of the "AI people" working in the field of education remain strikingly similar 25 years later (Knox, Williamson, and Bayne 2020). For forty years, AI-enabled research labs and commercial settings have seen the ongoing development of intelligent tutoring systems (du Boulay 2019). Around 2005, new areas of study in the fields of learning analytics and educational data mining arose. These areas of study were centered on the analysis of "big data" in education and the creation of new jobs for analytics specialists such as "education data scientists" (Fischer et al. 2020). As per the special issue of the British Journal of Educational Technology in 2019 that was devoted to learning analytics and AIed as a single research topic indicates that, while learning analytics and mining big educational data, whether at the institutional or individual level, are not exactly synonymous with AI, they are becoming more and more kin. Additionally, the field is changing and growing, with new roles becoming available for so-called "learning engineers," who have hybrid forms of expertise that cross the boundaries between the data, computing, and learning sciences (Williamson 2020).

Thousands of AI components will eventually come together to form a "marketplace" that will "enable system-level data collation and analysis that help us learn much more about learning itself and how to improve it," according to a significant report on the future of AIed by Luckin et al. (2016, 12). After the establishment of this market for AI components, Luckin and colleagues envisioned improved analytical capabilities for the assessment of teaching and learning at various levels as well as new AI-enabled tools for classroom use:

In her role as president of the International AI in Education Society, Luckin has adeptly converted AI-enhanced research and development as well as advocacy into mainstream, media-friendly forecasts that suggest that AI will revolutionize not only education but also human intelligence and learning, with an emphasis on augmentation.

This succinct summary demonstrates the contentious nature of AIed, with its convoluted history of approaches and fields, as well as the various claims made about how AI will help learning scientists create "transformative" or "revolutionary" understandings of human intelligence, learning, and cognition.

Perrotta and Selwyn (2020) draw attention to the way that machine learning, an applied artificial intelligence approach, is used in learning sciences research, superimposing algorithmic complexity on reductionist and contentious conceptions of human learning. They point out that applied AI methods of "automated knowledge discovery," like correlational analysis and pattern recognition, are predicated on an inductive, mechanical epistemology that holds that all patterns can be interpreted uniformly in all situations and cultures. Instead, they emphasize how AI-generated patterns are shaped by the particular contexts in which they are collected and are infused with professional, disciplinary, and financial constraints. They illustrate this point in their case study, which examines a dispute surrounding the application of predictive machine learning to the development of personalized and adaptive learning. The paper serves as a poignant reminder that, despite its appearance of objectivity, AIed is politically charged, represents specific sets of values, and involves shifting the balance of power in educational research to data science professionals who have specific ontological and epistemological philosophies. AI-enabled education is situated within a broader historical context of knowledge generation, theory development, and the establishment of epistemic proficiency in the learning sciences and educational data science. This expertise is linked to commercial and economic interests, but it cannot be reduced to them.

DISABLED STUDENTS

Throughout the world, the number of individuals with learning disabilities is 79.2 million, and there number is day by day growing continuously (UNICEF, 2021). When it comes to speaking, listening, thinking, reading, math, science, and spelling, and other learning problems, children with learning disabilities have substantial needs for special education. However, 2.3 million public school students in the America receive special education services due to learning disabilities; in countries with less developed socioeconomic status, this need is even more critical due to resource scarcity (National Center for Education Statistics, 2022). Compared to their peers, this group of students routinely performed worse on reading, science, math, and other subjects, suggesting that they had difficulties with writing, reading, or math reasoning.

Learning disabilities impact students' emotional and social capacities in addition to a wide range of academic skills, according to Ouherrou et al. (2019). Research has indicated that students who are having any learning disability or having multiple disabilities are experiencing more negative emotions like anxiety, depression and loneliness in comparsion to their same age group, who are not having learning disability.

Helping SWLDs achieve their academic goals will therefore contribute to their social and emotional development. Moreover, students majoring in STEM fields are disproportionately negatively impacted by learning disabilities. This is due to the fact that learning in these fields requires students to be able to process information in a variety of ways, such as absorbing, recalling, and applying, whatever they have grasped throughout there courses (Asghar et al., 2017).

Teachers support students with learning disabilities (SWLDs) in the classroom, but because each student has a unique presentation of their learning disability, it can be challenging to meet their needs. Teachers therefore require advanced tools, such as Artificial Intelligence (AI) applications, to assist them in identifying each student's unique needs and developing strategies to meet them. Moreover, it is imperative to provide assistance to students with learning disabilities (SWLDs) as their academic setbacks have a detrimental effect on their emotional health. We can reduce the risk of loneliness and depression for these students by using AI to support their academic endeavors.

AI has been used to assist SWLDs with diagnosis and intervention for a long time (Drigas & Ioannidou, 2013). Drigas and Ioannidou (2013) claim that dyslexia and other disabilities, such as short attention spans, can be detected or screened for using artificial intelligence (AI). Drigas & Ioannidou (2012) claim that artificial intelligence (AI) can automatically grade essays, identify the difficulties SWLDs have with reading and writing, create psychological profiles for SWLDs, and estimate spelling problems.

But the primary focus of these studies (Zvoncak et al., 2019; Rello et al., 2018; Rauschenberger et al., 2019) is on the diagnosis and screening for learning disabilities. While screening and diagnosis play a crucial role, they are insufficient for teachers to provide individualized lesson plans and support for students with disabilities (SWDs). It might be possible to create AI learning interventions for SWLDs (Drigas & Ioannidou, 2012, 2013). Several applications have been described in the literature as potentially offering speech therapy, personalized feedback, and social skill development (Drigas & Ioannidou, 2012, 2013). One such application is intelligent tutoring systems. In order to close the current gaps, it is imperative that researchers look more closely at the AI applications currently in use for SWLDs. They should also learn about the specific applications that are being used and how those technologies have been integrated to support SWLDs in terms of learning and intervention. Scholars have called for equitable uses of AI to advance learning for all (Zhai & Nehm, 2023).

Students With Learning Disabilities

Learning disabilities, also known as neurodevelopmental disorders, are not caused by environmental, cultural, or economic disadvantages, nor by visual, auditory, emotional, or motor disabilities. Instead, they stem from genetic or neurobiological factors that affect brain functions (Learning Disabilities Association of America, n.d.; Individuals with Disabilities Education Act, 2007). A significant piece of American legislation, the Individuals with Disabilities Education Act, offers a precise definition of learning disabilities. These are disorders that impact one or more of the basic psychological processes involved in reading, writing, listening, thinking, speaking, spelling, or performing mathematical calculations. Conditions such as dyslexia, minimal brain dysfunction, brain injury, perceptual disabilities, and developmental aphasia fall under this category. May show difficulty in thinking, speaking, listening, reading, writing, spelling or doing maths (Section 10 of the Disability Education Act, 2007). Learning disabilities are characterized by processing issues that hinder basic learning abilities such as reading, writing, and math, as well as more advanced skills like organization, scientific reasoning, attention, and memory (Learning Disabilities Association of America, n.d.). The Learning Disabilities Association of America categorizes learning disabilities into domains, including dyslexia (affecting reading and language-based processing), dysgraphia (impacting handwriting and fine motor skills), dyscalculia (impairing number comprehension and math learning), and non-verbal learning disabilities (affecting the interpretation of nonverbal cues).

Students' performance in math, reading, and writing can be significantly influenced by learning disabilities. Additionally, academic struggles can lead to low self-esteem, behavioral issues, and social difficulties, affecting students emotionally and socially. Supporting students with learning disabilities (SWLDs) in overcoming their academic challenges can promote both their academic success and their social and emotional development. Büttner and Hasselhorn (2011) found that these academic performances related to learning disabilities are not explained by external factors. Furthermore, researchers have noted that conditions other than learning disabilities can cause learning difficulties. However, the category of learning disabilities does not include conditions like attention deficit hyperactivity disorder (ADHD), Autism Spectrum Disorder (ASD), and Attention Deficit Disorder (ADD). Yet, students with these conditions may also have learning disabilities, placing them in both categories.

Academic performance is significantly affected for students with learning disabilities (SWLDs), and this impact is not due to external factors like inadequate instruction or physical disabilities. This indicates that SWLDs do not need physical accommodations, and their classroom challenges are not due to poor teaching. Instead, they need customized support, which can be best provided by teachers or advanced technology like AI. Teachers would need to meet individually with each student to evaluate their needs, select the most effective teaching methods, and adapt the curriculum to their learning styles.

While it would be time-consuming, AI could help save a teacher's time and effort. An AI-based program could collect data on students' needs and use it to identify the most effective tools and techniques for each student (Zingoni et al., 2021). Such a program could perform this task for multiple students simultaneously and more efficiently than a teacher, who would otherwise need to spend time individually with each student and possess the necessary expertise.

An AI-based mobile application could quickly tailor material to students' needs by capturing text with a camera and providing various tools for adaptation. In contrast, a teacher would need time to individually adapt materials for each student. This AI application would be more efficient both in terms of the time required and the number of students it could assist.

Artificial Intelligence for Learning Disabilities

Although ideas for artificial intelligence have been around for decades, the community cannot agree on a definition. As a result, definitions of artificial intelligence are multiplicity and domain-specific. Samoili et al. (2020) carried out a qualitative analysis of more than 50 documents defining AI in order to contribute to the understanding of the term. A group of high-level experts utilized the results to create an operational definition for AI. They came to the conclusion that artificial intelligence (AI) is humans-designed software and hardware that acts in the physical or digital realm by observing the environment through data collection, interpretation, reasoning, or processing of information, and then selecting the best course of action to follow in order to accomplish the stated goal (Samoili et al., 2020). The field of artificial intelligence (AI) has seen fluctuations in popularity over the years. However, in recent years, machine learning has gained significant attention from both academia and industry. This is because machine learning is a milestone development that allows a machine to "learn" from "experience" and apply what it has learned to solve new problems, much like humans do. (Thompson et al., n.d.). Due to the overwhelming interest in this new feature, various AI applications and technologies (such as computer vision and natural language processing) are being developed and used in every sphere of society, including education (Zhai et al., 2020). Chatbots, virtual assistants, intelligent tutors, facial recognition, adaptive learning tools, interactive robots, and mastery learning tools are some examples of these forms.

Due to the diversity in the nature and extent of AI applications in education, AI is a potent instrument for recognizing and providing appropriate support for the particular difficulties faced by SWLDs. The use of AI to enhance learning outcomes for students with learning disabilities has been the subject of increased publications in the literature in recent years. A review study by Poornappriya and Gopinath (2020) examined e-learning for learning and cognitive disorders as well as machine-learning applications for dyslexia prediction. Six of the 24 studies that were reviewed used external AI-based appearances to enhance learning. In particular, four of them concentrated on offering individualized or customized instruction, one on the impact of online learning activities, and one on machine learning interventions in general. We take a thorough tour in this article, revealing the complex web of factors that makes up AI-driven solutions for people with disabilities. Our common goal, which motivates us as we traverse this unexplored territory, is to use AI to advance accessibility, promote inclusion, and move people with disabilities closer to a bright future.

ASSISTIVE TECHNOLOGIES

AI-driven support systems come in many forms, such as computer vision, speech recognition, mobility assistance, and cognitive aids. The implementation of AI-powered assistive tools is causing a major revolution in the disability support field. These innovations are completely changing the lives of people with disabilities by lowering barriers, increasing their level of autonomy, and improving their general well-being.

Speech Recognition for Liberating Communication

An AI-based mobile application could quickly tailor material to students' needs by capturing text with a camera and providing various tools for adaptation. In contrast, a teacher would need time to individually adapt materials for each student. This AI application would be more efficient both in terms of the time required and the number of students it could assist.

Computer Vision for Illuminating the Visual Realm

Advancements in computer vision technology are revolutionizing AI-driven assistance, especially for individuals who cannot see or facing problem in visualising things. AI-enabled applications now offer real-time descriptions of the environment, obstacle identification, and autonomous navigation support by integrating image recognition, object detection, and scene analysis (Bharath, 2022 and Yang et al., 2022). These advancements allow individuals to navigate spaces independently, recognize objects, and interact with their surroundings in ways that were previously impossible. So, this helps these students in visualising things independently and helps them to become independent and functional.

Mobility Assistance for Independent Movement

Mobility is essential for independence, and AI-driven mobility assistance technologies are transforming how people with disabilities interact with their surroundings. Powered by sensor data and machine learning algorithms, these technologies provide different number of options for individuals in order to challenge mobility challenges. Innovations such as smart wheelchairs, which adapt to user preferences and navigate complex environments (Kumar and Jain, 2022), and exoskeletons that enhance walking abilities (Nazeer and Naseer, 2022), increase autonomy and enable individuals to confidently engage in a wider range of activities. Moreover, this makes feeling of independence among the disabled students and helps them to play their role as per the situation.

Cognitive Support for Nurturing Cognitive Autonomy

Cognitive impairments can present specific challenges that impact daily activities and communication. AI-powered cognitive support technologies leverage machine learning and natural language processing to enhance decision-making, memory, and communication. These systems assist with tasks such as scheduling, reminders, and generating contextually appropriate responses (Afonso-Jaco and Katz, 2022). By addressing cognitive gaps, these different technologies and applications help students to gain independence and autonomy and helps them to participate more actively and rigorously in the society to perform social interactions with other members and increase efficiency of their personal tasks.

User-Centric Design for Assistive AI

AI-powered assistive technologies are designed with the user's needs at the forefront. These solutions are continually refined based on user feedback to cater to the specific needs and preferences of individuals with disabilities. This ongoing improvement process ensures that the technologies effectively address functional limitations while aligning with users' goals and lifestyles. In this dynamic between AI and disability support, assistive technologies serve as powerful tools that eliminate barriers, enhance independence, and improve the quality of life for individuals with disabilities. The following sections of this article will explore how AI's transformative impact extends to ethical considerations, inclusive education, and advancements in healthcare, leading to more effective integration and empowerment for people with disabilities. This will also help us in understanding different technologies and their usage in order to provide every sort autonomy to students with learning disabilities. However, to the great extent, assistive technologies provide number of opportunities for disabled students which are very important for their gaining autonomy and development.

HEALTH INNOVATIONS

The integration of artificial intelligence and healthcare has yielded notable advancements in the areas of early detection, personalized treatment strategies, and rehabilitation for people with disabilities. This section explores how AI can improve patient outcomes by improving general well-being, developing tailored interventions, and improving diagnostic precision. An unparalleled era of potential has begun with the integration of AI and healthcare, particularly in the field of disability assistance. AI-driven developments in healthcare are revolutionizing the industry by offering early detection, specialized interventions, and individualized care for people with disabilities.

Precision Diagnosis

AI is important in disability support because it allows for accurate diagnosis. Artificial intelligence (AI) systems are capable of analyzing large amounts of complex medical data to find trends and differences that human analysts might miss. This accuracy covers a wide range of conditions, including degenerative conditions and neurodevelopmental disorders (Arumugam et al., 2022; Khoury et al., 2022; Wickramasinghe et al., 2022). Artificial Intelligence (AI) improves diagnostic accuracy, reduces the likelihood of misdiagnosis, and guarantees timely and appropriate interventions for each patient by interpreting complex connections in medical data.

Personalized Treatment Plans

AI has an impact on personalized care solutions in addition to diagnostics. By analyzing genetic markers, treatment responses, and personal health data, AI systems can recommend tailored strategies that improve therapeutic outcomes. This is especially important for people with disabilities, whose particular medical profiles frequently call for specialized care. AI supports healthcare professionals in creating interventions that are in line with each individual's unique needs and goals, from medication management to rehabilitative strategies (Barua et al., 2022).

Rehabilitation and Prosthetics

Artificial intelligence-driven advancements in prosthetics and rehabilitation have opened up new possibilities for people with disabilities that impact their ability to move or use their motor skills. Exoskeletons and prosthetic limbs driven by AI adjust to the movements of their users, offering intuitive and natural support. Moreover, AI-enhanced rehabilitation programs guarantee that treatment plans are dynamically modified in response to progress, fostering a more successful and efficient recovery (Nayak and Das, 2020; Malcangi, 2021; Shahabi et al., 2022). This customized method not only expedites recovery but also gives people the ability to reclaim a greater degree of functional independence.

Ethical Considerations in AI Healthcare

Even though AI has a lot of promise for the healthcare industry, ethical issues must come first. Concerns concerning consent, security, and privacy are brought up by the gathering, analyzing, and sharing of personal health data. AI-driven healthcare solutions must maintain ethical standards by finding a balance between individual autonomy and data-driven insights. Ensuring the rights and dignity of people with disabilities is contingent upon factors such as informed decision-making, data protection protocols, and transparency in AI algorithms.

Healthcare advancements provide evidence of the potential for improvement on the spectrum of AI's impact on disability empowerment. AI not only meets the special healthcare needs of people with disabilities but also helps to ensure a future in which health disparities are reduced and quality of life is maximized by providing individualized care, improving diagnostic accuracy, and customizing interventions.

INCLUSIVE EDUCATION

The goal of inclusive education is to provide all students with equal access and opportunities, regardless of their abilities, backgrounds, or disabilities. By offering a variety of tools and solutions customized to each student's unique learning needs, enhancing communication, and promoting greater participation from students with disabilities, artificial intelligence (AI) considerably advances inclusive education. The role AI plays in advancing inclusive education will be discussed in this section. Personalized learning pathways, tools for natural language processing, STEM (science, technology, engineering, and mathematics) inclusivity initiatives, and enhanced communication and engagement opportunities for students with disabilities will all be covered.

Personalized Learning Pathways

Artificial Intelligence plays a pivotal role in accurate diagnosis in the field of disability support. Artificial intelligence (AI) systems can detect patterns and discrepancies that conventional diagnostic techniques might miss by analyzing large and precise medical data sets. This accuracy covers a wide range of issues, including degenerative diseases and neurodevelopmental disorders (Barua et al., 2022; Furini et al., 2022; Kem, 2022; Yu et al., 2022). By deciphering intricate connections in medical data, AI improves diagnostic precision, reducing the likelihood of misdiagnosis and guaranteeing timely, appropriate interventions for each patient.

Language Processing Tools

Linguistic processing technologies driven by artificial intelligence are indispensable for students with diverse communication impairments. These technologies include text-to-speech converters, language translation programs, and speech recognition software. Technology that uses speech recognition makes it easier for students who have trouble speaking or hearing to express themselves. Additionally, text-to-speech solutions make written materials accessible to students who struggle with reading or who have visual impairments (Barua et al., 2022; Ingavélez-Guerra et al., 2022; Zdravkova, 2022; Sharma and Dash, 2023).

STEM Inclusivity Initiatives

AI is essential for improving inclusivity in STEM education. It makes it possible to create dynamic, adaptable educational materials that support different teaching philosophies. AI, for example, can create virtual laboratories, simulations, and 3D models, which enable students with physical disabilities to engage in hands-on STEM learning. Furthermore, according to research by Frisch-Villaronga and Poulsen (2022), Skowronek et al. (2022), and Siregar et al. (2023), AI-powered content can be customized to provide students who are struggling with STEM concepts with additional support in the form of clear instructions and visual aids. This fosters a more welcoming environment and encourages women and people with disabilities, two groups that are underrepresented in STEM fields to think about careers in the field.

Revolutionizing Communication and Interaction

AI-powered communication tools have significantly changed how students with disabilities interact with teachers and other students. AI-powered assistive technology and apps enable people with speech and motor impairments to communicate efficiently via text, symbols, or even eye tracking. Additionally, AI-based systems for sign language interpretation and recognition improve communication for students with hearing impairments or who are deaf (Hughes et al., 2022; Zdravkova, 2022; Zdravkova et al., 2022). By removing barriers to communication, these technologies enable students with disabilities to actively participate in group projects and classroom discussions.

AI plays an innovative and multifaceted role in advancing inclusive education. It gives teachers the resources they need to create individualized learning experiences, supports students with disabilities through initiatives for STEM inclusivity and language processing tools, and transforms the ways in which students with disabilities engage and communicate. By utilizing AI to its full potential, inclusive education can achieve its objective of providing all students, regardless of background or ability, with equal access to high-quality education. (0060)

ETHICAL CONSIDERATIONS

Concerning ethics, it is critical that we address these issues as AI technology develops. This section delves into the possible biases inherent in AI algorithms, the consequences for data privacy, and the balance between self-sufficiency and dependence on AI-driven solutions for people with disabilities. The use of AI in disability support raises a number of ethical issues that need to be carefully considered. The increasing incorporation of AI technologies into various aspects of people's lives, especially for those with disabilities, necessitates addressing potential roadblocks and challenges in order to guarantee that these advancements are not only effective but also compliant with fundamental ethical principles. This section explores the complex area of ethical issues surrounding AI in disability support, focusing on issues of autonomy, privacy, and bias.

Algorithm Bias

The possibility of algorithmic bias is one of the main ethical issues with AI. When AI systems learn from past data, the algorithms may reinforce and magnify preexisting biases if the data contains them. Bias may result in people with disabilities having less equal access to opportunities, services, or resources when it comes to disability support. It is imperative to thoroughly evaluate and reduce bias by utilizing strategies like algorithm auditing, data preprocessing, and fairness-aware algorithms (Tilmes, 2022; Edenberg and Wood, 2023)]. Artificial intelligence (AI) solutions have the potential to create a more equitable and inclusive environment for people with disabilities by proactively detecting and addressing bias.

Privacy and Data Security

Sensitive personal data collection and analysis is frequently necessary for the integration of AI. This could include mobility data, communication patterns, and health information for people with disabilities. Strong privacy safeguards are essential to preventing data breaches, unwanted access, and possible misuse of personal data (Müftüoğlu et al., 2022; Roemmich et al., 2023; Sharma et al., 2023). By putting robust encryption, data anonymization, and safe data storage procedures into place, people can benefit from AI-driven support while maintaining their privacy.

Autonomy and Independence

There is no denying that AI has the potential to increase a person's autonomy and independence if they have a disability. It's important to strike a careful balance between encouraging autonomy and preventing over-reliance on AI systems.

Although artificial intelligence (AI) technologies provide beneficial assistance, an excessive dependence on them may unintentionally reduce people's self-efficacy and ability to make decisions (Taeihagh, 2021; Wong, 2022). AI must be developed ethically such that it augments and empowers current capabilities rather than subsuming them. To guarantee that people comprehend the role of AI and maintain agency over their decisions and actions, open communication and user education are crucial.

As AI technologies advance, ethical issues need to be at the center of both development and application. Ensuring that AI-driven solutions for disabilities are in line with individual rights and societal values requires ongoing oversight, accountability systems, and adherence to established ethical frameworks. AI technologies are continuously being improved and made more ethically through collaborative efforts involving stakeholders like researchers, policymakers, ethicists, and people with disabilities. A comprehensive and proactive strategy is needed to navigate the ethical terrain of AI-driven disability support. AI technologies can genuinely become tools of empowerment, facilitating positive outcomes and opportunities for people with disabilities by addressing algorithmic bias, protecting privacy, balancing autonomy, and upholding ethical oversight.

CHALLENGES

As we navigate the increasingly complex terrain of artificial intelligence (AI), a myriad of issues demand careful consideration. These concerns span ethical implications, data privacy, equity in access, and the necessity of interdisciplinary collaboration. The transformative power of AI offers unprecedented opportunities for enhancing the lives of individuals with disabilities, but it also presents significant challenges that must be addressed to ensure that this potential is fully realized. Achieving a more inclusive future will require vigilance, thoughtful policy-making, and the active participation of diverse stakeholders.

One of the foremost challenges in integrating AI into disability support is ensuring ethical practices, particularly concerning algorithmic transparency and accountability. Algorithms are the backbone of AI systems, guiding decisions that can significantly impact individuals' lives. However, these algorithms are often complex and opaque, making it difficult for users and even developers to fully understand how decisions are made. Algorithmic transparency is essential for fostering trust in AI systems. It involves making the decision-making processes of AI systems clear and understandable to users. This transparency is critical in disability support, where the stakes are high, and the consequences of algorithmic decisions can be profound. For instance, AI-driven tools used in healthcare or employment screening must be designed so that users can understand how decisions are reached and, importantly, can contest those decisions if they appear biased or incorrect. Accountability is equally crucial. As AI systems become more autonomous, determining who is responsible when things go wrong becomes more challenging. This issue is particularly pressing in disability support, where errors or biases in AI systems can have serious implications for individuals' health, employment prospects, and overall well-being. Developers, companies, and policymakers must work together to establish clear lines of accountability, ensuring that those affected by AI decisions have recourse to address grievances and seek redress.

Another significant challenge in the integration of AI into disability support is balancing the benefits of AI-driven assistance with the need to maintain human autonomy. AI has the potential to greatly enhance the independence of individuals with disabilities by providing tailored support and facilitating daily activities. However, there is a risk that over-reliance on AI could erode personal autonomy, leading to a scenario where individuals become overly dependent on technology. Maintaining this balance requires a user-centric approach to AI design, where the needs and preferences of individuals with disabilities are prioritized. AI systems should be designed to augment human abilities rather than replace them. This means creating tools that empower users to make their own decisions and control the technology, rather than allowing the technology to dictate their actions. Furthermore, continuous communication between AI developers and end-users is essential. By engaging individuals with disabilities in the design and development process, AI systems can be tailored to meet their specific needs and preferences, ensuring that the technology remains a tool for empowerment rather than a source of dependency.

The widespread use of AI in disability support necessitates a comprehensive approach to data privacy and security. AI systems often rely on large datasets, including sensitive personal information, to function effectively. This reliance raises significant concerns about how this data is collected, stored, and used. Ensuring that sensitive personal data is handled with the utmost care is imperative. Data breaches can have severe consequences, particularly for individuals with disabilities, who may be more vulnerable to identity theft, discrimination, or other forms of exploitation. Therefore, robust data governance frameworks are essential to protect individuals' rights and foster trust in AI-driven solutions. Encryption techniques should be employed to safeguard data from unauthorized access, and strict compliance requirements should be established to ensure that data is only used for its intended purposes. Furthermore, individuals should have control over their data, with the ability to consent to its use and to withdraw that consent if they choose. Data privacy and security are not just technical issues but also ethical ones. The principles of transparency, accountability, and respect for individual autonomy must underpin all aspects of data governance in AI systems. By adhering to these principles, we can build AI-driven solutions that protect people's rights and enhance their lives everywhere.

While AI holds the potential to greatly benefit individuals with disabilities, it is crucial to address disparities in access to these technologies. The digital divide and unequal distribution of resources can prevent marginalized groups from fully benefiting from AI-driven disability assistance. This issue is particularly pressing in low-income communities and regions where access to technology and the internet is limited. Ensuring equitable access to AI-driven solutions requires concerted efforts at multiple levels. First, technology must be made affordable and accessible to all individuals, regardless of their socioeconomic status or geographic location. This may involve government subsidies, public-private partnerships, or other mechanisms to reduce the cost of technology and expand access to high-speed internet.

Second, training opportunities must be provided to ensure that individuals with disabilities can effectively use AI-driven tools. This includes not only technical training but also education on digital literacy and privacy rights. By equipping individuals with the skills they need to navigate the digital world, we can help them take full advantage of AI technologies and avoid being left behind.

Finally, it is essential to involve individuals with disabilities in the design and development of AI-driven solutions. By doing so, we can ensure that these technologies meet their needs and are accessible to all. This approach requires collaboration across sectors and disciplines, with researchers, policymakers, healthcare providers, technology developers, and individuals with disabilities working together to create inclusive solutions.

The effective use of AI in disability care requires collaboration across various sectors and disciplines. AI is a multidisciplinary field, and its successful integration into disability support depends on the contributions of diverse stakeholders. Researchers play a critical role in advancing the understanding of AI and its potential applications in disability support. They must work closely with individuals with disabilities to identify their needs and develop solutions that address those needs. Policymakers, in turn, must create frameworks that encourage innovation while protecting individuals' rights and ensuring ethical practices. Healthcare providers and technology developers must collaborate to create AI-driven tools that are both effective and accessible. This collaboration requires a deep understanding of both the technical aspects of AI and the practical needs of individuals with disabilities. By working together, these stakeholders can create solutions that are not only technologically advanced but also grounded in real-world experience and user feedback. Finally, individuals with disabilities must be involved in every stage of the design and development process. Their insights and experiences are invaluable in creating AI-driven solutions that are truly inclusive and responsive to their needs.

By addressing these challenges directly and embracing new trends, we can leverage AI's transformative power to build a society where individuals with disabilities not only overcome barriers but also achieve empowerment and inclusion. The future of AI in disability support is bright, but it will require ongoing vigilance, thoughtful policy-making, and a commitment to inclusivity to ensure that this technology fulfills its promise.

COUNTERING THE CHALLENGES: UNLOCKING AI'S TRANSFORMATIVE POWER IN DISABILITY SUPPORT

Artificial Intelligence (AI) holds immense potential to revolutionize accessibility and support for individuals with disabilities. However, harnessing this power requires addressing several significant challenges. By ensuring algorithmic transparency and accountability, safeguarding data privacy, bridging the digital divide, fostering interdisciplinary collaboration, and embracing emerging trends, we can create an inclusive society where people with disabilities thrive. This essay elaborates on these challenges and the strategies to counter them.

Algorithmic Transparency and Accountability

Ensuring ethical use of AI necessitates transparent algorithms and accountable systems. Transparency involves making the decision-making processes of AI systems understandable and accessible to all stakeholders. This can be achieved through regular audits and clear documentation, which provide insights into how algorithms operate and make decisions. Such transparency allows for the identification and correction of biases or errors, thereby enhancing trust and reliability.

Moreover, accountability is crucial. AI systems must be designed to allow for the attribution of responsibility. When an AI system makes an error or a decision that negatively impacts an individual, there should be a clear path to determine who or what is responsible. This can be achieved through robust governance frameworks and the involvement of diverse teams in AI development. Diverse teams can bring different perspectives and experiences, helping to anticipate and mitigate unintended consequences. Maintaining a balance between AI support and human autonomy ensures that while AI aids in decision-making, the ultimate control remains with humans, preserving individual rights and agency.

Data Privacy and Security

Safeguarding sensitive personal data is paramount in the use of AI for disability support. Individuals with disabilities often have to share extensive personal information, which, if mishandled, could lead to privacy breaches and misuse. Implementing robust data governance frameworks and encryption mechanisms is essential to protect against such breaches. These frameworks should include stringent access controls, regular security audits, and protocols for responding to data breaches.

Strict compliance with data protection laws, such as the General Data Protection Regulation (GDPR) in Europe, ensures that AI systems adhere to high standards of data privacy. Regular security assessments and updates to address new vulnerabilities are necessary to maintain the integrity of AI systems. Furthermore, transparent policies and obtaining user consent for data collection and use are crucial. Users should be fully informed about how their data will be used and have the ability to opt-out if they choose, fostering trust and confidence in AI solutions.

Bridging the Digital Divide

Promoting diversity in AI-driven disability support involves addressing access discrepancies. The digital divide—the gap between those who have access to modern information and communication technology and those who do not—can exacerbate inequalities, particularly for individuals with disabilities. Bridging this divide requires initiatives to improve digital literacy, provide affordable technology, and ensure equitable resource distribution.

Improving digital literacy involves providing training and education to help individuals with disabilities navigate and use AI technologies effectively. This can be achieved through collaborative efforts across sectors, including government, private sector, and non-profit organizations, to develop inclusive training programs. Additionally, providing affordable technology, such as subsidized devices and internet access, ensures that cost is not a barrier to accessing AI-driven solutions.

Equitable resource distribution is also critical. Resources should be allocated based on need, ensuring that marginalized and underserved populations benefit from AI advancements. This may involve targeted funding and support for communities with higher levels of disability or lower access to technology.

Interdisciplinary Collaboration

Tackling AI challenges in disability care requires interdisciplinary cooperation. The complex needs of individuals with disabilities cannot be addressed by a single discipline. Researchers, policymakers, healthcare providers, technologists, and people with disabilities must work together to co-create solutions.

Co-creation involves actively involving people with disabilities in the design and development of AI systems. Their insights and experiences are invaluable in creating solutions that are truly responsive to their needs. Defining ethical frameworks that guide the development and deployment of AI in disability support ensures that technologies align with community values and ethical standards.

Aligning technologies with community values involves understanding the cultural, social, and ethical contexts in which AI systems will be used. This requires continuous dialogue and collaboration among all stakeholders, ensuring that AI systems are designed to be inclusive and respectful of diverse perspectives.

Embracing Emerging Trends

Staying abreast of AI advancements and integrating innovative technologies can significantly enhance disability support. AI is a rapidly evolving field, and new developments can provide novel solutions to existing challenges. Encouraging creativity and fostering collaborations across disciplines leads to breakthrough solutions that can improve the quality of life for individuals with disabilities.

Continuous dialogue and adaptive strategies help navigate the evolving landscape of AI. Engaging with emerging trends, such as machine learning, natural language processing, and robotics, can provide new tools and approaches for disability support. For example, advancements in natural language processing can improve communication aids for individuals with speech impairments, while robotics can assist with physical tasks.

Adaptive strategies involve being flexible and responsive to new information and developments. This requires a commitment to ongoing learning and improvement, ensuring that AI systems remain at the cutting edge of technology and best practices. By embracing innovation, we can maximize AI's potential for empowerment and inclusion. however, addressing the challenges of algorithmic transparency and accountability, data privacy and security, bridging the digital divide, interdisciplinary collaboration, and embracing emerging trends is essential to unlocking AI's transformative power in disability support. Transparent, accountable AI systems, stringent data privacy measures, and efforts to bridge the digital divide are crucial steps. Interdisciplinary collaboration and embracing innovation are key to creating an inclusive society where people with disabilities thrive. By tackling these issues head-on and fostering creative partnerships, we can harness AI's potential to revolutionize accessibility and support, breaking barriers and paving the way for empowerment. The collective effort to address these challenges will not only enhance the lives of individuals with disabilities but also contribute to a more inclusive and equitable society for all.

CONCLUSION

Artificial Intelligence (AI) has significantly enhanced accessibility in education for students with learning disabilities by offering personalized learning experiences, adaptive learning platforms, and tailored educational content. AI-driven tools can identify the unique needs of each student and adjust the teaching methods accordingly, ensuring that all students can access the curriculum at their own pace. For instance, AI can provide real-time feedback and support, helping students understand complex concepts through interactive and engaging formats. Speech-to-text and text-to-speech technologies, powered by AI, enable students with reading and writing difficulties to participate fully in classroom activities. These technologies convert spoken words into written text and vice versa, allowing students to interact with educational materials in a way that suits their abilities. Additionally, AI-based applications can translate educational content into various formats, such as audiobooks, videos, or simplified text, making learning more accessible. Virtual tutors and AI-powered educational apps offer 24/7 assistance, giving students the flexibility to learn at their own pace and revisit challenging topics whenever necessary. AI can also help create a more inclusive classroom environment by providing teachers with insights into each student's progress and areas that need improvement. This data-driven approach allows educators to design more effective lesson plans and offer targeted support to students with learning disabilities. Moreover, AI can facilitate the development of individualized education plans (IEPs) by continuously monitoring students' performance and adjusting goals and strategies as needed. The use of AI in education also extends to the creation of accessible learning environments. For example, AI-powered classroom management systems can help teachers identify and mitigate potential barriers to learning, such as distractions or accessibility issues. These systems can suggest seating arrangements, assistive technologies, and other modifications to create an optimal learning environment for all students. Furthermore, AI can support the development of educational content that is universally designed, ensuring that it is accessible to students with diverse learning needs from the outset. This proactive approach to accessibility reduces the need for retrofitting and accommodations, making education more inclusive and equitable. In summary, AI has the potential to revolutionize accessibility in education for students with learning disabilities by offering personalized learning experiences, adaptive learning platforms, and tailored educational content. By leveraging AI, educators can create more inclusive and supportive learning environments that enable all students to reach their full potential.

AI in education empowers students with learning disabilities by fostering independence, boosting confidence, and enhancing academic performance. Through personalized learning experiences, AI helps students take control of their education, allowing them to progress at their own pace and according to their unique learning styles. This individualized approach reduces frustration and builds self-esteem, as students experience success and mastery of the material. AI tools can provide immediate feedback and support, helping students to understand and overcome their challenges. This real-time assistance enables students to correct mistakes and learn from them, fostering a growth mindset and resilience. AI-driven applications can also offer strategies and techniques for managing learning disabilities, such as organizational tools, memory aids, and problem-solving frameworks. These resources empower students to develop effective learning habits and skills that they can carry into adulthood. Moreover, AI can facilitate collaboration and communication between students, teachers, and parents. Through AI-powered platforms, students can share their progress, ask for help, and receive guidance from educators and caregivers. This collaborative approach ensures that students receive consistent support and encouragement, both at school and at home. AI can also enhance the role of teachers as facilitators and mentors, rather than just instructors. By automating routine tasks and providing data-driven insights, AI frees up teachers' time to focus on individualized instruction and mentorship. This shift in roles empowers students to take more responsibility for their learning, with teachers acting as guides and supporters. In addition, AI can help students with learning disabilities prepare for future careers by providing access to vocational training and skill development programs. AI-driven career counseling tools can match students with potential career paths based on their strengths, interests, and abilities. These tools can also offer resources and training opportunities to help students acquire the skills needed for their chosen careers. By providing personalized learning experiences, immediate feedback, and access to supportive resources, AI empowers students with learning disabilities to take control of their education and achieve their full potential. This empowerment extends beyond the classroom, as students develop the confidence and skills needed to succeed in all areas of life.

Further-more, AI plays a crucial role in promoting the inclusion of students with learning disabilities by creating supportive and equitable learning environments. By offering personalized and adaptive learning experiences, AI ensures that all students can participate fully in the educational process. This inclusivity extends to classroom activities, assessments, and social interactions, fostering a sense of belonging and community among all students. AI-powered tools can facilitate the integration of students with learning disabilities into mainstream classrooms by providing tailored support and accommodations. For example, AI-driven learning platforms can adjust the difficulty level of assignments and provide alternative ways to demonstrate knowledge, such as through multimedia projects or oral presentations. These adaptations ensure that students with learning disabilities can showcase their strengths and contribute meaningfully to classroom activities. AI can also support teachers in creating inclusive lesson plans and instructional strategies. By analyzing data on student performance and engagement, AI can identify patterns and trends that inform instructional decisions. This data-driven approach helps teachers design lessons that are accessible and engaging for all students, including those with learning disabilities. Additionally, AI can facilitate peer-to-peer learning and collaboration, promoting social inclusion and interaction among students. AI-powered collaboration tools can match students with complementary strengths and weaknesses, encouraging them to work together and support each other. This collaborative approach not only enhances academic performance but also fosters positive social relationships and mutual respect. Moreover, AI can help schools and districts implement inclusive policies and practices. AI-driven analytics can provide insights into the effectiveness of inclusion programs and identify areas for improvement. These insights can inform decision-making and resource allocation, ensuring that schools have the necessary support and infrastructure to meet the needs of all students. AI can also support professional development for teachers, providing training and resources on inclusive teaching practices and strategies. By equipping educators with the knowledge and skills needed to support students with learning disabilities, AI contributes to a more inclusive and equitable education system. In summary, AI promotes the inclusion of students with learning disabilities by creating supportive and equitable learning environments, facilitating the integration of students into mainstream classrooms, and supporting teachers in designing inclusive instruction. By fostering a sense of belonging and community, AI ensures that all students can participate fully in the educational process and achieve their full potential.

REFERENCES

Abhishek, S., Sathish, H., Kumar, A., & Anjali, T. (2022). Aiding the visually impaired using artificial intelligence and speech recognition technology. In: *2022 4th International Conference on Inventive Research in Computing Applications (ICIRCA)*, 21 Sep 2022; pp. 1356-1362, IEEE. DOI: 10.1109/ICIRCA54612.2022.9985659

Asghar, A., Sladeczek, I. E., Mercier, J., & Beaudoin, E. (2017). Learning in science, technology, engineering, and mathematics: Supporting students with learning disabilities. *Canadian Psychology*, *58*(3), 238–249. DOI: 10.1037/cap0000111

Baker, T., Smith, L., & Anissa, N. (2019). Educ-AI-tion rebooted? Exploring the future of artificial intelligence in schools and colleges. Retrieved from https://www .nesta.org. uk/report/education-rebooted/.

Bhatti, I., Mohi-U-din, S. F., Hayat, Y., & Tariq, M. (2024). Artificial Intelligence Applications for Students with Learning Disabilities: A Systematic Review. *European Journal of Science. Innovation and Technology*, *4*(2), 40–56.

Castaneda, L., & Selwyn, N. (2018). More than tools? Making sense of the ongoing digitizations of higher education. *International Journal of Educational Technology in Higher Education*, *15*(22). Advance online publication. https://doi.org/ DOI: 10.1186/s41239-018-0109-y

Drigas, A., & Ioannidou, R.-E. (2013). A review on artificial intelligence in special education. *Communications in Computer and Information Science*, *278*, 385–391. DOI: 10.1007/978-3-642-35879-1_46

Du Boulay, B. (2000). Can we learn from ITSs? In International conference on intelligent tutoring systems (pp. 9–17). Berlin, Heidelberg: Springer.

Holmes, W., Bialik, M., & Fadel, C. (2019). *Artificial intelligence in education: Promises and implications for teaching and learning*. Center for Curriculum Redesign.

Horáková, T., Houška, M., & Dömeová, L. (2017). Classification of the Educational Texts Styles with the Methods of Artificial Intelligence. *Journal of Baltic Science Education*, *16*(3), 324–336. DOI: 10.33225/jbse/17.16.324

Hwang, G. J., & Tu, Y. F. (2021). Roles and research trends of artificial intelligence in mathematics education: A bibliometric mapping analysis and systematic review. *Mathematics*, *9*(6), 584. Advance online publication. DOI: 10.3390/math9060584

Ijaz, K., Bogdanovych, A., & Trescak, T. (2017). Virtual worlds vs books and videos in history education. *Interactive Learning Environments*, *25*(7), 904–929. DOI: 10.1080/10494820.2016.1225099

Knox, J. (2020). Artificial intelligence and education in China. *Learning, Media and Technology*, *45*(3), 298–311. DOI: 10.1080/17439884.2020.1754236

Lawler, R. W., & Rushby, N. (2013). An interview with R obert L awler. *British Journal of Educational Technology*, *44*(1), 20–30. DOI: 10.1111/j.1467-8535.2012.01372.x

Luckin, R. (2020). "AI in Education Will Help us Understand How We Think." The Financial Times, March 10. https:// www.ft.com/content/4f24adca-5186-11ea-8841-482eed0038b1

Luckin, R., Holmes, W., Griffiths, M., & Forcier, L. B. (2016). *Intelligence Unleashed: An Argument for AI in Education*. Pearson Education.

McArthur, D., Lewis, M., & Bishary, M. (2005). The roles of artificial intelligence in education: Current progress and future prospects. *Journal of Educational Technology*, *1*(4), 42–80.

Ouyang, F., & Jiao, P. (2021). Artificial intelligence in education: The three paradigms. *Computers and Education: Artificial Intelligence*, *2*, 100020. DOI: 10.1016/j.caeai.2021.100020

Perrotta, C., & Selwyn, N. (2020). Deep Learning Goes to School: Toward a Relational Understanding of AI in Education. *Learning, Media and Technology*, *45*(3), 251–269. Advance online publication. DOI: 10.1080/17439884.2020.1686017

Poornappriya, T. S., & Gopinath, R. (2020). Application of machine learning techniques for improving learning disabilities. *International Journal of Electrical Engineering and Technology*, *11*(10), 403–411.

Rauschenberger, M., Lins, C., Rousselle, N., Hein, A., & Fudickar, S. (2019). Designing a new puzzle app to target dyslexia screening in pre-readers. *Proceedings of the 5th EAI International Conference on Smart Objects and Technologies for Social Good*, 155–159. DOI: 10.1145/3342428.3342679

Rello, L., Romero, E., Rauschenberger, M., Ali, A., Williams, K., Bigham, J. P., & White, N. C. (2018). Screening dyslexia for English using HCI measures and machine learning. *Proceedings of the 2018 International Conference on Digital Health*, 80–84. DOI: 10.1145/3194658.3194675

Samoili, S., López Cobo, M., Gómez, E., De Prato, G., Martínez-Plumed, F., & Delipetrev, B. (2020). *AI watch defining artificial intelligence towards an operational definition and taxonomy of artificial intelligence. Joint Research Centre*. JRC.

Spector, J. M., & Song, D. (1995). Automated instructional design advising. In *Automating instructional design: Computer-based development and delivery tools* (pp. 377–402). Springer Berlin Heidelberg.

Williamson, B., & Eynon, R. (2020). Historical threads, missing links, and future directions in AI in education. *Learning, Media and Technology, 45*(3), 223–235. DOI: 10.1080/17439884.2020.1798995

Yang, Q., Jin, W., Zhang, Q., Wei, Y., Guo, Z., Li, X., Yang, Y., Luo, Q., Tian, H., & Ren, T.-L. (2023). Mixed-modality speech recognition and interaction using a wearable artificial throat. *Nature Machine Intelligence, 5*(2), 169–180. DOI: 10.1038/s42256-023-00616-6

Zhai, X., Chu, X., Chai, C. S., Jong, M. S. Y., Istenic, A., Spector, M., Liu, J.-B., Yuan, J., & Li, Y. (2021). A Review of Artificial Intelligence (AI) in Education from 2010 to 2020. *Complexity, 2021*(1), 8812542. DOI: 10.1155/2021/8812542

Zhai, X., & Panjwani-Charania, S. (2023). AI for Students with Learning Disabilities. *Systematic Reviews*.

Zhai, X., Zhang, M., Li, M., & Zhang, X. (2019). Understanding the relationship between levels of mobile technology use in high school physics classrooms and the learning outcome. British Journal of Educational Technology. *Journal of the Council for Educational Technology, 50*(2), 750–766.

Chapter 9
AI Text Mining of Case Studies for Students With Disabilities Using Handy ICT Tools

Shigeru Ikuta
https://orcid.org/0000-0001-5065-190X
Otsuma Women's University, Japan

ABSTRACT

The author has conducted many case study activities for students with disabilities in collaboration with schoolteachers using handy tools such as a speaking-pen and dot-code reader. In these activities, tiny dot codes were used to link multimedia such as audio and video. Every year, the author compiled the case study activity reports sent by the schoolteachers and reported them in an online journal. In the present chapter paper, the context of the reports over a 10-year period was analyzed using AI text mining to obtain word cloud, the appearance frequency of words, and the co-occurrence of words and co-occurrence network. Dependency analysis was also performed to clarify the "modifier-modifier" relationship between two keywords in a sentence. Through this AI text mining, the role of schoolteachers and handy tools used will be clarified in enabling students with disabilities to realize activities that they were not able to do before.

DOI: 10.4018/979-8-3373-4576-5.ch009

INTRODUCTION

In some children, the loss of language is a major impairment. The inability to tell their wills and desires often leads to intolerable frustrations. Each student with autism spectrum disorder also has some problematic core verbal and nonverbal communication symptoms (e.g., a delay in learning to talk or a complete lack of verbal ability) (Hoffman, 2023; National Institute of Mental Health, 2025). The students labelled "reading-impaired" also have obvious troubles with learning sound-symbol correspondence, sounding out words, and spelling words (Moats & Tolman, n.d.; National Institute of Child Health and Human Development, 2020).

The teachers, especially at the schools for special needs education and the classes for special needs education at regular public schools, deeply feel that teaching aids and specific materials suitable for one student may not serve another student. Each student has individual hopes, needs, and desires, as well as a history of learning. Therefore, schoolteachers ideally should develop original, independent content suitable for each individual student. Given the challenges of doing so, easy-to-handle and less-costly software and hardware solutions are crucial to schoolteachers for conducting and developing activities with original self-made content for students in their class (Ikuta et al., 2013; Ikuta, 2019a; Ikuta, 2020). They also hope that newly developed software and tools and aids with information and communication technology (ICT) may effectively improve individual learning for the student with a disability. On the other hand, teachers have countless and profound questions about what kinds of tools and software they should use and how they should use them in the classrooms.

It's well-known that augmentative and alternative communication (AAC) (American Speech-Language-Hearing Association, n.d.; Ann et al., 2015; Beukelman & Light, 2020; Carpenter, et al., 2015; Mirenda, 2013; Ogletree, 2021; Polgar, et al., 2024; The ALS Association, n.d.) utilize assistive technology (AT) devices that range from no-tech to high-tech (Anson, 2018; Bugaj, 2023; Burns, 2021; Dell, et al., 2017; Green, 2018; QIAT Leadership Team, 2020; Viner, et al., 2020). Voice-output communication aids (VOCAs) (Assistive Technology Australia, n.d.; Assistive Technology Industry Association, n.d.; Mueller, 2013), also known as speech-generating devices (SGDs) (Communication Matters, n.d.), are commonly used AAC tools that utilize single-level or multilevel outputs to convey sounds. While a variety of VOCAs cater to students with varying abilities and needs, their low output numbers and short recording times severely hinder most devices.

More than 20 years ago, to address these problems, Shigeru Ikuta, the author of this chapter, organized a research project in collaboration with schoolteachers to create self-made teaching materials and conduct activities in their classes using ScanTalk dot codes, developed by Olympus Co. (1999). Such codes transform voices and sounds into two-dimensional dot codes directly placed on ordinary paper. In collaboration with schoolteachers, Ikuta created many skillful school activities (Ikuta et al., 2013). Students with severe hand, finger, or intellectual challenges, however, could not correctly trace long ScanTalk codes using the ScanTalk Reader.

As a result, Ikuta began utilizing the new multimedia-enabled dot codes (GridOnput) that Gridmark Inc. (n.d.) had independently developed to create original, self-made teaching materials overlayed with these tiny dots. By simply touching the "invisible" dot code on paper, using a simple tool such as a speaking pen or a dot-code reader, it is possible to play not only voices and sounds, but also multimedia sources such as photos, videos, and web pages. The Gridmark Inc. and the present author, Ikuta, have been developing the sheets with Post-it-like sticker icons overlaid with GridOnput dot codes, software to create original self-made teaching materials, and handy tools to reproduce such multimedia.

BACKGROUND

Japan has 1,191 *separated* schools for special needs education with 155,140 enrolled students and 89,018 permanent teachers in the 2024 academic year, as listed in Table 1 (Ministry of Education, Culture, Sports, Science and Technology, 2024). About half of these schools for special needs education cater to students with intellectual disabilities. Almost all of the schools for special needs education have three departments: elementary, junior high, and senior high; some schools also have a kindergarten department, and several schools have a high school department only.

Table 1. Basic information on education system for students with disabilities in Japan

Separated **schools for special needs education**	
Total number of schools	**1,191**
Total number of students	155,140
Total number of permanent teachers	89,018
Ordinary *elementary* school (including national, public and private)	
Total number of schools	18,824
Total number of students	5,941,729
Total number of permanent teachers	425,109
Number of students in home branch schools	
Elementary school	1,153
Junior high school	684

continued on following page

Table 1. Continued

Separated **schools for special needs education**	
Total number of schools	**1,191**
High school	622
Classroom for special needs education at public elementary schools	
Total number of classrooms	54,643
Total number of students	263,081

Outside of these separated schools for special needs education, Japanese *public* schools offer three assistance methods that vary depending on the severity of a student's disability. The lowest-needs group is taught in regular classrooms through various efforts, such as small-group instruction, team teaching that includes specialized education coordinators and external advisers, individual education support plans for each student, and instruction according to different achievement levels. The next approach involves implementing a resource room program, which is available a few times a week to students with disabilities. These students receive instruction in regular classrooms but are enrolled in the resource room program to receive specialized instruction. This approach is used with students who have speech or language impairment, autism, emotional disturbance, visual or hearing difficulties, attention deficit/hyperactivity disorder, or learning disabilities.

Another method used in schools involves classrooms for special needs students at regular public schools. These classes are limited to eight students in each and focus on those with relatively mild intellectual or physical/motor disabilities; autism/emotional disturbance; or health, visual, hearing, or speech/language impairment. Table 1 also reveals that a total of 54,643 classrooms with 263,081 students were designated for special needs education in public elementary schools. These classrooms primarily accommodated students with intellectual disabilities, comprising 22,609 classrooms with 113,573 students, and students with autism spectrum disorder and emotional disorders, comprising 26,035 classrooms with 140,726 students (Ministry of Education, Culture, Sports, Science and Technology, 2024).

Special needs education may also be established as a branch classroom in a hospital/home for sick children; the number of students in home branch schools (visiting classes) in the 2023 academic year was 1,153, 684, and 622 in elementary, junior high, and high school departments, respectively. (Isogai, 2017; Kawano, 2016; Ministry of Education, Culture, Sports, Science and Technology, 2015; Ministry of Education, Culture, Sports, Science and Technology, 2024; Ministry of Education, Culture, Sports, Science and Technology, n.d.).

Author Ikuta provides speaking pens and dot-code readers to schoolteachers for free, in addition to original Magical sheets overlaid with GridOnput dot codes. With these free materials, schoolteachers can create original teaching materials suited to each student in their classroom and conduct case study activities. Ikuta's research project has more than 300 schoolteachers who are eager to help students with various difficulties communicate their intentions and wishes to classmates and teachers.

In this paper, AI text mining techniques (User Local, n.d.) were used to analyze the context of reports published in an online journal, International Journal of Human Culture Studies (Int. J. Hum. Cult. Stud., n.d.), over a 10-year period and shared with schoolteachers across Japan. In addition, the role and usefulness of easy-to-use ICT tools in realizing reasonable accommodations will be clarified.

MAIN FOCUS OF THE CHAPTER

Multimedia-Enabled Dot Codes and Handy Tools

"Invisible" GridOnput dot codes (Gridmark, n.d.) is a novel two-dimensional code technology consisting of extremely small dots. Such dot codes, therefore, can invisibly overlay any graphically printed letters, photos, and illustrations with specially designed software (*GM Authoring Tool* developed by Gridmark Inc.). This dot overlay never affects the designed images. Letters, photos, and illustrations can be changed into information-trigger icons. Printing a document that includes the GridOnput dot codes requires an industry-standard cyan-magenta-yellow-black (CMYK) process.

The software *GM Authoring Tool* and the printer to print out the document with the dot codes are still costly. Therefore, Gridmark Inc. and Ikuta have created sheets overlaid with multimedia-enabled dot codes beforehand separately; the Magical sheet created by the present author has Post-it-like sticker icons and the controller icons with special functionality at the lower part that can change a mode, start recording voices/sounds and link them to each icon, delete the linked voices/sounds, and other functions. You can remove these sticker icons and paste them onto real items.

Some useful tools are the speaking pen (G-Speak) and the dot-code reader (G-Pen Blue) shown in Figure 1. They have an infrared camera (Ikuta et al., 2021a) built in that can read invisible dot codes on documents or Post-it-like sticker icons that are already covered in dot codes and play audio and video.

Figure 1. Speaking pen G-Speak and dot-code reader G-Pen Blue

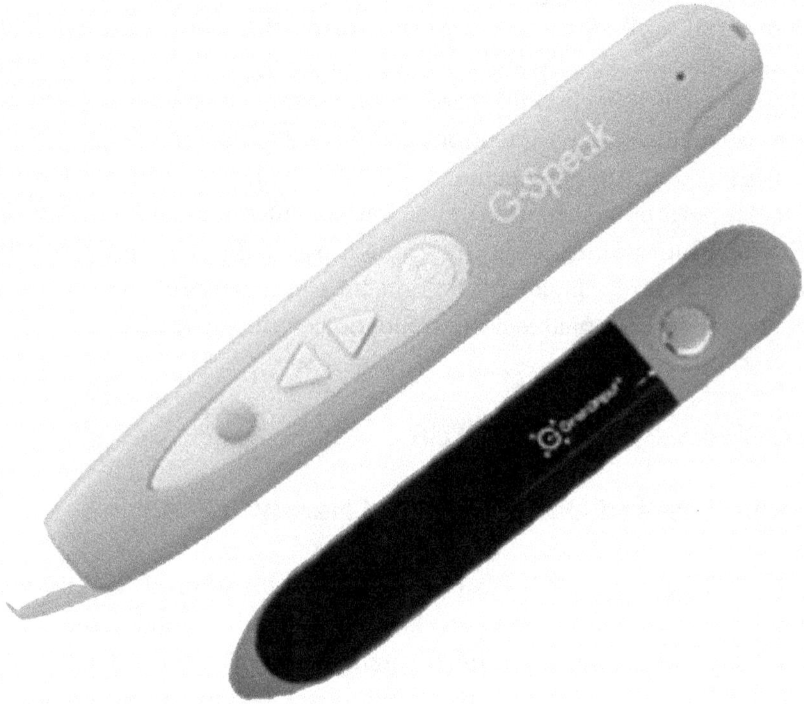

Five Software Packages to Create Self-made Teaching Materials

Gridmark Inc. has created and developed five software packages having the following functionalities in collaboration with Ikuta's project (Ikuta, et al., 2021a):

1. ***The GM Authoring Tool*** enables users to insert multimedia-enabled GridOnput dot codes into their designed documents at any desired location, size, and number. The resulting documents can be printed and used exactly as the Post-it-like sticker icons that Gridmark Inc. and Ikuta created.
2. ***Sound Linker*** enables users to effortlessly connect audio clips to each dot-code icon and generate content for a speaking pen using a personal computer running Windows OS. The recently updated software can now handle a new dot sticker, developed by Gridmark Inc., having 1,000 Post-it-like sticker icons. This software is capable of handling a maximum of 10 modes, allowing users

to link a maximum of 10 mediums, such as video clips, and a maximum of 10 audios to each sticker icon.

3. ***NANA*** allows users to easily link audio clips to each dot-code icon and create content for a speaking pen, with the help of a linkage table, filelist.csv. This filelist.csv file defines the relationship among the internal number of each dot-code icon, its mode, and the corresponding audio filename. The *NANA* program for macOS users was recently developed by the present author, Ikuta.
4. ***FileLinker*** allows users to create a standalone application that can reproduce multimedia (e.g., movies) with a speaking pen (G-Speak) connected to the personal computer on Windows OS.
5. ***BlueLinker*** allows users to easily create content that can replay multimedia (e.g., movies, photos, and Web pages) on iOS and iPad OS devices, such as iPhone and iPad, by touching the dot-code icons with the recently developed dot-code reader (G-Pen Blue) which is equipped with Bluetooth functionality. This software was recently widely updated from the previous one, *Gridmark Content Viewer (GCV)*, and is now uploaded to the Apple App Store. The new version of *GCV* has recently been developed also for macOS devices like MacBook Pro and MacBook Air.

The software (except *GM Authoring Tool*) is provided free of charge for schoolteachers and researchers. Users can ask Ikuta about trying them and refer to the published papers for detailed descriptions of each software (Ikuta et al., 2017; Ikuta, 2019a; Ikuta, 2020; Ikuta et al., 2021a).

Many teachers create a content for a speaking pen without using the *Sound Linker* or *NANA* software mentioned above, usually by recording voice/sound with the speaking pen's built-in microphone and linking it directly to a Post-it-like sticker icon with just a touch. This simple method is easy to use, but if users want to create content with clear, volume-adjusted audio files or with linking more than two voices/sounds per dot code icon, they will need to use software such as *Sound Linker* or *NANA*.

Case Study Activities

Ikuta has been working with schoolteachers for special needs students for over 20 years, conducting various case study activities using ICT tools such as a speaking pen and dot-code reader. He has published the results in numerous chapter papers in edited books published by IGI Global Scientific Publishing, including Ikuta, 2018, Ikuta et al., 2013, Ikuta et al., 2015, Ikuta et al., 2017, Ikuta, 2019a, and Ishitobi et al., 2019. In addition, from 2011 to 2020, he collected the case studies conducted by Japanese schoolteachers and published them in the online journal Int. J. Hum.

Cult. Stud. as reports to share with teachers in Japan. Over the 10-year period, he has compiled a total of 243 case studies (n=243) performed for students with disabilities.

AI Text Mining

AI text mining is an advanced discipline within data science that uses artificial intelligence (AI) and text data mining techniques to derive pertinent qualitative information from unstructured text data into a structured format to identify meaningful patterns and new insights (Genevieve, 2024; IBM, n.d.). In a typical document, "very common words" appear many times. However, because these words appear in any document, even if they occur frequently, they have little meaning and are not very important. If we simply rank the number of occurrences, we will mix in common words and fail to capture the text's characteristics. To solve this problem, text mining employs a mechanism in which "words that appear frequently in general documents are weighted lightly because they are not important," while "words that do not appear often in general documents but appear frequently in the document being investigated are given more weight." Generally, a statistical process known as the term frequency-inverse document frequency (TF-IDF) extracts such feature words (Leskovec et al., 2020; Ninja, 2023; Rajaraman & Ullman, 2011). AI text mining therefore calculates the "score" based on not only the number of occurrences but also the importance of the word. Words with high scores are considered to characterize the text.

The TF-IDF is also applied to the present AI text mining application developed by User Local (n.d.) to extract such feature words. Unlocking the full potential of the methodology requires a thorough understanding of the text-mining workflow, which includes understanding each step of the process, including data processing, and its significance to the overall outcome (China, 2023). The frequency and scored words, their word clouds, co-occurrence of words, its network, and dependency analysis were clarified in the present analysis.

According to Concetta & Wilkinson, 2014; Leskovec et al., 2020; Salloum et al., 2018, word clouds provide insights into the focus of textual materials and identify patterns and trends, or lack thereof; the more frequently words or the higher-scored words appear within the text, the bigger and bolder they appear in the generated visualizations.

The co-occurrence of words is defined as a relationship between two words/phrases in a sentence: the larger in their appearance frequency, the stronger in their relationship (Gupta, 2023; Zhao, et al., 2023). The co-occurrence network is a diagram in which lines are used to connect words that appear in a text with similar patterns of occurrence (Segev, 2022). We draw larger words that appear more frequently, and we use thick solid lines, thin solid lines, or dashed lines to define the strength of their relation within the text.

Dependency analysis extracts words from each phrase having a "modifier-modified" relationship and tallies the pairs of the target noun and other noun, verb, and/or adjective that modify it (IBM, 2021). The "scored value" is a uniquely calculated number determined by a combination of factors such as the number of occurrences and the percentage of all combinations. The higher the value, the more important the dependency relationship is. Co-occurrences and their dependency analysis not only allow users to clearly understand the relationship between two words but also the importance of that relationship.

SOLUTIONS AND RECOMMENDATIONS

From 2011 to 2020, schoolteachers sent the present author a total of 243 case study reports on the use of ICT tools, such as a speaking pen and dot code reader, for students with disabilities. The full text of these 243 reports was each categorized into the following eleven sections: number of reports sent by schoolteachers per year, school or organization where the case studies were conducted, prefecture where the school is located, department and its grade of the target students, types of disability of the target students, daily behavior of the target students, whether the target students can speak or not, activity scenes, handmade teaching materials created by teachers, practice and its content, and results and challenges obtained.

Number of Reports Sent by Schoolteachers per Year

The total of 243 case studies were conducted on students with disabilities for ten years, with 60 (24.7%) in 2016, followed by 52 in 2017, 47 in 2018, 23 in 2019, and 23 in 2014, etc. (see Table 2). We included some case studies for multiple students or entire classes/schools. In the early stages of this project, most case studies were conducted for elementary school students in public schools with the help of university students using a speaking pen, a dot-code reader, and eBooks and therefore were not included in the present analysis.

Table 2. Number of reports sent by schoolteachers per year

Year	Number of reports (%)
2011	3 (1.2%)
2012	2 (0.8%)
2013	1 (0.4%)
2014	23 (9.5%)
2015	12 (4.9%)
2016	60 (24.7%)
2017	52 (21.4%)
2018	47 (19.3%)
2019	23 (9.5%)
2020	20 (8.2%)

School or Organization Where the Case Studies Were Conducted and Its Department

Table 3 reveals that out of the 243 case studies, the majority (224) took place in special needs education schools, while only 13 took place in public school special needs classes. The elementary school department accounted for approximately half (50.2%) of the case studies conducted, followed by the junior high school department (27.8%) and the high school department (21.8%), with several case studies involving all students in grade or school.

Table 3. School or organization where the case studies were conducted

School or organization	Number
Separated school for special needs education	224
Class for special needs at public school	13
Education center at regional government	3
Child development support facility	1
Non-profit organization	1
Personal use	1

Prefecture Where the School is Located

The case study reports were sent to the author Ikuta by the schoolteachers in 23 of the 47 prefectures in Japan, but over 70% were by teachers in the near Tokyo (Kanto area) where Ikuta lives, as shown in Table 4. 59 reports (24.3%) were sent by the teachers in Chiba Prefecture, 52 reports (21.4%) by the teachers in Tochigi Prefecture, and 51 reports (21.0%) by the teachers in Tokyo, etc. Of course, the author has distributed a speaking pen, dot-code reader, and Post-it-like sticker icon sheet to any schoolteachers who requested them.

Table 4. Prefecture where the school is located

Prefecture	Number of case studies
Chiba	59 (24.3%)
Tochigi	52 (21.4%)
Tokyo	51 (21.0%)
Osaka	10 (4.1%)
Hyogo	9 (3.7%)
Aomori	7 (2.9%)
Fukuoka	7 (2.9%)
Saitama	7 (2.9%)
Oita	6 (2.5%)
Nagano	6 (2.5%)
Yamaguchi	5 (2.1%)
Kochi	4 (1.7%)
Kyoto	3 (1.2%)
Hiroshima	3 (1.2%)
Kanagawa	3 (1.2%)
Nara	2 (0.8%)
Gunma	2 (0.8%)
Ishikawa	2 (0.8%)
Wakayama	1 (0.4%)
Nagasaki	1 (0.4%)
Ibaraki	1 (0.4%)
Miyagi	1 (0.4%)
Shizuoka	1 (0.4%)

Types of Disability of the Target Students

Table 5 lists the types of disabilities among the target students in the 243 case studies. The students had a wide range of disabilities, some with multiple disabilities: 51.4% of the students had intellectual disabilities, 15.7% had autism spectrum disorder and 7.2% had Down's syndrome. 17 (5.3%) and 14 (4.4%) case studies were conducted on students from schools for the physically disabled and the visually impaired, respectively. A case study on a student with selective mutism was also carried out, thanks to the teachers' excellent ideas and ingenuity.

Table 5. Types of disability of the target students

Type of disability	Number of students
Intellectual disability ( )	164 (51.4%)
Autism spectrum disorder ( )	50 (15.7%)
Down syndrome ( )	23 (7.2%)
Physically disabled ( )	17 (5.3%)
Visual impairment ( )	14 (4.4%)
Multiple disabilities ( )	13 (4.1%)
ADHD ( )	5 (1.6%)
Upper and lower limb abolition ( )	4 (1.3%)
Learning disorder ( )	4 (1.3%)
Cerebral palsy ( )	3 (0.9%)
Fukuyama congenital muscular dystrophy ( )	2 (0.6%)
Trunk impairment (Core dysfunction) ( )	2 (0.6%)
Epilepsy ( )	2 (0.6%)
Delayed echolalia ( )	1 (0.3%)
Scoliosis ( )	1 (0.3%)
Developmental delay ( )	1 (0.3%)
Dysarthria ( )	1 (0.3%)
Acute encephalopathy aftereffect ( )	1 (0.3%)
Pervasive developmental disorder ( )	1 (0.3%)
Microcephaly ( )	1 (0.3%)
Academically slow ( )	1 (0.3%)
Selective mutism ( )	1 (0.3%)
Pierre-Robin syndrome ( )	1 (0.3%)
Stickler syndrome ( )	1 (0.3%)

continued on following page

Table 5. Continued

Type of disability	Number of students
Coffin-Lowry syndrome ( )	1 (0.3%)
Language disorder ( )	1 (0.3%)
Hyperacusis ( )	1 (0.3%)
Stuttering ( )	1 (0.3%)
Eating disorder ( )	1 (0.3%)

Table 6 shows the co-occurrence frequency of two words in the section of "types of disability of the target students." The co-occurrence frequency of two words, "intellectual disability" and "autism spectrum disorder" was 27, "Down syndrome" and "autism spectrum disorder" was 8, "Down syndrome" and "intellectual disability" was 6," "intellectual disability" and "physically disabled" was 5, and "intellectual disability" and "visual impairment" was 4, etc.

Table 6. Co-occurrence frequency of two words/phrases in "types of disability of the target students" section

Type of disability 1	Type of disability 2	Co-occurrence frequency
Intellectual disability	Autism spectrum disorder	27
Down syndrome	Autism spectrum disorder	8
Down syndrome	Intellectual disability	6
Intellectual disability	Physically disabled	5
Intellectual disability	Visual impairment	4
Upper and lower limb abolition	Multiple disabilities	4
Visual impairment	Multiple disabilities	3
Physically disabled	Multiple disabilities	3
Trunk impairment	Intellectual disability	2
Intellectual disability	Fukuyama congenital muscular dystrophy	2
Physically disabled	Visual impairment	2
Intellectual disability	Multiple disabilities	2

Table 7 provides the dependency analysis in the section of "types of disability of the target students." These data clearly show that a certain number of students have multiple disabilities. The co-occurrence network shown in Figure 2 also shows that "intellectual disability" located at the center clearly describes a co-occurrence relationship with other disabilities.

Table 7. Dependency analysis in "types of disability of the target students" section

Word 1	Word 2	Frequency
Intellectual disability	Autism spectrum disorder	21
Physically disabled	Intellectual disability	4
Intellectual disability	Down syndrome	3
Visual impairment	Physically disabled	2
Visual impairment	Intellectual disability	2
Intellectual disability	Language disorder	1
Intellectual disability	Stuttering	1
Intellectual disability	Trunk impairment (Core dysfunction)	1
Intellectual disability	Multiple disabilities	1
Intellectual disability	Physically disabled	1
Autism spectrum disorder	Down Syndrome	1

Figure 2. Co-occurrence network in "types of disability of the target students" section; upper is an original figure and lower with English words translated by the author (See also Table 5)

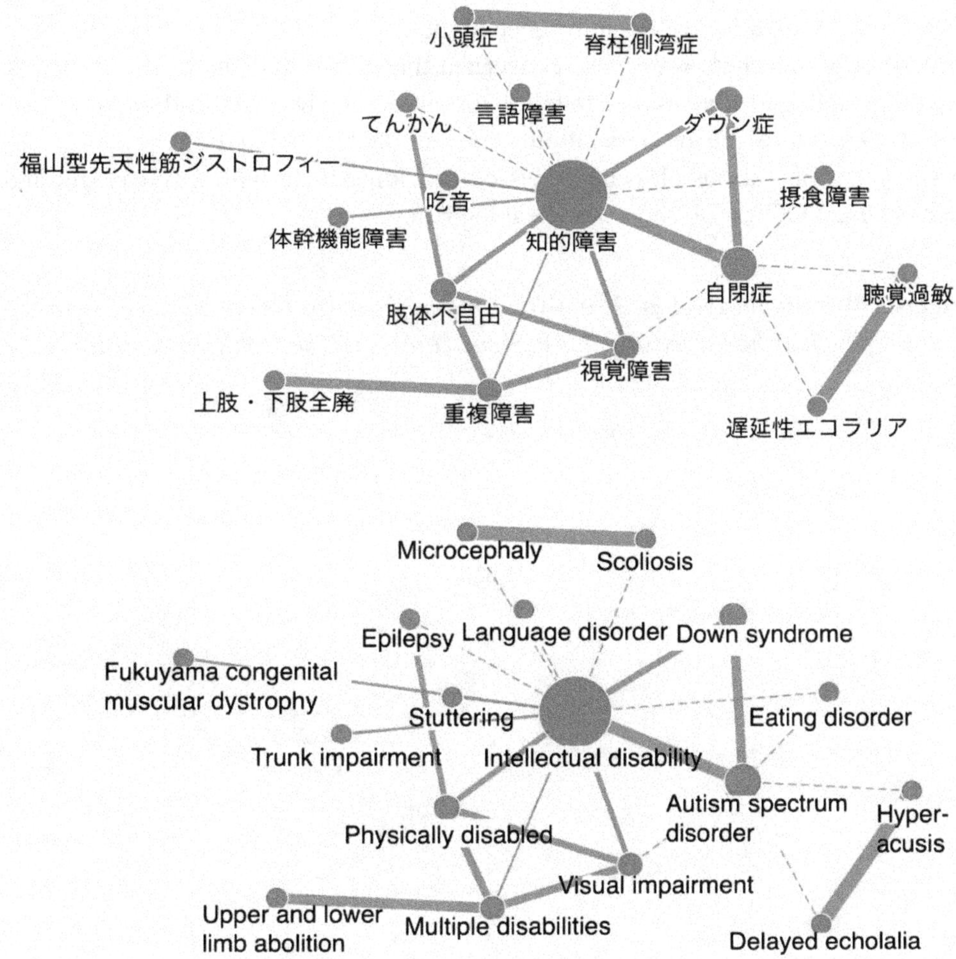

Whether the Target Students Can Speak or Not?

Figure 3 shows the word cloud created by AI text mining, based on the word frequency in the section, "Can target students speak or not?" In the center of the Figure 3, the word " (cannot speak)" is drawn largest, which corresponds to the fact that about half of the target students (51.2%) could not speak anything, and nearly 10% could only speak a few words and/or had unclear pronunciation, as listed in Table 8.

About 12.5% of the case studies were conducted for more than one student or many students together, and then, the lack of detailed information from the teachers who conducted the case studies made it unclear whether these students could speak or not. Therefore, we expect the percentage of students who could not speak at all or could only speak a few words to be even higher.

The schoolteachers were very concerned that many students could not speak anything at all and were unable to tell their wishes to others in the classroom or in society. Therefore, the teachers initially concentrated on facilitating these students' participation in various class activities by providing them with a convenient and easy-to-use VOCA tool, such as a speaking pen.

Figure 3. Word cloud developed from AI text mining based on the appearance frequency in the "Whether the target students can speak or not?" section (See also Table 8)

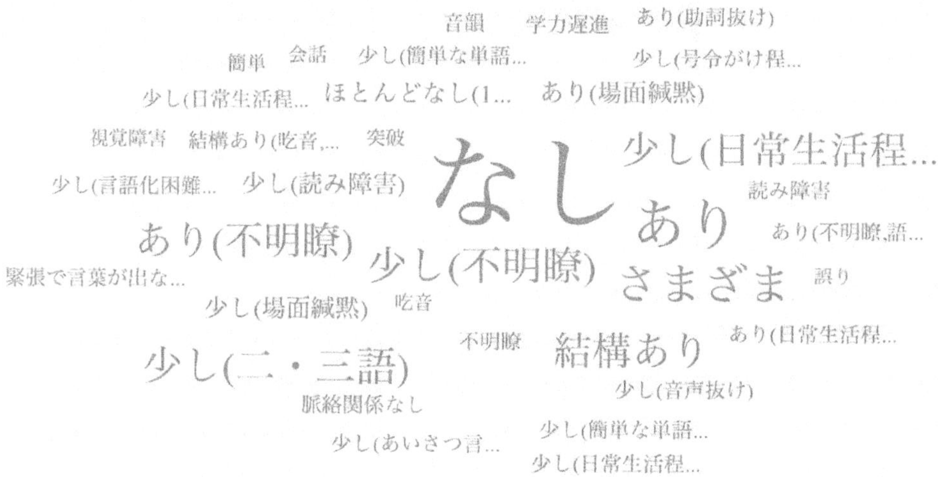

Table 8. Whether the target students can speak or not?

Can speak or not	Frequency	%
cannot speak	131	51.2%
no mention due to several students being conducted together	32	12.5%
can speak	25	9.8%
( ) a little (but ambiguity)	9	3.5%
( ) a little (few words only)	8	3.1%
( ) a little (daily words only)	7	2.7%

continued on following page

Table 8. Continued

Can speak or not	Frequency	%
( ) can speak, but ambiguous	7	2.7%
can speak some extent	6	2.3%
( ) can speak a little (reading disability)	2	0.8%
( ) can speak a little (selective mutism)	2	0.8%
(1) almost no speaking (one word only)	2	0.9%
( ) can speak, but selective mutism	2	0.8%
ambiguous speaking	2	0.8%

Daily Behavior of the Target Students

Figures 4 and 5 are word clouds, created through AI text mining, of the word frequency and scored value, respectively, in the "daily behavior of the target students" section; nouns are displayed in blue, verbs in red, and adjectives in green. The highest appearance frequency word is "be able to ( )," but the highest scored word is "speaking ( )."

Figure 4. Word cloud based on the appearance frequency in the "daily behavior of the target students" section (See also Table 9)

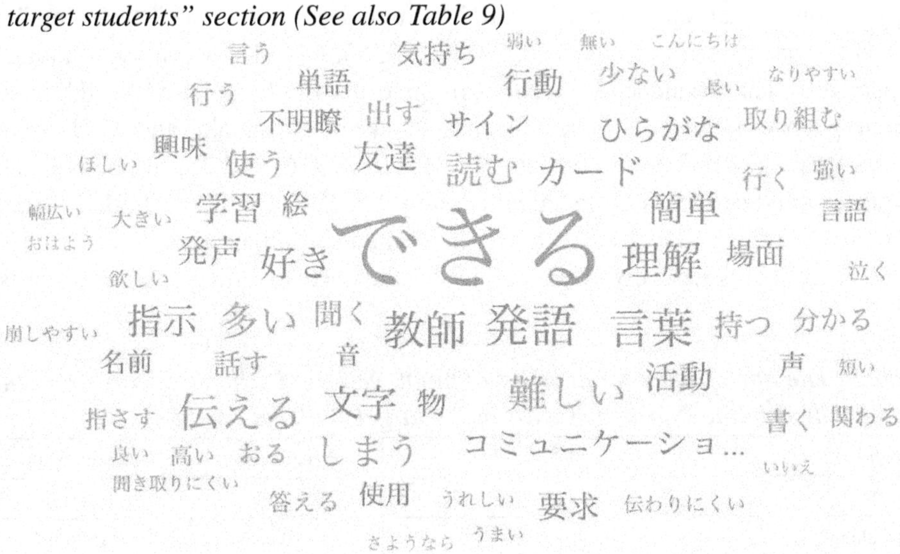

Figure 5. Scored word cloud in the "daily behavior of the target students" section (See also Table 9)

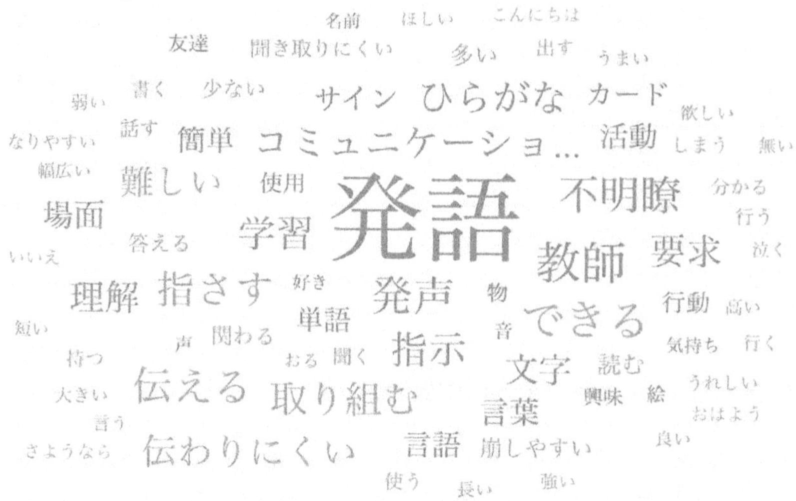

Table 9 shows the appearance frequency of nouns, verbs, and adjectives in the "daily behavior of the target students" section and their scored values. The frequency of nouns is in the order of "speaking," "understanding," "teacher," "vocabulary," "instruction," "character," "love," "card," "simplicity," "Hiragana," "learning," and "activity," and its frequency is 108, 93, 92, 90, 65, 64, 64, 59, 58, 49, 49, and 48, respectively. The frequency of verbs is in the order of "be able to," "tell," "read," "clean (put back)," "use," "hold," "listen to," "take out," "speak," and "understand," and its frequency is 289, 70, 56, 46, 35, 31, 29, 27, 26, and 25, respectively. The frequency of adjectives is in the order of "many," "difficult," "few," "high," "strong," "wanting," "large," "hard to tell," and "glad," and its frequency is 62, 61, 23, 15, 15, 14, 9, 8, and 6, respectively. (See Table 9 for the corresponding Japanese words.)

Table 9. The appearance frequencies of noun, verb and adjective words and their scored values in the "daily behavior of the target students" section

Word	Frequency	Scored value
[noun]		
speaking	108	1555.1
understanding	93	96.3
teacher	92	345.6

continued on following page

Table 9. Continued

Word	Frequency	Scored value
vocabulary	90	57.0
instruction	65	178.3
character	64	74.6
love	64	5.0
card	59	46.1
simplicity	58	47.8
Hiragana	49	147.3
learning	49	126.4
activity	48	47.8
pronunciation	47	233.1
communication	47	132.2
friend	47	10.7
demand	44	103.8
item	40	17.8
scene	39	64.2
sign	39	52.2
action	38	29.3
picture	33	7.1
ambiguity	31	207.9
word	31	47.5
interest	31	12.8
voice	31	4.3
speech	30	66.1
feeling	30	4.0
[verb]		
be able to	289	95.1
tell	70	75.7
read	56	14.3
clean, put back	46	3.3
use	35	2.8
hold	31	2.8
listen to	29	2.0
take out	27	3.0
speak	26	4.7

continued on following page

Table 9. Continued

Word	Frequency	Scored value
understand	25	2.3
[adjective]		
many	62	10.7
difficult	61	26.2
few	23	5.8
high	15	1.3
strong	15	1.0
wanting	14	0.2
large	9	0.9
hard to tell	8	31.8
glad	6	0.1

The frequency of co-occurrence two words is shown in Table 10; "be able to" and "understanding" is 65, "be able to" and "vocabulary" 50, "be able to" and "simplicity" 47, "be able to" and "instruction" 47, "be able to" and "teacher" 46, "instruction" and "understanding" 42, "be able to" and "speaking" 41, "be able to" and "tell" 35, etc. Figure 6 shows the co-occurrence network, which shows the target students' daily behavior and activities they had in the classroom.

Table 10. The frequency of co-occurrence words in the "daily behavior of the target students" section

Word-1	Word-2	Co-occurrence frequency
be able to	understanding	65
be able to	vocabulary	50
be able to	simplicity	47
be able to	instruction	47
be able to	teacher	46
instruction	understanding	42
be able to	speaking	41
be able to	tell	35
be able to	Hiragana	32
be able to	character	32
be able to	card	32
card	picture	32

continued on following page

Table 10. Continued

Word-1	Word-2	Co-occurrence frequency
speaking	vocabulary	26
Be able to	item	25
be able to	read	25
instruction	teach	25
be able to	activity	25

Figure 6. Co-occurrence network in the "daily behavior of the target students" section; upper is an original figure and lower with English words translated by the author (See also Table 9)

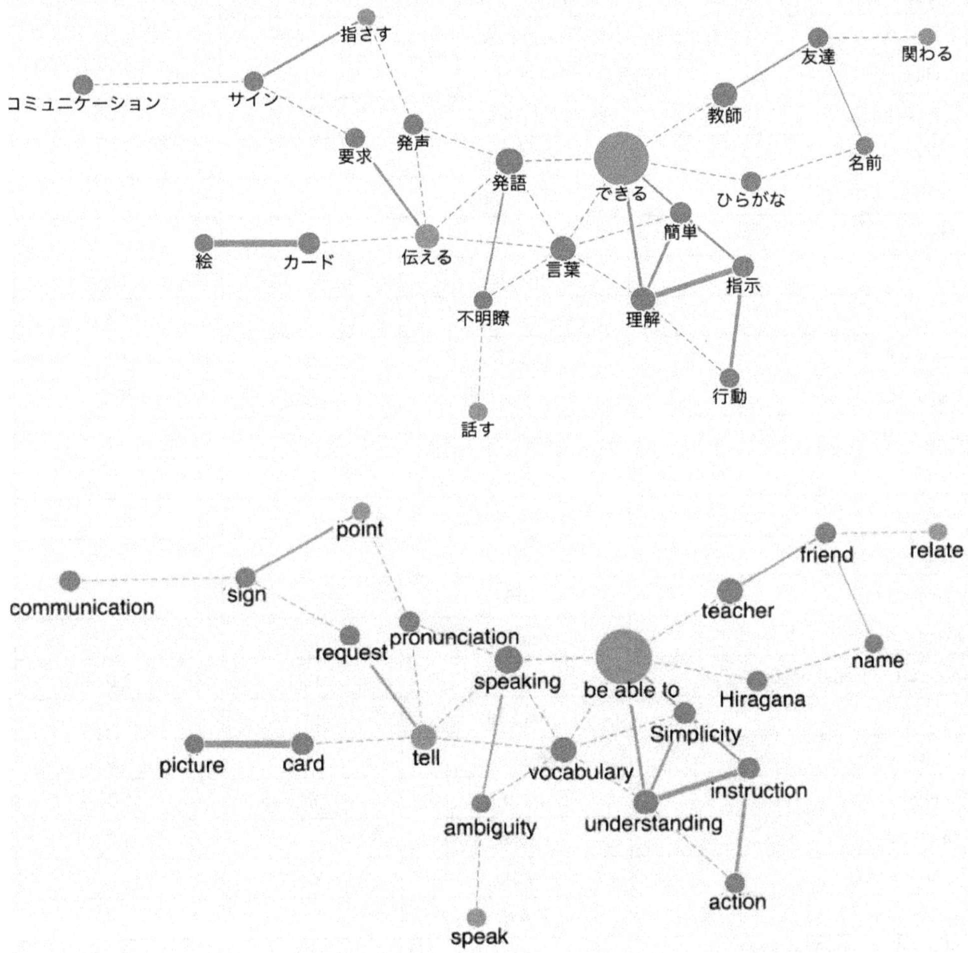

Table 11 shows the dependency analysis results which display the relationships in which nouns are modified by other nouns, verbs and adjectives in the "daily behavior of the target students" section. The two nouns "instruction" and "understanding" had the highest frequency at 22, the noun and verb "instruction" and "be able to" had the highest frequency at 14, and the noun and adjective "condition" and "easy to get sick," "love" and "glad," "relationship" and "glad," "understanding" and "difficult," had the same values being highest frequency at 4.

Table 11. Dependency analysis of a noun modified by other noun, verb, and adjective in the "daily behavior of the target students" section

Word-1	Word-2	Frequency	Scored value
[noun and noun]			
instruction	understanding	22	5.4
simplicity	instruction	14	3.2
teacher	instruction	9	1.4
understanding	action	8	1.9
pronunciation	ambiguity	7	1.8
vocabulary	instruction	7	0.9
simplicity	vocabulary	7	0.6
friend	teacher	7	0.6
support	necessity	6	3.5
understanding	possibility	6	2.2
instruction	possibility	6	2.2
instruction	action	6	1.1
gesture	sign	6	1.1
content	understanding	6	0.5
[noun and verb]			
instruction	be able to	14	0.7
voice	pronounce	13	6.5
request (wills and hopes)	tell	13	2.6
behavior	look at	11	2.2
understanding	be able to	10	0.4
pronunciation	tell	9	1.3
Hiragana	read	7	1.0
communication	build	6	3.8
vocabulary	tell	6	0.6

continued on following page

Table 11. Continued

Word-1	Word-2	Frequency	Scored value
ambiguity	be able to	6	0.1
[noun and adjective]			
condition	easy to get sick	4	4.0
love	glad	4	2.9
relationship	glad	4	2.9
understanding	difficult	4	0.3
love	wanting	3	1.5
upper limb	difficult	3	0.2
scene	many	3	0.2
play	many	3	0.2

The data in Figures 4, 5, and 6 and Tables 9, 10, and 11 clearly show that the schoolteachers tried to create original teaching materials suitable for each student, including those who could not speak, and help him/her to be able to participate in various school activities that they had been unable to carry out before.

Handmade Teaching Materials Created by Teachers

Figure 7 shows the word cloud based on the scored values, obtained from the "handmade teaching materials created by teachers" section. The highest scored word is "morning meeting (の)" indicating that many schoolteachers created the original handmade content available for "morning meeting" in classroom.

The appearance frequency of nouns is listed in Table 12; the most frequently used words were "presiding ( )" and "proceeding ( )" with 123 times, followed by "morning meeting (の)" 83 times, "teaching material ( )" 63 times, "after-classes homeroom (の)" 42 times, etc.

The co-occurrence frequency in the "handmade teaching materials created by teachers" section is listed in Table 13. The co-occurrence frequency of two noun keywords "presiding" and "proceeding" is 122 times, "morning meeting" and "presiding" 77 times, "morning meeting" and "proceeding" 77 times, "after-classes homeroom" and "proceeding" 40 times, "after-classes homeroom" and "presiding" 39 times, etc. In the co-occurrence frequency of noun and verb keywords, "English" and "learn" is 10 times, "Tama Animal Zoo" and "learn" 9 times, "teaching material" and "learn" 6 times, "presentation" and "do best" 5 times, "movie" and "learn" 5 times, "elementary school" and "learn" 5 times, etc.

Every class at the schools for special needs education in Japan holds a morning meeting and an after-class homeroom (afternoon meeting/farewell meeting) each day. In the "handmade teaching materials created by teachers" section, the scored word cloud for "morning meeting" was the largest, and the co-occurrence frequency of two words "presiding" and "proceeding" was the highest, which clearly shows that most teachers first tried to create a content like an interactive board with Post-it-like sticker icons linked to audio, so that even students who could not speak became able to be included in the meeting by using a speaking pen. Such an interactive board for the morning meeting, for example, included several steps which needed to be completed, such as today's date, today's weather, today's schedule, calling each student by name to check their health, and today's lunch menu, and so on. The data analyzed in this section revealed that many teachers also created content attached with Post-it-like sticker icons. These icons allowed students to select and share their current feelings and wishes with others, as well as learn Japanese Hiragana characters and words, including their sound-symbol correspondence, sounding out words, and spelling words.

Figure 7. Scored word cloud in the "handmade teaching materials created by teachers" section (see also Table 12)

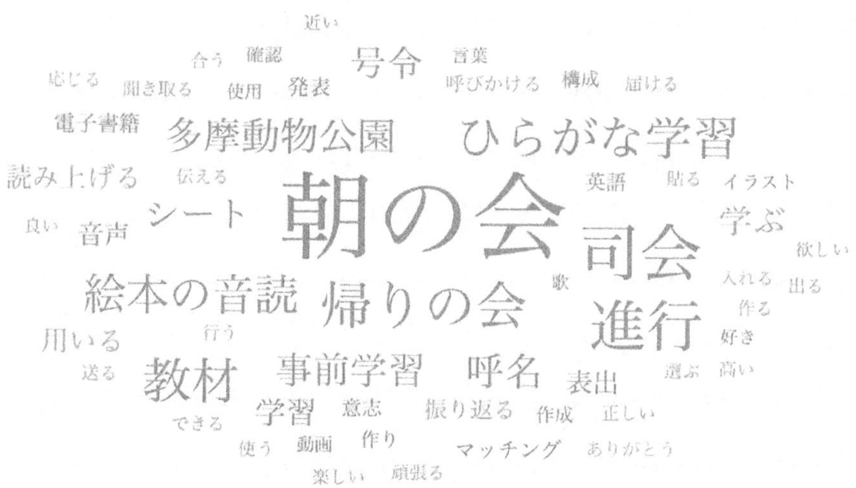

Table 12. Appearance frequency of the nouns in the "handmade teaching materials created by teachers" section

Word	Frequency
presiding	123
proceeding	123
の morning meeting	83
teaching material	63
の after-classes homeroom, afternoon meeting	42
sheet	38
presentation	24
Learning Hiragana	21
learning	21
voice/sound	18
English	18
movie	18
の reading picture books	17
calling his/her name	14
Tama Animal Zoo	14
illustration	14
order	12
matching	11
song	11

Table 13. Co-occurrence frequencies of "noun and noun" and "noun and verb" in the "handmade teaching materials created by teachers" section

Word-1	Word-2	Co-occurrence frequency
[noun and noun]		
presiding	proceeding	122
morning meeting	presiding	77
morning meeting	proceeding	77
after-classes homeroom	proceeding	40
after-classes homeroom	presiding	39
illustration	matching	10
teaching material	English	7

continued on following page

Table 13. Continued

Word-1	Word-2	Co-occurrence frequency
[noun and verb]		
English	learn	10
Tama Animal Zoo	learn	9
teaching material	learn	6
presentation	do best	5
movie	learn	5
elementary school	learn	5
teaching material	be able to	4

"Practice and its Content" and "Results and Challenges Obtained"

Table 14 shows the appearance frequency of words and their scored values on nouns, verbs, and adjectives for the 103,027 words text combined in "practice and its content" and "results and challenges obtained" sections.

The most frequently appeared *noun* was "speaking pen ( )" with 720 times and scored value was 12337.7. The second most frequently appearance noun was "card ( )" with 311 and scored value 702.8. The third most frequently appeared noun was "voice/sound ( )" with 306 and scored value 1431.1, etc. The most frequently appeared *verb* was "be able to ( )" with 724 times and scored value was 517.9. The second most frequently appeared verb was "perform ( )" with 163 and scored value 89.5. The third most frequently appeared verb was "use ( )" with 151 and scored value of 47.9, etc. The most frequently appeared *adjective* was "difficult ( )" with 78 and scored value was 41.3. The second most frequently appeared adjective was "many ( )" with 62 and scored value 10.7. The third most frequently appeared adjective was "good ( )" with 43 and scored value 0.7, etc.

Table 14. Appearance frequencies and their scored values of noun, verb and adjective words in the "practice and its content" and "results and challenges obtained" sections

word	frequency	Scored value
[noun]		
speaking pen	720	12337.7
card	311	702.8
voices/sounds	306	1431.1
use	261	800.9
learning	207	923.5
seal	199	797.2
teacher	186	877.4
touching	167	718.8
activity	157	327.6
scene	147	466.7
vocabulary	145	132.9
friend	138	81.3
processing	130	474.2
confirmation	128	142.0
presentation	124	199.5
[verb]		
be able to	724	517.9
perform	163	89.5
use	151	47.9
listen to	135	40.8
consider	123	39.1
go	117	24.9
work on	102	459.2
hold	95	24.3
understand	90	28.1
clean, put back	86	11.3
[adjective]		
difficult	78	41.3
many	62	10.7
good	43	0.7
happy, glad	27	1.9

continued on following page

Table 14. Continued

word	frequency	Scored value
pleasant	24	1.3
correct, proper	22	17.3
few	18	3.6
easy to understand	16	19.9

As shown in Table 15, the co-occurrence frequency of the two words "be able to" and "speaking pen" is 300 times, "use" and "speaking pen" 179, "be able to" and "voice/sound" 129, "voice/sound" and "replaying" 125, "voice/sound" and "speaking pen" 117, "seal" and "speaking pen" 114, and so on.

Table 16 displays the results of the dependency analysis of two keyword pairs, along with their scored values. The frequency and scored value of two *noun* keyword pair "speaking pen" and "use" are 98 and 37.0, respectively: followed by the pair "seal" and "touching" 59 and 21.1, the pair "speaking pen" and "touching" 39 and 9.3, the pair "voice/sound" and "replaying" 37 and 12.1, the pair "speaking" and "making use of" 35 and 12.2, etc. The frequency and scored value of *noun* and *verb* keyword pair "a speaking pen" and "use" are 64 and 27.4, respectively, followed by the pair "appearance" and "look at" 63 and 17.6, the pair "voice/sound" and "re-play" 37 and 10.3, the pair "seal" and "paste" 34 and 14.2, the pair "voice/sound" and "replay" 33 and 17.6, and so on. The frequency and scored value of *noun* and *adjective* keyword pairs of "voice/sound" and "faint" and "voice/sound" and "loud" have the same values of 3 and 1.1, and the following four pairs, "scene" and "many," "handling" and "difficult," "understanding" and "difficult," "pronunciation" and "difficult" have the same values of 3 and 0.2.

The co-occurrence network, generated by AI text mining, analyzed in the sections composed of "practice and its content" and "results and challenges obtained" is shown in Figure 8. This figure and the analysis data listed in Tables 12-16 clearly reveal the love and dreams of the schoolteachers, who created handmade teaching materials such as cards and sheets with multimedia-enabled dot codes directly overlaid or with Post-it-like sticker icons. They also attempted to assist students with a variety of disabilities in participating in various activities in their classes and school with the aid of the speaking pen.

Table 15. Co-occurrence frequencies of two words in a sentence in the "practice and its content" and "results and challenges obtained" sections

Word-1	Word-2	Co-occurrence frequency
be able to	speaking pen	300
use	speaking pen	179
be able to	voice/sound	129
voice/sound	replaying	125
voice/sound	speaking pen	117
seal	speaking pen	114
card	speaking pen	107
be able to	be able to	107
be able to	use	100
be able to	seal	100
seal	Touch, touching	95
be able to	understanding	92
touch, touching	speaking pen	90
speaking pen	speaking pen	90
teacher	speaking pen	88
be able to	touch, touching	82
appearance	look at	78
voice/sound	listen to	77
handling	speaking pen	76
seal	voice/sound	75

Table 16. Dependency analysis in the "practice and its content" and "results and challenges obtained" sections

Word-1	Word-2	Frequency	Scored value
[noun and noun]			
speaking pen	use	98	37.0
seal	touching	59	21.1
speaking pen	touching	39	9.3
voice/sound	replaying	37	12.1
speaking pen	making use of	35	12.2
speaking pen	replaying	22	4.4

continued on following page

Table 16. Continued

Word-1	Word-2	Frequency	Scored value
morning meeting	processing	22	3.9
morning meeting	after-classes homeroom	21	8.4
speaking pen	handling	20	4.0
speaking pen	recording	19	4.6
speaking pen	how to use	18	8.6
card	touching	17	1.8
friend	name	15	2.8
teacher	together	14	7.2
teaching material	idea	14	6.0
[noun and verb]			
speaking pen	use	64	27.4
appearance	look at	63	17.6
voice/sound	listen to	37	10.3
seal	paste	34	14.2
voice/sound	replay	33	17.6
behavior	look at	30	4.1
he/she oneself	be able to	26	1.0
[noun and adjective]			
voice/sound	faint	3	1.1
voice/sound	loud	3	1.1
scene	many	3	0.2
handling	difficult	3	0.2
understanding	difficult	3	0.2
pronunciation	difficult	3	0.2

Figure 8. Co-occurrence network in the "practice and its content" and "results and challenges obtained" sections; upper is an original figure and lower with English words translated by the author (See also Table 14)

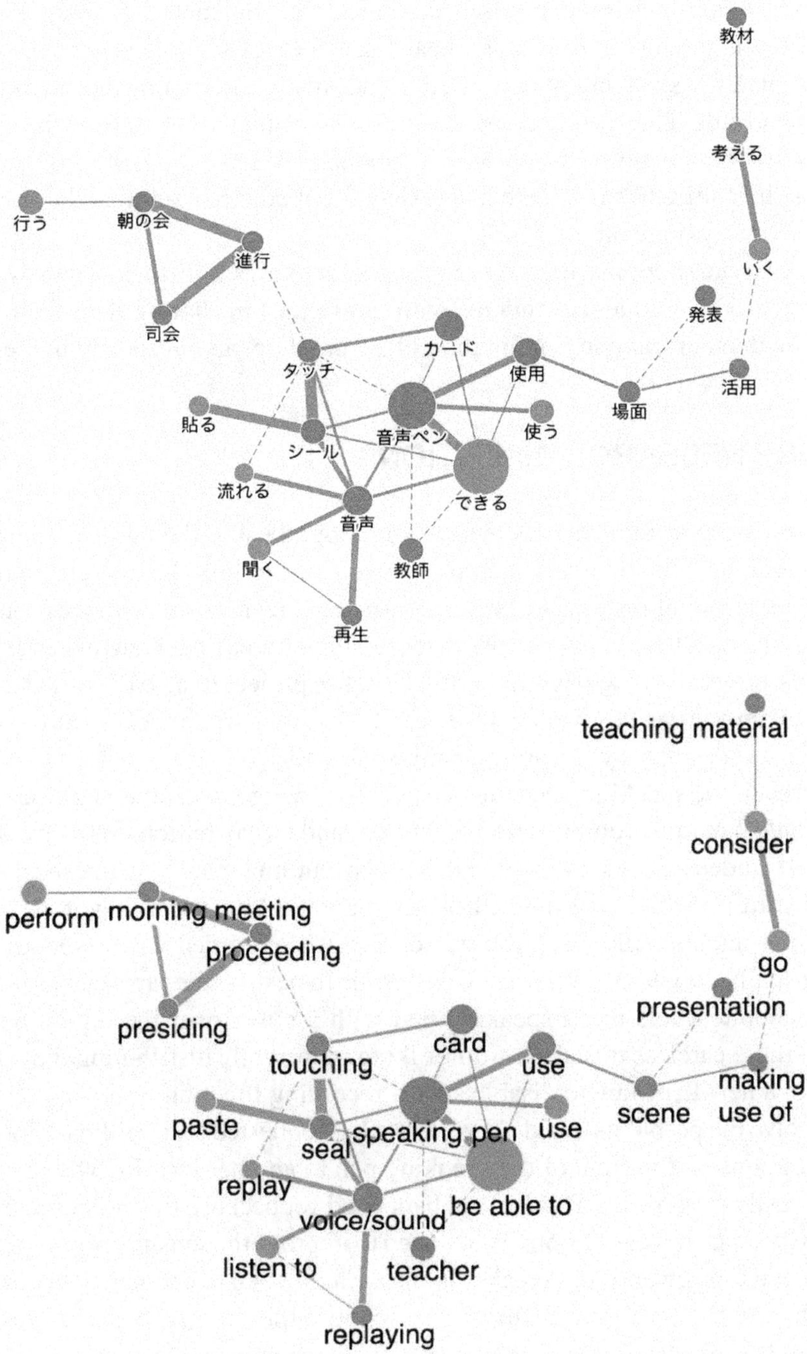

Original Handmade Teaching Materials and Handy Tools

The current AI text mining study, conducted on 243 case studies for students with disabilities, reveals that original handmade teaching materials using dot codes, created through the enthusiasm and heartfelt efforts of schoolteachers, along with handy tools like a speaking pen and the dot-code reader, are among the most effective content and aids. These aids enable students who cannot speak, those who can only speak a few words, those who speak with unclear pronunciation, or those who have reading difficulties to participate in a variety of school activities that they could not have previously done on their own.

There is much hope that the long-term school activities, with their original contents and handy tools, will assist students with disabilities in sharing their feelings and desires with others, and in finding their place in school and in society in the future.

FUTURE RESEARCH DIRECTIONS

Not only can schoolteachers record voice/sound using the built-in microphone in the speaking pen and touch the Post-it-like icons to link them to create original handmade teaching materials easily, but also can create more advanced ones with *Sound Linker* and/or *NANA* software; these software has been advanced from the assembly program at the beginning of the Ikuta's project to an easy-to-handle software that anyone can easily operate. The *NANA* software on macOS UNIX has also been created recently by the present author, Ikuta.

However, the speaking pen still faces the following issues: the placement of the power on/off button, volume up/down button, and replay button on the front of the device. If students accidentally hold this replay button for a while, the speaking pen starts recording audios with the built-in microphone. After recording, if the students would non-intentionally touch the sticker icon, the recorded voices/sounds (being noise, usually) would be overwritten and come to destroy the previous useful ones. Many schoolteachers use a speaking pen with a cover over the replay button to prevent these careless mistakes. Author Ikuta is currently distributing the speaking pen with a new firmware to disable such a recording function.

To solve the problems noted above, Ikuta has requested that Gridmark Inc. move all the buttons on the front of the speaking pen to another location where students cannot easily press them. This has not happened yet because the motherboard itself needs to be improved. Additionally, we need to improve the sensitivity of the infrared camera and the power of the speaker in the speaking pen to encourage better usage. To enable students with severe disabilities to touch the sticker icons more easily and confidently when using the speaking pen, we need enhanced and more accessible accessories, some of which schoolteachers have already developed and implemented in their activities (Ikuta et al., 2021b; Ikuta & Hisatsune, 2019b).

Students with disabilities can enhance their learning in their classes by using the dot-code reader, G-Pen Blue with Bluetooth functionality, to replay video clips on the iPad, iPhone, and MacBook. For example, using original handmade teaching materials, such as providing an example of mats and basketball model performance to students, has effectively promoted their practices in high school physical education classes. Another schoolteacher created content with Post-it-like sticker icons, linking video clips that expressed each phrase of the grade's song in sign language, by using the newly developed software *BlueLinker*. By touching the icon with the G-Pen Blue, the students could play the linked video on their iPad and iPhone screen; this content helped them learn sign language effectively.

To play the appropriate video clip, touching the Post-it-like sticker icon with a dot-code reader G-Pen Blue, may be better than operating the iPad screen with a finger or digital pen, especially as the students with disabilities often do not understand what they are doing with the iPad. Since there is one-to-one correspondence between the Post-it-like sticker icon and the linked multimedia, such as a video clip, touching the icon with G-Pen Blue to replay a video clip will not confuse students with disabilities. Gridmark Inc. recently uploaded *BlueLinker*, an easy-to-use content creation software, to the Apple App Store and anticipates further improvements in the future.

And finally, one aspect of the research might be most important of all; the case study reports of studies conducted by a large variety of schoolteachers needed to be gathered in a unified format; otherwise, AI text mining analysis would have been able to produce any useful, valuable information.

CONCLUSION

The author used the AI text mining method to analyze 243 case study activities conducted by teachers at schools for special needs education and special needs classes at public schools for students with disabilities. This analysis clarified the essence of these activities and the role of assistive technology tools such as a speaking pen and dot-code reader used in the studies.

The AI-generated Word Clouds allowed users to visualize unstructured text, clarified insights into the focus of the text material, and identified patterns and trends. In the "daily behavior of the target students" section, for example, the most frequently word was "be able to", while the highest scored word was "speaking"; these results clearly show that the teacher always cared about students who could not speak and wanted those students to "be able to" participate in various class activities that they were not able to do before by themselves.

Co-occurrence of words clearly defined the relationship between two words in a sentence. The co-occurrence network diagram also clearly showed the conjunctions that appeared in the text with similar occurrence patterns. The co-occurrence network obtained in the "daily behavior of the target students" section shown in Figure 6, for example, well represented the problems the target students had and the daily school activities that schoolteachers performed in their classes to solve or reduce their difficulties. The co-occurrence network, obtained in the "practice and its contents" and "results and challenges obtained" sections shown in Figure 8, also represented well the contents of the case study activities.

The co-occurrence frequency of "noun and noun" and "noun and verb" in the "handmade teaching materials created by teachers" section listed in Table 13 clearly indicated what the teachers hoped for and what they devised to solve or alleviate the difficulties faced by the target students. The co-occurrence frequency data, in the "practice and its content" and "results and challenges obtained" combined sections listed in Table 15, also clearly revealed that the schoolteachers were trying to help the students who had not been able to carry out on their own to do so without the help of teachers.

The use of AI text mining revealed that the schoolteachers' strongest concern was their worry about non-speaking students. Their top-priority was to help such students participate in their daily class activities, such as morning meetings and after-class homerooms, that previously they could not do without the help of teachers. To help students proceed with each step of morning meetings and after-class homerooms on their own, the schoolteachers created handmade cards and/or boards with dot codes directly overlaid or Post-it-like sticker icons. Some non-speaking students appeared to imitate speaking and listening by holding the speaking pen to their mouths and ears.

The present use of AI text mining also clearly showed that simple and convenient tools such as the speaking pen and dot-code reader were very effective in helping students who could only speak a few words to learn sound-symbol correspondence, sounding out words, and spelling words. The text mining technique includes advanced discipline information within data science. Text mining with artificial intelligence is now a useful tool to convert vast, unstructured texts into structured forms and generate new and invaluable insights.

This chapter paper focuses solely on case studies for students with disabilities, utilizing AI text mining. It fully revises the preliminary report in the online journal Int. J. Hum. Cult. Stud. (Ikuta, 2022) which included students from public schools, and publishes it as a scientific manuscript version.

ACKNOWLEDGMENT

The author, Shigeru Ikuta would like to express thanks for the support of "JSPS KAKENHI Grant Numbers: JP22530992 and JP16K04844" and the "Otsuma Grants-in-Aid for Individual Exploratory Research (Research Numbers: s2605, s2713, s2810, and s2912)." The author also thanks all the schoolteachers and students who joined the case study activities.

REFERENCES

American Speech-Language-Hearing Association. (n.d.). *Augmentative and Alternative Communication (AAC)*. https://www.asha.org/public/speech/disorders/AAc/

Ann, O. C., Theng, L. B., Seldon, H. L., & Putra, F. A. (2015). Critical Behavior Monitoring for Children with Special Needs in Preventing Physical Injury Using Kinect. In L. B. Theng (Ed.), Assistive Technologies for Physical and Cognitive Disabilities (pp. 211–249). IGI Global Scientific Publishing. DOI: 10.4018/978-1-4666-7373-1.ch011

Anson, D. K. (2018). *Assistive Technology for People with Disabilities*. Bloomsbury Publishing Inc. DOI: 10.5040/9798400615559

Assistive Technology Australia. (n.d.). *Browse Products: Communication - Voice Output Communication Aids VOCA (Recorded Speech)*. https://at-aust.org/items/2886

Assistive Technology Industry Association. (n.d.). *What is AT?*https://www.atia.org/home/at-resources/what-is-at/

Beukelman, D. R., & Light, J. C. (Eds.). (2020). *Augmentative & Alternative Communication: Supporting Children and Adults with Complex Communication Needs* (5th ed.). Paul H. Brookes Publishing Co., Inc.

Biemann, C., & Mehler, A. (Eds.). (2014). *Text Mining: From Ontology Learning to Automated Text Processing Applications*. Springer. DOI: 10.1007/978-3-319-12655-5

Bouck, E. C. (2016). Assistive Technology. SAGE Publications. DOI: 10.4135/9781071872765

Bugaj, C. (2023). *The New Assistive Tech: Make Learning Awesome for All!* International Society for Technology in Education.

Burns, M. (2021). EdTech Essentials: The top10 Technology Strategies for All Learning Environments. ASCD. *Top (Madrid)*, •••, 10.

Carpenter, L. A. B., Johnston, L. B., & Beard, L. A. (2015). *Assistive Technology: Access for All Students* (3rd ed.). Pearson.

China, C. R. (2023, August 28). *Leveraging user-generated social media content with text-mining examples.* https://www.ibm.com/think/topics/text-mining-use-cases

Communication Matters. (n.d.). *TYPES OF AAC.* https://www.communicationmatters.org.uk/what-is-aac/types-of-aac/

Concetta, A. D., & Wilkinson, K. (2014). Get Your Head into the Clouds: Using Word Clouds for Analyzing Qualitative Assessment Data. TECHTRENDS. *TechTrends, 58*(3), 38–44. DOI: 10.1007/s11528-014-0750-9

Dell, A. G., Newton, D. A., & Petroff, J. G. (2017). *Assistive Technology in the Classroom: Enhancing the School Experiences of Students with Disabilities* (3rd ed.). Pearson.

Genevieve, G. C. (2024, September 25). *AI and Text Mining for Searching and Screening the Literature.* https://libraryguides.mcgill.ca/text-mining

Green, J. L. (2018). *Assistive Technology in Special Education: Resources to Support Literacy, Communication, and Learning Differences* (3rd ed.). Routledge.

Gridmark Inc. (n.d.). *GridOnput.* https://gridmark.co.jp/en/

Gupta, K. (2023). An analysis of the co-occurrence of keywords on the topic sustainable development of libraries: A Scientometrics analysis. *Library Philosophy and Practice (e-journal).* 7868. https://digitalcommons.unl.edu/libphilprac/7868

Hoffman, M. (2023, January 12). *WebMD. What Are the Types of Autism Spectrum Disorders?* https://www.webmd.com/brain/autism/autism-spectrum-disorders#1

IBM. (2021, March 5). *Dependency analysis.* https://www.ibm.com/docs/en/wsr-and-r/8.5.6?topic=analysis-dependency

IBM. (n.d.). *What is text mining?* https://www.ibm.com/topics/text-mining

Ifukube, T. (2017). *Sound-Based Assistive Technology: Support to Hearing, Speaking and Seeing.* Springer International Publishing AG. DOI: 10.1007/978-3-319-47997-2

Ignatow, G., & Mihalcea, R. F. (Eds.). (2018). *An Introduction to Text Mining: Research Design, Data Collection, and Analysis.* SAGE Publications, Inc. DOI: 10.4135/9781506336985

Ikuta, S. (2018). Multimedia-Enabled Dot Codes as Communication Technologies. In M. Khosrow-Pour (Ed.), Encyclopedia of Information Science and Technology (4th ed., pp. 6464–6475). IGI Global Scientific Publishing. DOI: 10.4018/978-1-5225-2255-3.ch561

Ikuta, S. (Ed.). (2019a). *Handmade Teaching Materials for Students With Disabilities.* IGI Global. DOI: 10.4018/978-1-5225-6240-5

Ikuta, S. (Ed.). (2020). Handbook of Research on Software for Gifted and Talented School Activities in K-12 Classrooms. IGI Global. DOI: 10.4018/978-1-7998-1400-9

Ikuta, S. (2022). School activities using self-made teaching materials with voices and sounds: Extraction of outcomes and challenges through text mining. *Int. J. Hum. Cult. Stud.*, *32*, 399–411.

Ikuta, S., Endo, E., Nemoto, F., Kaiami, S., & Ezoe, T. (2013). School Activities Using Handmade Teaching Materials With Dot-Codes. In Barres, D. G., Carrion, Z. C., & Delgado, R. L.-C. (Eds.), *Technologies for Inclusive Education: Beyond Traditional Integration Approaches* (pp. 220–243). IGI Global Scientific Publishing. DOI: 10.4018/978-1-4666-2530-3.ch011

Ikuta, S., & Hisatsune, Y. (2019b). Handcrafted customized content and school activities with newly developed technologies. In Gronseth, S. L., & Dalton, E. M. (Eds.), *Universal access through inclusive instructional design: International perspectives on UDL* (pp. 164–172). Routledge. DOI: 10.4324/9780429435515-20

Ikuta, S., Ishitobi, R., Nemoto, F., Urushihata, C., Yamaguchi, K., & Nakui, H. (2017). Handmade content and school activities for autistic children with expressive language disabilities. In Kats, Y. (Ed.), *Supporting the Education of Children With Autism Spectrum Disorders* (pp. 85–115). IGI Global Scientific Publishing. DOI: 10.4018/978-1-5225-0816-8.ch006

Ikuta, S., Morton, D., Kasai, M., Nemoto, F., Ohtaka, M., & Horiuchi, M. (2015). School Activities With New Dot Code Handling Multimedia. In Lennex, L., & Nettleton, K. (Eds.), *Cases on Instructional Technology in Gifted and Talented Education* (pp. 314–340). IGI Global Scientific Publishing. DOI: 10.4018/978-1-4666-6489-0.ch015

Ikuta, S., Takagaki, Y., Sone, R., Okazaki, K., & Abe, S. (2021b). Collaborative Learning Community Facilitating Inclusive Learning Settings: Providing Reasonable Accommodations for Students with Disabilities. In AuCoin, D. (Ed.), *Building Integrated Collaborative Relationships for Inclusive Learning Settings* (pp. 181–214). IGI Global Scientific Publishing. DOI: 10.4018/978-1-7998-6816-3.ch008

Ikuta, S., Watanuki, M., & Abe, S. (2021a). Multimedia-Enabled Dot Codes as Communication Aids. In Khosrow-Pour, M. (Ed.), *Handbook of Research on Modern Educational Technologies, Applications, and Management* (pp. 331–345). IGI Global Scientific Publishing. DOI: 10.4018/978-1-7998-3476-2.ch020

Ishitobi, R., Taniuchi, M., Nemoto, F., Harada, K., Sugita, Y., Kanno, Y., Nakamura, Y., Tagami, K., Iijima, T., Tanaka, S., Takatsu, A., Yamashita, M., & Ikuta, S. (2019). Original teaching materials and school activities for students with an intellectual disability. In Ikuta, S. (Ed.), *Handmade Teaching Materials for Students With Disabilities* (pp. 111–131). IGI Global Scientific Publishing. DOI: 10.4018/978-1-5225-6240-5.ch005

Isogai, K. (2017). Recent Developments in Japan's Special Needs Education – Promoting an Inclusive Education System –. *NISE Bulletin, 16*, 28–32.

Kawano, K. (2016, November 1). *SAVVY Tokyo: Special Needs Education in Japan*. https://savvytokyo.com/special-needs-education-japan/

Krakower, B., & Plante, S. L. (2016). *Using Technology to Engage Students with Learning Disabilities*. Corwin. DOI: 10.4135/9781071800553

Kwartler, T. (2017). *Text Mining in Practice with R*. John Wiley & Sons. DOI: 10.1002/9781119282105

Lancioni, G. E., & Singh, N. N. (Eds.). (2014). *Assistive Technologies for People with Diverse Abilities*. Springer International Publishing AG. DOI: 10.1007/978-1-4899-8029-8

Leskovec, J., Rajaraman, A., & Ullman, J. D. (2020). *Mining of Massive Datasets* (3rd ed.). Cambridge University Press. DOI: 10.1017/9781108684163

Ministry of Education. (2015). Culture, Sports, Science and Technology. *Gide Book for Starting School: Procedures for Entering Japanese Schools*. https://www.mext.go.jp/component/a_menu/education/micro_detail/__icsFiles/afieldfile/2016/06/24/1358299_01.pdf

Mirenda, P. (2013). Augmentative and alternative communication. In Volkmar, F. R. (Ed.), *Encyclopedia of autism spectrum disorders* (pp. 328–333). Springer. DOI: 10.1007/978-1-4419-1698-3_486

Moats, L., & Tolman, C. (n.d.). *Types of Reading Disability*. https://www.readingrockets.org/article/types-reading-disability

Mueller, V. T. (2013). Voice Output Communication Aids. In F. R. Volkmar (Ed.), Encyclopedia of autism spectrum disorders. (pp. 3338–3341). Springer. DOI: 10.1007/978-1-4419-1698-3_1713

National Institute of Child Health and Human Development. (2020, March 5). *What are reading disorders?*https://www.nichd.nih.gov/health/topics/reading/conditioninfo/disorders

National Institute of Mental Health. (2025, January). *Autism Spectrum Disorder*. https://www.nimh.nih.gov/health/topics/autism-spectrum-disorders-asd/index.shtml

Ninja, N. (2023, June 30). *TF-IDF: Weighting Words in Text Analytics*. https://letsdatascience.com/tf-idf/

Ogletree, B. T. (Ed.). (2021). *Augmentative and Alternative Communication: Challenges and Solutions*. Plural Publishing.

Olympus Co. (1999). *ScanTalk, ScanTalk Reader, & Sound Print Kobo*. https://www.olympus.co.jp/jp/news/1999b/nr990823r300j.html

Polgar, J. M., Encarnação, P., Smith, E., & Cook, A. M. (2024). *Assistive Technology: Principals and Practice* (6th ed.). Elsevier.

QIAT Leadership Team. (2020). *The QIAT Companion: A Just-in-Time Resource for Implementing the Quality Indicators for Assistive Technology*. CAST, Inc.

Rajaraman, A., & Ullman, J. D. (2011). *Mining of Massive Datasets*. Cambridge University Press., DOI: 10.1017/CBO9781139058452

Salloum, S. A., Al-Emran, M., Monem, A. A., & Shaalan, K. (2018). Using Text Mining Techniques for Extracting Information from Research Articles. In Shaalan, K., Hassanien, A., & Tolba, F. (Eds.), *Intelligent Natural Language Processing: Trends and Applications. Studies in Computational Intelligence* (Vol. 740, pp. 373–397). Springer. DOI: 10.1007/978-3-319-67056-0_18

Segev, E. (Ed.). (2022). *Semantic Network Analysis in Social Sciences*. Routledge.

Sik-Lanyi, C., Hoogerwerf, E.-J., Miesenberger, K., & Cudd, P. (Eds.). (2015). *Assistive Technology: Building Bridges*. IOS Press.

Silton, N. R. (Ed.). (2015). *Recent Advances in Assistive Technologies to Support Children with Developmental Disorders*. IGI Global Scientific Publishing. DOI: 10.4018/978-1-4666-8395-2

The ALS Association. (n.d.), *Augmented and Alternative Communication*. https://www.als.org/navigating-als/living-with-als/therapies-care/augmentative-alternative-communication

User Local. (n.d.). *AI text mining (AI   )*. https://auth.userlocal.jp/login?return_url=https%3A%2F%2Ftextmining.userlocal.jp%2F&service=te

Viner, M., Singh, A., & Shaughnessy, M. F. (2020). Assistive technology to help students with disabilities. In Singh, A., Viner, M., & Yeh, C. J. (Eds.), *Special education design and development tools for school rehabilitation professionals* (pp. 240–267). IGI Global Scientific Publishing.

Wendt, O. (Ed.). (2011). *Assistive Technology: Principles and Applications for Communication Disorders and Special Education*. Brill.

Zhao, Y., Yin, J., Zhang, J., & Wu, L. (2023). Identifying the driving factors of word co-occurrence: A perspective of semantic relations. *Scientometrics*, *128*(12), 6471–6494. DOI: 10.1007/s11192-023-04851-x

KEY TERMS AND DEFINITIONS

AI Text Mining: AI text mining uses artificial intelligence (AI) and text data mining techniques to derive pertinent qualitative information from unstructured text data and convert it into a structured format to identify meaningful patterns and new insights. The context of each classified piece of data from 243 case studies conducted on students with disabilities was analyzed to reveal frequency and scored words, word clouds, co-occurrence of words and their dependencies, and co-occurrence networks.

Classroom for Special-Needs: This classroom in Japanese public schools is for students with relatively mild intellectual or physical/motor disabilities; autism/emotional disturbance; or health, visual, hearing, or speech/language impairment, and limited to eight students per class.

Co-Occurrence of Words: The co-occurrence of words is defined as a relationship between two words/phrases in a sentence: the larger in its appearance frequency, the stronger in their relationship.

Co-Occurrence Network: The co-occurrence network is a diagram in which lines are used to connect words that appear in a text with similar patterns of occurrence. Words that appear more frequently are drawn bigger, and the order of co-occurrence is drawn with thick solid lines > thin solid lines > dashed lines, defining their relation strength in the text.

Dependency Analysis: Dependency analysis extracts words from each phrase that has a "modifier-modified" relationship, and tallies pairs of the target noun and other noun, verb, and adjective that modify it. The "score" is a uniquely calculated number determined by a combination of factors such as the number of occurrences and the percentage of all combinations.

Dot-Code Reader: With this handy tool's Bluetooth functionality, touching multimedia-enabled dot codes overlaid and/or the Post-it-like sticker icon replays video clips, photos, and web pages on iPad, iPhone, and MacBook devices.

Post-it-Like Sticker Icon: This sticker icon, overlaid with multimedia-enabled dot codes, can be removed from a sheet and pasted to any item. Each sticker icon can link up to 10 media, such as video clips, in addition to 10 voices/sounds.

School for Special Needs Education: In Japan, there still exist more than 1,100 separated schools for special needs education, in which schoolteachers try to create original handmade teaching materials for each student with disabilities since he/she has different hopes and wills and learning styles.

Speaking Pen: With this handy tool, such as G-Speak or G-Talk, touching multimedia-enabled dot codes overlaid and/or a Post-it-like sticker icon replays the linked voice/sounds.

Word Cloud: Word clouds are used to provide insights into the focus of textual materials and identify patterns and trends or lack thereof; the more frequently words or the higher-scored words appear within the text, the bigger and bolder they appear in the visualizations generated.

Chapter 10
Critical Thinking Skills and Artificial Intelligence (AI)

Mehdi Kaddouri
https://orcid.org/0000-0001-7696-0276
Mohamed First University, Morocco

Ilham Chniete
https://orcid.org/0000-0003-1126-3028
Mohammed First University, Morocco

Khalid Mhamdi
https://orcid.org/0009-0007-3994-7743
Mohammed First University, Morocco

Abderrahmane Bouamri
National School of Agriculture, Meknes, Morocco

Khaoula Atmani
https://orcid.org/0009-0006-4069-2269
Mohammed First University, Morocco

ABSTRACT

This chapter explores the complex relationship between artificial intelligence (AI) and critical thinking skills in education. It examines how AI is reshaping learning and decision-making, while emphasizing critical thinking skills as essential for navigating these changes. AI offers opportunities through personalized learning and immersive scenarios, but faces limitations like algorithmic opacity and data bias that require ethical integration into education. The chapter addresses key areas: critical

DOI: 10.4018/979-8-3373-4576-5.ch010

thinking's role in the AI era, AI-critical thinking interactions, challenges posed by AI, and strategies for developing critical thinking skills. It focuses on pedagogical approaches fostering critical reflection and intellectual autonomy. The text advocates for a systemic approach where AI complements human cognitive capacities rather than replacing them. Through synergy between critical thinking and AI, educators can prepare learners for 21st-century challenges with discernment and responsibility.

INTRODUCTION

The rapid transformation of the informational environment described as "a key term to express organizational changes influenced by digital technologies" (Dethine et al., 2020, p. 20), continues to experience exponential growth (Reis et al., 2023), impacting all sectors of life, including manufacturing, service industries, healthcare, and education (Lamatsch, 2023). This transformation is primarily driven by the rise of digital technologies and the massive increase in available data (Junge, 2019; Kraus et al., 2021). While these technologies offer organizations scalability, agility, and cost-efficiency, they simultaneously reshape how information is produced, shared, and consumed (Plekhanov et al., 2022). This digital transformation impacts educational assessment strategies, presenting both challenges and opportunities for evaluating learning outcomes (Kaddouri et al., 2025). Consequently, they drive changes in value creation and the development of new business models, necessitating the acquisition of new skills and competencies. Furthermore, although digital technologies present undeniable potential for fostering skills such as problem-solving, critical thinking, creativity, and lifelong learning (Verschaffel et al., 2019), their impact contingent on numerous contextual, pedagogical, and equity-related factors. A critical and thoughtful approach is necessary to maximize their potential while minimizing associated risks. Today, the Internet of Things (IoT), artificial intelligence (AI), and blockchain are driving large-scale transformation within organizations of all sizes. These technologies serve as engines of the digital revolution, with the potential to propel profound social and economic changes while fostering significant advancements in analytical and cognitive activities within organizations and across industries (Gkrimpizi et al., 2023).

The education sector has not been exempt from this transformation (Mukul et al., 2023). The emergence of big data and artificial intelligence (AI) is enabling more flexible learning systems that are revolutionizing management and pedagogical practices in higher education (Jain & Jain, 2019); Rabeya et al., 2022; Singh et al., 2022). This transformation underscores the critical importance of collaboration among various stakeholders to clearly define what AI's role in information systems, its capabilities within universities (Mikalef et al., 2021), and its positioning as a key driver of development (Sych et al., 2021).

New learning fields are emerging where AI and open educational resources (OER) are establishing themselves as digital learning solutions (UNESCO, 2021b). Similarly, new international and intercultural dimensions are being integrated into higher education, alongside the establishment of common evaluation criteria to facilitate the mutual recognition of degrees and qualifications between educational institutions in different countries (Sych et al., 2021).

Nevertheless, adapting to these new digital realities and addressing the internationalization of the educational environment, with its transformative yet risky potential (Gkrimpizi et al., 2023), requires the development of key interpersonal and technical skills (Farias-Gaytan et al., 2023), as well as a shift in mindsets (Bereiter, 2005).

While students, facing fewer restrictions, become more active and autonomous in their learning (Sych et al., 2021), they must also adapt to a forward-looking educational environment that emphasizes developing learning-to-learn and thinking-to-think skills (Halpern et al., 2021). Educators, in turn, must not only think critically themselves but also teach their learners to do the same (Voinea et al., 2014), while demonstrating proficiency in emerging technologies (Sych et al., 2021). This "thinking-to-think" inherently refers to critical thinking, a skill increasingly essential in addressing the influx of information and combating the rapid spread of misinformation, which propagates faster than accurate information (Vosoughi et al., 2018). The urgent need to improve the teaching of this skill in university curricula remains a pressing issue. A survey conducted by Hart Research Associates (2018) underscores a significant gap between employers' expectations and university graduates' preparedness in this area. The findings reveal that 78% of business leaders consider critical thinking the most decisive skill for their employees, essential for solving complex problems and making informed decisions. In contrast, only 34% of university graduates believe they acquired adequate critical thinking skills during their studies.

The World Economic Forum's 2020 report highlights the ongoing struggle in educational systems to integrate critical thinking into curricula, leaving many graduates ill-equipped to analyze information and solve complex problems. This gap hinders students' employability and their ability to think independently in a professional world that increasingly values these skills. Critical thinking is crucial not only for career success but also for informed citizenship in a rapidly changing world. Research from NACE (2017) shows that 99.2% of employers regard critical thinking as the most relevant skill for employability. Graduates with strong critical thinking skills are more likely to succeed academically and professionally. Therefore, it is essential for learners to develop these skills, and universities must implement strategies that encourage independent thinking, decision-making, and active citizenship (Belmekki et al., 2024; Dumitru et al., 2023; Sellars et al., 2018).

In an era characterized by an influx of information and the transformative rise of AI technologies impacting vital sectors, particularly education, critical thinking has emerged as an indispensable skill. This highlights the need for a collaborative and thoughtful approach to integrate AI, ensuring its benefits are maximized while addressing the challenges and opportunities of an increasingly automated society. This chapter aims to examine how AI can be leveraged to enhance critical thinking among learners. It delves into the educational context where, the rapid proliferation of information, the growing risks of manipulation and misinformation, and the lack of transparency in AI systems present significant challenges.

This chapter aims to deepen our understanding of the interactions between artificial intelligence (AI) and critical thinking by exploring the complex dynamics between these two fields. It is organized into several key sections:

- Analyzing the critical thinking skills required in the AI era: an indispensable asset
- Exploring the interactions between AI and critical thinking skills
- Examining the specific challenges posed by AI in the development of critical thinking
- Proposing strategies to develop and strengthen critical thinking in the age of AI
- Looking ahead: future perspectives on the evolution of the relationship between AI and critical thinking

CRITICAL THINKING SKILLS IN THE AI ERA

This section explores the central role of critical thinking in a world transformed by artificial intelligence. The aim is to demonstrate how this skill, already essential for addressing the complex challenges of the 21st century, is strengthened and adapted in response to the rapid changes induced by AI. The constituent skills of critical thinking are analyzed, along with its strong connections to digital citizenship and its role in developing citizens who are equipped to engage actively and knowledgeably in today's connected society.

Critical Thinking: An Essential Skill in Facing the Challenges of the 21st Century

Critical thinking has become indispensable in the 21st century due to the complex challenges faced by modern societies. In an increasingly interconnected world undergoing rapid changes, there is a need for citizens capable of making informed decisions, innovating, and solving problems effectively (Bell et al., 2009). According to Trilling and Fadel (2009), critical thinking ranks first among the skills of the 21st century, followed by communication and collaboration, as well as creativity and innovation. These skills are deemed essential to *"unlock a life of learning and creative work"* (p. 49). Lennon (2014) argues that *"in the 21st century, critical thinking skills are essential due to the accelerating changes in technology, as the Internet allows students to access huge amounts of information in just a few seconds and with only a few keystrokes"* (p. 1). Today, critical thinking is seen as an essential tool for integrating AI into the teaching profession and for countering the threats posed by AI in the age of machine learning. *"Critical thinking [...] is expected to serve as a tool for integrating artificial intelligence into the teaching profession"* (UNESCO, 2019). Developing critical thinking skills is crucial for students and researchers to use AI effectively and to distinguish accurate information from misinformation.

Defining critical thinking is challenging due to its multidimensional nature and varying interpretations across fields like psychology, education, philosophy, and social sciences. It evolves over time and context, often encompassing skills like analysis and decision-making. Critical thinking has progressed through three phases: the philosophical focus on logic and reasoning (1970-1982), the integration of emotional, creative, and cultural elements (1980-1993), and the development of an integrated theory that combines rational and emotional reflection (since the 1990s) (Paul, 2011).

Initially associated with reflection, critical thinking finds its roots in the works of John Dewey, particularly "How We Think" and "Democracy and Education," where he identifies it as *"the method of intelligent learning and is used to reward the mind"* (Dewey, 1933, p. 12). Bloom and Anderson propose a taxonomy of cognitive skills in which critical thinking is identified as a hierarchy of analysis, evaluation, and creation processes (Wilson, 2016). Dumitru and Halpern (2023) base their reflection on a rich corpus of definitions and define critical thinking as a deliberate and dynamic cognitive process, characterized by awareness and self-direction, built on disciplinary and procedural knowledge, as well as metacognitive aspects. It can be cultivated through the development of skills and is facilitated by attitudes such as open-mindedness and flexibility. It encompasses intellectual skills such as analysis, reflection, and inference.

Component Skills of Critical Thinking

A clear definition of critical thinking skills, like any other skill to be taught, helps in better understanding what they entail and guides the development of educational programs, assessment strategies, and teaching methods aimed to prepare students to analyze complex situations, evaluate information, and face the challenges within their community. Certain skills frequently appear as common among theorists, such as analysis, evaluation, and inference. These three skills are mentioned by Facione (1990), Elder (2022), Paul (2011), Brookfield (1987), and others, and reappear as a shared theoretical foundation in contemporary models of critical thinking. Authors like Wade (1995) emphasize pragmatic and behavioral aspects such as relevant questioning, examining evidence, and avoiding oversimplifications.

Ennis (2011) distinguishes himself by introducing skills related to clarification (both basic and advanced) and showing particular attention to the early stages of critical reasoning. Facione (1990, 2013) and Lipman (2003) share similar skills, including analysis, evaluation, inference, explanation, and self-regulation (self-examination and self-correction), where self-reflection is crucial. The recent Australian Curriculum, Assessment and Reporting Authority (ACARA) model (2020) appears more practical and focused on addressing the concrete challenges faced by modern educational contexts, standing out with skills centered on problem-solving and investigating ideas. Other recent works, such as those by Funmi and Qian (2020), bring back skills such as "reflection" and "critique" in their lists, with a stronger emphasis on the introspective and metacognitive aspects of critical reasoning.

Figure 1. Main critical thinking skills studied

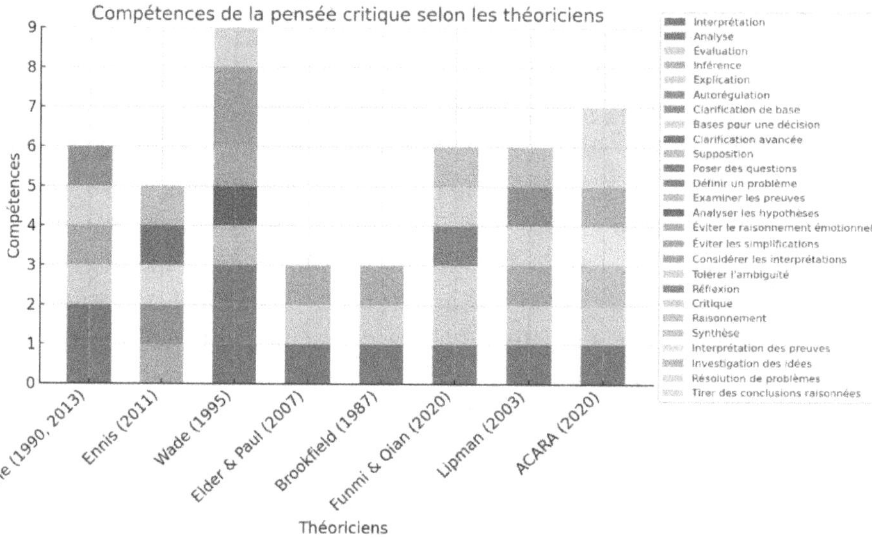

Figure1 reveals both the unity and multidimensionality of the concept of critical thinking. This multiplicity is relevant in an educational context increasingly influenced by AI. Like critical thinking, AI is not confined to a single domain of expertise and requires an interdisciplinary approach, where knowledge in data science, ethics, pedagogy, and psychology intersect. Critical thinking remains essential in interpreting and evaluating the relevance of the vast amounts of data generated and the rapid solutions based on the algorithms provided.

Ryan and Deci's (2000) theory highlights autonomy as a key psychological need for intellectual growth and learning motivation, often applied to technology adoption. Developing autonomy requires time, effort, and teacher support (Orakcı et al., 2019). The close relationship between critical thinking and autonomy means fostering autonomy boosts creative thinking and cognitive flexibility (Wu et al., 2020). Encouraging critical reflection on personal needs and beliefs enhances cognitive engagement and autonomy, further promoting cognitive abilities in critical thinking (Orakci, 2021; Raya et al., 2015). Little (1991) defines autonomy as encompassing detachment, critical reflection, decision-making, and independent action.

Autonomy is a capacity – for detachment, critical reflection, decision-making, and independent action. It presupposes, but also entails, that the learner will develop a particular kind of psychological relation to the process and content of his learning. The capacity for autonomy will be displayed both in the way the learner learns and in the way they transfer what has been learned to wider contexts (Little, 1991).

Autonomy relies on critical thinking, as it enables learners to reflect on their actions, evaluate options, and make independent decisions. This reflective process supports autonomous actions by allowing learners to justify their choices through rational evaluation (Little, 1991).

Critical Thinking and Digital Citizenship for a Connected Society

Critical thinking and digital citizenship are interconnected concepts essential for shaping informed and engaged citizens in the digital age. Critical thinking, a key digital competency, influences digital citizenship by fostering curiosity and autonomous reflection (Dewey, 1916). It continues to evolve as a critical element in global education, requiring attention from policymakers and educators (Ab Kadir, 2018; Schleicher, 2018). This competency helps learners make informed decisions, impacting both their futures and societies (Facione, 1990). Combined with problem-solving and creativity, critical thinking is a valuable skill sought by employers in a competitive labor market (Robles, 2012). It enables individuals to evaluate perspectives, make informed decisions in online interactions, and engage as active digital citizens, promoting ethical behavior and social responsibility (Kaur, 2018). Critical thinking is also vital for reconciliation and global peace, helping individuals question dominant ideologies and fostering better understanding of conflicts. It is an essential part of digital citizenship (Milenkova et al., 2021).

Digital citizenship is defined as a set of skills and behaviors necessary for interacting responsibly and critically in digital environments. It encompasses four main dimensions: digital ethics, which involves adoption respectful online behaviors; media and information literacy, which enables effective access to and evaluation of digital information; participation and active engagement in online communities; and critical thinking (Choi et al., 2021).

The concept refers to awareness, the development of critical attitudes, thinking, and opinions, as well as the strict fulfillment of responsibilities arising from different social roles. Digital citizenship is relevant to online information, knowledge of digital technology, creation of content in the digital environment, ethical rule compliance for online behavior. (Milenkova et al., 2021)

Digital citizenship involves individual responsibility and critical reflection on ethical and social values. Digital competence of teachers is fundamental in this context, as it enables educators to foster critical thinking skills among students in increasingly digitalized learning environments (Benali et al., 2018). This critical reflection is strengthened by digital tools, which not only enhance critical thinking but also promote citizen participation. Technology facilitates volunteering, collective problem-solving, and political actions by making collaboration and coordination more accessible. Consequently, the positive impact of digital tools on critical thinking contributes to greater civic engagement.

In conclusion, it is important to emphasize that critical thinking, far from being a static skill, evolves through its interaction with artificial intelligence, creating opportunities for mutual enrichment between humans and technology. The next section will delve into an in-depth analysis of the interactions between critical thinking and AI, exploring the dynamics of mutual stimulation and adaptation between these two fields.

INTERACTIONS BETWEEN AI AND CRITICAL THINKING

This section focuses on the interactions between artificial intelligence (AI) and critical thinking, which are crucial for optimizing educational and decision-making processes. Critical thinking is presented as an essential skill for evaluating and using AI effectively, particularly when addressing challenges such as biases and limitations in intelligent systems. Finally, the section explores the potential synergy between AI and critical thinking to enhance decision-making.

AI as a Catalyst for Reflective Processes

AI simulates human cognitive processes like analysis and problem-solving, offering unique opportunities to enhance learning by engaging critical thinking skills such as evaluation and argumentation. It fosters deep reflection and well-informed judgments. Marienko et al. (2022) show that AI promotes critical thinking by integrating realistic scenarios, and Danry's (2023) Wearable Reasoner tool corrects reasoning errors, improving decision-making. AI also supports educators by enhancing teaching practices. The intersection of emotional, relational, and digital dimensions necessitates a redesign of educational paradigms to effectively leverage AI as a catalyst for critical thinking (Kaddouri et al., 2024).

However, AI poses challenges, such as overreliance and reduced learner autonomy. Moustaghfir et al. (2024) note that AI can erode independence in analysis, compounded by filter bubbles (Pariser, 2011) and biased information (Aïmeur et al., 2023). For AI to develop critical thinking effectively, it must be integrated ethically, with teacher training to address biases, ethics, and AI's societal impact in digital literacy courses (Danday, 2021; Ng et al., 2021).

Mobilizing Critical Thinking to Evaluate and Use AI

AI excels in data processing and logical reasoning but struggles to assess complex contexts or consider ethical values, areas where human intelligence is crucial (Spector et al., 2019). Understanding AI's limitations and biases helps users identify flaws in reasoning or errors. Rusandi et al. (2023) highlight the role of critical thinking in distinguishing accurate from false information and using AI wisely in education. A notable example is Stanford's CRAFT project, which aims to equip students with critical thinking skills to evaluate AI, using resources co-designed with educators (Kaddouri et al., 2024).

The integration of critical thinking within the teaching profession is equally crucial. It allows educators to prepare students to be informed users of AI technologies while fostering a critical awareness of their potential effects (UNESCO, 2019). Teachers must demonstrate critical thinking to responsibly and securely incorporate AI tools into their educational practices, adhering to national and local policies while prioritizing safety, privacy, and stakeholder rights. They are also expected to critically assess the impact of AI on education, reflect on its societal implications, and engage in transformative actions to address the challenges associated with its use (Benali et al., 2023).

AI excels in data processing but struggles with complex contexts and ethical values, areas where human intelligence is essential (Spector et al., 2019). Understanding its biases helps users identify errors, which is why critical thinking is crucial for navigating AI, especially in education. Initiatives like Stanford's CRAFT project, which equips students with skills to evaluate AI (Kaddouri et al., 2024), highlight the importance of integrating critical thinking into teaching. Teachers must use AI responsibly, assessing its educational impact while remaining vigilant about its ethical implications (Benali et al., 2023; UNESCO, 2019). Ultimately, we must ask: Are we ready to use AI ethically?

AI enhances critical thinking by generating results that require evaluation. For instance, systems like Danry's (2023) help users identify logical flaws, while language learning tools like Quizlet encourage critical evaluation (Danday, 2021). Teaching critical thinking further equips users to assess AI content, particularly by identifying biases and limitations. Walter (2024) connects prompt design with critical thinking, explaining that effective prompts guide AI responses, and critical thinking allows users to evaluate their relevance and accuracy. This synergy ensures users interpret AI results ethically and strategically.

Towards a Synergy Between AI and Critical Thinking for Optimized Decision-Making

The introduction of AI has transformed decision-making processes within organizations and enabled human-AI collaboration in various ways. It is essential to recognize today that human skills, based on intuitive decisions, and those of AI, which rely on rational decisions, are complementary (Dietzmann et al., 2020; Gardner, 1999). Decisions can be fully delegated to AI, adopting a sequential human-AI decision-making model, or integrate contributions from both parties in an aggregated decision. This cooperation allows managers to use AI functionalities to perceive, process, and act autonomously, depending on the task's specificity and required speed (Parry et al., 2016). By emphasizing this complementarity, organizations can leverage human intuitive strengths while exploiting the analytical capabilities of AI for more informed decisions.

AI has become a priority in optimizing decision-making processes within organizations. It not only aids in data analysis but also accelerates and refines decisions. However, this should not undermine human skills. While AI performs tasks efficiently, it cannot replicate human adaptability, subjectivity, and continuous learning (Nassar, 2019; Scherer, 2015). The recognition of AI in academic contexts, such as ChatGPT in the Scopus Author Identifier, signals a shift in higher education, requiring a rethinking of educational practices (Popenici et al., 2017). This progress must be paired with ethical considerations to respect intellectual property and academic integrity, ensuring responsible AI use without threatening employment and human dynamics (Dwivedi et al., 2019; Pan, 2016; United Nations, 2019).

While AI holds considerable potential to enhance learning and optimize decision-making, it requires a measured and ethical approach. Encouraging collaboration between humans and machines can strengthen critical thinking, as long as intellectual autonomy is preserved and that the technology is integrated responsibly, with careful considering of its limitations and impacts on educational and social processes.

STUDY OF THE SPECIFIC CHALLENGES POSED BY AI

Section 4 examines the main challenges posed by AI across various fields. It addresses issues such as information overload in the digital age, the opacity and complexity of AI systems, and the ethical and social risks inherent in their use. The section also highlights the challenges faced by individuals, as informed citizens, in adapting to a complex environment influenced by AI technologies, while taking into consideration their impact on decisions, autonomy, and collective ethics.

Information Overload and Increasing Complexity

Concerns about information overload are not new. As early as the 16th century, the exponential increase in publications sparked criticism about the excessive proliferation of information. This phenomenon, seen as a potential source of confusion and intellectual distraction, marked the beginning of discussions around information management. By 1984, information overload had taken on a more formal dimension, recognized as an academic issue. This awareness grew between the 1950s and 1980s with the rise of scientific publications, generating an unprecedented influx of information (Bawden, 2016). This period thus laid the foundations for a growing inquiry into how to effectively manage an ever-increasing mass of data.

Information overload is influenced not only by environmental factors but also by individual characteristics. For example, certain personality traits, such as self-efficacy, affect one's ability to cope with an excess of data, either facilitating or exacerbating the feeling of overload (Johnson, 2014). Additionally, while it has often been assumed that age plays a decisive role in the perception of this overload, it appears that all generations are, in fact, affected by this phenomenon. Research shows that both young people and the elderly are exposed to similar levels of overload, although the impacts may vary across age groups. Thus, personal characteristics play a key role in how each individual processes and filters information.

The effects of information overload are evident at both individual and organizational levels. Information obesity, or the excessive accumulation of information, can lead to a form of anxiety that paralyzes decision-making, leaving the individual overwhelmed by an abundance of choices. In professional contexts, this overload has clear repercussions: it increases employee stress levels and can lead to a decline in performance, as processing too much information reduces focus and efficiency. From a mental health perspective, overload can lead to information fatigue syndrome, a state of exhaustion caused by excessive data, which affects not only psychological well-being but also the overall health of the individual. Therefore, information overload is a major challenge whose effects reverberate across various aspects of daily and professional life.

In the digital age, the overwhelming flow of information challenges cognitive processing, with short-term memory holding only about seven items at once and the brain's processing capacity limited to 126 bits per second (Csikszentmihalyi, 1990). Information overload, when information exceeds manageable levels, can reduce decision accuracy (Schroder, 1967) and become a barrier to efficiency (Edmunds et al., 2000). ICT tools help organize and prioritize data, but digital distractions like notifications and diverse formats increase anxiety and FOMO (Bawden, 2016; Tredinnick, 2018).

To manage this complexity, structured methods are essential. Cognitive overload, caused by too many choices and fragmented information, impairs decision-making. Ong et al. (2020) outline a six-step process for information synthesis, including filtering and interpretation. Effective filtering prevents "data smog" (Shenk, 1997) and maintains clarity (Bawden & Robinson, 2009), aiding decision-making and reducing the psychological impact of overload, as described in Simon's (1972) "bounded rationality".

Opacity of AI Systems and Difficulties of Interpretation

Danry (2023) emphasizes the need to develop more transparent systems and to promote users' critical reflection on AI's explanations and recommendations, through which they might be misled. Similarly, Carabantes (2023) explores the reasons why AI remains opaque at several levels and identifies three main layers of opacity: a technical layer related to complex computational methods that make AI systems difficult to understand, even for their designers; an institutional layer that maintains the opacity of algorithms for commercial reasons or to protect corporate and government data; and a cognitive opacity layer where the complexity of AI often exceeds the understanding capabilities of most individuals. However, some AI systems should simply not be used to make decisions with significant legal consequences due to their opacity, which could raise regulatory challenges: encouraging incorrect decisions, enabling prohibited decisions (such as those based on gender or race), and rendering decisions illegitimate due to the lack of transparency (Chesterman, 2021).

Ethical and Social Risks Related to the Use of AI

Users, faced with opaque AI, lack the necessary information to understand the decision-making process. This lack of explanation or access to the underlying mechanisms can lead to moral detachment. Users end up passively accepting AI decisions without questioning them, thereby reducing their ability to detect or respond to injustices or ethically problematic consequences (Khalili, 2023).

While transparency is often envisioned as a solution, it is not sufficient in some cases where opacity results from the intrinsic complexity of systems or their deliberately opaque design (Chesterman, 2021). Khalili (2023) argues that opaque AI technologies cater to the needs of users who do not seek to understand the decisions that influence their lives. Paradoxically, although AI research aims to mimic human intelligence, the adoption of human-mechanized behaviors could lead to the loss of its intrinsic qualities and dehumanize its interactions (Maroşan, 2019).

Thus, understanding the complex challenges posed by AI calls for rethinking educational strategies to strengthen critical thinking and enable ethical and informed interaction with information technologies. It becomes crucial to develop pedagogical approaches that equip individuals to manage information overload, decipher the opaque mechanisms of AI, and anticipate ethical and social risks, while preparing them to actively participate in shaping a responsible and inclusive digital future.

PROPOSALS DEVELOP CRITICAL THINKING IN THE AI AREA

Pedagogical strategies and technological tools play a crucial role in development critical thinking and artificial intelligence literacy. Educational approaches, adapted to the current challenges posed by AI, highlight the importance of teaching critical thinking while incorporating various pedagogical models. The integration of AI into learning environments acts as a catalyst for strengthening AI literacy.

Educational Approaches for Critical Thinking Adapted to the AI Challenge

Critical thinking in education, rooted in Dewey's pragmatism, aims to foster curiosity and intellectual independence, making students active participants in their learning and helping them solve real-world problems beyond mere knowledge transmission. Dewey acknowledges the difficulty of precisely defining "thinking" due to its varied usage, but explains it as going beyond the immediate, based on a foundation that allows one to accept or reject something as probable. He emphasizes that developing thinking skills is crucial in education because thinking is the method of intelligent learning (Dewey, 1916). For Dewey, thinking arises from situations where it influences outcomes, with the goal of reaching a conclusion based on existing information.

Current global education places a particular emphasis on developing critical thinking in students. This type of skill is considered essential to prepare them for the challenges of the 21st century, where the ability to analyze, evaluate, and synthesize information is crucial in the face of complex and changing environments (Sellars et al., 2018). Memorization, once valued, is now considered insufficient to meet current educational needs. Indeed, the focus should shift from simple memorization to the development of critical thinking skills, which are essential for independently analyzing, interpreting, and evaluating information.

Memorization and passive learning are no longer cited among the learning objectives of higher education as there is an increasing awareness that education should set critical thinking at its top priority.

Dumitru et al. (2023) suggest that to effectively develop critical thinking, regular and targeted instruction, such as a semester-long university course, is necessary. This type of in-depth training enables learners to apply critical thinking skills to real-world situations. However, the authors stress that continuous engagement is crucial for achieving these outcomes; isolated interventions alone are insufficient.

Several studies, including Sari and Prasetyo (2021), have examined strategies to promote critical thinking (CT). However, the lack of experiments in these studies limits conclusions on the effectiveness of these approaches. This raises the question of how CT teaching methods can be applied to maximize their impact. Pedagogical approaches for developing CT vary by discipline and objectives. The general approach teaches CT skills independently of a specific discipline, allowing students to apply transferable skills in different contexts. The infusion approach integrates CT within a specific discipline, focusing on its particular logic and methods for deeper understanding. The immersion approach embeds CT implicitly within the content without explicit mention. The mixed approach combines general CT skills with specific subject knowledge (Nejmaoui, 2019; Tiruneh et al., 2014). Teachers play a key role in teaching CT, with their training and practices influencing the success of these approaches. Teachers must be critical thinkers themselves to effectively teach CT, helping students engage in reflective and autonomous learning (Li, 2016; Christie et al., 2015). Azzimani and Kaddouri (2020) contribute to this discourse by examining the interconnections between technology, learning, and creativity through a semiotic lens, providing methodological insights into how technological tools can be thoughtfully integrated to support critical thinking development while maintaining pedagogical integrity.

Moreover, Pangh (2018) introduced the idea of teaching scaffolding to foster students' critical thinking in a digital context focused on AI. He cites several forms of scaffolding that teachers, educators, supervisors, and mentors can apply (Pangh, 2018):

- **Rapid Scaffolding:** The teacher provides useful context or cues and also asks specific questions to guide students toward a better understanding and handling of a topic.
- **Explicit Reflection:** In this case, the teacher helps students reflect on certain scenarios and potential pitfalls.

Bushuyev et al. (2024) introduced new concepts of critical thinking related to AI: "clip thinking" and "systems thinking." Clip thinking emphasizes detailed analysis of isolated problems, while systems thinking focuses on solving complex problems by considering interdependencies and the overall dynamics. Although more difficult to implement, systems thinking is crucial for addressing long-term complex challenges related to AI.

AI for the Development of Critical Thinking and Digital Literacy

Some researchers suggest limiting digital tools to foster critical thinking (Machete & Turpin, 2020), but adapting to AI is crucial for innovation. AI tools expose students to various perspectives, encouraging analytical thinking. They enhance debates, cooperative tasks, and self-assessments, helping students refine their reasoning and develop critical skills. Project-based learning with AI enables students to interpret complex data and draw conclusions, while immediate feedback from AI strengthens argumentation.

AI can significantly promote critical thinking by encouraging deep, particularly when combined with methods that enhance CT and understanding of AI contexts. AI literacy courses should include critical thinking to address ethical issues and societal impacts (Ng et al., 2021). In conclusion, education must prioritize critical thinking and AI literacy to tackle challenges like disinformation. Kaddouri et al. (2021) further elucidate the relationship between digital competencies and creative thinking processes, arguing that the cultivation of digital skills must be approached as a means to enhance critical and creative capacities rather than as an end in itself.

This section explored educational strategies and digital tools designed to foster critical thinking in the age of artificial intelligence. It emphasized the importance of critical education and innovative pedagogical approaches that encourages active student participation in addressing challenges posed by AI. AI, while serving as a tool to strengthen critical thinking, also presenting a phenomenon that must be critically analyzed.

TOWARDS A SYNERGY BETWEEN AI AND CRITICAL THINKING

A synergy between artificial intelligence and critical thinking paves the way for mutual enrichment: AI can foster the development of critical skills by creating interactive and complex learning environments, while critical thinking empowers individuals to evaluate and shape the impact of AI on our lives. This alliance offers the promise of a constructive coexistence, where human intelligence and technology work in harmony to address the challenges of the future with discernment and innovation.

Human-Machine Collaboration Models

In 2007, McCarthy predicted that AI would reach human-level intelligence in the 21st century, but noted that current systems remain fragile and struggle with "common sense" computing. Advances in machine vision (MV) and the Internet of Things (IoT) have given machines the ability to self-learn and analyze data, yet AI still falls short of human intelligence. Human thought is adaptable and flexible, whereas AI is constrained by data and predefined rules, limiting its capacity to handle complex, evolving contexts (Scherer, 2015).

AI's inability to autonomously revise concepts or think creatively further emphasizes the distinct role of human cognitive processes in reasoning and understanding (Nassar, 2019). The integration of AI with human critical thinking is essential, as it relies on adaptive reasoning that AI lacks. Xu et al. (2022) proposed a Human-Centered Artificial Intelligence (HCAI) approach, which stresses the need for human-centered design and interdisciplinary collaboration to create reliable, safe, and ethical AI systems.

Figure 2. The Human-Centered AI (HCAI) framework with specified design goals Xu et al. (2022)

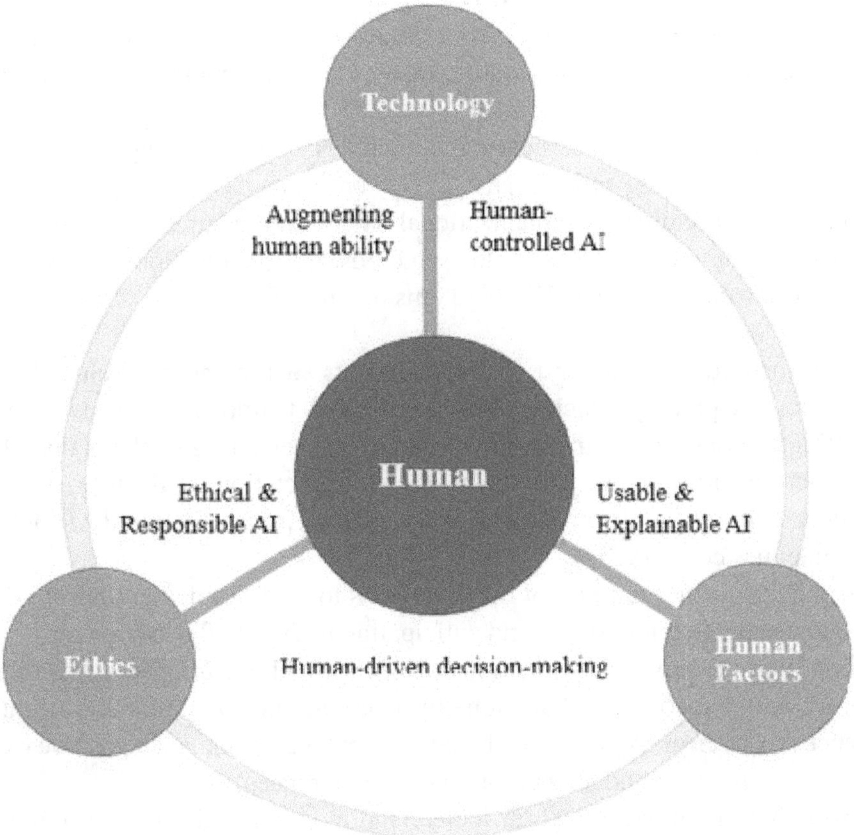

The approach focuses on human-centered design to develop AI systems that are usable, explainable, and support human decision-making (Human Factors). The goal is to create AI systems that enhance human capabilities while remaining under human control, rather than replacing them (Technology). Priority is given to fairness, accountability, and privacy protection, ensuring ethical AI and meaningful human oversight to guarantee safety and accountability (Ethics). The HCAI approach is based on the interdependence of these three areas and advocates for a synergy that places humans at the center of AI development. Educators' perceptions and attitudes toward AI tools like ChatGPT significantly influence their willingness to adopt and integrate these technologies into teaching practices aimed at developing critical thinking skills (Benali et al., 2024). To refocus AI on humans, Shneiderma (2020) proposed several approaches based on the principles of Human-Centered AI (HCAI):

- A bidimensional HCAI approach that integrates both high levels of human control and automation. Users retain meaningful control over critical decisions, even in highly automated systems
- A design approach that shifts from emulation to empowerment, designing AI as a tool to serve humans, rather than as an autonomous "teammate" that mimics them
- A three-tier governance structure that includes: an engineering team responsible for developing reliable and transparent systems; a management team that fosters a culture of organizational safety and ensures that ethical and safety values are central; a sector standards and certifications that validate and promote trustworthy HCAI systems that respect users

Having focused on broad and abstract concepts such as human values in this model, ethics, and privacy, which are therefore difficult to implement (Shneiderman, 2021), Bingley et al. (2022) translated these approaches into guidelines that align design practices more closely with the needs and expectations of the user, with the goal of enhancing development and user experience in Human-Centered AI (HCAI). These guidelines consist of:

Providing concrete examples of improvements for each guideline such as Algorithm adjustments (e.g for Alexa) and anticipating unexpected behaviors

Giving high priority to the functional aspects of AI, ensuring good usability, usefulness, and performance. Functionality is crucial not only to avoid negative experiences (e.g., errors, unexpected behaviors) but also to enhance positive experiences (e.g., efficiency and adaptation to user preferences)

Considering the impact of AI on society and individuals during development, giving it the same level of importance as functionality. Positive user experiences with AI are more when they also include social benefits

Prioritizing user understanding in AI design, adressing the need for personalization and tailored responses, while ensuring that AI explainable is and transparent

Adopting a proactive approach to ethics, privacy, and security, protecting users and ensuring compliance with human values. A significant degree of uncertainty remains among users regarding experiences with AI, which can limit satisfaction and trust

Stamboliev (2023) highlights the need for active human involvement in evaluating and deciding on AI systems, beyond technical skills. He criticizes the lack of critical reflection in digital literacy, similar to the past focus on technology over power and influence in media education. For AI to be truly beneficial, it must prioritize human well-being, with input from all societal stakeholders. This aligns with Human-Centered AI (HCAI), which emphasizes user needs in AI design (DeVito et al., 2017; Shneiderman, 2020). However, Bingley et al. (2022) note that this social aspect is often neglected by developers.

Literacy, initially focused on communication through writing, has expanded to include skills in areas like digital, computational, and scientific literacy to keep pace with a rapidly changing society. Digital literacy became essential with the rise of technology, requiring skills to use and evaluate information from digital sources (Long et al., 2020). In the AI era, literacy now extends to AI literacy, a concept introduced by Burgsteiner et al. (2016) and Kandlhofer et al. (2016), which involves understanding AI's societal implications and fostering critical evaluation skills (Yi, 2021). AI literacy is key for autonomous citizenship in an AI-driven world (Wong et al., 2020).AI literacy is based on foundations in functional, social, and technological literacy, and includes skills such as critical thinking, understanding social impacts, and the ability to use AI in an informed manner (Yi, 2021). It aims to educate individuals capable of fully participating in a society transformed by AI, promoting autonomy and independence (Su et al., 2023).

Ng et al. (2021) integrated AI literacy into contemporary digital literacy, making it a necessary skill in both professional contexts and everyday life. They included in AI literacy training: Bloom's Taxonomy model; technological and pedagogical knowledge (TPACK); as well as the concepts, practices, and perspectives of AI.

Figure 3. Foundation of IA literacy

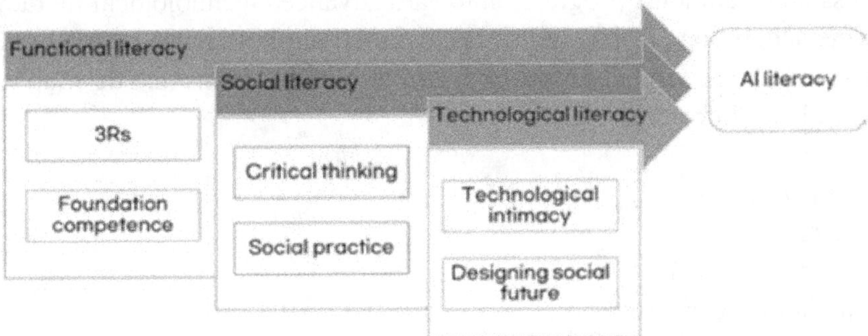

The development of other specific skills is also essential for 21st-century learners in the era of artificial intelligence (AI). Education 2030 and Futures Literacy highlight skills such as metacognition and anticipation of future changes as central elements of learning (Taguma et al., 2018). Metacognition, a key skill in AI literacy, is defined as the ability to think about one's own thinking and to manage cognitive processes effectively (Flavell, 1979). It allows learners to recognize their knowledge gaps, develop autonomous learning strategies, and adapt their learning to complex and uncertain environments, often referred to as VUCA (Volatile, Uncertain, Complex, Ambiguous (Characteristics of Complex and Changing Environments)), (Knox et al., 2023), an acronym for Volatile, Uncertain, Complex, Ambiguous. In addition, the skill of self-regulation helps learners select relevant information, access reliable sources, and evaluate the quality of educational resources related to AI.

At the same time, creative thinking is a reflective skill that enables the generation of innovative ideas and the combination of different elements to form a whole. This ability is crucial in problem-solving and critical thinking, as it leads to new solutions (Tso et al., 2020; DeSchryver et al., 2015). It is often associated with computational thinking, which applies systematic methods to solve complex problems. In this context, the act of creation involves cognitive engagement that unleashes creativity, allowing individuals to design new artifacts (Mishra, Yadav, and the Deep-Play research group, 2013, cited in Doleck et al., 2017).

To be truly transformative, AI literacy must also integrate a political dimension, allowing for an understanding of AI not just as a set of tools, but as a system of power (Stamboliev, 2023). In this regard, collaboration between journalists, academics, and the general public is essential to overcome problematic AI systems and address the asymmetry of access to information (Stamboliev, 2023). Several conceptual frameworks of AI literacy highlight essential skills for developing critical thinking (CT) in the AI era. Each framework addresses specific needs: some focus on a functional critical understanding of AI, while others aim for early ethical awareness and a complex progression toward advanced technological literacy and deeper metacognition. To strengthen critical thinking in the face of AI, Long and Magerko (2020) propose a framework based on five questions that develop fundamental skills for informed AI use:

a. What is AI?
b. What can AI do?
c. How does AI work?
d. How should AI be used?
e. How do people perceive AI?

These questions encourage a critical look at AI and contribute to developing skills for the reasoned evaluation of intelligent systems. The goal is to enable learners to assess AI systems, discern their limitations, and collaborate effectively with these tools, while maintaining the critical distance essential in a digital society.

Similarly, the "AI for K12" working group has formulated five guiding principles to promote a critical thinking through AI education in schools (Touretzky et al., 2019).

Figure 4. Core principles of AI and critical thinking

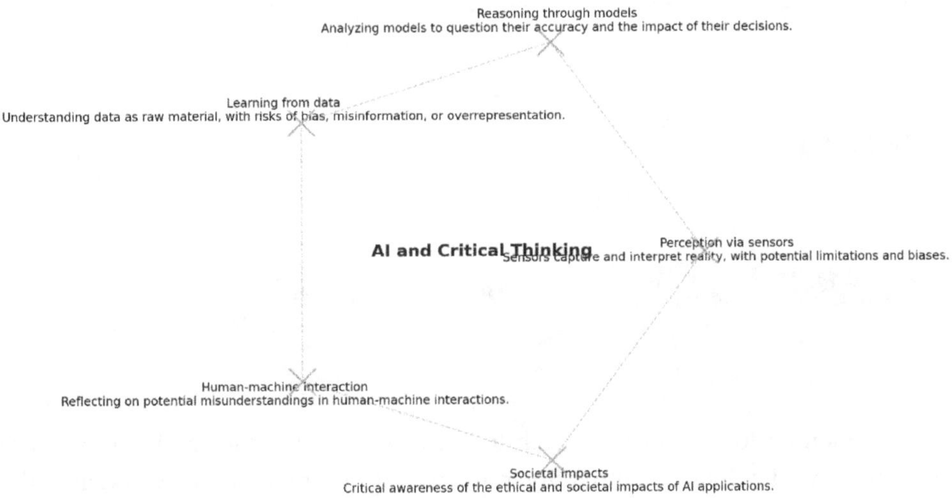

The first principle—computers perceive the world through sensors—encourages learners to explore how sensors capture and interpret reality, considering limitations and biases in the data. The second principle, that AI agents use models to reason, prompts students to analyze how models are created, their accuracy, and the impact of simplifications on AI decision-making. The third principle, that computers learn from data, teaches learners to critically assess datasets for risks of bias, misinformation, or overrepresentation and their effects on AI outcomes. Human-machine interaction presents challenges for AI developers, requiring mutual understanding and reflection on potential misinterpretations. Lastly, the final principle highlights the societal impacts of AI applications, emphasizing the need for critical awareness of ethics and responsibilities.

These principles can be used to develop critical thinking through activities that analyze AI systems. Learners could simulate decision-making scenarios to assess AI outcomes, biases, and limitations, and engage in ethical debates about AI's societal impact. Yi (2021) proposed a model of AI literacy that progresses from basic skills (functional literacy) to understanding social implications (social literacy), then to technological intimacy (technological literacy), and finally, to metacognition for anticipating future developments (AI literacy).

Figure 5. Competence and purpose of IA literacy (Yi, 2021)

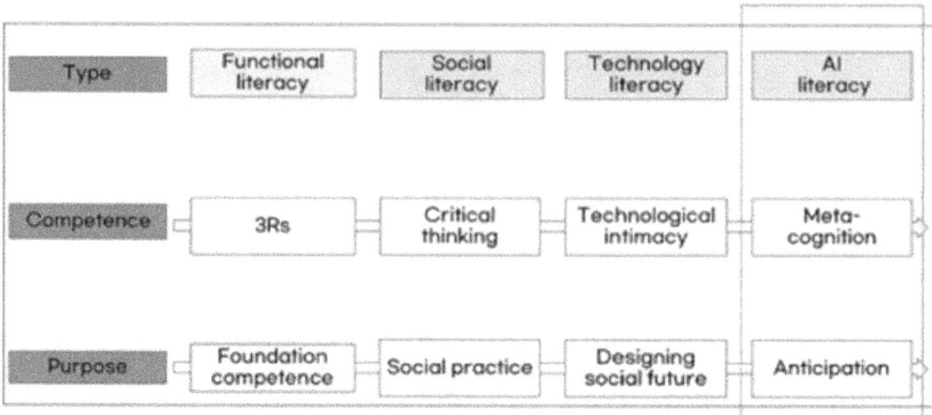

It is essential to continue research to identify the necessary skills in a future dominated by AI, which is profoundly transforming communication, work, and life. These skills, grouped under the term AI literacy, require continuous adaptation to new technologies and their potential impacts on society.

Innovation in AI-User Interfaces

Technological advances are redefining the tools for developing critical thinking and offering new approaches to enrich human reflection without replacing it. Critical thinking, as an individual's intellectual ability to analyze a problem using raw data and various solution strategies, is a skill that can be relatively easily improved through appropriate cognitive stimulation (Lestari et al., 2019). Thoughtfully designed interactive learning environments provide opportunities for active engagement and stimulate deep reflection and critical thinking in students (Yafie, 2020). The use of educational games, such as role-playing, has shown to have a positive impact on students' critical thinking and academic performance. Role-playing games, in particular, offer an interactive and immersive environment that forces participants to think critically, make complex decisions, and adopt different perspectives. This stimulates their ability to analyze situations, solve problems, and evaluate options—key skills for critical thinking (Rasyid et al., 2020). The digital tool screen can provide space and time to enhance reflective capacities by engaging users in systematic, sustained critical discourse based on interactive tasks (McCann et al., 2015).

Visionary for its time, Jonassen et al.'s study (1998) proposed a transformative use of technology, during an era when computers were primarily used for computer-assisted instruction limited to repetitive exercises or information delivery.

The groundbreaking concept of Mindtools suggested that, with specific types of software, computers could actively support critical thinking and deeper cognitive processing. These tools were designed not only to deliver content but to support learners in meaning-making, positioning them as active creators of knowledge. This approach laid a foundation for digital learning and the integration of critical thinking in modern educational tools.

Huang et al. (2016) developed an innovative project-based learning model in a cloud environment called Project-Based Cloud Learning (PBCL). The model leverages various Google tools and services to facilitate collaboration and real-time accessibility. Its goal is to stimulate students' critical thinking abilities. PBCL encourages learners to analyze and solve complex problems in teams, explore different perspectives, and engage in in-depth discussions, thus strengthening their critical thinking in a collaborative digital framework.

Danry (2023) implemented a wearable prototype system called Wearable Reasoner, designed to help identify fallacies in arguments. The integration of such AI systems to support critical thinking has been beneficial, but the author believes it is essential to design these systems in a way that does not replace human reflection but rather enriches it, especially as users can sometimes become overly dependent on the system to evaluate arguments. Moreover, the integration of AI in assessment and feedback opens up new possibilities to strengthen critical thinking. Various browser extensions, such as NewsGuard (Higdon et al., 2023) and Media Bias/Fact Check (Babaei et al., 2021), provide credibility assessments for news websites. These tools give users immediate insight into the reliability of the information source, helping them make informed decisions about the content they trust.

On the other hand, when AI "hallucinates," it can generate inaccurate or fabricated information in a convincing way (Athaluri et al., 2023). Alert systems that highlight potential biases in the data play an important educational and preventive role. They raise awareness among users, such as students, about AI's limitations, encouraging them to verify information. Bias indicators, commonly used in healthcare, promote critical vigilance, prompting users to question AI responses and identify biases. Providing explanatory feedback allows users to assess the logic behind AI recommendations, while AI tools could include follow-up questions to help users reflect and evaluate alternatives, ensuring the process remains efficient and non-burdensome.

Feedback is another key variable to consider. Appropriate, timely, and personalized formative feedback can enhance student engagement and critical thinking, as shown by Shute (2008). With AI, reflective questions can help students assess their own and peers' work, promoting active engagement and critical reflection while reducing reliance on teacher-only feedback, which is less effective in fostering critical thinking (Zou et al., 2022). Peer feedback encourages self-regulated learning and critical thinking (Winstone et al., 2019; Han et al., 2021). AI interfaces can guide students in providing constructive feedback, and interactive AI-based dashboards can offer real-time, personalized feedback, strengthening critical thinking (CT) by enabling students to analyze their learning process and self-regulate (Foung et al., 2022; Verbert et al., 2013).

AI also plays a crucial role in personalizing multimedia tools, such as videos, to meet individual learners' needs. By adapting content to students' levels and learning styles, AI supports knowledge construction (Verdugo et al., 2007). Yilmaz et al. (2016) highlight that videos help develop higher-order thinking skills, like reflective thinking. AI-powered chatbots, such as Alexa for Education or Google Assistant, provide dynamic audio feedback, fostering student engagement, self-regulation, and critical reflection (Johnson et al., 2016). Additionally, AI interfaces can offer varied interaction scenarios, where students make complex decisions and explore the consequences, encouraging active research and reflection.

Being closely related to critical thinking, autonomy has been the subject of several studies that explored the impact of AI tools on autonomous learning. These studies show that AI-based platforms such as chatbots and virtual assistants contribute to the development of autonomous skills. Dousay and Hall (2018) suggest that AI-based applications and platforms can offer personalized learning content, adapt to learners' progress, and provide real-time feedback, thereby promoting a personalized approach to autonomous learning. Virtual assistants and chatbots can simulate authentic classroom interactions and improve oral and listening skills. Tahir et al. (2023) revealed that the integration of Amazon Alexa and related activities significantly contributed to the development of autonomous learning skills and enhanced participants' critical and creative thinking abilities.

However, a good knowledge of AI alone does not facilitate the self-regulation process, as using a chatbot may change students' learning behaviors but not their cognition and perception of learning (Kumar, 2021). Immersive environments, on the other hand, allow students to explore ethical dilemmas and scenarios where judgment and critical analysis are essential. Such contexts contribute to better self-confidence, a more open mind, and the ability to reflect deeply when assessing nuanced situations and identifying the implications of their choices (Muthmainnah et al., 2022).

Transparency is a key concept across various disciplines, including computer science and social sciences, and is closely linked to explainability and openness (Larsson, 2017). Essential for trust and accountability, transparency is a core principle in the European Union's ethical guidelines for trustworthy AI (Larsson et al., 2020). In AI education, transparency refers to the ability of systems to explain and justify their decisions in an understandable way, crucial for AI acceptance and ethical applications (Touretzky et al., 2019). It requires traceability and human oversight to ensure responsible use (Larsson et al., 2020; Sperrle et al., 2021). The European

Union outlines seven key requirements for trustworthy AI, with transparency as the fourth pillar, encompassing data, system processes, and business models to ensure traceability, error identification, and improved transparency (Weiser, 2019).

Figure 6. Interrelationship of the seven requirements: all are of equal importance, support each other, and should be implemented and evaluated throughout the AI system's lifecycle

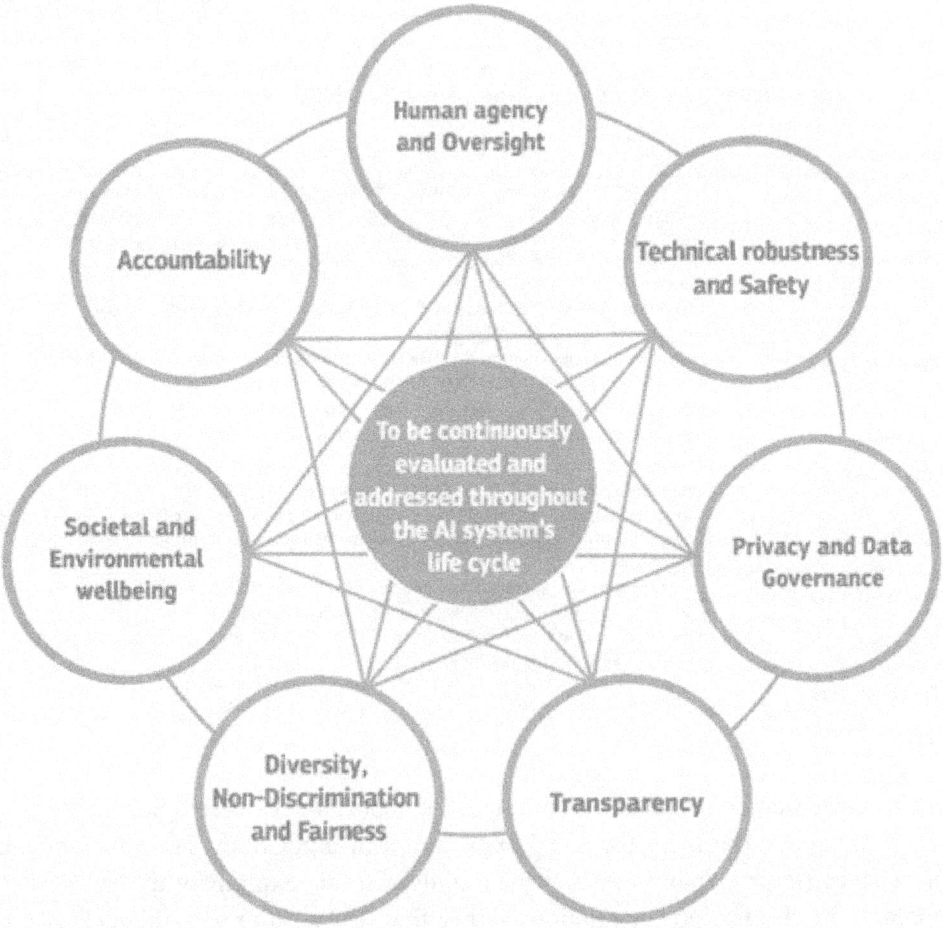

Explainability refers to clarifying the technical processes of AI systems and the human decisions behind them (Weiser, 2019). It ensures that AI decisions are understandable and traceable, though a trade-off may arise between explainability and accuracy. When AI significantly impacts people's lives, appropriate explanations should be provided, tailored to the stakeholder's expertise (e.g., citizen, regulator, or researcher). Explanations should also clarify how AI influences organizational decisions and business models. Explainability overlaps with algorithmic transparency, which focuses on algorithms, while transparency includes data, socio-technical systems, and societal implications (Larsson et al., 2020). There is a distinction between explainability (user understanding) and interpretability (Larsson et al., 2020). Felzmann et al. (2020) proposed a "Transparency by Design" approach to address the challenges of transparency in automated decision-making, offering nine principles covering technical, contextual, and stakeholder considerations.

Table 1. Transparency by design (Felzmann et al., 2020)

Principle	Description
Proactivity	Implement transparency measures from the beginning of the AI system development to avoid transparency being addressed only after the design phase.
Integration	Design transparency as an integrated process, considering the complexity of decisions to show how different parts of the system meet decision-making standards.
Public Orientation	Tailor communication based on the target audience, whether it's end-users, regulators, or the general public.
Data Processing	Provide an explanation of the data used and how it is processed, with a clear description of inspectable steps and moments for human intervention.
Decision-Making Standards	Explain and justify the normative criteria for decision-making to frame the implicit values embedded in the decision-making process.
Risk Disclosure	Explain the risks associated with AI, including potential biases and discrimination, as well as measures to mitigate these risks.
Inspectability	Ensure the possibility of audits by qualified third parties to verify the algorithm's behavior, providing appropriate documentation and Application Programming Interfaces (APIs).
Responsiveness	Be responsive to questions and concerns from stakeholders, facilitating access to contacts and providing serious, individualized responses.
Reporting	Regularly publish detailed reports on the use and performance of the AI system to continuously inform stakeholders.
Risk Disclosure	Explain the risks associated with AI, including potential biases and discrimination, as well as measures to mitigate these risks.

However, Stamboliev (2023) emphasizes the importance of developing AI literacy that goes beyond the mere technical explanation of algorithms. He criticizes the approach of transparency in AI (such as in algorithmic explainability or "XAI"), which could obscure power relations rather than truly illuminate them. It is not only about understanding how algorithms work, but also recognizing their impact on social and political relations. Critical thinking is therefore essential to assess the ideological issues hidden behind the discourses of transparency and technological neutrality (Stamboliev, 2023).

The complex and multifaceted nature of transparency highlights how challenging it is to integrate transparency into the design and implementation process of an AI system (Felzmann et al., 2020), requiring a nuanced approach. To effectively govern AI, a framework for transparency that takes into account technological, legal, and ethical dimensions is necessary. Research suggests that this multidisciplinary approach is the best way to balance conflicting interests in applied AI (Larsson et al., 2020). Human-machine collaboration and the need to develop appropriate skills are crucial in the age of AI. Although AI is advancing, it remains limited compared to the flexibility of human thinking. The Human-Centered AI (HCAI) approach proposes creating ethical systems and transparent AI-user interfaces that enhance human capabilities. Transparency in AI is vital for fostering critical engagement. It includes traceability and explainability of systems but must also consider the social and political implications of algorithms. AI literacy, which encompasses critical and social skills, is crucial in this regard.

CONCLUSION

This chapter has explored the complex interplay between artificial intelligence (AI) and critical thinking, emphasizing the challenges and opportunities this synergy presents within a rapidly evolving educational landscape. AI's ability to process vast amounts of data and simulate complex scenarios makes it a powerful tool for developing analytical and critical skills. However, its transformative potential is conditioned by significant limitations, such as algorithmic opacity and data biases, necessitating ethical, thoughtful and measured integration (Carabantes, 2023; Danry, 2023). In this context, critical thinking emerges as an indispensable skill, enabling users to evaluate AI tools critically and guard against the growing risks of misinformation, manipulation, and cognitive dependence (Rusandi et al., 2023). Its importance extends beyond education, becoming a societal imperative for digital citizenship and autonomous decision-making in a connected world (Milenkova et al., 2021; Xu et al., 2022). Moreover, the integration of AI into educational settings offers unparalleled opportunities for personalized learning and critical reflection, particularly through interactive and authentic scenarios (Marienko et al., 2022). However, this integration requires a rigorous ethical framework and tailored pedagogical strategies. AI, far from being a universal solution, must be employed as a complementary tool, guided by critical vigilance and ethical oversight (Shneiderman, 2021).

Finally, as AI extends beyond the educational sphere to influence social dimensions, such as digital citizenship and active participation in a connected society (Kaur, 2018; UNESCO, 2019), this chapter emphasizes the need for a systemic approach that harnesses the synergy between AI and critical thinking. This complementarity, rooted in ethical and pedagogical perspectives, forms a foundational pillar for reimagining educational practices. It aims to foster intellectual autonomy and prepare learners to address the complex challenges of the 21st century with discernment and responsibility. Ongoing research in this direction is essential to leverage AI's transformative potential in education while preserving human values and anticipating societal and ethical impacts (Marošan, 2019; Long et al., 2020).

REFERENCES

Ab Kadir, M. A. (2018). An inquiry into critical thinking in the Australian curriculum: Examining its conceptual understandings and their implications on developing critical thinking as a "general capability" on teachers' practice and knowledge. *Asia Pacific Journal of Education*, *38*(4), 533–549. DOI: 10.1080/02188791.2018.1535424

Athaluri, S. A., Manthena, S. V., Manoj, K., Yarlagadda, V., & Dave, T. (2023). Exploring the boundaries of reality: Investigating the phenomenon of artificial intelligence hallucination in scientific writing through ChatGPT references. *Cureus*, *15*(5), e37432. Advance online publication. DOI: 10.7759/cureus.37432 PMID: 37182055

Azzimani, T., & Kaddouri, E. M. (2020). Technology, Creativity, and Learning: Semiotic Perspective. In Tadlaoui, M. A., & Khaldi, M. (Eds.), (pp. 148–157). Advances in Educational Technologies and Instructional Design. IGI Global., DOI: 10.4018/978-1-7998-1492-4.ch006

Babaei, M., Kulshrestha, J., Chakraborty, A., Redmiles, E. M., Cha, M., & Gummadi, K. P. (2021). Analyzing biases in perception of truth in news stories and their implications for fact checking. *IEEE Transactions on Computational Social Systems*, *9*(3), 839–850. DOI: 10.1109/TCSS.2021.3096038

Bawden, D., & Robinson, L. (2020). Information overload: An overview. In *Oxford Encyclopedia of Political Decision Making*. Oxford University Press., DOI: 10.1093/acrefore/9780190228637.013.1360

Bell, L., Stevenson, H., & Neary, M. (2009). *The future of higher education: Policy*. Pedagogy and the Student Experience, Continuum International Publishing Group.

Belmekki, M., Belmekki, L., & Koumachi, B. (2024). The effect of project-based learning on the development of learners' critical thinking skills in higher education: A quasi-experimental study. *Revue Linguistique et Référentiels Interculturels*, *5*(1), 44–57. DOI: 10.34874/IMIST.PRSM/liri-v5i1.49980

Benali, M., Kaddouri, M., & Azzimani, T. (2018). Digital competence of Moroccan teachers of English. *International Journal of Education and Development Using Information and Communication Technology*, *14*, 99–120.

Benali, M., & Mak, J. (2024). Perception of Preservice Moroccan Teachers Regarding the Adoption of ChatGPT in Their Teaching Practices. In *Artificial Intelligence Applications in K-12*. Routledge. DOI: 10.4324/9781003440192-8

Bereiter, C. (2005). *Education and mind in the knowledge age*. Routledge. DOI: 10.4324/9781410612182

Bingley, W. J., Curtis, C., Lockey, S., Bialkowski, A., Gillespie, N., Haslam, S. A., Ko, R. K. L., Steffens, N., Wiles, J., & Worthy, P. (2022). Where is the human in human-centered AI? Insights from developer priorities and user experiences. *Computers in Human Behavior*, *141*, 107617–107617. DOI: 10.1016/j.chb.2022.107617

Brookfield, S. D. (1987). *Developing critical thinkers: Challenging adults to explore alternative ways of thinking and acting*. Jossey-Bass.

Burgsteiner, H., Kandlhofer, M., & Steinbauer, G. (2016). IRobot: Teaching the Basics of Artificial Intelligence in High Schools. Proceedings of the AAAI Conference on Artificial Intelligence, 30(1). DOI: 10.1609/aaai.v30i1.9864

Bushuyev, S., Bushuiev, D., Bushuieva, V., Bushuyeva, N., & Murzabekova, S. (2024). The erosion of competencies in managing innovation projects due to the impact of ubiquitous artificial intelligence systems. *Procedia Computer Science*, *231*, 403–408. DOI: 10.1016/j.procs.2023.12.225

Carabantes, M. (2023). Why artificial intelligence is not transparent: a critical analysis of its three opacity layers. Edward Elgar Publishing EBooks, 424–434. DOI: 10.4337/9781803928562.00045

Choi, M., & Cristol, D. (2021). Digital citizenship with intersectionality lens: Towards participatory democracy driven digital citizenship education. *Theory into Practice*, *60*(4), 361–370. DOI: 10.1080/00405841.2021.1987094

Danry, V. M. (2023). AI Enhanced Reasoning: Augmenting Human Critical Thinking with AI Systems. Mit.edu. https://hdl.handle.net/1721.1/151971

DeSchryver, M. D., & Yadav, A. (2015). Creative and computational thinking in the context of new literacies: Working with teachers to scaffold complex technology-mediated approaches to teaching and learning. *Journal of Technology and Teacher Education*, *23*(3), 411–431.

Dethine, B., Enjolras, M., & Monticolo, D. (2020). Digitalization and SMEs' export management: Impacts on resources and capabilities. *Technology Innovation Management Review*, *10*(4), 18–34. DOI: 10.22215/timreview/1344

Dewey, J. (1933). *How we think: A restatement of the relation of reflective thinking to the educative process*. D.C. Heath and Company.

Dietzmann, C., & Duan, Y. (2022). Artificial intelligence for managerial information processing and decision-making in the era of information overload. http://hdl.handle.net/10125/80060

Doleck, T., Bazelais, P., Lemay, D. J., Saxena, A., & Basnet, R. B. (2017). Algorithmic thinking, cooperativity, creativity, critical thinking, and problem solving: Exploring the relationship between computational thinking skills and academic performance. *Journal of Computers in Education*, *4*(4), 355–369. DOI: 10.1007/s40692-017-0090-9

Dousay, T. A., & Hall, C. (2018, June). Alexa, tell me about using a virtual assistant in the classroom. In EdMedia+ innovate learning (pp. 1413-1419). Association for the Advancement of Computing in Education (AACE). https://www.learntechlib.org/p/184359/

Dumitru, D., & Halpern, D. F. (2023). Critical Thinking: Creating Job-Proof Skills for the Future of Work. *Journal of Intelligence*, *11*(10), 194–194. DOI: 10.3390/jintelligence11100194 PMID: 37888426

Edmunds, A., & Morris, A. (2000). The problem of information overload in business organisations: A review of the literature. *International Journal of Information Management*, *20*(1), 17–28. DOI: 10.1016/S0268-4012(99)00051-1

Elder, L. (2022). *Critical Thinking*. Routledge., DOI: 10.4324/9781138609877-REE215-1

Ennis, R. (2011). Critical Thinking. *Inquiry (Upper Montclair, N.J.)*, *26*(2), 5–19. DOI: 10.5840/inquiryctnews201126215

Facione, P. A. (1990). *Critical thinking: A statement of expert consensus for purposes of educational assessment and instruction—The Delphi report*. California Academic Press.

Farias-Gaytan, S., Aguaded, I., & Ramirez-Montoya, M.-S. (2023). Digital transformation and digital literacy in the context of complexity within higher education institutions: A systematic literature review. *Humanities & Social Sciences Communications*, *10*(1), 386. Advance online publication. DOI: 10.1057/s41599-023-01875-9

Felzmann, H., Fosch-Villaronga, E., Lutz, C., & Tamò-Larrieux, A. (2020). Towards Transparency by Design for Artificial Intelligence. *Science and Engineering Ethics*, *26*(6), 3333–3361. DOI: 10.1007/s11948-020-00276-4 PMID: 33196975

Flavell, J. H. (1979). Metacognition and cognitive monitoring: A new area of cognitive–developmental inquiry. *The American Psychologist*, *34*(10), 906–911. DOI: 10.1037/0003-066X.34.10.906

Foung, D., & Kwan, J. (2022). Prevention is better than cure: Use of a dashboard in a university English course. In *Applications of machine learning and artificial intelligence in education* (pp. 162–176). IGI Global., DOI: 10.4018/978-1-7998-7776-9.ch007

Gkrimpizi, T., Peristeras, V., & Magnisalis, I. (2023). Classification of Barriers to Digital Transformation in Higher Education Institutions: Systematic Literature Review. *Education Sciences*, *13*(7), 746. DOI: 10.3390/educsci13070746

Halpern, D. F. (2013). *Thought and knowledge: An introduction to critical thinking*. Psychology press. DOI: 10.4324/9781315885278

Halpern, D. F., & Dunn, D. S. (2021). Critical Thinking: A Model of Intelligence for Solving Real-World Problems. *Journal of Intelligence*, *9*(2), 22–22. DOI: 10.3390/jintelligence9020022 PMID: 33916939

Han, Y., & Xu, Y. (2021). Student feedback literacy and engagement with feedback: A case study of Chinese undergraduate students. *Teaching in Higher Education*, *26*(2), 181–196. Advance online publication. DOI: 10.1080/13562517.2019.1648410

Higdon, N., & Maret, S. (2023). The Case Against NewsGuard. https://www.projectcensored.org/wp-content/uploads/2022/07/The_Case_Against_Newsguard.pdf

Huang, T.-C., Jeng, Y.-L., Hsiao, K.-L., & Tsai, B.-R. (2016). SNS collaborative learning design: Enhancing critical thinking for human–computer interface design. *Universal Access in the Information Society*, *16*(2), 303–312. DOI: 10.1007/s10209-016-0458-z

Jain, S., & Jain, R. (2019). Role Of Artificial Intelligence In Higher Education-An Empirical Investigation. IJRAR-International Journal of Research and Analytical Reviews, 6. https://new-artificial-intelligence.com/wp-content/uploads/2024/03/10.-Role-of-Artificial-Intelligence-in-Higher-Education-an-Empirical-Investigation-Article-Author-Suvrat-JainDr-Roshita-Jain.pdf

Johnson, G. M., & Cooke, A. (2016). Self-regulation of learning and preference for written versus audio-recorded feedback by distance education students. (2016). *Distance Education*, *37*(1), 107–120. Advance online publication. DOI: 10.1080/01587919.2015.1081737

Jonassen, D. H., Carr, C., & Hsiu-Ping, Y. (1998). Computers as mindtools for engaging learners in critical thinking. *TechTrends*, *43*(2), 24–32. DOI: 10.1007/BF02818172

Junge, A. L. (2019). Digital transformation technologies as an enabler for sustainable logistics and supply chain processes – an exploratory framework. *Brazilian Journal of Operations & Production Management, 16*(3), 462–472. DOI: 10.14488/BJOPM.2019.v16.n3.a9

Kaddouri, M., Benali, M., Azzimani, T., & Mimoun Elkhir, A. (2024). Emotional, Relational and Digitalisation: Towards a Redesign of the Educational Paradigm. International Journal of Research and Innovation in Social Science, VIII(IIIS), 4184–4197. DOI: 10.47772/IJRISS.2024.803302S

Kaddouri, M., Mhamdi, K., Chniete, I., Marhraoui, M., Khaldi, M., & Jmad, S. (2024). Adopting AI in Education: Technical Challenges and Ethical Constraints. In Sanmugam, M., Edwards, B. I., Mohd Barkhaya, N. M., & Khlaif, Z. (Eds.), (pp. 25–72). Advances in Educational Technologies and Instructional Design. IGI Global., DOI: 10.4018/979-8-3693-7255-5.ch002

Kaddouri, M., Mhamdi, K., Jabri, A., Boukare, M., & Jmad, S. (2025). Generative Artificial Intelligence and Assessment of Learning: Challenges and Perspectives. In Gregory, S. (Ed.), (pp. 277–326). Advances in Educational Technologies and Instructional Design. IGI Global., DOI: 10.4018/979-8-3693-6527-4.ch010

Kaddouri, M., & Tayalati, F. (2021, June). Compétences numériques et Créativité. OBTAIN 1st International Virtual Workshop on Digitalized Skills and Today's Job Market Needs. https://hal.science/hal-04270058

Kandlhofer, M., Steinbauer, G., Hirschmugl-Gaisch, S., & Huber, P. (2016). Artificial intelligence and computer science in education: From kindergarten to university. 2016 IEEE Frontiers in Education Conference (FIE), 1–9. DOI: 10.1109/FIE.2016.7757570

Kaur, M. K. (2018). Critical Thinking for Global Peace: A key for Sustainable Development. International Journal of Trend in Scientific Research and Development, Volume-2(Issue-3). https://www.ijtsrd.com/humanities-and-the-arts/education/11439/critical-thinking-for-global-peace-a-key-for-sustainable-development/ms-kuldeep-kaur

Knox, B. J., Sütterlin, S., & Lugo, R. (2023). Cognitive agility for improved understanding and self-governance: a human-centric AI enabler. Edward Elgar Publishing EBooks, 152–172. DOI: 10.4337/9781839106750.00019

Komolafe, B. F., & Qian, X. (2020). Critical thinking an antidote to artificial intelligence threat: An innovation in teacher education practices. *Proceeding of the 6th International Conference on Education*, 6(2), 51-56. https://doi.org/DOI: 10.17501/24246700.2020.6205

Kraus, S., Jones, P., Kailer, N., Weinmann, A., Chaparro-Banegas, N., & Roig-Tierno, N. (2021). Digital transformation: An overview of the current state of the art of research. *SAGE Open*, *11*(3), 21582440211047576. DOI: 10.1177/21582440211047576

Kumar, J. A. (2021). Educational chatbots for project-based learning: Investigating learning outcomes for a team-based design course. *International Journal of Educational Technology in Higher Education*, *18*(1), 65. Advance online publication. DOI: 10.1186/s41239-021-00302-w PMID: 34926790

Lamatsch, H. (2023). Transformation numérique de l'administration: La recherche d'efficacité et d'agilité. *Revue Défense Nationale*, *HS13*(HS13), 77–90. DOI: 10.3917/rdna.hs13.0077

Larsson, S. (2017). *Conceptions in the Code*. Oxford University Press., https://lup.lub.lu.se/search/publication/b7435f9d-f4b9-4fb3-8b5f-34d41c58d198 DOI: 10.1093/acprof:oso/9780190650384.001.0001

Larsson, S., & Heintz, F. (2020). Transparency in artificial intelligence. *Internet Policy Review*, *9*(2). Advance online publication. DOI: 10.14763/2020.2.1469

Lennon, N. K. (2014). How professors infuse critical thinking into college courses (Doctoral dissertation, Seton Hall University). https://www.proquest.com/openview/6c8fe9f36a915f710b59a34c4b6b45a2/1?pq-origsite=gscholar&cbl=18750

Lestari, S. W., Agung, L., & Musadad, A. A. (2019). Android based adventure games to enhance vocational high school students' critical thinking skills. Dans K. Saddhono, D. T. Ardianto, M. F. Hidayatullah, & V. R. Cahyani (Éds.), Proceedings of the 1st Seminar and Workshop on Research Design, for Education, Social Science, Arts, and Humanities (Vol. 115, pp. 115-120). SEWORD FRESSH. DOI: 10.4108/eai.27-4-2019.2286917

Lipman, M. (2003). *Thinking in education* (Vol. 304). Cambridge University Press. DOI: 10.1017/CBO9780511840272

Little, D. (1991). *Learner autonomy 1: Definitions, issues, and problems*. Authentik.

Long, D., & Magerko, B. (2020). *What is AI Literacy?* Competencies and Design Considerations., DOI: 10.1145/3313831.3376727

Machete, P., & Turpin, M. (2020). The Use of Critical Thinking to Identify Fake News: A Systematic Literature Review. In Hattingh, M., Matthee, M., Smuts, H., Pappas, I., Dwivedi, Y. K., & Mäntymäki, M. (Eds.), Lecture Notes in Computer Science: Vol. 12067. *Responsible Design, Implementation and Use of Information and Communication Technology. I3E 2020.* Springer., DOI: 10.1007/978-3-030-45002-1_20

Maroşan, M. I. (2019). Le devenir robot de l'humain. *Das Argument, 21*(2), 142–148.

McCann, S., & Camp Pendleton, C. A. (2015). Higher Order mLearning: Critical Thinking in Mobile Learning. MODSIM World, 208, 1-11. https://modsimworld.org/papers/2015/Higher_Order_mLearning.pdf

McCarthy, J. (2007). From here to human-level AI. *Artificial Intelligence, 171*(18), 1174–1182. DOI: 10.1016/j.artint.2007.10.009

Mikalef, P., & Gupta, M. (2021). Artificial intelligence capability: Conceptualization, measurement calibration, and empirical study on its impact on organizational creativity and firm performance. *Information & Management, 58*(3), 103434–103434. DOI: 10.1016/j.im.2021.103434

Milenkova, V., & Lendzhova, V. (2021). Digital Citizenship and Digital Literacy in the Conditions of Social Crisis. *Computers, 10*(4), 40–40. DOI: 10.3390/computers10040040

Mishra, P., & Yadav, A. (2013). Of art and algorithms: Rethinking technology & creativity in the 21st century. *TechTrends, 57*(3), 10–14. DOI: 10.1007/s11528-013-0655-z

Moustaghfir, S., & Brigui, H. (2024). Navigating critical thinking in the digital era: An informative exploration. *International Journal of Linguistics Literature & Translation, 7*(1), 137–143. DOI: 10.32996/ijllt.2024.7.1.11x

Mukul, E., & Büyüközkan, G. (2023). Digital transformation in education: A systematic review of education 4.0. *Technological Forecasting and Social Change, 194*, 122664. DOI: 10.1016/j.techfore.2023.122664

Muthmainnah, S., Ibna Seraj, P. M., & Oteir, I. (2022). P. M. I., & Oteir, I. (2022). Playing with AI to investigate human-computer interaction technology and improving critical thinking skills to pursue 21st century age. *Education Research International, 2022*, 1–17. DOI: 10.1155/2022/6468995

National Association of Colleges and Employers. (2017). Job outlook 2018. https://careerservices.wayne.edu/pdfs/2018-nacejob-outlook-survey.pdf

Ng, K., Lok, K., Wah, K., & Qiao, M. S. (2021). AI Literacy: Definition, Teaching, Evaluation and Ethical Issues. *Proceedings of the Association for Information Science and Technology, 58*(1), 504–509. DOI: 10.1002/pra2.487

Ong, D., Sands, P., Kilborn, A., & Parikh, J. Y. (2020). A beginner's guide to systematic reviews and meta-analyses. *British Journal of Hospital Medicine, 81*(9), 1–6. DOI: 10.12968/hmed.2020.0405 PMID: 33263480

Orakci, S., & Gelisli, Y. (2019). The Effect of the Application of Learning Activities Based on Learner Autonomy on the 6th Grade Students' English Achievements, Attitudes, and Learner Autonomy. *International Journal of Curriculum and Instruction, 11*(1), 269–292. https://eric.ed.gov/?id=EJ1217908

Paul, R. (2011). Critical thinking movement: 3 waves. *Retrieved, 18*, 2018.

Plekhanov, D., Franke, H., & Netland, T. H. (2023). Digital transformation: A review and research agenda. *European Management Journal, 41*(6), 821–844. DOI: 10.1016/j.emj.2022.09.007

Rabeya, M., Mahmud, M. S., Johora, S. F. T., & Sattar, A. (2022). A comparison of the application of artificial intelligence in the educational system. Dans *2022 International Conference on Emerging Trends in Computing and Engineering Applications (ETCEA)* (pp. 1-6). IEEE. DOI: 10.1109/ETCEA57049.2022.10009813

Rasyid, A., Iswari, R. I., Marwoto, P., & Rinto, . (2020). The effectiveness of mobile learning role play game (rpg) maker mv in improving students' critical thinking ability. *Journal of Physics: Conference Series, 1567*(4), 042088. DOI: 10.1088/1742-6596/1567/4/042088

Raya, J., & Vieira, F. (2015). Enhancing Autonomy in Language Education: A Case-Based Approach to Teacher and Learner Development. Oapen.org. https://doi.org/DOI: 1004875

Reis, J., & Melão, N. (2023). Digital transformation: A meta-review and guidelines for future research. *Heliyon, 9*(1), e12834–e12834. DOI: 10.1016/j.heliyon.2023.e12834 PMID: 36691547

Robles, A. C. M. O. (2012). Cyber Portfolio: The Innovative Menu for 21st Century Technology. *Online Submission, 2*(3), 143–150.

Rusandi, M. A., Ahman, , Saripah, I., Khairun, D. Y., & Mutmainnah, . (2023). No worries with ChatGPT: Building bridges between artificial intelligence and education with critical thinking soft skills. *Journal of Public Health (Oxford, England), 45*(3), e602–e603. DOI: 10.1093/pubmed/fdad049 PMID: 37099761

Saxena, D., & Sandul Yasobant. (2022). Information Overload. Springer EBooks, 566–568. DOI: 10.1007/978-3-319-32010-6_374

Schleicher, A. (2018). Educating Learners for Their Future, Not Our Past. *ECNU Review of Education, 1*(1), 58–75. DOI: 10.30926/ecnuroe2018010104

Sellars, M., Fakirmohammad, R., Bui, L., Fishetti, J., Niyozov, S., Reynolds, R., Thapliyal, N., Liu-Smith, Y.-L., & Ali, N. (2018). Conversations on Critical Thinking: Can Critical Thinking Find Its Way Forward as the Skill Set and Mindset of the Century? *Education Sciences*, *8*(4), 205–205. DOI: 10.3390/educsci8040205

Shneiderman, B. (2020). Human-Centered Artificial Intelligence: Three Fresh Ideas. AIS Electronic Library (AISeL). https://aisel.aisnet.org/thci/vol12/iss3/1/

Shneiderman, B. (2022). *Human-centered AI.* Oxford University Press., https://issues.org/wp-content/uploads/2021/01/56%E2%80%9361-Shneiderman-Human-Centered-AI-Winter-2021.pdf DOI: 10.1093/oso/9780192845290.001.0001

Shute, V. J. (2008). Focus on Formative Feedback. *Review of Educational Research*, *78*(1), 153–189. DOI: 10.3102/0034654307313795

Singh, S. V., & Hiran, K. K. (2022). The impact of AI on teaching and learning in higher education technology. *Journal of Higher Education Theory and Practice*, *22*(13).

Spector, J. M., & Ma, S. (2019). Inquiry and critical thinking skills for the next generation: From artificial intelligence back to human intelligence. *Smart Learn. Environ.*, *6*(1), 8. DOI: 10.1186/s40561-019-0088-z

Sperrle, F., El-Assady, M., Guo, G., Borgo, R., Chau, D. H., Endert, A., & Keim, D. (2021). A Survey of Human-Centered Evaluations in Human-Centered Machine Learning. *Computer Graphics Forum*, *40*(3), 543–568. DOI: 10.1111/cgf.14329

Stamboliev, E. (2023). Proposing a Postcritical AI Literacy: Why We Should Worry Less about Algorithmic Transparency and More about Citizen Empowerment. Media Theory, 7(1), 202–232. https://hal.science/hal-04221538

Su, J., Ng, K., & Kai, S. (2023). Artificial Intelligence (AI) Literacy in Early Childhood Education: The Challenges and Opportunities. *Computers and Education Artificial Intelligence*, *4*, 100124–100124. DOI: 10.1016/j.caeai.2023.100124

Sych, T., Khrykov, Y., & Ptakhina, O. (2021). Digital transformation as the main condition for the development of modern higher education. *Educational Technology Quarterly*, *2021*(2), 293–309. DOI: 10.55056/etq.27

Taguma, M., Feron, E., & Lim, M. H. (2018). *Future of education and skills 2030: Conceptual learning framework.* Organization of Economic Co-operation and Development.

Tahir, A., & Tahir, A. (2023). AI-driven Advancements in ESL Learner Autonomy: Investigating Student Attitudes Towards Virtual Assistant Usability. *Linguistic Forum -. Journal of Linguistics*, *5*(2), 50–56. DOI: 10.5281/zenodo.14776953

Touretzky, D., Gardner-McCune, C., Martin, F., & Seehorn, D. (2019, July). Envisioning AI for K-12: What should every child know about AI? *Proceedings of the AAAI Conference on Artificial Intelligence*, *33*(01), 9795–9799. DOI: 10.1609/aaai.v33i01.33019795

Touretzky, D. S. (2017). Computational thinking and mental models: From kodu to calypso.

Tredinnick, L. (2018). Information, communications and overload - Luke Tredinnick, Claire Laybats, 2018. Business Information Review. https://journals.sagepub.com/doi/full/10.1177/0266382118792762

Trilling, B., & Fadel, C. (2009). *21st century skills: Learning for life in our times*. John Wiley & Sons.

Tso, A. W., & Ho, W. (2020). Creativity and critical thinking in practice. June, 2019â.

UNESCO. (2021a). Rewired global declaration on connectivity for education. https://en.unesco.org/news/rewired-global-declaration-connectivity-education

UNESCO. (2021b). UNESCO strategy on technological innovation in education (2022-2025) (Document 212 EX/5.III.A). https://unesdoc.unesco.org/ark:/48223/pf0000378847_fre

Verbert, K., Duval, E., Klerkx, J., Govaerts, S., & Santos, J. L. (2013). Learning analytics dashboard applications. *The American Behavioral Scientist*, *57*(10), 1500–1509. DOI: 10.1177/0002764213479363

Verdugo, D., & Alonso Belmonte, I. (2007). Using digital stories to improve listening comprehension with Spanish young learners of English. *Language Learning & Technology*, *11*(1), 87–101. 10125/44090

Voinea, M., & Pălăşan, T. (2014). Teachers' professional identity in the 21st century Romania. *Procedia: Social and Behavioral Sciences*, *128*, 361–365. DOI: 10.1016/j.sbspro.2014.03.172

Vosoughi, S., Roy, D., & Aral, S. (2018). The spread of true and false news online. *Science*, *359*(6380), 1146–1151. DOI: 10.1126/science.aap9559 PMID: 29590045

Wade, C. (1995). Using writing to develop and assess critical thinking. *Teaching of Psychology*, *22*(1), 24–28. DOI: 10.1207/s15328023top2201_8

Walter, Y. (2024). Embracing the future of Artificial Intelligence in the classroom: The relevance of AI literacy, prompt engineering, and critical thinking in modern education. *International Journal of Educational Technology in Higher Education*, *21*(1), 15. Advance online publication. DOI: 10.1186/s41239-024-00448-3

Weiser, S. (2019, April 8). Requirements of Trustworthy AI - FUTURIUM - European Commission. FUTURIUM - European Commission.

Wilson, L. O. (2016). Anderson and Krathwohl Bloom's taxonomy revised understanding the new version of Bloom's taxonomy. *The Second Principle*, *1*(1), 1–8.

Winstone, N., & Boud, D. (2019). Exploring cultures of feedback practice: The adoption of learning-focused feedback practices in the UK and Australia. *Higher Education Research & Development*, *38*(2), 411–425. DOI: 10.1080/07294360.2018.1532985

Wu, Y., & Koutstaal, W. (2020). Charting the contributions of cognitive flexibility to creativity: Self-guided transitions as a process-based index of creativity-related adaptivity. *PLoS One*, *15*(6), e0234473. DOI: 10.1371/journal.pone.0234473 PMID: 32525947

Xia, Q., Chiu, T. K. F., Chai, C. S., & Xie, K. (2023). The mediating effects of needs satisfaction on the relationships between prior knowledge and self-regulated learning through artificial intelligence chatbot. *British Journal of Educational Technology*, *54*(4), 967–986. DOI: 10.1111/bjet.13305

Xu, W., Dainoff, M. J., Ge, L., & Gao, Z. (2022). Transitioning to Human Interaction with AI Systems: New Challenges and Opportunities for HCI Professionals to Enable Human-Centered AI. *International Journal of Human-Computer Interaction*, *39*(3), 494–518. DOI: 10.1080/10447318.2022.2041900

Yafie, E., Abu Samah, N., Mohamed, H., & Haqqi, Y. A. (2020). Collaborative Mobile Seamless Learning (CMSL) based on Android Apps to Improving Critical Thinking in Higher Education in the Post-Covid-19 Era. *Journal of Advanced Research in Dynamical and Control Systems*, *12*(SP7), 428–441. Advance online publication. DOI: 10.5373/JARDCS/V12SP7/20202125

Yi, Y. (2021). Establishing the concept of AI literacy. *JAHR*, *12*(2), 353–368. DOI: 10.21860/j.12.2.8

Yilmaz, F. G. K., & Keser, H. (2016). The impact of reflective thinking activities in e-learning: A critical review of the empirical research. *Computers & Education*, *95*, 163–173. DOI: 10.1016/j.compedu.2016.01.006

Zou, D., Xie, H., & Wang, F. L. (2022). Effects of technology enhanced peer, teacher and self-feedback on students' collaborative writing, critical thinking tendency and engagement in learning. *Journal of Computing in Higher Education*, *35*(1), 166–185. DOI: 10.1007/s12528-022-09337-y

Chapter 11
Critical Thinking and GenAI:
A Guide to Action

Silvio Andrae
https://orcid.org/0000-0002-8586-7812
Independent Researcher, Germany

ABSTRACT

Generative AI (GenAI) presents a dilemma: GenAI makes information more readily available but also reduces the likelihood that users will question or expand the information provided. This dilemma highlights the importance of fostering students' critical thinking skills. This chapter introduces a novel framework, the Learn, Evaluate, and Reflect (LER) methodology, designed to help individuals and organizations use GenAI effectively. This framework not only highlights the critical thinking processes needed to evaluate AI-generated results but also fosters collaboration between human intuition and machine intelligence, inviting everyone to be part of the AI discourse. This exploration reflects a broader imperative: cultivating an AI-literate society that values critical thinking as a core skill in the age of intelligent machines.

INTRODUCTION

Critical thinking has become a cornerstone of decision-making and problem-solving in companies. In an era of rapid technological advancement, global interconnectedness, and ever-changing market dynamics, organizations face complex, multifaceted problems requiring nuanced solutions. However, a lack of critical

DOI: 10.4018/979-8-3373-4576-5.ch011

thinking is often cited as a cause of ineffective strategies, ill-conceived actions, and avoidable crises.

Critical thinking is more than the ability to analyze information. It involves synthesizing various data points, evaluating their validity, and drawing informed conclusions that lead to action. This skill is invaluable for organizations when dealing with uncertainty, adapting to disruptive innovation, and addressing systemic issues such as climate change, digital transformation, and workforce diversity.

However, the proliferation of digital tools and data-driven technologies has, paradoxically, obscured the importance of critical thinking. Automation and artificial intelligence (AI) promise efficiency and scalability, but they often foster a false sense of security by encouraging reliance on algorithmic outcomes without critical examination. This over-reliance risks compounding errors, perpetuating biases, and overlooking contextual subtleties for which only human reasoning can account. Bozkurt et al. (2024) argue that GenAI 'reflects worldviews that can reinforce existing biases and marginalize diverse voices. Furthermore, as using GenAI reshapes education, it risks eroding essential human elements—creativity, critical thinking, and empathy—and could displace meaningful human interactions with algorithmic solutions.' (p.487)

As companies increasingly integrate generative AI (GenAI) into their workflows, the need to cultivate critical thinking as a complementary skill to technology application has never been more urgent.

Daniel Willingham (2019), a cognitive scientist and author, offers a pragmatic framework for understanding critical thinking. According to Willingham, critical thinking is characterized by three key attributes: novelty, self-direction, and efficacy.

- **Novelty**: Critical thinking involves novel problems that cannot be solved simply by repeating learned solutions. This attribute underscores the importance of adaptability when dealing with unique challenges and circumstances.
- **Self-regulation**: Effective critical thinking involves self-regulation, where individuals independently develop solutions without relying solely on predefined steps or templates. It is in sharp contrast to rote memorization or following rules.
- **Effectiveness**: To qualify as critical thinking, the process must lead to conclusions or actions that are logical, evidence-based, and likely to produce desired outcomes.

These attributes clarify the cognitive depth required for critical thinking and distinguish it from simple problem-solving. Critical thinking involves evaluating assumptions, challenging established norms, iterating solutions, and engaging in objective situational analysis and decision-making. It is inherently reflexive and iterative, requiring practitioners to constantly reevaluate their conclusions in light of new evidence (Priem, 2018).

BACKGROUND

This nuanced definition is particularly relevant in the context of GenAI, which often presents statistically coherent results but could be more logical and correct. Humans must apply critical thinking to assess AI-generated content's relevance, bias, and potential impact to ensure that it aligns with real-world goals and ethical standards.

Generative AI represents a critical advance in artificial intelligence, with the ability to create new content such as text, images, music, and code. Large language models (LLMs) like GPT-4 and image generation tools like DALL-E are being applied across industries, from content creation and customer service to medical diagnostics and scientific research.

GenAI has revolutionized how companies approach tasks requiring creativity, scalability, and personalization. Companies use GenAI to design marketing content, optimize customer support, and extract actionable insights from complex data sets (Feuerriegel et al., 2024). Researchers use GenAI for hypothesis generation (Lu et al., 2024), while educators use it to design innovative teaching materials (Mollick & Mollick, 2023) or to provide students with different perspectives and feedback (Hyde et al., 2024; Chiu, 2024).

Chiarello et al. (2024) use a dataset of over 3.8 million tweets. The authors group 31,747 tasks with a specific case study on ChatGPT to present a snapshot of the current situation. The results show a wide range of applications, from programming support to creative content creation, underscoring LLMs' versatility. The analysis identifies six application areas for ChatGPT: human resources, programming, social media, office automation, search engines, and education.

Ruiz-Rojas et al. (2024) investigate the effects of generative AI tools on critical thinking and collaboration among university students. Of a predominantly female sample, 87 percent of respondents report that they already have some knowledge of generative AI tools. About 38 percent use them occasionally. The most popular tools include Canva 2024 (33%), Chat PDF (26%), and YOU.COM (24%). In addition, 64% of respondents believe these tools significantly improve their critical thinking skills.

Despite their versatility, the GenAI has limitations. One of the main issues is the 'black-box' nature of these systems, where the processes that lead to their results are opaque even to their developers. This lack of transparency raises questions about accountability and trustworthiness. Furthermore, GenAI is prone to hallucinations—

producing plausible but false or fabricated information—which can undermine the credibility of its outputs (Jones, 2024).

Lee et al. (2025) surveyed 319 knowledge workers to understand the role of critical thinking in GenAI usage. The study, based on 936 first-hand examples of GenAI use in work tasks, found that user-specific factors, particularly a user's self-confidence and trust in GenAI, significantly influence the use of critical thinking in GenAI-supported tasks and the effort invested.

However, there are also ethical concerns. GenAI systems trained on biased datasets risk reinforcing harmful stereotypes, while their potential misuse for disinformation, plagiarism, and other unethical activities poses significant societal risks (Dabis & Csáki, 2024). Furthermore, the reliance of technology on vast computational resources raises ecological concerns (Bashir et al., 2024).

These challenges underscore the indispensable role of human oversight. With critical thinking, organizations can avoid blindly implementing GenAI outputs, which can lead to suboptimal or even harmful outcomes. A prerequisite is that learners in schools and universities receive appropriate training on how to use GenAI.

This chapter examines the interplay between critical thinking and GenAI and argues that the two must coexist for organizations and individuals to responsibly harness AI's full potential (Larson et al., 2024). The goal is to emphasize the irreplaceable value of human critical thinking in an AI-driven world and propose actionable strategies for integrating critical thinking into AI-related workflows.

This chapter introduces a novel framework, the Learn, Evaluate, Reflect (LER) methodology, designed to help individuals and organizations use GenAI effectively. This framework highlights the critical thinking processes needed to evaluate AI-generated results and promotes collaboration between human intuition and machine intelligence.

By the end of this chapter, readers will have a deeper understanding of:

- The basic principles of critical thinking and their relevance to GenAI.
- The potential and limitations of GenAI in different contexts.
- Practical approaches that ensure human oversight enhances rather than undermines AI-driven decision-making.

The discussion aims to empower practitioners, educators, and policymakers to navigate the GenAI landscape with a critical mindset to maximize the benefits of the technology while minimizing its risks.

In the following sections, the chapter provides a comprehensive overview of the GenAI taxonomy, examines its symbiotic relationship with critical thinking, and introduces the LER methodology as a structured approach to action. This exploration reflects a broader imperative: cultivating an AI-literate society that values critical thinking as a core skill in the age of intelligent machines.

UNDERSTANDING GENERATIVE AI

What is Generative AI? Overview and Definitions

Generative artificial intelligence (AI) is a fascinating class of AI systems that have the potential to inspire awe. These systems are designed to generate new content, from texts, images, and music to complex data models and simulations. Unlike traditional AI models, which focus on classification or regression tasks, generative AI produces output that has not been explicitly programmed or predefined, mirroring human creativity and adaptability.

At its core, GenAI uses deep learning (DL) techniques, specifically neural networks such as generative adversarial networks (GANs), variational autoencoders (VAEs), and large language models (LLMs). These models are trained on large datasets by exposing them to a variety of examples, allowing them to recognize patterns, structures, and relationships. Once trained, they can then use this knowledge to generate new, contextual content.

Key features of GenAI include:

- **Creativity**: Producing novel results, such as unique images or coherent texts.
- **Scalability**: GenAI can quickly produce large amounts of content tailored to specific requirements.
- **Adaptability**: By training with different data sets, these systems can be used for various applications, such as entertainment, health, and education.

GenAI has become more relevant due to technological advances, access to large data sets, and improved algorithms. However, the technology also raises critical questions about originality, reliability, and ethical issues. These concerns, as highlighted by Dabis & Csáki in 2024, should make us all pause and consider the potential misuse of this powerful technology.

A Taxonomy of GenAI

GenAI encompasses various applications, each tailored to specific tasks and domains. This section explores a taxonomy of GenAI based on its primary outputs.

Text Generation

Large Language Models (LLMs) such as OpenAI's ChatGPT and Google's Bard are among the best-known applications of GenAI. These models are trained on substantial text corpora, which makes them powerful for:

- **Conversational AI:** LLMs simulate human-like dialog and provide users with coherent, context-appropriate responses.
- **Content Creation:** Text generation models are revolutionizing content creation from writing emails and articles to composing poetry and stories.
- **Language Translation:** Models like DeepL use similar generative capabilities to deliver nuanced translations.

The strength of LLMs lies in their ability to synthesize large amounts of information and produce coherent results. However, their reliance on training data introduces bias, and their inability to recognize factual accuracy often results in logical inconsistencies or hallucinations (Xu et al., 2024).

Image and Video Generation

Generative AI models such as DALL-E, Stable Diffusion, and MidJourney have made great strides in visual content creation. These tools enable users to create high-quality images and videos based on text instructions. Applications include:

- **Art and Design:** Artists and designers use these tools to design and create unique images.
- **Marketing:** GenAI helps develop visual elements for advertising campaigns.
- **Healthcare:** AI-generated medical images are used for training and diagnosis.

These models often rely on GANs and diffusion algorithms to generate realistic or stylized images. At the same time, they offer unparalleled creative possibilities, but concerns about intellectual property and authenticity still need to be addressed, mainly when the models replicate existing artwork or images (Chesterman, 2024).

Code Generation

In software development, generative AI tools such as GitHub Copilot and Amazon CodeWhisperer have transformed how programmers write code. These systems generate code snippets or entire scripts based on natural language descriptions or partial code inputs (Rahman & Watanobe, 2023; Walter, 2024). The main benefits are:

- **Productivity:** Developers can accelerate programming tasks by automating routine programming activities.
- **Learning Support:** Novice programmers benefit from in-context code suggestions and explanations.
- **Error Reduction:** GenAI can detect potential errors and suggest fixes.

However, the limitations are noteworthy. The generated code may inherit vulnerabilities or inefficiencies from the training data, necessitating human review to ensure safety and optimal performance.

Domain-Specific Applications

Generative AI is evolving beyond the general app lications to specialized solutions tailored to the needs of specific industries. In healthcare, for example, this technology generates synthetic medical data for research purposes, simulates drug interactions, and creates diagnostic suggestions. Adaptive learning platforms use GenAI to develop customized lesson plans and personalized assessments in education. The financial industry benefits from AI's ability to create synthetic data for stress-testing models and simulating trading scenarios. In game development, procedural content generation enables the dynamic design of game environments and storylines, leading to innovative gaming experiences.

These domain-specific applications illustrate GenAI's immense versatility. However, they also show the need for expertise to critically validate AI results. Only through a combination of technological progress and human expertise can the potential of these technologies be used responsibly and effectively.

Strengths and Limitations of GenAI

Generative AI, with its unimagined possibilities for innovation, is a beacon of hope for the future. This section delves into its strengths and limitations, paving the way for a brighter tomorrow.

A key strength of GenAI is its ability to create content that appears novel and original. For example, text-generation tools can write articles on niche topics, and image-generation models can produce artwork in unique styles. However, behind this novelty often lies a fundamental limitation: the models do not 'create' in the human sense but recombine and extrapolate patterns from their training data.

While this imitation enables high-quality results, it raises questions about intellectual property and authenticity. The technology's reliance on training data means that AI can unintentionally reproduce copyrighted material or perpetuate existing biases in the data.

Generative AI models often produce factually incorrect or logically inconsistent results—a phenomenon known as a 'hallucination.' It happens because models prioritize statistical plausibility over factual accuracy. They have no fundamental understanding of the content they generate. For example, an LLM could confidently state a false historical fact or create a fictitious quote for a non-existent source. Such errors underscore the importance of human control over AI-generated results, reassuring us of our indispensable role in this process.

Mitigation strategies include fine-tuning the models with domain-specific data, integrating various review steps into workflows, and developing hybrid systems in which human critical thinking complements AI generation.

Generative AI models are only as good as the data on which they are trained. This dependency poses two significant challenges:

- **Data Bias:** If training data reflects societal biases, those biases will likely be reproduced in AI outputs. For example, text models may reinforce stereotypes, and image models may underrepresent minority groups.
- **Data Quality:** Poor quality data can lead to poor quality outputs, making model training a critical bottleneck.

Overcoming these challenges requires compiling diverse and representative data sets. Techniques for detecting and mitigating biases can also be used. Finally, models can be regularly adjusted to reflect evolving norms and knowledge, such as changes in societal attitudes or advancements in scientific understanding.

Understanding GenAI necessitates grappling with its dual nature: its capacity for unprecedented innovation and the limits that require careful monitoring. This chapter has outlined the basic concepts, applications, and challenges of GenAI, underscoring the pivotal role of critical thinking in maximizing its potential (Mogavi et al., 2024). The next chapter will explore how critical thinking can bridge the gap between human judgment and machine intelligence, empowering us to ensure the responsible and effective use of GenAI.

THE ROLE OF CRITICAL THINKING IN THE GENAI ERA

Why Critical Thinking Matters More Than Ever

In the era of GenAI, including ChatGPT, DALL-E, and GitHub Copilot, critical thinking has emerged as an essential skill. Successful critical thinking involves not only the ability to work cognitively in the face of novelty, self-regulation, and effectiveness (Willingham, 2019), but also a keen interest in building on reflectivity, embodiment, and emotion (Lindebaum & Fleming, 2024). It's not just about asking questions; successful critical thinking demands a commitment to thorough questioning (Larson et al., 2024; Andrae, 2025).

The increasing prevalence of AI systems capable of generating coherent, creative, and contextually relevant content presents opportunities and challenges. AI is excellent at processing and synthesizing vast amounts of data, enabling students to access a broader range of perspectives and information (Hyde et al., 2024). However, their outputs often require human scrutiny to ensure reliability, relevance, and ethical compliance. For Dabis and Csáki (2024), the key ethical dimensions associated with using GenAI in academia are identified: accountability, human oversight, transparency, or inclusivity.

The importance of critical thinking is underscored by the dual nature of GenAI. On one hand, these systems significantly enhance productivity, enabling professionals to accomplish in minutes what used to take hours. However, the manner in which GenAI presents information can lead users to accept it uncritically. This uncritical acceptance, in turn, can lead to a lack of genuine understanding of AI models, making their results susceptible to inaccuracies, biases, and even hallucinations. By exercising critical thinking, users can avoid passively accepting AI-generated content, thereby averting flawed decisions and unintended consequences (Lindebaum & Fleming, 2024). This emphasis on the potential pitfalls of uncritical acceptance should make readers more cautious and aware in their interactions with AI.

Critical thinking plays a pivotal role in enabling individuals to evaluate the validity and credibility of AI results. For instance, by encouraging students to ask the AI to identify errors in a text or to present counter-arguments to an argument, they can actively engage with the AI's outputs (Hyde et al., 2024). This ability to discern between plausible and factual information, to identify potential biases in data, and to question the ethical implications of AI-generated decisions, is not just a supplementary skill. It is an essential prerequisite for bridging the gap between human judgment and machine capabilities. By stressing this role, readers should feel more integral to the AI process, rather than passive recipients of its outputs.

The Interaction Between Human Cognition and Machine Output

The synergy between human cognition and GenAI is based on an iterative input, output, and feedback process. Humans provide prompts and context that guide the AI in content generation. The AI, in turn, produces results that humans evaluate, refine, and contextualize.

'When humans seek and critically reflect upon information provided by other humans, their assumptions regarding relevant source-related features (e.g., social boundedness, fallibility, empathy, fairness) are likely to differ compared to their assumptions regarding information received from 'traditional' machines. However, GenAI does not fall neatly into either one of these categories.' (Larson et al., 2024, p.376)

This interaction highlights the distinct yet complementary roles of humans and machines. AI systems do an excellent job at pattern recognition, data synthesis, and content generation at scale. However, they lack the cognitive and emotional depth required for nuanced understanding, ethical considerations, and values-driven decision-making (Dabis & Csáki, 2024).

For example:

- **Scenario 1**: A journalist uses an LLM to write an article. The AI creates a coherent narrative based on the available data. However, the journalist's role in verifying the facts, recognizing potential bias, and ensuring the article is consistent with journalistic ethics is crucial. This validation process is where human expertise shines.·
- **Scenario 2**: A marketing team uses DALL-E to create visual content. While the AI produces impressive visuals, the designers' role in ensuring the images align with brand identity and avoiding cultural insensitivity is indispensable. This oversight is a testament to the unique skills of human designers.

In both scenarios, the need for human interpretation, validation, and contextualization of AI-generated content is irreplaceable. The interaction underscores the importance of humans in viewing AI as a tool rather than a replacement for critical thinking and creativity.

Limits of AI as 'Machine Thinking'

Can AI really 'think'? Generative AI systems simulate thought processes but lack actual cognition. They work based on statistical associations and pattern recognition rather than understanding or reasoning. AI models produce results by analyzing training data and predicting the most likely sequence of words, pixels, or codes based on context. This process fundamentally differs from human reasoning, which involves introspection, creativity, and value judgments.

For example:

- AI can provide a plausible answer to a philosophical question, but it does not understand the abstract concepts or moral implications behind its words.
- An AI model can recommend a financial strategy based on historical data but does not understand the potential risks or ethical considerations involved.

'Machine thinking' risks confusing AI's computational processes with human cognition. While AI can mimic certain aspects of human thought, it lacks the self-awareness, empathy, and value-based reasoning that characterize critical thinking.

Outsourcing critical thinking to AI systems carries several risks:

Excessive cognitive trust in AI outputs. Users may place undue trust in AI content, assuming it is correct or unbiased. It can lead people to assume that the results are objective and coherent, ignoring the biases contained in the training data (Bender et al., 2021). This can lead to erroneous decisions, especially in high-stakes domains such as healthcare, law, and finance.

Excessive emotional trust. The GenAI output may exhibit human-like characteristics from its syntax, including greater empathy and readability than human experts (Chen et al., 2024). It can additionally evoke emotional trust in the user in addition to cognitive trust (Glikson & Woolley, 2020). As a result, the way GenAI presents information may reduce the likelihood of a user engaging in individual critical thinking.

Loss of cognitive skills. Reliance on AI tools can erode critical thinking skills as users become passive recipients of AI results rather than actively evaluating them (Lindebaum & Fleming, 2024). Using an experimental design, Putra and Abdunnafi (2024) compared two groups of fourth-year undergraduate students in an accredited accounting program: one group that used LLM and a control group that did not use LLM. The results show a significant decrease in critical thinking skills among students who used LLM, while the control group increased. These results suggest that over-reliance on LLM can hinder the development of important cognitive and professional skills.

Ethical blind spots. AI systems lack the moral judgment to cope with ethical dilemmas (including lying and strategic deception). Such behavior is not only observed when the models are instructed to deceive (Hagendorff, 2024). It also occurs when the AI systems are not instructed to do so (Scheurer et al., 2024). Thus, outsourcing critical thinking to AI could lead to decisions that contradict societal values or ethical norms.

Persistence of biases. AI models may reinforce stereotypes or perpetuate systemic inequalities when trained on biased data. Gender, race, and Western biases inherent in GenAI training data may be perpetuated (Bianchi et al., 2023). Critical thinking is important to recognize and eliminate these biases.

The consequences of uncritical trust in GenAI could be significant. It should be emphasized that students continue uncritically accepting GenAI results when they move outside the academic environment (Larson et al., 2024). Since business schools educate future leaders and managers who will encounter AI-generated results in their work (English, 2023), developing critical thinking skills is crucial.

Addressing these challenges requires a balanced approach to AI integration, one in which critical thinking remains at the core of human oversight and decision-making.

Key Attributes of Human Critical Thinking in Relation to AI

Critical thinking is crucial to responsibly navigating the complexities and challenges of GenAI. It starts with questioning fundamental assumptions underlying the results. This includes checking training data for representativeness and lack of bias to ensure that systematic distortions or exclusions do not distort the data sets. Algorithms must also be critically examined, as they may contain inherent assumptions that exclude specific perspectives or distort results. It is equally important to check input prompts and their context: Are they formulated, free of bias, and aligned with the desired objectives? For example, when using AI-generated forecasts, a financial analyst should question whether the underlying data includes relevant market anomalies or geopolitical risks. They should also ensure that the input prompts are clear and unambiguous, and that the context in which the AI operates is well-defined. This critical questioning can reveal potential errors and adjust the results to real-world conditions.

Another key aspect is recognizing biases and inaccuracies. GenAI, which relies on historical data, often reflects systematic biases, making critical thinking all the more important. Users should cross-check results with reliable sources, analyze patterns for potential biases, and apply their expertise to evaluate the credibility and relevance of AI-generated content. For example, a doctor using AI for diagnostic support must ensure that possible biases in the training data, such as overrepresentation of certain demographics, do not promote misdiagnoses or unequal treatment recommendations. Similarly, an educator using AI to develop teaching materials should be aware of potential biases in the historical data that could lead to a skewed representation of certain topics.

Furthermore, critical thinking requires assessing the logical consistency of AI results and the ability to solve problems that AI cannot handle. While AI is excellent at pattern recognition and content creation, it reaches its limits when interpreting context, unforeseen scenarios, and ethical value judgments. It can misunderstand contextual nuances, fail in novel situations, and cannot weigh competing values against each other. For example, educators using AI to create curricula must ensure the generated content is logically structured and aligned with educational objectives. Likewise, a policymaker using AI-generated projections must ensure that cultural sensitivities or political dynamics that the AI may have overlooked are considered.

Overall, critical thinking is not just a response to the limitations of GenAI, but a pathway to overcoming them. It is essential to maximize the potential of GenAI while recognizing and addressing its limitations. By questioning assumptions, identifying biases, and checking logical inconsistencies, humans can create a productive symbiosis between human judgment and machine intelligence. This symbiosis increases the innovative power of the technology and promotes ethical decision-making that considers both the strengths and weaknesses of GenAI, instilling a sense of optimism and hope for the future of AI.

LEVERAGING CRITICAL THINKING TO IMPROVE GENAI OUTPUTS

Human Intervention in AI Processes: Roles and Responsibilities

Human intervention is critical to the responsible and effective use of GenAI. While these systems can independently produce text, images, codes, and other outputs, they lack the judgment to recognize context, relevance, and ethical implications. Therefore, humans are versatile in guiding, refining, and monitoring AI processes.

Human intervention is not just critical, but empowering to the responsible and effective use of GenAI. These systems, while capable of independent generation of text, images, codes, and other results, lack the judgment to consider context, relevance, and ethical implications. Therefore, humans play a versatile and integral role in guiding, refining, and monitoring AI processes, which is essential to overcome GenAI's limitations.

A key role is played by so-called prompt engineers, who formulate precise inputs to guide GenAI in delivering context-dependent and high-quality results. The accuracy and quality of answers from systems like ChatGPT vary greatly depending on the input, available training data, and the complexity of the task. Prompt engineering (PE) presents an AI assistant with a problem, context, and constraints clearly and understandably to achieve precise results (Kocoń et al., 2023; Federiakin et al., 2024). It is especially relevant as current Large Language Models (LLMs) still struggle with in-depth comprehension and critical thinking (Roumeliotis & Tselikas, 2023).

In addition to prompt engineers, evaluators play a central role by critically examining AI-generated content's quality, relevance, and accuracy. Equally important are ethical reviewers, who ensure that the content is free of bias, adheres to ethical standards, and minimizes potential harm. Subject matter experts contribute to validating content through their expertise, especially in fields such as medicine, law, or education. In this context, the ability to contextualize is critical: expert knowledge makes it possible to incorporate relevant factors and details into the input, significantly increasing the chances of accurate and meaningful answers (Hié &

Thouary, 2023). Finally, feedback providers offer iterative feedback to optimize AI performance and refine its results.

Human actors have several responsibilities, each of which is crucial. They act as vigilant guardians of correctness by ensuring that AI-generated content is factually accurate and avoids logical errors. As bias detectors, they identify and mitigate distortions from flawed training data or algorithmic processes. Ethical stewards, in turn, uphold core values such as fairness, accountability, and transparency in the application of AI.

Human intervention is not just a check and balance, but a necessary and valued complement to address GenAI's limitations. It transforms raw data generated by AI into reliable, actionable insights and ensures that these technologies can be used responsibly and effectively.

The following example shows how to think through ethical dilemmas for students in the bachelor's program in Business Communication. The example is taken from Risvold et al. (2024). Before the lesson begins, students receive a specific prompt. They are instructed to copy and paste the prompt into their ChatGPT accounts. It is important to note that the rules and steps of the prompt tell the bot how to behave. Once the learner submits the prompt, ChatGPT will create an ethical dilemma, along with the three discussion questions and the required list of components that the learner must address. Until the learner has answered the questions and provided the information listed in the list, the system will continue to prompt the learner to fulfill all components. These components are listed a through d, as indicated below. Once the student has provided the required answers, ChatGPT becomes an expert debater and presents a response that challenges the student's position by offering the opposite perspective. The student then responds to this 'debate,' and ChatGPT grades the student's final answer.

Here is the prompt we use for this assignment:

Act as an expert professor in business ethics. Create an ethical dilemma that involves an entry-level finance employee.

Rule: The dilemma should be complex. Right versus wrong should not be explicit. Please do NOT provide analysis.

Now, please follow these steps:

1. Create three discussion questions.
2. After the user's response, create three more questions, UNLESS the response does NOT include all the following components:
   a) An overview of the ethical situation
   b) A list of options
   c) A list of stakeholders
   d) A recommended action

a) An overview of the ethical situation
b) A list of options
c) A list of stakeholders
d) A recommended action

3. If the responses are missing any of the components, please ask the user to provide the missing component.
4. If all the components are provided, then act as expert debater and present an opposite perspective.
5. Wait for a final statement from the user.
6. Once the user provides the final statement, evaluate the quality of the responses based on the detail of the user's responses, user's use of evidence, and ethical validity.

The benefit of having these conversations in class with ChatGPT is that students often move beyond the initial level of thinking about the ethics of the dilemma. Learners reach the secondary and tertiary levels of thinking. They ask themselves more sophisticated questions, which gives them a sense of accomplishment and boosts their confidence: Why is a particular reaction important? What are the implications of good or bad decisions? Which learned concepts can be applied to make ethical decisions and act ethically?

Evaluating GenAI Outputs: Strategies and Frameworks

Effectively evaluating GenAI outputs empowers you with a structured approach that combines technical analysis and critical thinking. This method ensures that the outputs meet desired quality standards and are aligned with intended objectives, giving you the confidence in your AI evaluation skills.

Strategies for evaluation include:

- **Fact checking**: Verifying the accuracy of information against trusted sources.
- **Contextual analysis**: Assessing whether the results are appropriate for the given context and target audience.
- **Uncovering biases**: Detecting and addressing patterns of unfairness or discrimination.
- **Relevance assessment**: Ensuring the results are directly aligned with the input prompts and objectives.
- **Ethical review**: Assessing AI-generated content's potential societal and moral implications.

There are several points of reference for the systematic evaluation of GenAI results:

- **LER methodology**: The LER (Learn-Evaluate-Reflect) approach emphasizes iterative evaluation to refine results and improve AI systems over time (Section 5).
- **HITL (Human-in-the-Loop)**: This dynamic framework wherein human evaluators intervene at critical points in the AI lifecycle to guide the results (Mosqueira-Rey et al., 2023).
- **PAIR (People + AI Research)**: This is a Google initiative that proposes human-centered evaluation metrics focusing on usability and interpretability (Ma et al., 2023).

These strategies and frameworks underscore the importance of your human critical thinking in bridging the gap between AI capabilities and human expectations, making you feel more valued and integral to the AI evaluation process.

Ethical Considerations: Trust, Accountability, and Transparency

Integrating AI into decision-making processes and content creation presents significant ethical challenges. Trust, accountability, and transparency must be addressed to ensure that AI systems are used responsibly (Dabis & Csáki, 2024).

Transparency is a cornerstone in maintaining trust in AI systems. Users' ability to understand the results and the process by which they are obtained is crucial. This understanding not only increases trust in the system's recommendations but also promotes responsible use of AI technologies. Consistency, reliability, and verifiability of results are equally important. Transparent processes for monitoring and optimizing the systems further help to ensure that all stakeholders can develop trust in the technology.

Responsibility for AI-supported decisions and content requires a clear division of roles between human actors and technology. Only if responsibilities are clearly defined can errors be traced and those responsible held accountable. Audit trails that document all decisions and processes also enable detailed retrospective analysis. It is complemented by ethical governance frameworks that ensure all AI applications are aligned with societal values and norms, providing a sense of security and confidence.

Companies must openly communicate their AI systems' capabilities and limitations. This includes disclosing the training data and algorithms so that users can better assess potential biases and restrictions. Inclusive design, which involves various stakeholders in developing and deploying AI, helps ensure that the systems consider society's diverse perspectives and needs.

Human-machine collaboration is a powerful tool in improving the quality of content and decisions. Case studies demonstrate that this collaboration can leverage GenAI's strengths while minimizing its weaknesses. This not only showcases the potential of AI technologies when used responsibly but also underscores the need for ethical considerations such as trust, accountability, and transparency to always be at the center of implementation.

Critical thinking remains essential to managing the complexity of ethical issues and ensuring that AI systems act as supportive tools rather than cause potential harm. The symbiotic relationship between human judgment and AI capabilities is ultimately key to fully realizing GenAI's transformative potential, empowering the audience and making them feel in control (Andrae, 2025).

THE LER METHODOLOGY: A NEW FRAMEWORK FOR ACTION

Introduction to LER: Learn, Evaluate, Reflect

As GenAI increasingly permeates organizational decision-making, education, and societal structures, a structured approach to engaging with AI is critical. The LER methodology—Learn, Evaluate, Reflect—not only provides a practical framework for harnessing critical thinking in human-AI collaboration (Valova et al., 2024), but also offers significant benefits such as improved decision-making and enhanced learning.

This chapter explores how LER empowers users to use GenAI outputs effectively. It focuses on understanding AI's capabilities and limitations, critically evaluating its results, and fostering adaptive human-AI interactions through reflected practices. By employing LER, individuals and organizations can build trust, enhance accountability, and most importantly, achieve meaningful outcomes in GenAI applications.

Learn: Acquiring Knowledge and Context

The learning phase of the LER framework is a crucial step that lays the foundation for understanding and interacting with GenAI. It focuses on acquiring basic knowledge about AI technologies, their possibilities, and their limitations. This knowledge is essential for making informed decisions about how to interact with GenAI.

Empower yourself by critically analyzing GenAI's strengths and weaknesses. GenAI's strengths lie primarily in its ability to process large amounts of data quickly and efficiently, generate diverse content such as texts or images with high precision, and promote human creativity by providing alternative perspectives.

At the same time, GenAI has significant limitations. It heavily depends on the quality of its training data, which may contain biases or inaccuracies. It also lacks contextual understanding and emotional intelligence, which makes it prone to logical inconsistencies, so-called hallucinations, or excessive generalizations. A sound understanding of these characteristics helps users develop a balanced perspective on GenAI, and neither trust the technology blindly nor show it excessive skepticism. Huber et al. (2024) recommend using gamified approaches to strengthen human judgment and domain-specific expertise through practical training.

The second central aspect of the learning phase is building a solid knowledge base:

1. Developing expertise is a key requirement for users to critically evaluate GenAI's results. Users need a deep understanding of their respective fields. For example, medical professionals using AI-based diagnostic tools must have sufficient medical knowledge to contextualize and validate the AI's recommendations meaningfully.
2. Socially critical thinking: Socially critical thinking enables users to interpret the content generated by GenAI with an awareness of social norms and values. It encourages them to question the apparent universal truths expressed by AI models. At the same time, this thinking helps to be aware of the dangers of possible misuse of GenAI by institutions or organizations (Larson et al., 2024).
3. Understanding of AI ethics is not just important, it's essential. Ethical knowledge is necessary to anticipate and avoid potential harm from using AI. It includes topics such as bias, fairness, and accountability. Users must know that moral and legal responsibility remains with humans even when AI systems are involved in decision-making (Dabis & Csáki, 2024).
4. Interdisciplinary awareness is key. Understanding GenAI's societal impact requires a combination of technological knowledge, philosophical reflection, and sociological understanding. This interdisciplinary awareness allows GenAI to be viewed in a broader context and its use to be aligned with ethical and social standards (Rakowski & Kowaliková, 2024).

The learning phase thus lays the foundation for the next phase of the LER framework, which focuses on evaluating GenAI spending using critical thinking. It promotes an in-depth understanding of the technology and enables users to apply GenAI effectively, responsibly, and context-sensitively.

Evaluate: Applying Critical Thinking to AI Outputs

The evaluation phase of the LER framework is GenAI's critical analysis of results. This phase empowers users to ensure that AI-generated content meets factual, ethical, and contextual expectations. By recognizing and addressing AI output's logical and methodological weaknesses, users take control of the process, enhancing the quality of the results.

A key aspect of the evaluation is identifying logical fallacies that can occur in AI-generated results. These include false causality, in which connections are interpreted as causal relationships when they are merely correlative. Equally common is overgeneralization, in which conclusions are drawn from limited or inadequate data. Another critical point is confirmation bias, in which existing beliefs are reinforced by selectively interpreting AI results.

In addition to logical fallacies, it is important to recognize AI systems' biases. One common source is bias in the training data, where certain demographic groups are over- or underrepresented. These inequalities are reflected in the results and can lead to systematic disadvantages. Algorithmic biases that arise unintentionally during model development can also influence the results. To identify and address these, users can [insert practical steps here]. Critical thinking enables users to identify these problems and improve the fairness and reliability of AI applications.

The evaluation phase also requires the development of appropriate metrics to measure the quality of the AI results. This is a crucial aspect of the process, as it allows users to play a significant role in determining the effectiveness of the AI system. Important criteria include:

1. **Accuracy and relevance**: The results must be consistent with the context and purpose of the original input. This is the only way to guarantee that the content meets requirements.
2. **Explainability**: The reasoning behind AI results should be clear and comprehensible to ensure trust and transparency. Users must be able to understand the processes behind the generated content.
3. **Cultural sensitivity**: Another criterion is to evaluate whether the content respects different cultural norms and values. This is especially important in global and diversified contexts, where cultural misunderstandings can have serious consequences.

Establishing solid evaluation metrics is key to promoting accountability in AI processes and reducing the gap between human expectations and machine performance. This phase highlights the need to consistently apply critical thinking to ensure AI-generated content's quality, relevance, and ethical appropriateness. It is how technology becomes an effective and responsible tool.

Reflect: Enhancing Human-AI Collaboration

The 'Reflect' phase within the LER framework is a powerful tool that empowers us to make iterative improvements and employ adaptive strategies to fully harness the potential of human-AI partnerships. This phase allows us to take control, conducting continuous reflection on the interaction between humans and AI to optimize the learning process and refine the results.

Iterative feedback loops play a central role here. Both humans and AI systems benefit from the continuous refinement of their collaboration. Human feedback leads to a steady improvement in AI performance as it helps the algorithms better adapt to users' needs and requirements. At the same time, the insights gained from AI provide valuable insights that can expand the expertise of the users and strengthen their decision-making. One example is a financial analyst who uses AI to analyze market trends: by continuously adjusting the model parameters based on new data and specific investment objectives, the analyst can continuously improve the relevance of the AI-based analyses.

Furthermore, reflection fosters a reciprocal relationship in which humans guide the AI systems and expand their knowledge with the insights gained from the AI. It creates a dynamic interaction in which both sides continuously develop and work together to find solutions to complex problems, inspiring us to keep pushing the boundaries of what's possible.

Another important aspect of the 'reflect' phase is adapting human skills to complement AI's strengths. While AI can process large amounts of data quickly and make accurate predictions, humans bring the creativity that AI cannot produce based on its training data. By contributing unconventional ideas and innovative approaches, humans play a crucial role in further refining the AI-supported results, making us feel valued and integral to the process.

The 'Reflect' phase also underscores the importance of human oversight in AI decision-making. Humans play a crucial role in addressing ethical dilemmas that AI cannot solve independently. While AI models can recognize patterns and make decisions based on data, they often need human intervention with complex ethical issues that arise in practical use cases. In this context, the human's role is to ensure that decisions are made on ethical principles.

Overall, reflection ensures that the interaction between humans and AI does not remain static but continues to evolve. This adaptability is crucial to address complex challenges while balancing efficiency and ethical considerations effectively. Only through continuous reflection can humans and AI work together in a symbiotic partnership that fully exploits both sides' potential.

Implementation in Education

The integration of the LER (learning, evaluating, reflecting) framework into curricula provides a crucial basis for preparing future generations for the challenges of a world shaped by AI (Dempere et al., 2024). Schools play a key role in teaching critical thinking as a fundamental skill that enables learners to engage responsibly and reflectively with AI's possibilities and limitations.

There are several core components to integrating LER into the school curriculum. First, students need to learn how to question and evaluate AI results based on real-world scenarios in critical thinking modules. This can be adapted for different age groups, with younger students focusing on simpler AI concepts and older students engaging with more complex scenarios. One example is reviewing GenAI-generated texts, such as essays, to question the quality and potential of such technologies regarding authenticity and accuracy. Another important building block is the promotion of AI literacy, which involves teaching basic knowledge about AI technologies. Early awareness of the capabilities and limitations of AI is crucial to enable students to use the technology responsibly and critically. Complementing this, using interactive learning methods, such as AI tools in the classroom, enables experiential learning and collaborative problem-solving, which is particularly beneficial for developing practical skills in AI analysis (Xu, 2023).

In higher education, applying the LER framework is gaining importance in ensuring that graduates from different disciplines not only understand the technological possibilities of GenAI but can also use it responsibly. In profession-specific courses of study, such as law, medicine, or engineering, the integration of LER ensures that students understand both the technical and ethical implications of AI in their respective fields. For instance, in a law course, students could evaluate the use of AI in legal research and its potential impact on the justice system. In medicine, students could learn to critically assess the use of AI in diagnosis and treatment. It empowers them to use AI in a way that meets the requirements of their professional discipline. In addition, the university provides a valuable platform for addressing ethical and political issues around the use of AI, such as courses on AI ethics, governance, and policy that help students understand the broader societal implications of AI. In addition, by promoting interdisciplinary research in AI, the foundation for innovation and critical analysis is laid, enabling future leaders to use AI responsibly and ethically soundly (Rejeb et al., 2024).

However, it's important to note that implementing the LER framework in education may also present some challenges. For instance, there may be a lack of resources or expertise in AI education, or resistance to change from traditional teaching methods. Overcoming these challenges will require a concerted effort from educators, policymakers, and other stakeholders. Overall, implementing the LER framework in education ensures that future generations develop not only the technical skills to work with AI but also the critical thinking skills needed to address the ethical, social, and policy challenges associated with the technology. This comprehensive preparation empowers learners to maximize the potential of GenAI while recognizing its limitations and acting responsibly. The LER framework enables users to balance the benefits of AI and the necessary ethical considerations, thus promoting a future-oriented and human-centered use of technology.

CHALLENGES AND FUTURE DIRECTION

Overcoming Barriers to Critical Thinking in AI Contexts

Generative AI, a transformative force in industry and personal productivity, holds immense potential that can be fully realized by overcoming challenges related to human engagement. The power of critical thinking, central to the responsible use of GenAI, is hindered by significant obstacles.

Cognitive overload. The vast possibilities of GenAI can overwhelm users. AI systems generate extensive data and recommendations and require users to sift through complex results while considering the decision-making objectives. For example, a lawyer using AI to analyze a contract could be cognitively overwhelmed when reviewing the system's nuanced suggestions. Interfaces must, above all, be clear and concise to avoid cognitive overload. Graduated levels of detail—starting with summaries and the option to drill down into the details—can reduce mental strain.

Moreover, the integration of visual aids such as graphics and diagrams can significantly enhance users' ability to process large amounts of information. Liang and Wu (2024) view ChatGPT as a valuable tool for learners of English as a foreign language (EFL) to enhance cognition. They stress the crucial role of maintaining a balance between technology and human thought processes in the development of critical thinking skills, reassuring us about the continued importance of human cognition in the AI era.

Automation bias, a tendency to favor the decisions made by AI systems over human judgment, can be a significant challenge. This bias can lead users to assume that AI-generated results are inherently correct, especially in high-stakes areas like healthcare or finance. However, unquestioned trust in AI can lead to adverse outcomes. Training programs that promote skepticism and critical evaluation of AI results are crucial. For example, a doctor using AI for diagnostic purposes must cross-check the suggestions generated by the AI with traditional diagnostic methods to ensure accuracy.

Another challenge is the limited user knowledge of AI, which exacerbates the difficulties in critically handling GenAI. Many users need to understand the underlying principles of AI, leading to unrealistic expectations or uncritical acceptance of the results. Governments, academic institutions, and private organizations must collaborate through educational initiatives to integrate AI literacy into the curricula of schools and workplace training programs. Equally important is the need for developers to design user-friendly documentation and instructions that demystify AI processes, providing users with the support and guidance they need.

Improving AI literacy empowers users to approach AI with informed skepticism and fosters a culture of critical inquiry. 'The better students are at communicating with AI, the more likely it is that they will have seamless and rewarding learning experiences as they use AI to deepen their understanding of complex concepts, find solutions to problems, or explore new areas of knowledge'. (Hié & Thouary, 2023).

Munn and Henrickson (2024) develop a framework contributing to a more comprehensive understanding of LLMs. It is designed to promote textual literacy to support the development of technical literacy in formal or public pedagogical spaces. The framework includes four methods of inquiry for critically examining LLMs:

'*Tell me my story* employs more personal language to probe a model's ability to act in empathetic or therapeutic ways. *Tell me our story* uses thorny questions to test the system's ability to accurately reproduce knowledge and extrapolate from its temporally and epistemically limited training data. And *Tell me 'their' story* intentionally pursues 'marginal' (in this case Indigenous) knowledge to reveal the dominant viewpoints and begin a broader conversation about the biases and ideologies baked into these models.' (Munn & Henrickson, 2024)

Lee and Low (2024) suggest that teachers model how students can use GenAI meaningfully and ethically. Another suggestion could be to use formative assessments with clear guidelines for using GenAI that focus more on the learning process than the product itself. However, it's important to note that there may be challenges in implementing these strategies, such as ensuring students understand the ethical implications of using GenAI. Chan's (2023) 3R framework encourages students to report using GenAI tools, revise their results, and reflect on the process. This framework views AI-assisted writing as fundamental writing that leads to specific writing goals. Another ethical safeguard could be requiring students to declare the originality of their work, as this has proven to be an effective means of preventing academic dishonesty in the past (Borup, 2023).

Future Trends in GenAI Development

The future of GenAI is promising, as it is poised to evolve into a tool that enhances human intelligence rather than replacing it. Exciting trends are emerging to address the challenges of logical reasoning and foster collaboration between humans and AI, instilling optimism in the AI community.

Despite recent progress, GenAI struggles with logical consistency and reasoning. Large language models (LLMs) like ChatGPT can mimic reasoning by recognizing patterns but often cannot perform rigorous deductive or causal analysis (Li et al., 2024). 'Have modern chatbots passed the Turing Test? Moreover, should we grant them thinking status, as Turing proposed? Surprisingly, given the Turing Test's broad cultural importance, there is little agreement in the AI community on the criteria for passing and much doubt about whether having conversational skills that can fool a human reveals anything about a system's underlying intelligence or 'thinking status'.' (Mitchell, 2024).

Developments in logical AI:

1. **Neuro-symbolic approaches**: Combining neural networks with symbolic reasoning improves AI's ability to handle structured logic. For example, hybrid models can integrate rule-based systems to validate inferences against predefined logical frameworks.
2. **Advances in reinforcement learning**: AI systems trained with reinforcement learning algorithms are beginning to simulate step-by-step thinking, enabling them to solve problems logically.

These advancements are crucial in bridging the gap between machine outcomes and human-like thinking as AI evolves. They promise to significantly reduce errors such as hallucinations or overgeneralizations, providing reassurance about the progress in AI development.

The next phase of GenAI is set to foster symbiotic relationships between humans and machines. AI will not be viewed as a replacement for human cognition, but as a collaborator that augments human strengths with computational efficiency. This inclusive vision of AI's future includes:

- **Adaptive interfaces**: AI systems tailored to users' individual preferences and levels of knowledge will improve collaboration.
- **Collaborative problem solving**: Future AI systems can be integrated into human teams and contribute analytical insights while adapting to the team's evolving needs.

In urban planning, for example, AI could simulate sustainable development scenarios while human planners interpret and implement solutions based on nuanced sociopolitical factors.

The Role of Policymakers and Educators in Promoting Critical Thinking

Building a society capable of responsibly using GenAI requires coordinated efforts from policymakers and educators. These two groups play a central role in fostering a culture of critical thinking that empowers people to use AI ethically and responsibly.

Policymakers must take decisive action to create an ethical and transparent environment for using GenAI. First, they must develop robust standards and frameworks to ensure that AI is aligned with societal values. Transparency, accountability, and fairness should be emphasized to prevent the technology from being used in ways that negatively impact society. Another important step is the regulation and oversight of AI systems. Regular audits help identify biases and inaccuracies and ensure that AI applications meet ethical standards. One example is the European Union's AI Act, which provides risk-based classification to ensure that high-risk AI systems are subject to more stringent scrutiny. Ferdaus et al. (2024) emphasize that a combination of ethical oversight, industry accountability, regulation, and public participation is needed to guide the development of AI in the right direction. In addition, policymakers should launch public education campaigns to help citizens develop a critical understanding of AI and the importance of scrutinizing AI-generated information.

Educators, on the other hand, must integrate critical thinking into curricula at all levels of education. It can be done through specialized critical thinking modules that teach students to evaluate the credibility and relevance of AI-generated content, for example, by comparing it with verified data sources. It is also important that educational programs foster interdisciplinary learning by combining AI with traditional disciplines such as philosophy, ethics, and logic. This approach enriches students' understanding of the societal implications of AI and fosters their ability to question the technology in a social context. Another key aspect is experiential learning, in which students use interactive platforms to work directly with AI tools. It allows them to experience first-hand how AI is used in various areas, such as the creative writing task, and to recognize the strengths and weaknesses of the technology themselves. Doshi and Hauser (2024) point out that access to AI-powered ideas can boost the creative process, but it could also limit the collective novelty of content.

Given AI's dynamic nature, lifelong learning programs are also of great importance. Universities and training institutes should offer continuous professional development courses to help professionals familiarize themselves with the latest developments in

GenAI and develop their skills. In this way, educational institutions can produce a generation of professionals capable of using AI technically and ethically to address the complex challenges of an increasingly AI-driven world.

In summary, critical thinking and GenAI must go hand in hand to meet the demands of an increasingly AI-driven world. Overcoming cognitive overload and limited AI knowledge requires targeted measures such as user-friendly AI designs, sound educational programs, and legal frameworks. Policymakers and educators have an indispensable role in ensuring that these advances align with societal goals. Only by fostering a culture of critical engagement can GenAI be used as an innovation tool that both realizes its benefits and balances its limitations. A cross-disciplinary approach and proactive strategies will enable society to reap the full benefits of GenAI while ensuring ethical use.

CONCLUSION

Integrating GenAI into business practice has brought transformative capabilities that enable unprecedented efficiency, creativity, and problem-solving. This technological marvel, as this book chapter makes clear, has the potential to inspire a sense of wonder and excitement. However, the actual benefits of GenAI depend to a large extent on the critical thinking skills of human users. Only by adequately handling and incorporating human judgment can the full impact of GenAI be realized, adding a sense of awe to the audience's perception.

One key point is the complementarity of critical thinking and GenAI. While AI can process and analyze enormous amounts of data quickly, it remains dependent on data input and has limitations in interpretation and contextualization. Critical thinking is, therefore, indispensable for evaluating, questioning, and supplementing the results of AI. It serves as a necessary counterweight to the limitations of AI and ensures that the content provided by GenAI is both logically and ethically consistent. Only by applying critical thinking can biases, inaccuracies, and potential ethical dilemmas in the AI's results be identified and corrected promptly. However, it should also be noted that greater trust in GenAI is associated with less critical thinking, while greater self-confidence is associated with more critical thinking. Qualitatively, GenAI shifts the nature of critical thinking toward information verification, response integration, and task management (Lee et al., 2025).

The taxonomy of GenAI, which ranges from text generation to domain-specific applications, shows the versatility of this technology. GenAI can be used in various areas, from automated content creation to the analysis of complex scientific data. Understanding its diverse capabilities and limitations is crucial to using these technologies effectively and responsibly. In this way, AI tailored to specific fields of application can be used to develop creative and efficient solutions. At the same time, however, it requires critical understanding to maximize its effectiveness and applicability.

The LER ('Learn, Evaluate, Reflect') framework provides a structured approach that promotes collaboration between humans and AI. It emphasizes continuous improvement and the ethical use of GenAI. Through constant exchange and reflection, humans and AI can improve together and maximize AI's benefits without losing sight of its potential risks. The iterative nature of the LER approach ensures that human users not only act as passive users of AI but also as active shapers and refiners of its results.

Ultimately, the symbiosis between humans and AI is the key to the further development of GenAI. AI should not be seen as a replacement for human cognition but as a tool that complements it. Humans with critical thinking skills can guide, interpret, and, if necessary, adjust GenAI's results. Such a partnership can maximize the efficiency and precision of GenAI while maintaining the crucial human perspective. In this context, Tang et al. (2024) emphasize the potential of ChatGPT and similar models for automating and scaling critical thinking assessments.

The insights illustrate that human capabilities remain central in an increasingly technologized world. Despite GenAI's advanced capabilities, critical thinking remains essential for the responsible use of this technology. While GenAI can be seen as both an opportunity and a challenge for critical thinking, human judgment ensures that technology is innovative and ethical (Thiga, 2024; Yang, 2024).

The LER methodology—learning, evaluating, and reflecting—provides a practice-oriented framework that enables critical thinking to be effectively linked to using GenAI. This approach is applicable in various fields, from education to business, and offers concrete steps that enable users to develop a balanced and informed approach to AI technologies.

The first phase, 'Learn,' lays the foundation by equipping users with the knowledge to understand GenAI's capabilities and limitations. Users must be aware of the potential weaknesses of AI systems, particularly the possibility of hallucinations or distortions in the AI's results (Jones, 2024). By being aware that AI is not a flawless source, users can take a critical look at the content generated and use it more cautiously. Continuous learning is also crucial as AI technologies continue to evolve. To this end, companies should provide training programs that enable employees to adapt to new GenAI capabilities. This stress on continuous learning can motivate the audience to stay updated with the latest AI technologies.

The 'evaluate' phase is about critically analyzing the results of GenAI. Users should implement structured evaluation frameworks based on relevance, accuracy, and logical consistency metrics. One example is a journalist who uses GenAI to create content and compares it with trusted sources to ensure its credibility. Detecting biases and logical errors is also important to verify the quality of AI decisions. Tools such as SHAP and LIME help identify potential results errors and minimize risks. Furthermore, 'what-if' analyses, which involve feeding different inputs into the AI system to predict how it might respond, can help predict how AI systems might respond to different inputs. This scenario planning builds confidence in the technology and helps users better assess possible outcomes.

The final phase, 'reflect,' fosters continuous improvement and adaptation. Through iterative feedback loops, organizations can ensure that users provide regular feedback on GenAI results, improving system performance. It is crucial that human judgment remains integrated into the decision-making process and is not replaced by AI. This emphasis on human judgment not only maintains accountability but also engages the audience in the responsible use of AI. It is the only way to maintain accountability and build greater trust in the technology.

The LER methodology ensures that GenAI is used technologically, ethically, and responsibly. It emphasizes the need to continuously engage with AI's challenges and constantly question its use to realize its full potential while maintaining its limits.

As GenAI advances, its role in society will become increasingly significant. However, this progress should not come at the expense of human thought and judgment. The key to a responsible approach to GenAI lies in fostering a symbiotic relationship between humans and machines, in which each complements the strengths of the other. Critical thinking plays a dual role in this context. On the one hand, it protects against the potential pitfalls of AI misuse and ensures that AI systems are ethical, correct, and aligned with corporate values. On the other hand, it acts as a catalyst for innovation. By questioning assumptions and exploring alternative perspectives, critical thinking not only safeguards against misuse but also drives the innovative use of GenAI, inspiring the audience and helping solve complex problems.

Despite their advanced capabilities, GenAI systems need more true understanding and thought. They mimic human-like responses but cannot emulate human intuition, creativity, or ethical judgment. This paradox highlights the irreplaceable value of human cognition, especially in contexts that require nuanced decisions. As GenAI becomes more prevalent in healthcare, education, and governance, the ethical questions surrounding its use are also becoming more pressing. Issues such as data privacy, accountability, and the potential for abuse emphasize the need for a human-centered approach in which policymakers, educators, and industry leaders must work together to establish frameworks that promote transparency and fairness.

Given the rapid development of GenAI, it is necessary to prepare future generations for the challenges of an AI-driven world. Schools and universities should incorporate AI literacy and critical thinking into their curricula so that students learn to evaluate GenAI outputs and recognize low-quality or inaccurate information. Socially critical thinking will support students in identifying missing perspectives and marginalized voices in AI outputs and reduce the potential harm of biases. This will strengthen individual judgment and the ability to understand AI's social and ethical implications.

Collaboration across disciplines, such as computer science, philosophy, and sociology, is crucial to gaining a broader perspective and bridging the gap between technological expertise and ethical considerations. At the same time, the dynamic nature of AI also requires lifelong learning to keep pace with continuous developments.

In conclusion, critical thinking remains central in the age of GenAI. While AI systems offer unparalleled efficiency and scalability, they are ultimately tools that require human oversight and judgment. By fostering a culture of critical engagement and incorporating methods such as LER, individuals, and organizations can responsibly and effectively harness GenAI's potential.

'The future of learning and human development depends on our collective ability to make these decisions with foresight and care; not as passive consumers, but as active shapers of technology's role in our lives.' (Bozkurt et al., 2024, p.512)

The key to success lies in balancing AI innovation and human thinking to ensure that technology serves humanity and does not replace its insights.

REFERENCES

Andrae, S. (2025). Critical thinking in the age of algorithms. In Aldosemani, T. I., Lytras, M. D., & Ordóñez de Pablos, P. (Eds.), *Fostering teacher skills and critical thinking in modern education* (pp. 221–258). IGI Global Publishing., DOI: 10.4018/979-8-3373-1692-5.ch010

Bashir, N., Donti, P., Cuff, J., Sroka, S., Ilic, M., Sze, V., ... (2024). The climate and sustainability implications of generative AI. An MIT exploration of generative AI. https://mit-genai.pubpub.org/pub/8ulgrckc/release/2?readingCollection=9434a92e

Bender, E. M., Gebru, T., McMillan-Major, A., & Shmitchell, S. (2021). On the dangers of stochastic parrots: Can language models be too big? *Proceedings of the 2021 ACM Conference on Fairness, Accountability, and Transparency*, 610-623. https://doi.org/DOI: 10.1145/3442188.3445922

Bianchi, F., Kalluri, P., Durmus, E., Ladhak, F., Cheng, M., & Nozza, D.. (2023). Easily accessible text-to-image generation amplifies demographic stereotypes at large scale. In *FAccT '23: Proceedings of the 2023 ACM conference on fairness, accountability, and transparency*, 1493–1504. https://doi.org/DOI: 10.1145/3593013.3594095

Borup, J. (2023). This was written by a human: A real educator's thoughts on teaching in the age of Chatgpt. EDUCAUSE Review. https://er.educause.edu/articles/2023/3/this-was-written-by-a-human-a-real-educators-thoughts-onteaching-in-the-age-of-chatgpt

Bozkurt, A., Xiao, J., Farrow, R., Bai, J. Y. H., Nerantzi, C., Moore, S., Dron, J., Stracke, C. M., Singh, L., Crompton, H., Koutropoulos, A., Terentev, E., Pazurek, A., Nichols, M., Sidorkin, A. M., Costello, E., Watson, S., Mulligan, D., Honeychurch, S., & Asino, T. I. (2024). The manifesto for teaching and learning in a time of Generative AI: A critical collective stance to better navigate the future. *Open Praxis*, *16*(4), 487–513. DOI: 10.55982/openpraxis.16.4.777

Chan, C. B. (2023). Grading generative AI-based assignments using a 3R framework. In Proceedings for IEEE International Conference on Teaching, Assessment and Learning for Engineering, 28 Nov-–1 Dec. Auckland. https://doi.org/DOI: 10.1109/TALE56641.2023.10398408

Chen, D., Parsa, R., Hope, A., Hannon, B., Mak, E., Eng, L., Liu, F.-F., Fallah-Rad, N., Heesters, A. M., & Raman, S. (2024). Physician and artificial intelligence chatbot responses to cancer questions from social media. *JAMA Oncology*, *10*(7), 956–960. DOI: 10.1001/jamaoncol.2024.0836 PMID: 38753317

Chesterman, S. (2024). Good models borrow, great models steal: Intellectual property rights and generative AI. *Policy and Society*, •••, puae006. Advance online publication. DOI: 10.1093/polsoc/puae006

Chiarello, F., Giordano, V., Spada, I., Barandoni, S., & Fantoni, G. (2024). Future applications of generative large language models: A data-driven case study on ChatGPT. *Technovation, 133*, 103002. DOI: 10.1016/j.technovation.2024.103002

Dabis, A., & Csáki, C. (2024). AI and ethics: Investigating the first policy responses of higher education institutions to the challenge of generative AI. *Humanities & Social Sciences Communications, 11*(1), 1006. DOI: 10.1057/s41599-024-03526-z

Dempere, J., Modugu, K., Hesham, A., & Ramasamy, L. K. (2024). The impact of ChatGPT on higher education. *Frontiers in Education, 8*, 1206936. DOI: 10.3389/feduc.2023.1206936

Doshi, A. R., & Hauser, O. P. (2024). Generative AI enhances individual creativity but reduces the collective diversity of novel content. *Science Advances, 10*(28), eadn5290. Advance online publication. DOI: 10.1126/sciadv.adn5290 PMID: 38996021

English, L. 2023. What are the new must-have leadership skills in today's AI world? Medium. August 31, 2023. https://larry-english.medium.com/what-are-the-new-must-have-leadership-skills-in-todays-ai-world-56654dd1b62f

Federiakin, D., Molerov, D., Zlatkin-Troitschanskaia, O., & Maur, A. (2024). Prompt engineering as a new 21st century skill. *Frontiers in Education, 9*, 1366434. Advance online publication. DOI: 10.3389/feduc.2024.1366434

Ferdaus, M. M., Abdelguerfi, M., Ioup, E., Niles, K. N., Pathak, K., & Sloan, S. (2024). Towards trustworthy AI: A review of ethical and robust large language models. *arXiv*.https://doi.org//arXiv.2407.13934DOI: 10.48550

Feuerriegel, S., Hartmann, J., Janiesch, C., & Zschech, P. (2024). Generative AI. *Business & Information Systems Engineering, 66*(1), 111–126. DOI: 10.1007/s12599-023-00834-7

Glikson, E., & Woolley, A. (2020). Human trust in artificial intelligence: Review of empirical research. *The Academy of Management Annals, 14*(2), 627–660. DOI: 10.5465/annals.2018.0057

Hagendorff, T. (2024). Deception abilities emerged in large language models. *Proceedings of the National Academy of Sciences of the United States of America, 121*(24), e2317967121. DOI: 10.1073/pnas.2317967121 PMID: 38833474

Hié, A., & Thouary, C. (2023). How AI is reshaping higher education. October 17, 2023. https://www.aacsb.edu/insights/articles/2023/10/how-ai-is-reshaping-higher-education

Huber, S. E., Kiili, K., Nebel, S., Ryan, R. M., Sailer, M., & Ninaus, M. (2024). Leveraging the potential of large language models in education through playful and game-based learning. *Educational Psychology Review*, *36*(1), 25. DOI: 10.1007/s10648-024-09868-z

Hyde, S. J., Busby, A., & Bonner, R. L. (2024). Tools or fools: Are we educating managers or creating tool-dependent robots? *Journal of Management Education*, *48*(4), 708–734. DOI: 10.1177/10525629241230357

Jones, N. (2024). 'In awe': Scientists impressed by latest ChatGPT model o1. *Nature, 634*, 275–276. c10.1038/d41586-024-03169-9

Kocoń, J., Cichecki, I., Kaszyca, O., Kochanek, M., Szydło, D., Baran, J., Bielaniewicz, J., Gruza, M., Janz, A., Kanclerz, K., Kocoń, A., Koptyra, B., Mieleszczenko-Kowszewicz, W., Miłkowski, P., Oleksy, M., Piasecki, M., Radliński, Ł., Wojtasik, K., Woźniak, S., & Kazienko, P. (2023). ChatGPT: Jack of all trades, master of none. *Information Fusion*, *99*, 101861. DOI: 10.1016/j.inffus.2023.101861

Larson, B. Z., Moser, C., Caza, A., Muehlfeld, K., & Colombo, L. A. (2024). Critical thinking in the Age of Generative AI. *Academy of Management Learning & Education*, *23*(3), 373–378. DOI: 10.5465/amle.2024.0338

Lee, C. C., & Low, M. Y. H. (2024). Using GenAI in education: The case for critical thinking. *Frontiers in Artificial Intelligence*, *7*, 1–3. DOI: 10.3389/frai.2024.1452131 PMID: 39554991

Lee, H.-P., Sarkar, A., Tankelevitch, L., Drosos, I., Rintel, S., & Banks, R.. (2025). The impact of Generative AI on critical thinking: Self-Reported reductions in cognitive effort and confidence effects from a survey of knowledge workers. *CHI '25: Proceedings of the 2025 CHI Conference on Human Factors in Computing Systems*, 1121, 1–22. https://doi.org/DOI: 10.1145/3706598.3713778

Li, Q., Fu, L., Zhang, W., Chen, X., Yu, J., Xia, W., ... (2024). Adapting large language models for education: Foundational capabilities, potentials, and challenges. *arXiv*. https://doi.org//arXiv.2401.08664DOI: 10.48550

Liang, W., & Wu, Y. (2024). Exploring the use of ChatGPT to foster EFL learners' critical thinking skills from a post-humanist perspective. *Thinking Skills and Creativity*, *54*, 101645. DOI: 10.1016/j.tsc.2024.101645

Lindebaum, D., & Fleming, P. (2024). ChatGPT undermines human reflexivity, scientific responsibility and responsible management research. *British Journal of Management, 35*(2), 566–575. DOI: 10.1111/1467-8551.12781

Lu, C., Lu, C., Lange, R. T., Foerster, J., Clune, J., & Ha, D. (2024). The AI scientist: Towards fully automated open-ended scientific discovery. *arXiv.*https://doi.org//arXiv.2408.06292DOI: 10.48550

Ma, Q., Wu, T., & Koedinger, K. (2023). Is AI the better programming partner? Human-Human Pair Programming vs. Human-AI pAIr Programming. *arXiv.*https://doi.org//arXiv.2306.05153DOI: 10.48550

Mitchell, M. (2024). The Turing Test and our shifting conceptions of intelligence. *Science, 385*(6710), eadq9356. Advance online publication. DOI: 10.1126/science.adq9356 PMID: 39146414

Mogavi, R. H., Deng, C., Kim, J. J., Zhou, P. Z., Kwon, Y. D., & Metwally, A. H. S.. (2024). ChatGPT in education: A blessing or a curse? A qualitative study exploring early adopters' utilization and perceptions. *Computers in Human Behavior: Artificial Humans, 2*(1), 100027. DOI: 10.1016/j.chbah.2023.100027

Mollick, E. R., & Mollick, L. (2023). Using AI to implement effective teaching strategies in classrooms: Five strategies, including prompts. The Wharton School Research Paper, http://dx.doi.org/DOI: 10.2139/ssrn.4391243

Mosqueira-Rey, E., Hernández-Pereira, E., Alonso-Ríos, D., Bobes-Bascarán, J., & Fernández-Leal, A. (2023). Human-in-the-loop machine learning: A state of the art. *Artificial Intelligence Review, 56*(4), 3005–3054. DOI: 10.1007/s10462-022-10246-w

Munn, L., & Henrickson, L. (2024). Tell me a story: A framework for critically investigating AI language models. *Learning, Media and Technology*, 1–17. Advance online publication. DOI: 10.1080/17439884.2024.2327024

Priem, R. L. (2018). Toward becoming a complete teacher of strategic management. *Academy of Management Learning & Education, 17*(3), 374–388. DOI: 10.5465/amle.2017.0237

Putra, I. M., & Abdunnafi, F. I. (2024). Understanding the unexpected: The adverse influence of large language models on critical thinking and professional skepticism in accounting education. https://ssrn.com/abstract=4914889 DOI: 10.2139/ssrn.4914889

Rahman, M. M., & Watanobe, Y. (2023). ChatGPT for education and research: Opportunities, threats, and strategies. *Applied Sciences (Basel, Switzerland), 13*(9), 5783. DOI: 10.3390/app13095783

Rakowski, R., & Kowaliková, P. (2024). The political and social contradictions of the human and online environment in the context of artificial intelligence applications. *Humanities & Social Sciences Communications*, *11*(1), 289. DOI: 10.1057/s41599-024-02725-y

Rejeb, A., Rejeb, K., Appolloni, A., Treiblmaier, H., & Iranmanesh, M. (2024). Exploring the impact of ChatGPT on education: A web mining and machine learning approach. *International Journal of Management Education*, *22*(1), 100932. DOI: 10.1016/j.ijme.2024.100932

Risvold, W., Stratton, M., & Geddy, M. (2024). How to evaluate critical thinking in the age of AI. February 14, 2024. https://www.aacsb.edu/insights/articles/2024/02/how-to-evaluate-critical-thinking-in-the-age-of-ai

Roumeliotis, K. I., & Tselikas, N. D. (2023). ChatGPT and Open-AI models: A preliminary review. *Future Internet*, *15*(6), 192. DOI: 10.3390/fi15060192

Ruiz-Rojas, L. I., Salvador-Ullauri, L., & Acosta-Vargas, P. (2024). Collaborative working and critical thinking: Adoption of generative artificial intelligence tools in higher education. *Sustainability (Basel)*, *16*(13), 5367. DOI: 10.3390/su16135367

Scheurer, J., Balesni, M., & Hobbhahn, M. (2024). Large language models can strategically deceive their users when put under pressure. *arXiv.*https://doi.org//arXiv.2311.07590DOI: 10.48550

Tang, T., Sha, J., Zhao, Y., Wang, S., Wang, Z., & Shen, S. (2024). Unveiling the efficacy of ChatGPT in evaluating critical thinking skills through peer feedback analysis: Leveraging existing classification criteria. *Thinking Skills and Creativity*, *53*, 101607. DOI: 10.1016/j.tsc.2024.101607

Thiga, M. N. (2024). Generative AI and the development of critical thinking. *Iconic Research and Engineering Journals*, *7*(9). https://www.irejournals.com/formatedpaper/1705580.pdf

Valova, I., Mladenova, T., & Kanev, G. (2024). Students' perception of ChatGPT usage in education. *International Journal of Advanced Computer Science and Applications*, *15*(1), 466–473. DOI: 10.14569/IJACSA.2024.0150143

Walter, Y. (2024). Embracing the future of artificial intelligence in the classroom: The relevance of AI literacy, prompt engineering, and critical thinking in modern education. *International Journal of Educational Technology in Higher Education*, *21*(1), 15. DOI: 10.1186/s41239-024-00448-3

Wang, S., Xu, T., Li, H., Zhang, C., Liang, J., Tang, J., ... (2024). Large language models for education: A survey and outlook. *arXiv.*https://doi.org//arXiv.2403.18105DOI: 10.48550

Willingham, D. T. (2019). How to teach critical thinking. Occasional Paper Series. http://www.danielwillingham.com/uploads/5/0/0/7/5007325/willingham_2019_nsw_critical_thinking2.pdf

Xu, E., Wang, W., & Wang, Q. (2023). The effectiveness of collaborative problem-solving in promoting students' critical thinking: A meta-analysis based on empirical literature. *Humanities & Social Sciences Communications*, *10*(1), 16. DOI: 10.1057/s41599-023-01508-1 PMID: 37192950

Xu, Z., Jain, S., & Kankanhalli, M. (2024). Hallucination is inevitable: An innate limitation of large language models. *arXiv*. https://doi.org//arXiv.2401.11817DOI: 10.48550

Yang, X., Wang, Q., & Lyu, J. (2024). Assessing ChatGPT's educational capabilities and application potential. *ECNU Review of Education*, *7*(3). Advance online publication. DOI: 10.1177/20965311231210006

Zhang, H., Xie, J., Wu, C., Cai, J., Kim, C., & Carroll, J. M. (2024). The future of learning: Large language models through the lens of students. *arXiv*. https://doi.org//arXiv.2407.12723DOI: 10.1145/3686852.3687069

Chapter 12
Enhancing Critical Thinking:
The Role of AI in Modern Education

Andi Asrifan
https://orcid.org/0000-0002-9934-6129
Universitas Negeri Makassar, Indonesia

K. Khristianto
https://orcid.org/0000-0002-6565-2670
Universitas Muhammadiyah Purwokerto, Indonesia

Arif Budiman
UIN Sunan Kalijaga, Indonesia

Purwani Indri Astuti
Univet Bantara Sukoharjo, Indonesia

Ahmad Rossydi
Politeknik Penerbangan Makassar, Indonesia

ABSTRACT

This chapter examines the transformative impact of Artificial Intelligence (AI) on the enhancement of critical thinking skills in educational environments. It emphasizes that AI-driven learning platforms, like Knewton and Carnegie Learning, offer tailored and interactive experiences that enhance student engagement and inquiry. By accommodating distinct learning styles and providing customized feedback, these platforms promote students' abilities to analyze, evaluate, and synthesize material proficiently. The chapter also addresses the potential challenges of over-reliance

DOI: 10.4018/979-8-3373-4576-5.ch012

on AI, emphasizing the need for a balanced approach that promotes independent problem-solving skills. The use of AI in education improves academic achievement and equips students with vital abilities for informed decision-making and effective problem-solving in a complicated modern society.

UNDERSTANDING CRITICAL THINKING

1.1 Definition and Importance

Critical thinking is the capacity to analyze, assess, and integrate knowledge logically and contemplatively (Woldt & Nenad, 2021; Indrašienė et al., 2021). It entails scrutinizing assumptions, recognizing biases, and evaluating the soundness of arguments. Critical thinking enables individuals to make educated judgments, resolve intricate problems, and manage the extensive information faced in everyday life. This talent is crucial for academic achievement and vital for personal and professional growth.

Critical thinking is essential in the realm of education. It promotes profound engagement with content, establishing a learning environment that values inquiry and exploration. Instead of passively receiving information, students who engage in critical thinking learn to interrogate the material, seek evidence, and derive logical conclusions (Calma & Cotronei-Baird, 2021). This active participation improves understanding and memory, resulting in a deeper grasp of topics.

Furthermore, critical thinking is essential in equipping pupils with the intricacies of the contemporary world. In an age marked by swift technological progress and an excessive influx of information, the capacity to distinguish reliable sources from falsehoods is essential. Students possessing robust critical thinking abilities are more adept at addressing issues, making informed decisions, and contributing significantly to society (Southworth, 2022; Tariq, 2024). They grow proficient in assessing the consequences of their decisions, whether in personal relationships, civic duties, or professional pursuits.

Critical thinking is crucial in daily life outside the classroom. It allows individuals to tackle problems methodically, evaluate various viewpoints, and reach sound decisions. In a polarized environment, critical thinking promotes open-mindedness and empathy, facilitating productive discourse and collaboration (Huston, 2022; Canova & Ma'rof, 2023). It forces individuals to interrogate their own convictions and contemplate divergent perspectives, which is crucial for personal development and societal advancement.

Moreover, the significance of critical thinking encompasses the workplace, where employers are progressively in search of persons capable of critical and innovative thought. In a multinational market, the capacity to assess intricate circumstances, devise inventive solutions, and communicate proficiently is important. As automation and artificial intelligence transform employment environments, critical thinking persists as a distinctly human capability that robots cannot readily copy (George, 2023).

1.2 Historical Context

Critical thinking has evolved due to different educational frameworks and philosophical orientations (Holdo, 2023; Anggraeni et al., 2023). Philosophers like Socrates, Plato, and Aristotle founded rational inquiry and discourse in ancient Greece. Socrates' Socratic questioning stressed the importance of conversation and critical study of convictions, demanding deep thought and rationale. Through inquiry and discourse, critical thinking became a fundamental part of education. Scholasticism brought religious doctrine and classical text analysis to schooling in the Middle Ages. Aquinas and others promoted critical thinking in this era. However, dogma often limited critical thinking (Mascarenhas et al., 2023). The Renaissance revived humanism and empirical observation, encouraging inquisitive learning. Descartes and Bacon promoted critical analysis and evidence-based reasoning through systematic skepticism and the scientific method. The Enlightenment shaped critical thought. John Locke and Immanuel Kant stressed the importance of individual cognition and skepticism towards authority in their philosophy of reason (Chandratreya, 2025). This time laid the groundwork for modern education, encouraging independent thought and diverse perspectives.

Educational philosophies changed critical thinking in the 20th century. Educational reformer John Dewey believed that experiential learning and reflective thinking should help pupils engage thoughtfully with their surroundings (Castagno et al., 2022). Progressive education adopted Dewey's critical thinking philosophy, encouraging pupils to analyze real-world problems and collaborate on solutions.

In the 21st century, technological innovation and globalization provided new challenges and opportunities for critical thinking in education (Thornhill-Miller et al., 2023). The digital age has made a lot of data available, making it necessary to tell fact from fiction. Critical thinking is vital to solving complex social issues, thus educational systems include it.

Critical thinking is a crucial ability in global education. Every school level includes it, showing a shared commitment to educating and engaging individuals (Shutaleva, 2023). To understand the significance of AI in modern education, one must acknowledge the historical context, which defines current practices and emphasizes the need to acquire critical thinking skills in a changing educational environment.

Since 2023, generative AI tools have swiftly proliferated in the educational sector. Platforms such as ChatGPT are currently employed to enhance critical thinking via Socratic questioning, allowing students to engage with intricate subjects interactively. Microsoft Copilot has been included into productivity suites, assisting students in composing essays, analyzing data, and collaboratively reflecting on modifications. Google Gemini, integrated into Google Workspace, facilitates individualized learning by producing study guides and feedback customized to student contributions. These tools not only optimize assignments but also promote metacognitive reflection, enabling learners to assess, enhance, and justify their ideas—an indispensable practice in fostering higher-order thinking across several disciplines.

1.3 Key Components of Critical Thinking

Critical thinking requires sophisticated cognitive processes for effective reasoning and problem-solving (Van Le & Chong, 2024). Understanding its core elements—analysis, assessment, inference, and reasoning—lays the groundwork for educational critical thinking.

The first step is analysis, which involves breaking down complex data into its basic components (Ates et al., 2022; González-Granadillo, 2021). This skill helps people spot correlations, patterns, and assumptions. Critical thinkers assess a study article's technique, facts, and conclusions to determine how they support the main point. This analytical strategy encourages students to question the content and deepen their understanding.

Evaluation assesses knowledge's credibility and relevance after analysis (Teixeira et al., 2021). People must analyze arguments, biases, and sources for this component. In a time of rampant misinformation, critical thinking is crucial. A critical thinker evaluates sources, cross-checks information, and considers plausible explanations for contradicting news stories. This evaluation method promotes decision-making and encourages discerning, evidence-based thinking.

Critical thinking requires inference, or drawing logical inferences from facts (Kaczkó & Ostendorf, 2023). This skill requires synthesizing knowledge from several sources and drawing inferences from its implications. Critical thinkers can assess experimental data's relevance to theories and applications in science. Inference encourages creative problem-solving by transcending direct evidence.

Deductive and inductive reasoning allow humans to produce logical arguments and wise conclusions (van et al., 2021; Rantala, 2024). Deductive reasoning applies broad principles to specific cases, while inductive reasoning draws general conclusions from specific facts. Critical thinking requires both styles of reasoning to form hypotheses, examine assumptions, and draw conclusions. Critical thinkers employ reasoning to communicate their opinion, anticipate counterarguments, and defend it in a discussion.

THE RISE OF AI IN EDUCATION

2.1 Overview of AI Technologies

Artificial Intelligence (AI) has swiftly revolutionized multiple areas, including education (Ahmad et al., 2021; George & Wooden, 2023). The incorporation of AI technologies in educational environments has created opportunities for individualized learning, increased engagement, and higher administrative efficiency. This section offers a summary of the AI tools and technologies presently influencing the educational scene.

Recent AI education initiatives have prioritized the incorporation of critical thinking into AI literacy. The AI4K12 initiative, revised in 2024, broadened its "Five Big Ideas" structure to incorporate ethical reasoning and data bias awareness, ensuring that pupils comprehend AI while critically evaluating its societal implications. The Indonesian Ministry of Education launched the "AI Kompeten Merdeka" program, integrating AI utilization with Kurikulum Merdeka principles to promote independent learning and digital citizenship. The EU's Digital Education Action Plan 2023–2030 advocates for the proper integration of AI in educational institutions, emphasizing the importance of teacher training and fair access to AI-enhanced learning resources among member states.

Intelligent Tutoring Systems (ITS)

Intelligent Tutoring Systems are AI-based platforms that deliver customized instruction and feedback to learners (Baig et al., 2024). These systems adjust to personal learning preferences and speeds, providing customized activities and materials. Platforms like Carnegie Learning employ AI algorithms to evaluate student performance in real time, modifying task complexity according to students' comprehension of ideas. This tailored method not only improves student engagement but also cultivates critical thinking by presenting learners with suitably difficult tasks.

Learning Management Systems (LMS) with AI Capabilities

Contemporary LMSs, including Canvas and Moodle, are progressively integrating AI functionalities to improve the educational experience (Alier et al., 2025). These systems can examine student data to discern patterns in learning habits, allowing instructors to intervene when students face difficulties. AI-driven analytics can offer insights into student engagement, enabling educators to customize their instructional approaches to enhance critical thinking growth.

Natural Language Processing (NLP) Tools

Natural Language Processing technologies are employed to improve communication and understanding in educational environments (Bauer et al., 2023; Kasthuri & Balaji, 2023). Applications such as Grammarly and Turnitin utilize natural language processing to deliver immediate feedback on writing, assisting students in enhancing their analytical and evaluative abilities. These tools promote critical thinking in students by providing suggestions for clarity, coherence, and reasoning, thereby enhancing their writing and refining their ideas.

AI-Powered Assessment Tools

Artificial intelligence technologies are transforming evaluation methodologies via automated grading and feedback systems (Kamalov et al., 2023). Platforms such as Gradescope utilize artificial intelligence to optimize the grading process for assignments and examinations, enabling educators to concentrate more on delivering substantive feedback. These tools can evaluate student responses, detect prevalent misconceptions, and recommend specific resources for enhancement, fostering critical thinking by prompting students to contemplate their learning.

Virtual Learning Environments (VLEs)

Artificial intelligence augments virtual learning settings, rendering them more interactive and engaging (Seo et al., 2021). Tools such as Knewton and DreamBox Learning employ AI algorithms to generate adaptive learning experiences that react to student requirements in real-time. These platforms promote investigation and inquiry, cultivating critical thinking as students engage with intricate topics and scenarios.

Chatbots and Virtual Assistants

AI-driven chatbots and virtual assistants, exemplified by those embedded in platforms such as Microsoft Teams and Google Classroom, offer prompt assistance to students (Jose, 2024; Kavitha et al., 2024). They can respond to inquiries, direct users to resources, and enhance communication between students and educators. This accessibility promotes students to solicit assistance and participate in critical discourse regarding their education.

2.2 AI's Role in Personalized Learning

Personalized learning is an educational methodology that customizes training to address the varied needs, abilities, and interests of individual students. Artificial Intelligence (AI) is essential in enhancing personalized learning experiences, allowing educators to develop more effective and engaging educational settings (Ellikkal & Rajamohan, 2024). By utilizing AI technologies, educators can gain insights into student needs and modify their teaching tactics accordingly.

Adaptive Learning Systems

AI-driven adaptive learning systems lead the way in personalized education (Ezzaim et al., 2024). These systems evaluate student performance data instantaneously, modifying the difficulty and kind of content delivered according to individual advancement. Platforms such as DreamBox Learning and Knewton employ algorithms to evaluate a student's strengths and weaknesses, delivering tailored lessons that suitably challenge them. This adaptive method facilitates students' mastery of concepts at their own pace while promoting critical thinking through the introduction of progressively complicated questions as they progress.

Data-Driven Insights

Artificial intelligence technology can analyze extensive datasets to produce insights regarding student learning behaviors (Sajja et al., 2024). Through the analysis of data from evaluations, exchanges, and engagement metrics, AI can discern trends that guide instructional choices. Educators can utilize these insights to customize their pedagogical approaches, thereby addressing particular learning deficiencies and fostering critical thinking. If a learner persistently encounters difficulties with a specific topic, AI can suggest tailored resources or interventions to facilitate their improvement.

Customized Learning Pathways

Artificial intelligence facilitates the development of customized educational trajectories that correspond to the individual interests and objectives of each student (Ellikkal & Rajamohan, 2024). By evaluating students' preferences and learning modalities, AI may recommend pertinent resources, activities, and projects that align with individual learners. This customisation cultivates a sense of ownership in the learning process, encouraging students to engage more profoundly with the content. A student pursuing environmental science may receive customized tasks that enable them to investigate real-world sustainability concerns, so improving their critical thinking abilities.

Intelligent Tutoring Systems

Intelligent Tutoring Systems (ITS) offer individualized assistance by replicating one-on-one tutoring interactions (Baillifard et al., 2024; Alam, 2023). These technologies provide instantaneous feedback, directing students through problem-solving methodologies and prompting them to contemplate their rationale. Platforms like as Carnegie Learning modify their instructional approaches according to student feedback, encouraging learners to engage in critical analysis of their errors and grasp the fundamental principles. This prompt feedback mechanism is essential for cultivating critical thinking abilities, as it compels pupils to scrutinize their cognitive processes and implement modifications.

Enhanced Engagement and Motivation

The capacity of AI to tailor learning experiences markedly improves student engagement and motivation (Alam, 2023). Students are more likely to remain engaged and invested in their learning when they get content that aligns with their interests and is provided at an appropriate level of difficulty. This intrinsic drive is vital for cultivating critical thinking, as students are more predisposed to investigate, interrogate, and contest concepts when they possess a personal connection to the content.

2.3 AI as a Teaching Assistant

The incorporation of Artificial Intelligence (AI) in education has provided novel methods to assist educators, improving their capacity to deliver curriculum and evaluate student performance efficiently (Hooda et al., 2022). AI functions as an effective teaching assistant, optimizing administrative duties, delivering tailored feedback, and enhancing the learning experience. This chapter examines AI's capacity to revolutionize educators' function and enhance educational results.

Automating Administrative Tasks

A primary benefit of AI in education is its capacity to automate repetitive administrative activities (Ahmad et al., 2021; George & Wooden, 2023). Evaluating assignments, overseeing attendance, and arranging course materials can be labor-intensive for educators. AI-driven systems, including Gradescope and Turnitin, can automate the evaluation of multiple-choice assessments and written assignments, delivering immediate feedback to students. Minimizing administrative responsibilities enables educators to concentrate on instruction and student engagement, so cultivating a more participatory learning atmosphere.

Personalized Feedback and Support

Artificial intelligence can deliver tailored feedback to pupils, aiding them in recognizing their strengths and areas needing enhancement (Hooda et al., 2022). Intelligent teaching systems, like Carnegie Learning, evaluate student responses and provide customized recommendations for additional study. This prompt feedback mechanism enables pupils to contemplate their learning and implement requisite modifications, fostering critical thinking. Furthermore, AI can discern patterns in student performance, allowing educators to act promptly when pupils encounter difficulties, so ensuring that no learner lags behind.

Enhancing Content Delivery

Artificial intelligence technology can improve the dissemination of educational content by offering dynamic and interactive learning experiences (Sajja et al., 2024). Virtual teaching assistants, such as chatbots, can respond to student inquiries instantaneously, directing them through course content and resources. These AI-powered tools can enhance discussions, offer supplementary context, and motivate students to investigate subjects more thoroughly. AI enhances information accessibility and engagement, fostering a more stimulating learning environment that promotes critical inquiry.

Data-Driven Insights for Educators

Artificial intelligence can evaluate extensive datasets to furnish educators with significant information regarding student performance and engagement (Ouyang et al., 2023; Kim et al., 2022). By monitoring variables such as participation rates, assignment completion, and assessment scores, AI can assist educators in identifying patterns and modifying their teaching tactics accordingly. This data-centric methodology empowers educators to make educated choices regarding curriculum development and teaching strategies, hence improving the educational experience for students.

Supporting Diverse Learning Needs

Artificial intelligence can significantly assist in addressing varied learning requirements in the classroom (Ahmad et al., 2021; Dimitriadou & Lanitis, 2023). Through the analysis of individual student data, AI can assist instructors in identifying kids who may need supplementary support, including those with learning difficulties or language obstacles. AI solutions can deliver tailored resources and interventions, guaranteeing that all students have the support necessary for success. This inclusivity cultivates a more equal educational atmosphere, enabling every student to cultivate critical thinking abilities.

INTEGRATING AI TO FOSTER CRITICAL THINKING

3.1 AI-Driven Learning Platforms

AI-driven learning platforms are transforming education by offering interactive and tailored experiences that improve critical thinking skills (Onesi-Ozigagun et al., 2024). These platforms utilize sophisticated algorithms and data analytics to foster compelling learning environments that promote students' abilities to analyze, evaluate, and synthesize information. This section examines some notable AI-powered learning platforms and their roles in promoting critical thinking.

Knewton is an adaptive learning platform that customizes educational content according to individual student performance and learning preferences (Osipovskaya & Dmitrieva, 2022). Knewton customizes lessons to address the distinct needs of each student by analyzing data from evaluations and interactions. This tailored method not only aids students in comprehending intricate concepts but also stimulates critical thinking by presenting challenges that necessitate profound analysis and reasoning. Knewton's capacity to dynamically modify information cultivates a growth mentality, enabling students to confront progressively challenging material as they advance.

Carnegie Learning integrates artificial intelligence with cognitive science to develop an all-encompassing mathematics education platform (Bahassi et al., 2024). The Intelligent Tutoring System offers immediate feedback and tailored assistance, enabling students to solve issues at their own speed. The platform fosters critical thinking by providing students with open-ended questions and real-world scenarios that necessitate the creative application of mathematical principles. Carnegie Learning fosters discovery and inquiry, enabling students to cultivate problem-solving abilities vital for achievement in academic and real-world contexts.

DreamBox Learning is an adaptive mathematics program tailored for K-8 pupils, utilizing artificial intelligence to generate individualized learning experiences (Foster, 2024). The platform perpetually evaluates student advancement and modifies assignment complexity accordingly. DreamBox prioritizes critical thinking by integrating interactive, game-like components that necessitate students to engage in strategic thought and decision-making grounded in their comprehension of mathematical principles. This captivating method not only improves pupils' mathematics abilities but also cultivates a passion for learning and discovery.

Socratic by Google is an AI-driven mobile application that assists students with homework by offering explanations and resources customized to their inquiries (Labadze et al., 2023; Labadze et al., 2023). Socratic employs image recognition and natural language processing, enabling students to capture images of difficulties or input queries, thereby obtaining immediate feedback and assistance. This interactive platform fosters critical thinking by urging students to investigate various solutions and comprehend the foundational principles instead of merely supplying responses. Socratic cultivates an environment of inquiry, enabling students to assume responsibility for their education.

Edmodo is a social learning platform that use AI to enhance cooperation and communication between students and educators (Saqr et al., 2023; Maqbool et al., 2024). Edmodo fosters critical engagement with information and peers by offering tools for conversation, peer criticism, and project-based learning. The platform's AI capabilities can evaluate student interactions and provide resources or discussion topics that encourage a more profound examination of themes. This collaborative setting fosters critical thinking by prompting students to express their views, question assumptions, and gain insights from varied perspectives.

3.2 Case Studies of Successful Integration

The incorporation of Artificial Intelligence (AI) in educational environments has produced encouraging outcomes in enhancing critical thinking among students (Saritepeci & Yildiz Durak, 2024). This section examines various case studies of educational institutions and programs that have successfully utilized AI technologies to improve critical thinking skills, illustrating the transformative capabilities of these advances.

The Summit Public Schools Model

Summit Public Schools, a charter school network in California and Washington, has adopted an AI-driven personalized learning platform known as Summit Learning (Morris et al., 2022; Peterson & Shakeel, 2024). This platform enables students to establish personal learning objectives and advance autonomously. Summit Learning employs data analytics to offer customized tools and exams that encourage students to engage in critical thinking around their education. Educators have insights about student performance, allowing them to initiate discussions and interventions that enhance comprehension. The approach has demonstrated substantial enhancements in student engagement and critical thinking abilities, as students are motivated to assume responsibility for their educational journey.

The New York City Department of Education's AI Initiative

In 2020, the New York City Department of Education initiated a program to incorporate AI tools into schools around the city (Wang & Cheng, 2021; Schiff, 2021). A prominent initiative involves the deployment of AI-driven chatbots to aid students with assignments and deliver instantaneous feedback. These chatbots facilitate interaction with students, encouraging critical thinking over their responses and the exploration of alternate solutions. The program has resulted in heightened student engagement and enhanced problem-solving abilities, as students communicate their reasoning and assess their comprehension of intricate ideas.

The University of Southern California's (USC) AI-Enhanced Learning

The University of Southern California has established an AI-augmented educational framework in its School of Education, emphasizing teacher preparation and student involvement (Alqahtani & Wafula, 2024). The application employs AI algorithms to assess student interactions and deliver tailored feedback on instructional techniques. The AI system facilitates the development of essential critical thinking abilities for prospective educators by simulating classroom scenarios. This method not only improves the pedagogical abilities of prospective educators but also equips them to cultivate critical thinking in their students, so generating a ripple effect within the educational system.

The International School of Amsterdam

The International School of Amsterdam has used AI tools in its curriculum to enhance inquiry-based learning (Jeon et al., 2024). Utilizing technologies such as Knewton and Google Classroom, educators may deliver tailored learning experiences that motivate students to investigate subjects thoroughly. The institution prioritizes project-based learning, enabling students to utilize AI tools for researching, analyzing, and presenting their conclusions on real-world problems. This method has led to increased student engagement and enhanced critical thinking abilities, as students acquire tools to tackle complicated issues and interact efficiently.

The AI4K12 Initiative

The AI4K12 effort, a partnership of multiple educational groups, seeks to include AI instruction into K-12 curricula throughout the United States (Li et al., 2024). The initiative supplies materials and frameworks for educators to foster the cultivation of critical thinking abilities through AI-related initiatives and conversations. Institutions engaged in this effort have indicated heightened student enthusiasm for STEM disciplines and improved problem-solving skills when learners apply AI principles to practical situations.

Integrate Concrete Classroom Vignettes

An English teacher at a rural Indonesian junior high school employed the Socratic method to assist students facing difficulties in argumentative writing. Permitting learners to capture images of prompts and obtain guided feedback facilitated a more profound investigation of claims and evidence. A student remarked, "Socratic enabled me to recognize that my rationale did not substantiate my argument." Simultaneously, in a U.S. middle school, DreamBox was employed in mathematics instruction to customize problem sets according to individual proficiency levels. A teacher said, "Students initiated discussions on strategies and interrogated one other's reasoning—AI enhanced their introspective problem-solving abilities." These examples underscore AI's function in initiating critical discourse and investigation.

3.3 Designing AI-Enhanced Curriculum

Integrating Artificial Intelligence (AI) tools into the curriculum offers educators a distinctive opportunity to cultivate critical thinking abilities in pupils (Walter, 2024; Muthmainnah et al., 2022). To proficiently develop an AI-enhanced curriculum, educators must adhere to many principles that foster engagement, inquiry, and analytical abilities. This section delineates essential ways for incorporating AI tools into educational methodologies.

Identify Learning Objectives

Prior to the integration of AI tools, instructors must explicitly delineate the learning objectives pertaining to critical thinking. These objectives should concentrate on competencies such as analysis, evaluation, inference, and reasoning. By setting explicit objectives, educators can identify suitable AI tools that correspond with these aims, guaranteeing that technology augments rather than undermines the educational process (Shankar et al., 2024).

Select Appropriate AI Tools

Educators ought to select AI technologies that are intuitive and pertinent to their discipline. Platforms such as Knewton, DreamBox Learning, and Socratic provide interactive functionalities that enhance critical thinking via tailored learning experiences. It is crucial to assess the functionalities of these tools, confirming they offer real-time feedback, adaptive learning trajectories, and avenues for collaborative problem-solving (Zamiri & Esmaeili, 2024; Strielkowski et al., 2024).

Integrate Project-Based Learning

Artificial intelligence techniques can be seamlessly incorporated into project-based learning frameworks, wherein students tackle real-world challenges necessitating critical thinking (Kong et al., 2024). Educators can develop projects that employ AI technologies to evaluate data, simulate scenarios, or generate answers. Students could utilize AI-powered data analysis tools to examine environmental challenges, prompting them to assess evidence and formulate informed opinions.

Foster Collaborative Learning

Promoting collaboration among students fosters critical thinking by enabling the exchange of varied viewpoints and the challenge of each other's ideas (Liang & Fung, 2021). Educators can utilize AI tools that enhance collaborative efforts, such as platforms like Google Classroom or Edmodo. By assigning group tasks that necessitate the utilization of AI for research and analysis, instructors can cultivate a climate conducive to the flourishing of critical thinking through discourse and debate.

Encourage Reflection and Metacognition

Incorporating opportunities for reflection is essential for cultivating critical thinking skills. Educators may utilize AI technologies that encourage students to contemplate their learning processes, including digital journals or discussion boards. Educators facilitate the development of metacognitive abilities crucial for critical thinking by prompting students to scrutinize their cognitive processes and assess their problem-solving strategies (Xu et al., 2023; Akcaoğlu et al., 2023).

Provide Continuous Feedback

Artificial intelligence tools provide instantaneous feedback, which is essential for cultivating critical thinking (Muthmainnah et al., 2022; Ruiz-Rojas et al., 2024). Educators should utilize these qualities to deliver constructive feedback on student work, assisting them in enhancing their reasoning and analytical skills. Consistent feedback enables students to see their strengths and weaknesses, fostering a growth mentality.

Professional Development for Educators

For the successful integration of AI technologies into the curriculum, educators must possess the requisite skills and knowledge (Southworth et al., 2023; Ng et al., 2023). Educational institutions ought to offer professional development opportunities centered on artificial intelligence technologies and their role in enhancing critical thinking. This training enables instructors to adopt AI tools and adjust their teaching practices accordingly securely.

Teacher or Student Testimonials

A student in California stated, "Utilizing an AI chatbot in our science lesson enabled me to scrutinize my assumptions and evaluate many hypotheses before selecting one." A fellow participant in a Malaysian STEM program remarked, "The AI feedback was immediate and explicit, yet it compelled me to evaluate the structure of my arguments critically." These perspectives highlight how AI promotes reflection, inquiry, and enhanced cognitive engagement in education.

CHALLENGES AND LIMITATIONS OF AI IN EDUCATION

4.1 Technological Barriers

The incorporation of Artificial Intelligence (AI) in education presents significant potential for improving learning experiences and cultivating critical thinking (Walter, 2024). Nevertheless, educational institutions have numerous technological obstacles that may impede the successful integration of AI technologies. Comprehending these issues is essential for educators and administrators aiming to utilize AI in their classrooms.

Infrastructure Constraints

A fundamental difficulty faced by schools is insufficient technology infrastructure. Numerous educational institutions, especially in underfunded regions, are deficient in the requisite technology and software to facilitate AI applications. (Kunjumuhammed, 2024) Inadequate internet connectivity, obsolete computers, and restricted access to contemporary technologies can hinder the implementation of AI tools. In the absence of a robust infrastructure, the promised advantages of AI remain unfulfilled, placing students and educators at a disadvantage.

Concerns Regarding Data Privacy and Security

The implementation of AI in education frequently entails the aggregation and examination of extensive student data. This engenders substantial apprehensions about data privacy and security. Educational institutions must comply with intricate laws, including the Family Educational Rights and Privacy Act (FERPA) in the United States, which regulates the management of student data (Giuffrida & Hall, 2023). Ensuring AI systems adhere to these regulations while safeguarding sensitive data presents a significant problem. A breach of data security may result in significant repercussions, including the erosion of trust among students and parents, along with possible legal implications.

Integration with Existing Systems

The incorporation of AI technology into current educational frameworks can be intricate and labor-intensive (Giuffrida & Hall, 2023). Numerous educational institutions employ diverse Learning Management Systems (LMS) and instructional software that may lack compatibility with emerging AI technologies. The absence of interoperability might generate information silos, hindering educators' capacity to access and utilize data efficiently. Educational institutions must allocate time and money to ensure the seamless integration of AI technologies with existing systems to optimize their efficacy.

Educator Training and Professional Development

Educators need training to use AI technologies effectively. However, many instructors lack the skills and support to use AI in their lessons. Instructors often feel unprepared to use AI technologies due to professional development programs that don't keep up with AI technology (Giuffrida & Hall, 2023). Teacher opposition to new technology and insufficient training may prevent teachers from using AI to promote critical thinking.

Educational institutions may struggle to incorporate AI technologies due to cultural opposition (Giuffrida & Hall, 2023). Some instructors may doubt AI's efficacy or worry about its effects on their jobs. Reluctance may stem from a lack of understanding AI's potential benefits or job security concerns. Addressing this hesitation requires a coordinated effort to educate stakeholders about AI's benefits and foster innovation in educational institutions.

4.2 Teacher Training and Adaptation

As Artificial Intelligence (AI) technologies become more prevalent in educational environments, extensive professional development for educators is critical (Giuffrida & Hall, 2023). The effective utilization of AI tools necessitates that educators modify their educational approaches and adopt innovative tactics that foster critical thinking. This part examines the difficulties related to teacher training and the significance of continuous professional development in enabling the effective incorporation of AI in education.

Comprehending AI Technologies

Educators' insufficient knowledge of AI technologies and classroom applications is a significant difficulty (Giuffrida & Hall, 2023). Many educators may lack formal training in AI or have limited familiarity with its functionalities. This knowledge deficit may result in trepidation or reluctance to use AI tools. Professional development programs should emphasize equipping educators with a comprehensive understanding of AI technologies, encompassing their mechanisms, possible advantages, and practical applications in enhancing critical thinking.

Enhancing Pedagogical Skills

Incorporating AI into the curriculum necessitates that educators reevaluate their instructional methodologies. Conventional pedagogical approaches may not adequately utilize AI tools to improve educational results. Professional development must prioritize the cultivation of pedagogical skills compatible with AI-enhanced learning settings (Giuffrida & Hall, 2023). Educators require training in designing classes that integrate AI technologies, foster inquiry-based learning, and enable collaborative problem-solving. This pedagogical shift is crucial for optimizing AI's capacity to enhance critical thinking in students.

Ongoing Learning and Adaptation

The swift progression of technical innovation indicates that AI tools are perpetually developing (Giuffrida & Hall, 2023). Educators must participate in ongoing education to remain informed about the newest advancements and optimal methodologies in AI integration. Professional development programs must be continuous, offering educators opportunity to acquire knowledge about emerging AI tools, exchange experiences, and interact with colleagues. This culture of perpetual learning compels educators to modify their instructional methods and embrace creative strategies that foster critical thinking.

Addressing Concerns and Resistance

Certain educators may express apprehensions regarding the ramifications of AI in education, encompassing matters relating to data privacy, employment security, and the possibility of technology supplanting conventional teaching positions. Professional development programs must tackle these issues by promoting candid dialogues regarding the function of AI in education (Cohen et al., 2024). By underscoring that AI serves as an auxiliary instrument for educators rather than a substitute, training can mitigate apprehensions and foster a more favorable disposition towards technology integration.

Collaboration with AI Specialists

Educational institutions may work with AI professionals and educational technologists to enhance professional development (Kim et al., 2022; Ramírez-Montoya et al., 2021). These professionals can provide valuable AI system knowledge and practical instructor training. Workshops, webinars, and collaborative projects can help educators use AI in their classrooms.

Socratic (mobile-based) and WhatsApp-integrated AI bots work well in low-bandwidth areas to overcome infrastructure constraints. These technologies work on basic cellphones and are suited for rural or under-resourced educational institutions. The implementation should prioritize mobile-first and offline content options. Google's Teachable Machine and Microsoft's AI for Educators offer free, self-directed courses to make teacher training easier. Educational institutions may use these in professional development programs. For colleges with restricted resources or external funding, many tools are free or offer educational discounts.

4.3 Dependence on Technology

With the growing use of AI in education, concerns about overreliance on technology have arisen (Zhai et al., 2024; Shah & Asad, 2024). AI tools can improve learning and critical thinking, but overuse may reduce students' ability to think critically and solve problems independently. This section discusses the risks of overusing AI in education and its consequences on critical thinking.

AI tools may impair students' problem-solving skills (Zhai et al., 2024). Students may lose interest in critical thinking if they rely on AI for answers. Students may miss opportunities to study, evaluate options, and improve their thinking if they rely on AI-driven platforms for rapid feedback or complex problem-solving. As students prioritize quick answers above deep understanding, this dependency may lead to a shallow understanding of subjects.

Decreased Engagement in Learning

Excessive dependence on AI may also reduce student involvement in the educational process (Gawlik-Kobylińska, 2024; Zhai et al., 2024). When AI systems automate tasks like grading or supplying answers, students may transform into passive consumers of information instead of active participants in their education. This passivity may impede their motivation to investigate subjects thoroughly, pose inquiries, and participate in debates that foster critical thinking. Insufficient engagement might inhibit curiosity and creativity, vital critical thinking elements.

Impeded Social Contact and Collaboration

AI tools may occasionally obstruct social contact and collaboration among students. Students who depend on technology for solutions may forfeit significant opportunities to communicate with peers, exchange ideas, and participate in substantive debates. Collaborative learning experiences are essential for cultivating critical thinking abilities, since they prompt students to express their ideas, question assumptions, and evaluate varied views (Herrera-Pavo, 2024; Hursen, 2024). Excessive reliance on AI may result in social isolation and a reduced ability for collaboration and communication.

The Potential for Disinformation and Prejudice Exists

AI systems are not flawless; they may propagate biases and inaccuracies inherent in their training data (Gray et al., 2024). If students depend exclusively on AI for information, they may unintentionally accept biased or erroneous content without critical assessment. This dependence can impede their capacity to evaluate reputable sources, assess arguments, and formulate educated conclusions. Instructing pupils to evaluate information, including that derived by AI, critically, is crucial for cultivating critical thinking abilities.

Balancing Technology and Traditional Learning

To alleviate the hazards linked to reliance on AI, educators must achieve equilibrium between technological and conventional learning approaches (Strielkowski et al., 2024; Yu, 2024). Although AI can augment educational experiences, it must not supplant essential instructional methodologies that foster critical thinking. Educators ought to promote student participation in experiential activities, dialogues, and analytical exercises that necessitate autonomous reasoning and cooperation. By incorporating AI as an auxiliary resource rather than a dependency, educators can facilitate the development of critical thinking skills essential for success in a progressively intricate world.

THE FUTURE OF CRITICAL THINKING AND AI IN EDUCATION

5.1 Emerging Trends in AI and Education

As Artificial Intelligence (AI) advances, its incorporation into education is anticipated to intensify, introducing novel patterns that will influence the future of learning (Strielkowski et al., 2024). These advancements are poised to improve critical thinking abilities in pupils while reshaping the educational environment. This section examines new trends in artificial intelligence technology and their ramifications for education.

Customized Educational Experiences

A prominent development in AI is the enhancement of customized educational experiences. Future AI systems will utilize advanced algorithms to more effectively examine individual learning styles, preferences, and performance data (Gligorea et al., 2023; Sajja et al., 2024). This will facilitate the development of highly tailored educational trajectories that adjust in real-time to accommodate each student's distinct requirements. Consequently, students will interact with knowledge that suitably challenges them, promoting critical thinking through investigation and a greater comprehension of intricate ideas.

Advanced Data Analytics for Educators

Emerging AI technologies will furnish educators with sophisticated data analytics capabilities that yield profound insights into student performance and engagement (Hooda et al., 2022). Utilizing big data, instructors may discern trends, forecast learning results, and customize their educational approaches accordingly. This data-centric methodology will enable educators to intervene preemptively when students encounter difficulties, fostering critical thinking development during the educational journey. Improved analytics will promote more efficient collaboration among educators, enabling them to exchange best practices and techniques for cultivating critical thinking.

AI-Enhanced Collaborative Learning Environments

We can expect AI-enhanced collaborative learning platforms to encourage peer-to-peer interaction and teamwork in education (Mohanty et al., 2024). AI will match students with similar skills and interests, encouraging collaborative problem-solving and critical thinking. Through group projects and conversations, students will learn to articulate their opinions, question assumptions, and analyze other perspectives, which are essential to critical thinking.

AI and VR/AR will change education (AlGerafi et al., 2023). Students can participate in realistic simulations and scenarios that require critical thinking and decision-making using these immersive technologies. Virtually, students could study history, science, or complex technology. Students will be more engaged and learn more by using critical thinking in real-world circumstances.

Ethical AI and Digital Citizenship Education: Education will emphasize ethical AI and digital citizenship as AI becomes more prevalent. Teachers must teach kids about biases, data protection, and AI ethics. Students will learn how to critically use technology and make educated decisions in an AI-dominated world by being aware of these obstacles.

Technology will accelerate, requiring lifelong study and adaptation. Future educational frameworks will emphasize critical thinking to help students adapt to new technologies and job markets. AI will help this shift by providing individualized educational experiences that improve skills and critical thinking (Muthmainnah et al., 2022).

5.2 The Role of Educators in an AI-Driven World

As AI changes education, instructors' duties change (Bozkurt et al., 2021). AI is turning teachers into facilitators, advisers, and mentors, and it can help teachers teach critical thinking.

Facilitator: AI-enhanced classrooms require teachers to facilitate, guide, and interact with students rather than merely teach. AI can assist teachers in assessing student requirements and adapting support (Chounta et al., 2022). Educators may develop critical thinking by supporting student autonomy in learning as students analyze, inquire, and interact with knowledge. As AI technology advances, educators must learn to curate and analyze the available AI resources (Kamalov et al., 2023). To achieve educational goals and increase critical thinking, educators must carefully evaluate AI tools and platforms. High-quality materials help instructors promote inquiry and analysis.

AI Integration into Education

Teachers must grasp AI integration (Chounta et al., 2022; Ruiz-Rojas, 2023). AI-powered classrooms enable customized learning, data analysis, and collaboration. AI-powered platforms can assist teachers and students in solving key problems. AI can help teachers develop curious, deep learning environments.

Digital Literacy and Ethics

Schools must teach pupils these skills in an AI-centric future. Teachers should discuss AI's effects on data protection, bias, and technology ethics. Through critical discourse, teachers can help students grasp AI and its societal implications and navigate the digital environment responsibly (Chan, 2023; Grassini, 2023). AI tools can boost student collaboration, but instructors must actively foster teamwork and communication. Teachers should assign collaborative, idea-sharing, and intellectually challenging assignments. Encourage students to explain their opinions, evaluate other perspectives, and engage in constructive discourse to encourage critical thinking (Xu et al., 2023).

Instructors need lifelong learning and professional development to succeed in AI-driven education. This involves training, AI technology updates, and best practices exchange. With ongoing learning and improvement, instructors can employ AI to increase critical thinking and fulfill students' needs. Summit Learning educators said, “With AI-generated feedback, students began to take ownership of their learning—posing more complex inquiries and independently reassessing their reasoning.” USC academics said, “AI simulations in our teacher training program sparked introspective debates surrounding classroom decision-making." A middle school teacher in Indonesia said, "Despite limited internet availability, AI tools like as Socratic have enabled pupils in crafting more powerful arguments in English composition." A student said, "It was not only about receiving the answer—it was about comprehending the rationale behind that answer." An CEO said, "We demand targeted training and defined standards to guarantee that AI enhances—not supplants—our educational mission."

5.3 Lifelong Learning and Critical Thinking

Critical thinking skills contribute to personal and professional success in the fast-paced digital economy, outside formal education (González-Pérez & Ramírez-Montoya, 2022; Rajaram, 2023). Critical thinking requires lifelong learning. This section discusses how non-school skills assist society.

Handling Change

Complex and ambiguous modern life requires swift adaptation to new knowledge, technology, and difficulties. Critical thinking lets people assess, analyze, and draw conclusions. These lifelong skills enhance personal and professional decision-making (Gouthro, 2022). Critical thinking can select job winners in the fast-changing sector. Lifelong learning improves problem-solving by expanding perspectives. Critical thinking solves problems. Workshops, online courses, and community activities boost critical thinking (Pacholek et al., 2023). Continuous exposure to new ideas and problems encourages creativity and resourcefulness, which are crucial in personal and professional life.

Knowledgeable Citizenship

Strong democracies need knowledgeable citizenry. Critical thinking allows social reflection, information appraisal, and civic debate. Citizens may learn their roles through lifelong ethics, social responsibility, and contemporary challenges programmes (Benavot et al., 2022). Critical thinking can help educated, energetic individuals alter things. Lifelong learning boosts resilience and career growth. Novel learning experiences force people to grow and leave their comfort zones (Chalkley et al., 2022). Critical thinking facilitates learning, reflection, and adaptability. You need resilience to endure life's uncertainty and attain goals. Online and digital technology simplify lifetime learning. AI-driven tools let students learn critical thinking and explore their interests at their own pace (Strielkowski et al., 2024;

Dandachi, 2024). These tools make critical thinking a lifelong goal through targeted and professional education.

CONCLUSION

In conclusion, the use of Artificial Intelligence (AI) in education offers a transformative chance to improve critical thinking skills in pupils. As discussed in the previous chapters, critical thinking is vital for managing the intricacies of contemporary life, allowing individuals to examine, assess, and integrate information proficiently. The emergence of AI-driven educational platforms, such as Knewton and Carnegie Learning, illustrates the capability of technology to customize learning experiences according to individual styles and speeds. These platforms offer customized material while also presenting students with open-ended questions and real-world settings, promoting enhanced engagement and inquiry.

It is essential to recognize the potential dangers linked to over dependence on AI technologies. Although these tools can augment learning, overreliance may undermine students' autonomous problem-solving abilities and reduce their involvement in the educational process. Consequently, educators must achieve equilibrium between utilizing AI for individualized learning and promoting active engagement and critical evaluation.

The effective incorporation of AI in education depends on a cooperative strategy among educators, AI specialists, and policymakers. By cultivating a climate that prioritizes critical thinking and innovation, we can equip students to excel in a more intricate world, providing them with the skills essential for informed decision-making and proficient problem-solving. It is essential to consistently assess and modify our educational methods to fully leverage AI's potential while fostering the critical thinking skills necessary for individual and social progress.

REFERENCES

Ahmad, S. F., Rahmat, M. K., Mubarik, M. S., Alam, M. M., & Hyder, S. I. (2021). Artificial intelligence and its role in education. *Sustainability (Basel), 13*(22), 12902. DOI: 10.3390/su132212902

Akcaoğlu, M., Mor, E., & Külekçi, E. (2023). The mediating role of metacognitive awareness in the relationship between critical thinking and self-regulation. *Thinking Skills and Creativity, 47*, 101187. Advance online publication. DOI: 10.1016/j.tsc.2022.101187

Alam, A. (2023). Harnessing the Power of AI to Create Intelligent Tutoring Systems for Enhanced Classroom Experience and Improved Learning Outcomes. In *Intelligent Communication Technologies and Virtual Mobile Networks* (pp. 571–591). Springer Nature Singapore., DOI: 10.1007/978-981-99-1767-9_42

AlGerafi, M. A. M., Zhou, Y., Oubibi, M., & Wijaya, T. T. (2023). Unlocking the potential: A comprehensive evaluation of augmented reality and virtual reality in education. *Electronics (Basel), 12*(18), 3953. Advance online publication. DOI: 10.3390/electronics12183953

Alier, M., Pereira, J., García-Peñalvo, F. J., Casañ, M. J., & Cabré, J. (2025). LAMB: An open-source software framework to create artificial intelligence assistants deployed and integrated into learning management systems. *Computer Standards & Interfaces, 92*, 103940. DOI: 10.1016/j.csi.2024.103940

Alqahtani, N., & Wafula, Z. (2024). Artificial Intelligence Integration: Pedagogical Strategies and Policies at Leading Universities. *Innovative Higher Education*. Advance online publication. DOI: 10.1007/s10755-024-09749-x

Anggraeni, D. M., Prahani, B. K., Suprapto, N., Shofiyah, N., & Jatmiko, B. (2023). Systematic review of problem based learning research in fostering critical thinking skills. *Thinking Skills and Creativity, 49*, 101334. DOI: 10.1016/j.tsc.2023.101334

Ates, H. C., Nguyen, P. Q., Gonzalez-Macia, L., Morales-Narváez, E., Güder, F., Collins, J. J., & Dincer, C. (2022). End-to-end design of wearable sensors. *Nature Reviews. Materials, 7*(11), 887–907. DOI: 10.1038/s41578-022-00460-x PMID: 35910814

Bahassi, H., Azmi, M., & Khiat, A. (2024). Cognitive systems for education: Architectures, innovations, and comparative analyses. *Procedia Computer Science, 238*, 436–443. Advance online publication. DOI: 10.1016/j.procs.2024.06.045

Baig, A., Cressler, J. D., & Minsky, M. (2024). The future of AI in education: Personalized learning and intelligent tutoring systems. *AlgoVista. Journal of AI & Computer Science, 1*(2).

Baillifard, A., Gabella, M., Lavenex, P. B., & Martarelli, C. S. (2024). Effective learning with a personal AI tutor: A case study. *Education and Information Technologies*, •••, 1–16. DOI: 10.1007/s10639-024-12888-5

Bauer, E., Greisel, M., Kuznetsov, I., Berndt, M., Kollar, I., Dresel, M., Fischer, M. R., & Fischer, F. (2023). Using natural language processing to support peer-feedback in the age of artificial intelligence: A cross-disciplinary framework and a research agenda. *British Journal of Educational Technology, 54*(5), 1222–1245. DOI: 10.1111/bjet.13336

Benavot, A., Hoppers, C. O., Lockhart, A. S., & Hinzen, H. (2022). Reimagining adult education and lifelong learning for all: Historical and critical perspectives. *International Review of Education, 68(2), 165-194.* https://doi.org/ springer.comDOI: 10.1007/s11159-022-09955-9

Bozkurt, A., Karadeniz, A., Baneres, D., Guerrero-Roldán, A. E., & Rodríguez, M. E. (2021). Artificial intelligence and reflections from educational landscape: A review of AI Studies in half a century. *Sustainability (Basel), 13*(2), 800. DOI: 10.3390/su13020800

Calma, A., & Cotronei-Baird, V. (2021). Assessing critical thinking in business education: Key issues and practical solutions. *International Journal of Management Education, 19*(3), 100531. DOI: 10.1016/j.ijme.2021.100531

Canova, R., & Ma'rof, A. A. (2023). Empowering Students With Ideological and Political Education and Bridging the Gap in Modern Democracies' Ideological Division. In *Social Psychology Theories and Methods in Education (pp. 159-181).* IGI Global. DOI: DOI: 10.4018/978-1-6684-8837-9.ch008

Castagno, A. E., Ingram, J. C., Camplain, R., & Blackhorse, D. (2022). "We constantly have to navigate": Indigenous students' and professionals' strategies for navigating ethical conflicts in STEMM. *Cultural Studies of Science Education, 17*(3), 683–700. DOI: 10.1007/s11422-021-10081-5

Chalkley, A. E., Mandelid, M. B., Thurston, M., Daly-Smith, A., Singh, A., Huiberts, I., Archbold, V. S. J., Resaland, G. K., & Tjomsland, H. E. (2022). "Go beyond your own comfort zone and challenge yourself": A comparison on the use of physically active learning in Norway, the Netherlands and the UK. *Teaching and Teacher Education, 118*, 103825. DOI: 10.1016/j.tate.2022.103825

Chan, C. K. Y. (2023). A comprehensive AI policy education framework for university teaching and learning. *International Journal of Educational Technology in Higher Education*, *20*(1), 38. DOI: 10.1186/s41239-023-00408-3

Chandratreya, A. (2025). Epistemology in Research: Understanding the Foundations of Knowledge. In *Enhancing Research for Academicians in Higher Education (pp. 125-160).* IGI Global Scientific Publishing. DOI: DOI: 10.4018/979-8-3693-4496-5.ch008

Chounta, I. A., Bardone, E., Raudsep, A., & Pedaste, M. (2022). Exploring teachers' perceptions of artificial intelligence as a tool to support their practice in Estonian K-12 education. *International Journal of Artificial Intelligence in Education*, *32*(3), 725–755. DOI: 10.1007/s40593-021-00243-5

Cohen, B., Hu, A., Patino, D., & Coffman, J. (2024). This Is Going on Your Permanent Record: A Legal Analysis of Educational Data in the Cloud. *ACM Journal on Responsible Computing*, *1*(3), 1–27. DOI: 10.1145/3675230

Dandachi, I. E. (2024). AI-powered personalized learning: Toward sustainable education. In *Navigating the Intersection of Business, Sustainability and Technology (pp. 109-118).* Singapore: Springer Nature Singapore. https://doi.org/DOI: 10.1007/978-981-99-8572-2_5

Dimitriadou, E., & Lanitis, A. (2023). *A critical evaluation, challenges, and future perspectives of using artificial intelligence and emerging technologies in smart classrooms*. Smart Learning Environments., DOI: 10.1186/s40561-023-00231-3

Ellikkal, A., & Rajamohan, S. (2024). *AI-enabled personalized learning: empowering management students for improving engagement and academic performance*. Vilakshan-XIMB Journal of Management., DOI: 10.1108/XJM-02-2024-0023

Ezzaim, A., Dahbi, A., Aqqal, A., & Haidine, A. (2024). AI-based learning style detection in adaptive learning systems: A systematic literature review. *Journal of Computers in Education*, •••, 1–39. DOI: 10.1007/s40692-024-00328-9

Foster, M. E. (2024). Evaluating the Impact of Supplemental Computer-Assisted Math Instruction in Elementary School: A Conceptual Replication. *Journal of Research on Educational Effectiveness*, *17*(1), 94–118. Advance online publication. DOI: 10.1080/19345747.2023.2174919

Gawlik-Kobylińska, M. (2024). Harnessing Artificial Intelligence for Enhanced Scientific Collaboration: Insights from Students and Educational Implications. *Education Sciences*, *14*(10), 1132. Advance online publication. DOI: 10.3390/educsci14101132

George, A. S. (2023). *Future economic implications of artificial intelligence*. Partners Universal International Research Journal.

George, B., & Wooden, O. (2023). Managing the strategic transformation of higher education through artificial intelligence. *Administrative Sciences*, *13*(9), 196. Advance online publication. DOI: 10.3390/admsci13090196

Giuffrida, I., & Hall, A. (2023). Technology integration in higher education and student privacy beyond learning environments—A comparison of the UK and US perspective. *British Journal of Educational Technology*, *54*(6), 1587–1603. Advance online publication. DOI: 10.1111/bjet.13375

Gligorea, I., Cioca, M., Oancea, R., Gorski, A. T., Gorski, H., & Tudorache, P. (2023). Adaptive learning using artificial intelligence in e-learning: A literature review. *Education Sciences*, *13*(12), 1216. DOI: 10.3390/educsci13121216

González-Granadillo, G., González-Zarzosa, S., & Diaz, R. (2021). Security information and event management (SIEM): Analysis, trends, and usage in critical infrastructures. *Sensors (Basel)*, *21*(14), 4759. Advance online publication. DOI: 10.3390/s21144759 PMID: 34300500

González-Pérez, L. I., & Ramírez-Montoya, M. S. (2022). Components of Education 4.0 in 21st century skills frameworks: Systematic review. *Sustainability (Basel)*, *14*(3), 1493. Advance online publication. DOI: 10.3390/su14031493

Gouthro, P. A. (2022). Lifelong learning in a globalized world: The need for critical social theory in adult and lifelong education. *International Journal of Lifelong Education*, *41*(1), 107–121. DOI: 10.1080/02601370.2022.2033863

Grassini, S. (2023). Shaping the future of education: Exploring the potential and consequences of AI and ChatGPT in educational settings. *Education Sciences*, *13*(7), 692. Advance online publication. DOI: 10.3390/educsci13070692

Gray, M., Samala, R., Liu, Q., Skiles, D., Xu, J., Tong, W., & Wu, L. (2024). Measurement and mitigation of bias in artificial intelligence: A narrative literature review for regulatory science. *Clinical Pharmacology and Therapeutics*, *115*(4), 687–697. DOI: 10.1002/cpt.3117 PMID: 38018360

Herrera-Pavo, M. (2021). Collaborative learning for virtual higher education. *Learning*. https://doi.org/DOI: 10.1016/j.lcsi.2020.100437

Holdo, M. (2023). Critical reflection: John Dewey's relational view of transformative learning. *Journal of Transformative Education*, *21*(1), 9–25. Advance online publication. DOI: 10.1177/15413446221086727

Hooda, M., Rana, C., Dahiya, O., Rizwan, A., & Hossain, M. S. (2022). Artificial intelligence for assessment and feedback to enhance student success in higher education. *Mathematical Problems in Engineering*, *2022*(1), 5215722. DOI: 10.1155/2022/5215722

Hursen, C. (2021, September). The effect of problem-based learning method supported by web 2.0 tools on academic achievement and critical thinking skills in teacher education. *Technology*, *26*(3), 515–533. Advance online publication. DOI: 10.1007/s10758-020-09458-2

Huston, T. (2022). Social Media for Teaching Empathy, Civil and Moral Development, and Critical Thinking. In *Exploring Ethical Problems in Today's Technological World* (pp. 120–140). IGI Global., DOI: 10.4018/978-1-6684-5892-1.ch007

Indrašienė, V., Jegelevičienė, V., Merfeldaitė, O., Penkauskienė, D., Pivorienė, J., Railienė, A., Sadauskas, J., & Valavičienė, N. (2021). Linking critical thinking and knowledge management: A conceptual analysis. *Sustainability (Basel)*, *13*(3), 1476. DOI: 10.3390/su13031476

Jeon, I. S., Kang, S. J., & Kang, S. J. (2024). A Staged Framework for Computer Vision Education: Integrating AI, Data Science, and Computational Thinking. *Applied Sciences (Basel, Switzerland)*, *14*(21), 9792. Advance online publication. DOI: 10.3390/app14219792

Jose, J. (2024). The impact of integrating Microsoft Teams–Reading Progress as an Artificial Intelligence (AI) platform for promoting learners' reading aloud skills. *Education and Information Technologies*. Advance online publication. DOI: 10.1007/s10639-024-13074-3

Kaczkó, É., & Ostendorf, A. (2023). Critical thinking in the community of inquiry framework: An analysis of the theoretical model and cognitive presence coding schemes. *Computers & Education*, *193*, 104662. Advance online publication. DOI: 10.1016/j.compedu.2022.104662

Kamalov, F., Santandreu Calonge, D., & Gurrib, I. (2023). New era of artificial intelligence in education: Towards a sustainable multifaceted revolution. *Sustainability (Basel)*, *15*(16), 12451. Advance online publication. DOI: 10.3390/su151612451

Kasthuri, E., & Balaji, S. (2023). Natural language processing and deep learning chatbot using long short term memory algorithm. *Materials Today: Proceedings*, *81*, 690–693. Advance online publication. DOI: 10.1016/j.matpr.2021.04.154

Kavitha, R. K., Krupa, C. R., & Kaarthiekheyan, V. (2025). AI-Powered Digital Solutions for Smart Learning: Revolutionizing Education. In *Cybersecurity and Data Science Innovations for Sustainable Development of HEICC (pp. 213-227).* CRC Press. https://doi.org/DOI: 10.1201/9781032711300

Kim, J., Lee, H., & Cho, Y. H. (2022). Learning design to support student-AI collaboration: Perspectives of leading teachers for AI in education. *Education and Information Technologies*, *27*(5), 6069–6104. Advance online publication. DOI: 10.1007/s10639-021-10831-6

Kong, S. C., Cheung, M. Y. W., & Tsang, O. (2024). Developing an artificial intelligence literacy framework: Evaluation of a literacy course for senior secondary students using a project-based learning approach. *Computers and Education: Artificial Intelligence*, *6*, 100214. DOI: 10.1016/j.caeai.2024.100214

Kunjumuhammed, S. K. (2024). Artificial Intelligence in Addressing Educational Inequality Dimensions in Higher Education Institutions (HEIs): A Critical Review. Risks and Challenges of AI-Driven *Finance: Bias, Ethics, and Security, 146-164.* DOI: DOI: 10.4018/979-8-3693-2185-0.ch007

Labadze, L., Grigolia, M., & Machaidze, L. (2023). Role of AI chatbots in education: Systematic literature review. *International Journal of Educational Technology in Higher Education*, *20*(1), 56. DOI: 10.1186/s41239-023-00426-1

Labadze, L., Grigolia, M., & Machaidze, L. (2023). Role of AI chatbots in education: systematic. https://doi.org/DOI: 10.1186/s41239-023-00426-1

Li, L., Fengchao, Y., & Zhang, E. (2024). A systematic review of learning task design for K-12 AI education: Trends, challenges, and opportunities. *Computers and Education: Artificial Intelligence*, *100217*, 100217. Advance online publication. DOI: 10.1016/j.caeai.2024.100217

Liang, W., & Fung, D. (2021). Fostering critical thinking in English-as-a-second-language classrooms: Challenges and opportunities. *Thinking Skills and Creativity*, *39*, 100769. Advance online publication. DOI: 10.1016/j.tsc.2020.100769

Maqbool, M. A., Asif, M., Imran, M., Bibi, S., & Almusharraf, N. (2024). Emerging e-learning trends: A study of faculty perceptions and impact of collaborative techniques using fuzzy interface system. *Social Sciences & Humanities Open*, *10*, 101035. DOI: 10.1016/j.ssaho.2024.101035

Mascarenhas, O. A., Thakur, M., & Kumar, P. (2023). Critical Thinking for Understanding Fallibility and Falsifiability of Our Knowledge. In *A Primer on Critical Thinking and Business Ethics: Recent Conceptualizations of Critical Thinking (Volume 1) (pp. 187-216)*. Emerald Publishing Limited. https://doi.org/DOI: 10.1108/978-1-83753-308-420231007

Mascarenhas, O. A., Thakur, M., & Kumar, P. (2023). History of Critical Thinking and Some Models of Critical Thinking. In *A Primer on Critical Thinking and Business Ethics: Recent Conceptualizations of Critical Thinking (Volume 1) (pp. 41-80)*. Emerald Publishing Limited. https://doi.org/DOI: 10.1108/978-1-83753-308-420231003

Mohanty, R. N., Thomas, A., & Kori, A. (2024). Next-Generation Innovative Teaching Ecosystems for Futuristic Management Education. In *Global Higher Education Practices in Times of Crisis: Questions for Sustainability and Digitalization (pp. 5-28)*. Emerald Publishing Limited. https://doi.org/DOI: 10.1108/978-1-83797-052-020241002

Morris, P., Park, C., & Auld, E. (2022). Covid and the future of education: Global agencies 'building back better'. *Compare: A Journal of Comparative Education*, *52*(5), 691–711. DOI: 10.1080/03057925.2022.2066886

Muthmainnah, I. S., Ibna Seraj, P. M., & Oteir, I. (2022). P. M., & Oteir, I. (2022). Playing with AI to Investigate Human-Computer Interaction Technology and Improving Critical Thinking Skills to Pursue 21st Century Age. *Education Research International*, *6468995*(1), 1–17. DOI: 10.1155/2022/6468995

Ng, D. T. K., Leung, J. K. L., Su, J., Ng, R. C. W., & Chu, S. K. W. (2023). Teachers' AI digital competencies and twenty-first century skills in the post-pandemic world. *Educational Technology Research and Development*, *71*(1), 137–161. DOI: 10.1007/s11423-023-10203-6 PMID: 36844361

Onesi-Ozigagun, O., Ololade, Y. J., Eyo-Udo, N. L., & Ogundipe, D. O. (2024). Revolutionizing education through AI: A comprehensive review of enhancing learning experiences. *International Journal of Applied Research in Social Sciences*, *6*(4), 589–607. DOI: 10.51594/ijarss.v6i4.1011

Osipovskaya, E., & Dmitrieva, S. (2022). The Issue of Adaptive Learning as Educational Innovation. In *Technology, Innovation and Creativity in Digital Society: XXI Professional Culture of the Specialist of the Future (pp. 606-617)*. Springer International Publishing. https://doi.org/ [HTML]DOI: 10.1007/978-3-030-89708-6_50

Ouyang, F., Wu, M., Zheng, L., Zhang, L., & Jiao, P. (2023). Integration of artificial intelligence performance prediction and learning analytics to improve student learning in online engineering course. *International Journal of Educational Technology in Higher Education, 20(1), 4.* https://doi.org/ springer.comDOI: 10.1186/s41239-022-00372-4

Pacholek, K., Prostean, M., Burris, S., Cockburn, L., Nganji, J., Nadège, A. N., & Mbibeh, L. (2021). A WhatsApp community forum for improving critical thinking and practice skills of mental health providers in a conflict zone. *Interactive Learning Environments, 31*(4), 2471–2489. DOI: 10.1080/10494820.2021.1890622

Peterson, P. E., & Shakeel, M. D. (2024). The nation's charter report card: A new ranking of states by charter student performance. *Journal of School Choice, 18*(1), 30–66. Advance online publication. DOI: 10.1080/15582159.2023.2273607

Rajaram, K. (2023). Future of learning: Teaching and learning strategies. In *Learning Intelligence: Innovative and Digital Transformative Learning Strategies: Cultural and Social Engineering Perspectives (pp. 3-53).* Singapore: Springer Nature Singapore. https://doi.org/DOI: 10.1007/978-981-19-9201-8_1

Ramírez-Montoya, M. S., Andrade-Vargas, L., Rivera-Rogel, D., & Portuguez-Castro, M. (2021). Trends for the future of education programs for professional development. *Sustainability (Basel), 13*(13), 7244. DOI: 10.3390/su13137244

Rantala, K., Alasuutari, N., & Kuorikoski, J. (2024). The logic of regulatory impact assessment: From evidence to evidential reasoning. *Regulation & Governance, 18*(2), 534–550. DOI: 10.1111/rego.12542

Ruiz-Rojas, L. I., Acosta-Vargas, P., De-Moreta-Llovet, J., & Gonzalez-Rodriguez, M. (2023). Empowering education with generative artificial intelligence tools: Approach with an instructional design matrix. *Sustainability (Basel), 15*(15), 11524. DOI: 10.3390/su151511524

Ruiz-Rojas, L. I., Salvador-Ullauri, L., & Acosta-Vargas, P. (2024). Collaborative working and critical thinking: Adoption of generative artificial intelligence tools in higher education. *Sustainability (Basel), 16*(13), 5367. Advance online publication. DOI: 10.3390/su16135367

Sajja, R., Sermet, Y., Cikmaz, M., Cwiertny, D., & Demir, I. (2024). Artificial intelligence-enabled intelligent assistant for personalized and adaptive learning in higher education. *Information (Basel), 15*(10), 596. Advance online publication. DOI: 10.3390/info15100596

Saqr, R. R., Al-Somali, S. A., & Sarhan, M. Y. (2023). Exploring the acceptance and user satisfaction of AI-driven e-learning platforms (Blackboard, Moodle, Edmodo, Coursera and edX): An integrated technology model. *Sustainability (Basel), 16*(1), 204. Advance online publication. DOI: 10.3390/su16010204

Saritepeci, M., & Yildiz Durak, H. (2024). Effectiveness of artificial intelligence integration in design-based learning on design thinking mindset, creative and reflective thinking skills: An experimental study. *Education and Information Technologies, 29*(18), 25175–25209. Advance online publication. DOI: 10.1007/s10639-024-12829-2

Schiff, D. (2021). Out of the laboratory and into the classroom: the future of artificial intelligence in education. *AI & society*. https://doi.org/springer.comDOI: 10.1007/s00146-020-01033-8

Seo, K., Tang, J., Roll, I., Fels, S., & Yoon, D. (2021). The impact of artificial intelligence on learner–instructor interaction in online learning. *International Journal of Educational Technology in Higher Education, 18*(1), 1–23. DOI: 10.1186/s41239-021-00292-9 PMID: 34778540

Shah, S. S., & Asad, M. M. (2024). Impact of critical thinking approach on learners' dependence on innovative transformation through artificial intelligence. In *The Evolution of Artificial Intelligence in Higher Education: Challenges, Risks, and Ethical Considerations (pp. 161-182)*. Emerald Publishing Limited. https://doi.org/DOI: 10.1108/978-1-83549-486-820241010

Shankar, S. K., Pothancheri, G., Sasi, D., & Mishra, S. (2024). Bringing teachers in the loop: Exploring perspectives on integrating generative AI in technology-enhanced learning. *International Journal of Artificial Intelligence in Education*, •••, 1–26. DOI: 10.1007/s40593-024-00428-8

Shutaleva, A. (2023). Ecological culture and critical thinking: Building of a sustainable future. *Sustainability (Basel), 15*(18), 13492. Advance online publication. DOI: 10.3390/su151813492

Southworth, J. (2022). Bridging critical thinking and transformative learning: The role of perspective-taking. *Theory and Research in Education, 20*(1), 44–63. Advance online publication. DOI: 10.1177/14778785221090853

Southworth, J., Migliaccio, K., Glover, J., Reed, D., McCarty, C., Brendemuhl, J., & Thomas, A. (2023). Developing a model for AI Across the curriculum: Transforming the higher education landscape via innovation in AI literacy. *Computers and Education: Artificial Intelligence, 4*, 100127. DOI: 10.1016/j.caeai.2023.100127

Strielkowski, W., Grebennikova, V., Lisovskiy, A., Rakhimova, G., & Vasileva, T. (2024). AI-driven adaptive learning for sustainable educational transformation. *Sustainable Development*. Advance online publication. DOI: 10.1002/sd.3221

Tariq, M. U. (2024). Enhancing students and learning achievement as 21st-century skills through transdisciplinary approaches. In *Transdisciplinary Approaches to Learning Outcomes in Higher Education* (pp. 220–257). IGI Global., DOI: 10.4018/979-8-3693-3699-1.ch007

Teixeira, R., Nogal, M., & O'Connor, A. (2021). Adaptive approaches in metamodel-based reliability analysis: A review. *Structural Safety*, *89*, 102019. Advance online publication. DOI: 10.1016/j.strusafe.2020.102019

Thornhill-Miller, B., Camarda, A., Mercier, M., Burkhardt, J. M., Morisseau, T., Bourgeois-Bougrine, S., Vinchon, F., El Hayek, S., Augereau-Landais, M., Mourey, F., Feybesse, C., Sundquist, D., & Lubart, T. (2023). Creativity, critical thinking, communication, and collaboration: Assessment, certification, and promotion of 21st century skills for the future of work and education. *Journal of Intelligence*, *11*(3), 54. DOI: 10.3390/jintelligence11030054 PMID: 36976147

van Baalen, S., Boon, M., & Verhoef, P. (2021). From clinical decision support to clinical reasoning support systems. *Journal of Evaluation in Clinical Practice*, *27*(3), 520–528. DOI: 10.1111/jep.13541 PMID: 33554432

Van Le, H., & Chong, S. L. (2024). The dynamics of critical thinking skills: A phenomenographic exploration from Malaysian and Vietnamese undergraduates. *Thinking Skills and Creativity*, *51*, 101445. Advance online publication. DOI: 10.1016/j.tsc.2023.101445

Walter, Y. (2024). Embracing the future of Artificial Intelligence in the classroom: The relevance of AI literacy, prompt engineering, and critical thinking in modern education. *International Journal of Educational Technology in Higher Education*, *21*(1), 15. DOI: 10.1186/s41239-024-00448-3

Wang, T. & Cheng, E. C. K. (2021). An investigation of barriers to Hong Kong K-12 schools incorporating Artificial Intelligence in education. *Computers and Education: Artificial Intelligence*. https://doi.org/.DOI: 10.1016/j.caeai.2021.100031

Woldt, J. L., & Nenad, M. W. (2021). Reflective writing in dental education to improve critical thinking and learning: A systematic review. *Journal of Dental Education*, *85*(6), 778–785. Advance online publication. DOI: 10.1002/jdd.12561 PMID: 33576055

Xu, E., Wang, W., & Wang, Q. (2023). The effectiveness of collaborative problem solving in promoting students' critical thinking: A meta-analysis based on empirical literature. *Humanities & Social Sciences Communications*, *10*(1), 1–11. DOI: 10.1057/s41599-023-01508-1 PMID: 37192950

Yu, H. (2024). The application and challenges of ChatGPT in educational transformation: New demands for teachers' roles. *Heliyon*, *10*(2), e24289. Advance online publication. DOI: 10.1016/j.heliyon.2024.e24289 PMID: 38298626

Zamiri, M., & Esmaeili, A. (2024). Strategies, methods, and supports for developing skills within learning communities: A systematic review of the literature. *Administrative Sciences*, *14*(9), 231. Advance online publication. DOI: 10.3390/admsci14090231

Zhai, C., Wibowo, S., & Li, L. D. (2024). *The effects of over-reliance on AI dialogue systems on students' cognitive abilities: a systematic review*. Smart Learning Environments., DOI: 10.1186/s40561-024-00316-7

Chapter 13
Navigating the AI Era:
Enhancing Critical Thinking Skills for Global Challenges

Andi Asrifan
https://orcid.org/0000-0002-9934-6129
Universitas Negeri Makassar, Indonesia

Agnes Widyaningrum
Universitas Stikubank Semarang, Indonesia

Ratu Bulkis Ramli
Universitas Musamus, Indonesia

Riyanti Riyanti
https://orcid.org/0000-0002-0640-6920
Universitas Muhammadiyah Palopo, Indonesia

Sultan Sultan
https://orcid.org/0000-0003-3306-9306
Universitas Muhammadiyah Palopo, Indonesia

ABSTRACT

This chapter examines the vital junction between artificial intelligence (AI) and critical thinking, highlighting the imperative to improve critical thinking abilities to effectively manage the complexities of contemporary society. As AI technologies are progressively incorporated into several sectors, the capacity to assess, evaluate, and synthesize information is essential for effective decision-making. The chapter examines the progression of AI, its applications in everyday life, and the ethical implications that emerge from its utilization. It underscores the significance of cultivating critical thinking using educational methodologies, including Socratic

DOI: 10.4018/979-8-3373-4576-5.ch013

seminars, case studies, and problem-based learning. By fostering a culture of inquiry and adaptation, humans may more effectively tackle global concerns such as climate change and inequality, utilizing AI as a means for inventive solutions. The chapter ultimately promotes a proactive educational strategy that emphasizes critical thinking in the era of AI.

UNDERSTANDING AI AND ITS IMPACT

1.1 The Evolution of Artificial Intelligence

Outstanding accomplishments and groundbreaking innovations define AI's progress. From the mid-20th century to today, AI has changed the connection between technology and users. This section covers AI's evolution, primitive progress, AI winters, and machine learning and deep learning's recent resurrection. This history is crucial to understanding AI's impact across businesses and predicting its future.

Artificial intelligence (AI) has undergone several decades of milestones and transformational advancements that have changed our understanding of technology and its possibilities. In the mid-20th century, Alan Turing and John McCarthy laid the groundwork for artificial intelligence, a transformative field. Turing's foundational paper, "Computing Machinery and Intelligence," proposed machines that can emulate human intelligence, while McCarthy introduced the term "artificial intelligence" at the 1956 Dartmouth Conference, often considered AI's inception.

Early artificial intelligence research focused on symbolic thinking and rule-based systems, which used logical deduction to solve problems. These early technologies, called "expert systems," were limited and heavily reliant on human expertise for information. They struggled to adapt to new situations and learn from experience, culminating in the "AI winter" of the 1970s and 1980s, when funding and excitement in the field plummeted (Villar et al., 2021).

Processor improvements, data availability, and machine learning advancements revived AI in the late 1990s and early 2000s (Khan et al., 2021). Machine learning, an AI discipline, lets systems learn from data instead of rules. The development of algorithms that could recognize patterns, anticipate, and improve over time led to widespread applications in many industries.

In the 2010s, deep learning used multi-layered neural networks to analyse complex data (Sarker, 2021; Shao et al., 2022). Picture and audio recognition, natural language processing, and autonomous systems have advanced because to this technology. Deep learning helped Google, Amazon, and Facebook create advanced virtual assistants, recommendation systems, and other features.

Today, artificial intelligence influences our communication, work, and decision-making. AI affects self-driving cars and smart household products. This rapid rise raises ethical and social questions that require serious examination. Understanding AI growth is crucial for maximizing its promise and overcoming its challenges. This foundation will be vital when we investigate AI and critical thinking convergence in later chapters.

Franco-Mariscal et al. (2024) conducted a mixed-methods study with Spanish secondary school science educators to evaluate the ENCIC-CT model's critical thinking benefits. Structured, inquiry-based methods significantly enhanced students' scientific analysis and evaluation skills, according to classroom observations, teacher interviews, and student assessments. The research found obstacles like teacher implementation variability and the Spanish education system's contextual uniqueness that may limit generalizability. This study underscores the need of fostering critical thinking within topic frameworks and broader validation across educational and cultural contexts.

1.2 AI in Daily Life

AI has transformed our technology use and affected many industries (Rashid & Kausik, 2024). AI improves healthcare, finance, and education efficiency, outcomes, and methodologies.

Artificial intelligence is changing healthcare and research. Machine learning algorithms find patterns in large datasets that humans miss, enabling early diagnosis and customised treatment (Asif et al., 2024). AI-driven diagnostic devices can precisely analyze X-rays and MRIs, helping doctors diagnose cancer and fractures. AI chatbots also answer health issues quickly, improving communication and relieving healthcare providers.

Finance uses AI to improve decision-making and reduce risk. AI-based automated trading systems analyze market patterns and execute deals faster than human traders (Pik et al., 2025; Leahy, 2024). Fraud detection relies on AI to analyze transactions for anomalies and identify potential fraud in real time. This proactive technique protects clients and maintains financial institution confidence and security.

AI is changing education for students and teachers. Intelligent tutoring systems tailor support and resources to each student's learning style (Bradáč et al., 2022; Lin et al., 2023). Duolingo uses AI to adjust language exercise difficulty based on user performance, keeping learners engaged and challenged. AI-driven data also help educators track student progress and identify areas that need more help, improving learning.

Beyond these areas, AI applications include daily conveniences like Siri and Alexa, which use natural language processing to understand and respond to human commands (Buhalis & Moldavska, 2022). These tools improve our efficiency by setting reminders and managing smart home devices.

It's crucial to carefully evaluate AI's effects as it permeates daily life. Data privacy, algorithmic bias, and technology dependence necessitate informed conversation and deliberate decision-making. Understanding AI's role in human life helps us overcome its hurdles and use its powers to solve global issues (Kulkov et al. 2024). In the following chapters, we will use this perspective to analyze AI and critical thinking.

Thinking about AI's role in society today is important given its history. Since AI is now part of many industries, it's a relatable issue. AI improves efficiency and decision-making in almost every area, from predictive diagnosis to personalized learning. These advances are valuable, yet also raise ethical and social issues.

1.3 Ethical Considerations

Responsible AI application in higher education requires ethical frameworks based on openness, accountability, justice, and beneficence. AI systems used in education, evaluation, and decision-making must disclose their data sources, algorithms, and limits. Institutions and developers are accountable for AI outcomes, especially when mistakes affect student learning or growth. Justice promotes equal access, eliminating algorithmic bias and ensuring student diversity. Beneficence requires institutions to use AI to improve student learning. These ideas build trust and link AI deployment to education.

Due to the widespread use of artificial intelligence (AI), ethical issues arise that demand careful consideration (Jedličková, 2024). The ethical implications of AI are complex, notably with bias, privacy, and job loss. A responsible and equitable AI environment requires addressing these issues.

Bias is a major AI ethical issue. Artificial intelligence systems use large datasets of historical data and social norms (Varona & Suárez, 2022; Norori et al., 2021). AI systems may unintentionally reinforce race, gender, and socioeconomic status biases in their decision-making if these datasets contain them. Critics say facial recognition technology makes more mistakes when identifying people of color, reinforcing structural disadvantages. Open and accountable AI systems require developers to find and fix algorithm biases.

AI makes privacy an ethical issue. AI system expansion often requires collecting and analyzing large amounts of personal data. Online habit tracking and health monitoring may compromise privacy to improve services and insights (Bhatt et al., 2023)—data collection raises ethical questions about consent, ownership, and exploitation. Finding a balance between data use for innovation and privacy is crucial.

To address these concerns, strict data protection rules and ethical data management are necessary.

AI's expansion threatens jobs (Mirbabaie et al., 2022; Tong, 2021). As automation and AI technologies improve at human jobs, job displacement and economic inequality issues grow. AI can boost productivity and create new jobs, but it may also upend the workforce. Displacement in manufacturing, transportation, and customer service may need proactive staff retraining and reskilling. In an AI-driven economy, policymakers, businesses, and schools must collaborate to help workers adjust to new jobs (Adel, 2024).

THE IMPORTANCE OF CRITICAL THINKING

2.1 Defining Critical Thinking

Critical thinking is essential for processing complex information and making educated decisions (Thornhill-Miller et al., 2023). Understanding critical thinking is crucial for addressing global issues in an AI-driven and data-driven future. Critical thinking involves examining, assessing, and inferring to solve problems rationally.

Critical thinking begins with analysis. Deconstructing complex information into its basic components helps explain its structure and relationships (Franco-Mariscal et al., 2024). This method requires identifying relevant facts, acknowledging assumptions, and identifying data patterns. Critical thinkers examine a news article's sources, proof, and context. This analytical strategy clarifies main points and reveals biases or reasoning errors.

Second, appraisal assesses information's credibility and significance. Consider sources' credibility, arguments' coherence, and opposing views. Critical information evaluation is crucial in an age of quick deception. Critical thinkers weigh the pros and cons of other viewpoints, taking into account the author's credentials, research methodologies, and possible motivations (Campo et al., 2023). This evaluation method improves understanding and decision-making on complex topics.

The third step, inference, involves drawing conclusions from data analysis. At this level, people must synthesize data and draw judgments beyond the local circumstances. Inferences can predict future events or suggest solutions (Kuperberg, 2021). A corporate manager may examine market trends and consumer feedback to predict a new product's success. Strategic planning and problem-solving require informed decisions.

The literature discusses AI's role in critical thinking from several angles. AI advocates say technology can increase metacognition by providing instant, personalized feedback and enabling data-informed reflection (Vashishth et al., 2024). They highlight AI's ability to provide inquiry-based learning and customized instruction. Critics say overreliance on AI could reduce cognitive engagement and encourage learners to accept AI outputs without question (Andrae, 2025). Some experts worry about algorithmic bias and human judgment loss. This disparity shows that AI can be a powerful instructional tool and a cognitive reliance.

2.2 The Role of Critical Thinking in Problem Solving

Critical thinking is fundamental to effective problem-solving and decision-making processes (Moustaghfir & Brigui, 2024). Critical thinking is vital for managing uncertainty and making informed decisions in a time marked by swift technological progress and intricate global issues. Critical thinking improves our ability to develop successful solutions by promoting a methodical method for discovering, analyzing, and resolving issues.

The essence of issue-solving lies in the precise definition of the problem. Critical thinking drives individuals to explore thoroughly, transcending superficial symptoms to identify fundamental causes (Van Le & Chong, 2024). In a corporate context, a decrease in sales may initially seem to be a simple problem. Through critical analysis, a team may identify underlying issues such as changes in consumer behavior, poor marketing methods, or heightened competition. By precisely delineating the problem, critical thinkers can formulate targeted tactics that tackle the fundamental causes instead of merely alleviating the symptoms.

Upon defining the problem, critical thinking enables the investigation of possible solutions. This procedure entails generating a variety of alternatives and assessing their viability and potential effects. Critical thinkers evaluate the merits and drawbacks of each option, taking into account aspects such as resource availability, time limitations, and potential dangers (Michel-Villarreal et al., 2023; Ruiz-Rojas et al., 2024). This evaluative method guarantees that conclusions rely on evidence and rational judgment instead of intuition or prejudice. For instance, when confronted with a decision regarding the adoption of new technology, a critical thinker will evaluate the anticipated advantages against the expenses and any disruptions to current procedures.

Furthermore, critical thinking improves collaboration and communication throughout the problem-solving process (Xu et al., 2023). Incorporating varied viewpoints enhances the overall comprehension of the matter being addressed. Critical thinkers foster open debate, challenge assumptions, and invite constructive feedback, creating an environment where innovative solutions might develop. This cooperative method is especially beneficial in interdisciplinary teams, where diverse knowledge can result in more effective problem-solving results.

Ultimately, critical thinking facilitates the assessment of executed solutions. Following the implementation of a decision and solution, critical thinkers consistently evaluate its efficacy (Rivas et al., 2022). They collect data, evaluate results, and contemplate the decision-making process, recognizing insights gained and opportunities for enhancement. This iterative method not only improves future problem-solving endeavors but also cultivates a culture of perpetual learning.

2.3 Critical Thinking in the Age of Information Overload

In the contemporary digital environment, individuals are overwhelmed by an incessant flow of information from diverse sources, such as social media, news organizations, and online platforms (Ochonogor, 2021). This syndrome, commonly known as information overload, presents considerable critical thinking and decision-making hurdles. In navigating this intricate environment, establishing ways to identify genuine information is crucial for making educated decisions and effectively tackling global concerns.

One of the initial ways to address information overload is to develop a critical attitude (Panda & Kaur, 2024). This entails examining information with skepticism and inquisitiveness instead of accepting it uncritically. Critical thinkers ought to inquire: Who is the author? What is their area of expertise? What evidence substantiates their assertions? By critically interrogating the information encountered, individuals can more effectively evaluate its reliability and pertinence.

Assessing the sources of information is a crucial method. In an age of quick misinformation dissemination, identifying reputable sources is essential. Credible sources generally possess defined editorial standards, rigorous fact-checking protocols, and transparency concerning their methodologies (Ye, 2023; Sánchez et al., 2024). Individuals ought to emphasize information from reputable organizations, scholarly journals, and acknowledged specialists in the domain. Moreover, cross-referencing information from several sources can enhance its accuracy and yield a more thorough comprehension of the subject.

Enhancing media literacy skills is essential in the era of information saturation. Media literacy comprises critically examining media information, understanding its purpose, and recognizing bias (Polanco-Levicán & Salvo-Garrido2022; Luo et al., 2022). Individuals should be aware of the strategies utilized in media, such as sensationalism or emotional appeals, which can distort facts and impact opinions. By strengthening media literacy abilities, individuals can better manage the intricacies of information intake and make more informed judgments.

Additionally, the "CRAAP" test—an acronym representing Currency, Relevance, Authority, Accuracy, and Purpose—can function as an effective framework for assessing material. This strategy prompts individuals to evaluate the timeliness of the information, its relevance to their requirements, the author's legitimacy, the content's veracity, and the intent behind its development. Through the methodical application of this test, individuals can discern erroneous information and concentrate on stuff that satisfies their critical criteria.

Finally, it is imperative to engage in mindfulness when consuming information. Establishing boundaries around media consumption, such as restricting time allocated to social media or selectively curating news feeds, helps mitigate feelings of being overwhelmed. Engaging with information deliberately and purposefully enables individuals to process content more efficiently and improves their critical thinking skills (Muthmainnah et al., 2022; Ienca, 2023).

INTEGRATING AI WITH CRITICAL THINKING

3.1 AI as a Tool for Enhancing Critical Thinking

As artificial intelligence (AI) advances, it offers distinctive chances to improve critical thinking abilities, especially in data processing and decision-making. Utilizing AI technologies enables individuals and businesses to traverse intricate information environments more efficiently, facilitating more educated and nuanced choices (Marengo, 2024).

AI mostly aids in data analysis by efficiently and precisely processing extensive volumes of information. Conventional data analysis techniques frequently falter when confronted with the vast data produced in the contemporary digital world. AI algorithms can analyze extensive datasets, uncovering patterns and trends that may not be readily discernible to human analysts (Jejeniwa et al., 2024). AI may examine patient records and clinical data in healthcare to identify correlations between symptoms and diagnoses, resulting in more precise and prompt treatments. Through the automation of these procedures, AI liberates critical thinkers to concentrate on analyzing outcomes and formulating strategic decisions derived from the insights created by the data.

Furthermore, AI systems can improve decision-making through the provision of predictive insights. Machine learning algorithms can evaluate historical data to predict future events, allowing firms to make proactive rather than reactive decisions (Aljohani, 2023). In finance, AI-driven models can forecast market movements, assisting investors in making informed decisions regarding asset allocation. Integrating predictive analytics into decision-making enables individuals to evaluate prospective risks and advantages more efficiently, resulting in more informed plans.

AI can also promote improved collaboration and communication across teams. AI-driven platforms can consolidate and integrate information from many sources, offering team members a holistic perspective of pertinent data (Akter et al., 2023; Nguyen-Trung et al., 2024). This capacity promotes educated discourse and stimulates critical thinking, enabling team members to participate with a common comprehension of the pertinent topics. In project management, AI tools assist teams in monitoring progress, pinpointing bottlenecks, and optimizing resource allocation, hence enhancing problem-solving and decision-making efficacy.

Moreover, AI can enhance critical thinking by delivering immediate feedback and insights. In educational contexts, AI-based tutoring systems can assess student performance and provide tailored recommendations for enhancement (Vashishth et al., 2024). This prompt feedback mechanism compels learners to contemplate their comprehension and modify their strategies, promoting an environment of critical inquiry and perpetual learning.

Nonetheless, although AI can augment critical thinking, it is essential to acknowledge its constraints. Artificial intelligence is not flawless and can be affected by biases inherent in the data it analyzes. Consequently, critical thinkers must maintain vigilance, interrogating AI-generated ideas and employing them as a resource rather than a conclusive solution. Integrating the analytical capabilities of AI with human discernment enables individuals to address intricate difficulties more efficiently (Kase et al., 2022; Zarei et al., 2024).

Examining the convergence of AI and critical thinking under constructivist theory illustrates how learners actively construct knowledge through engagement with AI tools. Constructivism underscores the significance of meaning-making via exploration, reflection, and collaboration—tenets bolstered by adaptive AI platforms that react to student input and facilitate inquiry. Conversely, connectivism emphasizes the significance of digital networks in the construction of knowledge, situating AI as a component inside learners' cognitive ecosystems. AI enhances critical thinking by aggregating varied knowledge sources, promoting pattern recognition, and facilitating discernment in managing complexity. Both frameworks emphasize AI's capacity to augment—rather than supplant—human reasoning via guided discovery and informed decision-making.

3.2 Limitations of AI in Critical Thinking

Although artificial intelligence (AI) provides significant advantages in improving critical thinking and decision-making, it is crucial to acknowledge its limitations (Muthmainnah et al., 2022; Walter, 2024). Comprehending these limitations is essential to maintain human oversight in the problem-solving process, especially in an age of growing technological dependence.

A key drawback of AI is its reliance on the quality and availability of data. AI algorithms derive knowledge from past data, and their outputs are contingent upon the quality of the training data (Sarker, 2021). Biased, incomplete, or unrepresentative data might result in AI generating skewed outcomes that may perpetuate existing biases or yield incorrect findings. Facial recognition algorithms exhibit elevated error rates for individuals from underprivileged communities, owing to insufficient variety in the training datasets. This underscores the imperative of human supervision in curating and validating data to guarantee that AI systems operate equitably and efficiently.

Furthermore, AI does not possess the capacity to comprehend context like humans do. Although AI can identify patterns and correlations, it lacks the deep comprehension of human emotions, cultural dynamics, and ethical issues that are frequently essential in decision-making (Baranidharan & Dhakshayini, 2024). In a healthcare context, an AI may provide treatment exclusively based on statistics, disregarding a patient's individual circumstances, preferences, or emotional well-being. This constraint highlights the significance of human discernment in understanding AI-generated insights and making judgments that consider the wider context.

Artificial intelligence has difficulties in intricate problem-solving situations characterized by uncertainty or necessitating innovation (Henriksen et al., 2024). Although AI is proficient at processing organized data and executing repetitive activities, it lacks the capability to address unstructured challenges that need original thinking or ethical reasoning. For instance, when tackling social challenges like poverty or climate change, critical thinking necessitates a comprehensive approach that considers diverse stakeholders, ethical ramifications, and enduring consequences—domains where AI may be inadequate.

Furthermore, dependence on AI may result in cognitive complacency, causing individuals to rely excessively on technology for decision-making. This dependence can erode critical thinking abilities, as individuals may accept AI advice without scrutinizing their validity or considering opposing perspectives. It is essential to foster a culture of critical inquiry that motivates individuals to actively engage with AI outputs instead of passively accepting them (Andrae, 2025).

3.3 Case Studies: AI in Action

Artificial intelligence (AI) has become a transformational influence in multiple domains, improving critical thinking and refining decision-making processes. Analyzing real-world case studies provides insights into the effective integration of

AI across several sectors, illustrating its capacity to enhance human judgment and improve outcomes (Theodorakopoulos et al., 2024; Hao et al., 2024).

A prominent instance is within the healthcare sector, where AI has played a crucial role in diagnoses and patient management. IBM's Watson Health exhibits this integration by employing natural language processing and machine learning to examine extensive volumes of medical literature, patient records, and clinical trial data (Joshi, 2025; Martínez-García & Hernández-Lemus, 2022). In one instance, Watson aided oncologists in cancer diagnosis by offering evidence-based therapy options customized for particular patients. Through the synthesis of intricate data, Watson empowers healthcare providers to make better educated decisions, hence enhancing patient outcomes. This partnership between AI and healthcare professionals illustrates how AI may augment critical thinking by delivering actionable insights, enabling human practitioners to utilize their experience and empathy.

In finance, AI-driven algorithms are transforming risk assessment and investment strategies (Oyeniyi et al., 2024). For example, companies such as BlackRock employ AI to evaluate market patterns and identify portfolio risks. Through the analysis of vast information encompassing economic indicators and previous market performance, AI models may discern prospective investment possibilities and risks that human experts may overlook. This method enables financial professionals to make data-driven judgments, hence improving their analytical skills. Moreover, AI systems may perpetually learn from fresh data, adjusting investment strategies in real-time, hence enhancing proactive decision-making in a swiftly evolving market landscape (Samara et al., 2024).

The education sector has shown substantial progress due to AI integration. Platforms such as Coursera and Khan Academy utilize AI algorithms to tailor educational experiences for learners (Song et al., 2024). Through the analysis of individual performance data, these platforms can provide customized learning trajectories, resources, and evaluations. This tailored method increases student involvement and enables educators to make educated choices on instructional tactics. Educators, by understanding student development and learning styles, can employ critical thinking to modify their teaching techniques, guaranteeing that all students have the necessary support for success (El-Sabagh, 2021).

Although AI tools such as Khan Academy are primarily intended for K-12 education, their significance in higher education is evident in their capacity to provide scalable, adaptive learning paradigms. In K-12 environments, AI modifies content difficulty according to real-time performance, promoting early autonomous thinking. This principle is applicable to higher education via analogous adaptive platforms such as ALEKS or Smart Sparrow, which facilitate personalized learning in extensive university courses. In contrast to K-12 education, university students are anticipated to engage more seriously with AI input, utilizing it for discipline-specific challenges.

The alteration in cognitive requirements underscores the necessity for contextual adjustment at various educational tiers.

Furthermore, in the domain of environmental sustainability, AI is employed to address climate change. Google's AI for Environmental Insights exemplifies the application of machine learning to scrutinize urban data, offering municipalities actionable intelligence regarding energy consumption, emissions, and resource management (Casali et al., 2022). AI empowers city planners with data-driven insights, enhancing their capacity to make informed decisions that foster sustainability and tackle environmental issues.

To more accurately represent the higher education setting, generic examples such as Coursera or Watson should be substituted with more specific institutional instances. At Universitas Indonesia, artificial intelligence-based plagiarism detection and academic writing tools are incorporated into undergraduate thesis supervision, fostering ethical scholarship and critical evaluation. At Aalto University in Finland, AI tutors assist engineering students by providing real-time feedback on problem sets, thereby promoting analytical reasoning. Arizona State University employs adaptive learning platforms to tailor instruction in large-enrollment courses, thereby improving student engagement and reflective learning. These examples provide tangible insights into the influence of AI on the development of critical thinking in various higher education settings.

DEVELOPING CRITICAL THINKING SKILLS

4.1 Educational Approaches

The cultivation of critical thinking abilities is vital for equipping students to manage the intricacies of contemporary society, especially within an AI-driven framework (Walter, 2024). Educators are essential in cultivating these skills through diverse pedagogical approaches that promote inquiry, analysis, and reflection. An examination of excellent educational methodologies demonstrates their capacity to foster critical thinking in pupils.

A well-acknowledged approach is project-based learning (PBL). This method involves students in practical projects that necessitate the exploration of intricate questions, the resolution of challenges, and the production of concrete results. Through collaborative project work, students acquire the skills to analyze information, assess sources, and integrate their results into cohesive presentations or deliverables (Ruiz-Rojas et al., 2024). Project-based Learning (PBL) cultivates critical thinking while augmenting collaboration and communication skills, equipping students with the skills to work well in varied settings.

An additional useful tactic is the Socratic method, which prioritizes dialogue and inquiry. This method involves educators guiding discussions through the use of open-ended questions that compel students to engage in critical thinking and express their rationale. Through polite discourse and considering many perspectives, students cultivate the capacity to understand arguments and assess evidence (Bächtold et al., 2023). This approach fosters intellectual curiosity and enables students to become more reflective thinkers, adept at scrutinizing their preconceptions and biases.

Inquiry-based learning is a strategy that fosters critical thinking by motivating students to pose questions and investigate subjects of interest. In this methodology, educators assist students in developing their inquiries, performing research, and deriving conclusions from their results. This technique enables students to assume control of their education, cultivating a sense of autonomy and accountability. Through inquiry, students acquire the skills to assess source credibility, examine evidence, and formulate coherent arguments, vital critical thinking elements (Sönmez et al., 2021).

Moreover, integrating technology and digital literacy into the curriculum is essential in the age of AI. Educators can utilize digital tools to instruct students on navigating online material, evaluating its authenticity, and participating in critical conversations regarding digital content (Gouseti et al., 2024). Utilizing platforms that facilitate collaborative learning, such as discussion boards or virtual classrooms, can improve students' capacity to express their ideas and interact with varied perspectives. Instructing kids on how to differentiate credible material from misinformation is essential for cultivating their critical thinking abilities.

Ultimately, reflection and metacognition are vital components in fostering critical thinking. Educators can prompt students to contemplate their learning processes, evaluate their comprehension, and recognize areas for enhancement. By cultivating metacognitive awareness, students improve their capacity to assess their cognitive processes, hence augmenting their critical thinking skills across diverse contexts (Le & Nguyen, 2024).

The incorporation of AI in higher education prompts significant inquiries over academic freedom, especially in relation to educators' autonomy in choosing curriculum, teaching methodologies, and research trajectories. Although AI might enhance instructional efficiency and automate evaluations, it may also homogenize educational trajectories, thus constraining innovative pedagogical methods. The function of academics is transforming from content providers to learning facilitators and AI interpreters, necessitating new digital competencies. In research, AI expedites data analysis and literature synthesis while simultaneously presenting ethical dilemmas, including algorithmic bias and authorship attribution in AI-generated content. Universities must reconcile innovation with measures that safeguard academic autonomy and research integrity.

Artificial intelligence is progressively utilized to improve student support services in higher education. AI-driven chatbots, shown by "AskUNM" at the University of New Mexico, offer round-the-clock support for administrative inquiries, aiding students in managing enrollment, deadlines, and campus resources. Predictive analytics technologies detect at-risk students through the analysis of engagement data, facilitating prompt interventions by academic advisers. Virtual advising platforms tailor course suggestions according to academic performance and career objectives. These technologies enhance operational efficiency and cultivate a more responsive and inclusive academic environment. When ethically applied, AI can substantially enhance student retention, contentment, and overall achievement in academic environments.

4.2 Practical Exercises and Techniques

Fostering critical thinking abilities in students necessitates their involvement in practical tasks and exercises that encourage investigation, analysis, and reflection (Yusuf et al., 2024). Incorporating practical exercises into the educational process enables instructors to cultivate dynamic environments that foster the active development of students' critical thinking skills (Ruiz-Rojas et al., 2024; Shutaleva, 2023; Franco-Mariscal et al., 2024). Presented are various efficient methods and activities aimed at cultivating these fundamental talents.

1. **Socratic Seminars:** This method entails guiding discussions centered on a particular text or subject, wherein students are prompted to pose inquiries and examine various viewpoints. Students examine a chosen literary work or article and, thereafter, participate in a group discussion, making inquiries and addressing one another's perspectives. This practice enhances active listening, critical inquiry, and the capacity to express and justify one's perspectives, all of which are essential elements of critical thinking.
2. **Case Studies:** Examining real-world case studies enables students to employ critical thinking skills in intricate situations. Educators can provide students with a case that necessitates problem identification, factor analysis, and solution proposal. This activity pushes students to assess facts, contemplate other perspectives, and formulate cogent arguments. Case studies can be derived from diverse domains, including business, healthcare, and environmental research, rendering them pertinent and captivating.
3. **Debates:** Facilitating structured debates on contentious subjects promotes students' study, analysis, and defense of their viewpoints. By formulating arguments for both perspectives of an issue, students gain insight into contrasting opinions and cultivate critical thinking regarding their convictions. This activity increases

critical thinking and improves public speaking and persuasive communication skills.

4. **Problem-Based Learning (PBL):** In PBL situations, students collaborate in groups to address real-world challenges. They are assigned to diagnose the issue, investigate possible remedies, and deliver their conclusions. This experiential method promotes teamwork and compels students to utilize critical thinking abilities in practical contexts, enhancing the relevance and effect of learning.
5. **Reflection Journals:** Promoting the use of reflection diaries among students helps enhance their metacognitive abilities. Students can utilize these diaries to record their reflections on acquired knowledge, unresolved inquiries, and interrelations among various concepts. Reflective writing fosters self-evaluation and critical examination of one's learning journey, enabling pupils to enhance their awareness of cognitive patterns.
6. **Mind Mapping:** This graphic brainstorming method assists students in structuring their thoughts and ideas around a common theme. By creating mind maps, students can visually depict the relationships among various concepts, facilitating their analysis and synthesis of knowledge. This practice fosters creativity and aids pupils in cultivating a more thorough comprehension of intricate subjects.
7. **Role-Playing:** Participating in role-playing activities enables pupils to adopt diverse perspectives and examine various events. By adopting roles in a simulated environment, students can cultivate empathy, evaluate diverse perspectives, and enhance critical thinking abilities while managing intricate interpersonal dynamics.

4.3 Lifelong Learning and Adaptation

The imperative for ongoing education and flexibility has never been more essential in a progressively AI-oriented society. As technological breakthroughs transform businesses, work positions, and cultural norms, individuals must have a lifelong learning attitude to succeed in this evolving landscape (Gamberini & Pluchino, 2024). Embracing lifelong learning and flexibility promotes critical thinking abilities and prepares individuals to negotiate the intricacies of the contemporary terrain.

Lifelong learning is the continual pursuit of information and skills throughout an individual's life, transcending formal education (Matsumoto-Royo et al., 2021). The capacity to learn and adapt is crucial in a dynamic information landscape. This continuous quest for information enables individuals to be apprised of evolving technology, industrial trends, and societal transformations. Professionals in sectors such as healthcare, technology, and finance must consistently refresh their expertise to maintain competitiveness and efficacy. Through lifelong learning, individuals can cultivate critical thinking abilities that allow them to evaluate new information, determine its significance, and implement it in practical contexts (Patel et al., 2024).

Adaptability is an essential element for flourishing in an AI-driven environment. As automation and AI technologies persist in altering employment responsibilities, humans must be prepared to accept change and adapt their skill sets accordingly (Trenerry et al., 2021; Li, 2022). This adaptability necessitates a proactive learning strategy, where individuals actively pursue opportunities to gain new skills and investigate other career trajectories. A marketing professional must acquire knowledge of data analytics and AI-driven marketing tools to maintain relevance in their industry. By fostering a flexible mentality, individuals can adeptly manage job transitions and capitalize on emerging possibilities in a dynamic environment.

Furthermore, the incorporation of AI across diverse sectors requires a cooperative strategy for addressing challenges. Lifelong learners are more inclined to interact with varied perspectives, promoting teamwork and collaboration (Zamiri & Esmaeili, 2024). Critical thinking flourishes in settings that facilitate the exchange of ideas, the questioning of assumptions, and mutual learning. Active participation in collaborative learning enhances critical thinking abilities and fosters creative solutions to complicated challenges.

Moreover, cultivating a culture of curiosity and inquiry is vital for enhancing lifelong learning and adaptation. Promoting inquiry, soliciting feedback, and investigating novel concepts fosters an environment conducive to the flourishing of critical thinking (Salmon & Barrera, 2021; van den Berg & du Plessis, 2023). Organizations can foster this culture by offering access to professional development opportunities, mentorship programs, and resources that promote continual learning.

FACING GLOBAL CHALLENGES WITH CRITICAL THINKING AND AI

5.1 Identifying Global Challenges

In a more interconnected society, various significant global issues necessitate urgent attention and innovative solutions. Challenges such as climate change, inequality, and public health threaten society's stability and require a collaborative approach that integrates critical thinking and contemporary technologies like artificial intelligence (AI) (Ziervogel et al., 2022). Understanding these challenges is the first step toward developing effective ways to alleviate them.

Climate change constitutes a major challenge of our day. As global temperatures rise due to greenhouse gas emissions, the consequences manifest in extreme weather events, rising sea levels, and disruptions to ecosystems. The complexity of climate change requires analytical reasoning to examine its various causes and effects, as well as to evaluate potential remedies. Artificial intelligence can enhance our understanding of climate dynamics by analyzing large datasets related to weather patterns, carbon emissions, and land use (Chen et al., 2023; Pimenow et al., 2024). By employing AI, scholars can develop predictive models that inform policy decisions, improve resource management, and promote sustainable practices.

Inequality constitutes a significant global challenge that threatens social cohesion and economic stability. Both nationally and globally, economic disparities exacerbate difficulties related to access to education, healthcare, and employment opportunities (Panneer et al., 2022). Critical thinking is essential for identifying the root causes of inequality and evaluating the effectiveness of various solutions. Artificial Intelligence can substantially aid in alleviating inequality by providing data-driven insights into social disparities and enabling targeted interventions. AI algorithms can analyze demographic data to identify disadvantaged communities, allowing policymakers to allocate resources more effectively and develop projects that promote equity.

Public Health is a crucial field that has garnered heightened attention, particularly in light of the COVID-19 pandemic. Global health difficulties encompass infectious diseases, mental health crises, and access to healthcare (Sheridan et al., 2021). Critical thinking is vital for evaluating health information, understanding public health policy implications, and combating misinformation. Artificial intelligence technologies can enhance the monitoring of disease outbreaks, predict health trends, and tailor treatment strategies (Zhao et al., 2024). By analyzing huge datasets from many sources, AI can aid public health professionals in making informed decisions and efficiently allocating resources.

The analysis of global challenges such as climate change, inequality, and public health underscores the imperative for critical thinking and the integration of AI in developing effective solutions. By understanding the complexities of these issues, individuals and organizations can employ critical thinking to evaluate facts, assess potential solutions, and implement strategies that address the root causes of these challenges. In the era of AI, fostering collaboration between critical thinkers and AI technology is essential for creating a sustainable and equitable future. The next parts will examine the synergy between critical thinking and AI in generating innovative solutions to pressing global issues.

5.2 Collaborative Problem Solving

Resolving intricate global issues like climate change, inequality, and public health necessitates cooperative problem-solving that utilizes the capabilities of interdisciplinary teams. By integrating varied knowledge and viewpoints, these teams can employ critical thinking and artificial intelligence (AI) to create new solutions that are both efficient and sustainable (Joksimovic et al., 2023; Kulkov et al., 2024).

Interdisciplinary collaboration unites people from diverse fields—such as scientists, engineers, social scientists, policymakers, and business leaders—who provide distinctive insights and methodologies for problem-solving (Witti et al., 2023). Diversity of thought is crucial for addressing complex situations that cannot be solved with a singular disciplinary perspective. Climate change covers environmental science, economics, sociology, and technology. A multidisciplinary team may evaluate the environmental consequences of policy decisions while assessing their economic viability and social ramifications, resulting in more holistic and effective tactics.

Critical thinking is essential in this collaborative process. Team members must participate in transparent discourse, interrogate preconceptions, and jointly assess evidence. Encouraging an environment that values inquiry and constructive criticism allows interdisciplinary teams to examine diverse viewpoints and develop innovative solutions (Lorenzetti et al., 2022). This collaborative critical thinking process enables teams to recognize potential shortcomings in their methods and enhance their tactics through shared ideas.

AI functions as a potent instrument to enhance the capacities of interdisciplinary teams (Bouschery et al., 2023). Through the analysis of extensive data sets, AI can reveal patterns and trends that guide decision-making. In public health, AI algorithms may evaluate health data from various populations to detect outbreaks, assess risk factors, and forecast future health trends. This data-centric methodology enables teams to make educated decisions and deploy resources efficiently. Furthermore, AI can enable simulations and modeling, permitting teams to evaluate the potential results of different interventions prior to execution.

The incorporation of AI improves communication and collaboration among team members. AI-driven systems can facilitate information dissemination, allowing team members to instantaneously obtain pertinent data and insights (Aldoseri et al., 2024; Mudunuri et al., 2025). This accessibility promotes a more unified approach to problem-solving, enabling team members to enhance one another's ideas and discoveries. Moreover, AI tools facilitate the visualization of intricate data, enhancing interdisciplinary teams' ability to convey their findings to stakeholders and the public.

In summary, collaborative problem-solving among interdisciplinary teams is essential for tackling complex global issues. By integrating critical thinking with AI's analytical capabilities, these teams may formulate novel solutions informed by varied views and data-driven insights. In the AI era, addressing complex issues necessitates collaboration among experts from several disciplines to develop effective and sustainable ways of confronting contemporary concerns. This collaborative method promotes problem-solving abilities and guarantees that solutions are fair, inclusive, and attuned to the requirements of varied populations.

5.3 Future Perspectives

The interaction among artificial intelligence (AI), critical thinking, and global problem-solving is expected to evolve substantially. The swift progress in AI technology, along with a growing acknowledgment of the need for critical thinking, will influence how individuals and organizations tackle intricate global issues (Kopalle et al., 2022). Several significant patterns and forecasts can be discerned concerning this dynamic interaction.

Enhanced Decision-Making Capabilities

In the future, AI is anticipated to assume a more essential role in decision-making processes across multiple sectors (Al-Surmi et al., 2022). As AI systems advance, they will evaluate extensive datasets with enhanced precision and rapidity, yielding insights that facilitate critical thinking. This collaboration will enable decision-makers to evaluate a broader spectrum of data-driven alternatives, resulting in better-informed and effective solutions to critical challenges such as climate change, public health, and social injustice.

Increased Demand for Critical Thinking Skills

As artificial intelligence assumes an increasing number of regular activities, the necessity for critical thinking skills will rise. Individuals must cultivate the capacity to analyze AI-generated insights, scrutinize assumptions, and make ethical decisions informed by intricate facts. Educational systems are expected to evolve to prioritize critical thinking and analytical skills, hence preparing future generations to effectively traverse an AI-driven environment (Moustaghfir & Brigui, 2024). This emphasis on critical thinking will cultivate a culture of lifelong learning, as individuals acknowledge the necessity to always adapt and enhance their talents.

Collaborative AI-Human Partnerships

The future will witness the development of collaborative alliances between AI systems and human specialists (Järvelä et al., 2023). Instead of supplanting human judgment, AI will boost critical thinking through data analysis and predicted insights that improve decision-making. This collaboration will be especially beneficial in interdisciplinary teams, where varied skills may be integrated with AI capabilities to address complex difficulties. These relationships will foster a comprehensive approach to problem-solving, utilizing the advantages of both human intuition and computer intelligence.

Ethical Considerations and Accountability

As artificial intelligence increasingly addresses global concerns, ethical considerations will become paramount (Borenstein & Howard, 2021). The demand for openness, accountability, and equity in AI systems will propel dialogues over ethical AI development. Critical thinking is imperative for assessing the ramifications of AI technology and guaranteeing its responsible utilization. Stakeholders will progressively require that AI systems be developed to reduce prejudice and enhance equity, underscoring the significance of critical thinking in ethical decision-making.

Global Collaboration and Knowledge Sharing

The future of AI and critical thinking will likely entail more global collaboration and knowledge exchange. As nations encounter common difficulties, the capacity to consolidate resources, information, and experience will be essential. Artificial intelligence can enhance this collaboration by facilitating real-time communication and data exchange across international boundaries (Singh, 2023). This connection will improve collaborative problem-solving, enabling states to tackle global challenges more efficiently and fairly.

In summary, the future interaction among AI, critical thinking, and global problem-solving possesses significant potential for tackling the intricate difficulties of our era. By leveraging AI's capabilities while emphasizing critical thinking and ethical considerations, individuals and organizations can create new solutions that foster sustainability, justice, and resilience. In navigating this dynamic world, cultivating a culture of collaboration, ongoing education, and critical inquiry will be vital for establishing a superior future for all.

CONCLUSION

In the swiftly changing environment influenced by artificial intelligence (AI), the significance of critical thinking is paramount. In confronting intricate global concerns, the capacity to assess, appraise, and synthesize information is crucial for effective decision-making. Critical thinking is an essential talent that enables individuals to effectively traverse the extensive data and information available today, allowing them to identify reputable sources and make informed decisions.

The incorporation of AI across diverse areas, like healthcare and finance, illustrates how technology can augment critical thinking. AI technologies such as IBM's Watson Health support healthcare practitioners by analyzing vast medical data, thus enhancing diagnosis precision and therapy suggestions. In finance, AI algorithms evaluate market patterns to guide investment strategies, enabling experts to make data-driven judgments. These instances demonstrate AI's capacity to enhance human judgment, promoting a collaborative atmosphere conducive to critical thinking.

Furthermore, as AI assumes more everyday activities, the necessity for critical thinking skills will escalate. Educational systems must evolve to prioritize these competencies, equipping future generations to analyze AI-generated insights and make ethical choices. This transition will foster a culture of perpetual learning, wherein individuals consistently enhance their analytical skills in reaction to a constantly evolving technology environment.

Ethical considerations about AI implementation will significantly influence the future of critical thinking. As stakeholders require transparency and accountability in AI systems, critical thinking will facilitate ethical decision-making, guaranteeing responsible and equitable use of technology.

In conclusion, the interaction between AI and critical thinking offers significant prospects for tackling the complex challenges of our era. By emphasizing critical inquiry and ethical considerations, we may leverage AI's advantages to create innovative solutions that foster sustainability, justice, and resilience in our global community.

REFERENCES

Adel, A. (2024). *The convergence of intelligent tutoring, robotics, and IoT in smart education for the transition from industry 4.0 to 5.0.* Smart Cities., DOI: 10.3390/smartcities7010014

Akter, S., Hossain, M. A., Sajib, S., Sultana, S., Rahman, M., Vrontis, D., & McCarthy, G. (2023). A framework for AI-powered service innovation capability: Review and agenda for future research. *Technovation*, *125*, 102768. DOI: 10.1016/j.technovation.2023.102768

Al-Surmi, A., Bashiri, M., & Koliousis, I. (2022). AI based decision making: Combining strategies to improve operational performance. *International Journal of Production Research*, *60*(14), 4464–4486. DOI: 10.1080/00207543.2021.1966540

Aldoseri, A., Al-Khalifa, K. N., & Hamouda, A. M. (2024). AI-Powered Innovation in Digital Transformation: Key Pillars and Industry Impact. *Sustainability (Basel)*, *16*(5), 1790. Advance online publication. DOI: 10.3390/su16051790

Aljohani, A. (2023). Predictive analytics and machine learning for real-time supply chain risk mitigation and agility. *Sustainability (Basel)*, *15*(20), 15088. Advance online publication. DOI: 10.3390/su152015088

Andrae, S. (2025). Critical Thinking in the Age of Algorithms. In *Fostering Teacher Skills and Critical Thinking in Modern Education* (pp. 221–258). IGI Global Scientific Publishing., DOI: 10.4018/979-8-3373-1692-5.ch010

Asif, S., & Wenhui, Y., ur-Rehman, S., ul-ain, Q., Amjad, K., Yueyang, Y., ... & Awais, M. (2024). Advancements and prospects of machine learning in medical diagnostics: Unveiling the future of diagnostic precision. *Archives of Computational Methods in Engineering*, •••, 1–31.

Bächtold, M., Pallarès, G., De Checchi, K., & Munier, V. (2023). Combining debates and reflective activities to develop students' argumentation on socioscientific issues. *Journal of Research in Science Teaching*, *60*(4), 761–806. DOI: 10.1002/tea.21816

Baranidharan, S., & Dhakshayini, K. N. (2024). Exploring the Influence of Emotional Intelligence on Decision-Making Across Diverse Domains: A Systematic Literature Review. *Neuroleadership Development and Effective Communication in Modern Business, 70-91*. DOI: DOI: 10.4018/979-8-3693-4350-0.ch004

Bhatt, P., Vemprala, N., Valecha, R., Hariharan, G., & Rao, H. R. (2023). User privacy, surveillance and public health during COVID-19–an examination of twitterverse. *Information Systems Frontiers*, *25*(5), 1667–1682. DOI: 10.1007/s10796-022-10247-8 PMID: 35125937

Borenstein, J., & Howard, A. (2021). Emerging challenges in AI and the need for AI ethics education. *AI and Ethics*, *1*(1), 61–65. Advance online publication. DOI: 10.1007/s43681-020-00002-7 PMID: 38624388

Bouschery, S. G., Blazevic, V., & Piller, F. T. (2023). Augmenting human innovation teams with artificial intelligence: Exploring transformer-based language models. *Journal of Product Innovation Management*, *40*(2), 139–153. DOI: 10.1111/jpim.12656

Bradáč, V., Smolka, P., Kotyrba, M., & Průdek, T. (2022). Design of an intelligent tutoring system to create a personalized study plan using expert systems. *Applied Sciences (Basel, Switzerland)*, *12*(12), 6236. Advance online publication. DOI: 10.3390/app12126236

Buhalis, D., & Moldavska, I. (2022). Voice assistants in hospitality: Using artificial intelligence for customer service. *Journal of Hospitality and Tourism Technology*, *13*(3), 386–403. DOI: 10.1108/JHTT-03-2021-0104

Campo, L., Galindo-Domínguez, H., Bezanilla, M. J., Fernández-Nogueira, D., & Poblete, M. (2023). Methodologies for fostering critical thinking skills from university students' points of view. *Education Sciences*, *13*(2), 132. DOI: 10.3390/educsci13020132

Casali, Y., Aydin, N. Y., & Comes, T. (2022). Machine learning for spatial analyses in urban areas: A scoping review. *Sustainable Cities and Society*, *85*, 104050. Advance online publication. DOI: 10.1016/j.scs.2022.104050

Chen, L., Chen, Z., Zhang, Y., Liu, Y., Osman, A. I., Farghali, M., Hua, J., Al-Fatesh, A., Ihara, I., Rooney, D. W., & Yap, P. S. (2023). Artificial intelligence-based solutions for climate change: A review. *Environmental Chemistry Letters*, *21*(5), 2525–2557. DOI: 10.1007/s10311-023-01617-y

Cheok, A. D., Edirisinghe, C., & Shrestha, M. L. (2024). *The Rise of Machines: Future of Work in the Age of AI*. CRC Press.

El-Sabagh, H. A. (2021). Adaptive e-learning environment based on learning styles and its impact on development students' engagement. *International Journal of Educational Technology in Higher Education*, *18*(1), 53. DOI: 10.1186/s41239-021-00289-4

Franco-Mariscal, A. J., Cano-Iglesias, M. J., España-Ramos, E., & Blanco-López, Á. (2024). The ENCIC-CT model for the development of critical thinking. In *Critical thinking in science education and teacher training* (pp. 3–42). Springer Nature Switzerland., DOI: 10.1007/978-3-031-78578-8_1

Gamberini, L., & Pluchino, P. (2024). Industry 5.0: A comprehensive insight into the future of work, social sustainability, sustainable development, and career. *Australian Journal of Career Development*, *33*(1), 5–14. DOI: 10.1177/10384162241231118

Gouseti, A., Lakkala, M., Raffaghelli, J., Ranieri, M., Roffi, A., & Ilomäki, L. (2024). Exploring teachers' perceptions of critical digital literacies and how these are manifested in their teaching practices. *Educational Review*, *76*(7), 1751–1785. DOI: 10.1080/00131911.2022.2159933

Hao, X., Demir, E., & Eyers, D. (2024). Exploring collaborative decision-making: A quasi-experimental study of human and Generative AI interaction. *Technology in Society*, *78*, 102662. Advance online publication. DOI: 10.1016/j.techsoc.2024.102662

Henriksen, D., Mishra, P., & Stern, R. (2024). Creative Learning for Sustainability in a World of AI: Action, Mindset, Values. *Sustainability (Basel)*, *16*(11), 4451. Advance online publication. DOI: 10.3390/su16114451

Ienca, M. (2023). On artificial intelligence and manipulation. *Topoi*, *42*(3), 833–842. Advance online publication. DOI: 10.1007/s11245-023-09940-3

Järvelä, S., Nguyen, A., & Hadwin, A. (2023). Human and artificial intelligence collaboration for socially shared regulation in learning. *British Journal of Educational Technology*, *54*(5), 1057–1076. DOI: 10.1111/bjet.13325

Jedličková, A. (2024). Ethical approaches in designing autonomous and intelligent systems: A comprehensive survey towards responsible development. *AI & Society*. Advance online publication. DOI: 10.1007/s00146-024-02040-9

Jejeniwa, T. O., Mhlongo, N. Z., & Jejeniwa, T. O.Temitayo Oluwaseun JejeniwaNoluthando Zamanjomane MhlongoTitilola Olaide Jejeniwa. (2024). A comprehensive review of the impact of artificial intelligence on modern accounting practices and financial reporting. *Computer Science & IT Research Journal*, *5*(4), 1031–1047. DOI: 10.51594/csitrj.v5i4.1086

Joksimovic, S., Ifenthaler, D., Marrone, R., De Laat, M., & Siemens, G. (2023). Opportunities of artificial intelligence for supporting complex problem-solving: Findings from a scoping review. *Computers and Education: Artificial Intelligence*, *4*, 100138. DOI: 10.1016/j.caeai.2023.100138

Joshi, H. (2025). AI and Chronic Diseases From Data Integration to Clinical Implementation. In *Generative AI Techniques for Sustainability in Healthcare Security* (pp. 17–40). IGI Global Scientific Publishing., DOI: 10.4018/979-8-3693-6577-9.ch002

Kase, S. E., Hung, C. P., Krayzman, T., Hare, J. Z., Rinderspacher, B. C., & Su, S. M. (2022). The future of collaborative human-artificial intelligence decision-making for mission planning. *Frontiers in Psychology*, *13*, 850628. DOI: 10.3389/fpsyg.2022.850628 PMID: 35444590

Khan, F. H., Pasha, M. A., & Masud, S. (2021). Advancements in microprocessor architecture for ubiquitous AI—An overview on history, evolution, and upcoming challenges in AI implementation. *Micromachines*, *12*(6), 665. Advance online publication. DOI: 10.3390/mi12060665 PMID: 34204065

Kopalle, P. K., Gangwar, M., Kaplan, A., Ramachandran, D., Reinartz, W., & Rindfleisch, A. (2022). Examining artificial intelligence (AI) technologies in marketing via a global lens: Current trends and future research opportunities. *International Journal of Research in Marketing*, *39*(2), 522–540. DOI: 10.1016/j.ijresmar.2021.11.002

Kulkov, I., Kulkova, J., Rohrbeck, R., Menvielle, L., Kaartemo, V., & Makkonen, H. (2024). Artificial intelligence-driven sustainable development: Examining organizational, technical, and processing approaches to achieving global goals. *Sustainable Development, 32(3), 2253-2267*. DOI: DOI: 10.1002/sd.2773

Kuperberg, G. R. (2021, January). (2021). Tea with milk? A hierarchical generative framework of sequential event comprehension. *Topics in Cognitive Science*, *13*(1), 256–298. Advance online publication. DOI: 10.1111/tops.12518 PMID: 33025701

Le, H. V., & Nguyen, L. Q. (2024). Promoting L2 learners' critical thinking skills: The role of social constructivism in reading class. *Frontiers in Education*, *9*, 1241973. Advance online publication. DOI: 10.3389/feduc.2024.1241973

Leahy, E. (2024). AI-Powered Bitcoin Trading: Developing an Investment Strategy with Artificial Intelligence.

Li, L. (2022). Reskilling and upskilling the future-ready workforce for industry 4.0 and beyond. *Information Systems Frontiers*. Advance online publication. DOI: 10.1007/s10796-022-10308-y PMID: 35855776

Lin, C. C., Huang, A. Y. Q., & Lu, O. H. T. (2023). *Artificial intelligence in intelligent tutoring systems toward sustainable education: a systematic review*. Smart Learning Environments., DOI: 10.1186/s40561-023-00260-y

Lorenzetti, L., Jacobsen, M., Lorenzetti, D. L., Nowell, L., Pethrick, H., Clancy, T., ... & Oddone Paolucci, E. (2022). Fostering learning and reciprocity in interdisciplinary research. *Small Group Research, 53(5), 755-777.*https://doi.org/ Luo, Y. F., Yang, S. C., & Kang, S. (2022). New media literacy and news trustworthiness: An application of importance–performance analysis. *Computers & Education.*https://doi.org/DOI: 10.1177/10464964221089836

Marengo, A. (2024). Navigating the nexus of AI and IoT: A comprehensive review of data analytics and privacy paradigms. *Internet of Things.*https://doi.org/DOI: 10.1016/j.iot.2024.101318

Martínez-García, M., & Hernández-Lemus, E. (2022). Data integration challenges for machine learning in precision medicine. *Frontiers in Medicine*, *8*, 784455. Advance online publication. DOI: 10.3389/fmed.2021.784455 PMID: 35145977

Matsumoto-Royo, K., Ramírez-Montoya, M. S., & Conget, P. (2021). Opportunities to develop lifelong learning tendencies in practice-based teacher education: Getting ready for education 4.0. *Future Internet*, *13*(11), 292. Advance online publication. DOI: 10.3390/fi13110292

Michel-Villarreal, R., Vilalta-Perdomo, E., Salinas-Navarro, D. E., Thierry-Aguilera, R., & Gerardou, F. S. (2023). Challenges and opportunities of generative AI for higher education as explained by ChatGPT. *Education Sciences*, *13*(9), 856. DOI: 10.3390/educsci13090856

Mirbabaie, M., Brünker, F., Möllmann, N. R. J., & Stieglitz, S. (2022). The rise of artificial intelligence–understanding the AI identity threat at the workplace. *Electronic Markets*, *32*(1), 73–99. Advance online publication. DOI: 10.1007/s12525-021-00496-x

Moustaghfir, S., & Brigui, H. (2024). Navigating Critical Thinking in the Digital Era: An Informative Exploration. *International Journal of Linguistics, Literature and Translation, 7(1), 137-143*. DOI: DOI: 10.32996/ijllt

Mudunuri, L. N. R., Hullurappa, M., Vemula, V. R., & Selvakumar, P. (2025). AI-powered leadership: Shaping the future of management. In *Navigating Organizational Behavior in the Digital Age With AI* (pp. 127–152). IGI Global Scientific Publishing., DOI: 10.4018/979-8-3693-8442-8.ch006

Muthmainnah, I. S., Ibna Seraj, P. M., & Oteir, I. (2022). P. M., & Oteir, I. (2022). Playing with AI to Investigate Human-Computer Interaction Technology and Improving Critical Thinking Skills to Pursue 21st Century Age. *Education Research International*, *6468995*(1), 1–17. DOI: 10.1155/2022/6468995

Nguyen-Trung, K., Saeri, A. K., & Kaufman, S. (2024). Applying ChatGPT and AI-Powered Tools to Accelerate Evidence Reviews. *Human Behavior and Emerging Technologies, 2024*(1), 8815424. DOI: 10.1155/2024/8815424

Norori, N., Hu, Q., Aellen, F. M., Faraci, F. D., & Tzovara, A. (2021). Addressing bias in big data and AI for health care: A call for open science. *Patterns (New York, N.Y.), 2*(10), 100347. DOI: 10.1016/j.patter.2021.100347 PMID: 34693373

Ochonogor, C. I. (2021). *Digital media revolution and information overload in Nigerian cyberspace: The challenges and prospects*. Media and Communication in Nigeria., DOI: 10.4324/9781003208747-22

Oyeniyi, L. D., Ugochukwu, C. E., & Mhlongo, N. Z.Lawrence Damilare OyeniyiChinonye Esther UgochukwuNoluthando Zamanjomane Mhlongo. (2024). Transforming financial planning with AI-driven analysis: A review and application insights. *Finance & Accounting Research Journal*, *6*(4), 626–647. DOI: 10.51594/farj.v6i4.1037

Panda, S., & Kaur, N. (2024). Empowered Minds: Navigating Digital Seas With Emerging Information Literacy Framework. In *Examining Information Literacy in Academic Libraries (pp. 48-82).* IGI Global. https://doi.org/DOI: 10.3390/healthcare10050770

Panneer, S., Kantamaneni, K., Palaniswamy, U., Bhat, L., Pushparaj, R. R. B., Nayar, K. R., . . . Rice, L. (2022, April). Health, economic and social development challenges of the COVID-19 pandemic: strategies for multiple and interconnected issues. *In Healthcare (Vol. 10, No. 5, p. 770).* MDPI. https://doi.org/DOI: 10.3390/healthcare10050770

Patel, N. S., Puah, S., & Kok, X. F. K. (2024). Shaping future-ready graduates with mindset shifts: Studying the impact of integrating critical and design thinking in design innovation education. *Frontiers in Education*, *9*, 1358431. Advance online publication. DOI: 10.3389/feduc.2024.1358431

Pik, J., Chan, E. P., Broad, J., Sun, P., & Singh, V. (2025). *Hands-On AI Trading with Python*. QuantConnect and AWS.

Pimenow, S., Pimenowa, O., & Prus, P. (2024). Challenges of Artificial Intelligence Development in the Context of Energy Consumption and Impact on Climate Change. *Energies*, *17*(23), 5965. Advance online publication. DOI: 10.3390/en17235965

Polanco-Levicán, K., & Salvo-Garrido, S. (2022). Understanding social media literacy: A systematic review of the concept and its competences. *International Journal of Environmental Research and Public Health*, *19*(14), 8807. DOI: 10.3390/ijerph19148807 PMID: 35886657

Rashid, A. B., & Kausik, A. K. (2024). *AI revolutionizing industries worldwide: A comprehensive overview of its diverse applications*. Hybrid Advances., DOI: 10.1016/j.hybadv.2024.100277

Rivas, S. F., Saiz, C., & Ossa, C. (2022). Metacognitive strategies and development of critical thinking in higher education. *Frontiers in Psychology*, *13*, 913219. Advance online publication. DOI: 10.3389/fpsyg.2022.913219 PMID: 35783800

Rojas, R. V. B. (2024). *Artificial Intelligence: Genesis, Development, and Future*. Revolutionizing Communication., DOI: 10.1201/9781003473633

Ruiz-Rojas, L. I., Salvador-Ullauri, L., & Acosta-Vargas, P. (2024). Collaborative working and critical thinking: Adoption of generative artificial intelligence tools in higher education. *Sustainability (Basel)*, *16*(13), 5367. Advance online publication. DOI: 10.3390/su16135367

Salmon, A. K., & Barrera, M. X. (2021). Intentional questioning to promote thinking and learning. *Thinking Skills and Creativity*, *40*, 100822. Advance online publication. DOI: 10.1016/j.tsc.2021.100822

Samara, F. Y. A., Taha, A. H. A., Massa, N. M., Jamie, T. N. A., Harara, F. E., Abu-Nasser, B. S., & Abu-Naser, S. S. (2024). The Role of AI in Enhancing Business Decision-Making: Innovations and Implications.

Sánchez Gonzales, H. M., Sánchez González, M., & Martos Moreno, J. (2024). The Methodology Used by Fact-Checkers. An In-Depth Analysis of Commonly Used Strategies. *Journalism Practice*, •••, 1–24. DOI: 10.1080/17512786.2024.2340522

Sarker, I. H. (2021). Deep learning: A comprehensive overview on techniques, taxonomy, applications and research directions. *SN Computer Science*, *2*(6), 420. Advance online publication. DOI: 10.1007/s42979-021-00815-1 PMID: 34426802

Sarker, I. H. (2021). Machine learning: Algorithms, real-world applications and research directions. *SN Computer Science*, *2*(3), 160. Advance online publication. DOI: 10.1007/s42979-021-00592-x PMID: 33778771

Shao, Z., Zhao, R., Yuan, S., Ding, M., & Wang, Y. (2022). Tracing the evolution of AI in the past decade and forecasting the emerging trends. *Expert Systems with Applications*, *209*, 118221. DOI: 10.1016/j.eswa.2022.118221

Sheridan Rains, L., Johnson, S., Barnett, P., Steare, T., Needle, J. J., Carr, S., & Simpson, A. (2021). Early impacts of the COVID-19 pandemic on mental health care and on people with mental health conditions: Framework synthesis of international experiences and responses. *Social Psychiatry and Psychiatric Epidemiology*, *56*(1), 13–24. DOI: 10.1007/s00127-020-01924-7 PMID: 32804258

Shutaleva, A. (2023). Ecological culture and critical thinking: building of a sustainable future. Sustainability. https://doi.org/mdpi.comDOI: 10.3390/su151813492

Singh, J. (2023). Autonomous Vehicle Swarm Robotics: Real-Time Coordination Using AI for Urban Traffic and Fleet Management. *Journal of AI-Assisted Scientific Discovery.*

Song, C., Shin, S. Y., & Shin, K. S. (2024). Implementing the Dynamic Feedback-Driven Learning Optimization Framework: A Machine Learning Approach to Personalize Educational Pathways. *Applied Sciences (Basel, Switzerland)*, *14*(2), 916. Advance online publication. DOI: 10.3390/app14020916

Sönmez, E., Kabataş Memiş, E., & Yerlikaya, Z. (2019). The effect of practices based on argumentation-based inquiry approach on teacher candidates' critical thinking. *Educational Studies*, *47*(1), 59–83. DOI: 10.1080/03055698.2019.1654364

Stokel-Walker, C. (2024). *How AI Ate the World: A Brief History of Artificial Intelligence–and Its Long Future*. Canbury Press.

Targowski, A. (Ed.). (2021). *The Strategies of Informing Technology in the 21st Century*. IGI Global.

Theodorakopoulos, L., Theodoropoulou, A., & Stamatiou, Y. (2024). A state-of-the-art review in big data management engineering: Real-life case studies, challenges, and future research directions. *Eng*.https://doi.org/DOI: 10.3390/eng5030068

Thornhill-Miller, B., Camarda, A., Mercier, M., Burkhardt, J. M., Morisseau, T., Bourgeois-Bougrine, S., Vinchon, F., El Hayek, S., Augereau-Landais, M., Mourey, F., Feybesse, C., Sundquist, D., & Lubart, T. (2023). Creativity, critical thinking, communication, and collaboration: Assessment, certification, and promotion of 21st century skills for the future of work and education. *Journal of Intelligence*, *11*(3), 54. DOI: 10.3390/jintelligence11030054 PMID: 36976147

Tong, S., Jia, N., Luo, X., & Fang, Z. (2021). The Janus face of artificial intelligence feedback: Deployment versus disclosure effects on employee performance. *Strategic Management Journal*, *42*(9), 1600–1631. Advance online publication. DOI: 10.1002/smj.3322

Trenerry, B., Chng, S., Wang, Y., Suhaila, Z. S., Lim, S. S., Lu, H. Y., & Oh, P. H. (2021). Preparing workplaces for digital transformation: An integrative review and framework of multi-level factors. *Frontiers in Psychology*, *12*, 620766. DOI: 10.3389/fpsyg.2021.620766 PMID: 33833714

van Assen, M., Muscogiuri, E., Tessarin, G., & De Cecco, C. N. (2022). Artificial intelligence: A century-old story. In *Artificial Intelligence in Cardiothoracic Imaging* (pp. 3–13). Springer International Publishing., DOI: 10.1007/978-3-030-92087-6_1

van den Berg, G., & du Plessis, E. (2023). ChatGPT and generative AI: Possibilities for its contribution to lesson planning, critical thinking and openness in teacher education. *Education Sciences*, *13*(10), 998. Advance online publication. DOI: 10.3390/educsci13100998

Van Le, H., & Chong, S. L. (2024). The dynamics of critical thinking skills: A phenomenographic exploration from Malaysian and Vietnamese undergraduates. *Thinking Skills and Creativity*, *51*, 101445. Advance online publication. DOI: 10.1016/j.tsc.2023.101445

Varona, D., & Suárez, J. L. (2022). Discrimination, bias, fairness, and trustworthy AI. *Applied Sciences (Basel, Switzerland)*, *12*(12), 5826. Advance online publication. DOI: 10.3390/app12125826

Vashishth, T. K., Sharma, V., Sharma, K. K., Kumar, B., Panwar, R., & Chaudhary, S. (2024). AI-driven learning analytics for personalized feedback and assessment in higher education. In *Using traditional design methods to enhance AI-driven decision making* (pp. 206–230). IGI Global., DOI: 10.4018/979-8-3693-0639-0.ch009

Villar, R. C., Nashwan, A. J., Mathew, R. G., Mohamed, A. S., Munirathinam, S., Abujaber, A. A., Al-Jabry, M. M., & Shraim, M. (2021). The lived experiences of frontline nurses during the coronavirus disease 2019 (COVID-19) pandemic in Qatar: A qualitative study. *Nursing Open*, *8*(6), 3516–3526. DOI: 10.1002/nop2.901 PMID: 33949145

Walter, Y. (2024). Embracing the future of Artificial Intelligence in the classroom: The relevance of AI literacy, prompt engineering, and critical thinking in modern education. *International Journal of Educational Technology in Higher Education*, *21*(1), 15. DOI: 10.1186/s41239-024-00448-3

Witti, M. J., Zottmann, J. M., Wershofen, B., Thistlethwaite, J. E., Fischer, F., & Fischer, M. R. (2023). FINCA–a conceptual framework to improve interprofessional collaboration in health education and care. *Frontiers in Medicine*, *10*, 1213300. DOI: 10.3389/fmed.2023.1213300 PMID: 37849484

Xu, E., Wang, W., & Wang, Q. (2023). The effectiveness of collaborative problem solving in promoting students' critical thinking: A meta-analysis based on empirical literature. *Humanities & Social Sciences Communications*, *10*(1), 1–11. DOI: 10.1057/s41599-023-01508-1 PMID: 37192950

Ye, Q. (2023). Comparison of the transparency of fact-checking: A global perspective. *Journalism Practice*, *17*(10), 2263–2282. Advance online publication. DOI: 10.1080/17512786.2023.2211555

Yusuf, A., Bello, S., Pervin, N., & Tukur, A. K. (2024). Implementing a proposed framework for enhancing critical thinking skills in synthesizing AI-generated texts. *Thinking Skills and Creativity*, *53*, 101619. Advance online publication. DOI: 10.1016/j.tsc.2024.101619

Zamiri, M., & Esmaeili, A. (2024). Strategies, methods, and supports for developing skills within learning communities: A systematic review of the literature. *Administrative Sciences*, *14*(9), 231. Advance online publication. DOI: 10.3390/admsci14090231

Zarei, E., Yazdi, M., Moradi, R., & BahooToroody, A. (2024). Expert judgment and uncertainty in sociotechnical systems analysis. In Safety causation analysis in sociotechnical systems: advanced models and techniques (pp. 487-530). Cham: Springer Nature Switzerland.

Zhao, A. P., Li, S., Cao, Z., Hu, P. J. H., Wang, J., Xiang, Y., Xie, D., & Lu, X. (2024). AI for science: Predicting infectious diseases. *Journal of Safety Science and Resilience = An Quan Ke Xue Yu Ren Xing (Ying Wen)*, *5*(2), 130–146. Advance online publication. DOI: 10.1016/j.jnlssr.2024.02.002

Ziervogel, G., Enqvist, J., Metelerkamp, L., & van Breda, J. (2022). Supporting transformative climate adaptation: Community-level capacity building and knowledge co-creation in South Africa. *Climate Policy*, *22*(5), 607–622. DOI: 10.1080/14693062.2020.1863180

Compilation of References

Ab Kadir, M. A. (2018). An inquiry into critical thinking in the Australian curriculum: Examining its conceptual understandings and their implications on developing critical thinking as a "general capability" on teachers' practice and knowledge. *Asia Pacific Journal of Education*, *38*(4), 533–549. DOI: 10.1080/02188791.2018.1535424

Abdelwahab, H. R., Rauf, A., & Chen, D. (2023). Business students' perceptions of Dutch higher educational institutions in preparing them for artificial intelligence work environments. *Industry and Higher Education*, *37*(1), 22–34. DOI: 10.1177/09504222221087614

Abhishek, S., Sathish, H., Kumar, A., & Anjali, T. (2022). Aiding the visually impaired using artificial intelligence and speech recognition technology. In: *2022 4th International Conference on Inventive Research in Computing Applications (ICIRCA)*, 21 Sep 2022; pp. 1356-1362, IEEE. DOI: 10.1109/ICIRCA54612.2022.9985659

Academy Victoria. (2024). *Enhancing differentiation in the classroom using generative artificial intelligence*. Academy Victoria. Retrieved from https://www.academy.vic.gov.au/resources/enhancing-differentiation-classroom-using-generative-artificial-intelligence

Adel, A. (2024). *The convergence of intelligent tutoring, robotics, and IoT in smart education for the transition from industry 4.0 to 5.0*. Smart Cities., DOI: 10.3390/smartcities7010014

Aeni, N., Khang, A., Al Yakin, A., Yunus, M., & Cardoso, L. (2024). Revolutionized teaching by incorporating artificial intelligence chatbot for higher education ecosystem. In *AI-Centric Modeling and Analytics* (pp. 43–76). CRC Press.

Ahmad, S. F., Rahmat, M. K., Mubarik, M. S., Alam, M. M., & Hyder, S. I. (2021). Artificial intelligence and its role in education. *Sustainability (Basel)*, *13*(22), 12902. DOI: 10.3390/su132212902

Ajzen, I. (1991). The theory of planned behavior. *Organizational Behavior and Human Decision Processes, 50*(2), 179–211. DOI: 10.1016/0749-5978(91)90020-T

Akcaoğlu, M., Mor, E., & Külekçi, E. (2023). The mediating role of metacognitive awareness in the relationship between critical thinking and self-regulation. *Thinking Skills and Creativity, 47*, 101187. Advance online publication. DOI: 10.1016/j.tsc.2022.101187

Akter, S., Hossain, M. A., Sajib, S., Sultana, S., Rahman, M., Vrontis, D., & McCarthy, G. (2023). A framework for AI-powered service innovation capability: Review and agenda for future research. *Technovation, 125*, 102768. DOI: 10.1016/j.technovation.2023.102768

Al Shehab, N. A. (2022). Under the COVID pandemic: is it the springtime for forensic accounting field to blossom? In Accounting, Finance, Sustainability, Governance and Fraud (pp. 11-32). Springer. DOI: 10.1007/978-981-19-1036-4_2

Alabdulkareem, A., Alhakbani, N., & Al-Nafjan, A. (2022). A systematic review of research on robot-assisted therapy for children with autism. *Sensors (Basel), 22*(3), 944. DOI: 10.3390/s22030944 PMID: 35161697

Alam, A. (2023). Harnessing the power of AI to create intelligent tutoring systems for enhanced classroom experience and improved learning outcomes. In *Intelligent Communication Technologies and Virtual Mobile Networks* (pp. 571–591). Springer Nature Singapore. DOI: 10.1007/978-981-99-1767-9_42

Alateyyat, S., & Soltan, M. (2024). Utilizing Artificial Intelligence in Higher Education: A Systematic Review. 2024 ASU International Conference in Emerging Technologies for Sustainability and Intelligent Systems, ICETSIS 2024, Al-haimi, B., Hujainah, F., Nasir, D., & Alhroob, E. (2021). Higher education institutions with artificial intelligence: roles, promises, and requirements. Applications of artificial intelligence in business, education and healthcare, 221-238. DOI: 10.1007/978-3-030-72080-3_13

Aldoseri, A., Al-Khalifa, K. N., & Hamouda, A. M. (2024). AI-Powered Innovation in Digital Transformation: Key Pillars and Industry Impact. *Sustainability (Basel), 16*(5), 1790. Advance online publication. DOI: 10.3390/su16051790

AlGerafi, M. A. M., Zhou, Y., Oubibi, M., & Wijaya, T. T. (2023). Unlocking the potential: A comprehensive evaluation of augmented reality and virtual reality in education. *Electronics (Basel), 12*(18), 3953. Advance online publication. DOI: 10.3390/electronics12183953

Alier, M., Pereira, J., García-Peñalvo, F. J., Casañ, M. J., & Cabré, J. (2025). LAMB: An open-source software framework to create artificial intelligence assistants deployed and integrated into learning management systems. *Computer Standards & Interfaces*, *92*, 103940. DOI: 10.1016/j.csi.2024.103940

Aljohani, A. (2023). Predictive analytics and machine learning for real-time supply chain risk mitigation and agility. *Sustainability (Basel)*, *15*(20), 15088. Advance online publication. DOI: 10.3390/su152015088

Al-Mseidin, K. I., Al-Zu'bi, M. A., Al-Mawadieh, R. S. M., & Alelaimat, A. M. (2023). The Integration of AI Applications in Psychological and Educational Counselling for University Students: Opportunities and Challenges. 2023 24th International Arab Conference onInformation Technology, ACIT 2023, Al-Saiari, M. A., Al-Mughairi, Y. M., Al-Mashaikhi, B. N., & Mudhsh, B. A. (2024). Investigating the Impact of Training Program on Generative AI Applications in Improving University Teaching. Qubahan Academic Journal, 4(3), 315-332. DOI: 10.48161/qaj.v4n3a760

Almusaed, A., Almssad, A., Yitmen, I., & Homod, R. Z. (2023). Enhancing student engagement: Harnessing "AIED"'s power in hybrid education—A review analysis. *Education Sciences*, *13*(7), 632. DOI: 10.3390/educsci13070632

Alqahtani, N., & Wafula, Z. (2024). Artificial Intelligence Integration: Pedagogical Strategies and Policies at Leading Universities. *Innovative Higher Education*. Advance online publication. DOI: 10.1007/s10755-024-09749-x

Al-Surmi, A., Bashiri, M., & Koliousis, I. (2022). AI based decision making: Combining strategies to improve operational performance. *International Journal of Production Research*, *60*(14), 4464–4486. DOI: 10.1080/00207543.2021.1966540

American Speech-Language-Hearing Association. (n.d.). *Augmentative and Alternative Communication (AAC)*. https://www.asha.org/public/speech/disorders/AAc/

Americans with Disabilities Act of 1990, no. 42, United States Congress (1990).

Anderson, L. W., & Krathwohl, D. R. (Eds.). (2001). *A taxonomy for learning, teaching, and assessing: A revision of Bloom's taxonomy of educational objectives*. Allyn & Bacon.

Anderson, P., & Rainie, L. (2018). *The Future of AI in Higher Education: Insights from 2030*. Pew Research Center.

Andrae, S. (2025). Critical thinking in the age of algorithms. In Aldosemani, T. I., Lytras, M. D., & Ordóñez de Pablos, P. (Eds.), *Fostering teacher skills and critical thinking in modern education* (pp. 221–258). IGI Global Publishing., DOI: 10.4018/979-8-3373-1692-5.ch010

Angelone, L., & Burton, B. (2024). MagicSchool: An exploration of the use of Generative AI by southwest Ohio teachers. *Ohio Journal of Teacher Education, 39*(1), Article 4. https://www.exhibit.xavier.edu/ojte/vol39/iss1/4

Anggraeni, D. M., Prahani, B. K., Suprapto, N., Shofiyah, N., & Jatmiko, B. (2023). Systematic review of problem based learning research in fostering critical thinking skills. *Thinking Skills and Creativity, 49*, 101334. DOI: 10.1016/j.tsc.2023.101334

Ann, O. C., Theng, L. B., Seldon, H. L., & Putra, F. A. (2015). Critical Behavior Monitoring for Children with Special Needs in Preventing Physical Injury Using Kinect. In L. B. Theng (Ed.), Assistive Technologies for Physical and Cognitive Disabilities (pp. 211–249). IGI Global Scientific Publishing. DOI: 10.4018/978-1-4666-7373-1.ch011

Anson, D. K. (2018). *Assistive Technology for People with Disabilities*. Bloomsbury Publishing Inc. DOI: 10.5040/9798400615559

Anthropic. (2024). Claude [AI assistant]. https://www.anthropic.com

Anuradha, J., Dhiman, T., Ramachandran, V., Arulalan, K. V., & Tripathy, B. K. (2010). Diagnosis of ADHD using SVM algorithm. In *Proceedings of the Third Annual ACM Bangalore Conference* (pp. 1–4). Association for Computing Machinery. DOI: 10.1145/1754288.1754317

Aoun, J. E. (2017). *Robot-proof: Higher Education in the Age of Artificial Intelligence*. MIT Press. DOI: 10.7551/mitpress/11456.001.0001

Arnold, M. (2020). The role of experiential learning in fostering AI ethics in education. *AI & Society, 35*(4), 771–783. DOI: 10.1007/s00146-020-00981-0

Asghar, A., Sladeczek, I. E., Mercier, J., & Beaudoin, E. (2017). Learning in science, technology, engineering, and mathematics: Supporting students with learning disabilities. *Canadian Psychology, 58*(3), 238–249. DOI: 10.1037/cap0000111

Ashaari, M. A., Singh, K. S. D., Abbasi, G. A., Amran, A., & Liebana-Cabanillas, F. J. (2021). Big data analytics capability for improved performance of higher education institutions in the Era of IR 4.0: A multi-analytical SEM & ANN perspective. *Technological Forecasting and Social Change, 173*, C7–C121119. DOI: 10.1016/j.techfore.2021.121119

Asif, S., & Wenhui, Y., ur-Rehman, S., ul-ain, Q., Amjad, K., Yueyang, Y., ... & Awais, M. (2024). Advancements and prospects of machine learning in medical diagnostics: Unveiling the future of diagnostic precision. *Archives of Computational Methods in Engineering*, •••, 1–31.

Asrifan, A., & Dewi, A. C. (2024). AI-driven classroom conversations: Revolutionizing Education 5.0 for enhanced student engagement in speaking skills. *JETAL: Journal of English Teaching & Applied Linguistics*, *5*(2), 117–131. DOI: 10.36655/jetal.v5i2.1482

Asselborn, T., Chapatte, M., & Dillenbourg, P. (2020). Extending the spectrum of dysgraphia: A data driven strategy to estimate handwriting quality. *Scientific Reports*, *10*(1), 3140. DOI: 10.1038/s41598-020-60011-8 PMID: 32081940

Assim, M., Al-Bahri, H., Zafar, Q., Shahada, M., & Al-Ammary, J. (2021). Remote Teaching during COVID-19 pandemic in Higher Education Institutions in the Kingdom of Bahrain: Challenges and Innovative Solutions. 2021 Sustainable Leadership and Academic Excellence International Conference, SLAE 2021, Ateeq, A., Alaghbari, M. A., Alzoraiki, M., Milhem, M., & Hasan Beshr, B. A. (2024). Empowering academic success: integrating AI tools in university teaching for enhanced assignment and thesis guidance. 2024 ASU International Conference in Emerging Technologies for Sustainability and Intelligent Systems, ICETSIS 2024.

Assistive Technology Australia. (n.d.). *Browse Products: Communication - Voice Output Communication Aids VOCA (Recorded Speech)*. https://at-aust.org/items/2886

Assistive Technology Industry Association. (n.d.). *What is AT?* https://www.atia.org/home/at-resources/what-is-at/

Ates, H. C., Nguyen, P. Q., Gonzalez-Macia, L., Morales-Narváez, E., Güder, F., Collins, J. J., & Dincer, C. (2022). End-to-end design of wearable sensors. *Nature Reviews. Materials*, *7*(11), 887–907. DOI: 10.1038/s41578-022-00460-x PMID: 35910814

Athaluri, S. A., Manthena, S. V., Manoj, K., Yarlagadda, V., & Dave, T. (2023). Exploring the boundaries of reality: Investigating the phenomenon of artificial intelligence hallucination in scientific writing through ChatGPT references. *Cureus*, *15*(5), e37432. Advance online publication. DOI: 10.7759/cureus.37432 PMID: 37182055

Awesomegpts.ai. (2024). Scholar GPT. https://www.awesomegpts.ai

Azzimani, T., & Kaddouri, E. M. (2020). Technology, Creativity, and Learning: Semiotic Perspective. In Tadlaoui, M. A., & Khaldi, M. (Eds.), (pp. 148–157). Advances in Educational Technologies and Instructional Design. IGI Global., DOI: 10.4018/978-1-7998-1492-4.ch006

Babaei, M., Kulshrestha, J., Chakraborty, A., Redmiles, E. M., Cha, M., & Gummadi, K. P. (2021). Analyzing biases in perception of truth in news stories and their implications for fact checking. *IEEE Transactions on Computational Social Systems*, *9*(3), 839–850. DOI: 10.1109/TCSS.2021.3096038

Bächtold, M., Pallarès, G., De Checchi, K., & Munier, V. (2023). Combining debates and reflective activities to develop students' argumentation on socioscientific issues. *Journal of Research in Science Teaching*, *60*(4), 761–806. DOI: 10.1002/tea.21816

Bahassi, H., Azmi, M., & Khiat, A. (2024). Cognitive systems for education: Architectures, innovations, and comparative analyses. *Procedia Computer Science*, *238*, 436–443. Advance online publication. DOI: 10.1016/j.procs.2024.06.045

Baig, A., Cressler, J. D., & Minsky, M. (2024). The future of AI in education: Personalized learning and intelligent tutoring systems. *AlgoVista. Journal of AI & Computer Science*, *1*(2).

Baillifard, A., Gabella, M., Lavenex, P. B., & Martarelli, C. S. (2024). Effective learning with a personal AI tutor: A case study. *Education and Information Technologies*, ●●●, 1–16. DOI: 10.1007/s10639-024-12888-5

Bakare, O. D., & Jatto, O. V. (2023). In Keengwe, J. (Ed.), *"The potential impact of Chatbots on student engagement and learning outcomes" in Creative AI tools and ethical implications in teaching and learning* (pp. 212–229). IGI Global.

Baker, T., Smith, L., & Anissa, N. (2019). Educ-AI-tion rebooted? Exploring the future of artificial intelligence in schools and colleges

Baker, T., Smith, L., & Anissa, N. (2019). Educ-AI-tion rebooted? Exploring the future of artificial intelligence in schools and colleges. Retrieved from https://www.nesta.org. uk/report/education-rebooted/.

Bali, M. (2023, September 18). What I mean when I say critical AI literacy. *Mahabali.* https://blog.mahabali.me/educational-technology-2/what-i-mean-when-i-say-critical-ai-literacy/

Bana e Costa, C. A., & Oliveira, M. D. (2012). A multicriteria decision analysis model for faculty evaluation. *Omega*, *40*(4), 424–436. DOI: 10.1016/j.omega.2011.08.006

Baranidharan, S., & Dhakshayini, K. N. (2024). Exploring the Influence of Emotional Intelligence on Decision-Making Across Diverse Domains: A Systematic Literature Review. *Neuroleadership Development and Effective Communication in Modern Business, 70-91*. DOI: DOI: 10.4018/979-8-3693-4350-0.ch004

Barbhuiya, R. K. (2023). Introduction to Artificial Intelligence: Current Developments, Concerns and Possibilities for Education. *Indian Journal of Educational Technology*, *5*(2), 266.

Barua, P. D., Vicnesh, J., Gururajan, R., Oh, S. L., Palmer, E., Azizan, M. M., Kadri, N. A., & Acharya, U. R. (2022). Artificial intelligence enabled personalised assistive tools to enhance Education of children with neurodevelopmental disorders—A review. *International Journal of Environmental Research and Public Health*, *19*(3), 1192. DOI: 10.3390/ijerph19031192 PMID: 35162220

Bashir, N., Donti, P., Cuff, J., Sroka, S., Ilic, M., Sze, V., ... (2024). The climate and sustainability implications of generative AI. An MIT exploration of generative AI. https://mit-genai.pubpub.org/pub/8ulgrckc/release/2?readingCollection=9434a92e

Bates, T., Cobo, C., Mariño, O., & Wheeler, S. (2020). Can artificial intelligence transform higher education? *International Journal of Educational Technology in Higher Education*, *17*(1), 1–12. DOI: 10.1186/s41239-020-00218-x

Bauer, E., Greisel, M., Kuznetsov, I., Berndt, M., Kollar, I., Dresel, M., Fischer, M. R., & Fischer, F. (2023). Using natural language processing to support peer-feedback in the age of artificial intelligence: A cross-disciplinary framework and a research agenda. *British Journal of Educational Technology*, *54*(5), 1222–1245. DOI: 10.1111/bjet.13336

Bawden, D., & Robinson, L. (2020). Information overload: An overview. In *Oxford Encyclopedia of Political Decision Making*. Oxford University Press., DOI: 10.1093/acrefore/9780190228637.013.1360

Bayne, S. (2015). Teacherbot: Interventions in automated teaching. *Teaching in Higher Education*, *20*(4), 455–467. DOI: 10.1080/13562517.2015.1020783

Bearman, M., Ryan, J., & Ajjawi, R. (2023). Discourses of artificial intelligence in higher education: A critical literature review. *Higher Education*, *86*(2), 369–385. DOI: 10.1007/s10734-022-00937-2

Becker, K. P., Parker, J. L., & Richter, D. (2024). *Framework for the future: Building AI literacy in higher education* (v. 1.0). Moxie. https://moxielearn.ai/wp-content/uploads/2024/06/Ai-literacies-white-paper.docx.pdf

Bednar, D. A. (2024, November). *Things as they really are 2.0.* https://www.churchofjesuschrist.org/study/broadcasts/worldwide-devotional-for-young-adults/2024/11/13bednar?lang=eng

Bell, L., Stevenson, H., & Neary, M. (2009). *The future of higher education: Policy.* Pedagogy and the Student Experience, Continuum International Publishing Group.

Belmekki, M., Belmekki, L., & Koumachi, B. (2024). The effect of project-based learning on the development of learners' critical thinking skills in higher education: A quasi-experimental study. *Revue Linguistique et Référentiels Interculturels*, *5*(1), 44–57. DOI: 10.34874/IMIST.PRSM/liri-v5i1.49980

Benali, M., Kaddouri, M., & Azzimani, T. (2018). Digital competence of Moroccan teachers of English. *International Journal of Education and Development Using Information and Communication Technology*, *14*, 99–120.

Benali, M., & Mak, J. (2024). Perception of Preservice Moroccan Teachers Regarding the Adoption of ChatGPT in Their Teaching Practices. In *Artificial Intelligence Applications in K-12*. Routledge. DOI: 10.4324/9781003440192-8

Benavot, A., Hoppers, C. O., Lockhart, A. S., & Hinzen, H. (2022). Reimagining adult education and lifelong learning for all: Historical and critical perspectives. *International Review of Education, 68(2), 165-194.* https://doi.org/ springer.comDOI: 10.1007/s11159-022-09955-9

Bender, E. M., Gebru, T., McMillan-Major, A., & Shmitchell, S. (2021). On the dangers of stochastic parrots: Can language models be too big? *Proceedings of the 2021 ACM Conference on Fairness, Accountability, and Transparency*, 610-623. https://doi.org/DOI: 10.1145/3442188.3445922

Benfatto, M. N., Seimyr, G. Ö., Ygge, J., Pansell, T., Rydberg, A., & Jacobson, C. (2016). Screening for dyslexia using eye tracking during reading. PLoS One, 11(12), e0165508. https://doi.org/ al.pone.0165508DOI: 10.1371/journ

Benhayoun, L., & Lang, D. (2021). Does higher education properly prepare graduates for the growing artificial intelligence market? Gaps' identification using text mining. *Human Systems Management*, *40*(5), 639–651. DOI: 10.3233/HSM-211179

Bentur, A., Getz, D., & Shacham, O. K. (2021). System Analysis of Technology Transfer Policies and Models in Higher Education. In International Series in Operations Research and Management Science (Vol. 309, pp. 241-262). Springer. DOI: 10.1007/978-3-030-74051-1_8

Bereiter, C. (2005). *Education and mind in the knowledge age*. Routledge. DOI: 10.4324/9781410612182

Beukelman, D. R., & Light, J. C. (Eds.). (2020). *Augmentative & Alternative Communication: Supporting Children and Adults with Complex Communication Needs* (5th ed.). Paul H. Brookes Publishing Co., Inc.

Bhardwaj, S., & Sharma, I. (2025). Exploring the effects of AI-powered personalized classroom management strategies. In *AI Applications and Strategies in Teacher Education* (pp. 21–42). IGI Global.

Bhatia, A., Bhatia, P., & Sood, D. (2024). Leveraging AI to transform online higher education: Focusing on personalized learning, assessment, and student engagement. *International Journal of Management and Humanities (IJMH, 11*(1).

Bhattacharjee, K. K. (2019). Research output on the usage of artificial intelligence in indian higher education - a scientometric study. IEEE International Conference on Industrial Engineering and Engineering Management C7 - 8978798, Cankaya, B., Roberts, R., Douglas, S., Vigness, R., & Oztekin, A. (2024). What postpones degree completion? Discovering key predictors of undergraduate degree completion through explainable artificial intelligence (XAI). Journal of Marketing Analytics. DOI: 10.1057/s41270-024-00290-6

Bhatti, I., Mohi-U-din, S. F., Hayat, Y., & Tariq, M. (2024). Artificial Intelligence Applications for Students with Learning Disabilities: A Systematic Review. *European Journal of Science. Innovation and Technology*, *4*(2), 40–56.

Bhatt, P., Vemprala, N., Valecha, R., Hariharan, G., & Rao, H. R. (2023). User privacy, surveillance and public health during COVID-19–an examination of twitterverse. *Information Systems Frontiers*, *25*(5), 1667–1682. DOI: 10.1007/s10796-022-10247-8 PMID: 35125937

Bianchi, F., Kalluri, P., Durmus, E., Ladhak, F., Cheng, M., & Nozza, D.. (2023). Easily accessible text-to-image generation amplifies demographic stereotypes at large scale. In *FAccT '23: Proceedings of the 2023 ACM conference on fairness, accountability, and transparency*, 1493–1504. https://doi.org/DOI: 10.1145/3593013.3594095

Biemann, C., & Mehler, A. (Eds.). (2014). *Text Mining: From Ontology Learning to Automated Text Processing Applications*. Springer. DOI: 10.1007/978-3-319-12655-5

bin Salem, I. (2024). Integrating artificial intelligence in personalized learning: A future-oriented approach to enhance student engagement and achievement. *International Journal of Post Axial: Futuristic Teaching and Learning*, 111–119.

Bingley, W. J., Curtis, C., Lockey, S., Bialkowski, A., Gillespie, N., Haslam, S. A., Ko, R. K. L., Steffens, N., Wiles, J., & Worthy, P. (2022). Where is the human in human-centered AI? Insights from developer priorities and user experiences. *Computers in Human Behavior*, *141*, 107617–107617. DOI: 10.1016/j.chb.2022.107617

Binns, R., Veale, M., Van Kleek, M., & Shadbolt, N. (2018). "It's reducing a human being to a percentage": Perceptions of justice in algorithmic decisions. *Proceedings of the 2018 CHI Conference on Human Factors in Computing Systems*. https://doi.org/DOI: 10.1145/3173574.3173951

Boddington, P. (2017). *Towards a code of ethics for artificial intelligence*. Springer. DOI: 10.1007/978-3-319-60648-4

Bodily, R., & Verbert, K. (2017). Review of research on student-facing learning analytics dashboards and educational recommender systems. *IEEE Transactions on Learning Technologies, 10*(4), 405–418. DOI: 10.1109/TLT.2017.2740172

Borenstein, J., & Howard, A. (2021). Emerging challenges in AI and the need for AI ethics education. *AI and Ethics, 1*(1), 61–65. Advance online publication. DOI: 10.1007/s43681-020-00002-7 PMID: 38624388

Borup, J. (2023). This was written by a human: A real educator's thoughts on teaching in the age of Chatgpt. EDUCAUSE Review. https://er.educause.edu/articles/2023/3/this-was-written-by-a-human-a-real-educators-thoughts-onteaching-in-the-age-of-chatgpt

Bostrom, N. (2006). *AI set to exceed human brain power*. CNN.

Botrel, L., Holz, E., & Kübler, A. (2015). Brain painting V2: Evaluation of P300-based brain-computer interface for creative expression by an end-user following the user centered design. *Brain Computer Interfaces (Abingdon, England), 2*(2–3), 135–149. DOI: 10.1080/2326263X.2015.1100038

Bouck, E. C. (2016). Assistive Technology. SAGE Publications. DOI: 10.4135/9781071872765

Bouschery, S. G., Blazevic, V., & Piller, F. T. (2023). Augmenting human innovation teams with artificial intelligence: Exploring transformer-based language models. *Journal of Product Innovation Management, 40*(2), 139–153. DOI: 10.1111/jpim.12656

Bowen, J. A., & Watson, C. E. (2024). *Teaching with AI: A Practical Guide to a New Era of Human Learning*. Johns Hopkins University Press. DOI: 10.56021/9781421449227

Bozkurt, A., Karadeniz, A., Baneres, D., Guerrero-Roldán, A. E., & Rodríguez, M. E. (2021). Artificial intelligence and reflections from educational landscape: A review of AI Studies in half a century. *Sustainability (Basel), 13*(2), 800. DOI: 10.3390/su13020800

Bozkurt, A., Xiao, J., Farrow, R., Bai, J. Y. H., Nerantzi, C., Moore, S., Dron, J., Stracke, C. M., Singh, L., Crompton, H., Koutropoulos, A., Terentev, E., Pazurek, A., Nichols, M., Sidorkin, A. M., Costello, E., Watson, S., Mulligan, D., Honeychurch, S., & Asino, T. I. (2024). The manifesto for teaching and learning in a time of Generative AI: A critical collective stance to better navigate the future. *Open Praxis, 16*(4), 487–513. DOI: 10.55982/openpraxis.16.4.777

Bradáč, V., Smolka, P., Kotyrba, M., & Průdek, T. (2022). Design of an intelligent tutoring system to create a personalized study plan using expert systems. *Applied Sciences (Basel, Switzerland), 12*(12), 6236. Advance online publication. DOI: 10.3390/app12126236

Brey, P. (2012). Anticipating ethical issues in emerging IT. *Ethics and Information Technology, 14*(4), 305–317. DOI: 10.1007/s10676-012-9293-y

Brookfield, S. D. (1987). *Developing critical thinkers: Challenging adults to explore alternative ways of thinking and acting*. Jossey-Bass.

Brown, T. B., Mann, B., Ryder, N., Subbiah, M., Kaplan, J., Dhariwal, P., Neelakantan, A., Shyam, P., Sastry, G., Askell, A., & Agarwal, S. Herbert-Voss., Krueger, G., Henighan, T., Child, R., Ramesh, A., Ziegler, D. M., Wu, J., Winter, C., … Amodei, D. (2020). Language models are few-shot learners. Cornell University. http://arxiv.org/abs/2005.14165

Bryan, C., & Clegg, K. (Eds.). (2019). *Innovative assessment in higher education: A handbook for academic practitioners*. Routledge. DOI: 10.4324/9780429506857

Bugaj, C. (2023). *The New Assistive Tech: Make Learning Awesome for All!* International Society for Technology in Education.

Buhalis, D., & Moldavska, I. (2022). Voice assistants in hospitality: Using artificial intelligence for customer service. *Journal of Hospitality and Tourism Technology, 13*(3), 386–403. DOI: 10.1108/JHTT-03-2021-0104

Burgsteiner, H., Kandlhofer, M., & Steinbauer, G. (2016). IRobot: Teaching the Basics of Artificial Intelligence in High Schools. Proceedings of the AAAI Conference on Artificial Intelligence, 30(1). DOI: 10.1609/aaai.v30i1.9864

Burns, M. (2021). EdTech Essentials: The top10 Technology Strategies for All Learning Environments. ASCD. *Top (Madrid)*, •••, 10.

Bushuyev, S., Bushuiev, D., Bushuieva, V., Bushuyeva, N., & Murzabekova, S. (2024). The erosion of competencies in managing innovation projects due to the impact of ubiquitous artificial intelligence systems. *Procedia Computer Science, 231*, 403–408. DOI: 10.1016/j.procs.2023.12.225

Bush, V. (1945). As we may think. *Atlantic Monthly*, *176*(1), 101–108.

Butler-Ulrich, T., Hughes, J., & Morrison, L. (2024). Creativity and Generative AI for Preservice Teachers. In L. Barlach (Ed.), *Creativity in Contemporaneity* (working title). IntechOpen. DOI: 10.5772/intechopen.1007517

Calma, A., & Cotronei-Baird, V. (2021). Assessing critical thinking in business education: Key issues and practical solutions. *International Journal of Management Education*, *19*(3), 100531. DOI: 10.1016/j.ijme.2021.100531

Cambridge Dictionary. (n.d.). Logic. In dictionary.cambridge.org. Retrieved March 8, 2025, from https://dictionary.cambridge.org/us/dictionary/english/logic

Campo, L., Galindo-Domínguez, H., Bezanilla, M. J., Fernández-Nogueira, D., & Poblete, M. (2023). Methodologies for fostering critical thinking skills from university students' points of view. *Education Sciences*, *13*(2), 132. DOI: 10.3390/educsci13020132

Canova, R., & Ma'rof, A. A. (2023). Empowering Students With Ideological and Political Education and Bridging the Gap in Modern Democracies' Ideological Division. In *Social Psychology Theories and Methods in Education (pp. 159-181)*. IGI Global. DOI: DOI: 10.4018/978-1-6684-8837-9.ch008

Carabantes, M. (2023). Why artificial intelligence is not transparent: a critical analysis of its three opacity layers. Edward Elgar Publishing EBooks, 424–434. DOI: 10.4337/9781803928562.00045

Carpenter, L. A. B., Johnston, L. B., & Beard, L. A. (2015). *Assistive Technology: Access for All Students* (3rd ed.). Pearson.

Casali, Y., Aydin, N. Y., & Comes, T. (2022). Machine learning for spatial analyses in urban areas: A scoping review. *Sustainable Cities and Society*, *85*, 104050. Advance online publication. DOI: 10.1016/j.scs.2022.104050

Castagno, A. E., Ingram, J. C., Camplain, R., & Blackhorse, D. (2022). "We constantly have to navigate": Indigenous students' and professionals' strategies for navigating ethical conflicts in STEMM. *Cultural Studies of Science Education*, *17*(3), 683–700. DOI: 10.1007/s11422-021-10081-5

Castaneda, L., & Selwyn, N. (2018). More than tools? Making sense of the ongoing digitizations of higher education. *International Journal of Educational Technology in Higher Education*, *15*(22). Advance online publication. https://doi.org/ DOI: 10.1186/s41239-018-0109-y

Chaka, C. (2023). Fourth industrial revolution—A review of applications, prospects, and challenges for artificial intelligence, robotics and blockchain in higher education. *Research and Practice in Technology Enhanced Learning*, *18*, C7–C2. DOI: 10.58459/rptel.2023.18002

Chalkley, A. E., Mandelid, M. B., Thurston, M., Daly-Smith, A., Singh, A., Huiberts, I., Archbold, V. S. J., Resaland, G. K., & Tjomsland, H. E. (2022). "Go beyond your own comfort zone and challenge yourself": A comparison on the use of physically active learning in Norway, the Netherlands and the UK. *Teaching and Teacher Education*, *118*, 103825. DOI: 10.1016/j.tate.2022.103825

Chan, C. B. (2023). Grading generative AI-based assignments using a 3R framework. In Proceedings for IEEE International Conference on Teaching, Assessment and Learning for Engineering, 28 Nov-–1 Dec. Auckland. https://doi.org/DOI: 10.1109/TALE56641.2023.10398408

Chan, C. K. Y. (2023). A comprehensive AI policy education framework for university teaching and learning. *International Journal of Educational Technology in Higher Education*, *20*(1), 38. DOI: 10.1186/s41239-023-00408-3

Chan, C. K. Y., & Hu, W. (2023). Students' voices on generative AI: Perceptions, benefits, and challenges in higher education. *International Journal of Educational Technology in Higher Education*, *20*(1), 43. DOI: 10.1186/s41239-023-00411-8

Chandratreya, A. (2025). Epistemology in Research: Understanding the Foundations of Knowledge. In *Enhancing Research for Academicians in Higher Education (pp. 125-160)*. IGI Global Scientific Publishing. DOI: DOI: 10.4018/979-8-3693-4496-5.ch008

Chang, V., Ansari, Y., & Arami, M. (2024). ChatGPT in Higher Education: A Risk Management Approach to Academic Integrity, Critical Thinking, and Workforce Readiness. *Proceedings of the 6th International Conference on Finance, Economics, Management and IT Business, FEMIB 2024*. DOI: 10.5220/0012764100003717

Chan, K. S., & Zary, N. (2019). Applications and challenges of implementing artificial intelligence in medical education: Integrative review. *JMIR Medical Education*, *5*(1), e13930. DOI: 10.2196/13930 PMID: 31199295

Chassignol, M., Khoroshavin, A., Klimova, A., & Bilyatdinova, A. (2018). Artificial Intelligence trends in education: A narrative overview. *Procedia Computer Science*, *136*, 16–24. DOI: 10.1016/j.procs.2018.08.233

Chaudhry, M. A., & Kazim, E. (2022). Artificial Intelligence in Education (AIEd): A high-level academic and industry note 2021. *AI and Ethics*, *2*(1), 157–165. DOI: 10.1007/s43681-021-00074-z PMID: 34790953

Chen, D., Parsa, R., Hope, A., Hannon, B., Mak, E., Eng, L., Liu, F.-F., Fallah-Rad, N., Heesters, A. M., & Raman, S. (2024). Physician and artificial intelligence chatbot responses to cancer questions from social media. *JAMA Oncology*, *10*(7), 956–960. DOI: 10.1001/jamaoncol.2024.0836 PMID: 38753317

Chen, L., Chen, P., & Lin, Z. (2020). Artificial intelligence in education: A review. *IEEE Access : Practical Innovations, Open Solutions*, *8*, 75264–75278. DOI: 10.1109/ACCESS.2020.2988510

Chen, L., Chen, Z., Zhang, Y., Liu, Y., Osman, A. I., Farghali, M., Hua, J., Al-Fatesh, A., Ihara, I., Rooney, D. W., & Yap, P. S. (2023). Artificial intelligence-based solutions for climate change: A review. *Environmental Chemistry Letters*, *21*(5), 2525–2557. DOI: 10.1007/s10311-023-01617-y

Chen, X., Xie, H., Zou, D., & Hwang, G.-J. (2020). Application and theory gaps during the rise of artificial intelligence in *Education.Computers and Education: Artificial Intelligence*, *1*, 100002. DOI: 10.1016/j.caeai.2020.100002

Chen, Y., Jensen, S., Albert, L. J., Gupta, S., & Lee, T. (2023). Artificial intelligence (AI) student assistants in the classroom: Designing chatbots to support student success. *Information Systems Frontiers*, *25*(1), 161–182. DOI: 10.1007/s10796-022-10291-4

Cheok, A. D., Edirisinghe, C., & Shrestha, M. L. (2024). *The Rise of Machines: Future of Work in the Age of AI*. CRC Press.

Chergarova, V., Tomeo, M., Provost, L., De la Peña, G., Ulloa, A., & Miranda, D. (2023). Case study: Exploring the role of current and potential usage of generative artificial intelligence tools in higher education. *Issues in Information Systems*, *24*(2), 282–292. DOI: 10.48009/2_iis_2023_125

Chesterman, S. (2024). Good models borrow, great models steal: Intellectual property rights and generative AI. *Policy and Society*, •••, puae006. Advance online publication. DOI: 10.1093/polsoc/puae006

Chiarello, F., Giordano, V., Spada, I., Barandoni, S., & Fantoni, G. (2024). Future applications of generative large language models: A data-driven case study on ChatGPT. *Technovation*, *133*, 103002. DOI: 10.1016/j.technovation.2024.103002

Children's Online Privacy Protection Act of 1998, 15 U.S.C. §§ 6501-6506 (1998).

China, C. R. (2023, August 28). *Leveraging user-generated social media content with text-mining examples.* https://www.ibm.com/think/topics/text-mining-use-cases

Chin, D. B., Dohmen, I. M., Cheng, B. H., Oppezzo, M. A., Chase, C. C., & Schwartz, D. L. (2010). Preparing students for future learning with teachable agents. *Educational Technology Research and Development, 58*, 649–669.

Choi, M., & Cristol, D. (2021). Digital citizenship with intersectionality lens: Towards participatory democracy driven digital citizenship education. *Theory into Practice, 60*(4), 361–370. DOI: 10.1080/00405841.2021.1987094

Chounta, I. A., Bardone, E., Raudsep, A., & Pedaste, M. (2022). Exploring teachers' perceptions of artificial intelligence as a tool to support their practice in Estonian K-12 education. *International Journal of Artificial Intelligence in Education, 32*(3), 725–755. DOI: 10.1007/s40593-021-00243-5

Churches, A. (2008). *Bloom's digital taxonomy.* http://burtonslifelearning.pbworks.com/w/file/fetch/26327358/BloomDigitalTaxonomy2001.pdf

Cision, P. R. Newswire. (2023). *State of the media report.* Cision. https://www.cision.com/resources/guides- and-reports/2024-state-of-the-media-report/

Civil Rights Act of 1964, Title VI, 42 U.S.C. § 2000d et seq. (1964).

Cohen, B., Hu, A., Patino, D., & Coffman, J. (2024). This Is Going on Your Permanent Record: A Legal Analysis of Educational Data in the Cloud. *ACM Journal on Responsible Computing, 1*(3), 1–27. DOI: 10.1145/3675230

Communication Matters. (n.d.). *TYPES OF AAC.* https://www.communicationmatters.org.uk/what-is-aac/types-of-aac/

Concetta, A. D., & Wilkinson, K. (2014). Get Your Head into the Clouds: Using Word Clouds for Analyzing Qualitative Assessment Data. TECHTRENDS. *TechTrends, 58*(3), 38–44. DOI: 10.1007/s11528-014-0750-9

Connell, J., & Malik, A. (2021). Higher Education. In The Fourth Industrial Revolution: What does it mean for Australian Industry? (pp. 161-181). Springer Nature. DOI: 10.1007/978-981-16-1614-3_10

Copyright Act of 1976, 17 U.S.C. § 101 et seq. (1976).

Cotton, D. R. E., Cotton, P. A., & Shipway, J. R. (2023). ChatGPT, educational integrity, and assessment design: Creative possibilities and ethical implications. *Assessment & Evaluation in Higher Education, 48*(1), 1–14. DOI: 10.1080/02602938.2023.2195289

Council of Chief State School Officers. (2013). *InTASC Model Core Teaching Standards and Learning Progressions for educators 1.0.* https://ccsso.org/resource-library/intasc-model-core-teaching-standards-and-learning-progressions-educators-10

Crawford, C., Cowling, M., & Allen, W. (2023). Leadership is needed for ethical ChatGPT: Character, assessment, and learning using artificial intelligence (AI). *Journal of Applied Learning & Teaching, 6*(1), 10–22. DOI: 10.37074/jalt.2023.6.1.5

Crompton, H., & Burke, D. (2021). Artificial intelligence in higher education: The state of the field. *International Journal of Educational Technology in Higher Education.* https://educationaltechnologyjournal.springeropen.com/articles/10.1186/s41239-021-00235-x

Crompton, H., & Burke, D. (2023). Artificial intelligence in higher education: The state of the field. *International Journal of Educational Technology in Higher Education, 20*(1), 22. DOI: 10.1186/s41239-023-00392-8

Dabis, A., & Csáki, C. (2024). AI and ethics: Investigating the first policy responses of higher education institutions to the challenge of generative AI. *Humanities & Social Sciences Communications, 11*(1), 1006. DOI: 10.1057/s41599-024-03526-z

Dandachi, I. E. (2024). AI-powered personalized learning: Toward sustainable education. In *Navigating the Intersection of Business, Sustainability and Technology (pp. 109-118).* Singapore: Springer Nature Singapore. https://doi.org/DOI: 10.1007/978-981-99-8572-2_5

Danry, V. M. (2023). AI Enhanced Reasoning: Augmenting Human Critical Thinking with AI Systems. Mit.edu. https://hdl.handle.net/1721.1/151971

Davis, F. D. (1989). Perceived usefulness, perceived ease of use, and user acceptance of information technology. *Management Information Systems Quarterly, 13*(3), 319–340. DOI: 10.2307/249008

De Freitas, J., Agarwal, S., Schmitt, B., & Haslam, N. (2023). Psychological factors underlying attitudes toward AI tools. *Nature Human Behaviour, 7*(11), 1845–1854. DOI: 10.1038/s41562-023-01734-2 PMID: 37985913

Del Pino, J. S., Gheorghiu, R., & Roman, A. (2012). The rest of me. *Futures, 44*(8), 730–734. DOI: 10.1016/j.futures.2012.04.011

Della Ventura, M. (2017). Creating inspiring learning environments by means of digital technologies: A case study of the effectiveness of WhatsApp in music education. In E-Learning, & E-Education (Eds.), Online training (pp. 36–45). Springer. DOI: 10.4108/eai.26-7-2017.152906

Della Ventura, M. (2018). Twitter as a music education tool to enhance the learning process: Conversation analysis. In *New Media for Educational Change: Selected Papers from HKAECT 2018 International Conference* (pp. 81-88). Springer Singapore.

Dell, A. G., Newton, D. A., & Petroff, J. G. (2017). *Assistive Technology in the Classroom: Enhancing the School Experiences of Students with Disabilities* (3rd ed.). Pearson.

Dempere, J., Modugu, K., Hesham, A., & Ramasamy, L. K. (2024). The impact of ChatGPT on higher education. *Frontiers in Education*, *8*, 1206936. DOI: 10.3389/feduc.2023.1206936

Denga, E. M. & Denga, S. W. (2024). Revolutionizing Education: The Power of Technology. In *Revolutionizing Curricula Through Computational Thinking, Logic, and Problem Solving* (pp. 167-188). IGI Global.

Deng, Y., Wang, W., & Zhang, Z. (2023). Exploring the application of generative AI in higher education: Opportunities and challenges. *Educational Technology Research and Development*. Advance online publication. DOI: 10.1007/s11423-023-10182-y

DeSchryver, M. D., & Yadav, A. (2015). Creative and computational thinking in the context of new literacies: Working with teachers to scaffold complex technology-mediated approaches to teaching and learning. *Journal of Technology and Teacher Education*, *23*(3), 411–431.

Dethine, B., Enjolras, M., & Monticolo, D. (2020). Digitalization and SMEs' export management: Impacts on resources and capabilities. *Technology Innovation Management Review*, *10*(4), 18–34. DOI: 10.22215/timreview/1344

Dewey, J. (1933). *How we think: A restatement of the relation of reflective thinking to the educative process*. D.C. Heath and Company.

Dewey, J. (1938). *Experience and education*. Kappa Delta Pi.

Dianova, V. G., & Schultz, M. D. (2023). Discussing ChatGPT's implications for industry and higher education: The case for transdisciplinarity and digital humanities. *Industry and Higher Education*, *37*(5), 593–600. DOI: 10.1177/09504222231199989

Dietzmann, C., & Duan, Y. (2022). Artificial intelligence for managerial information processing and decision-making in the era of information overload. http://hdl.handle.net/10125/80060

Dillenbourg, P., Zufferey, G., Alavi, H., Jermann, P., Do-Lenh, S., & Bonnard, Q. (2011). *Classroom orchestration: The third circle of usability*. CSCL.

Dimitriadou, E., & Lanitis, A. (2023). *A critical evaluation, challenges, and future perspectives of using artificial intelligence and emerging technologies in smart classrooms*. Smart Learning Environments., DOI: 10.1186/s40561-023-00231-3

Dogru, T., Line, N., Hanks, L., Acikgoz, F., Abbott, J., Bakir, S., Berbekova, A., Bilgihan, A., Iskender, A., Kizildag, M., Lee, M., Lee, W., McGinley, S., Mody, M., Onder, I., Ozdemir, O., & Suess, C. (2024). The implications of generative artificial intelligence in academic research and higher education in tourism and hospitality. *Tourism Economics*, *30*(5), 1083–1094. DOI: 10.1177/13548166231204065

Doleck, T., Bazelais, P., Lemay, D. J., Saxena, A., & Basnet, R. B. (2017). Algorithmic thinking, cooperativity, creativity, critical thinking, and problem solving: Exploring the relationship between computational thinking skills and academic performance. *Journal of Computers in Education*, *4*(4), 355–369. DOI: 10.1007/s40692-017-0090-9

Doshi, A. R., & Hauser, O. P. (2024). Generative AI enhances individual creativity but reduces the collective diversity of novel content. *Science Advances*, *10*(28), eadn5290. Advance online publication. DOI: 10.1126/sciadv.adn5290 PMID: 38996021

Dousay, T. A., & Hall, C. (2018, June). Alexa, tell me about using a virtual assistant in the classroom. In EdMedia+ innovate learning (pp. 1413-1419). Association for the Advancement of Computing in Education (AACE). https://www.learntechlib.org/p/184359/

Drigas, A., & Ioannidou, R.-E. (2013). A review on artificial intelligence in special education. *Communications in Computer and Information Science*, *278*, 385–391. DOI: 10.1007/978-3-642-35879-1_46

Du Boulay, B. (2000). Can we learn from ITSs? In International conference on intelligent tutoring systems (pp. 9–17). Berlin, Heidelberg: Springer.

Duan, Y., Edwards, J. S., & Dwivedi, Y. K. (2019). Artificial intelligence for decision making in the era of Big Data – evolution, challenges and research agenda. *International Journal of Information Management*, *48*, 63–71. DOI: 10.1016/j.ijinfomgt.2019.01.021

Dumitru, D., & Halpern, D. F. (2023). Critical Thinking: Creating Job-Proof Skills for the Future of Work. *Journal of Intelligence*, *11*(10), 194–194. DOI: 10.3390/jintelligence11100194 PMID: 37888426

Eaton, L. (2024, June 20). AI plagiarism considerations part 2: When students use AI. *AI EduSimplified.* https://aiedusimplified.substack.com/p/ai-plagiarism-considerations-part-a27

Eaton, S. E. (2023). Postplagiarism: Transdisciplinary ethics and integrity in the age of artificial intelligence and neurotechnology. *International Journal for Educational Integrity, 19*(1), 23. DOI: 10.1007/s40979-023-00144-1

Edmunds, A., & Morris, A. (2000). The problem of information overload in business organisations: A review of the literature. *International Journal of Information Management, 20*(1), 17–28. DOI: 10.1016/S0268-4012(99)00051-1

Edutopia. (2024). *Using AI tools for differentiated instruction*. Edutopia. Retrieved from https://www.edutopia.org/article/using-ai-tools-differentiated-instruction

Edutopia. (n.d.). *AI tools for lesson planning: Streamlining teacher workflows*. Retrieved from https://www.edutopia.org/article/ai-tools-lesson-planning

Edwards, S. (2017). Reflecting differently. New dimensions: reflection-before-action and reflection-beyond-action. *International Practice Development Journal, 7*(1).

Eguchi, A. (2016). RoboCupJunior for promoting STEM education, 21st century skills, and technological advancement through robotics competition. *Robotics and Autonomous Systems, 75*, 692–699. DOI: 10.1016/j.robot.2015.05.013

Egunjobi, D., & Adeyeye, O. J. (2024). Revolutionizing Learning: The Impact of Augmented Reality (AR) and Artificial Intelligence (AI on Education). ResearchGate, Oct.

Elder, L. (2022). *Critical Thinking*. Routledge., DOI: 10.4324/9781138609877-REE215-1

Ellikkal, A., & Rajamohan, S. (2024). *AI-enabled personalized learning: Empowering management students for improving engagement and academic performance*. Vilakshan-XIMB Journal of Management.

Ellikkal, A., & Rajamohan, S. (2024). *AI-enabled personalized learning: empowering management students for improving engagement and academic performance*. Vilakshan-XIMB Journal of Management., DOI: 10.1108/XJM-02-2024-0023

El-Sabagh, H. A. (2021). Adaptive e-learning environment based on learning styles and its impact on development students' engagement. *International Journal of Educational Technology in Higher Education, 18*(1), 53. DOI: 10.1186/s41239-021-00289-4

Engelbart, D. C. (1963). A conceptual framework for the augmentation of man's intellect. In Howerton, P. W., & Weeks, D. C. (Eds.), *Vistas in information handling* (pp. 1–29). Spartan Books.

English, L. 2023. What are the new must-have leadership skills in today's AI world? Medium. August 31, 2023. https://larry-english.medium.com/what-are-the-new-must-have-leadership-skills-in-todays-ai-world-56654dd1b62f

Ennis, R. (2011). Critical Thinking. *Inquiry (Upper Montclair, N.J.)*, *26*(2), 5–19. DOI: 10.5840/inquiryctnews201126215

Estevez, J., Garate, G., & Graña, M. (2019). Gentle introduction to artificial intelligence for high-school students using scratch. *IEEE Access : Practical Innovations, Open Solutions*, *7*, 179027–179036. DOI: 10.1109/ACCESS.2019.2956136

Ewing, M. E. (2023, September). Navigating ethical implications for AI-driven PR practice. *Public Relations Society of America*. https://www.prsa.org/article/navigating-ethical-implications-for-ai-driven-pr-practice

Ezzaim, A., Dahbi, A., Aqqal, A., & Haidine, A. (2024). AI-based learning style detection in adaptive learning systems: A systematic literature review. *Journal of Computers in Education*, •••, 1–39. DOI: 10.1007/s40692-024-00328-9

Facione, P. A. (1990). *Critical thinking: A statement of expert consensus for purposes of educational assessment and instruction—The Delphi report*. California Academic Press.

Fahmy, Y. (2024). *Student Perception on AI-Driven Assessment: Motivation, Engagement and Feedback Capabilities* (Bachelor's thesis, University of Twente).

Family Educational Rights and Privacy Act of 1974, 20 U.S.C. § 1232g (1974).

Farias-Gaytan, S., Aguaded, I., & Ramirez-Montoya, M.-S. (2023). Digital transformation and digital literacy in the context of complexity within higher education institutions: A systematic literature review. *Humanities & Social Sciences Communications*, *10*(1), 386. Advance online publication. DOI: 10.1057/s41599-023-01875-9

Fazil, A. W., Hakimi, M., Shahidzay, A. K., & Hasas, A. (2024). Exploring the Broad Impact of AI Technologies on Student Engagement and Academic Performance in University Settings in Afghanistan. *RIGGS: Journal of Artificial Intelligence and Digital Business*, *2*(2), 56–63. DOI: 10.31004/riggs.v2i2.268

Federiakin, D., Molerov, D., Zlatkin-Troitschanskaia, O., & Maur, A. (2024). Prompt engineering as a new 21st century skill. *Frontiers in Education*, *9*, 1366434. Advance online publication. DOI: 10.3389/feduc.2024.1366434

Felzmann, H., Fosch-Villaronga, E., Lutz, C., & Tamò-Larrieux, A. (2020). Towards Transparency by Design for Artificial Intelligence. *Science and Engineering Ethics*, *26*(6), 3333–3361. DOI: 10.1007/s11948-020-00276-4 PMID: 33196975

Ferdaus, M. M., Abdelguerfi, M., Ioup, E., Niles, K. N., Pathak, K., & Sloan, S. (2024). Towards trustworthy AI: A review of ethical and robust large language models. *arXiv.*https://doi.org//arXiv.2407.13934DOI: 10.48550

Ferguson, R., & Clow, D. (2019). Learning analytics: AI's role in higher education. *EDUCAUSE Review*, *54*(2), 24–34.

Feuerriegel, S., Hartmann, J., Janiesch, C., & Zschech, P. (2024). Generative AI. *Business & Information Systems Engineering*, *66*(1), 111–126. DOI: 10.1007/s12599-023-00834-7

Fitria, T. N. (2021, December). Artificial intelligence (AI) in education: Using AI tools for teaching and learning process. In *Prosiding Seminar Nasional & Call for Paper STIE AAS* (Vol. 4, No. 1, pp. 134-147). Freire, P. (1970). *Pedagogy of the oppressed* (M. B. Ramos, Trans.). Herder and Herder.

Flavell, J. H. (1979). Metacognition and cognitive monitoring: A new area of cognitive–developmental inquiry. *The American Psychologist*, *34*(10), 906–911. DOI: 10.1037/0003-066X.34.10.906

Floridi, L. (2023). *The ethics of artificial intelligence: Principles, challenges, and opportunities*. Oxford University Press. DOI: 10.1093/oso/9780198883098.001.0001

Floridi, L., & Cowls, J. (2019). A unified framework of five principles for AI in society. *Harvard Data Science Review*. Advance online publication. DOI: 10.1162/99608f92.8cd550d1

Foltynek, T., Bjelobaba, S., Glendinning, I., Khan, Z. R., Santos, R., Pavletic, P., & Kravjar, J. (2023). ENAI Recommendations on the ethical use of Artificial Intelligence in Education. *International Journal for Educational Integrity*, *19*(1), 1–4. DOI: 10.1007/s40979-023-00133-4

Foster, D., White, L., Erdil, D. C., Adams, J., Argüelles, A., Hainey, B., . . . Stott, L. (2019). Toward a cloud computing learning community. Annual Conference on Innovation and Technology in Computer Science Education, ITiCSE, Gallastegui, L. M. G., & Forradellas, R. F. R. (2021). Business methodology for the application in university environments of predictive machine learning models based on an ethical taxonomy of the student's digital twin. Administrative Sciences, 11(4 C7 - 118). DOI: 10.1145/3344429.3372506

Foster, M. E. (2024). Evaluating the Impact of Supplemental Computer-Assisted Math Instruction in Elementary School: A Conceptual Replication. *Journal of Research on Educational Effectiveness*, *17*(1), 94–118. Advance online publication. DOI: 10.1080/19345747.2023.2174919

Foung, D., & Kwan, J. (2022). Prevention is better than cure: Use of a dashboard in a university English course. In *Applications of machine learning and artificial intelligence in education* (pp. 162–176). IGI Global., DOI: 10.4018/978-1-7998-7776-9.ch007

Franco-Mariscal, A. J., Cano-Iglesias, M. J., España-Ramos, E., & Blanco-López, Á. (2024). The ENCIC-CT model for the development of critical thinking. In *Critical thinking in science education and teacher training* (pp. 3–42). Springer Nature Switzerland., DOI: 10.1007/978-3-031-78578-8_1

Gamberini, L., & Pluchino, P. (2024). Industry 5.0: A comprehensive insight into the future of work, social sustainability, sustainable development, and career. *Australian Journal of Career Development*, *33*(1), 5–14. DOI: 10.1177/10384162241231118

Gao, P., Li, J., & Liu, S. (2021). An introduction to key technology in artificial intelligence and big data driven e-learning and e-education. *Mobile Networks and Applications*, *26*(5), 2123–2126. DOI: 10.1007/s11036-021-01777-7

Gautam, D. (2024). Revolutionizing education through innovative technological solutions. As the editors of *Transforming Learning. Power and Education*, •••, 60.

Gawlik-Kobylińska, M. (2024). Harnessing Artificial Intelligence for Enhanced Scientific Collaboration: Insights from Students and Educational Implications. *Education Sciences*, *14*(10), 1132. Advance online publication. DOI: 10.3390/educsci14101132

Genevieve, G. C. (2024, September 25). *AI and Text Mining for Searching and Screening the Literature.*https://libraryguides.mcgill.ca/text-mining

George, A. S. (2023). *Future economic implications of artificial intelligence*. Partners Universal International Research Journal.

George, B., & Wooden, O. (2023). Managing the strategic transformation of higher education through artificial intelligence. *Administrative Sciences*, *13*(9), 196. Advance online publication. DOI: 10.3390/admsci13090196

Ge, X., Yin, Y., & Feng, S. (2018). Application research of computer artificial intelligence in college student sports autonomous learning. *Kuram Ve Uygulamada Egitim Bilimleri*, *18*(5), 2143–2154.

Ge, X., Yin, Y., & Feng, S. (2018). Application research of computer artificial intelligence in college student sports autonomous learning. *Kuram Ve Uygulamada EgitimBilimleri*, *18*(5), 2143–2154.

Giuffrida, I., & Hall, A. (2023). Technology integration in higher education and student privacy beyond learning environments—A comparison of the UK and US perspective. *British Journal of Educational Technology*, *54*(6), 1587–1603. Advance online publication. DOI: 10.1111/bjet.13375

Gkrimpizi, T., Peristeras, V., & Magnisalis, I. (2023). Classification of Barriers to Digital Transformation in Higher Education Institutions: Systematic Literature Review. *Education Sciences*, *13*(7), 746. DOI: 10.3390/educsci13070746

Gligorea, I., Cioca, M., Oancea, R., Gorski, A. T., Gorski, H., & Tudorache, P. (2023). Adaptive learning using artificial intelligence in e-learning: A literature review. *Education Sciences*, *13*(12), 1216. DOI: 10.3390/educsci13121216

Glikson, E., & Woolley, A. (2020). Human trust in artificial intelligence: Review of empirical research. *The Academy of Management Annals*, *14*(2), 627–660. DOI: 10.5465/annals.2018.0057

Golowko, N., Tamla, P., & Stein, H. BÃ¶hm, T., Hemmje, M., & Onete, C. B. (2019). On the trail of future management topics with digital technology - How can artificial intelligence influence the didactic content of higher education in economics? Proceedings of the 33rdInternational Business Information Management Association Conference, IBIMA 2019: Education Excellence and Innovation Management through Vision 2020, Guizzo, D. (2024). Ceremonial Economics: A Social-Institutional Analysis of Universities, Disciplines, and Academic Positioning. Journal of Economic Issues, 58(2), 397-423.DOI: 10.1080/00213624.2024.2343246

González-Granadillo, G., González-Zarzosa, S., & Diaz, R. (2021). Security information and event management (SIEM): Analysis, trends, and usage in critical infrastructures. *Sensors (Basel)*, *21*(14), 4759. Advance online publication. DOI: 10.3390/s21144759 PMID: 34300500

González-Pérez, L. I., & Ramírez-Montoya, M. S. (2022). Components of Education 4.0 in 21st century skills frameworks: Systematic review. *Sustainability (Basel)*, *14*(3), 1493. Advance online publication. DOI: 10.3390/su14031493

Google. (2024). Gemini. https://gemini.google.com

Gouseti, A., Lakkala, M., Raffaghelli, J., Ranieri, M., Roffi, A., & Ilomäki, L. (2024). Exploring teachers' perceptions of critical digital literacies and how these are manifested in their teaching practices. *Educational Review*, *76*(7), 1751–1785. DOI: 10.1080/00131911.2022.2159933

Gouthro, P. A. (2022). Lifelong learning in a globalized world: The need for critical social theory in adult and lifelong education. *International Journal of Lifelong Education*, *41*(1), 107–121. DOI: 10.1080/02601370.2022.2033863

Grassini, S. (2023). Shaping the future of education: Exploring the potential and consequences of AI and ChatGPT in educational settings. *Education Sciences*, *13*(7), 692. Advance online publication. DOI: 10.3390/educsci13070692

Gray, M., Samala, R., Liu, Q., Skiles, D., Xu, J., Tong, W., & Wu, L. (2024). Measurement and mitigation of bias in artificial intelligence: A narrative literature review for regulatory science. *Clinical Pharmacology and Therapeutics*, *115*(4), 687–697. DOI: 10.1002/cpt.3117 PMID: 38018360

Green, J. L. (2018). *Assistive Technology in Special Education: Resources to Support Literacy, Communication, and Learning Differences* (3rd ed.). Routledge.

Gridmark Inc. (n.d.). *GridOnput*. https://gridmark.co.jp/en/

Gupta, K. (2023). An analysis of the co-occurrence of keywords on the topic sustainable development of libraries: A Scientometrics analysis. *Library Philosophy and Practice (e-journal)*. 7868. https://digitalcommons.unl.edu/libphilprac/7868

Haddaway, N. R., Page, M. J., Pritchard, C. C., & McGuinness, L. A. (2022). PRISMA 2020: An R package and Shiny app for producing PRISMA 2020-compliant flow diagrams, with interactivity for optimized digital transparency and Open Synthesis. *Campbell Systematic Reviews*, *18*(2), e1230. DOI: 10.1002/cl2.1230 PMID: 36911350

Hagendorff, T. (2024). Deception abilities emerged in large language models. *Proceedings of the National Academy of Sciences of the United States of America*, *121*(24), e2317967121. DOI: 10.1073/pnas.2317967121 PMID: 38833474

Hakimi, M., Zarinkhail, M. S., Ghafory, H., & Hamidi, S. A. (2024). Revolutionizing Technology Education with Artificial Intelligence and Machine Learning: A Comprehensive Systematic Literature Review. *TIERS Information Technology Journal*, *5*(2), 94–110. DOI: 10.38043/tiers.v6i2.5640

Halpern, D. F. (2013). *Thought and knowledge: An introduction to critical thinking*. Psychology press. DOI: 10.4324/9781315885278

Halpern, D. F., & Dunn, D. S. (2021). Critical Thinking: A Model of Intelligence for Solving Real-World Problems. *Journal of Intelligence*, *9*(2), 22–22. DOI: 10.3390/jintelligence9020022 PMID: 33916939

Han, Y., & Xu, Y. (2021). Student feedback literacy and engagement with feedback: A case study of Chinese undergraduate students. *Teaching in Higher Education*, *26*(2), 181–196. Advance online publication. DOI: 10.1080/13562517.2019.1648410

Hao, X., Demir, E., & Eyers, D. (2024). Exploring collaborative decision-making: A quasi-experimental study of human and Generative AI interaction. *Technology in Society*, *78*, 102662. Advance online publication. DOI: 10.1016/j.techsoc.2024.102662

Hart, S. A. (2016). Precision education initiative: Moving toward personalized education. *Mind, Brain and Education : the Official Journal of the International Mind, Brain, and Education Society*, *10*(4), 209–211. DOI: 10.1111/mbe.12109 PMID: 28642807

Harvey, F., & Kotting, J. (2011). Teaching mapping for digital natives: New pedagogical ideas for undergraduate cartography education. *Cartography and Geographic Information Science*, *38*(3), 269–277. DOI: 10.1559/1523040638269

Hashmi, N., & Bal, A. S. (2024). Generative AI in higher education and beyond. *Business Horizons*, *67*(5), 607–614. DOI: 10.1016/j.bushor.2024.05.005

Heffernan, N. T., & Heffernan, C. L. (2014). The ASSISTments ecosystem: Building a platform that brings scientists and teachers together for minimally invasive research on human learning and teaching. *International Journal of Artificial Intelligence in Education*, *24*(4), 470–497. DOI: 10.1007/s40593-014-0024-x

Henderson, L. H., Wersun, A., Wilson, J., Mo-ching Yeung, S., & Zhang, K. (2019). Principles for responsible management education in 2068. *Futures*, *111*, 81–89. DOI: 10.1016/j.futures.2019.05.005

Henriksen, D., Mishra, P., & Stern, R. (2024). Creative Learning for Sustainability in a World of AI: Action, Mindset, Values. *Sustainability (Basel)*, *16*(11), 4451. Advance online publication. DOI: 10.3390/su16114451

Herrera-Pavo, M. (2021). Collaborative learning for virtual higher education. *Learning*. https://doi.org/DOI: 10.1016/j.lcsi.2020.100437

Hié, A., & Thouary, C. (2023). How AI is reshaping higher education. October 17, 2023. https://www.aacsb.edu/insights/articles/2023/10/how-ai-is-reshaping-higher-education

Higdon, N., & Maret, S. (2023). The Case Against NewsGuard. https://www.projectcensored.org/wp-content/uploads/2022/07/The_Case_Against_Newsguard.pdf

Hinojo-Lucena, F. J., Aznar-Díaz, I., Cáceres-Reche, M. P., & Romero-Rodríguez, J. M. (2019). Artificial intelligence in higher education: A bibliometric study on its impact in the scientific literature. *Education Sciences*, *9*(1), 51. DOI: 10.3390/educsci9010051

Hoffman, M. (2023, January 12). *WebMD. What Are the Types of Autism Spectrum Disorders?*https://www.webmd.com/brain/autism/autism-spectrum-disorders#1

Holdo, M. (2023). Critical reflection: John Dewey's relational view of transformative learning. *Journal of Transformative Education*, *21*(1), 9–25. Advance online publication. DOI: 10.1177/15413446221086727

Holmes, W., Bialik, M., & Fadel, C. (2019). Artificial Intelligence in Education: Promises and Implications for Teaching and Learning. Center for Curriculum Redesign. Scopus Index.

Holmes, W. (2020). Artificial intelligence in education: Promises and implications for teaching and learning. *Learning, Media and Technology*, *45*(2), 189–206. DOI: 10.1080/17439884.2020.1695763

Holmes, W., Bialik, M., & Fadel, C. (2019). *Artificial intelligence in education: Promises and implications for teaching and learning*. Center for Curriculum Redesign., Retrieved from https://curriculumredesign.org/wp-content/uploads/AI-in-education.pdf

Holmes, W., Borenstein, J., & Howard, A. (2021). Unpacking the role of AI ethics online education for science and engineering students. *International Journal of STEM Education*, *8*(1), 23–45. DOI: 10.1186/s40594-021-00235-x

Holmes, W., Persson, J., Chounta, I.-A., Wasson, B., & Dimitrova, V. (2022). *Artificial intelligence and Education. A critical view through the lens of human rights, democracy, and the rule of law*. Council of Europe.

Holmes, W., & Porayska-Pomsta, K. (2019). Ethics in AIED: Who cares? *International Journal of Artificial Intelligence in Education*, *29*(2), 1–21.

Holmes, W., & Tuomi, I. (2022). State of the art and practice in AI in education. *European Journal of Education*, *57*(4), 542–570. DOI: 10.1111/ejed.12533

Holstein, K., Hong, G., Tegene, M., McLaren, B. M., & Aleven, V. (2018). The classroom as a dashboard: Co-designing wearable cognitive augmentation for K-12 teachers. In Proceedings of the 8th international conference on learning analytics and knowledge -LAK '18 (pp. 79–88). Association for Computing Machinery. DOI: 10.1145/3170358.3170377

Hooda, M., Rana, C., Dahiya, O., Rizwan, A., & Hossain, M. S. (2022). Artificial intelligence for assessment and feedback to enhance student success in higher education. *Mathematical Problems in Engineering*, *2022*(1), 5215722. DOI: 10.1155/2022/5215722

Horáková, T., Houška, M., & Dömeová, L. (2017). Classification of the Educational Texts Styles with the Methods of Artificial Intelligence. *Journal of Baltic Science Education*, *16*(3), 324–336. DOI: 10.33225/jbse/17.16.324

Horowitz, M. C., & Kahn, L. (2021). What influences attitudes about artificial intelligence adoption: Evidence from US local officials. *PLoS One*, *16*(10), e0257732. DOI: 10.1371/journal.pone.0257732 PMID: 34669734

Hou, J., & Wan, J. (2024). Theme Mining and Evolutionary Analysis of Artificial Intelligence Integration in Higher Education Research. *Lecture Notes in Business Information Processing*, *516*, 108–119. DOI: 10.1007/978-3-031-60260-3_10

Hsiang, S., & Hsu, Y. (2024). *Innovative teaching: How pre-service teachers use artificial intelligence to teach science to fourth graders. Computers in Education Research Journal, 15*(2), 123-134. Retrieved from https://www.cedtech.net/download/innovative-teaching-how-pre-service-teachers-use-artificial-intelligence-to-teach-science-to-fourth-15686.pdf

Hsu, T.-C., Abelson, H., & Van Brummelen, J. (2022). The effects on secondary school students of applying experiential learning to the conversational AI learning curriculum. *International Review of Research in Open and Distance Learning*, *23*(1), 82–103. DOI: 10.19173/irrodl.v22i4.5474

Huang, T.-C., Jeng, Y.-L., Hsiao, K.-L., & Tsai, B.-R. (2016). SNS collaborative learning design: Enhancing critical thinking for human–computer interface design. *Universal Access in the Information Society*, *16*(2), 303–312. DOI: 10.1007/s10209-016-0458-z

Huber, S. E., Kiili, K., Nebel, S., Ryan, R. M., Sailer, M., & Ninaus, M. (2024). Leveraging the potential of large language models in education through playful and game-based learning. *Educational Psychology Review*, *36*(1), 25. DOI: 10.1007/s10648-024-09868-z

Humble, N., & Mozelius, P. (2019, October). Artificial intelligence in education—A promise, a threat or a hype. In *Proceedings of the european conference on the impact of artificial intelligence and robotics* (pp. 149-156).

Hursen, C. (2021, September). The effect of problem-based learning method supported by web 2.0 tools on academic achievement and critical thinking skills in teacher education. *Technology*, *26*(3), 515–533. Advance online publication. DOI: 10.1007/s10758-020-09458-2

Hussain, A. (2017). Ada—Bolton College's latest digital assistant. Blogtext. http://www.aftab hussa in.com/ada.html

Hussain, M., Zhu, W., Zhang, W., & Abidi, S. M. R. (2020). Student Engagement Predictions in an e-Learning System and Their Impact on Student Course Assessment Scores. *Computational Intelligence and Neuroscience*, *2020*, 1–8. DOI: 10.1155/2020/6342365 PMID: 30369946

Huston, T. (2022). Social Media for Teaching Empathy, Civil and Moral Development, and Critical Thinking. In *Exploring Ethical Problems in Today's Technological World* (pp. 120–140). IGI Global., DOI: 10.4018/978-1-6684-5892-1.ch007

Hwang, G. J. (2014). Definition, framework, and research issues of smart learning environments-a context-aware ubiquitous learning perspective. *Smart Learning Environments*, *1*(1), 4. DOI: 10.1186/s40561-014-0004-5

Hwang, G. J., & Tu, Y. F. (2021). Roles and research trends of artificial intelligence in mathematics education: A bibliometric mapping analysis and systematic review. *Mathematics*, *9*(6), 584. Advance online publication. DOI: 10.3390/math9060584

Hwang, G. J., Xie, H., Wah, B. W., & Gašević, D. (2020). Vision, challenges, roles and research issues of Artificial Intelligence in Education. *Computers and Education: Artificial Intelligence*, *1*, 100001. DOI: 10.1016/j.caeai.2020.100001

Hwang, G.-J., & Chang, C.-Y. (2021). A review of opportunities and challenges of chatbots in education. *Interactive Learning Environments*, •••, 1–14. DOI: 10.1080/10494820.2021.1952615

Hyde, S. J., Busby, A., & Bonner, R. L. (2024). Tools or fools: Are we educating managers or creating tool-dependent robots? *Journal of Management Education*, *48*(4), 708–734. DOI: 10.1177/10525629241230357

IBM. (2021, March 5). *Dependency analysis*. https://www.ibm.com/docs/en/wsr-and-r/8.5.6?topic=analysis-dependency

IBM. (n.d.). *What is text mining?* https://www.ibm.com/topics/text-mining

Ibrahim, O., Sundgren, D., & Larsson, A. (2014). An integrated decision support system framework for strategic planning in higher education institutions. *Lecture Notes in Business Information Processing, 180*, 237–245. DOI: 10.1007/978-3-319-07179-4_27

Ienca, M. (2023). On artificial intelligence and manipulation. *Topoi, 42*(3), 833–842. Advance online publication. DOI: 10.1007/s11245-023-09940-3

Ifukube, T. (2017). *Sound-Based Assistive Technology: Support to Hearing, Speaking and Seeing*. Springer International Publishing AG. DOI: 10.1007/978-3-319-47997-2

Ignatow, G., & Mihalcea, R. F. (Eds.). (2018). *An Introduction to Text Mining: Research Design, Data Collection, and Analysis*. SAGE Publications, Inc. DOI: 10.4135/9781506336985

Ijaz, K., Bogdanovych, A., & Trescak, T. (2017). Virtual worlds vs books and videos in history education. *Interactive Learning Environments, 25*(7), 904–929. DOI: 10.1080/10494820.2016.1225099

Ikuta, S. (2018). Multimedia-Enabled Dot Codes as Communication Technologies. In M. Khosrow-Pour (Ed.), Encyclopedia of Information Science and Technology (4th ed., pp. 6464–6475). IGI Global Scientific Publishing. DOI: 10.4018/978-1-5225-2255-3.ch561

Ikuta, S. (Ed.). (2020). Handbook of Research on Software for Gifted and Talented School Activities in K-12 Classrooms. IGI Global. DOI: 10.4018/978-1-7998-1400-9

Ikuta, S. (2022). School activities using self-made teaching materials with voices and sounds: Extraction of outcomes and challenges through text mining. *Int. J. Hum. Cult. Stud., 32*, 399–411.

Ikuta, S. (Ed.). (2019a). *Handmade Teaching Materials for Students With Disabilities*. IGI Global. DOI: 10.4018/978-1-5225-6240-5

Ikuta, S., Endo, E., Nemoto, F., Kaiami, S., & Ezoe, T. (2013). School Activities Using Handmade Teaching Materials With Dot-Codes. In Barres, D. G., Carrion, Z. C., & Delgado, R. L.-C. (Eds.), *Technologies for Inclusive Education: Beyond Traditional Integration Approaches* (pp. 220–243). IGI Global Scientific Publishing. DOI: 10.4018/978-1-4666-2530-3.ch011

Ikuta, S., & Hisatsune, Y. (2019b). Handcrafted customized content and school activities with newly developed technologies. In Gronseth, S. L., & Dalton, E. M. (Eds.), *Universal access through inclusive instructional design: International perspectives on UDL* (pp. 164–172). Routledge. DOI: 10.4324/9780429435515-20

Ikuta, S., Ishitobi, R., Nemoto, F., Urushihata, C., Yamaguchi, K., & Nakui, H. (2017). Handmade content and school activities for autistic children with expressive language disabilities. In Kats, Y. (Ed.), *Supporting the Education of Children With Autism Spectrum Disorders* (pp. 85–115). IGI Global Scientific Publishing. DOI: 10.4018/978-1-5225-0816-8.ch006

Ikuta, S., Morton, D., Kasai, M., Nemoto, F., Ohtaka, M., & Horiuchi, M. (2015). School Activities With New Dot Code Handling Multimedia. In Lennex, L., & Nettleton, K. (Eds.), *Cases on Instructional Technology in Gifted and Talented Education* (pp. 314–340). IGI Global Scientific Publishing. DOI: 10.4018/978-1-4666-6489-0.ch015

Ikuta, S., Takagaki, Y., Sone, R., Okazaki, K., & Abe, S. (2021b). Collaborative Learning Community Facilitating Inclusive Learning Settings: Providing Reasonable Accommodations for Students with Disabilities. In AuCoin, D. (Ed.), *Building Integrated Collaborative Relationships for Inclusive Learning Settings* (pp. 181–214). IGI Global Scientific Publishing. DOI: 10.4018/978-1-7998-6816-3.ch008

Ikuta, S., Watanuki, M., & Abe, S. (2021a). Multimedia-Enabled Dot Codes as Communication Aids. In Khosrow-Pour, M. (Ed.), *Handbook of Research on Modern Educational Technologies, Applications, and Management* (pp. 331–345). IGI Global Scientific Publishing. DOI: 10.4018/978-1-7998-3476-2.ch020

Individuals with Disabilities Education Act, 20 U.S.C. § 1400 (2004).

Indrašienė, V., Jegelevičienė, V., Merfeldaitė, O., Penkauskienė, D., Pivorienė, J., Railienė, A., Sadauskas, J., & Valavičienė, N. (2021). Linking critical thinking and knowledge management: A conceptual analysis. *Sustainability (Basel)*, *13*(3), 1476. DOI: 10.3390/su13031476

Isogai, K. (2017). Recent Developments in Japan's Special Needs Education – Promoting an Inclusive Education System –. *NISE Bulletin*, *16*, 28–32.

Ivanov, S. (2023). The dark side of artificial intelligence in higher education. *Service Industries Journal*, *43*(15-16), 1055–1082. DOI: 10.1080/02642069.2023.2258799

Ivanov, S., Soliman, M., Tuomi, A., Alkathiri, N. A., & Al-Alawi, A. N. (2024). Drivers of generative AI adoption in higher education through the lens of the Theory of Planned Behaviour. *Technology in Society*, *77*, C7–C102521. DOI: 10.1016/j.techsoc.2024.102521

Jain, S., & Jain, R. (2019). Role Of Artificial Intelligence In Higher Education-An Empirical Investigation. IJRAR-International Journal of Research and Analytical Reviews, 6. https://new-artificial-intelligence.com/wp-content/uploads/2024/03/10.-Role-of-Artificial-Intelligence-in-Higher-Education-an-Empirical-Investigation-Article-Author-Suvrat-JainDr-Roshita-Jain.pdf

Järvelä, S., Nguyen, A., & Hadwin, A. (2023). Human and artificial intelligence collaboration for socially shared regulation in learning. *British Journal of Educational Technology*, *54*(5), 1057–1076. DOI: 10.1111/bjet.13325

Jedličková, A. (2024). Ethical approaches in designing autonomous and intelligent systems: A comprehensive survey towards responsible development. *AI & Society*. Advance online publication. DOI: 10.1007/s00146-024-02040-9

Jejeniwa, T. O., Mhlongo, N. Z., & Jejeniwa, T. O.Temitayo Oluwaseun JejeniwaNoluthando Zamanjomane MhlongoTitilola Olaide Jejeniwa. (2024). A comprehensive review of the impact of artificial intelligence on modern accounting practices and financial reporting. *Computer Science & IT Research Journal*, *5*(4), 1031–1047. DOI: 10.51594/csitrj.v5i4.1086

Jeon, I. S., Kang, S. J., & Kang, S. J. (2024). A Staged Framework for Computer Vision Education: Integrating AI, Data Science, and Computational Thinking. *Applied Sciences (Basel, Switzerland)*, *14*(21), 9792. Advance online publication. DOI: 10.3390/app14219792

Jha, C. K., & Sachan, A. (2023). Blockchain and artificial intelligence technology in professional services. In *Fostering Sustainable Development in the Age of Technologies* (pp. 43–50). Emerald Publishing., DOI: 10.1108/978-1-83753-060-120231005

Jia, J., & Zhang, S. (2011). Notice of Retraction: Study on the management model of foreign language teaching reform of higher education. 2011 2nd International Conference on Artificial Intelligence, Management Science and Electronic Commerce, AIMSEC 2011 -Proceedings C7 - 6009850, 5800-5803. DOI: 10.1109/AIMSEC.2011.6009850

Jiang, Y. (2023). Optimization of Automatic Scheduling Algorithms for Biotechnology Course Allocation in Higher Education Institutes. *Journal of Commercial Biotechnology*, *28*(5), 153–167. DOI: 10.5912/jcb1193

Johnson, G. M., & Cooke, A. (2016). Self-regulation of learning and preference for written versus audio-recorded feedback by distance education students. (2016). *Distance Education*, *37*(1), 107–120. Advance online publication. DOI: 10.1080/01587919.2015.1081737

Joksimovic, S., Ifenthaler, D., Marrone, R., De Laat, M., & Siemens, G. (2023). Opportunities of artificial intelligence for supporting complex problem-solving: Findings from a scoping review. *Computers and Education: Artificial Intelligence, 4*, 100138. DOI: 10.1016/j.caeai.2023.100138

Jonassen, D. H., Carr, C., & Hsiu-Ping, Y. (1998). Computers as mindtools for engaging learners in critical thinking. *TechTrends, 43*(2), 24–32. DOI: 10.1007/BF02818172

Jones, N. (2024). 'In awe': Scientists impressed by latest ChatGPT model o1. *Nature, 634*, 275–276. c10.1038/d41586-024-03169-9

Jose, J. (2024). The impact of integrating Microsoft Teams–Reading Progress as an Artificial Intelligence (AI) platform for promoting learners' reading aloud skills. *Education and Information Technologies*. Advance online publication. DOI: 10.1007/s10639-024-13074-3

Joseph, S., Tahir, A., Bibi, F., Hamid, K., Iqbal, M. W., Ruk, S. A., & Ahmad, S. Z. (2024). A review analysis on using "AIED" to improve student engagement in hybrid education. *Bulletin of Business and Economics (BBE, 13*(2), 424–435.

Joshi, H. (2025). AI and Chronic Diseases From Data Integration to Clinical Implementation. In *Generative AI Techniques for Sustainability in Healthcare Security* (pp. 17–40). IGI Global Scientific Publishing., DOI: 10.4018/979-8-3693-6577-9.ch002

Junge, A. L. (2019). Digital transformation technologies as an enabler for sustainable logistics and supply chain processes – an exploratory framework. *Brazilian Journal of Operations & Production Management, 16*(3), 462–472. DOI: 10.14488/BJOPM.2019.v16.n3.a9

Kaczkó, É., & Ostendorf, A. (2023). Critical thinking in the community of inquiry framework: An analysis of the theoretical model and cognitive presence coding schemes. *Computers & Education, 193*, 104662. Advance online publication. DOI: 10.1016/j.compedu.2022.104662

Kaddouri, M., & Tayalati, F. (2021, June). Compétences numériques et Créativité. OBTAIN 1st International Virtual Workshop on Digitalized Skills and Today's Job Market Needs. https://hal.science/hal-04270058

Kaddouri, M., Benali, M., Azzimani, T., & Mimoun Elkhir, A. (2024). Emotional, Relational and Digitalisation: Towards a Redesign of the Educational Paradigm. International Journal of Research and Innovation in Social Science, VIII(IIIS), 4184–4197. DOI: 10.47772/IJRISS.2024.803302S

Kaddouri, M., Mhamdi, K., Chniete, I., Marhraoui, M., Khaldi, M., & Jmad, S. (2024). Adopting AI in Education: Technical Challenges and Ethical Constraints. In Sanmugam, M., Edwards, B. I., Mohd Barkhaya, N. M., & Khlaif, Z. (Eds.), (pp. 25–72). Advances in Educational Technologies and Instructional Design. IGI Global., DOI: 10.4018/979-8-3693-7255-5.ch002

Kaddouri, M., Mhamdi, K., Jabri, A., Boukare, M., & Jmad, S. (2025). Generative Artificial Intelligence and Assessment of Learning: Challenges and Perspectives. In Gregory, S. (Ed.), (pp. 277–326). Advances in Educational Technologies and Instructional Design. IGI Global., DOI: 10.4018/979-8-3693-6527-4.ch010

Kamalov, F., Santandreu Calonge, D., & Gurrib, I. (2023). New era of artificial intelligence in education: Towards a sustainable multifaceted revolution. *Sustainability (Basel)*, *15*(16), 12451. Advance online publication. DOI: 10.3390/su151612451

Kandlhofer, M., Steinbauer, G., Hirschmugl-Gaisch, S., & Huber, P. (2016). Artificial intelligence and computer science in education: From kindergarten to university. 2016 IEEE Frontiers in Education Conference (FIE), 1–9. DOI: 10.1109/FIE.2016.7757570

Kaplan, A., & Haenlein, M. (2019). Siri, siri, in my hand: Who's the fairest in the land? On the interpretations, illustrations, and implications of artificial intelligence. *Business Horizons*, *62*(1), 15–25. DOI: 10.1016/j.bushor.2018.08.004

Kärki, K. (2024). Digital distraction, attention regulation, and inequality. *Philosophy & Technology*, *37*(1), 8. DOI: 10.1007/s13347-024-00698-z

Karpouzis, K., Zhang, Y., Li, H., & Chen, J. (2024). *Generative AI for lesson planning: Customizing education for diverse classrooms*. Retrieved from https://arxiv.org/abs/2403.12071

Kase, S. E., Hung, C. P., Krayzman, T., Hare, J. Z., Rinderspacher, B. C., & Su, S. M. (2022). The future of collaborative human-artificial intelligence decision-making for mission planning. *Frontiers in Psychology*, *13*, 850628. DOI: 10.3389/fpsyg.2022.850628 PMID: 35444590

Kasthuri, E., & Balaji, S. (2023). Natural language processing and deep learning chatbot using long short term memory algorithm. *Materials Today: Proceedings*, *81*, 690–693. Advance online publication. DOI: 10.1016/j.matpr.2021.04.154

Kaur, K., & Dahiya, O. (2023). Role of Educational Data Mining and Learning Analytics Techniques Used for Predictive Modeling. Proceedings of 2023 3rd International Conference on Innovative Practices in Technology and Management, ICIPTM 2023, Kavitha, K., & Joshith, V. P. (2024). Factors Shaping the Adoption of AI Tools among Gen Z: An Extended UTAUT2 Model Investigation Using CB-SEM. Bulletin of Science, Technology andSociety. DOI: 10.1109/ICIPTM57143.2023.10117779

Kaur, M. K. (2018). Critical Thinking for Global Peace: A key for Sustainable Development. International Journal of Trend in Scientific Research and Development, Volume-2(Issue-3). https://www.ijtsrd.com/humanities-and-the-arts/education/11439/critical-thinking-for-global-peace-a-key-for-sustainable-development/ms-kuldeep-kaur

Kavitha, R. K., Krupa, C. R., & Kaarthiekheyan, V. (2025). AI-Powered Digital Solutions for Smart Learning: Revolutionizing Education. In *Cybersecurity and Data Science Innovations for Sustainable Development of HEICC (pp. 213-227).* CRC Press. https://doi.org/DOI: 10.1201/9781032711300

Kawano, K. (2016, November 1). *SAVVY Tokyo: Special Needs Education in Japan.* https://savvytokyo.com/special-needs-education-japan/

Kaya, F., Aydin, F., Schepman, A., Rodway, P., Yetişensoy, O., & Demir Kaya, M. (2024). The roles of personality traits, AI anxiety, and demographic factors in attitudes toward artificial intelligence. *International Journal of Human-Computer Interaction*, *40*(2), 497–514. DOI: 10.1080/10447318.2022.2151730

Kay, J. (2012). AI and education: Grand challenges. *IEEE Intelligent Systems*, *27*(5), 66–69. DOI: 10.1109/MIS.2012.92

Kessler, G. (2018). Technology and the future of language teaching. *Foreign Language Annals*, *51*(1), 205–218. DOI: 10.1111/flan.12318

Khan, S. (2024, September 4). Khan Academy founder Sal Kahn on the future of learning [WorkLab: The Podcast]. YouTube. https://www.youtube.com/playlist?list=PLFPUGjQjckXFuFOmH4VE0nOf2gtXJjv6U

Khan, F. H., Pasha, M. A., & Masud, S. (2021). Advancements in microprocessor architecture for ubiquitous AI—An overview on history, evolution, and upcoming challenges in AI implementation. *Micromachines*, *12*(6), 665. Advance online publication. DOI: 10.3390/mi12060665 PMID: 34204065

Khreisat, M. N., Khilani, D., Rusho, M. A., Karkkulainen, E. A., Tabuena, A. C., & Uberas, A. D. (2024). Ethical Implications Of AI Integration In Educational Decision Making: Systematic Review. *Educational Administration: Theory and Practice*, *30*(5), 8521–8527.

Kim, J., Lee, H., & Cho, Y. H. (2022). Learning design to support student-AI collaboration: Perspectives of leading teachers for AI in education. *Education and Information Technologies*, *27*(5), 6069–6104. Advance online publication. DOI: 10.1007/s10639-021-10831-6

Kim, J., & Lee, S. (2024). Pre-service teachers' dual perspectives on generative AI: Benefits, challenges, and integrating into teaching and learning. *Journal of Educational Technology and Pedagogy*, *29*(1), 78–92. https://www.researchgate.net/publication/381851959_Pre-service_teachers%27_dual_perspectives_on_generative_AI_Benefits_challenges_and_integrating_into_teaching_and_learning

Kim, J., Merrill, K., Xu, K., & Sellnow, D. D. (2020). My teacher is a machine: Understanding students' perceptions of AI teaching assistants in online education. *International Journal of Human-Computer Interaction*, *36*(20), 1902–1911. DOI: 10.1080/10447318.2020.1801227

Knox, B. J., Sütterlin, S., & Lugo, R. (2023). Cognitive agility for improved understanding and self-governance: a human-centric AI enabler. Edward Elgar Publishing EBooks, 152–172. DOI: 10.4337/9781839106750.00019

Knox, J. (2020). Artificial intelligence and education in China. *Learning, Media and Technology*, *45*(3), 298–311. DOI: 10.1080/17439884.2020.1754236

Kocoń, J., Cichecki, I., Kaszyca, O., Kochanek, M., Szydło, D., Baran, J., Bielaniewicz, J., Gruza, M., Janz, A., Kanclerz, K., Kocoń, A., Koptyra, B., Mieleszczenko-Kowszewicz, W., Miłkowski, P., Oleksy, M., Piasecki, M., Radliński, Ł., Wojtasik, K., Woźniak, S., & Kazienko, P. (2023). ChatGPT: Jack of all trades, master of none. *Information Fusion*, *99*, 101861. DOI: 10.1016/j.inffus.2023.101861

Koedinger, K. R., & Corbett, A. (2006). *Cognitive tutors: Technology bringing learning sciences to the classroom.* na.

Kolb, D. A. (1984). *Experiential learning: Experience as the source of learning and development.* Prentice Hall.

Komolafe, B. F., & Qian, X. (2020). Critical thinking an antidote to artificial intelligence threat: An innovation in teacher education practices. *Proceeding of the 6th International Conference on Education*, 6(2), 51-56. https://doi.org/DOI: 10.17501/24246700.2020.6205

Kondratenko, Y. P., & Shevcenkc, A. I. (2024). *Research tendencies and prospect domains for AI development and implementation*. River Publishers. DOI: 10.1201/9788770046947

Kong, S. C., Cheung, M. Y. W., & Tsang, O. (2024). Developing an artificial intelligence literacy framework: Evaluation of a literacy course for senior secondary students using a project-based learning approach. *Computers and Education: Artificial Intelligence*, *6*, 100214. DOI: 10.1016/j.caeai.2024.100214

Kopalle, P. K., Gangwar, M., Kaplan, A., Ramachandran, D., Reinartz, W., & Rindfleisch, A. (2022). Examining artificial intelligence (AI) technologies in marketing via a global lens: Current trends and future research opportunities. *International Journal of Research in Marketing*, *39*(2), 522–540. DOI: 10.1016/j.ijresmar.2021.11.002

Krakower, B., & Plante, S. L. (2016). *Using Technology to Engage Students with Learning Disabilities*. Corwin. DOI: 10.4135/9781071800553

Kraus, S., Jones, P., Kailer, N., Weinmann, A., Chaparro-Banegas, N., & Roig-Tierno, N. (2021). Digital transformation: An overview of the current state of the art of research. *SAGE Open*, *11*(3), 21582440211047576. DOI: 10.1177/21582440211047576

Kulkov, I., Kulkova, J., Rohrbeck, R., Menvielle, L., Kaartemo, V., & Makkonen, H. (2024). Artificial intelligence-driven sustainable development: Examining organizational, technical, and processing approaches to achieving global goals. *Sustainable Development, 32(3), 2253-2267*. DOI: DOI: 10.1002/sd.2773

Kumar, A., Diwan, V., & Joshi, R. (2021). Applications of Artificial Intelligence in Education. *Journal of Computer Science and Technology*, *21*(1), 36–45. DOI: 10.1166/jcst.2021.1234

Kumar, J. A. (2021). Educational chatbots for project-based learning: Investigating learning outcomes for a team-based design course. *International Journal of Educational Technology in Higher Education*, *18*(1), 65. Advance online publication. DOI: 10.1186/s41239-021-00302-w PMID: 34926790

Kumar, P., & Lohan, A. (2024). Evaluating ChatGPT adoption through the lens of the technology acceptance model: Perspectives from higher education. International Journal of Technological Learning. *Innovation and Development*, *15*(4), 370–383. DOI: 10.1504/IJTLID.2024.140316

Kumar, P., Sharma, R., & Kaur, G. (2022). Student perceptions of AI in higher education: Opportunities and challenges. *Journal of Educational Technology Systems*, *50*(3), 345–362. DOI: 10.1177/00472395211052198

Kumar, R., Banerjee, M., & Gupta, A. (2021). The Role of Artificial Intelligence in Education: Current Developments and Future Trends. *Journal of Educational Technology & Society*, *24*(3), 103–114. https://www.j-ets.net/ETS/journals/24_3/8.pdf

Kumar, S., Rao, P., Singhania, S., Verma, S., & Kheterpal, M. (2024). Will artificial intelligence drive the advancements in higher education? A tri-phased exploration. *Technological Forecasting and Social Change*, *201*, C7–C123258. DOI: 10.1016/j.techfore.2024.123258

Kunjumuhammed, S. K. (2024). Artificial Intelligence in Addressing Educational Inequality Dimensions in Higher Education Institutions (HEIs): A Critical Review. Risks and Challenges of AI-Driven *Finance: Bias, Ethics, and Security, 146-164*. DOI: DOI: 10.4018/979-8-3693-2185-0.ch007

Kuperberg, G. R. (2021, January). (2021). Tea with milk? A hierarchical generative framework of sequential event comprehension. *Topics in Cognitive Science*, *13*(1), 256–298. Advance online publication. DOI: 10.1111/tops.12518 PMID: 33025701

Kwartler, T. (2017). *Text Mining in Practice with R*. John Wiley & Sons. DOI: 10.1002/9781119282105

Labadze, L., Grigolia, M., & Machaidze, L. (2023). Role of AI chatbots in education: Systematic literature review. *International Journal of Educational Technology in Higher Education*, *20*(1), 56. DOI: 10.1186/s41239-023-00426-1

Lamatsch, H. (2023). Transformation numérique de l'administration: La recherche d'efficacité et d'agilité. *Revue Défense Nationale*, *HS13*(HS13), 77–90. DOI: 10.3917/rdna.hs13.0077

Lan, A. S., Waters, A. E., Studer, C., & Baraniuk, R. G. (2014). Sparse factor analysis for learning and content analytics. *Journal of Machine Learning Research*, *15*(1), 1959–2008.

Lancioni, G. E., & Singh, N. N. (Eds.). (2014). *Assistive Technologies for People with Diverse Abilities*. Springer International Publishing AG. DOI: 10.1007/978-1-4899-8029-8

LaPierre, J. (2021, January 18). *Educational games and AI*. Blogtext. Filament Games. https://www.filam entga mes.com/ blog/educa tiona l-games-and-ai/

Larson, B. Z., Moser, C., Caza, A., Muehlfeld, K., & Colombo, L. A. (2024). Critical thinking in the Age of Generative AI. *Academy of Management Learning & Education*, *23*(3), 373–378. DOI: 10.5465/amle.2024.0338

Larsson, S. (2017). *Conceptions in the Code*. Oxford University Press., https://lup.lub.lu.se/search/publication/b7435f9d-f4b9-4fb3-8b5f-34d41c58d198 DOI: 10.1093/acprof:oso/9780190650384.001.0001

Larsson, S., & Heintz, F. (2020). Transparency in artificial intelligence. *Internet Policy Review*, *9*(2). Advance online publication. DOI: 10.14763/2020.2.1469

Lawler, R. W., & Rushby, N. (2013). An interview with R obert L awler. *British Journal of Educational Technology*, *44*(1), 20–30. DOI: 10.1111/j.1467-8535.2012.01372.x

Leahy, E. (2024). AI-Powered Bitcoin Trading: Developing an Investment Strategy with Artificial Intelligence.

Lee, C. C., & Low, M. Y. H. (2024). Using GenAI in education: The case for critical thinking. *Frontiers in Artificial Intelligence*, *7*, 1–3. DOI: 10.3389/frai.2024.1452131 PMID: 39554991

Lee, H.-P., Sarkar, A., Tankelevitch, L., Drosos, I., Rintel, S., & Banks, R.. (2025). The impact of Generative AI on critical thinking: Self-Reported reductions in cognitive effort and confidence effects from a survey of knowledge workers. *CHI '25: Proceedings of the 2025 CHI Conference on Human Factors in Computing Systems*, 1121, 1–22. https://doi.org/DOI: 10.1145/3706598.3713778

Lee, Y.-F., Hwang, G.-J., & Chen, P.-Y. (2022). Impacts of an AI-based chatbot on college students' after-class review, academic performance, self-efficacy, learning attitude, and motivation. *Educational Technology Research and Development*, *70*(5), 1843–1865. DOI: 10.1007/s11423-022-10142-8

Le, H. V., & Nguyen, L. Q. (2024). Promoting L2 learners' critical thinking skills: The role of social constructivism in reading class. *Frontiers in Education*, *9*, 1241973. Advance online publication. DOI: 10.3389/feduc.2024.1241973

Lennon, N. K. (2014). How professors infuse critical thinking into college courses (Doctoral dissertation, Seton Hall University). https://www.proquest.com/openview/6c8fe9f36a915f710b59a34c4b6b45a2/1?pq-origsite=gscholar&cbl=18750

Leskovec, J., Rajaraman, A., & Ullman, J. D. (2020). *Mining of Massive Datasets* (3rd ed.). Cambridge University Press. DOI: 10.1017/9781108684163

Lestari, S. W., Agung, L., & Musadad, A. A. (2019). Android based adventure games to enhance vocational high school students' critical thinking skills. Dans K. Saddhono, D. T. Ardianto, M. F. Hidayatullah, & V. R. Cahyani (Éds.), Proceedings of the 1st Seminar and Workshop on Research Design, for Education, Social Science, Arts, and Humanities (Vol. 115, pp. 115-120). SEWORD FRESSH. DOI: 10.4108/eai.27-4-2019.2286917

Lewin, K. (1946). Action research and minority problems. *The Journal of Social Issues*, *2*(4), 34–46. DOI: 10.1111/j.1540-4560.1946.tb02295.x

Li, H., Xu, T., Zhang, C., Chen, E., Liang, J., Fan, X., . . . Wen, Q. (2024). Bringing generative AI to adaptive learning in education. arXiv preprint arXiv:2402.14601.

Liang, W., & Fung, D. (2021). Fostering critical thinking in English-as-a-second-language classrooms: Challenges and opportunities. *Thinking Skills and Creativity*, *39*, 100769. Advance online publication. DOI: 10.1016/j.tsc.2020.100769

Liang, W., & Wu, Y. (2024). Exploring the use of ChatGPT to foster EFL learners' critical thinking skills from a post-humanist perspective. *Thinking Skills and Creativity*, *54*, 101645. DOI: 10.1016/j.tsc.2024.101645

Lieu, J. (2018). *Eyes to the front camera: Chinese facial recognition tech targets inattentive students*. Blogtext. Mashable. https://masha ble.com/artic le/chine se-facial-recognition-class

Li, L. (2022). Reskilling and upskilling the future-ready workforce for industry 4.0 and beyond. *Information Systems Frontiers*. Advance online publication. DOI: 10.1007/s10796-022-10308-y PMID: 35855776

Li, L., Fengchao, Y., & Zhang, E. (2024). A systematic review of learning task design for K-12 AI education: Trends, challenges, and opportunities. *Computers and Education: Artificial Intelligence*, *100217*, 100217. Advance online publication. DOI: 10.1016/j.caeai.2024.100217

Li, M. (2011). On constructing the practical teaching system of taxation major in newly-built academies. 2011 2nd International Conference on Artificial Intelligence, Management Science and Electronic Commerce, AIMSEC 2011 - Proceedings C7 - 6011012, Li, Z. (2011). China's Higher Education Quality Management based on Six-Sigma Management principles. 2011 2nd International Conference on Artificial Intelligence, Management Science and Electronic Commerce, AIMSEC 2011 - Proceedings C7 - 6010499, Liwång, H. (2022). Defense development: The role of co-creation in filling the gap between policy-makers and technology development. *Technology in Society*, *68*, C7–C101913. DOI: 10.1016/j.techsoc.2022.101913

Lin, C. C., Huang, A. Y. Q., & Lu, O. H. T. (2023). *Artificial intelligence in intelligent tutoring systems toward sustainable education: a systematic review*. Smart Learning Environments., DOI: 10.1186/s40561-023-00260-y

Lindebaum, D., & Fleming, P. (2024). ChatGPT undermines human reflexivity, scientific responsibility and responsible management research. *British Journal of Management*, *35*(2), 566–575. DOI: 10.1111/1467-8551.12781

Lipman, M. (2003). *Thinking in education* (Vol. 304). Cambridge University Press. DOI: 10.1017/CBO9780511840272

Little, D. (1991). *Learner autonomy 1: Definitions, issues, and problems*. Authentik.

Liu, C.-C., & Gu, X.-Q. (2024). Developing frames for change: How generative AI impacts the broad practices of teacher educators. In M. Searson, E. Langran, & J. Trumble (Eds.), *Exploring new horizons: Generative artificial intelligence and educator education* (pp. 225-237). Association for the Advancement of Computing in Education (AACE). https://www.learntechlib.org/p/223928/

Loeckx, J. (2016). Blurring boundaries in education: Context and impact of MOOCs. *International Review of Research in Open and Distance Learning, 17*(3), 92–121. DOI: 10.19173/irrodl.v17i3.2395

Long, D., & Magerko, B. (2020). What is AI literacy: Competencies and design considerations. In *CHI '20: Proceedings of the 2020 CHI Conference on Human Factors in Computing Systems* (pp. 1-16). Association for Computing Machinery. DOI: 10.1145/3313831.3376727

Lorenzetti, L., Jacobsen, M., Lorenzetti, D. L., Nowell, L., Pethrick, H., Clancy, T., ... & Oddone Paolucci, E. (2022). Fostering learning and reciprocity in interdisciplinary research. *Small Group Research, 53(5), 755-777.*https://doi.org/ Luo, Y. F., Yang, S. C., & Kang, S. (2022). New media literacy and news trustworthiness: An application of importance–performance analysis. *Computers & Education.*https://doi.org/DOI: 10.1177/10464964221089836

Luan, J., & Zhang, Z. (2011). Notice of Retraction: On the innovation of science and technology management in Chinese universities and colleges. 2011 2nd International Conference on Artificial Intelligence, Management Science and Electronic Commerce, AIMSEC 2011 -Proceedings C7 - 6010728, 1278-1281. DOI: 10.1109/AIMSEC.2011.6010728

Luckin, R. (2020). "AI in Education Will Help us Understand How We Think." The Financial Times, March 10. https:// www.ft.com/content/4f24adca-5186-11ea-8841-482eed0038b1

Luckin, R., Holmes, W., Griffiths, M., & Forcier, L. B. (2016). *Intelligence unleashed: An argument for AI in education*. Pearson Education. Retrieved from https://www.pearson.com/content/dam/one-dot-com/one-dot-com/global/Files/about-pearson/innovation/open-ideas/Intelligence-Unleashed.pdf

Luckin, R., Holmes, W., Griffiths, M., & Forcier, L. B. (2020). Intelligence Unleashed: An argument for AI in Education. Pearson. Scopus Index.

Luckin, R. (2017). *Towards AI-powered education: Notes from the frontiers of AI and education*. Pearson.

Luckin, R., Cukurova, M., Kent, C., & Du Boulay, B. (2022). Empowering educators to be AI-ready. *Computers and Education: Artificial Intelligence*, *3*, 100076.

Luckin, R., Holmes, W., Griffiths, M., & Forcier, L. B. (2016). *Intelligence Unleashed: An Argument for AI in Education*. Pearson Education.

Luckin, R., Holmes, W., Griffiths, M., & Forcier, L. B. (2016). *Intelligence Unleashed: An argument for AI in education*. Pearson.

Lu, H., Li, Y., Chen, M., Kim, H., & Serikawa, S. (2018). Brain intelligence: Go beyond artificial intelligence. *Mobile Networks and Applications*, *23*, 368–375.

Lu, H., Li, Y., Chen, M., Kim, H., & Serikawa, S. (2020). Brain Intelligence: Go Beyond Artificial Intelligence. *Mobile Networks and Applications*, *25*(4), 1333–1342. DOI: 10.1007/s11036-019-01445-5

Lu, L., Zhang, H., & Wang, W. (2021). Gamification in education: AI-enabled learning systems for improving student engagement. *Computers & Education: Artificial Intelligence*, *2*, 100027. DOI: 10.1016/j.caeai.2021.100027

Luo, P. (2011a). Notice of Retraction: Analysis on the international competitiveness of China's trade in higher education service. 2011 2nd International Conference on Artificial Intelligence, Management Science and Electronic Commerce, AIMSEC 2011 - ProceedingsC7 - 6011368, 2807-2810. DOI: 10.1109/AIMSEC.2011.6011368

Luo, P. (2011b). Opening drives and policy proposals for China higher education service trade.2011 2nd International Conference on Artificial Intelligence, Management Science and Electronic Commerce, AIMSEC 2011 - Proceedings C7 - 6010834, Majumdar, R., Flanagan, B., & Ogata, H. (2021). E-book technology facilitating university education during COVID-19: Japanese experience. Canadian Journal of Learning and Technology, 47(4 Special Issue). DOI: 10.21432/cjlt28038

Luttrell, R., Wallace, A., McCollough, C., & Lee, J. (2020). The digital divide: Addressing artificial intelligence in communication education. *Journalism & Mass Communication Educator*, *75*(4), 470–482. DOI: 10.1177/1077695820925286

Lu, Y. (2019). Artificial Intelligence: A survey on evolution, models, applications and future trends. *Journal of Management Analytics*, *6*(1), 1–29. DOI: 10.1080/23270012.2019.1570365

MacCarthy, M., & Propp, K. (2018). *AI and the Future of Work: Perspectives from Higher Education*. Brookings Institution Press.

Machete, P., & Turpin, M. (2020). The Use of Critical Thinking to Identify Fake News: A Systematic Literature Review. In Hattingh, M., Matthee, M., Smuts, H., Pappas, I., Dwivedi, Y. K., & Mäntymäki, M. (Eds.), Lecture Notes in Computer Science: Vol. 12067. *Responsible Design, Implementation and Use of Information and Communication Technology. I3E 2020.* Springer., DOI: 10.1007/978-3-030-45002-1_20

Madden, M., Calvin, A., Hasse, A., & Lenhart, A. (2024). *The dawn of the AI era: Teens, parents, and the adoption of generative AI at home and school.* Common Sense., https://www.commonsensemedia.org/sites/default/files/research/report/2024-the-dawn-of-the-ai-era_final-release-for-web.pdf

Magic School AI. (n.d.). *Lesson Plan Generator: Creating standards-aligned content for educators.* Retrieved from https://www.magicschool.ai/tools/lesson-plan-generator

Makinde, A. I., Adeleye, S. A., Oronti, A. O., & Jimoh, I. T. (2024). Revolutionizing education. *Artificial Intelligence for Wireless Communication Systems: Technology and Applications*, 103.

Maqbool, M. A., Asif, M., Imran, M., Bibi, S., & Almusharraf, N. (2024). Emerging e-learning trends: A study of faculty perceptions and impact of collaborative techniques using fuzzy interface system. *Social Sciences & Humanities Open, 10*, 101035. DOI: 10.1016/j.ssaho.2024.101035

Marengo, A. (2024). Navigating the nexus of AI and IoT: A comprehensive review of data analytics and privacy paradigms. *Internet of Things.*https://doi.org/DOI: 10.1016/j.iot.2024.101318

Maroşan, M. I. (2019). Le devenir robot de l'humain. *Das Argument, 21*(2), 142–148.

Martínez-García, M., & Hernández-Lemus, E. (2022). Data integration challenges for machine learning in precision medicine. *Frontiers in Medicine, 8*, 784455. Advance online publication. DOI: 10.3389/fmed.2021.784455 PMID: 35145977

Mascarenhas, O. A., Thakur, M., & Kumar, P. (2023). Critical Thinking for Understanding Fallibility and Falsifiability of Our Knowledge. In *A Primer on Critical Thinking and Business Ethics: Recent Conceptualizations of Critical Thinking (Volume 1) (pp. 187-216).* Emerald Publishing Limited. https://doi.org/DOI: 10.1108/978-1-83753-308-420231007

Mascarenhas, O. A., Thakur, M., & Kumar, P. (2023). History of Critical Thinking and Some Models of Critical Thinking. In *A Primer on Critical Thinking and Business Ethics: Recent Conceptualizations of Critical Thinking (Volume 1) (pp. 41-80)*. Emerald Publishing Limited. https://doi.org/DOI: 10.1108/978-1-83753-308-420231003

Matsumoto-Royo, K., Ramírez-Montoya, M. S., & Conget, P. (2021). Opportunities to develop lifelong learning tendencies in practice-based teacher education: Getting ready for education 4.0. *Future Internet*, *13*(11), 292. Advance online publication. DOI: 10.3390/fi13110292

McArthur, D., Lewis, M., & Bishary, M. (2005). The roles of artificial intelligence in education: Current progress and future prospects. *Journal of Educational Technology*, *1*(4), 42–80.

McCann, S., & Camp Pendleton, C. A. (2015). Higher Order mLearning: Critical Thinking in Mobile Learning. MODSIM World, 208, 1-11. https://modsimworld.org/papers/2015/Higher_Order_mLearning.pdf

McCarthy, J. (2007). From here to human-level AI. *Artificial Intelligence*, *171*(18), 1174–1182. DOI: 10.1016/j.artint.2007.10.009

McGuire, L. S., & Alaraj, A. (2018). Competency assessment in virtual reality-based simulation in neurosurgical training. In *Comprehensive healthcare simulation: Neurosurgery* (pp. 153–157). Springer. DOI: 10.1007/978-3-319-75583-0_12

McLuhan, M. (1964). *Understanding media: The extensions of man*. McGraw-Hill.

Mendez, J. I., Ponce, P., Medina, A., Peffer, T., Meier, A., & Molina, A. (2021). A smooth and accepted transition to the future of cities based on the standard ISO 37120, artificial intelligence, and gamification constructors. 2021 IEEE European Technology and Engineering Management Summit, E-TEMS 2021 - Conference Proceedings.

Metz, C. (2021, March 15). Who is making sure the a.I. machines Aren't racist? Online article. *The New York Times*. https:// www.nytim es.com/2021/03/15/technology/ artificial -intelligence-google-bias. Html

Meyer, M., Smith, A., & Williams, J. (2023). AI in academics: Enhancing productivity and quality through AI tools. *Journal of Academic Research and Innovation*, *10*(1), 45–62. DOI: 10.1016/j.jari.2023.03.001

Miao, F., & Holmes, W. (2021). AI and education: Guidance for policy-makers. UNESCO. https://unesd oc.unesco.org/ark:/48223/ pf000 0376709

Michel-Villarreal, R., Vilalta-Perdomo, E., Salinas-Navarro, D. E., Thierry-Aguilera, R., & Gerardou, F. S. (2023). Challenges and opportunities of generative AI for higher education as explained by ChatGPT. *Education Sciences*, *13*(9), 856. DOI: 10.3390/educsci13090856

Microsoft. (2024). Microsoft Copilot (Version 1.0) [Computer software]. Microsoft. https://www.microsoft.com

Mikalef, P., & Gupta, M. (2021). Artificial intelligence capability: Conceptualization, measurement calibration, and empirical study on its impact on organizational creativity and firm performance. *Information & Management*, *58*(3), 103434–103434. DOI: 10.1016/j.im.2021.103434

Milenkova, V., & Lendzhova, V. (2021). Digital Citizenship and Digital Literacy in the Conditions of Social Crisis. *Computers*, *10*(4), 40–40. DOI: 10.3390/computers10040040

Mills, K., Ruiz, P., Lee, K., Coenraad, M., Fusco, J., Roschelle, J., & Weisgrau, J. (2024). *AI Literacy: A Framework to Understand, Evaluate, and Use Emerging Technology*. Digital Promise., DOI: 10.51388/20.500.12265/218

Ministry of Education. (2015). Culture, Sports, Science and Technology. *Gide Book for Starting School: Procedures for Entering Japanese Schools*. https://www.mext.go.jp/component/a_menu/education/micro_detail/__icsFiles/afieldfile/2016/06/24/1358299_01.pdf

Mirbabaie, M., Brünker, F., Möllmann, N. R. J., & Stieglitz, S. (2022). The rise of artificial intelligence–understanding the AI identity threat at the workplace. *Electronic Markets*, *32*(1), 73–99. Advance online publication. DOI: 10.1007/s12525-021-00496-x

Mirenda, P. (2013). Augmentative and alternative communication. In Volkmar, F. R. (Ed.), *Encyclopedia of autism spectrum disorders* (pp. 328–333). Springer. DOI: 10.1007/978-1-4419-1698-3_486

Mishra, P. (2025). Revolutionizing education with AI and ML. In *Internet of Behavior-Based Computational Intelligence for Smart Education Systems* (pp. 53–94).

Mishra, P., & Heath, M. K. (2024). The (Neil) Postman Always Rings Twice: 5 Questions on AI and Education. In M. Searson, E. Langran, & J. Trumble (Eds.), *Exploring new horizons: Generative artificial intelligence and teacher education* (pp. 14-24). Association for the Advancement of Computing in Education (AACE).

Mishra, P., & Yadav, A. (2013). Of art and algorithms: Rethinking technology & creativity in the 21st century. *TechTrends*, *57*(3), 10–14. DOI: 10.1007/s11528-013-0655-z

Mitchell, M. (2024). The Turing Test and our shifting conceptions of intelligence. *Science*, *385*(6710), eadq9356. Advance online publication. DOI: 10.1126/science.adq9356 PMID: 39146414

Moats, L., & Tolman, C. (n.d.). *Types of Reading Disability*. https://www.readingrockets.org/article/types-reading-disability

Mogavi, R. H., Deng, C., Kim, J. J., Zhou, P. Z., Kwon, Y. D., & Metwally, A. H. S.. (2024). ChatGPT in education: A blessing or a curse? A qualitative study exploring early adopters' utilization and perceptions. *Computers in Human Behavior: Artificial Humans*, *2*(1), 100027. DOI: 10.1016/j.chbah.2023.100027

Mohanty, R. N., Thomas, A., & Kori, A. (2024). Next-Generation Innovative Teaching Ecosystems for Futuristic Management Education. In *Global Higher Education Practices in Times of Crisis: Questions for Sustainability and Digitalization (pp. 5-28)*. Emerald Publishing Limited. https://doi.org/DOI: 10.1108/978-1-83797-052-020241002

Molenaar, I. (2022). Towards hybrid human-AI educational scenarios. *European Journal of Education*, *57*(4). Advance online publication. DOI: 10.1111/ejed.12527

Mollick, E. (2024, November 24). Getting started with AI: Good enough prompting. *One Useful Thing*. https://www.oneusefulthing.org/p/getting-started-with-ai-good-enough

Mollick, E. R., & Mollick, L. (2023). Using AI to implement effective teaching strategies in classrooms: Five strategies, including prompts. The Wharton School Research Paper, http://dx.doi.org/DOI: 10.2139/ssrn.4391243

Mollick, E. (2024). *Co-Intelligence: Living and working with AI*. Penguin.

Moon, J. A. (2004). *A handbook of reflective and experiential learning: Theory and practice*. Routledge.

Moriarty-Mclaughlin, F. (2020). *More colleges eye AI to track, monitor students*. The College Fix. https://www.theco llege fix.com/more-colleges-eye-ai-to-track-monitor-students/

Morris, P., Park, C., & Auld, E. (2022). Covid and the future of education: Global agencies 'building back better'. *Compare: A Journal of Comparative Education*, *52*(5), 691–711. DOI: 10.1080/03057925.2022.2066886

Mosqueira-Rey, E., Hernández-Pereira, E., Alonso-Ríos, D., Bobes-Bascarán, J., & Fernández-Leal, A. (2023). Human-in-the-loop machine learning: A state of the art. *Artificial Intelligence Review*, *56*(4), 3005–3054. DOI: 10.1007/s10462-022-10246-w

Moursund, D. G. (2006). Brief introduction to educational implications of Artificial Intelligence.

Moustaghfir, S., & Brigui, H. (2024). Navigating Critical Thinking in the Digital Era: An Informative Exploration. *International Journal of Linguistics, Literature and Translation, 7(1), 137-143.* DOI: DOI: 10.32996/ijllt

Moustaghfir, S., & Brigui, H. (2024). Navigating critical thinking in the digital era: An informative exploration. *International Journal of Linguistics Literature & Translation*, *7*(1), 137–143. DOI: 10.32996/ijllt.2024.7.1.11x

Mudunuri, L. N. R., Hullurappa, M., Vemula, V. R., & Selvakumar, P. (2025). AI-powered leadership: Shaping the future of management. In *Navigating Organizational Behavior in the Digital Age With AI* (pp. 127–152). IGI Global Scientific Publishing., DOI: 10.4018/979-8-3693-8442-8.ch006

Mueller, V. T. (2013). Voice Output Communication Aids. In F. R. Volkmar (Ed.), Encyclopedia of autism spectrum disorders. (pp. 3338–3341). Springer. DOI: 10.1007/978-1-4419-1698-3_1713

Mukul, E., & Büyüközkan, G. (2023). Digital transformation in education: A systematic review of education 4.0. *Technological Forecasting and Social Change*, *194*, 122664. DOI: 10.1016/j.techfore.2023.122664

Munn, L., & Henrickson, L. (2024). Tell me a story: A framework for critically investigating AI language models. *Learning, Media and Technology*, 1–17. Advance online publication. DOI: 10.1080/17439884.2024.2327024

Muthmainnah, S., Ibna Seraj, P. M., & Oteir, I. (2022). P. M. I., & Oteir, I. (2022). Playing with AI to investigate human-computer interaction technology and improving critical thinking skills to pursue 21st century age. *Education Research International*, *2022*, 1–17. DOI: 10.1155/2022/6468995

Nan, Y. (2011). Research on evaluation of higher education investment efficiency. 2011 2ndInternational Conference on Artificial Intelligence, Management Science and ElectronicCommerce, AIMSEC 2011 - Proceedings C7 – 6010724.

National Association of Colleges and Employers. (2017). Job outlook 2018. https://careerservices.wayne.edu/pdfs/2018-nacejob-outlook-survey.pdf

National Institute of Child Health and Human Development. (2020, March 5). *What are reading disorders?*https://www.nichd.nih.gov/health/topics/reading/conditioninfo/disorders

National Institute of Mental Health. (2025, January). *Autism Spectrum Disorder.* https://www.nimh.nih.gov/health/topics/autism-spectrum-disorders-asd/index.shtml

Ng, D. T. K., Leung, J. K. L., Su, J., Ng, R. C. W., & Chu, S. K. W. (2023). Teachers' AI digital competencies and twenty-first century skills in the post-pandemic world. *Educational Technology Research and Development*, *71*(1), 137–161. DOI: 10.1007/s11423-023-10203-6 PMID: 36844361

Ng, K., Lok, K., Wah, K., & Qiao, M. S. (2021). AI Literacy: Definition, Teaching, Evaluation and Ethical Issues. *Proceedings of the Association for Information Science and Technology*, *58*(1), 504–509. DOI: 10.1002/pra2.487

Nguyen, A., Kremantzis, M., Essien, A., Petrounias, I., & Hosseini, S. (2024). Enhancing student engagement through artificial intelligence (AI): Understanding the basics, opportunities, and challenges. *Journal of University Teaching & Learning Practice*, *21*(06). Advance online publication. DOI: 10.53761/caraaq92

Nguyen, D. P., Phan, L. T., Ho, H. X., & Le, A. N. H. (2022). Human resource management practices in higher education: A literature review using co-word analysis. *International Journal of Management Education*, *16*(1), 40–61. DOI: 10.1504/IJMIE.2022.10043292

Nguyen-Trung, K., Saeri, A. K., & Kaufman, S. (2024). Applying ChatGPT and AI-Powered Tools to Accelerate Evidence Reviews. *Human Behavior and Emerging Technologies*, *2024*(1), 8815424. DOI: 10.1155/2024/8815424

Ninja, N. (2023, June 30). *TF-IDF: Weighting Words in Text Analytics.* https://letsdatascience.com/tf-idf/

Norori, N., Hu, Q., Aellen, F. M., Faraci, F. D., & Tzovara, A. (2021). Addressing bias in big data and AI for health care: A call for open science. *Patterns (New York, N.Y.)*, *2*(10), 100347. DOI: 10.1016/j.patter.2021.100347 PMID: 34693373

Nursalim, A., Judijanto, L., & Asfahani, A. (2022). Educational revolution through the application of AI in the digital era. *Journal of Artificial Intelligence and Development*, *1*(1), 31–40.

Nwana, H. S. (1990). Intelligent tutoring systems: An overview. *Artificial Intelligence Review*, *4*(4), 251–277. DOI: 10.1007/BF00168958

Nye, B. D., Graesser, A. C., & Hu, X. (2014). AutoTutor and family: A review of 17 years of natural language tutoring. *International Journal of Artificial Intelligence in Education, 24*(4), 427–469. DOI: 10.1007/s40593-014-0029-5

Ochonogor, C. I. (2021). *Digital media revolution and information overload in Nigerian cyberspace: The challenges and prospects*. Media and Communication in Nigeria., DOI: 10.4324/9781003208747-22

Ogletree, B. T. (Ed.). (2021). *Augmentative and Alternative Communication: Challenges and Solutions*. Plural Publishing.

Olympus Co. (1999). *ScanTalk, ScanTalk Reader, & Sound Print Kobo*. https://www.olympus.co.jp/jp/news/1999b/nr990823r300j.html

Onesi-Ozigagun, O., Ololade, Y. J., Eyo-Udo, N. L., & Ogundipe, D. O. (2024). Revolutionizing education through AI: A comprehensive review of enhancing learning experiences. *International Journal of Applied Research in Social Sciences, 6*(4), 589–607. DOI: 10.51594/ijarss.v6i4.1011

Ong, D., Sands, P., Kilborn, A., & Parikh, J. Y. (2020). A beginner's guide to systematic reviews and meta-analyses. *British Journal of Hospital Medicine, 81*(9), 1–6. DOI: 10.12968/hmed.2020.0405 PMID: 33263480

Open, A. I. (2023). How can educators respond to students presenting AI-generated content as their own? Retrieved September 2, 2023 from https://help.openai.com/en/articles/8313351-how-can-educators-respond-to-students-presenting-ai-generated-content-as-their-own

Orakci, S., & Gelisli, Y. (2019). The Effect of the Application of Learning Activities Based on Learner Autonomy on the 6th Grade Students' English Achievements, Attitudes, and Learner Autonomy. *International Journal of Curriculum and Instruction, 11*(1), 269–292. https://eric.ed.gov/?id=EJ1217908

Oregon State University Ecampus. (2024). *Bloom's taxonomy revisited (Version 2.0)*. https://ecampus.oregonstate.edu/faculty/artificial-intelligence-tools/blooms-taxonomy-revisited-v2-2024.pdf

Osipovskaya, E., & Dmitrieva, S. (2022). The Issue of Adaptive Learning as Educational Innovation. In *Technology, Innovation and Creativity in Digital Society: XXI Professional Culture of the Specialist of the Future (pp. 606-617)*. Springer International Publishing. https://doi.org/ [HTML]DOI: 10.1007/978-3-030-89708-6_50

Ouyang, F., Wu, M., Zheng, L., Zhang, L., & Jiao, P. (2023). Integration of artificial intelligence performance prediction and learning analytics to improve student learning in online engineering course. *International Journal of Educational Technology in Higher Education, 20(1), 4.* https://doi.org/ springer.comDOI: 10.1186/s41239-022-00372-4

Ouyang, F., & Jiao, P. (2021). AI in education: The three paradigms of AI integration. *Journal of Educational Technology Development and Exchange, 14*(2), 37–54. DOI: 10.18785/jetde.1402.03

Ouyang, F., & Jiao, P. (2021). Artificial intelligence in education: The three paradigms. *Computers and Education: Artificial Intelligence, 2*, 100020. DOI: 10.1016/j.caeai.2021.100020

Oyeniyi, L. D., Ugochukwu, C. E., & Mhlongo, N. Z.Lawrence Damilare OyeniyiChinonye Esther UgochukwuNoluthando Zamanjomane Mhlongo. (2024). Transforming financial planning with AI-driven analysis: A review and application insights. *Finance & Accounting Research Journal, 6*(4), 626–647. DOI: 10.51594/farj.v6i4.1037

Pacholek, K., Prostean, M., Burris, S., Cockburn, L., Nganji, J., Nadège, A. N., & Mbibeh, L. (2021). A WhatsApp community forum for improving critical thinking and practice skills of mental health providers in a conflict zone. *Interactive Learning Environments, 31*(4), 2471–2489. DOI: 10.1080/10494820.2021.1890622

Page, M. J., McKenzie, J. E., Bossuyt, P. M., Boutron, I., Hoffmann, T. C., Mulrow, C. D., Shamseer, L., Tetzlaff, J. M., Akl, E. A., Brennan, S. E., Chou, R., Glanville, J., Grimshaw, J. M., Hróbjartsson, A., Lalu, M. M., Li, T., Loder, E. W., Mayo-Wilson, E., McDonald, S., & Moher, D. (2021). The PRISMA 2020 statement: An updated guideline for reporting systematic reviews. *BMJ (Clinical Research Ed.), 372*, n71. Advance online publication. DOI: 10.1136/bmj.n71 PMID: 33782057

Painter, D. L., & Howell, C. (2020). Community engagement in the liberal arts: How service hours and reflections influence course value. *Journal of Experiential Education, 43*(4), 416–430. DOI: 10.1177/1053825920931563

Panda, S., & Kaur, N. (2024). Empowered Minds: Navigating Digital Seas With Emerging Information Literacy Framework. In *Examining Information Literacy in Academic Libraries (pp. 48-82).* IGI Global. https://doi.org/DOI: 10.3390/healthcare10050770

Pan, Y., & Yang, P. (2021). The role of AI assisted socio-cultural frameworks in academic change and higher education growth. *International Journal of Technology Management, 86*(2-4), 196–213. DOI: 10.1504/IJTM.2021.118316

Patel, N. S., Puah, S., & Kok, X. F. K. (2024). Shaping future-ready graduates with mindset shifts: Studying the impact of integrating critical and design thinking in design innovation education. *Frontiers in Education*, *9*, 1358431. Advance online publication. DOI: 10.3389/feduc.2024.1358431

Paul, R. (2011). Critical thinking movement: 3 waves. *Retrieved*, *18*, 2018.

Pavlik, J. V. (2023). Collaborating with ChatGPT: Considering the implications of generative artificial intelligence for journalism and media education. *Journalism & Mass Communication Educator*, *78*(1), 84–93. DOI: 10.1177/10776958221149577

Pedro, F., Subosa, M., Rivas, A., & Valverde, P. (2019). Artificial intelligence in education: Challenges and opportunities for sustainable development.

Peng, C., Zhou, X., & Liu, S. (2022). An introduction to artificial intelligence and machine learning for online education. *Mobile Networks and Applications*, *27*(3), 1147–1150. DOI: 10.1007/s11036-022-01953-3

Pérez, J. Q., Daradoumis, T., & Puig, J. M. M. (2020). Rediscovering the use of chatbots in education: A systematic literature review. *Computer Applications in Engineering Education*, *28*(6), 1549–1565. DOI: 10.1002/cae.22326

Perplexity.ai. (2024). Perplexity [AI assistant].https://Perplexity.ai

Perrotta, C., & Selwyn, N. (2020). Deep Learning Goes to School: Toward a Relational Understanding of AI in Education. *Learning, Media and Technology*, *45*(3), 251–269. Advance online publication. DOI: 10.1080/17439884.2020.1686017

Peterson, P. E., & Shakeel, M. D. (2024). The nation's charter report card: A new ranking of states by charter student performance. *Journal of School Choice*, *18*(1), 30–66. Advance online publication. DOI: 10.1080/15582159.2023.2273607

Pik, J., Chan, E. P., Broad, J., Sun, P., & Singh, V. (2025). *Hands-On AI Trading with Python*. QuantConnect and AWS.

Pimenow, S., Pimenowa, O., & Prus, P. (2024). Challenges of Artificial Intelligence Development in the Context of Energy Consumption and Impact on Climate Change. *Energies*, *17*(23), 5965. Advance online publication. DOI: 10.3390/en17235965

Pinar, W. F. (2023). Understanding Curriculum: Interview with Prof. William F. Pinar. *Journal of Higher Education Policy and Leadership Studies*, *4*(4), 180–184. DOI: 10.61186/johepal.4.4.180

Plato. (2007). *The Republic* (D. Lee, Trans.; 2nd ed.). Penguin. (Original work published ca. 380 B.C.E.).

Plekhanov, D., Franke, H., & Netland, T. H. (2023). Digital transformation: A review and research agenda. *European Management Journal, 41*(6), 821–844. DOI: 10.1016/j.emj.2022.09.007

Polanco-Levicán, K., & Salvo-Garrido, S. (2022). Understanding social media literacy: A systematic review of the concept and its competences. *International Journal of Environmental Research and Public Health, 19*(14), 8807. DOI: 10.3390/ijerph19148807 PMID: 35886657

Polgar, J. M., Encarnação, P., Smith, E., & Cook, A. M. (2024). *Assistive Technology: Principals and Practice* (6th ed.). Elsevier.

Poole, D. I., Goebel, R. G., & Mackworth, A. K. (1998). *Computational intelligence and knowledge*. Oxford University Press.

Poornappriya, T. S., & Gopinath, R. (2020). Application of machine learning techniques for improving learning disabilities. *International Journal of Electrical Engineering and Technology, 11*(10), 403–411.

Popenici, S. A. D., & Kerr, S. (2017). Exploring the impact of artificial intelligence on teaching and learning in higher education. *Research and Practice in Technology Enhanced Learning, 12*(1), 22. DOI: 10.1186/s41039-017-0062-8 PMID: 30595727

Pratama, M. P., Sampelolo, R., & Lura, H. (2023). Revolutionizing education: Harnessing the power of artificial intelligence for personalized learning. *Klasikal: Journal of Education. Language Teaching and Science, 5*(2), 350–357.

Praveen, J. V. S. (2024). Understanding the potential impact of AI-powered classroom management on student engagement, and overall learning outcomes. *Global Journal of Business and Integral Security, 1*(2).

Prichard, B. S. (2024). The CLAIM Method: A Roadmap for AI Integration in Education. Presentation for Morehead State University Faculty. The CLAIM Method: A Roadmap for AI Integration in Education.

Priem, R. L. (2018). Toward becoming a complete teacher of strategic management. *Academy of Management Learning & Education, 17*(3), 374–388. DOI: 10.5465/amle.2017.0237

Prud'homme-Genereux, A. (2024). Writing case studies using generative AI: Interactive role play. Faculty Focus. https://www.facultyfocus.com/articles/teaching-with-technology-articles/writing-case-studies-using-generative-ai-interactive-role-play/

Putra, I. M., & Abdunnafi, F. I. (2024). Understanding the unexpected: The adverse influence of large language models on critical thinking and professional skepticism in accounting education. https://ssrn.com/abstract=4914889 DOI: 10.2139/ssrn.4914889

QIAT Leadership Team. (2020). *The QIAT Companion: A Just-in-Time Resource for Implementing the Quality Indicators for Assistive Technology*. CAST, Inc.

Quezada Castro, G. A., Castro Arellano, M. P., & Quezada Castro, M. P. (2022). Artificial intelligence and legal education: Its incorporation during the Covid-19 pandemic. *Revista Venezolana de Gerencia*, *27*(8), 750–764. DOI: 10.52080/rvgluz.27.8.2

Rabeya, M., Mahmud, M. S., Johora, S. F. T., & Sattar, A. (2022). A comparison of the application of artificial intelligence in the educational system. Dans *2022 International Conference on Emerging Trends in Computing and Engineering Applications (ETCEA)* (pp. 1-6). IEEE. DOI: 10.1109/ETCEA57049.2022.10009813

Rahman, M. M., Alam, G. M., Aziz, N. A. B. A., Bashir, K., & Kader, R. (2024). Whether mismatch finds match in the digitalized era: A comparison of five types of graduates to align business education and banking jobs. *Industry and Higher Education*, *38*(6), 547–561. Advance online publication. DOI: 10.1177/09504222241249900

Rahman, M. M., & Watanobe, Y. (2023). ChatGPT for education and research: Opportunities, threats, and strategies. *Applied Sciences (Basel, Switzerland)*, *13*(9), 5783. DOI: 10.3390/app13095783

Rajaram, K. (2023). Future of learning: Teaching and learning strategies. In *Learning Intelligence: Innovative and Digital Transformative Learning Strategies: Cultural and Social Engineering Perspectives (pp. 3-53).* Singapore: Springer Nature Singapore. https://doi.org/DOI: 10.1007/978-981-19-9201-8_1

Rajaram, A., Olory, C., Leduc, V., Evaristo, G., Coté, K., Isenberg, J., Isenberg, J. S., Dai, D. L., Karamchandani, J., Chen, M. F., Maedler-Kron, C., & Fiset, P. O. (2022). An integrated virtual pathology education platform developed using Microsoft Power Apps and Microsoft Teams. *Journal of Pathology Informatics*, *13*, 100117. Advance online publication. DOI: 10.1016/j.jpi.2022.100117 PMID: 36268098

Rakhra, M., Gopinadh, G., Addepalli, N. S., Singh, G., Aliraja, S., Reddy, V. S. G., & Reddy, M. N. (2021). E-Commerce Assistance with a Smart Chatbot using Artificial Intelligence. Proceedings of 2021 2nd International Conference on Intelligent Engineering and Management, ICIEM 2021 C7 - 9445316, Rasiah, R., Turner, J. J., & Ho, Y. F. (2019). The impact of emotional intelligence on work performance: Perceptions and reflections from academics in Malaysian higher education obitat endiaest que. *Contemporary Economics*, *13*(3), 269–282. DOI: 10.5709/ce.1897-9254.312

Rakowski, R., & Kowaliková, P. (2024). The political and social contradictions of the human and online environment in the context of artificial intelligence applications. *Humanities & Social Sciences Communications*, *11*(1), 289. DOI: 10.1057/s41599-024-02725-y

Ramesh, D., & Sanampudi, S. K. (2021). An automated essay scoring systems: A systematic literature review. *Artificial Intelligence Review*, *55*(3), 2495–2527. DOI: 10.1007/s10462-021-10068-2 PMID: 34584325

Ramírez-Montoya, M. S., Andrade-Vargas, L., Rivera-Rogel, D., & Portuguez-Castro, M. (2021). Trends for the future of education programs for professional development. *Sustainability (Basel)*, *13*(13), 7244. DOI: 10.3390/su13137244

Rana, H., Rajiv, R., & Lal, M. (2021). The Potential of Artificial Intelligence for Enhancing Student Support Services in Higher Education. *Journal of Computing in Higher Education*, *33*(1), 274–292. DOI: 10.1007/s12528-021-09270-6

Rantala, K., Alasuutari, N., & Kuorikoski, J. (2024). The logic of regulatory impact assessment: From evidence to evidential reasoning. *Regulation & Governance*, *18*(2), 534–550. DOI: 10.1111/rego.12542

Rashid, A. B., & Kausik, A. K. (2024). *AI revolutionizing industries worldwide: A comprehensive overview of its diverse applications*. Hybrid Advances., DOI: 10.1016/j.hybadv.2024.100277

Rasul, T., Nair, S., Kalendra, D., Balaji, M. S., Santini, F. D. O., Ladeira, W. J.,… Hossain, M. U. (2024). Enhancing academic integrity among students in GenAI Era: A holistic framework.International Journal of Management Education, 22(3 C7 - 101041).DOI: 10.1016/j.ijme.2024.101041

Rasyid, A., Iswari, R. I., Marwoto, P., & Rinto, . (2020). The effectiveness of mobile learning role play game (rpg) maker mv in improving students' critical thinking ability. *Journal of Physics: Conference Series*, *1567*(4), 042088. DOI: 10.1088/1742-6596/1567/4/042088

Rauschenberger, M., Lins, C., Rousselle, N., Hein, A., & Fudickar, S. (2019). Designing a new puzzle app to target dyslexia screening in pre-readers. *Proceedings of the 5th EAI International Conference on Smart Objects and Technologies for Social Good*, 155–159. DOI: 10.1145/3342428.3342679

Raya, J., & Vieira, F. (2015). Enhancing Autonomy in Language Education: A Case-Based Approach to Teacher and Learner Development. Oapen.org. https://doi.org/DOI: 1004875

Ray, S., & Sikdar, D. P. (2024). AI-driven flipped classroom: Revolutionizing education through digital pedagogy. *Psychology (Irvine, Calif.)*, *7*(2), 169–179.

Razia, B., Awwad, B., & Taqi, N. (2023). The relationship between artificial intelligence (AI) and its aspects in higher education. *Development and Learning in Organizations*, *37*(3), 21–23. DOI: 10.1108/DLO-04-2022-0074

Rehman, A. U., Behera, R. K., Islam, M. S., Abbasi, F. A., & Imtiaz, A. (2024). Assessing the usage of ChatGPT on life satisfaction among higher education students: The moderating role of subjective health. *Technology in Society*, *78*, C7–C102655. DOI: 10.1016/j.techsoc.2024.102655

Reis, J., & Melão, N. (2023). Digital transformation: A meta-review and guidelines for future research. *Heliyon*, *9*(1), e12834–e12834. DOI: 10.1016/j.heliyon.2023.e12834 PMID: 36691547

Rejeb, A., Rejeb, K., Appolloni, A., Treiblmaier, H., & Iranmanesh, M. (2024). Exploring the impact of ChatGPT on education: A web mining and machine learning approach. *International Journal of Management Education*, *22*(1), 100932. DOI: 10.1016/j.ijme.2024.100932

Rello, L., Romero, E., Rauschenberger, M., Ali, A., Williams, K., Bigham, J. P., & White, N. C. (2018). Screening dyslexia for English using HCI measures and machine learning. *Proceedings of the 2018 International Conference on Digital Health*, 80–84. DOI: 10.1145/3194658.3194675

Renz, A., & Hilbig, R. (2020). Prerequisites for artificial intelligence in further education: Identification of drivers, barriers, and business models of educational technology companies. *International Journal of Educational Technology in Higher Education*, *17*(1), 14. DOI: 10.1186/s41239-020-00193-3

Rhoads, M. (2023). *AI for educators: Learning strategies, teacher efficiencies, and a vision for an artificial intelligence future*. EduMatch Publishing.

Richter, T. T., & Langesee, L. M. (2024). Supporting virtual learning and international academic visits with AI. IDIMT 2024: Changes to ICT, Management, and business processes through AI - 32nd Interdisciplinary Information Management Talks.

Rigopoulos, G., & Karadimas, N. V. (2017). Military student assignment using Nex-Class decision support system. Proceedings - 2016 3rd International Conference on Mathematics and Computers in Sciences and in Industry, MCSI 2016 C7 – 7815147.

Risvold, W., Stratton, M., & Geddy, M. (2024). How to evaluate critical thinking in the age of AI. February 14, 2024. https://www.aacsb.edu/insights/articles/2024/02/how-to-evaluate-critical-thinking-in-the-age-of-ai

Rivas, S. F., Saiz, C., & Ossa, C. (2022). Metacognitive strategies and development of critical thinking in higher education. *Frontiers in Psychology*, *13*, 913219. Advance online publication. DOI: 10.3389/fpsyg.2022.913219 PMID: 35783800

Rizvi, S. (2023). Revolutionizing student engagement: Artificial intelligence's impact on specialized learning motivation. *International Journal of Advanced Engineering Research and Science*, *10*(09), 27–31. DOI: 10.22161/ijaers.109.4

Roberts, A., & Ryan, T. (2017). AI and the Future of Higher Education: Planning for Education 4.0. *Journal of Higher Education Theory and Practice*, *17*(6), 45–58.

Robles, A. C. M. O. (2012). Cyber Portfolio: The Innovative Menu for 21st Century Technology. *Online Submission*, *2*(3), 143–150.

Rodrigues, F., & Oliveira, P. (2014). A system for formative assessment and monitoring of students' progress. *Computers & Education*, *76*, 30–41. DOI: 10.1016/j.compedu.2014.03.001

Rojas, R. V. B. (2024). *Artificial Intelligence: Genesis, Development, and Future*. Revolutionizing Communication., DOI: 10.1201/9781003473633

Roll, I., & Wylie, R. (2016). Evolution and revolution in artificial intelligence in education. *International Journal of Artificial Intelligence in Education*, *26*(2), 582–599. DOI: 10.1007/s40593-016-0110-3

Rosário, A., Moreira, C., & Macedo, P. (2021). Competitive dynamics of strategic groups in the Portugueses Banking Industrry, Cuadernos de Gestión, 21(2), 1-15. ISSN: 1131-6837. DOI: 10.5295/cdg.180975ac

Rosário, A. T., Lopes, P. R., & Rosário, F. S. (2023). Metaverse in Marketing: Challenges and Opportunities. In Khang, A., Shah, V., & Rani, S. (Eds.), *Handbook of Research on AI-Based Technologies and Applications in the Era of the Metaverse* (pp. 204–227). IGI Global., DOI: 10.4018/978-1-6684-8851-5.ch010

Rosário, A., & Casaca, J. (2023). Relationship marketing and customer retention - A systematic literature review. *Studies in Business and Economics*, *18*(3), 44–66. DOI: 10.2478/sbe-2023-0044

Rose, D. H. (2016). *Universal design for learning: Theory and practice*. CAST Professional Publishing.

Roumeliotis, K. I., & Tselikas, N. D. (2023). ChatGPT and Open-AI models: A preliminary review. *Future Internet*, *15*(6), 192. DOI: 10.3390/fi15060192

Ruiz-Rojas, L. I., Acosta-Vargas, P., De-Moreta-Llovet, J., & Gonzalez-Rodriguez, M. (2023). Empowering education with generative artificial intelligence tools: Approach with an instructional design matrix. *Sustainability (Basel)*, *15*(15), 11524. DOI: 10.3390/su151511524

Ruiz-Rojas, L. I., Salvador-Ullauri, L., & Acosta-Vargas, P. (2024). Collaborative working and critical thinking: Adoption of generative artificial intelligence tools in higher education. *Sustainability (Basel)*, *16*(13), 5367. DOI: 10.3390/su16135367

Rusandi, M. A., Ahman, , Saripah, I., Khairun, D. Y., & Mutmainnah, . (2023). No worries with ChatGPT: Building bridges between artificial intelligence and education with critical thinking soft skills. *Journal of Public Health (Oxford, England)*, *45*(3), e602–e603. DOI: 10.1093/pubmed/fdad049 PMID: 37099761

Russell, S. J., & Norvig, P. (2016). *Artificial intelligence: A modern approach*. Pearson Education Limited.

Sadegh-Zadeh, S. A., Movahhedi, T., Hajiyavand, A. M., & Dearn, K. D. (2023, December). Exploring undergraduates' perceptions of and engagement in an AI-enhanced online course. [). Frontiers Media SA.]. *Frontiers in Education*, *8*, 1252543. DOI: 10.3389/feduc.2023.1252543

Sajja, R., Sermet, Y., Cikmaz, M., Cwiertny, D., & Demir, I. (2024). Artificial intelligence-enabled intelligent assistant for personalized and adaptive learning in higher education. *Information (Basel)*, *15*(10), 596. Advance online publication. DOI: 10.3390/info15100596

Sakasa, T., & Mawela, T. (2023). AIOps in Higher Education Institutions. Lecture Notes inBusiness Information Processing.

Salinas-Navarro, D. E., Vilalta-Perdomo, E., Michel-Villarreal, R., & Montesinos, L. (2024). Using generative artificial intelligence tools to explain and enhance experiential learning for authentic assessment. *Education Sciences*, *14*(1), 83. DOI: 10.3390/educsci14010083

Salloum, S. A., Al-Emran, M., Monem, A. A., & Shaalan, K. (2018). Using Text Mining Techniques for Extracting Information from Research Articles. In Shaalan, K., Hassanien, A., & Tolba, F. (Eds.), *Intelligent Natural Language Processing: Trends and Applications. Studies in Computational Intelligence* (Vol. 740, pp. 373–397). Springer. DOI: 10.1007/978-3-319-67056-0_18

Salmon, A. K., & Barrera, M. X. (2021). Intentional questioning to promote thinking and learning. *Thinking Skills and Creativity*, *40*, 100822. Advance online publication. DOI: 10.1016/j.tsc.2021.100822

Samara, F. Y. A., Taha, A. H. A., Massa, N. M., Jamie, T. N. A., Harara, F. E., Abu-Nasser, B. S., & Abu-Naser, S. S. (2024). The Role of AI in Enhancing Business Decision-Making: Innovations and Implications.

Samman, A. M. A. (2024). Harnessing Potential: Meta-Analysis of AI Integration in Higher Education. 2024 ASU International Conference in Emerging Technologies for Sustainabilityand Intelligent Systems, ICETSIS 2024, Schön, E. M., Buchem, I., Sostak, S., & Rauschenberger, M. (2023). Shift Toward Value-Based Learning: Applying Agile Approaches in Higher Education. Lecture Notes in Business Information Processing.

Samoili, S., López Cobo, M., Gómez, E., De Prato, G., Martínez-Plumed, F., & Delipetrev, B. (2020). *AI watch defining artificial intelligence towards an operational definition and taxonomy of artificial intelligence. Joint Research Centre*. JRC.

Sánchez Gonzales, H. M., Sánchez González, M., & Martos Moreno, J. (2024). The Methodology Used by Fact-Checkers. An In-Depth Analysis of Commonly Used Strategies. *Journalism Practice*, •••, 1–24. DOI: 10.1080/17512786.2024.2340522

Saqr, R. R., Al-Somali, S. A., & Sarhan, M. Y. (2023). Exploring the acceptance and user satisfaction of AI-driven e-learning platforms (Blackboard, Moodle, Edmodo, Coursera and edX): An integrated technology model. *Sustainability (Basel)*, *16*(1), 204. Advance online publication. DOI: 10.3390/su16010204

Sari, E., & Yalçın, S. S. (2024). Interplay of paternal caregiving and screen use habits on early childhood development and children's tantrums. *Italian Journal of Pediatrics*, *50*(1), 230. DOI: 10.1186/s13052-024-01802-x PMID: 39501365

Saritepeci, M., & Yildiz Durak, H. (2024). Effectiveness of artificial intelligence integration in design-based learning on design thinking mindset, creative and reflective thinking skills: An experimental study. *Education and Information Technologies*, *29*(18), 25175–25209. Advance online publication. DOI: 10.1007/s10639-024-12829-2

Saritepeci, M., & Yildiz Durak, H. (2024). The impact of AI integration on design-based learning: Enhancing creativity and reflective thinking in education. *Journal of Educational Technology Research and Development*, *72*(1), 123–145. DOI: 10.1007/s11423-024-01234-5

Sarker, I. H. (2021). Deep learning: A comprehensive overview on techniques, taxonomy, applications and research directions. *SN Computer Science*, *2*(6), 420. Advance online publication. DOI: 10.1007/s42979-021-00815-1 PMID: 34426802

Sarker, I. H. (2021). Machine learning: Algorithms, real-world applications and research directions. *SN Computer Science*, *2*(3), 160. Advance online publication. DOI: 10.1007/s42979-021-00592-x PMID: 33778771

Sathy, V., & Hogan, K. A. (2023, November). How to Make Your Teaching More Inclusive: Advice Guide. *The Chronicle of Higher Education*. https://www-chronicle-com.msu.idm.oclc.org/article/how-to-make-your-teaching-more-inclusive/

Saxena, D., & Sandul Yasobant. (2022). Information Overload. Springer EBooks, 566–568. DOI: 10.1007/978-3-319-32010-6_374

Schaffer, S. (1999). Enlightened automata. In W. Clark, J. Golinski, & S. Schaffer (Eds.), The sciences in enlightened Europe. The University of Chicago Press. https://press.uchic ago.edu/ucp/books/ book/chica go/S/bo362 3650. Html

Scherer, R., Siddiq, F., & Tondeur, J. (2019). The role of ICT in higher education: A qualitative review of the literature. *Technology, Pedagogy and Education*, *28*(2), 123–144.

Schiff, D. (2021). Out of the laboratory and into the classroom: the future of artificial intelligence in education. *AI & society*. https://doi.org/springer.comDOI: 10.1007/s00146-020-01033-8

Schiff, D. (2022). Education for AI, not AI for education: The role of education and ethics in national AI policy strategies. *International Journal of Artificial Intelligence in Education*, *32*(3), 527–563. https://doi.org/10crti.1007/s40593-021-00270-2. DOI: 10.1007/s40593-021-00270-2

Schleicher, A. (2018). Educating Learners for Their Future, Not Our Past. *ECNU Review of Education*, *1*(1), 58–75. DOI: 10.30926/ecnuroe2018010104

Searson, M. Langran, E., & Trumble J. (Eds). (2024). *Exploring new horizons: Generative artificial intelligence and educator education.* Association for the Advancement of Computing in Education (AACE). https://www.learntechlib.org/p/223928/

Segev, E. (Ed.). (2022). *Semantic Network Analysis in Social Sciences*. Routledge.

Selber, S. (2004). *Multiliteracies for a Digital Age*. Southern Illinois University Press.

Sellars, M., Fakirmohammad, R., Bui, L., Fishetti, J., Niyozov, S., Reynolds, R., Thapliyal, N., Liu-Smith, Y.-L., & Ali, N. (2018). Conversations on Critical Thinking: Can Critical Thinking Find Its Way Forward as the Skill Set and Mindset of the Century? *Education Sciences*, *8*(4), 205–205. DOI: 10.3390/educsci8040205

Selwyn, N. (2019). *Should robots replace teachers? AI and the future of education*. Polity Press.

Seo, K., Tang, J., Roll, I., Fels, S., & Yoon, D. (2021). The impact of artificial intelligence on learner–instructor interaction in online learning. *International Journal of Educational Technology in Higher Education, 18*(1), 1–23. DOI: 10.1186/s41239-021-00292-9 PMID: 34778540

Sequeira, R., Reis, A., Branco, F., & Alves, P. (2024). Roadmap for Implementing Business Intelligence Systems in Higher Education Institutions: Validation of a Case Study at the University of Trás-os-Montes and Alto Douro. *ICSBT International Conference on Smart Business Technologies*. DOI: 10.1007/978-3-031-67904-9_4

Shah, S. S., & Asad, M. M. (2024). Impact of critical thinking approach on learners' dependence on innovative transformation through artificial intelligence. In *The Evolution of Artificial Intelligence in Higher Education: Challenges, Risks, and Ethical Considerations (pp. 161-182)*. Emerald Publishing Limited. https://doi.org/ DOI: 10.1108/978-1-83549-486-820241010

Shankar, S. K., Pothancheri, G., Sasi, D., & Mishra, S. (2024). Bringing teachers in the loop: Exploring perspectives on integrating generative AI in technology-enhanced learning. *International Journal of Artificial Intelligence in Education*, •••, 1–26. DOI: 10.1007/s40593-024-00428-8

Shao, Z., Zhao, R., Yuan, S., Ding, M., & Wang, Y. (2022). Tracing the evolution of AI in the past decade and forecasting the emerging trends. *Expert Systems with Applications*, *209*, 118221. DOI: 10.1016/j.eswa.2022.118221

Sharma, S., & Lenka, U. (2024). How does transformational leadership impact organizational unlearning: Insights from persistence theories. *Journal of Organizational Change Management*, *37*(1), 150–172. DOI: 10.1108/JOCM-07-2023-0302

Sharma, S., Singh, G., Sharma, C. S., & Kapoor, S. (2024). Artificial intelligence in Indian higher education institutions: A quantitative study on adoption and perceptions. *International Journal of System Assurance Engineering and Management*. Advance online publication. DOI: 10.1007/s13198-023-02193-8

Sheridan Rains, L., Johnson, S., Barnett, P., Steare, T., Needle, J. J., Carr, S., & Simpson, A. (2021). Early impacts of the COVID-19 pandemic on mental health care and on people with mental health conditions: Framework synthesis of international experiences and responses. *Social Psychiatry and Psychiatric Epidemiology*, *56*(1), 13–24. DOI: 10.1007/s00127-020-01924-7 PMID: 32804258

Shneiderman, B. (2020). Human-Centered Artificial Intelligence: Three Fresh Ideas. AIS Electronic Library (AISeL). https://aisel.aisnet.org/thci/vol12/iss3/1/

Shneiderman, B. (2022). *Human-centered AI*. Oxford University Press., https://issues.org/wp-content/uploads/2021/01/56%E2%80%9361-Shneiderman-Human-Centered-AI-Winter-2021.pdf DOI: 10.1093/oso/9780192845290.001.0001

Shutaleva, A. (2023). Ecological culture and critical thinking: Building of a sustainable future. *Sustainability (Basel)*, *15*(18), 13492. Advance online publication. DOI: 10.3390/su151813492

Shute, V. J. (2008). Focus on Formative Feedback. *Review of Educational Research*, *78*(1), 153–189. DOI: 10.3102/0034654307313795

Siemens, G. (2020). The Future of AI in Higher Education: Perspectives from Leaders. Chronicle of Higher Education.

Sik-Lanyi, C., Hoogerwerf, E.-J., Miesenberger, K., & Cudd, P. (Eds.). (2015). *Assistive Technology: Building Bridges*. IOS Press.

Silton, N. R. (Ed.). (2015). *Recent Advances in Assistive Technologies to Support Children with Developmental Disorders*. IGI Global Scientific Publishing. DOI: 10.4018/978-1-4666-8395-2

Singh, J. (2023). Autonomous Vehicle Swarm Robotics: Real-Time Coordination Using AI for Urban Traffic and Fleet Management. *Journal of AI-Assisted Scientific Discovery*.

Singh, S. V., & Hiran, K. K. (2022). The impact of AI on teaching and learning in higher education technology. *Journal of Higher Education Theory and Practice*, *22*(13).

Singh, V. V., Kumar, N., Singh, S., Kaul, M., Gupta, A. K., & Kapur, P. K. (2024). Assessment of artificial intelligence-based digital learning systems in higher education amid the pandemic using analytic hierarchy. *International Journal of System Assurance Engineering and Management*, *15*(8), 4069–4084. DOI: 10.1007/s13198-024-02411-x

Sirisubsatid, S. (2018). The new era of language teaching: Case study of peer teaching method in German language class. Proceedings of 2018 5th International Conference on Business and Industrial Research: Smart Technology for Next Generation of Information, Engineering, Business and Social Science, ICBIR 2018.

Siskind, D., Conlin, D., Hestenes, L., Kim, S. A., Barnes, A., & Yaya-Bryson, D. (2022). Balancing technology and outdoor learning: Implications for early childhood teacher educators. *Journal of Early Childhood Teacher Education*, *43*(3), 389–405. DOI: 10.1080/10901027.2020.1859024

Slade, S., & Prinsloo, P. (2013). Learning analytics: Ethical issues and dilemmas. *The American Behavioral Scientist*, *57*(10), 1510–1529. DOI: 10.1177/0002764213479366

Slimi, Z., & Carballido, B. V. (2023a). Navigating the Ethical Challenges of Artificial Intelligence in Higher Education: An Analysis of Seven Global AI Ethics Policies. TEM Journal, 12(2), 590-602. https://doi.org/DOI: 10.18421/TEM122-02

Slimi, Z., & Carballido, B. V. (2023b). Systematic Review: AI's Impact on Higher Education -Learning, Teaching, and Career Opportunities. TEM Journal, 12(3), 1627-1637.https://doi.org/DOI: 10.18421/TEM123-44

Sloane, M. (2021). Silicon Valley's quest to make ethical AI: Lessons from hubris and limits. *Patterns (New York, N.Y.)*, *2*(6), 100243. DOI: 10.1016/j.patter.2021.100243

Song, N. (2024). Higher education crisis: Academic misconduct with generative AI. Journal of Contingencies and Crisis Management, 32(1 C7 - e12532). DOI: 10.1111/1468-5973.12532

Song, S., Xie, T., & Yang, H. (2011). Notice of Retraction: The research and practice on long-term guarantee system of teaching quality in local colleges. 2011 2nd International Conferenceon Artificial Intelligence, Management Science and Electronic Commerce, AIMSEC 2011 -Proceedings C7 - 6009751, 5959-5962. DOI: 10.1109/AIMSEC.2011.6009751

Song, C., Shin, S. Y., & Shin, K. S. (2024). Implementing the Dynamic Feedback-Driven Learning Optimization Framework: A Machine Learning Approach to Personalize Educational Pathways. *Applied Sciences (Basel, Switzerland)*, *14*(2), 916. Advance online publication. DOI: 10.3390/app14020916

Songer, N. B., Newstadt, M. R., Lucchesi, K., & Ram, P. (2020). Navigated learning: An approach for differentiated classroom instruction built on learning science and data science foundations. *Human Behavior and Emerging Technologies*, *2*(1), 93–105. DOI: 10.1002/hbe2.169

Sönmez, E., Kabataş Memiş, E., & Yerlikaya, Z. (2019). The effect of practices based on argumentation-based inquiry approach on teacher candidates' critical thinking. *Educational Studies*, *47*(1), 59–83. DOI: 10.1080/03055698.2019.1654364

Southworth, J. (2022). Bridging critical thinking and transformative learning: The role of perspective-taking. *Theory and Research in Education*, *20*(1), 44–63. Advance online publication. DOI: 10.1177/14778785221090853

Southworth, J., Migliaccio, K., Glover, J., Reed, D., McCarty, C., Brendemuhl, J., & Thomas, A. (2023). Developing a model for AI Across the curriculum: Transforming the higher education landscape via innovation in AI literacy. *Computers and Education: Artificial Intelligence*, *4*, 100127. DOI: 10.1016/j.caeai.2023.100127

Spector, J. M., & Ma, S. (2019). Inquiry and critical thinking skills for the next generation: From artificial intelligence back to human intelligence. *Smart Learn. Environ.*, *6*(1), 8. DOI: 10.1186/s40561-019-0088-z

Spector, J. M., & Song, D. (1995). Automated instructional design advising. In *Automating instructional design: Computer-based development and delivery tools* (pp. 377–402). Springer Berlin Heidelberg.

Sperling, K., Stenliden, L., Nissen, J., & Heintz, F. (2022). Still w(AI)ting for the automation of teaching: An exploration of machine learning in Swedish primary education using actor-network- theory. *European Journal of Education*, *57*(4), 584–600. DOI: 10.1111/ejed.12526

Sperrle, F., El-Assady, M., Guo, G., Borgo, R., Chau, D. H., Endert, A., & Keim, D. (2021). A Survey of Human-Centered Evaluations in Human-Centered Machine Learning. *Computer Graphics Forum*, *40*(3), 543–568. DOI: 10.1111/cgf.14329

Sri Tulasi, T., & Inayath Ahamed, S. B. (2024). Artificial Intelligence Effects on Student Learning Outcomes in Higher Education. Proceedings of 9th International Conference on Science, Technology, Engineering and Mathematics: The Role of Emerging Technologies in Digital Transformation, ICONSTEM 2024, Suhasini, B., & Santhosh Kumar, N. (2019). Emerging trends and future perspective of human resource reskilling in higher education. International Journal of Recent Technology and Engineering, 8(2 Special Issue 4), 351-353.DOI: 10.35940/ijrte.B1067.0782S419

Stahl, G., Koschmann, T., & Suthers, D. (2006). *Computer-supported collaborative learning: An historical perspective*. Cambridge Handbook of the Learning Sciences.

Stamboliev, E. (2023). Proposing a Postcritical AI Literacy: Why We Should Worry Less about Algorithmic Transparency and More about Citizen Empowerment. Media Theory, 7(1), 202–232. https://hal.science/hal-04221538

Stein, S. J., Goodchild, A., Moskal, A., Terry, S., & McDonald, J. (2021). Student perceptions of student evaluations: Enabling student voice and meaningful engagement. *Assessment & Evaluation in Higher Education, 46*(6), 837–851. DOI: 10.1080/02602938.2020.1824266

Stiles, J., & Jernigan, T. L. (2010). The basics of brain development. *Neuropsychology Review, 20*(4), 327–348. DOI: 10.1007/s11065-010-9148-4 PMID: 21042938

Stokel-Walker, C. (2024). *How AI Ate the World: A Brief History of Artificial Intelligence–and Its Long Future*. Canbury Press.

Strielkowski, W., Grebennikova, V., Lisovskiy, A., Rakhimova, G., & Vasileva, T. (2024). AI-driven adaptive learning for sustainable educational transformation. *Sustainable Development*. Advance online publication. DOI: 10.1002/sd.3221

Su, J., Ng, K., & Kai, S. (2023). Artificial Intelligence (AI) Literacy in Early Childhood Education: The Challenges and Opportunities. *Computers and Education Artificial Intelligence, 4*, 100124–100124. DOI: 10.1016/j.caeai.2023.100124

Sun, Y. M. (2011). Reform of the basic education of OFFICE software in university. 2011 2ndInternational Conference on Artificial Intelligence, Management Science and Electronic Commerce, AIMSEC 2011 - Proceedings C7 - 6009816, Swiontek, F., Lawson-Body, A., & Lawson-Body, L. (2019). The use of machine learning in higher education. *Issues in Information Systems, 20*(2), 56–61. DOI: 10.48009/2_iis_2019_56-61

Sych, T., Khrykov, Y., & Ptakhina, O. (2021). Digital transformation as the main condition for the development of modern higher education. *Educational Technology Quarterly, 2021*(2), 293–309. DOI: 10.55056/etq.27

Taguma, M., Feron, E., & Lim, M. H. (2018). *Future of education and skills 2030: Conceptual learning framework*. Organization of Economic Co-operation and Development.

Tahir, A., & Tahir, A. (2023). AI-driven Advancements in ESL Learner Autonomy: Investigating Student Attitudes Towards Virtual Assistant Usability. *Linguistic Forum -. Journal of Linguistics, 5*(2), 50–56. DOI: 10.5281/zenodo.14776953

Tan, W., & Zhang, J. (2011). Notice of Retraction: A strategic vision on interactive development for higher education under economic integration: Set Chengdu-Chongqing area as an example. 2011 2nd International Conference on Artificial Intelligence, Management Science and Electronic Commerce, AIMSEC 2011 - Proceedings C7 - 6011171, 1857-1860.DOI: 10.1109/AIMSEC.2011.6011171

Tang, T., Sha, J., Zhao, Y., Wang, S., Wang, Z., & Shen, S. (2024). Unveiling the efficacy of ChatGPT in evaluating critical thinking skills through peer feedback analysis: Leveraging existing classification criteria. *Thinking Skills and Creativity*, *53*, 101607. DOI: 10.1016/j.tsc.2024.101607

Targowski, A. (Ed.). (2021). *The Strategies of Informing Technology in the 21st Century*. IGI Global.

Tariq, M. U. (2024). Harnessing Persuasive Technologies for Enhanced Learner Engagement and Motivation. In M. Sanmugam, D. Lim, N. Mohd Barkhaya, W. Wan Yahaya, & Z. Khlaif (Eds.), *Power of Persuasive Educational Technologies in Enhancing Learning* (pp. 30-62). IGI Global. https://doi.org/DOI: 10.4018/979-8-3693-6397-3.ch002

Tariq, M. U. (2024). Enhancing students and learning achievement as 21st-century skills through transdisciplinary approaches. In *Transdisciplinary Approaches to Learning Outcomes in Higher Education* (pp. 220–257). IGI Global., DOI: 10.4018/979-8-3693-3699-1.ch007

Tariq, M. U. (2024). Generative AI in Curriculum Development in Higher Education. In Fields, Z. (Ed.), *Impacts of Generative AI on Creativity in Higher Education* (pp. 227–258). IGI Global., DOI: 10.4018/979-8-3693-2418-9.ch009

Tariq, M. U. (2025). *AI-Driven Learning and Engagement in Higher Education*. IGI Global., DOI: 10.4018/979-8-3693-4074-5

Tariq, M. U., & Sergio, R. P. (2025). Innovative Assessment Techniques in Physical Education: Exploring Technology-Enhanced and Student-Centered Models for Holistic Student Development. In Garcia, M. (Ed.), *Global Innovations in Physical Education and Health* (pp. 85–112). IGI Global., DOI: 10.4018/979-8-3693-3952-7.ch004

Taş, N. (2023). Revolutionizing education: Applications of artificial intelligence. *ISTES Books*, 21–30.

Tatar, D., Roschelle, J., Vahey, P., & Penuel, W. R. (2003). Handhelds go to school: Lessons learned. *Computer*, *36*(9), 30–37. DOI: 10.1109/MC.2003.1231192

TeachHub. (2023, November). *AI-powered lesson planning: Revolutionizing the way teachers create content*. Retrieved from https://www.teachhub.com/teaching-strategies/2023/11/ai-powered-lesson-planning-revolutionizing-the-way-teachers-create-content

Teixeira, R., Nogal, M., & O'Connor, A. (2021). Adaptive approaches in metamodel-based reliability analysis: A review. *Structural Safety*, *89*, 102019. Advance online publication. DOI: 10.1016/j.strusafe.2020.102019

The ALS Association. (n.d.), *Augmented and Alternative Communication.* https://www.als.org/navigating-als/living-with-als/therapies-care/augmentative-alternative-communication

The Teaching Factor. (2024, February 25). *10 ways teachers can use AI tools to support the diverse learners in their classroom. The Teaching Factor*. Retrieved from https://theteachingfactor.wordpress.com/2024/02/25/10-ways-teachers-can-use-ai-tools-to-support-the-diverse-learners-in-their-classroom

Theodorakopoulos, L., Theodoropoulou, A., & Stamatiou, Y. (2024). A state-of-the-art review in big data management engineering: Real-life case studies, challenges, and future research directions. *Eng*.https://doi.org/DOI: 10.3390/eng5030068

Thiga, M. N. (2024). Generative AI and the development of critical thinking. *Iconic Research and Engineering Journals*, *7*(9). https://www.irejournals.com/formatedpaper/1705580.pdf

Thomas, M., & Porayska-Pomsta, K. (2022). *Neurocomputational methods: From models of brain and cognition to artificial intelligence in education.* Cambridge University Press. DOI: 10.1017/9781108399838.037

Thornhill-Miller, B., Camarda, A., Mercier, M., Burkhardt, J. M., Morisseau, T., Bourgeois-Bougrine, S., Vinchon, F., El Hayek, S., Augereau-Landais, M., Mourey, F., Feybesse, C., Sundquist, D., & Lubart, T. (2023). Creativity, critical thinking, communication, and collaboration: Assessment, certification, and promotion of 21st century skills for the future of work and education. *Journal of Intelligence*, *11*(3), 54. DOI: 10.3390/jintelligence11030054 PMID: 36976147

Tong, S., Jia, N., Luo, X., & Fang, Z. (2021). The Janus face of artificial intelligence feedback: Deployment versus disclosure effects on employee performance. *Strategic Management Journal*, *42*(9), 1600–1631. Advance online publication. DOI: 10.1002/smj.3322

Topol, E. J. (2019). High-performance medicine: The convergence of human and artificial intelligence. *Nature Medicine*, *25*(1), 44–56. DOI: 10.1038/s41591-018-0300-7 PMID: 30617339

Tossell, C. C., Tenhundfeld, N. L., Momen, A., Cooley, K., & de Visser, E. J. (2024). Student perceptions of ChatGPT use in a college essay assignment: Implications for learning, grading, and trust in artificial intelligence. *IEEE Transactions on Learning Technologies, 17*, 1069–1081. Advance online publication. DOI: 10.1109/TLT.2024.3355015

Touretzky, D. S. (2017). Computational thinking and mental models: From kodu to calypso.

Touretzky, D., Gardner-McCune, C., Martin, F., & Seehorn, D. (2019, July). Envisioning AI for K-12: What should every child know about AI? *Proceedings of the AAAI Conference on Artificial Intelligence, 33*(01), 9795–9799. DOI: 10.1609/aaai.v33i01.33019795

Tran, M. T. T. (2021). Microsoft Teams in the context of freshmen ELF learning. *AsiaCALL Online Journal, 12*, 12–23.

Tredinnick, L. (2018). Information, communications and overload - Luke Tredinnick, Claire Laybats, 2018. Business Information Review. https://journals.sagepub.com/doi/full/10.1177/0266382118792762

Trenerry, B., Chng, S., Wang, Y., Suhaila, Z. S., Lim, S. S., Lu, H. Y., & Oh, P. H. (2021). Preparing workplaces for digital transformation: An integrative review and framework of multi-level factors. *Frontiers in Psychology, 12*, 620766. DOI: 10.3389/fpsyg.2021.620766 PMID: 33833714

Trilling, B., & Fadel, C. (2009). *21st century skills: Learning for life in our times.* John Wiley & Sons.

Tripathi, S. (2024). Paradigm shift in higher education model by using artificial intelligence: challenges and future perspectives in India and Oman. In Incorporating Ai Technology in the Service Sector: Innovations in Creating Knowledge, Improving Efficiency, and Elevating Quality of Life (pp. 215-238). Apple Academic Press. DOI: 10.1201/9781003378068-10

Tsai, C. L., Ku, H. Y., & Campbell, A. (2021). Impacts of course activities on student perceptions of engagement and learning online. *Distance Education, 42*(1), 106–125. DOI: 10.1080/01587919.2020.1869525

Tso, A. W., & Ho, W. (2020). Creativity and critical thinking in practice. June, 2019â.

Tutors, A. I. (2023). *Modern Education: An Overview*. Education Today.

Tyson, L., & Zysman, J. (2023, February 8). Artificial intelligence and education: A reading list. *JSTOR Daily*. https://daily.jstor.org/artificial-intelligence-and-education-a-reading-list/

U.S. Copyright Office. (2023, March 16). Copyright registration guidance: Works containing material generated by artificial intelligence. *Federal Register*, *88*(51), 16190–16194. https://www.federalregister.gov/documents/2023/03/16/2023-05321/copyright-registration-guidance-works-containing-material-generated-by-artificial-intelligence

UNESCO. (2020). Education in a post-COVID world: Nine ideas for public action. https://unesdoc.unesco.org/ark:/48223/pf0000373717

UNESCO. (2021a). Rewired global declaration on connectivity for education. https://en.unesco.org/news/rewired-global-declaration-connectivity-education

UNESCO. (2021b). UNESCO strategy on technological innovation in education (2022-2025) (Document 212 EX/5.III.A). https://unesdoc.unesco.org/ark:/48223/pf0000378847_fre

Urtasun, A. (2023). Empowering undergraduates through machine learning. *Industry and Higher Education*, *37*(3), 443–447. DOI: 10.1177/09504222221124498

User Local. (n.d.). *AI text mining (AI).* https://auth.userlocal.jp/login?return_url=https%3A%2F%2Ftextmining.userlocal.jp%2F&service=te

Usher, M., & Barak, M. (2024). Ethical AI for teaching and learning. *Journal of Experiential Learning*, *10*(3), 123–142.

Vallis, C., Wilson, S., Gozman, D., & Buchanan, J. (2024). Student perceptions of AI-generated avatars in teaching business ethics: We might not be impressed. *Post-digital Science and Education*, *6*(2), 537–555. DOI: 10.1007/s42438-023-00407-7

Valova, I., Mladenova, T., & Kanev, G. (2024). Students' perception of ChatGPT usage in education. *International Journal of Advanced Computer Science and Applications*, *15*(1), 466–473. DOI: 10.14569/IJACSA.2024.0150143

van Assen, M., Muscogiuri, E., Tessarin, G., & De Cecco, C. N. (2022). Artificial intelligence: A century-old story. In *Artificial Intelligence in Cardiothoracic Imaging* (pp. 3–13). Springer International Publishing., DOI: 10.1007/978-3-030-92087-6_1

van Baalen, S., Boon, M., & Verhoef, P. (2021). From clinical decision support to clinical reasoning support systems. *Journal of Evaluation in Clinical Practice*, *27*(3), 520–528. DOI: 10.1111/jep.13541 PMID: 33554432 van den Berg, G., & du Plessis, E. (2023). ChatGPT and generative AI: Possibilities for its contribution to lesson planning, critical thinking and openness in teacher education. *Education Sciences, 13*(10), 998. Advance online publication. DOI: 10.3390/educsci13100998

Van Dijk, J. A. G. M. (2006). Digital divide research, achievements and shortcomings. *Poetics, 34*(4-5), 221–235. DOI: 10.1016/j.poetic.2006.05.004

Van Le, H., & Chong, S. L. (2024). The dynamics of critical thinking skills: A phenomenographic exploration from Malaysian and Vietnamese undergraduates. *Thinking Skills and Creativity, 51*, 101445. Advance online publication. DOI: 10.1016/j.tsc.2023.101445

VanLehn, K. (2011). The relative effectiveness of human tutoring, intelligent tutoring systems, and other tutoring systems. *Educational Psychologist, 46*(4), 197–221. DOI: 10.1080/00461520.2011.611369

Varona, D., & Suárez, J. L. (2022). Discrimination, bias, fairness, and trustworthy AI. *Applied Sciences (Basel, Switzerland), 12*(12), 5826. Advance online publication. DOI: 10.3390/app12125826

Vashishth, T. K., Sharma, V., Sharma, K. K., Kumar, B., Chaudhary, S., & Panwar, R. (2024). Transforming classroom dynamics: The social impact of AI in teaching and learning. In *AI-Enhanced Teaching Methods* (pp. 322–346). IGI Global. DOI: 10.4018/979-8-3693-2728-9.ch015

Vashishth, T. K., Sharma, V., Sharma, K. K., Kumar, B., Panwar, R., & Chaudhary, S. (2024). AI-driven learning analytics for personalized feedback and assessment in higher education. In *Using traditional design methods to enhance AI-driven decision making* (pp. 206–230). IGI Global., DOI: 10.4018/979-8-3693-0639-0.ch009

Vengathattil, S. (2025). Future-Proofing AI Talent in The United States: The Role of Academia in Meeting Industry Demands. *International Journal of Management Science and Information Technology, 5*(1), 210–217. DOI: 10.35870/ijmsit.v5i1.3837

Verbert, K., Duval, E., Klerkx, J., Govaerts, S., & Santos, J. L. (2013). Learning analytics dashboard applications. *The American Behavioral Scientist, 57*(10), 1500–1509. DOI: 10.1177/0002764213479363

Verbert, K., Govaerts, S., Duval, E., Santos, J. L., Van Assche, F., Parra, G., & Klerkx, J. (2014). Learning dashboards: An overview and future research opportunities. *Personal and Ubiquitous Computing, 18*, 1499–1514.

Verdugo, D., & Alonso Belmonte, I. (2007). Using digital stories to improve listening comprehension with Spanish young learners of English. *Language Learning & Technology, 11*(1), 87–101. 10125/44090

Verma, N., Getenet, S., Dann, C., & Shaik, T. (2023). Designing an artificial intelligence tool to understand student engagement based on teacher's behaviours and movements in video conferencing. *Computers and Education: Artificial Intelligence, 5*, 100187. DOI: 10.1016/j.caeai.2023.100187

Viegas, C. V., Bond, A. J., Vaz, C. R., Borchardt, M., Pereira, G. M., Selig, P. M., & Varvakis, G. (2016). Critical attributes of Sustainability in Higher Education: A categorisation from literature review. *Journal of Cleaner Production, 126*, 260–276. DOI: 10.1016/j.jclepro.2016.02.106

Villar, R. C., Nashwan, A. J., Mathew, R. G., Mohamed, A. S., Munirathinam, S., Abujaber, A. A., Al-Jabry, M. M., & Shraim, M. (2021). The lived experiences of frontline nurses during the coronavirus disease 2019 (COVID-19) pandemic in Qatar: A qualitative study. *Nursing Open, 8*(6), 3516–3526. DOI: 10.1002/nop2.901 PMID: 33949145

Viner, M., Singh, A., & Shaughnessy, M. F. (2020). Assistive technology to help students with disabilities. In Singh, A., Viner, M., & Yeh, C. J. (Eds.), *Special education design and development tools for school rehabilitation professionals* (pp. 240–267). IGI Global Scientific Publishing.

Vinichenko, M. V., Melnichuk, A. V., & Karácsony, P. (2020). Technologies of improving the university efficiency by using artificial intelligence: Motivational aspect. *Entrepreneurship and Sustainability Issues, 7*(4), 2696–2714. DOI: 10.9770/jesi.2020.7.4(9)

Voinea, M., & Pălăşan, T. (2014). Teachers' professional identity in the 21st century Romania. *Procedia: Social and Behavioral Sciences, 128*, 361–365. DOI: 10.1016/j.sbspro.2014.03.172

Vosoughi, S., Roy, D., & Aral, S. (2018). The spread of true and false news online. *Science, 359*(6380), 1146–1151. DOI: 10.1126/science.aap9559 PMID: 29590045

Wade, C. (1995). Using writing to develop and assess critical thinking. *Teaching of Psychology, 22*(1), 24–28. DOI: 10.1207/s15328023top2201_8

Wadhwa, R., Rabby, F., Bansal, R., & Hundekari, S. (2024). Drivers and impact of artificial intelligence on student engagement. In *AI Algorithms and ChatGPT for Student Engagement in Online Learning* (pp. 161–170). IGI Global. DOI: 10.4018/979-8-3693-4268-8.ch011

Walczak, K., & Cellary, W. (2023). Challenges for higher education in the era of widespread access to Generative AI. *Economics and Business Review, 9*(2), 71–100. DOI: 10.18559/ebr.2023.2.743

Walker, T. (2023, February 3). Cellphone bans in school are back. How far will they go? NEA Today. https://www.nea.org/nea-today/all-news-articles/cellphone-bans-school-are-back-how-far-will-they-go

Walter, Y. (2024). Embracing the future of Artificial Intelligence in the classroom: The relevance of AI literacy, prompt engineering, and critical thinking in modern education. *International Journal of Educational Technology in Higher Education, 21*(1), 15. Advance online publication. DOI: 10.1186/s41239-024-00448-3

Wang, H. C., & Wang, F. (2010). Development of an interactive multimedia E-learning environment based on wireless PDA. Proceedings of the International Conference on E-Business and E-Government, ICEE 2010 C7 - 5592284, Wang, J. Q. (2011). Notice of Retraction: Evaluation and analysis on adverse effects of the mass higher education in China. 2011 2nd International Conference on Artificial Intelligence, Management Science and Electronic Commerce, AIMSEC 2011 - Proceedings C7 - 6009823,5557-5560. DOI: 10.1109/AIMSEC.2011.6009823

Wang, T. & Cheng, E. C. K. (2021). An investigation of barriers to Hong Kong K-12 schools incorporating Artificial Intelligence in education. *Computers and Education: Artificial Intelligence*. https://doi.org/.DOI: 10.1016/j.caeai.2021.100031

Wang, F. H. (2017). An exploration of online behaviour engagement and achievement in flipped classroom supported by learning management system. *Computers & Education, 114*, 79–91. DOI: 10.1016/j.compedu.2017.06.012

Wang, S., Gorbunova, N. V., Masalimova, A. R., Bírová, J., & Sergeeva, M. G. (2017). Formation of academic mobility of future foreign language teachers by means of media education technologies. *Eurasia Journal of Mathematics, Science and Technology Education, 14*(3), 959–976.

Warnick, B. (2002). *Critical literacy in a digital era: Technology, rhetoric, and the public interest*. Erlbaum Associates.

Warwick, K., & Shah, H. (2016). Can machines think? A report on Turing test experiments at the Royal Society. *Journal of Experimental & Theoretical Artificial Intelligence, 28*(6), 989–1007. DOI: 10.1080/0952813X.2015.1055826

Watters, A. (2021). *Teaching machines: The history of personalized learning*. MIT Press. DOI: 10.7551/mitpress/12262.001.0001

Weiser, S. (2019, April 8). Requirements of Trustworthy AI - FUTURIUM - European Commission. FUTURIUM - European Commission.

Wendt, O. (Ed.). (2011). *Assistive Technology: Principles and Applications for Communication Disorders and Special Education.* Brill.

Williamson, B. (2017). Big data in education: The digital future of learning, policy, and practice. *Sage (Atlanta, Ga.).* Advance online publication. DOI: 10.4135/9781529714920

Williamson, B., & Eynon, R. (2020). Historical threads, missing links, and future directions in AI in education. *Learning, Media and Technology*, *45*(3), 223–235. DOI: 10.1080/17439884.2020.1798995

Willingham, D. T. (2019). How to teach critical thinking. Occasional Paper Series. http://www.danielwillingham.com/uploads/5/0/0/7/5007325/willingham_2019_nsw_critical_thinking2.pdf

Wilson, L. O. (2016). Anderson and Krathwohl Bloom's taxonomy revised understanding the new version of Bloom's taxonomy. *The Second Principle*, *1*(1), 1–8.

Winstone, N., & Boud, D. (2019). Exploring cultures of feedback practice: The adoption of learning-focused feedback practices in the UK and Australia. *Higher Education Research & Development*, *38*(2), 411–425. DOI: 10.1080/07294360.2018.1532985

Wiryawan, D., Ramadhan, W., Krisnata, F., & Dhiya'Ulhaq, F. (2024). Data Security Framework with Cognitive Theory on Higher Education. 2024 ASU International Conference in Emerging Technologies for Sustainability and Intelligent Systems, ICETSIS 2024, Xia, C. (2011). Notice of Retraction: Study on management methods of college English course grade evaluation. 2011 2nd International Conference on Artificial Intelligence, Management Science and Electronic Commerce, AIMSEC 2011 - Proceedings C7 - 6010493, 4792-4795. DOI: 10.1109/AIMSEC.2011.6010493

Witti, M. J., Zottmann, J. M., Wershofen, B., Thistlethwaite, J. E., Fischer, F., & Fischer, M. R. (2023). FINCA–a conceptual framework to improve interprofessional collaboration in health education and care. *Frontiers in Medicine*, *10*, 1213300. DOI: 10.3389/fmed.2023.1213300 PMID: 37849484

Woldt, J. L., & Nenad, M. W. (2021). Reflective writing in dental education to improve critical thinking and learning: A systematic review. *Journal of Dental Education*, *85*(6), 778–785. Advance online publication. DOI: 10.1002/jdd.12561 PMID: 33576055

Wood, D., & Moss, S. H. (2024). Evaluating the impact of students' generative AI use in educational contexts. *Journal of Research in Innovative Teaching & Learning*. https://www.emerald.com/insight/2397-7604.htm

Wu, X., Zhang, Y., Li, H., & Chen, J. (2024). *Artificial intelligence in personalized learning: A review of smart education systems*. Retrieved from https://arxiv.org/abs/2402.01666

Wu, Y., & Koutstaal, W. (2020). Charting the contributions of cognitive flexibility to creativity: Self-guided transitions as a process-based index of creativity-related adaptivity. *PLoS One*, *15*(6), e0234473. DOI: 10.1371/journal.pone.0234473 PMID: 32525947

Xia, Q., Chiu, T. K. F., Chai, C. S., & Xie, K. (2023). The mediating effects of needs satisfaction on the relationships between prior knowledge and self-regulated learning through artificial intelligence chatbot. *British Journal of Educational Technology*, *54*(4), 967–986. DOI: 10.1111/bjet.13305

Xu, E., Wang, W., & Wang, Q. (2023). The effectiveness of collaborative problem-solving in promoting students' critical thinking: A meta-analysis based on empirical literature. *Humanities & Social Sciences Communications*, *10*(1), 16. DOI: 10.1057/s41599-023-01508-1 PMID: 37192950

Xu, W., Dainoff, M. J., Ge, L., & Gao, Z. (2022). Transitioning to Human Interaction with AI Systems: New Challenges and Opportunities for HCI Professionals to Enable Human-Centered AI. *International Journal of Human-Computer Interaction*, *39*(3), 494–518. DOI: 10.1080/10447318.2022.2041900

Xu, Z. (2024). AI in education: Enhancing learning experiences and student outcomes. *Applied Computing Engineering*, *51*(1), 104–111. DOI: 10.54254/2755-2721/51/20241187

Yafie, E., Abu Samah, N., Mohamed, H., & Haqqi, Y. A. (2020). Collaborative Mobile Seamless Learning (CMSL) based on Android Apps to Improving Critical Thinking in Higher Education in the Post-Covid-19 Era. *Journal of Advanced Research in Dynamical and Control Systems*, *12*(SP7), 428–441. Advance online publication. DOI: 10.5373/JARDCS/V12SP7/20202125

Yang, C., & Stivers, A. (2024). Investigating AI languages' ability to solve undergraduate finance problems. *Journal of Education for Business*, *99*(1), 44–51. DOI: 10.1080/08832323.2023.2253963

Yang, Q., Jin, W., Zhang, Q., Wei, Y., Guo, Z., Li, X., Yang, Y., Luo, Q., Tian, H., & Ren, T.-L. (2023). Mixed-modality speech recognition and interaction using a wearable artificial throat. *Nature Machine Intelligence*, *5*(2), 169–180. DOI: 10.1038/s42256-023-00616-6

Yang, X., Wang, Q., & Lyu, J. (2024). Assessing ChatGPT's educational capabilities and application potential. *ECNU Review of Education*, *7*(3). Advance online publication. DOI: 10.1177/20965311231210006

Yannier, N., Hudson, S. E., & Koedinger, K. R. (2020). Active learning is about more than hands-on: A mixed-reality AI system to support STEM education. *International Journal of Artificial Intelligence in Education*, *30*(1), 74–96. DOI: 10.1007/s40593-020-00194-3

Yee, K., Johnson, A., & Thompson, R. (2024). AI hacks for educators: Practical tools to enhance teaching and learning efficiency. *Journal of Educational Technology Innovation*, *15*(2), 89–105. DOI: 10.1234/jeti.2024.567

Ye, Q. (2023). Comparison of the transparency of fact-checking: A global perspective. *Journalism Practice*, *17*(10), 2263–2282. Advance online publication. DOI: 10.1080/17512786.2023.2211555

Yilmaz, F. G. K., & Keser, H. (2016). The impact of reflective thinking activities in e-learning: A critical review of the empirical research. *Computers & Education*, *95*, 163–173. DOI: 10.1016/j.compedu.2016.01.006

Yi, Y. (2021). Establishing the concept of AI literacy. *JAHR*, *12*(2), 353–368. DOI: 10.21860/j.12.2.8

Yuan, C., Pang, J., & Zheng, C. (2011). Notice of Retraction: The study of the governance mechanisms of higher education quality based on the educational purposes. 2011 2ndInternational Conference on Artificial Intelligence, Management Science and Electronic Commerce, AIMSEC 2011 - Proceedings C7 - 6009715, 6017-6020. DOI: 10.1109/AIMSEC.2011.6009715

Yu, H. (2024). The application and challenges of ChatGPT in educational transformation: New demands for teachers' roles. *Heliyon*, *10*(2), e24289. Advance online publication. DOI: 10.1016/j.heliyon.2024.e24289 PMID: 38298626

Yunusaliyev, M., Yuldashev, I., & Yusupov, A. (2024, May). Revolutionizing the present education system through AI-driven learning platform with hybrid techniques. In *2024 4th International Conference on Advance Computing and Innovative Technologies in Engineering (ICACITE)* (pp. 523–527). IEEE. DOI: 10.1109/ICACITE60783.2024.10616605

Yusof, M. H. M., & Khalid, I. A. (2021). Precision education reviews: a case study on predicting student's performance using feed forward neural network. 2021 International Conferenceof Technology, Science and Administration, ICTSA 2021 C7 - 9406525, Závadský, J., Závadská, Z., & Osvaldová, Z. (2024). Differences in ai utilization between students and teachers in higher education institution: an empirical study. IDIMT 2024: Changes to ICT, Management, and Business Processes through AI - 32ndInterdisciplinary Information Management Talks.

Yusuf, A., Bello, S., Pervin, N., & Tukur, A. K. (2024). Implementing a proposed framework for enhancing critical thinking skills in synthesizing AI-generated texts. *Thinking Skills and Creativity*, *53*, 101619. Advance online publication. DOI: 10.1016/j.tsc.2024.101619

Zamiri, M., & Esmaeili, A. (2024). Strategies, methods, and supports for developing skills within learning communities: A systematic review of the literature. *Administrative Sciences*, *14*(9), 231. Advance online publication. DOI: 10.3390/admsci14090231

Zarei, E., Yazdi, M., Moradi, R., & BahooToroody, A. (2024). Expert judgment and uncertainty in sociotechnical systems analysis. In Safety causation analysis in sociotechnical systems: advanced models and techniques (pp. 487-530). Cham: Springer Nature Switzerland.

Zawacki-Richter, O., Marín, V. I., Bond, M., & Gouverneur, F. (2019). Systematic review of research on artificial intelligence applications in higher education –Where are the educators? *International Journal of Educational Technology in Higher Education*, *16*(1), 39. DOI: 10.1186/s41239-019-0171-0

Zhai, C., Wibowo, S., & Li, L. D. (2024). *The effects of over-reliance on AI dialogue systems on students' cognitive abilities: a systematic review*. Smart Learning Environments., DOI: 10.1186/s40561-024-00316-7

Zhai, X., Chu, X., Chai, C. S., Jong, M. S. Y., Istenic, A., Spector, M., Liu, J.-B., Yuan, J., & Li, Y. (2021). A Review of Artificial Intelligence (AI) in Education from 2010 to 2020. *Complexity*, *2021*(1), 8812542. DOI: 10.1155/2021/8812542

Zhai, X., Li, M., & Chen, X. (2021). Automated essay scoring with content-based relevance feedback. *British Journal of Educational Technology*, *52*(3), 1103–1118. DOI: 10.1111/bjet.13078

Zhai, X., & Panjwani-Charania, S. (2023). AI for Students with Learning Disabilities. *Systematic Reviews*.

Zhai, X., Zhang, M., Li, M., & Zhang, X. (2019). Understanding the relationship between levels of mobile technology use in high school physics classrooms and the learning outcome. British Journal of Educational Technology. *Journal of the Council for Educational Technology*, *50*(2), 750–766.

Zhang, H., Xie, J., Wu, C., Cai, J., Kim, C., & Carroll, J. M. (2024). The future of learning: Large language models through the lens of students. *arXiv*. https://doi.org//arXiv.2407.12723DOI: 10.1145/3686852.3687069

Zhang, L., Ma, Z., Ji, X., & Wang, C. (2020). Blockchain: Application in the System of Teaching Informatization Management of Higher Education. Proceedings - 2020 3rd InternationalConference on Smart BlockChain, SmartBlock 2020 C7 - 9415687, Zhao, J. Y., & Ma, X. H. (2011). New era school status management analysis. 2011 2ndInternational Conference on Artificial Intelligence, Management Science and Electronic Commerce, AIMSEC 2011 - Proceedings C7 - 6011025, Zhu, C. Z. G., Hall, C. M., Fong, L. H. N., Lin, F., & Naderi Koupaei, S. (2024). Examining the effects of ChatGPT on tourism and hospitality student responses through integrating technology acceptance model. International Journal of Tourism Research, 26(4 C7 -e2727). DOI: 10.1002/jtr.2727

Zhang, X., & Wang, L. (2024). Supporting learning with AI-generated images: A research-backed guide. *Journal of Educational Technology*, *32*(4), 256–271. https://link.springer.com/article/10.1007/s10956-024-10159-z

Zhao, A. P., Li, S., Cao, Z., Hu, P. J. H., Wang, J., Xiang, Y., Xie, D., & Lu, X. (2024). AI for science: Predicting infectious diseases. *Journal of Safety Science and Resilience = An Quan Ke Xue Yu Ren Xing (Ying Wen)*, *5*(2), 130–146. Advance online publication. DOI: 10.1016/j.jnlssr.2024.02.002

Zhao, H., Li, G., & Feng, W. (2018). *Research on application of artificial intelligence in medical education. In 2018 international conference on engineering simulation and intelligent control (ESAIC)*. IEEE.

Zhao, Y., Yin, J., Zhang, J., & Wu, L. (2023). Identifying the driving factors of word co-occurrence: A perspective of semantic relations. *Scientometrics*, *128*(12), 6471–6494. DOI: 10.1007/s11192-023-04851-x

Zharmukhanbetov, S., & Singh, C. P. (2023, November). Enhancing flipped classroom engagement and personalized learning through AI-powered adaptive content delivery. In *2023 3rd International Conference on Technological Advancements in Computational Sciences (ICTACS)* (pp. 1411–1416). IEEE. DOI: 10.1109/ICTACS59847.2023.10389841

Zhou, Z., & Yu, G. (2020). The impact of MOOCs on teacher education: An exploratory study on their integration into teacher education programs. *Journal of Educational Technology & Society*, *23*(1), 133–145.

Zhu, L. (2011). Notice of Retraction: Reflections on the education reforms for newly established local undergraduate colleges. 2011 2nd International Conference on Artificial Intelligence, Management Science and Electronic Commerce, AIMSEC 2011 - Proceedings C7 - 6010705,1340-1342. DOI: 10.1109/AIMSEC.2011.6010705

Ziervogel, G., Enqvist, J., Metelerkamp, L., & van Breda, J. (2022). Supporting transformative climate adaptation: Community-level capacity building and knowledge co-creation in South Africa. *Climate Policy*, *22*(5), 607–622. DOI: 10.1080/14693062.2020.1863180

Zou, D., Xie, H., & Wang, F. L. (2022). Effects of technology enhanced peer, teacher and self-feedback on students' collaborative writing, critical thinking tendency and engagement in learning. *Journal of Computing in Higher Education*, *35*(1), 166–185. DOI: 10.1007/s12528-022-09337-y

About the Contributors

Michael W. Kessinger is an Associate Professor in Education Leadership at Morehead State University. He is the program leader for K-12 Administration and Leadership. Dr. Kessinger is a retired P-12 educator where he was a high school math and computer science teacher, Assistant Principal. He later moved to the central office where he held various administrative positions such as District Technology Coordinator, Assessment Coordinator, Professional Development Coordinator, School Food Service Director, Director of Finance, and Assistant Superintendent. He earned his Doctor of Education in Administration and Supervision from the University of Kentucky; Education Specialist and Master in Secondary Education from Morehead State University (KY); and the Bachelors of Science from the University of Wisconsin - Eau Claire in Mathematics and Psychology. Dr. Kessinger has authored and coauthored several chapters in books related to school safety, instructional leadership, special and gifted education, technology, and school administration.

Gera Nelson is an assistant professor at Morehead State University, where she teaches graduate and undergraduate literacy classes, in addition to coordinating the Study Abroad Programs to Brazil and Ireland. Additionally, Dr. Nelson has taught P-12 education for over 20 years in Georgia and Kentucky. She has earned a Doctoral Degree in Curriculum and instruction - Literacy (Georgia Southern University), a master's in Middle School Education (Georgia Southwestern State University), and a bachelor's degree in journalism (FAFI -BH University in Brazil).

Lesia Lennex is a Professor of Education at Morehead State University in the Department of Middle Grades and Secondary Education. She teaches P-12 curriculum and instruction, and edtech. Her research areas include P16 3D technologies, technology issues and integration for P16 schools, biology and social studies curriculum, and ethnobotany. Dr. Lennex was awarded both MSU's Distinguished Researcher and an Adron Doran Fellowship. Lennex is professionally committed to scholarly productions and leadership with the Society for Information Technology and Teacher Education (SITE). She has served as Chair of the special interest groups (SIG) Social Studies Education, Science Education, and Information Technology Education. Lennex is a Master Reviewer for Quality Matters P-12, higher education, and continuing professional education courses. Dr. Lennex took her Doctorate in Curriculum and Instruction, Social Studies education, with supporting areas in botany and American history from the University of Tennessee, Knoxville. She also holds a BA in Anthropology (minor Zooarchaeology) and MS in Curriculum and Instruction, Social Studies education (minor Historical Archaeology).

Kimberely Fletcher Nettleton earned a doctorate in education in curriculum and instruction from the University of Kentucky. She is currently an Associate Professor in the College of Education and the Director of University Assessment at Morehead State University. She has mentored over 76 students in action research, reviewed and edited several articles and programs, and has presented at numerous conferences.

***

Andi Asrifan is an accomplished educator and academic leader with a Doctorate in Education, specializing in English Language Education from Universitas Negeri Makassar. With a strong academic foundation, he holds a Master's degree in the same field and a Bachelor's degree in Secondary Education. His dissertation focused on developing bilingual educational materials, reflecting his commitment to enhancing language education. Dr. Asrifan has extensive experience in various educational roles, including serving as the Head of the International Affairs Office at Politeknik Negeri Nunukan and as the Head of the Institute for Student Development and Alumni at Universitas Muhammadiyah Sidenreng Rappang. He is also an active member of several professional organizations, including the Linguistics Society of Indonesia and TEFLIN. In addition to his administrative roles, Dr. Asrifan is a passionate advocate for educational innovation and has participated in numerous international conferences and webinars, sharing his insights on language teaching and curriculum development. His dedication to professional development is evident through his participation in various training programs.

Arif Budiman, S.S., M.A., is a dedicated lecturer in English Literature at the Faculty of Adab and Cultural Sciences, UIN Sunan Kalijaga, Yogyakarta. He holds a Bachelor's degree in English Literature from Universitas Sebelas Maret (UNS), followed by a Master's and Doctorate in Linguistics from Gadjah Mada University (UGM). His doctoral dissertation focused on the grammatical and semantic analysis of cleft sentences in the Indonesian translation of the Qur'an, showcasing his expertise in linguistics and translation studies. Dr. Budiman has contributed significantly to academic discourse, with several published works in various journals. His research interests include linguistic politeness in multicultural preaching, linguistic landscapes, and anthropological linguistics. Notable publications include "A Linguistic Landscape in a Thailand Chinatown Area" and "Metaphor Play between Jokowi and Prabowo in the Last Battle," reflecting his engagement with contemporary linguistic issues in Indonesia. Dr. Budiman aims to bridge the gap between linguistics and cultural studies through his teaching and research, fostering a deeper understanding of language in its social context. His commitment to education and research continues to inspire students and colleagues alike in linguistics and translation.

Ratu Bulkis Ramli, M.Pd, serves as a lecturer in Indonesian Language and Literature Education at Musamus University in Merauke. Her academic journey includes obtaining a Bachelor's degree from Universitas Cokroaminoto Palopo and a Master's degree from Universitas Negeri Makassar. Ratu's scholarly pursuits are deeply rooted in the fields of education, language, culture, and literature, reflecting her commitment to advancing knowledge and fostering critical thinking among students. Her research contributions are notable, encompassing various contemporary issues in education, such as digital literacy and the integration of cultural elements in teaching. Ratu has been involved in significant research projects, including the analysis of language crime practices and the implementation of innovative teaching methodologies like Project Based Learning (PJBL). Her works aim to enhance students' 21st-century skills and promote a multidisciplinary approach to learning. In addition to her academic responsibilities, Ratu is an accomplished writer, with a portfolio that includes poetry and short stories, as well as educational literature. Her publications, such as "Guru Penggerak di Indonesia" and "Profesi Keguruan: Menjadi Guru Transformatif di Era Merdeka Belajar," showcase her dedication to addressing educational challenges and advocating for transformative teaching practices. Ratu's leadership skills and passion for literature further contribute to her role as an influential educator in the region.

Casey Cosgriff, Ph.D. is an Assistant Professor teaching special education in the Teacher Education Program in the Volgenau College of Education. He has eight years of experience as a middle school special educator, focusing on students with autism, and twelve years in higher education. His research and teaching interests span communication, collaboration, assistive technologies, including GenAI, assessment, postsecondary transition, self-determination, and advocacy for individuals with disabilities

Shigeru Ikuta is now a Senior Chief Researcher at Institute of Human Culture Studies, Otsuma Women's University, Japan. He is an education technologist, teacher educator in Science, and special educator with a focus on student learning and development on the basis of communication aids. He completed his graduate work and earned a doctorate in science at Tohoku University in Sendai, Japan. He had been working as a Professor of Computation Chemistry at Tokyo Metropolitan University for twenty-nine years. He moved to University of Tsukuba and has started collaborative works with schoolteachers, affiliated with the University. He has been conducting many school activities in cooperation with the schoolteachers all over the world for more than 19 years using original handmade teaching materials with dot codes, eBooks with Media Overlays, and Augmented Reality in supporting the students' learning both at the special needs and general public schools. He is honored to be an Emeritus Professor of Otsuma Women's University and Tokyo Metropolitan University.

Purwani Indri Astuti, S.S., M.Hum., is a prominent academic figure serving as a Senior Lecturer (Lektor Kepala) at Univet Bantara Sukoharjo. Born on January 17, 1969, in Surakarta, she completed her Bachelor's degree in English Literature from Universitas Sebelas Maret (UNS) in 1993 and subsequently obtained her Master's degree in Translation Linguistics from the same institution in 2008. Currently, she is pursuing her Doctorate, having commenced her studies in 2019. Her extensive teaching career began with tutoring positions at LPIA and LTI in Surakarta, before she joined Univet Bantara in 1995. Purwani has a strong research background, having received competitive research grants from DP2M Ditjen Dikti in 2011 and 2013, alongside participating in various internal research initiatives. In addition to her academic responsibilities, she has engaged in community service projects, securing funding for outreach activities in 2013. Purwani has also enhanced her professional development through various training sessions, including research reviewing and academic assessment. Her commitment to education and research significantly contributes to her students' learning experiences and the academic community at large.

Mehdi Kaddouri is a professor at Mohammed First University, Morocco, specializing in educational technology and digital learning. He earned his PhD from Paul Valéry University of Montpellier (France). Currently, he serves as the Director of the CEDUC-URL-CNRST-19 Laboratory and heads the E-learning Center at Mohammed First University. His research focuses on the integration of technology in education, digital practices in learning environments, and educational semiotics. Through his academic work, Dr. Kaddouri examines educational technology implementation, digital learning processes, and semiotic approaches in education, contributing to the understanding of digital transformation in educational settings and its impact on teaching and learning practices in higher education.

Fehmina Khalique, Professor OB & HR, Lloyd Business School, Greater Noida, is a Ph.D. and MBA in human resource management and also Editor for Lloyd Business Review Journal. She is associated with academics for the past 17 years with 4 years of industry experience and enjoys being a corporate trainer, counsellor, and consultant. Her research interest lies in cross-cultural management, international management, human resource management, and human capital management. She has several high-quality research papers to her credit and has co-authored a book with a reputed publisher. In her free time, she likes to do some social work and deliver free career counselling sessions for students.

Mohd. Azmi Khan is a Faculty in the Department of Business Administration, Aligarh Muslim University, Aligarh. He has more than 5 years of teaching experience and holds a Ph.D. in Business Administration from Aligarh Muslim University. Dr. Khan has qualified Junior Research Fellow (JRF) entrance exam in Management and National Eligibility Test (NET) in Commerce conducted by University Grants Commission. He has more than four years of teaching experience in the field of Management. Throughout his career, he has published various research papers, book chapters and research articles in Scopus indexed, UGC care listed and peer reviewed journals.

Nusrat Khan is an expert in the area of HR and OB. She has worked with national and International NGOs. She also worked as a researcher for projects with an internationally recognized Distinguished Professor of Western Kentucky University, Kentucky, USA. She has also worked for the corporates both nationally and internationally. She has taught in several well-known universities. While working in these universities she had held several administrative duties as well. She is presently working as a Professor at GD Goenka University in the School of Management. At GD Goenka University she has also been serving as Head Post Graduate Programmes, MBA Admission head, HR Area Head, Teaching various management subjects, also served as a class teacher, handling mentees, had been a member of the Internal Quality Assurance Cell (IQAC) as prescribed by National Assessment and Accreditation Council (NAAC), Member of the Departmental Research Committee for Doctor of Philosophy (Ph.D.) program of G.D. Goenka University, Member of the Examination Moderation Committee, served as an Associate editor of GD Goenka Journal. She is also a Mendeley Advisor from Mendeley (Elsevier UK).

Khristianto is a senior lecturer at the Faculty of Cultural Sciences and Communication, Universitas Muhammadiyah Purwokerto. He completed his undergraduate studies in English Literature at Universitas Sebelas Maret (UNS) Surakarta, Indonesia and earned his master's degree in Applied Linguistics from Universitas Negeri Yogyakarta (UNY), Yogyakarta, Indonesia. He has a wealth of experience in both research and teaching. His research interests include gender ideology in women's writings, discourse analysis on multimodalities, and Javanese grammar. He has led numerous studies, such as analyzing gender ideology in online media and examining the concept of animacy in the Javanese language. He has also published extensively in national and international journals, with works focusing on topics such as cultural translation, multimodal meanings, and political discourse analysis. In addition to research, Khristianto has been actively involved in community service, focusing on language education for teachers. His dedication to both academia and community service has contributed significantly to advancing linguistic studies and education in Indonesia. His most recent publications explore contemporary issues in discourse, including modality in social media and linguistic landscapes in urban settings.

Khalid Mhamdi is a researcher at Mohammed Premier University (Oujda, Morocco) specializing in Communication and Educational Technologies. His research focuses on e-learning implementation, learner autonomy, and AI in education. He has published on organizational practices during COVID-19 online learning, quality management in higher education, and language learning platforms. Currently teaches graduate courses in knowledge management and e-learning while leading workshops on educational innovation.

David Lynn Painter (Ph.D., University of Florida) is an Associate Professor of Communication at Rollins College. David has authored more than 30 publications in scholarly volumes and more than 45 papers competitively that were selected for presentation at national and international conferences. David's research focuses on the representation of minorities in the media, political communication, and social media marketing while his teaching interests center on experiential service-learning and other high impact practices.

Daryl R. Privott, Ph.D. is an Associate Professor in the Adult & Higher Education Program in the Volgenau College of Education. Dr. Privott is a first-generation college graduate and his research interests are higher education leadership/ administration, higher education law, higher education facilities management, first-generation college students/graduates, Generative Artificial Intelligence (GenAI)

LLM's, adult education, teaching & learning, inclusion, equity and diversity (IED) and ethics.

Nasir Rasheed is a dedicated research scholar in the Department of Education at the University of Kashmir, pursuing a Ph.D. with a focus on Educational Technology. A Gold Medalist with a B.Ed. and M.Ed. from the University of Kashmir, he also holds an M.A. in Sociology and an M.Sc. in Environmental Science from IGNOU. Nasir has qualified CTET and UGC NET multiple times, authored eight research papers and two book chapters and serves as a reviewer for journals, including IGI Global. He has taught at Kendriya Vidyalaya and in SED JK. Reach him at na sirrasheededucation@gmail.com & nasir.edscholar@kashmiruniversity.net

Riyanti, S.E., M.Ak is a dedicated lecturer at Universitas Muhammadiyah Palopo, specializing in Accounting. She holds a Bachelor's degree in Accounting from STIE Muhammadiyah Palopo and a Master's degree in Accounting from Universitas Hasanuddin. With expertise in computer accounting, financial reporting, and project management, she has a strong foundation in the field's academic and practical aspects. In addition to her teaching responsibilities, Riyanti has contributed to academic research, particularly in the area of financial accounting. She has published the book Akuntansi Keuangan Syariah: Relevansi Standar Akuntansi Syariah Dalam Menjalankan Bisnis Syariah, reflecting her commitment to advancing knowledge in Islamic accounting standards. Her research is indexed in SINTA and Google Scholar, showcasing her active engagement in scholarly activities. Previously, she worked as an accounting tutor at Shifu Accounting, where she honed her skills in teaching and mentoring students. She is proficient in Indonesian and English, enabling her to engage with a diverse academic audience. Passionate about education and financial accounting, Riyanti continues to explore innovative approaches in accounting education and research.

Albérico Travassos Rosário, Ph.D. Marketing and Strategy of the Universities of Aveiro (UA), Minho (UM) and Beira Interior (UBI). With affiliation to the GOVCOPP research center of the University of Aveiro. Master in Marketing and Degree in Marketing, Advertising and Public Relations, degree from ISLA Campus Lisbon-European University I Laureate International Universities. Has the title of Marketing Specialist and teaches with the category of Assistant Professor at IADE-Faculty of Design, Technology and Communication of the European University and as a visiting Associate Professor at the Santarém Higher School of Management and Technology (ESGTS) of the Polytechnic Institute of Santarém. He taught at IPAM-School of Marketing I Laureate International Universities, ISLA- Higher Institute of Management and Administration of Santarém (ISLA-Santarém), was Director of the Commercial Management Course, Director of the Professional Technical Course (TeSP) of Sales and Commercial Management, Chairman of the Pedagogical Council and Member of the Technical Council and ISLA-Santarém Scientific Researcher. He is also a marketing and strategy consultant for SMEs.

Ahmad Rossydi is an associate professor and lecturer at Politeknik Penerbangan Makassar. He earned his bachelor's degree in English language teaching from the University of Pancasakti Tegal and completed his master's and doctoral degrees in English language teaching from the Postgraduate Program of Universitas Negeri Makassar, Indonesia. His research interests encompass a wide range of topics, including language teacher cognition, learning strategies, technology-based learning approaches, curriculum and materials development, and teacher professional development. With a passion for advancing educational practices, Ahmad has contributed significantly to the academic community through his innovative research and dedication to improving teaching methodologies. His work aims to bridge the gap between theoretical knowledge and practical application, ensuring that educators are well-equipped to meet the evolving demands of modern education.

Kartikay Saini, an ex Naval Commander of the Indian Navy, is the Chairman of Scottish High International School, India. He is the former Chairman of Special Olympics of India and Board Member of Special Olympics Worldwide, Washington. With more than 36 years of experience in the Corporate, Defence and the Education world, Cdr Saini had been recognised worldwide and felicitated at House of Commons London, the President of Mauritius,, the Govt of Sri Lanka, the Presient of Dominican Republic, Education world, Forbes Magazine among others.Presently he is a research scholar at GD Goenka University.

Sultan Se. M. Ak is a dedicated academic and researcher in the field of accounting, currently serving as a lecturer. With expertise in financial management, taxation, and risk management, he has contributed extensively to the academic landscape through publications in books and journals. His research covers diverse topics, including tax compliance, financial literacy, fraud prevention, corporate social responsibility, and the economic impact of government expenditures. Sultan has authored books such as Praktikum Akuntansi (2020) and Dasar Dasa Perpajakan (2025), alongside numerous journal articles that address contemporary challenges in accounting and finance. His recent works explore themes like financial behavior among millennials, tax knowledge's impact on compliance, and accounting students' readiness for Society 5.0. Committed to enhancing financial literacy and ethical financial practices, Sultan actively engages in research on economic growth, capital expenditures, and the role of Islamic banking in corporate social responsibility.

His scholarly contributions aim to bridge the gap between theory and real-world financial management challenges. Based in Palopo, Indonesia, Sultan is passionate about education, academic integrity, and the evolution of accounting practices in a digitalized world. He continues to shape the future of financial research through his impactful studies and teaching endeavors.

Muhammad Usman Tariq has more than 16+ year's experience in industry and academia. He has authored more than 200+ research articles, 110+ case studies, 115+ book chapters and several books other than 4 patents. He is founder and CEO of The Case HQ, a unique repository for courses, narrative and video case studies. He has been working as a consultant and trainer for industries representing six sigma, quality, health and safety, environmental systems, project management, and information security standards. His work has encompassed sectors in aviation, manufacturing, food, hospitality, education, finance, research, software and transportation. He has diverse and significant experience working with accreditation agencies of ABET, ACBSP, AACSB, WASC, CAA, EFQM and NCEAC. Additionally, Dr. Tariq has operational experience in incubators, research labs, government research projects, private sector startups, program creation and management at various industrial and academic levels. He is Certified Higher Education Teacher from Harvard University, USA, Certified Online Educator from HMBSU, Certified Six Sigma Master Black Belt and has been awarded PFHEA, SFSEDA, SMIEEE, and CMBE.

Agnes Widyaningrum is an accomplished English lecturer with over 20 years of experience in private higher education. She holds a Ph.D. in English education from Universitas Negeri Semarang (UNNES), where she specialized in the cognitive task-based approach for teaching young learners. Her academic journey also includes a focus on English skills during her postgraduate studies. Throughout her career, Agnes has been deeply committed to enhancing students' literacy and language skills through innovative, technology-driven teaching methods. She has actively participated in curriculum development and academic research, contributing to effective communication strategies for business purposes and cross-cultural integration in education. Agnes has held significant leadership roles, including Dean of the Faculty of Law and Language and Head of the English Literature Department at UNISBANK. During her tenure, she successfully implemented government-aligned changes in student outcomes and received a grant for her "OBE-Based Curriculum" initiative in 2020. Her dedication to education and research continues to shape the future of English language teaching in Indonesia.

Index

Symbols

21st Century Skills 27, 374, 440, 446, 477

A

Accessibility 7, 10, 18, 20, 21, 22, 23, 38, 122, 135, 136, 151, 158, 160, 216, 218, 246, 267, 271, 277, 286, 289, 290, 359, 418, 421, 466
Active Learning 49, 65, 82, 84, 85, 87, 93, 97, 438
Adaptive Learning 3, 9, 20, 35, 36, 40, 41, 47, 53, 61, 99, 100, 101, 103, 104, 107, 108, 115, 120, 124, 129, 133, 151, 166, 168, 197, 199, 201, 223, 238, 242, 250, 251, 273, 276, 289, 290, 291, 383, 418, 419, 422, 426, 439, 440, 443, 444, 446, 459, 460
AI in Special Education 53
AI Literacy 2, 52, 63, 64, 71, 84, 100, 103, 114, 125, 126, 136, 144, 149, 166, 171, 189, 190, 191, 192, 193, 195, 196, 228, 249, 251, 349, 351, 355, 356, 357, 358, 362, 363, 370, 371, 373, 375, 397, 399, 404, 410, 417, 445, 446, 478
AI-Powered Tools 3, 16, 78, 108, 214, 244, 291, 421
Artificial Intelligence 1, 2, 9, 10, 12, 25, 26, 27, 28, 29, 30, 31, 32, 33, 34, 35, 37, 39, 40, 41, 42, 43, 44, 45, 46, 48, 50, 53, 55, 57, 58, 59, 60, 61, 63, 78, 94, 95, 96, 97, 99, 100, 101, 102, 108, 112, 123, 129, 132, 133, 134, 137, 151, 186, 193, 194, 195, 196, 199, 200, 201, 202, 207, 225, 226, 227, 230, 231, 232, 233, 234, 235, 237, 251, 252, 254, 255, 256, 257, 258, 259, 260, 261, 262, 263, 264, 265, 266, 267, 268, 269, 270, 271, 272, 274, 276, 279, 280, 281, 282, 283, 286, 289, 292, 293, 294, 302, 328, 334, 337, 338, 340, 341, 344, 349, 351, 352, 355, 363, 365, 366, 367, 368, 369, 370, 371, 372, 373, 374, 375, 378, 379, 381, 406, 407, 408, 409, 410, 413, 415, 417, 418, 419, 420, 421, 422, 423, 425, 426, 427, 429, 432, 436, 437, 438, 439, 440, 441, 442, 444, 445, 446, 449, 450, 451, 452, 456, 457, 458, 460, 462, 464, 465, 466, 467, 468, 471, 472, 473, 474, 475, 476, 477, 478
Artificial Intelligence in Higher Education 28, 94, 132, 252, 254, 255, 256, 257, 262, 368, 445
Assessment 6, 27, 28, 31, 32, 33, 40, 45, 52, 58, 60, 64, 73, 75, 76, 81, 86, 87, 88, 91, 92, 93, 94, 96, 115, 118, 120, 121, 128, 132, 133, 135, 136, 139, 140, 143, 145, 154, 156, 157, 162, 164, 172, 173, 174, 179, 182, 183, 184, 199, 200, 201, 208, 210, 214, 215, 217, 218, 223, 243, 250, 262, 272, 330, 338, 341, 342, 359, 367, 369, 391, 406, 416, 418, 421, 432, 441, 444, 446, 455, 459, 477, 478

B

Business 1, 28, 30, 33, 38, 39, 59, 114, 126, 195, 227, 228, 229, 230, 231, 232, 233, 234, 235, 236, 240, 241, 242, 243, 244, 245, 246, 247, 248, 249, 250, 251, 252, 253, 254, 255, 256, 257, 260, 261, 262, 263, 264, 338, 339, 361, 362, 367, 374, 387, 390, 402, 403, 407, 438, 439, 443, 462, 466, 470, 476

C

Classroom for Special Needs 298
Content Creation 65, 66, 72, 119, 122, 141, 199, 201, 327, 379, 382, 388, 392, 402
Co-occurrence Network 295, 302, 307, 314, 322, 328, 334
Co-occurrence of words 295, 302, 328, 334
Critical Thinking 11, 38, 39, 49, 55, 65,

72, 81, 82, 89, 90, 91, 93, 103, 114, 120, 124, 125, 138, 139, 140, 141, 142, 145, 147, 148, 149, 150, 153, 154, 155, 157, 160, 161, 167, 170, 171, 174, 203, 217, 219, 240, 250, 255, 337, 338, 339, 340, 341, 342, 343, 344, 345, 346, 347, 349, 350, 351, 352, 353, 355, 356, 357, 358, 359, 360, 362, 363, 365, 366, 367, 368, 369, 370, 371, 372, 373, 374, 375, 376, 377, 378, 379, 380, 381, 384, 385, 386, 387, 388, 389, 391, 392, 393, 394, 395, 397, 398, 401, 402, 403, 404, 405, 406, 408, 409, 410, 411, 413, 414, 415, 416, 417, 418, 419, 420, 421, 422, 423, 424, 425, 426, 427, 429, 430, 431, 432, 433, 434, 435, 436, 437, 438, 441, 442, 443, 444, 445, 446, 447, 449, 450, 451, 452, 453, 454, 455, 456, 457, 458, 459, 460, 461, 462, 463, 464, 465, 466, 467, 468, 469, 470, 471, 472, 473, 474, 476, 477, 478, 479

D

Data-Driven Insights 35, 61, 123, 199, 201, 280, 290, 419, 421, 460, 465, 466
Dependency Analysis 295, 302, 303, 307, 308, 316, 317, 322, 326, 330, 335
Dot Code 297, 301, 303, 331

E

Education 1, 2, 3, 4, 5, 7, 8, 9, 10, 11, 13, 14, 15, 16, 17, 22, 23, 24, 25, 26, 27, 28, 29, 30, 31, 32, 33, 34, 35, 36, 37, 38, 39, 40, 42, 43, 45, 46, 49, 50, 51, 52, 53, 54, 55, 56, 57, 58, 59, 60, 61, 64, 65, 66, 67, 68, 69, 70, 71, 72, 73, 74, 75, 76, 77, 78, 79, 81, 82, 84, 86, 90, 92, 93, 94, 95, 96, 97, 99, 100, 102, 104, 105, 106, 107, 108, 109, 110, 111, 112, 114, 115, 120, 121, 122, 123, 124, 125, 126, 127, 128, 129, 130, 131, 132, 133, 134, 135, 136, 137, 138, 139, 140, 145, 146, 148, 149, 150, 152, 158, 159, 160, 161, 162, 163, 165, 166, 167, 168, 169, 172, 173, 175, 176, 178, 181, 182, 183, 184, 187, 191, 192, 193, 194, 195, 196, 199, 200, 201, 205, 207, 209, 210, 217, 218, 219, 221, 225, 226, 227, 228, 229, 230, 231, 232, 233, 234, 235, 237, 238, 239, 240, 241, 242, 243, 244, 245, 246, 247, 248, 249, 250, 251, 252, 253, 254, 255, 256, 257, 258, 259, 260, 261, 262, 263, 264, 265, 267, 268, 269, 270, 271, 272, 273, 274, 275, 276, 278, 280, 281, 282, 283, 285, 287, 289, 290, 291, 292, 293, 294, 296, 297, 298, 304, 318, 327, 329, 330, 331, 332, 334, 335, 337, 338, 339, 340, 341, 343, 345, 346, 349, 350, 351, 354, 355, 356, 360, 363, 364, 365, 366, 367, 368, 369, 370, 371, 372, 373, 374, 375, 376, 378, 379, 381, 383, 389, 393, 397, 398, 401, 403, 404, 406, 407, 408, 409, 410, 411, 413, 414, 415, 417, 418, 419, 420, 422, 423, 424, 427, 428, 429, 430, 431, 432, 433, 434, 435, 436, 437, 438, 439, 440, 441, 442, 443, 444, 445, 446, 451, 452, 459, 460, 461, 462, 463, 465, 468, 470, 471, 472, 473, 474, 475, 476, 477, 478
Educational Technology 25, 26, 27, 30, 34, 94, 96, 97, 133, 134, 169, 176, 225, 226, 255, 256, 260, 272, 292, 293, 294, 370, 373, 375, 410, 438, 439, 440, 442, 443, 444, 445, 446, 471, 472, 478
Educator Training 104, 114, 168, 428
Ethical AI Integration 43, 93, 200
Ethical Considerations 45, 66, 75, 85, 90, 92, 105, 109, 111, 114, 125, 126, 135, 138, 145, 146, 147, 148, 149, 150, 160, 161, 171, 172, 174, 182, 190, 199, 200, 201, 217, 219, 220, 224, 248, 251, 252, 268, 278, 280, 282, 346, 386, 392, 393, 396, 398, 405, 445, 452, 468, 469
Ethical Implementation 65, 253

Experiential Learning Theory 63, 64, 66, 76, 92

F

Formative Assessment 6, 32, 156

G

Generative AI 26, 27, 59, 97, 133, 135, 136, 137, 140, 145, 148, 151, 181, 188, 189, 192, 193, 194, 195, 196, 225, 254, 257, 262, 263, 265, 377, 378, 379, 381, 382, 383, 384, 386, 398, 406, 407, 408, 410, 416, 445, 472, 473, 474, 478
Global Challenges 449, 464, 465, 468

H

Handy Tool 335
Higher Education 3, 10, 25, 26, 27, 28, 30, 33, 34, 58, 59, 60, 94, 97, 99, 100, 115, 121, 123, 124, 126, 127, 129, 131, 132, 133, 134, 165, 192, 194, 195, 199, 227, 228, 229, 230, 231, 232, 233, 234, 235, 237, 238, 239, 240, 244, 245, 251, 252, 253, 254, 255, 256, 257, 258, 259, 260, 261, 262, 263, 264, 292, 338, 339, 346, 350, 365, 367, 368, 370, 373, 375, 376, 397, 407, 408, 410, 437, 439, 440, 441, 442, 443, 444, 445, 446, 452, 459, 460, 461, 462, 471, 474, 476, 478
Human-AI Collaboration 346, 393, 396
Human-Centered AI 353, 354, 363, 366, 373, 375

I

Instructional Materials 184, 200, 201, 211, 213
InTASC Standards 162

L

Learning Disabilities 5, 53, 54, 165, 166, 168, 267, 269, 270, 271, 273, 274, 275, 276, 278, 289, 290, 291, 292, 293, 294, 298, 332
LER Methodology 380, 392, 393, 403, 404

M

Multimedia 81, 170, 263, 291, 295, 297, 299, 300, 301, 323, 327, 331, 332, 335, 360

P

Pedagogical Strategies 103, 349, 363, 437
Personalized Feedback 103, 108, 112, 128, 141, 142, 156, 172, 239, 243, 247, 270, 274, 360, 421, 453, 478
Personalized Learning 3, 10, 16, 23, 24, 34, 50, 53, 58, 59, 60, 64, 99, 101, 102, 104, 106, 108, 111, 112, 114, 115, 117, 118, 120, 122, 123, 127, 135, 136, 140, 158, 159, 163, 168, 174, 176, 182, 207, 208, 218, 226, 228, 241, 243, 249, 250, 252, 267, 268, 269, 270, 271, 280, 281, 289, 290, 337, 360, 363, 419, 423, 438, 439, 452, 459

S

School for Special Needs Education 304, 335
Student Engagement 7, 11, 16, 25, 28, 31, 35, 36, 58, 59, 60, 86, 100, 104, 107, 108, 115, 122, 129, 133, 147, 151, 160, 165, 172, 210, 228, 239, 242, 243, 244, 252, 359, 360, 413, 417, 418, 420, 421, 424, 425, 460
Student Perceptions 1, 7, 30, 33, 97
Students 1, 3, 5, 6, 7, 8, 9, 10, 11, 12, 13, 14, 15, 16, 17, 18, 20, 22, 23, 24, 26, 27, 28, 30, 31, 32, 35, 36, 37, 38, 39, 40, 41, 42, 43, 44, 45, 46, 47, 48, 49, 50, 51, 52, 53, 54, 55, 56, 57, 58, 61,

63, 64, 65, 66, 67, 68, 69, 70, 71, 72, 73, 74, 75, 76, 77, 78, 79, 80, 81, 82, 83, 84, 85, 86, 87, 88, 89, 90, 91, 92, 93, 95, 97, 100, 101, 102, 103, 104, 105, 107, 108, 109, 111, 112, 113, 115, 116, 117, 118, 119, 120, 121, 122, 123, 124, 125, 126, 127, 131, 135, 136, 138, 140, 141, 142, 143, 144, 145, 146, 147, 148, 149, 150, 151, 153, 154, 155, 156, 157, 158, 160, 161, 162, 163, 164, 165, 166, 167, 168, 169, 170, 171, 172, 173, 174, 176, 180, 182, 184, 185, 191, 192, 194, 200, 201, 202, 203, 204, 205, 206, 207, 208, 209, 210, 211, 212, 213, 214, 216, 217, 218, 219, 220, 222, 223, 227, 228, 238, 239, 240, 241, 242, 243, 244, 245, 246, 247, 248, 249, 250, 251, 252, 253, 254, 260, 264, 265, 267, 268, 269, 270, 271, 273, 274, 275, 276, 277, 278, 279, 280, 281, 282, 289, 290, 291, 292, 294, 295, 296, 297, 298, 299, 301, 302, 303, 304, 306, 307, 309, 310, 311, 312, 314, 316, 317, 318, 323, 326, 327, 328, 329, 330, 331, 332, 334, 339, 341, 344, 345, 346, 349, 350, 351, 357, 358, 359, 360, 368, 370, 372, 376, 377, 379, 385, 387, 390, 391, 397, 399, 401, 404, 410, 411, 413, 414, 416, 417, 418, 419, 420, 421, 422, 423, 424, 425, 426, 427, 428, 429, 431, 432, 433, 434, 435, 436, 438, 439, 442, 446, 447, 451, 459, 460, 461, 462, 463, 470, 471, 479

T

Teacher Education 58, 134, 192, 194, 199, 200, 201, 366, 369, 438, 441, 474, 478
Teacher Preparation 139, 200, 201, 424
Technology Integration 430, 440
Theory of Planned Behavior 85, 94, 265

W

Word Cloud 295, 309, 317, 318, 335

www.ingramcontent.com/pod-product-compliance
Lightning Source LLC
LaVergne TN
LVHW080615300926
849162LV00005B/1164